Actuarial practice in social security

QUANTITATIVE METHODS IN
SOCIAL PROTECTION SERIES

Actuarial practice in social security

Pierre Plamondon, Anne Drouin,
Gylles Binet, Michael Cichon,
Warren R. McGillivray,
Michel Bédard, Hernando Perez-Montas

A joint technical publication of the
International Labour Office (ILO) and the
International Social Security Association (ISSA)

 International Labour Office • Geneva

Copyright © International Labour Organization 2002
First published 2002

Publications of the International Labour Office enjoy copyright under Protocol 2 of the Universal Copyright Convention. Nevertheless, short excerpts from them may be reproduced without authorization, on condition that the source is indicated. For rights of reproduction or translation, application should be made to the Publications Bureau (Rights and Permissions), International Labour Office, CH-1211 Geneva 22, Switzerland. The International Labour Office welcomes such applications.

Libraries, institutions and other users registered in the United Kingdom with the Copyright Licensing Agency, 90 Tottenham Court Road, London W1T 4LP [Fax: (+44) (0) 20 7 631 5500; email: cla@cla.co.uk], in the United States with the Copyright Clearance Center, 222 Rosewood Drive, Danvers, MA 01923 [Fax: (+1) (978) 750 4470; email: info@copyright.com] or in other countries with associated Reproduction Rights Organizations, may make photocopies in accordance with the licences issued to them for this purpose.

Plamondon, P.; Drouin, A.; Binet, G.; Cichon, M.; McGillivray, W.R.; Bédard, M.; Perez-Montas, H.
Actuarial practice in social security
Quantitative Methods in Social Protection Series
Geneva, International Labour Office/International Social Security Association, 2002
Guide: actuarial valuation, social security, social security financing. 02.13.2

ISBN 92-2-110863-5

The designations employed in ILO publications, which are in conformity with United Nations practice, and the presentation of material therein do not imply the expression of any opinion whatsoever on the part of the International Labour Office concerning the legal status of any country, area or territory or of its authorities, or concerning the delimitation of its frontiers.
The responsibility for opinions expressed in signed articles, studies and other contributions rests solely with their authors, and publication does not constitute an endorsement by the International Labour Office of the opinions expressed in them.
Reference to names of firms and commercial products and processes does not imply their endorsement by the International Labour Office, and any failure to mention a particular firm, commercial product or process is not a sign of disapproval.
ILO publications can be obtained through major booksellers or ILO local offices in many countries, or direct from ILO Publications, International Labour Office, CH-1211 Geneva 22, Switzerland. Catalogues or lists of new publications are available free of charge from the above address, or by email: pubvente@ilo.org
Visit our website: www.ilo.org/publns

Printed in Europe by the Alden Group, Oxford

FOREWORD

The actuarial analysis of social protection schemes requires the actuary to deal with complex demographic, economic, financial, institutional and legal aspects that all interact with each other. Frequently, these issues retain their complexity at the national level, becoming ever more sophisticated as social protection schemes evolve in the context of a larger regional or subregional arrangement. National or regional disparities in terms of coverage, benefit formulae, funding capabilities, investment possibilities, demographic evolution and economic soundness and stability complicate the actuarial analysis still further.

Under this framework, social protection actuaries are obliged to gather, analyse and project into the future delicate balances in the demographic, economic, financial and actuarial fields. This exercise requires the handling of reliable statistical information, the formulation of prudent and safe, though realistic, actuarial assumptions and the design of sophisticated models to ensure consistency between the objectives and the means of the social protection scheme, together with numerous other variables of the national social, economic, demographic and financial environments. Only with the help of sound financial analysis can decision-makers, the social partners and the population in general decide democratically how to enhance and modernize their social protection schemes.

Good governance, sound economic, financial and actuarial strategies and democratic choices of feasible alternatives are the prerequisites for well-founded social protection schemes that efficiently contribute to decent work and national social and economic development. In this sense, this volume in particular and the series of quantitative analysis in the social protection field as a whole constitute a contribution to the Decent Work initiative of the International Labour Office (ILO), conceived as a core part of a new development paradigm.

There are, at present, no compendiums of methods at the international level to address and orient the practice of social security actuaries. The

Foreword

aim of this publication is, therefore, to fill this gap in order to support present and future generations of social protection actuaries. Lessons from the vast international experience of the ILO, the International Social Security Association (ISSA) as well as other organizations are brought together in this volume, with a pragmatic and result-oriented approach.

This volume is the fourth in the Quantitative Methods in Social Protection series being developed by the Financial, Actuarial and Statistical Branch of the Social Protection Sector of the ILO, together with the ISSA. The volumes already published or in preparation in this series are:

- *Actuarial mathematics of social security pensions*
- *Modelling in health care finance: A compendium of quantitative techniques for health care financing*
- *Social budgeting*
- *Social security statistics*
- *Financing of social protection*

The issues approached in these volumes complement each other and together they represent a set of quantitative tools to orient the busy professional and decision-maker. It is also intended that this set of volumes become standard training material at the college, university and professional level for quantitative specialists working in the social protection field.

This series has also been designed to promote the technical exchange and permanent enhancement of quantitative tools. The ILO and ISSA consider this volume and the quantitative series elaborated by the Financial, Actuarial and Statistical Branch as dynamic references, requiring constant criticism and updating. In order to assure this dynamism, the ILO and ISSA welcome all comments and feedback on relevant theoretical issues or empirical experiences.[1]

Assane Diop *Dalmer D. Hoskins*
Executive Director *Secretary General*
Social Protection Sector *International Social Security Association*
International Labour Office *Geneva, Switzerland*
Geneva, Switzerland

---

[1]Please send all comments and feedback to the Secretariat of the Financial Actuarial and Statistical Branch at: antosik@ilo.org

CONTENTS

Foreword	v
Acknowledgements	xix
About the authors	xxi
List of acronyms	xxv
Introduction	xxvii

Part I   The scope and context of actuarial work in social security   1

1   The global picture   3
  1.1   The need for social security-specific actuarial models   3
  1.2   The nature of the interrelationships between social security schemes and their demographic, economic and fiscal environments   7
    1.2.1   Democratic and behavioural linkages   7
    1.2.2   Economic linkages   9
    1.2.3   Fiscal linkages   11
    1.2.4   The social security actuary's central role in social governance   13

2   The role of actuaries in social security   14
  2.1   The valuation of a new scheme   14
    2.1.1   Legal versus actual coverage   15
    2.1.2   Benefit provisions   15
    2.1.3   Financing provisions   16
  2.2   Periodic review of an ongoing scheme   17
    2.2.1   Analysis of past results   17
    2.2.2   Revision of assumptions and methods   18
    2.2.3   Revision of financial projections   18
    2.2.4   Financing recommendations   19
    2.2.5   Other recommendations   19

Contents

	2.3	Actuarial considerations at the reform stage	19
		2.3.1 Amendments to a scheme	20
		2.3.2 Structural reform of a system	20
	2.4	Short-term projections	21
	2.5	Ad hoc actuarial support and other related fields	21
		2.5.1 Ad hoc support	22
		2.5.2 Statistical reports	22
		2.5.3 Performance indicators	22
		2.5.4 Social security agreements	22
	2.6	Organization of actuarial services	23

Part II The valuation of public pension schemes — **25**

3	**The characteristics of public pension schemes**		**27**
	3.1	Broad coverage and mandatory participation	27
		3.1.1 The open-group method	27
		3.1.2 Links with the general context	28
		3.1.3 Relevance of the scheme's experience	28
		3.1.4 No underwriting	28
	3.2	Government sponsorship	29
	3.3	Self-financing	29
	3.4	Funding flexibility	30
	3.5	Redistribution mechanisms	31
		3.5.1 Between earnings classes	31
		3.5.2 Between workers with different career patterns	32
		3.5.3 In favour of married insured persons and large families	32
		3.5.4 Between generations	32
4	**The actuarial valuation process**		**34**
5	**Financial systems**		**38**
	5.1	Pattern of expenditure of a pension scheme	38
	5.2	Sources of revenue	39
	5.3	Objectives of the financial system	40
	5.4	Types of financial systems	41
		5.4.1 PAYG	42
		5.4.2 Full funding	45
		5.4.3 Partial funding	46
6	**Actuarial modelling for public pensions**		**56**
	6.1	Definition of the actuarial model	56
	6.2	Deterministic versus stochastic models	57

	6.3	Modelling social security pensions: the objectives	59
	6.4	Modelling social security pensions: the structure	62
		6.4.1 The demographic environment	63
		6.4.2 The economic environment	63
		6.4.3 The future development of the scheme	63
7	**The data and information base for the valuation**		**69**
	7.1	Sources of statistical information	69
	7.2	Legal provisions of the scheme	72
		7.2.1 Coverage	72
		7.2.2 Contingencies covered	73
		7.2.3 Covered earnings	74
		7.2.4 Eligibility conditions	75
		7.2.5 Amount of benefit	75
		7.2.6 Financing provisions	79
	7.3	General demographic and economic data	80
	7.4	Scheme-specific data	81
		7.4.1 Appraisal of the institution's data maintenance system	81
		7.4.2 Database on the insured population	82
		7.4.3 Database on beneficiaries	88
8	**The analysis of past experience**		**90**
	8.1	Financial statements	90
		8.1.1 Cash versus accrual basis	91
		8.1.2 Financial reporting	91
	8.2	Experience analysis and key indicators	93
	8.3	The analysis of administrative expenses	95
	8.4	The analysis of investment performance	96
	8.5	Determining the value of the reserve	99
		8.5.1 Value of investments	99
		8.5.2 Smoothing techniques	100
		8.5.3 Adjustment of particular items	100
9	**Demographic and macroeconomic frames for projections**		**102**
	9.1	Projection of the general population	102
		9.1.1 Fertility	103
		9.1.2 Mortality	103
		9.1.3 Migration	104
		9.1.4 A standard population projection model	105
	9.2	The macroeconomic frame	107
		9.2.1 Economic growth	110
		9.2.2 Labour force, employment and unemployment	112

Contents

	9.2.3	Wages	112
	9.2.4	Inflation	114
	9.2.5	Interest rates	114
	9.2.6	Other considerations	115

10 Scheme-specific assumptions — **117**
- 10.1 Development of the insured population — 117
  - 10.1.1 Coverage rate — 117
  - 10.1.2 Components of the insured population — 119
  - 10.1.3 New entrants and re-entrants — 121
- 10.2 Projection of insurable earnings — 124
  - 10.2.1 Earnings growth — 124
  - 10.2.2 Earnings distribution — 126
  - 10.2.3 Total versus insurable earnings — 129
  - 10.2.4 Density of contributions — 129
- 10.3 Accumulation of insurance credits — 130
- 10.4 Mortality rates — 131
- 10.5 Retirement behaviour — 131
- 10.6 Invalidity incidence and termination — 132
- 10.7 Entitlement to survivors' benefits — 134
  - 10.7.1 Probability of having a spouse at time of death — 136
  - 10.7.2 Average age of spouse — 136
  - 10.7.3 Number and age of children — 136
- 10.8 Rate of pension indexing — 137
- 10.9 Investment return — 138
  - 10.9.1 General level of interest rates — 138
  - 10.9.2 Return by type of investment — 140
- 10.10 Contribution collection rate — 140
- 10.11 Future level of administrative expenses — 142

11 Results and sensitivity analysis — **146**
- 11.1 Valuation results — 146
- 11.2 Calculation of indicators — 149
  - 11.2.1 Demographic indicators — 149
  - 11.2.2 Financial indicators — 150
- 11.3 Sensitivity analysis — 152
- 11.4 Reconciliation of results with the previous valuation — 156

12 The valuation of modifications to a scheme — **158**
- 12.1 Modifications to benefits — 158

		12.1.1	Eligibility conditions (contribution requirements)	158
		12.1.2	Retirement age	159
		12.1.3	The pension formula	161
		12.1.4	Adjustments to pensions in payment	162
		12.1.5	Level of minimum and maximum pensions	163
		12.1.6	Earnings test at retirement	163
		12.1.7	A more stringent definition of invalidity	164
		12.1.8	Survivors' benefits	165
	12.2	Modifications to contributions		165
		12.2.1	Modifications to the contribution rate	166
		12.2.2	Extensions of the salary base	166
	12.3	Other considerations		167
	12.4	Presenting the effect of modifications		167

13 Structural reform considerations — **170**

	13.1	Converting a DB scheme into a DC scheme		170
		13.1.1	Valuation of a scheme's liability at conversion	172
		13.1.2	Specific considerations in the context of a reform	176
	13.2	The Swedish pension reform		176
		13.2.1	Description of the new scheme	176
		13.2.2	The intervention of the actuary	177
	13.3	Converting a provident fund into a DB scheme		179
		13.3.1	General considerations	179
		13.3.2	Differences between provident funds and pension schemes	180
		13.3.3	Alternatives to moving from a provident fund to a pension scheme	183
		13.3.4	Countries that have changed from provident funds to pension schemes	186

Part III The valuation of employment injury benefits — **189**

14 Financial and rating systems — **191**

14.1	Financial systems		192
	14.1.1	Sources of funds	192
	14.1.2	Basic concepts	193
	14.1.3	PAYG method of financing	196
	14.1.4	Full funding	197
	14.1.5	Mixed systems	199
	14.1.6	The actuary and the financial system	201
14.2	Rating systems		202
	14.2.1	Uniform rates	203

Contents

	14.2.2	Differential rates	203
14.3	Experience-rating systems		207
	14.3.1	Nature of experience rating	207
	14.3.2	Prospective programmes	208
	14.3.3	Retrospective programmes	208
Annex 14A	Demonstration of the principle that the contribution rate under a fully funded system and the ultimate PAYG cost rate can be equal		209

15 Temporary incapacity cash benefits — 212

- 15.1 Legislative provisions — 212
- 15.2 Methodology for financial projections — 213
  - 15.2.1 Benefits related to injuries that occurred before the valuation date — 214
  - 15.2.2 Benefits related to injuries occurring after the valuation date — 216
- 15.3 Assumptions — 217
  - 15.3.1 Duration of incapacity — 218
  - 15.3.2 Evolution of the number of benefit recipients — 220
  - 15.3.3 The continuation table — 221
  - 15.3.4 Basic amount of benefits — 223
  - 15.3.5 Number of new injuries — 224
- 15.4 Analysis of experience deviations — 225
  - 15.4.1 Projection — 225
  - 15.4.2 Sources of deviations — 226
- Annex 15A Table 15A.1 Illustration of formula 15.3 — 232

16 Permanent incapacity and survivorship benefits — 233

- 16.1 Legislative provisions — 233
  - 16.1.1 Permanent incapacity benefits — 233
  - 16.1.2 Survivorship benefits — 235
- 16.2 Methodology for financial projections — 235
  - 16.2.1 Pensions in payment at the valuation date — 236
  - 16.2.2 Present value of new awards at date of award — 238
  - 16.2.3 Future awards for past injuries — 239
  - 16.2.4 Future awards for future injuries — 240
  - 16.2.5 Successive liabilities — 241
- 16.3 Assumptions — 242
  - 16.3.1 Terminations of pensions in payment — 243
  - 16.3.2 Future awards — 248
  - 16.3.3 Basic amount of benefits related to new awards — 251
- Annex 16A Cash flow of new awards in terms of financial years — 252
- Annex 16B Technical note on mortality tables by degree of impairment — 252
- Annex 16C Table 16C. A Partial permanent incapacity terminations — 254

17	Medical expenses and rehabilitation benefits	256
17.1	Legislative provisions	256
	17.1.1 Medical expenses	256
	17.1.2 Rehabilitation	257
17.2	Database and statistical reports for actuarial valuations	258
	17.2.1 Description of the database	258
	17.2.2 Statistical reporting	260
17.3	Methodology for financial projections	260
	17.3.1 Benefits related to injuries that occurred before the valuation date	261
	17.3.2 Benefits related to injuries occurring after the valuation date	266
17.4	Assumptions	267
	17.4.1 Raw data	267
	17.4.2 Observed development factors	270
	17.4.3 Graduated development factors	274
	17.4.4 Tests	276

Part IV	The valuation of short-term cash benefits	279

18	Sickness and maternity benefits	281
18.1	The financial system	281
18.2	Data requirements	282
	18.2.1 For sickness cash benefits	282
	18.2.2 For maternity allowances	282
18.3	Cost projections	283
	18.3.1 The general formula	283
	18.3.2 Special considerations for sickness benefits	285
	18.3.3 Special considerations for maternity benefits	286
	18.3.4 Possible refinements	287

19	Unemployment insurance	288
19.1	Introduction	288
	19.1.1 UI and the insurance concepts	288
	19.1.2 Expertise and background required of a UI actuary	289
19.2	UI projections in general	291
	19.2.1 Data sources	291
19.3	Business cycles and stability	292
	19.3.1 The desirability of premium financing for UI (for macroeconomic stabilization)	292
	19.3.2 A discussion of business cycles	292
19.4	The projection of benefits	294
19.5	Financing	302

Contents

		19.5.1	The desirability of premium financing, and some characteristics	302
		19.5.2	Projecting revenues	304
		19.5.3	Projecting reserves and recommending premium rates	305
		19.5.4	Some thoughts on experience rating	306
	19.6	Validation of results		307
	19.7	Conclusion		307

Part V The actuarial report — 309

20 Presentation of the methodology and results — 311
- 20.1 Standard structure of the actuarial report — 311
  - 20.1.1 Executive summary — 311
  - 20.1.2 Economic, demographic and governance context — 311
  - 20.1.3 Analysis of the present situation and performance — 312
  - 20.1.4 Actuarial projections — 314
  - 20.1.5 Conclusions and recommendations — 316
- 20.2 Communicating the results — 317

21 A practical exercise: The Demoland case — 318
- 21.1 Introducing Demoland — 318
- 21.2 The Demoland valuation report — 319

Technical Brief I	Examples of tables used for the collection of social security data	373
Technical Brief II	ILO social security Conventions and Recommendations	413
Technical Brief III	The main characteristics of DC schemes	423
Technical Brief IV	Advanced topics on the valuation of employment injury benefits	440

List of symbols — 471

Glossary of terms — 483

Bibliography — 488

Index — 495

List of tables

7.1	Average earnings of active contributors (the Demoland case)	85
15.1	Form of experience data	218
15.2	Illustration of formula 15.3	219
15.3	Illustration of formula 15.2	220
15.4	Probability of a benefit recipient in the valuation year being a benefit recipient in year t after the valuation year	221
15.5	Continuation table for temporary incapacity benefits	222
15.6	Projection of benefit days	224
15.7	Projected actuarial liability for the injury years up to 1998	225
15.8	Example of an experience analysis	228
15.9	Sources of surpluses and deficits	229
15.10	Revised projections at 31 December 1999	229
15.11	Revised projected actuarial liability for the injury years up to 1998	230
16.1	Illustration of an adjustment to a population mortality table	244
16.2	Terminations of partial incapacity pensions	246
16.3	Example: New awards of permanent incapacity benefits per 100,000 injuries	249
17.1	Example: Payments in current monetary values	268
17.2	Example: Variations in general prices	270
17.3	Example: Observed development factors	271
17.4	Example: Average development factors	273
17.5	Graduated development factors	275
17.6	Development factors	276
20.1	Standard content of an actuarial report	312
TBI.1	General information	374
TBI.2	General population: Number of people at mid-year, historical and future	375
TBI.3	General population: Fertility rates and sex ratio of newborns, historical and future	376
TBI.4	General population: Mortality rates, historical and future	377
TBI.5	General population: Net migration (net number of migrants), historical and future	378
TBI.6	General population: Marriage rate by sex and age group, historical and future	379
TBI.7	Labour force: Average number of people, historical and future	380
TBI.8	Labour force: Labour force participation rates, historical and future	382
TBI.9	Total employment: Average number of people, historical and future	383
TBI.10	Employees: Average number of people, historical and future	385
TBI.11	Self-employment: Average number of people, historical and future	387
TBI.12	Unemployment: Average number of people, historical and future	389
TBI.13	Unemployment: Unemployment rates, historical and future	391
TBI.14	Wages: Total compensation of employees (current prices), historical	392
TBI.15	Wages: Wage share of gross domestic product (GDP)	392

List of tables

TBI.16	Wages: Average wages for the economy and by sector	392
TBI.17	Gross domestic product (GDP) by economic sector	392
TBI.18	Gross domestic product (GDP) sectoral deflators	393
TBI.19	Gross domestic product (GDP) by expenditure components	393
TBI.20	Gross domestic product (GDP) expenditure deflators	393
TBI.21	Primary income distribution (current prices)	394
TBI.22	Inflation and interest rates	395
TBI.23	Exchange rates (annual average)	395
TBI.24	General government revenue and expenditure	396
TBI.25	Social security legal provisions	397
TBI.26	Social security financial reporting	397
TBI.27	Insured population: Number of people, historical	398
TBI.28	Insured population: Age distribution at valuation date	398
TBI.29	Insured population: Development of density factors	399
TBI.30	Insured population: Insurable earnings and lower and upper limits, historical	400
TBI.31	Insured population: Monthly insurable earnings in year of valuation	400
TBI.32	Insured population: Past insurable credits of active insured persons as of valuation date	401
TBI.33	Insured population: Past insurable credits of inactive insured persons as of valuation date	401
TBI.34	Insured population: New entrants, historical	402
TBI.35	Insured population: New entrants' age distribution in three years prior to valuation date	402
TBI.36	Long-term benefit branch: Historical number of beneficiaries and expenditure	403
TBI.37	Long-term benefit branch: Pensions in payment at valuation date	404
TBI.38	Long-term benefit branch: New benefit cases in three years prior to valuation date	406
TBI.39	Long-term benefit branch: Pensioners' cohort tables	409
TBIII.1	Minimum pension provisions in selected countries	436
TBIV.1	Illustration of rate calculation	442
TBIV.2	Example of the balancing process	443
TBIV.3	Database for the calculation of rate relativities of year t	447
TBIV.4	Table of adjustment to the basic rate	449
TBIV.5	Prospective rating and balancing	450
TBIV.6	Temporary incapacity benefit payments	463
TBIV.7	Permanent incapacity benefit awards	465
TBIV.8	Permanent incapacity terminations	465

List of figures

1.1	Structural long-term relationships in SEA models	6
5.1	Typical evolution of expenditure under a public pension scheme	39

List of figures

5.2	Reserve accumulation in a public pension scheme	42
5.3	Contribution rates under the scaled premium system	47
5.4	Contribution rates for Demoland	49
5.5	Reserve ratios for Demoland	50
5.6	Contribution rate under the GAP system	50
6.1	The ILO projection model for pensions	60
9.1	A standard population projection model	106
9.2	The general frame for labour force projections	111
9.3	Determination of the average wage in the economy	113
10.1	Classification of insured persons in the total population	120
10.2	Effect of a ceiling on insurable earnings	129
14.1	Benefit payments of an injury year	194
14.2	Benefit payments related to all injury years	194
14.3	Reserve as a percentage of covered earnings	199
14.4	Comparison of reserve levels under the full-funding and mixed systems	200
16.1	Observed recovery rates	247
17.1	Ratio of development factors	274
17.2	Development factors	275
TBIV.1	Credibility curve: Limited fluctuations approach	446
TBIV.2	Credibility curve: Bühlmann approach	446

List of boxes

1.1	Interactions between social security and the general context	8
5.1	Basic formulae on financing	43
5.2	Actuarial balance sheet of the Kuwait Public Institution for Social Security as of 30 June 1995	46
5.3	Application of the reserve ratio system to the Demoland case	49
5.4	Financial systems in selected countries	51
6.1	An example of the stochastic approach to project the rate of return	58
6.2	The mathematics of a typical social security pension model	64
7.1	Sources of information for the actuarial valuation of a social insurance pension scheme	70
7.2	Particular issues related to legal provisions	73
7.3	Typical categories of insured persons under a social insurance pension scheme	74
7.4	Typical pension formulae	76
7.5	Typical formulae for the determination of reference earnings	77
7.6	Considerations for defining the basis for indexing social security benefits	79
7.7	Checklist of the data to be collected for building the demographic and macroeconomic frames for an actuarial valuation	80
7.8	Breakdown of insured persons under a pension scheme	82
7.9	Past service of the insured population (the Demoland case)	88

List of boxes

8.1	Typical balance sheet of a social security institution	92
8.2	Typical income statement of a social security scheme	92
8.3	Typical administrative expenses of a social security institution	95
8.4	Calculation of the rate of return of a pension fund	97
8.5	A smoothing technique to estimate the value of a social security reserve	99
8.6	Example: Adjusted reserve as of 31 December 1999	101
9.1	The United Nations methodology for mortality projections	104
9.2	Basic macroeconomic relationships for the determination of actuarial assumptions on employment, wages and interest rates	108
10.1	Illustrative methods to calculate effective coverage rates	119
10.2	Mathematical example of the treatment of new entrants and re-entrants	122
10.3	Definition of a salary scale	123
10.4	Simple methods for constructing a salary scale	125
10.5	Parametric or non-parametric distributions?	128
10.6	Determination of retirement take-up rates	133
10.7	Determination of invalidity incidence rates with limited experience data	135
10.8	Biometric data for survivors' benefit calculations (the Demoland case)	137
10.9	Setting assumptions on future investment return	139
10.10	Social security investments in the Caribbean	141
10.11	An example of a contribution collection pattern	143
11.1	Valuation results under status quo projections (the Demoland case)	147
11.2	Summary of factors influencing the financial equilibrium of a pension scheme	153
11.3	Sensitivity tests performed in the 1997 report of the Quebec Pension Plan	154
11.4	Reconciliation between two valuations (the Demoland case)	155
12.1	Increasing the retirement age (the Demoland case)	160
12.2	The effect of a modification to the minimum pension (the Demoland case)	168
13.1	The Chilean pension reform	171
13.2	Two World Bank concepts: the implicit pension debt and the pension debt overhang	172
13.3	An example of apportionment of credits	173
14.1	Example of a constant EIOD record	195
14.2	Full funding versus terminal funding	197
14.3	Illustration of formula 14.5	204
15.1	Numerical example	226
16.1	Alternative estimation of new awards	250
17.1	Averaging of observed past payments	264
18.1	Cost calculation for short-term benefits	284
TBIV.1	Calculation of rate relativities	441
TBIV.2	Illustration of an experience-rating plan for small employers	449
TBIV.3	Illustration of an experience-rating plan for middle-sized employers	451

ACKNOWLEDGEMENTS

This volume is very much the result of a team effort. The authors would like to express their sincere thanks to all those people who shared their time and energy by closely collaborating with them during the drafting process, by providing additional information, or as reviewers of the text.

Pierre Hébert and Lalina Montgrain-Lévesque of the Commission de la santé et de la sécurité du travail in Quebec, Canada, collaborated with Gylles Binet on the drafting of Part III on employment injury benefits. Kenichi Hirose, actuary in the ILO's Social Security Department, is the author of box 5.4, a description of the financial systems in operation in three countries, and box 6.2, on the mathematical description of the ILO pension model. Derek Osborne, actuarial officer for the National Insurance Board of the Bahamas, is the author of box 10.10, on social security investments in the Caribbean. Pascale Lapierre and Isabelle Beaudry of the ILO's Social Security Department collaborated on the revision of formulae, the glossary and the bibliography, and made useful comments during the drafting process.

The authors would also like to thank Florian Léger, John Woodall and Wolfgang Scholz for taking the time to read the draft version of the book, for improving its content and for making it generally more accessible and uniform.

ABOUT THE AUTHORS

Pierre Plamondon is a Fellow of the Canadian Institute of Actuaries (FCIA) and of the Society of Actuaries (FSA). After acquiring experience in an insurance company and an actuarial consultancy group in Quebec, he joined the Quebec Pension Commission in 1985, where he was Chief of the Valuation Department between 1990 and 1998. He was responsible for the actuarial valuation of the Quebec Pension Plan, the publication of official statistics for the scheme and the technical support for the development of supplemental (occupational) pension plans in Quebec. In 1998, he joined the Financial, Actuarial and Statistical Branch of the ILO's Social Security Department as actuarial coordinator. He has realized various actuarial assignments for the ILO: in Barbados, Bulgaria, Burkina Faso, Côte d'Ivoire, Cyprus, Guyana, and Trinidad and Tobago. He has coordinated a study on the investment of social security reserves and initiated the development of a model for the projection of national populations in the context of AIDS.

Anne Drouin has been working as an ILO social security specialist, advising ILO constituents in East Asia, since 1999. Prior to that, she was a social security actuary with the Financial, Actuarial and Statistical Branch of the ILO's Social Security Department, working with a number of countries in the Caribbean, Central America, Eastern Europe, as well as in Mongolia and Thailand. Before joining the ILO, she worked for three years as an actuary with the Canada Life Assurance Company in Toronto, Canada. In 1999, she became an FCIA and FSA. She completed her Bachelor of Sciences with the actuarial programme of the Mathematics Department of the University of Laval in 1985 and has a Masters in International Development Studies from the University of Ottawa (1992). She has participated in the publication of a number of papers and ILO reports on social security, pensions and other actuarial topics.

About the authors

Gylles Binet works as an actuary at Quebec's Commission de la santé et de la sécurité du travail (CSST). He studied at Laval University and is an FCIA and FSA. He has acquired experience in many branches of social security in the province of Quebec, including the Quebec Pension Plan, the public no-fault automobile insurance system (bodily injury), the health insurance system and the workers' compensation scheme. He was also involved in private pension and insurance matters while working for an insurance company, in an actuarial consultant firm and in the Office of the Superintendent of Insurance of Quebec. As a professor at Laval University in Quebec, he used his diversified background in teaching and research activities. Since joining the CSST in 1983, he has been responsible for actuarial valuations required by the law, and has been a speaker at meetings of the Canadian Institute of Actuaries on matters regarding the workers' compensation system in Canada. He has been involved in actuarial projects under the authority of international development organizations and the ILO in Asia, Latin America and the Middle East.

Michael Cichon holds a Masters degree in Pure and Applied Mathematics (Technical University, Aachen, Germany), a Masters degree in Public Administration (Harvard University) and a Ph.D. in Health Economics (University of Göttingen, Germany). He is a member of the German Actuarial Association (DAV), and worked in the Planning Department of the German Ministry of Labour and Social Affairs in Bonn as an actuary for eight years before joining the Social Security Department of the ILO in 1986 as senior actuary and health economist. Between 1993 and 1995, he served as social security specialist in the ILO's multidisciplinary advisory team for Central and Eastern Europe in Budapest. In 1995, he was appointed Chief of the Financial, Actuarial and Statistical Branch of the ILO's Social Security Department. He writes on financial and economic issues related to social security, with occasional excursions into governance. He has undertaken technical cooperation assignments in more than 15 ILO member countries.

Warren R. McGillivray is Chief of the Studies and Operations Branch of the ISSA in Geneva. From 1969 to 1975, he was lecturer in Statistics at the University of Dar es Salaam, Tanzania, and senior lecturer in Actuarial Science at the University of Lagos, Nigeria. Subsequently, he joined the ILO in Geneva as senior actuary in the Social Security Department (1976–79). He was later regional adviser for Asia and the Pacific located in Bangkok (1980–85), Head of the Actuarial Section of the Social Security Department (1985–89) and Director of the ILO Office for the South Pacific, located in Fiji (1989–93). He has undertaken numerous social security advisory missions and participated in projects involving financial studies, actuarial valuations and various aspects of social security policy and planning. He has written a number of articles on social security financing and actuarial topics. He received his Bachelor and Masters degrees from the University of Saskatchewan, Canada, and is an FSA.

Michel Bédard is chief actuary for the unemployment insurance programme with the Department of Human Resources Development in Canada. After studying Actuarial Science at Laval University in Quebec, Canada, he became an FCIA in 1980. He began his career in pension supervision for the Canadian government, before becoming associated with the Canadian unemployment insurance programme in the 1970s. He is recognized as a leading expert on unemployment insurance in Canada, both in the projecting field as well as in programme design, operations and principles. He has written study material on this topic for the Society of Actuaries as well as reports for the ILO. He has also made presentations to foreign delegations interested in the Canadian unemployment insurance experience. He holds a Bachelor of Arts degree, a *Licence* in Business Administration and has trained in computer science.

Hernando Perez-Montas studied Actuarial Science at the University of Madrid from 1961 to 1963 and holds a Masters in demography from the London School of Economics. He has carried out actuarial assignments on pensions and cash-benefit schemes in Latin America and the Caribbean as a consultant for the ILO, the World Bank and other international organizations, as well as in a personal capacity. He has also prepared valuations and studies dealing with health insurance, unemployment and complementary pension schemes. From 1969 to 1971, he was stationed in Washington, DC, as a principal specialist in social security for the Organization of American States, for which he undertook assignments in Colombia, Costa Rica, Ecuador, Panama, Paraguay and Venezuela. He has also undertaken assignments in several anglophone schemes in the Caribbean, for the ILO between 1983 and 1987 and as a private consultant between 1998 and 2000. He also lectures at special seminars for the ISSA. He has been a Vice-President of the Committee of Actuaries and Statisticians of the ISSA, as well as a President of the Inter-American Commission of Actuaries of the Permanent Inter-American Social Security Committee (CPISS, Mexico). Since 1989, he has been a member of the Committee of Actuaries of the United Nations Pension Fund, and presides over a pension fund consulting firm in the Dominican Republic.

LIST OF ACRONYMS

ABO	Accumulated benefit obligation
AFP	Private pension fund management company (Chile)
AIDS	Acquired immune deficiency syndrome
COLA	Cost-of-living adjustments
CPI	Consumer price index
CPISS	Permanent Inter-American Social Security Committee (Mexico)
CSST	Commission de la santé et de la sécurité du travail (Canada)
DB	Defined-benefit (scheme)
DC	Defined-contribution (scheme)
EIOD	Employment injury occupational diseases
FCIA	Fellow of the Canadian Institute of Actuaries
FSA	Fellow of the Society of Actuaries
GAP	General average premium
GDP	Gross domestic product
ILO	International Labour Office/Organization
ILO FACTS	International Financial and Actuarial Service of the ILO
ILO-PENS	ILO pension model
IMF	International Monetary Fund
ISSA	International Social Security Association

Lost of acronyms

MAE	Maximum assessable earnings
MPCC	Maximum per claim cost
MPIC	Maximum per incident cost
NBER	National Bureau of Economic Research
NIB	National Insurance Board (of Demoland)
NIF	National Insurance Fund (of Demoland)
NIS	National Insurance Scheme (of Demoland)
OASDI	Old-Age, Survivors, and Disability Insurance (United States)
OECD	Organisation for Economic Co-operation and Development
PAYG	Pay-as-you-go
PBO	Projected benefit basis
SEA	Socio-economic actuarial (model)
UI	Unemployment insurance

INTRODUCTION

The objective of this volume is to provide a practical tool for actuaries involved in the valuation of social security schemes. Not all the mathematical background needed to carry out such valuations has been given in this book, as the theory has already been covered by other publications. Rather, this publication should be viewed as a step-by-step guide and as a reminder of the considerations that the actuary working in social security should always bear in mind.

Social security schemes cover many risks, including those for old age, survivors, disability, sickness, maternity, employment injury, unemployment and medical care. With the exception of medical care, which is covered by another volume in the series, this publication considers all these risks and provides different methodologies adapted to each one.

The technical material on valuation covers the whole range of topics with which an actuary working on a fully comprehensive scheme must deal. It is recognized that few schemes worldwide will include provisions of every kind, and that those in less developed countries will omit a good many. Nevertheless, every social security actuary should find it of interest to study the full range of techniques applicable to the various branches.

This book is divided into five sections. Part I provides a general background to the particular context of actuarial practice in social security, showing how the work of the social security actuary is linked with the demographic and economic context of a country. It also presents the various roles of actuaries practising in the field and shows how their work is usually organized. Part II covers the valuation of pensions. It presents a step-by-step account of the usual process of the actuarial valuation and tries, at each stage, to give appropriate examples to illustrate the work concretely. Part III covers the valuation of employment injury benefits. Special techniques adapted to the field are explained and illustrated through various applications. Part IV looks at the valuation of short-

Introduction

term cash benefits (sickness, maternity and unemployment insurance). Where techniques are similar or when the demographic and economic context elaborated for the valuation of pensions can be used, Part IV uses some of the material used in previous sections of the book. Part V is concerned with the standard content of the actuarial report for social security valuations. After giving a general description, it presents a typical actuarial report of a small country, Demoland. (Throughout the book, a number of examples are taken from the Demoland report as practical demonstrations of various aspects of actuarial work.)

PART I

THE SCOPE AND CONTEXT OF ACTUARIAL WORK IN SOCIAL SECURITY

THE GLOBAL PICTURE 1

National social protection systems are no economic, demographic, social or fiscal islands. Most countries redistribute between 5 and 30 per cent of their gross domestic product (GDP) through national social transfer systems, fuelled by general revenues, payroll taxes or social security contributions. Redistributive mechanisms of this order need to be sensitive to the economic and fiscal environments in which they operate. They are obviously influenced by the economy and public budgets upon which they, in turn, have a significant impact. Furthermore, social transfer or social security systems[1] are influenced by the demographic structure and development of the society they serve as well as by fiscal realities. Meaningful actuarial work, which in itself is only one tool in national financial, fiscal and social governance, has to be fully cognizant of the economic, demographic and fiscal environments in which national social security systems operate, which has not always been the case. This chapter sets out the interrelationships between social security systems and their environments as well as their relevance for actuarial work.

1.1 THE NEED FOR SOCIAL SECURITY-SPECIFIC ACTUARIAL MODELS

Models are crucial instruments in actuarial work. Since the early days of the profession, about 150 years ago, actuaries have built models for relatively small population subgroups in societies (such as groups of insured persons of an insurance company). For these groups, demographic trends and key economic variables (such as wages and interest-rate developments) can, with some justification, be considered independent. A small, well-to-do group of insured persons might well enjoy long-term stable wage increases close to, or even higher than, interest rates, while in the economy at large such a long-term development would be rather unusual. By the same token, a small insurance scheme could experience rapid increases in the insured population, while at the same time unemployment in the economy at large might be on the rise. Mortality rates in the group of well-off people might be declining and be much lower than in the population at large.

Actuarial models for the demographic and financial projections of public pension schemes were generally derived from models that had been applied to occupational pension schemes covering relatively small groups of workers and that were based on exogenous and independent demographic and economic variables and assumptions, including:

I Demographic variables

- the rate of increase of the insured population;
- invalidity rates;
- mortality rates;
- the age of children.

II Economic variables

- the initial salary scale by age and sex;
- the rate of increase of insured wages;
- inflation rates;
- long-term interest-rate developments;
- long-term trends in contribution density (which was, inter alia, an indicator for the annual "employment intensity" of the individual).

III Social (behavioural) variables

- marriage rates;
- the age differential between husbands and wives;
- retirement rates;
- the age pattern of new entrants into the scheme.

Clearly, assumptions relating to these variables that were appropriate for small occupational schemes – islands in a society – were inappropriate for economy-wide and society-wide social security pension schemes. Furthermore, in public schemes the independence of many of the variables cannot be assumed. In selecting the assumptions, then, orientation was sought from the past experience of the scheme or from the experience of similar schemes, but not always from the national socio-economic situation and prospects.

In practice, this sometimes led to unsatisfactory results in actuarial valuations. For example, insured populations that were projected to grow at the same rate as the general population eventually exceeded the employed labour force, and sometimes even the entire labour force; reserves rapidly became a major source of investment capital, but the resulting effect on interest rates was not taken into account; and wages were sometimes projected to grow at rates quite different from overall economic growth. The exogenous demographic assumptions sometimes failed to take into account the effect of increasing wealth on mortality and fertility rates. Economic analysis focused on the short term and did not take into account long-term economic scenarios or economic development paths. Few social scientists took a long-term view of labour force participation rates, retirement rates or even marriage breakdown rates.

Uncertainties about the future development of the variables that determine the volume of pensions and other social transfers, and their complex interrelationships and interactions with the demographic, economic and fiscal environments, make actuarial projections a difficult and complex undertaking. But these projections are vital, despite the many uncertainties and stringent or fuzzy relationships it is necessary to seek out to take them into account.

Social security schemes, notably pension schemes (where actuarial work is most relevant) are long-term societal commitments, many of which have to be honoured by future generations. Such schemes should only be introduced if we at least try – to the best of our knowledge – to assess what these future burdens might be. Academic complaints about imperfect models do not help policy-makers and planners map out the future shape of societies. Models should combine social, economic, demographic and actuarial knowledge to develop a long-term vision of economic and social transfer systems, which we call here *socio-economic actuarial (SEA) models*.

Some of the typical interrelationships that SEA models need to take into account and that have to be explored by social security actuaries around the world in much more detail and in more quantitative terms are described in figure 1.1.

Over the past decade the ILO's International Financial and Actuarial Service (ILO FACTS) has begun to develop a new family of models. The ILO model family has only just begun to take the above relationships into consideration, and there is still a long way to go. For the time being, our understanding of many of the relationships is rudimentary, but that is no reason to ignore them. Lack of knowledge may, to some extent, be substituted by a careful analysis of alternative scenarios and hypotheses, while at the same time research should continue. In any case, building an intelligent set of assumptions for actuarial models in social security models that attempts to look decades into the future, remains an art rather than a scientific skill.

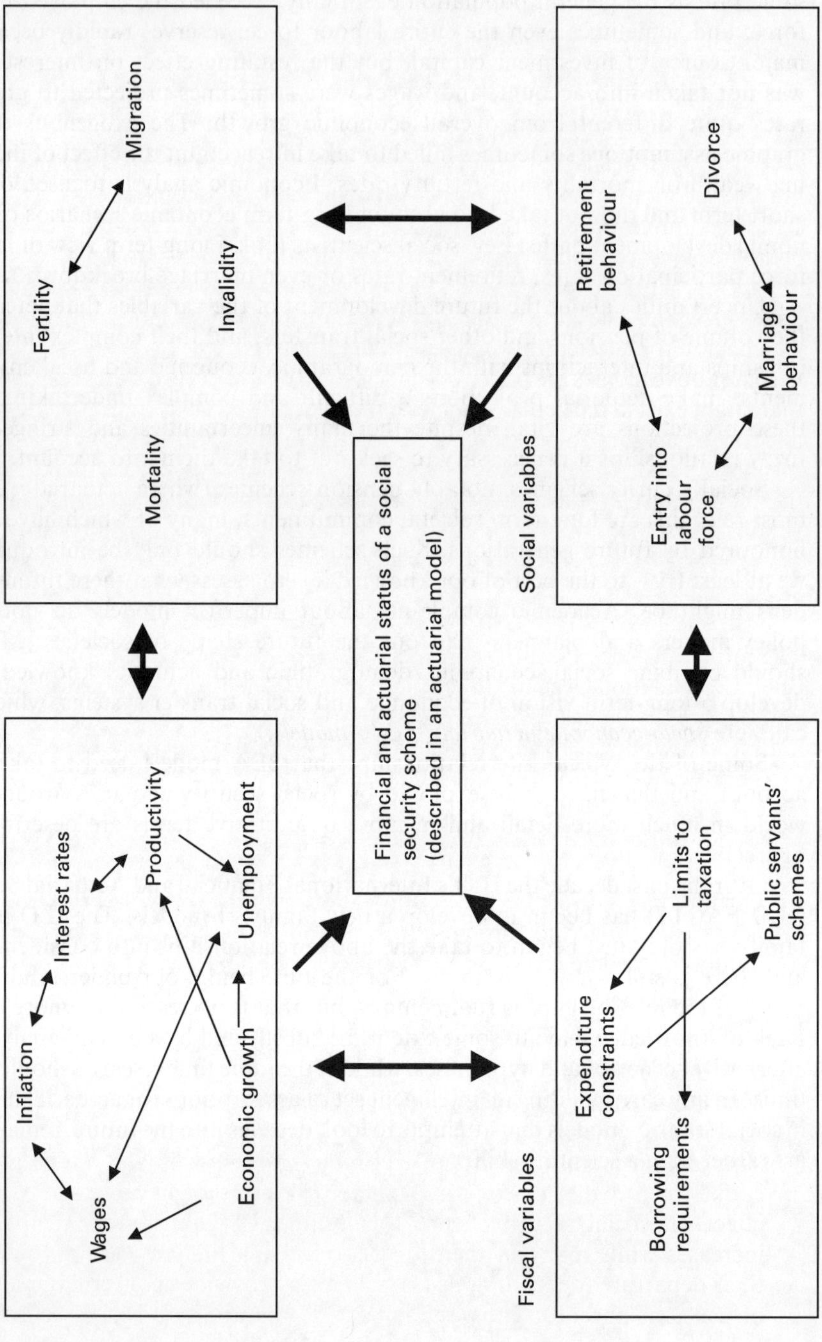

Actuarial practice in social security

Figure 1.1 Structural long-term relationships in SEA models

Demographic variables
- Fertility
- Migration
- Mortality
- Invalidity

Social variables
- Retirement behaviour
- Divorce
- Entry into labour force
- Marriage behaviour

Economic variables
- Inflation
- Interest rates
- Productivity
- Unemployment
- Wages
- Economic growth

Fiscal variables
- Expenditure constraints
- Limits to taxation
- Public servants' schemes
- Borrowing requirements

Financial and actuarial status of a social security scheme (described in an actuarial model)

1.2 THE NATURE OF THE INTERRELATIONSHIPS BETWEEN SOCIAL SECURITY SCHEMES AND THEIR DEMOGRAPHIC, ECONOMIC AND FISCAL ENVIRONMENTS

A list of key interrelationships between social security schemes and their demographic, economic, fiscal and social environments is given in box 1.1. The list serves a double purpose. Firstly, it is a checklist for establishing exogenous demographic, economic and budgetary assumptions that have a crucial impact on actuarial projections. Secondly, it serves as a list of potential variables affecting the future financial equilibrium of social security scheme, which should be tested through sensitivity analysis.

The above factors are only a crude selection of a variety of other relationships that might exist in particular schemes. However, the box can serve as a first guideline for the actuary to reflect on the potential interrelationships for modelling a specific scheme. The following paragraphs provide some more explanations for the main interrelationships. More details can be found in Chapter 9 and in Scholz et al. (2000).

1.2.1 Demographic and behavioural linkages

The future of a social security scheme is closely linked to the development of the general population. Ageing affects, in particular, pensions and health schemes, and is generally the result of decreasing fertility rates combined with the improving life expectancy. The development of the general population directly affects the number of contributors and beneficiaries.

Each actuarial valuation must, therefore, reflect the impact of the key characteristics of the future evolution of the general population:

- Fertility has a direct impact on the labour supply but with a time lag until newborns enter the labour force; labour supply affects the potential number of people covered by social security;
- Increasing life expectancy implies that old-age pensions and health benefits are paid for longer periods, and health benefits for the elderly might be substantially more costly than for the young;
- Migration usually has a lesser impact, depending on the magnitude and age structure of migrants as well as on their pattern of migration. For example, if migration mainly consists of incoming workers who will later leave the country before they reach retirement age, then this might cause a net positive effect on social security, since the number of contributors temporarily increases while many of them do not receive a lifetime pension owing to their departure (depending on the scheme's provisions concerning payment of pensions abroad). Thus, the impact of migration on social security can

Box 1.1 Interactions between social security and the general context

Influencing factor	Influenced variable
Demography on social security	
Population structure and development	• number of contributors; number of beneficiaries
Social security on demography	
Benefit structure and level	• number of children (through maternity and parental benefits); number of older people (through health care benefits and lower old-age poverty)
Economy on social security	
Employment	• number of contributors
Wages	• contribution income; level of earnings-related benefits
Inflation	• indexation of benefits
Interest rates and financial markets	• investment income
Social security on the economy	
Contributions	• disposable income; wages; labour cost, employment, productivity; labour supply
Benefit levels and provisions	• income distribution; consumption; productivity
Reserves	• savings, capital stock and growth
Public budgets on social security	
Public servants' schemes	• number of contributors and beneficiaries in a general scheme
Expenditure constraints	• income from public subsidies
Publicly accepted limits of taxation	• contribution income (if contributions are perceived to be taxes)
Public borrowing requirements	• investment returns
Social security on public budgets	
Annual cash flows	• potential public borrowing; potential volume of subsidies required
Benefit levels and administration	• public expenditure through social assistance
Social behaviour on social security	
Labour force participation rates	• number of contributors and beneficiaries
Retirement behaviour	• number of beneficiaries and benefit amounts
Marriage and child-bearing behaviour	• number of beneficiaries
Divorce	• number of beneficiaries
Social security on social behaviour	
Benefit levels and structure	• number of beneficiaries; labour force participation

only be determined with a consistent view on social security provisions and the existence of international social protection agreements.
- The actuary should be aware of the influence of urbanization on the social security coverage of the general population: coverage is usually higher where a large proportion of the population lives in urban areas as opposed to a predominantly rural population.[2]

Decent social protection benefits will reduce old-age poverty and make people healthier, which will raise life expectancy. Attractive maternity and parental benefits may also induce more couples to have more children, although it is not clear whether social policy can really influence people's reproductive behaviour. Likewise, in the case of divorce it is uncertain whether fair pension-splitting arrangements actually influence formal divorce behaviour; people might agree to remain in pro-forma marriages if the benefit protection for divorced people is deemed insufficient.

The impact of pension levels on retirement behaviour seems unquestionable; people will obviously retire when they can afford to retire. As schemes mature and average benefit levels increase, the actuary should expect that retirement rates at certain ages will increase. Benefit levels and benefit conditions will also have an impact on the incidence of invalidity, levels of which might be expected to be higher if alternative benefits, such as unemployment benefits, are considered unattractive.

1.2.2 Economic linkages[3]

Social security systems usually serve two basic functions, that of:

- alleviating poverty by providing a safety net to individuals facing destitution; and
- maintaining income for individuals during periods of economic inactivity.

It is widely recognized that social and economic developments must proceed together by way of carefully designed benefit protection in line with available resources. Social security enhances economic development by providing a benefit delivery system that provides:

- health services that improve the health of workers and their families and hence have an impact on productivity;
- income-replacement benefits (such as old-age and invalidity pensions, sickness and unemployment benefits) that affect the income distribution and, inter alia, permit the maintenance of consumption levels for people during inactive phases of their lives;

- anti-poverty benefits that help reduce poverty and maintain social peace, which is a crucial prerequisite for economic growth.

Reserves held by social security schemes may also have an important and positive impact on the economy. Social security reserves can be used as an instrument to direct investments to particular purposes defined by national economic policy, which may have a positive impact on economic growth. It is less clear, however, whether social security funding does increase the overall national level of savings. Countries with high levels of funding of the national pension systems (such as the United States) may still have a lower overall savings rate than a country with a low level of overall pension funding (such as Germany).

The level of contributions levied on the gross income of workers directly affects their disposable income available for consumption. This indirectly affects domestic demand for goods and services, which, in turn, affects GDP and the level of employment. Formal-sector employment may also be negatively affected as workers may decide to escape to the informal sector to avoid paying contributions, which is a behavioural pattern that reduces productivity in the economy. To the extent that social security taxes and contributions are perceived to increase labour costs, they may also have a negative impact on the demand for labour. However, if one considers overall labour costs as the critical determinant for the demand for labour, the actual allocation of those costs to wages and social security taxes or contributions may be irrelevant as long as increasing social security costs can be financed by reductions in disposable wages. Understandably, a growing economy with real wage increases offers more potential for financing social security benefits than a contracting economy where real wages are falling.

Most of the economic literature suggests that employer payroll taxes are passed back to labour in the form of lower wages or lower benefits. The wage rates that an employer pays must eventually reflect the total payroll costs for workers. These payroll costs will include the employer's contributions to pension and insurance plans, whether public (payroll taxes) or private. For example, an employer might be prepared to trade off higher nominal wages for lower pension contributions. Similarly, faced with higher taxes for public pensions, workmen's compensation or for unemployment insurance (UI), an employer might offer lower wages to workers or seek to reduce payroll-related costs (for example, for private pensions or insurance, etc.). Exceptions to this could occur in the case of abrupt rises in payroll costs, outside the employer's control (for contributions to public social security programmes, for example). Then, the employer might not be able to offset those increases immediately through lower wages or through some other reduction in payroll costs. The employer would temporarily be faced with higher costs and lower profitability. Another exception would be the situation of workers being paid the minimum legal wage and benefits. In this case, an individual employer might not be able to adopt any offsetting reductions, although the employer could seek to exert pressure on public decision-makers to change either the minimum wage rate or the level of the payroll tax.

On the microeconomic level, social security benefits certainly have an impact on individual behaviour. Generous benefit levels may induce people to leave the labour market. In countries with excess labour demand, this in itself may not affect total employment and the level of GDP but it might lead to higher social security contributions and taxes, which, in turn, might influence the economy through lower disposable incomes and, consequently, inflationary pressures.

The net impact of social security on the economy and, in particular, the numerical size of that impact is not a priori clear for all countries at different stages of economic development. The fact is that actuaries need to be aware of these effects and to build coherent economic scenarios when developing the economic assumptions for their projections. Economic expertise should be sought. And yet, alternative scenarios will probably still have to be built, since complex possible future developments are unlikely to be captured in just one scenario.

1.2.3 Fiscal linkages

There are a large number of financial links between government budgets and all major social security schemes. They are explored in more detail in the recent ILO publication on pensions (Gillion et al., 2000).

Many government budgets have substantially benefited from the existence of national pension schemes. Young pension schemes normally produce large surpluses in their early years, as that is a period when substantial contributions are collected but no, or few, pensions are paid out. These surpluses might simply have been absorbed into the general government budget either through straight transfers (as was the case in Central and Eastern Europe) or through lending (as was the case in many African schemes). On the other hand, governments often subsidize social security systems, even if they are formally independent financial institutions. Direct government involvement in financing pensions is not limited to full financing of pension benefits as occurs, for example, in Denmark. Governments may also subsidize social security pension schemes through general subsidies or specific transfers. The public financing of transition costs – which fall due when a country is changing its social security pension scheme from a pay-as-you-go (PAYG) or partially funded defined-benefit (DB) scheme to a fully funded defined-contribution (DC) scheme – is another form of explicit government financing of a national social security scheme.

In addition to direct financial costs, governments may bear indirect costs or be liable for potential costs. Government participation in the financing of pensions, for example, is becoming increasingly important, especially following the reforms that mandated some national pension provisions to private entities.

Actuarial practice in social security

This type of reform confirms the explicit role of the government as a financial guarantor (or ultimate underwriter) of social security and private pension schemes. This contingent liability through underwriting of social security or private pension schemes can take several explicit and implicit forms. An explicit form occurs when the social insurance law stipulates that the government will cover potential deficits of a social security scheme. The latter are often linked with an obligation of the scheme to reduce the deficit, either through increasing contributions or through expenditure reductions. In other cases, governments might guarantee minimum pension levels by complementing social security or private pension benefits. An implicit guarantee is given if – owing to public political pressure – the government must bail out non-performing, private, community-based or social security schemes. A form of indirect bailing out of failing public and private pension schemes is the increased payment of social assistance benefits in case pension systems are not in a financial position to pay benefits in full, or when benefits are provided at a low level. Governments under political pressure and with sufficient resources would probably also bail out informal-sector, community-based schemes. Thus, through explicit or implicit financial guarantees, governments provide reinsurance for public and private social transfer systems. Even if they do not directly finance pension or social security benefits, they underwrite multiple risks and remain the ultimate guarantor of national social security schemes.

Even if governments farm out some of the social security benefit delivery to the private or parastatal sector and accept no open financial liabilities, these benefit costs will still have an impact on the government budget. Contributing and tax-paying citizens demand that governments provide – directly or indirectly – a certain range and quality of services or provide re-insurance of essential levels of social protection, and they naturally want to minimize the cost of these services in terms of overall taxes and contributions. There is no rule as to what the acceptable limits of overall taxation plus contribution payments are, but there are limits in each society, indicated by increasing resistance to tax and contribution payments. If, for example, pension costs were to increase steeply, the accompanying higher contribution rates would de facto crowd out other social or public spending, since it may be politically impossible to increase overall revenues to the same extent.

While it may not always be possible to build all these interdependencies into actuarial models, it still remains the responsibility of the social security actuary to warn the government of the potential effects that budgetary decisions might have on a social security scheme and, ultimately, on the government budget. Failing to report likely skyrocketing future needs for the public subsidies of a pension scheme (under legal status quo conditions) at an early stage could subject the long-term financial stability of a scheme to a substantial political risk, as the government might find itself unable to honour its legal commitments.

1.2.4 The social security actuary's central role in social governance

The actuary needs to check the plausibility of the many demographic, economic, fiscal and social assumptions that go into the modelling process. It is the actuary who has to judge whether the vision of the future development of a given society and economy that underlies all these assumptions is consistent and realistic. It is the actuary who has to alert the government and the governors of individual social security schemes to obvious inconsistencies and incompatibilities in national social, economic and fiscal policies. It is necessary for the actuary to indicate overly promising financing, under-financing, too low benefit levels, as well as the misallocation of resources and risks for future government budgets. The actuary needs to act as the guardian of financial rationality in the social policy formulation process.

Notes

[1] The term social security as used here encompasses all social transfers in kind and in cash that are organized by state or parastatal organizations or are agreed upon through collective bargaining processes. Benefits include cash transfers, such as pensions, short-term cash benefits (sickness and maternity benefits, unemployment benefits), as well as benefits in kind, such as health services. This book does not deal with social assistance benefits and health services, which are examined in two other volumes in the Quantitative Methods in Social Protection series (see Scholz et al., 2000, and Cichon et al., 1999).

[2] Cf. ILO: *Introduction to social security* (Geneva, 1984), p. 123.

[3] This chapter discusses only broadly the economic context of actuarial practice in social security. The reader is encouraged to consult the following publications for more in-depth discussions: W. Scholz et al.: *Social budgeting* (Geneva, ILO/ISSA, 2000); ILO: *Introduction to social security* (Geneva, 1984); L. Thompson: *Older and wiser: The economics of public pensions* (Washington, DC, The Urban Institute Press, 1998); N. Barr: *The economics of the welfare state* (London, Weidenfeld and Nicolson, 1993, 2nd ed.); H.J. Aaron: *Economic effects of social security* (Washington, DC, The Brookings Institution, 1982); Social Security Council: *Planning and financing in the nineties*, Proceedings of the Sixth Seminar for Actuaries in Social Security (Zoetermeer, The Netherlands, 1992).

THE ROLE OF ACTUARIES IN SOCIAL SECURITY 2

From the very beginning of the operation of a social security scheme, the actuary plays a crucial role in analysing its financial status and recommending appropriate action to ensure its viability. More specifically, the work of the actuary includes assessing the financial implications of establishing a new scheme, regularly following up its financial status and estimating the effect of various modifications that might have a bearing on the scheme during its existence.

This chapter presents a discussion of these various areas of intervention and the ways in which actuarial services are usually organized in the public sector.

2.1 THE VALUATION OF A NEW SCHEME

The actuarial valuation carried out at the inception of a scheme should answer one of the following two questions:

- How much protection can be provided with a given level of financial resources?
- What financial resources are necessary to provide a given level of protection?

The uncertainties associated with the introduction of a social security scheme require the intervention of, among other specialists, the actuary, which usually starts during the consultation process that serves to set the legal bases of the scheme. This process may be lengthy, as negotiations take place among the various interest groups, i.e. the government, workers and employers. Usually, each interest group presents a set of requests relating to the extent of the benefit protection that should be offered and to the amount of financial resources that should be allocated to cover the risks. This is where the work of the actuary becomes crucial, since it consists of estimating the long-term financial implications of proposals, ultimately providing a solid quantitative framework that will guide future policy decisions.

The difficulty of valuating a new scheme relates to the high level of uncertainty associated with the development of assumptions that cannot be based on the scheme's specific experience. For example, assumptions are necessary to simulate the compliance of workers and employers with the payment of contributions or to project retirement behaviour. These assumptions are highly relevant to the future financial situation of the scheme, and their development in the context of an initial valuation remains a tedious exercise. Various approaches exist to set these assumptions, such as extrapolating from past general economic/demographic statistics or using the experience of the scheme in other countries with similar characteristics. But, in the end, it is the judgement of the actuary that is essential.

2.1.1 Legal versus actual coverage

"Who will be covered?" One preoccupation of the actuary concerns the definition of the covered population and the way that the coverage is enforced. Coverage may vary according to the risk covered. A number of countries have started by covering only government employees, gradually extending coverage to private-sector employees, and eventually to the self-employed. A gradual coverage allows the administrative structure to develop its ability to support a growing insured population and to have real compliance with the payment of contributions. Some categories of workers, such as government employees, present no real problem of compliance because the employer's administrative structure assures a regular and controlled payment of contributions. For other groups of workers, the situation may be different. These issues will have an impact on the basic data that the actuary will need to collect on the insured population and on the assumptions that will have to be set on the future evolution of coverage and on the projected rate of compliance.

2.1.2 Benefit provisions

"What kind of benefit protection will be provided?" Social security schemes include complex features, and actuaries are usually required, along with policy analysts, to ensure consistency between the various rules and figures. The following design elements will affect the cost of the scheme and require the intervention of the actuary:

- What part of workers' earnings will be subject to contributions and used to compute benefits? (This refers to the floor and ceiling of earnings adopted for the scheme.)
- What should be the earnings replacement rate in computing benefits?
- Should the scheme allow for cross-subsidization between income groups through the benefit formula?

Actuarial practice in social security

- What will be the required period of contribution as regards eligibility for the various benefits?
- What is the normal retirement age?
- How should benefits be indexed?

As the answers to these questions will each have a different impact on the cost of the scheme, the actuary is asked to cost the various benefit packages. The actuary should ensure that discussions are based on solid quantitative grounds and should try to reach the right balance between generous benefits and pressure on the scheme's costs.

At this stage, it is usual to collect information on the approaches followed in other countries. Such comparisons inform the policy analysts on the extent of possible design features. Furthermore, mistakes made in other countries can, hopefully, be avoided.

2.1.3 Financing provisions

"Who pays and how much?" The financial resources of a social insurance scheme come from contributions, investment earnings on the scheme's assets and sometimes from government subsidies. Contributions are generally shared between employers and employees, except under employment injury schemes, which are normally fully financed by employers.

The actuarial valuation provides a projection of the scheme's expenditure, such that different schedules of contribution rates can be assessed on the basis of different financing methods. If the primary focus of policy-makers is expressed in terms of a given maximum contribution rate to be levied on salaries, then the actuary needs to suggest alternative benefit designs that will allow the total cost to stand at an affordable level. But if the primary objectives are set in terms of a given level of benefit protection, then the actuary needs to recommend alternative contribution rate schedules.

With long-term benefits, costs will escalate because of the maturing process of the scheme. In the actuarial valuation of a new scheme, the actuary focuses particular attention on this process in order to make everyone aware of the expected future increases in contribution rates. It is important that the actuarial projections be performed with a horizon of 50 years and more to provide policy-makers with a complete picture of the future pattern of increasing expenditure.

This issue is related to determining a funding objective for the scheme or, alternatively, the level of reserves set aside to support the scheme's future obligations. The funding objective may be set in the law. If not, then the actuary will recommend one. In the case of a sickness benefits scheme, for example, the optimal level of reserves to be maintained has to be established, taking into account possibly unfavourable, short-term experience. In the case of a pension scheme, however, the funding objective will be placed in a longer-term context and may consider, for example, the need to smooth future contribution rate increases. Different financing mechanisms are available to match these funding objectives. For example, the pension law may provide for a scaled contribution rate to allow for a substantial accumulation of reserves during the first 20 years and thereafter a gradual move towards a PAYG system with minimal long-term reserves. In the case of employment injury schemes, transfers between different generations of employers tend to be avoided; hence, these schemes require a higher level of funding.

The actuarial report presents the viability of the scheme under various economic and demographic scenarios, giving the financiers of the system an evaluation of the risk they face with regard to the sufficiency of the legal or recommended contribution rates. The report also informs the general population on the extent of funds raised under the social security system and how these funds are expected to be used for investment purposes and for meeting future benefit obligations.

2.2 PERIODIC REVIEW OF AN ONGOING SCHEME

For a social insurance scheme, the periodical review is like a personal health check-up; it acts as the monitoring tool for the scheme's financial aspects, providing an opportunity for rapid adjustments to be made if actual experience is deviating from what has been projected. In fact, it is not so much the actual numbers included in an actuarial report that are important but how they change from one valuation to the next. The reader of an actuarial report should know that long-term projections will change at each review. What is important is the direction they are moving in.

The law governing social security pensions usually requires that an actuarial review of a social security system be undertaken every three to five years. As mentioned in the introduction of the 1995 actuarial report of the Government Actuary of the United Kingdom:

> The major purpose of the five-yearly reviews by the Government Actuary of the operation of the Social Security Acts is to establish the rates of contribution likely to be required in future years to meet the cost of the benefits provided for under the National Insurance Scheme.

Unlike pension schemes, the review for work injury and UI schemes is often made on an annual basis.

2.2.1 Analysis of past results

The periodical actuarial review starts with a comparison of the scheme's actual demographic and financial experience against the projections made in the previous review. The experience analysis serves to identify items of revenue or expenditure that have evolved differently than predicted in the assumptions and to assess the extent of the gap. It focuses on the number of contributors and beneficiaries, average insurable earnings and benefits, the investment return on the scheme's assets and the level of administrative expenses. Each of these items is separated and analysed by its main components, showing, for example, a difference in the number of new retirees, unexpected increases in average insurable earnings, higher indexing of pensions than projected, etc. The actuary determines the causes of the discrepancies, which may result in some actuarial assumptions being adjusted in the ongoing review.

2.2.2 Revision of assumptions and methods

The experience analysis and the revised economic and demographic prospects indicate areas of adjustment to the actuarial assumptions[1] used in the previous valuation. For example, a recent change in retirement behaviour may induce a new future expected retirement pattern. A slowdown in the economy will require a database revision of the number of workers contributing to the scheme. However, as actuarial projections for pensions are performed over a long period, a change in recently observed data will not necessarily require any modifications to be made to long-term assumptions. The actuary looks primarily at consistency between assumptions, and should not give undue weight to recent short-term conjectural effects.

In addition to revising assumptions, the periodical actuarial review is the appropriate time to improve the actuarial model used for projections. Some refinements may be introduced to account for the availability of a more extensive database, for example.

2.2.3 Revision of financial projections

Based on the revised assumptions and methods, projections are produced according to the updated provisions of the law. In that respect, the actuary ensures that all legal modifications since the last valuation have been taken into account. Sensitivity tests showing the variability of results under different demographic and economic scenarios complete the actuarial projections.

On the investment side, the actuary is usually involved in the establishment and revision of the investment policy. The assumption that the actuary uses for the accumulation of social security reserves must reflect the investment policy. The actuary should make people aware of the fact that the contribution rates have been determined with the expectation of a specific level of investment return. A change in the investment policy thus has an effect on the amount of contributions required by the scheme, and the actuary has a role in explaining these consequences.

2.2.4 Financing recommendations

The nature of the actuary's recommendations on financing depends on the provisions of the law concerning the determination of contribution rates. If the law is silent in this regard, the periodical actuarial review sets a scale of contribution rates that will ensure the financial viability of the scheme, given that present benefit provisions are maintained indefinitely. If the law does not specify the rule for the determination of contribution rates, the actuarial report normally recommends such a rule to ensure that the scheme remain in actuarial balance.

If contribution rates are already specified in the law, the actuarial review represents the tool for measuring the long-term financial balance of the social security scheme. In this case, the report shows the evolution of social security funds (the reserve) with the use of the legal contribution rates, and comments on their sufficiency. A projected financial imbalance will necessitate measures to restore the financial equilibrium of the scheme. These measures may include modifications to financing provisions (a rise in contribution rates or an extension of the contributory salary base) and/or modifications to benefit provisions.

The periodic review confirms whether the funding objectives of the scheme are being met or not, taking into account the scheme's maturity.

2.2.5 Other recommendations

The observed level of coverage, the actual replacement rate of benefits, the part of total earnings subject to contributions are all parameters that are usually analysed in the actuarial report. For example, the analysis may lead to a recommendation concerning the design of the benefit formula. The actuary will also address the issue of redistribution between people of different earnings classes and generations. The recent evolution of earnings subject to contributions may show distortions, such as, for example, when comparing the level of basic insurable earnings with the national minimum wage or when comparing the earnings ceiling with the average earnings of insured persons. The indexing mechanisms used to revalue past earnings or to adjust pensions in payment may be inadequate and may lead to a gradual decrease in the real value of benefits. Eligibility conditions may be too generous for some types of benefits and too stringent for others and, as a consequence, they will distort the attribution of benefits or cause unnecessary costs. All these possible weaknesses usually give rise to a recommendation by the actuary.

2.3 ACTUARIAL CONSIDERATIONS AT THE REFORM STAGE

In a reform process, the actuary's intervention depends on the nature and extent of the reforms to be made. Often, legal modifications to an ongoing scheme are aimed at consolidating the scheme's long-term viability. They usually concern the scheme's coverage, the level of benefits or the financing provisions. However, a government may contemplate instituting a structural reform to modify the mechanisms for providing economic security, which means completely reformulating benefit provisions or adding new insurance or savings mechanisms. The context of these two types of reform is addressed below.

2.3.1 Amendments to a scheme

Modifications to an ongoing scheme may concern benefit eligibility conditions, the amount of benefits, the admission of a new category of insured person, the introduction of protection against new contingencies, or new financing provisions. The actuarial valuation serves to measure the financial impact of such measures on the contribution rates. Modifications to other components of the retirement package (such as mandatory occupational schemes) may also require a review of the benefit provisions of the social security scheme. This would imply an evaluation by the actuary of joint replacement rates and of other social protection measures.

The law governing social insurance often requires that a special actuarial report accompany any proposed modification. This is necessary in order to show decision-makers the financial impact of the proposed legislative change. Sometimes, the periodical actuarial review itself will include the valuation of the actuary's recommended modifications. The actuarial report proposing consolidation measures shows the long-term demographic and financial development prospects, given that the proposed amendments are adopted. These projections are compared with those produced under the status quo legal provisions. It should be noted that the introduction of a new covered contingency or the extension of coverage to new categories of workers will require many of the issues described previously on the valuation of a new scheme to be taken into account.

2.3.2 Structural reform of a system

Structural reforms may be of several types. In Chile, for example, a DB pension scheme has been converted into a DC scheme. In this type of reform, the attention of the actuary focuses mainly on the investment of contributions, the determination of individual annuity factors, the presence of minimum benefit guarantees and the acknowledgement by the new system of past rights acquired under the former scheme. Actuarial support is thus essential to estimate the amount of total accrued liability under the former scheme and to determine the various scenarios of recognition of these past rights by the new system. Transition considerations are crucial.

In other types of reforms (in Poland and Sweden, for example), the PAYG scheme is transformed into a notional DC scheme. Even if the contribution rate becomes the fixed parameter, this kind of arrangement keeps many of its DB

The role of actuaries in social security

characteristics. In these types of reforms, actuaries are involved in determining the annuity factors that will be used at the time of retirement for the conversion of accumulated funds into periodic payments. They also analyse the balance between contributions and the level of benefits offered by the scheme.

Other structural reforms, encountered in some African or Caribbean countries, for example, are aimed at converting a provident fund (DC type) into a social insurance scheme of the DB type. In this instance, the actuary studies various alternatives in using accumulated individual balances under the former system and converts them into past service equivalents under the new DB scheme.

2.4 SHORT-TERM PROJECTIONS

Every year, social security institutions must submit to their governments a proposed budget of their revenue and expenditure for the coming year, for which the actuary prepares short-term projections of contributions, investment income, benefits and administrative expenditure. These projections are also used by the social security institution or centralized units of the government for planning purposes. For example, social security institution managers use these figures to determine the human resources and computer capacity needed for the treatment of claims and the collection of contributions. Short-term projections normally provide monthly cash-flow projections, and are a useful tool for investment managers having to take liquidity requirements into account in their short-term investment strategies.

Short-term projections differ substantially from typical long-term actuarial valuations in terms of methodology and assumption refinements. The exercise requires the input of an actuary, who must work in close collaboration with government economists, accountants and investment managers. Unlike a periodical actuarial valuation, assumptions are set within a short-term horizon (usually established according to the government's own economic forecasts) and try to reflect more precisely than the periodic actuarial valuation the scheme's monthly revenue and expenditure.

2.5 AD HOC ACTUARIAL SUPPORT AND OTHER RELATED FIELDS

In addition to the clearly defined actuarial assignments that take place at critical times in the existence of a social security scheme, the actuarial team in the public sector also assumes a wide range of other functions to support the management of the social security scheme and the minister responsible for social policy. The team is also involved in communicating social security financial matters to the public.

2.5.1 Ad hoc support

The actuarial team working in a social insurance institution may be asked to advise, on an ad hoc basis, on the effects of various modifications related to benefit and financing provisions. These requests may come from the management of the social security institution or from the government. A flexible actuarial projection model must be available and readily adaptable for this purpose. In some cases, actuaries are part of a team of research and policy advisory services through which they report to the ministerial authorities on various improvements in social security programmes.

2.5.2 Statistical reports

Actuaries need to maintain a statistical database for their valuations. As actuaries are aware of the available statistics, take a critical approach to them and possess a mathematical and statistical background, they are generally involved in the preparation of the social insurance annual statistical reports that are made available to the public. These reports are used by various government bodies and the general public, and serve as research material for academic studies.

2.5.3 Performance indicators

A social insurance institution must monitor the efficiency of its contribution collection, its benefit delivery and its administration in general. The development of performance indicators with regard to the design of the scheme, its administration and its financing serves these purposes. These indicators are calculated from the administrative and financial data of the scheme and make use of economic data. They are followed over time and indicate when and if it is necessary to take action. As they require the manipulation of statistics and because some indicators are directly related to the evolution of the financial status of the scheme, the involvement of the actuary is usually required.

2.5.4 Social security agreements

Actuaries are involved in the negotiation and administration of social security agreements. These agreements are established for migrant workers, primarily to allow the recognition of insurance periods realized in a country by the social insurance scheme of another country. The primary objective of a social security agreement is the coordination of national laws. These agreements are generally based on the following principles: equal treatment of nationals and non-nationals, reciprocity, maintenance of acquired rights and maintenance of rights in the course of acquisition.

The negotiation of social security agreements requires legal expertise. However, it also involves calculations concerning eligibility and benefit determination and requires a good knowledge of the operations of the social security institutions of both countries. So actuaries are frequently called on to participate in the negotiation of such arrangements. The work of the actuary focuses first on comparing and checking the compatibility of the design of both social security schemes. Once compatibility has been assessed, the actuary is primarily involved in the calculation aspects of the agreement (totalization and proration) and in explaining the benefit provisions and financing features of the national schemes.

2.6 ORGANIZATION OF ACTUARIAL SERVICES

Social security actuarial work can be performed through various types of organizations. During the discussions surrounding the inception of a new scheme, governments usually use external actuarial services, mainly because the administrative structure of the scheme is not yet in place. Once the scheme has been established, the financial and other quantitative issues require day-to-day actuarial support, and a social security institution often chooses to rely on its own actuarial resources.

Government actuarial services may be established for the benefit of a specific institution administering a social insurance scheme. In this case, beyond actuarial matters concerning the scheme, the government actuarial services also execute other financial and statistical tasks related to the scheme because of the quantitative background of its resources. They perform the "number-crunching" for the institution. For example, the Office of the Chief Actuary of the Social Security Administration of the United States employs several actuaries who prepare long-term projections for the annual actuarial review of the Old-Age, Survivors, and Disability Insurance (OASDI), short-term projections and various actuarial or statistical studies. In Japan, actuaries work in two divisions within the country's Ministry of Health and Welfare: one team produces actuarial valuations, statistical reports and other policy papers related to public pension schemes and is concerned with the supervision of contracted-out occupational schemes; the other team supervises top-up occupational schemes. Actuaries are also employed in Japan's Ministry of Labour for the valuation of UI and employment injury schemes.

Another way of organizing government actuarial services is to centralize the actuarial expertise into a single department, which performs most of the actuarial work required by the government. This type of arrangement exists in the United Kingdom and Canada. Centralized units are responsible for the valuation of the social security pension scheme, the valuation of civil servants' pension plans, the supervision of occupational pension schemes and the supervision of financial institutions. They thus require their actuaries to have the full range of actuarial skills, since these units are an amalgamation of several specialist actuarial departments. In Canada, however, a separate actuarial department is responsible for the actuarial valuation of the UI scheme at the federal level.

Some international organizations have their own actuaries to support their action in the field of social security. This is the case at the ILO and the World Bank. Owing to the limited financial resources of these organizations, they usually complete their actuarial team by relying on a network of actuaries from various countries for a certain number of ad hoc assignments.

Government auditing procedures often require that the work of government actuaries be audited by competent external professionals as a means of ensuring the quality and independence of the actuarial work undertaken. External auditing may be done by private consulting firms, by international organizations providing actuarial expertise or by actuarial associations.

Notes

[1] The main assumptions used for an actuarial valuation are discussed in Chapters 9 and 10.

PART II

THE VALUATION OF PUBLIC PENSION SCHEMES

THE CHARACTERISTICS OF PUBLIC PENSION SCHEMES 3

Public pension schemes have certain characteristics that differentiate them from occupational schemes and which may affect the way an actuarial valuation is conducted. This chapter focuses on some of the characteristics of a social security scheme that may influence actuarial practice in the pension field. For some items, a comparison is made with occupational pensions.

3.1 BROAD COVERAGE AND MANDATORY PARTICIPATION

3.1.1 The open-group method

Social security schemes are generally set up to cover a large part of the labour force. The scheme may be universal, meaning that it applies to almost all the workers in a country, or it may cover some defined sectors or categories of employment. But more usually it covers a large group of workers. Once the intended covered population has been defined, participation in the scheme is usually mandatory (some schemes may permit voluntary coverage, but they do not represent a large part of the total coverage). Mandatory coverage ensures a continuous flow of new entrants into the scheme as the number of employed people is normally assumed to increase over time.

In order to demonstrate the long-term financial developments of the scheme – i.e. that long-term funds will be sufficient to finance the incoming pensions on a continuous basis – the actuarial valuation projects revenue and expenditure, taking into consideration the people who will enter the scheme in the future. The procedure used is called the "projection method" or the "open-group method".

In an occupational pension scheme, on the other hand, the actuarial valuation is usually made on the basis of a closed group of participants. The actuarial valuation considers only those people who have acquired rights under the scheme before the valuation date. Costs are calculated on an individual basis and the contributions necessary to finance a worker's pension are distributed over the working lifetime of that individual.

3.1.2 Links with the general context

Because of the size of the scheme and the fact that participation is mandatory, some workers will leave and then re-enter the social security scheme during the course of their careers. Re-entry may be with a different employer, but the social security scheme will fully recognize the past insurance history of the individual, as long as the old and the new jobs are part of the covered employment defined in the law. This continuity in coverage and the movement of participants in and out of the workforce compels the actuary to use a model that must be consistent with the general economic context of the country. The model has to take into account the evolution of the total population and of the total workforce. By contrast, an occupational scheme does not recognize a new employee's former pension plan, unless the pension plans of the two employers are part of the same multi-employer plan. There exist transfer agreements between pension plans, but they do not work on the basis of direct recognition of past insurance history.

3.1.3 Relevance of the scheme's experience

The broad coverage offered by a social security scheme means that more credibility may be attributed to the experience observed under the scheme itself. Assumptions concerning mortality rates, invalidity incidence, or retirement rates, for example, may often be based on the scheme's own statistics. The size of the scheme also has the advantage of leading to more predictability for some variables. Fewer fluctuations in experience imply that the actuary will have to use fewer margins for conservatism in the assumptions and will often reduce the need for important contingency reserves. The existence of a single scheme for a large number of participants also leads to economies of scale. This is reflected in, for example, the provision for administrative expenses that the actuary will project.

3.1.4 No underwriting

The fact that participation in a social security scheme is mandatory means that there is no underwriting of insurance risks as in individual life insurance. Underwriting relates to the need to study personal characteristics of a potential insured person in order to refer this insured person to an appropriate risk class and consequently to charge this person a premium related to, for example, the individual's health status. Social security is intended to cover everyone who falls under the legal definition of a covered person. Hence, mortality and invalidity experiences under a social security scheme include a greater proportion of "bad risks" in comparison to individual insurance. Actuarial assumptions, therefore, have to be established with appropriate probabilities of risk occurrence, reflecting the higher risk associated with coverage of non-underwritten cases.

3.2 GOVERNMENT SPONSORSHIP

An occupational pension plan may be sponsored by an employer, a group of employers or by a union, and pensions promised by the plan are supported by the accumulated reserves, the solvency of the employer, or sometimes by a system of plan termination insurance to which all plan sponsors contribute. There is thus a certain element of risk associated with the termination of an occupational scheme if the accumulated reserves (or the financial capacity of the employer) cannot support the totality of the rights accrued under the scheme.

Under a public pension scheme, there is normally no risk associated with the termination of the plan. The power of the government to increase taxes can always be used if the scheme experiences financial hardship. This does not mean that promised pensions are always paid at the level initially contemplated (the government may decide to reduce benefits to help the scheme's financing), but it means that there is not the same need to accumulate a reserve equal to the value of the accrued rights under the scheme. In the case of lack of funds, the contribution rate may be increased or other taxes may be levied by the government. The choice of a level of reserve to be accumulated under a social security scheme then becomes one of economic utility and intergenerational equity, rather than a means of increasing the security of benefits.

Government sponsorship also means that part of the population associates the payment of contributions with taxes, which may make the collection of contributions more difficult to enforce. Contribution compliance then becomes a critical assumption for the actuary. Current behaviour as regards the payment of contributions must be compared with the legal provisions concerning who should be covered. Investigation may be necessary as to the reasons for an eventual discrepancy between the legal and actual extent of coverage. Assumptions must be made on the future evolution of coverage, based on the current contribution collection procedures and on any institutional plan aimed at improving compliance.

3.3 SELF-FINANCING

Generally speaking, a public pension scheme is autonomous in terms of financing. Consequently, the financiers of the scheme and their share of the costs are well identified, and a specific account exists to receive contributions and pay all benefits and administrative expenses under the scheme. This also means that the work of the actuary will mainly consist of projecting the level of that account and of recommending a scale of contribution rates that will assure the maintenance of sufficient reserves to face the scheme's future expenditure. For that purpose, the operations of that account must be isolated from the operations of other social security schemes as well as from the government's own operations.

However, keeping these accounts separate is not always straightforward. Countries provide a certain number of different social security schemes, including short-term, long-term and employment injury benefits. These different branches operate under different financial systems and reserve objectives. The reserve objectives of short-term benefits (for example, to face fluctuations in experience) differ from those of a pension scheme (for example, long-term viability or equalization of contribution rates for various generations). In order to be able to recommend an appropriate financing strategy for the pension scheme, the actuary must be able to isolate the operations of the pension scheme from the operations of the other public programmes. Otherwise, there may be cross-subsidization between schemes, since contribution rates for the pension scheme in excess of the PAYG rate will create the illusion of an excess reserve that can be used to finance deficits in the short-term branches. Ensuring that the accounts of different schemes are kept separate is thus necessary, and the actuary needs to explain the reasons behind this requirement.

3.4 FUNDING FLEXIBILITY

There is a wide range of possible funding levels for a social security pension scheme, extending from the virtual absence of reserve (the PAYG system) to the accumulation of reserves equal to the value of total accrued rights under the scheme (full funding). As mentioned earlier, the ability of the scheme to meet its future financial commitments is not related to the amount of reserves in the social security account but more to its continuous capacity to raise contributions from present and future workers and employers.

When compared with the situation of occupational schemes, the level of funding under a social security scheme is not motivated by possible tax advantages. Occupational pension schemes may have tax incentives to increase the level of funding:[1]

- Employer contributions are usually tax-deductible (in the form of an allowable business expense against profits);
- The reduction of the unfunded liability may improve the after-tax profit (as a result of the application of accounting rules);
- No tax is usually payable on the investment income of the pension fund.

The funding objective of a social security scheme reflects other considerations. Firstly, a reserve may be set up to attenuate the effect of a short-term economic downturn on the contributory basis of the scheme. For example, a scheme may maintain a reserve equal to one or two years of benefits in order to be able to maintain the contribution rate at its current level when a recession brings high unemployment and slows down employment and wage growth.

Secondly, the reserve may represent a way of equalizing contribution rates of various generations of contributors. For a young scheme, the contribution rate necessary to finance current pensions is very low. In that case, it may be desirable to set the contribution rate at a level higher than the PAYG rate to avoid sharp future rises in the contribution rate. Several countries face a situation where a large number of people are currently at working age and will reach retirement age in the next few decades, leaving the following smaller generations with high social security costs. Some of those countries may decide to increase the contribution rate more rapidly (before the "baby-boom" generation retires) in order to increase the reserve and allow the contribution rates of future generations to be maintained at lower levels.

Thirdly, the maintenance of social security reserves may be desirable in an environment where wage increases are low and interest rates high. When the salary base is increasing rapidly, the PAYG financing strategy assures a continuous flow of income into the scheme and may be more advantageous than raising social security reserves on which returns are far from guaranteed. However, several countries facing chronic unemployment may find it attractive to search the alternative source of funds that represent investment earnings. Maintaining reserves may be the answer to a changing economic environment.

Fourthly, governments may decide to raise reserves as a way of financing the economic development of the country. Social security reserves represent public savings that can be used to finance infrastructures and projects. Opinions on this issue vary widely. Generally speaking, the existence of social security reserves should have a social utility. However, this objective should not be detrimental to the yield and security objectives that should stand behind the investment of social security reserves. The political sensitivity related to the maintenance of social security reserves is a factor that should be considered when establishing a funding objective.

3.5 REDISTRIBUTION MECHANISMS

3.5.1 Between earnings classes

The benefit formula of a social security scheme is usually biased in favour of workers with low earnings. It may take the form of a different replacement rate applicable to different earnings classes or it may result from the use of a flat-rate benefit that represents a larger proportion of low salaries. The use of a floor and/or a ceiling on contributory earnings may also contribute to the redistribution of benefits in favour of low-earning participants. These features of a social insurance scheme require that each actuarial review analyse the extent of the redistribution and its evolution over the years. The incidence of inflation, salary increases and the regularity of the adjustment of the scheme's parameters (such as the earnings ceiling) may modify over time the income redistribution among people of different earnings levels. A ceiling that is not periodically adjusted to reflect general wage increases will gradually make the benefits insignificant for high-earning participants. The actuary needs to investigate the evolution of replacement rates calculated for different classes of earnings and must be alert to any evolution contrary to the objectives of the scheme.

3.5.2 Between workers with different career patterns

The pension formula of a social insurance scheme normally provides for the exclusion of part of the contributory history during which earnings were lower. For example, the scheme may take into account only 80 per cent of the whole career of an individual in the computation of the average career earnings used in the benefit formula. This will be of benefit, for example, to people having undergone spells of unemployment. Some intervals, such as periods of invalidity or periods during which a person takes care of young children, may give rise to special credits to avoid any reduction in the pension associated with these episodes. These characteristics of a social insurance scheme affect the modelling of the actuarial valuation and require some adjustments in the treatment of scheme's data on past credits of insured persons.

3.5.3 In favour of married insured persons and large families

Pensions to widows, widowers and orphans as well as family supplements added to a retirement pension favour married people and those with children. In analysing a pension scheme, the actuary will try to obtain a picture of the current family situation of participants and will set assumptions on the evolution of these patterns.

3.5.4 Between generations

Redistribution can also result from intergenerational transfers. Some cohorts of people participating in a social security pension scheme may receive benefits loosely related to the value of contributions paid on their behalf because the cost of this cohort's pension may be spread over different generations of participants. This practice has the advantage, at the inception of a new social security scheme, of providing pensions to the first generations of insured persons at a level higher than would otherwise have been possible (grand-fathering provisions). This allows the problem of old-age poverty to be tackled from the inception of the scheme.

The extent of intergenerational transfers is related to the financial systems in use. The PAYG system is the one that leads to the majority of such transfers. Each generation's contributions serve, in fact, to pay for the benefits of the previous generations of participants. At the other extreme, occupational pension schemes provide for a full funding of pensions on an individual basis, financed during the working lifetime of the worker. In a fully funded scheme, the termination of the plan, in theory, should not affect the payment of future benefits accrued on the date of termination. On reaching retirement, the total present value of the pension of a participant is in reserve and no other participant will have to contribute further in order to assure the service of the periodic pension payments.

Contributors to a social security scheme generally accept that the first generations of pensioners in the scheme will receive relatively larger benefits. However, account must be taken, too, of the willingness of future generations of contributors to continue financing a scheme on that basis. The level of contribution rates must be set so as to preserve an acceptable ratio of benefits to contributions for each generation. The level of the pension scheme's contribution rate must also be compared with the present and future total contribution burden put on workers and employers by various public programmes. These are all considerations that might influence the choice of a financing strategy for the pension scheme.

Notes

[1] See Z. Bodie, O.S. Mitchell and J.A. Turner: *Securing employer-based pensions: An international perspective* (Philadelphia, Pension Research Council, 1996).

THE ACTUARIAL VALUATION PROCESS 4

The actuarial valuation of a social security scheme is a lengthy exercise. It is usually organized in a series of steps that are generally the same for all practitioners. These steps are presented here as much as possible in the chronological order in which they are usually taken. The importance of each stage obviously varies depending on the valuation's objectives and on the place of the valuation in the life of the scheme. For the valuation of a new scheme, it may be necessary to spend moretime designing the statistical base and building the model. On the other hand, regular valuations of a long-standing scheme normally put more emphasis on refining the actuarial assumptions and analysing the scheme's past experience.

Preparatory work

The objectives and scope of the actuarial valuation are first identified. The valuation may take the form of a periodic actuarial review or a scheme's reform. The terms of reference may include the regular actuarial review, plus some specific points for analysing, such as benefit adjustments or the financing strategy. One base scenario is selected and serves as the reference in comparisons of the various scenarios to be modelled. The valuation date is fixed and the length of the projection period is determined with regard to the objectives of the valuation.

A study of the scheme's provisions is undertaken at this stage as a guide to the following step – data collection. It includes a careful examination of eligibility conditions for entitlement to benefits, benefit formulae, indexing provisions, definition on insurable earnings, contribution rates and financing rules.

Data collection and analysis

The actuary then initiates the collection of input data that will feed the model. The data come principally from the scheme's administrative files, but statistics concerning general demographic and economic variables must be sought from the national statistical office or from other sources. The format and level of disaggregation of data have to be consistent with the scheme's provisions and the structure of the model. The data are analysed in detail for their consistency and validation tests are performed. In case of insufficient, unreliable or deficient data, the actuary may have to use alternative sources, which may include the conducting of surveys.

Financial statements and additional data collected on the various components of revenue and expenditure will allow an analysis of past experience and a reconciliation of the projections of the previous report. If there are significant differences, explanations must be sought before actuarial assumptions or parameters can be set. This reconciliation exercise can also serve as a test for the model, that is, trying to reproduce the current status of the scheme from the situation at the time of the last valuation date.

Model building and adjustments

Having in mind the objectives of the valuation and the database, it is now time to build the model or to update the one used for the last valuation. Important decisions to be made at this point concern the choice of computer support and programming language. How these are decided will depend on the data available, the objectives of the valuation and the possible need to simulate various scenarios. Most of the time, a model already exists and will just need to be adjusted to take into account legislative modifications made since the last valuation.

For the first valuation of the scheme, a generic model may be available. In this case, there will be a need to set the basic parameters, notably concerning the eligibility conditions for benefits, the benefit formula, the earnings floor and ceiling and the contribution rates, if specified by law.

Selection of assumptions and indicators

Assumptions are determined on the evolution of the general population (fertility, mortality, migration rates), economic development (growth, labour force, wages, interest rates) and scheme-specific variables (retirement behaviour, invalidity incidence, family characteristics, etc.). Different assumptions may be necessary for the different scenarios under study. For example, a simulation to measure the impact of an increase in the normal retirement age will normally require a new assumption on retirement rates.

Most assumptions refer to variables that are not independent. It is thus important that a set of assumptions selected for a specific scenario be internally consistent. There are many interdependencies that have to be taken into account when a set of assumptions is built. A few are mentioned here.

Economic, demographic and scheme-related assumptions are interdependent. Economic growth and technological developments (as expressed, for example, in the productivity growth ratio) determine demand for employment and wage levels. Employment demand can only be satisfied if the demographic development and labour force participation rates generate enough labour supply. Employment then determines the number of potential insured persons. Contribution income depends on insurable wages. Insurable wages ultimately depend on the share of wages in GDP (the sharing of income between capital and labour). Nominal wages will, in turn, depend on inflation rates in the long run. The same goes for nominal interest rates.

Retirement behaviour depends on the level of unemployment in the country, so do apparently invalidity rates. Even fertility and mortality patterns observed over long periods are not independent of long-term economic performance.

It is at this stage that the actuary selects the indicators that will be used for analysing results, including demographic ratios, financial ratios, PAYG cost rates, the general average premium (GAP), reserve ratios, etc.

Feeding of the model

It is now time to put into the model the data collected and the actuarial assumptions. The entry of data may be done with the help of clerical personnel but it needs to be closely supervised and validated by the actuary. A decision must be taken on which basis (whether monthly or annual) will be used for the entry of data and for the presentation of results.

Base run and results analysis

The following results obtained from the model for the first projection year will have to be validated by the actuary against the database and financial statements:

- the total contribution income and benefit expenditure of the first projection year;
- the initial number of contributors;
- the number of beneficiaries in payment on the valuation date;
- average contributory earnings and average pensions;
- the number of new beneficiaries of each type for the first year of projection;
- the age distribution of new old-age pensioners.

In addition, validation checks will have to be made concerning the projected figures on:

- the evolution over the years of the number of beneficiaries who were in payment on the valuation date and the evolution of the number of new incoming beneficiaries, for each type of benefit;

- the evolution of the ratio of beneficiaries to contributors and its comparison with the general population dependency ratio, with due consideration of the scheme's eligibility conditions;
- the evolution of the replacement ratios for each benefit and a comparison with the legal provisions concerning the benefit formula;
- the evolution of the PAYG rates generated by the model, a comparison with those projected in the last valuation and an explanation of any differences.

Sensitivity testing

In a deterministic model, sensitivity tests are the only means of estimating a range of realistic results. In this exercise, the most sensitive demographic and economic assumptions are modified and the model is run for every chosen assumption to measure its impact. Alternatively, blocks of assumptions may be tested in order to arrive at a limited set of consistent scenarios.

Additional simulations

Additional scenarios may concern modifications to benefit provisions, changes in financing strategy or modifications to the covered population. For the analysis of alternative reform scenarios, appropriate modifications are made to the base model. Minor modifications can be easy to handle, but more fundamental changes to the scheme may require the complete redesigning of the model. It is for this reason that the initial step concerning the valuation objectives and its scope is of utmost importance.

Writing of the report

The actuarial report contains information on the valuation's aims, the methodology and assumptions used by the actuary, an analysis of past results and the results of the projection concerning the base projections, alternative scenarios and sensitivity tests. It usually contains a series of recommendations, firstly on the financing of the scheme, but also on matters concerning benefit provisions and coverage. The report should be written clearly, using language that can be easily understood by readers unfamiliar with actuarial terminology.

Presentation of findings and recommendations

One important part of the valuation process consists of explaining the content of the report and presenting its main recommendations to political representatives and those responsible for the management of social security. This represents an opportunity to explain in more detail specific parts of the report that may appear overly technical, and to obtain feedback on the recommendations. A policy dialogue might follow in order to define the implementation of reforms or policies.

FINANCIAL SYSTEMS 5

The financing of a pension scheme refers to the orderly mechanisms by which resources are raised to support the scheme's expected future expenditure. This chapter shows how the financing of a public pension scheme can be organized. It starts by explaining the pattern of expenditure generally encountered under this type of scheme, followed by a description of the sources of revenue on which the financing may be based. A number of financial systems whereby an equilibrium between revenue and expenditure can be reached are presented in this chapter.

5.1 PATTERN OF EXPENDITURE OF A PENSION SCHEME

From the early years of its existence and until a pension scheme reaches a state of maturity, it experiences a pattern of increasing expenditures, resulting from the following factors:

- the number of pensioners increases each year as new cohorts qualify;
- the average length of service of new pensioners increases;
- the earnings on which pensions are based increase;
- longevity increases, affecting the average duration of payment;
- pensions are indexed.

After a period of 65 to 70 years, under stable conditions, the cost of a scheme expressed as a percentage of insured earnings normally stabilizes, since the first generation of young new entrants to the scheme has passed through the various stages of participation. A person enters the scheme around the age of 20, contributes to it for 40 years, becomes a pensioner and eventually dies, upon which a survivor's pension is awarded. On the death of the survivor or survivors all benefits related to the participant are ended.

Figure 5.1 Typical evolution of expenditure under a public pension scheme (as a percentage of total insured earnings)

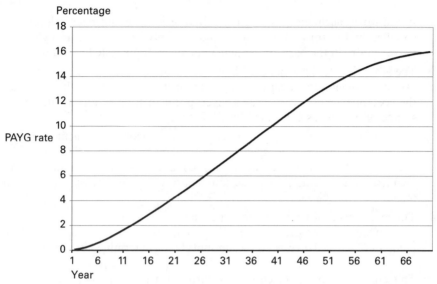

Looking at the shape of the curve in figure 5.1, one can conclude that there exist a large number of possible methods of raising the necessary resources for financing the expenditure. The financial system chosen by the actuary represents a systematic way of ensuring that the scheme's expenditure is met at all times.

5.2 SOURCES OF REVENUE

The resources necessary to meet the scheme's expenditure may come from a variety of sources. Revenues of a social security pension scheme may come from:

- employers' and workers' contributions;
- general or earmarked taxes;
- investment income;
- other revenues (usually marginal).

The choice made concerning the sources of revenue of a specific scheme may depend on the structure of the economy, the fiscal environment as well as political considerations. The weight of each of these sources of revenue may vary over time. According to the American Academy of Actuaries, there are four primary mechanisms for setting the level of revenue of a social insurance scheme:

1. A statutory mechanism, where contribution income and benefit levels are specified by law for all future years and can only be changed through legislative action on the basis of financing adequacy to be tested by the actuary;
2. The administrative mechanism, where contribution income or benefit levels may be changed periodically through administrative action on the basis that the cost of benefits accrued at a given point in time should relate to the source of income as calculated by the actuary;
3. The automatic mechanism, where contribution income or benefit levels are adjusted automatically as specified by the law to maintain financing adequacy; the latter being ensured through automatic adjustments recommended by the actuarial calculations relating to the cost of benefits and income;
4. The mechanism of government guarantee, where an excess of expenditures over income under the scheme other than government subsidies will be paid out of general income; these amounts being determined by the actuary.[1]

This chapter does not discuss cost-sharing, for example, between workers and employers. Rather, the discussion of the financial systems in this chapter takes into consideration a global contribution rate that will be shared later among different groups according to economic and political considerations.

When the government is involved in the financing of social security, it is important that the actuary carefully describe the impact (direct and indirect) of that involvement. In some cases, the contribution of the government to the scheme consists of paying a direct percentage of the covered payroll, to which must be added the contribution of the government as an employer of the civil servants covered by social security. If, in addition, social security reserves are invested in government securities, positive cash flows to the government will result from the fact that annual surpluses of the scheme purchase new government securities. However, negative cash flows will result from the payment of interest by the government to the scheme on the securities held by social security. As part of establishing a financing strategy, the actuary may have to recommend particular action to avoid any excessive future financial burden on the government budget.

5.3 OBJECTIVES OF THE FINANCIAL SYSTEM

The fundamental objective of the financial system of a pension scheme is to accumulate revenue systematically to provide security for the benefits provided by the scheme and to allocate this income in an orderly and rational manner over time. Under an appropriate financial system, a scheme ensures that financing resources will be available to meet the projected benefits and administrative expenditure. The financial system determines the manner by which contributions will be collected and accumulated over time.

The choice of an appropriate financial system for pension schemes must reflect the long-term nature of the benefits and the desire to reach, in the long run, a stable contribution rate. As a consequence, the financial system will determine the pace and amount of accumulation of reserve funds.

There is sometimes confusion between the contribution rate of a scheme and its cost. The cost of a scheme refers to its level of expenditure, which can be expressed in nominal amounts, as a percentage of earnings or as a percentage of GDP, for example. However, the cost itself is not affected by the choice of a financial system. The cost of a scheme and its contribution rate will only be equal in the particular case of the PAYG financial system, as will be seen later.

In the context of a new scheme, the financing of long-term benefits must take into account the fact that a certain period is required for the build-up of entitlements. An insured person usually needs to contribute to a scheme for a minimal period (usually ranging from ten to 15 years) before the individual is able to draw a pension. The career pattern of insured persons is of particular importance for the financing of pensions.

Reserve funds are usually allowed to develop because they are necessary for maintaining a stable contribution rate. The financing method will be directly determined by the funding objective, if any, which can take various forms depending on the expected level and stability of the contribution rate. Figure 5.2 presents the factors contributing to the accumulation of the reserve, and shows that the level of the contribution rate will affect the reserve accumulation. However, if the financial system is designed so that the reserve level is the fixed parameter (reserve ratio system), then the contribution rate becomes the variable that assures the equilibrium. The figure also reveals that the level and characteristics of the reserve will determine the rate of return and the investment income that it will generate. In some financial systems aiming at higher funding, investment income is a critical element of the equilibrium.

5.4 TYPES OF FINANCIAL SYSTEMS

Financial systems for public pensions can ensure actuarial equilibrium in a variety of ways. As already mentioned, public pension schemes are assumed to be indefinitely in operation and there is generally no risk that the sponsor of the scheme will go bankrupt. The actuarial equilibrium is based on the open-group approach, whereby it is assumed that there will be a continuous flow of new entrants into the scheme. The actuary thus has more flexibility in designing the financial system appropriate for a given scheme. The final choice of a financial system will often be made taking into consideration non-actuarial constraints, such as the capacity of the economy to absorb a given level of contri-

Actuarial practice in social security

Figure 5.2 Reserve accumulation in a public pension scheme

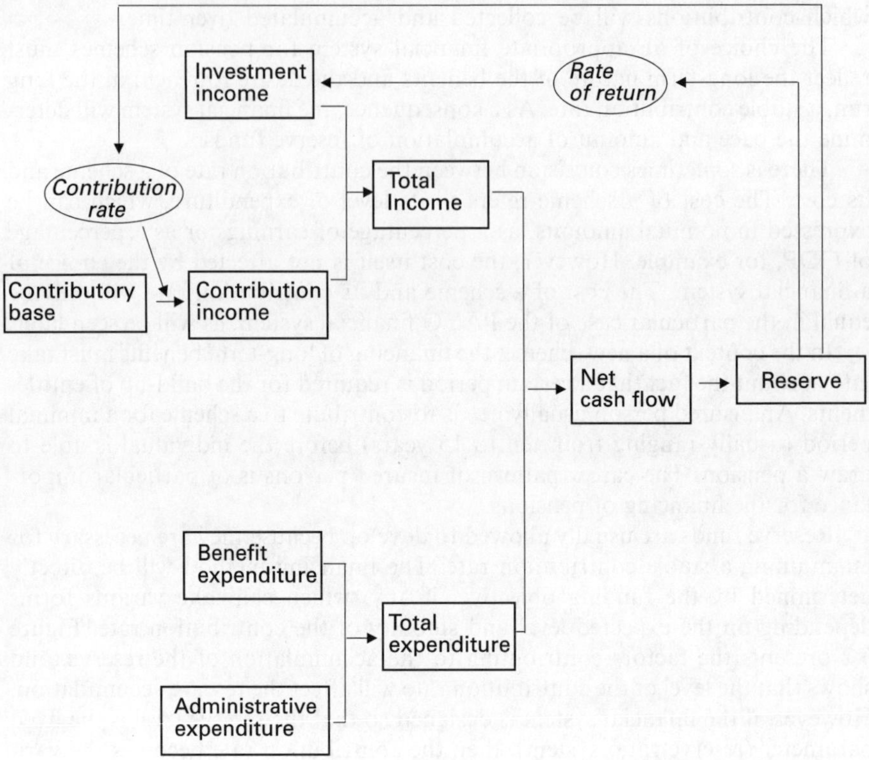

bution rate, the capacity of the country to invest productively social security reserves, the cost of other public schemes, etc.

This section presents a comparison of the most common financial systems in application, with a description of systems currently in operation in a selection of countries.

5.4.1 PAYG

Under the PAYG[2] method of financing, no funds are, in principle, set aside in advance, and the cost of annual benefits and administrative expenses is fully met from current contributions collected in the same year. Given the pattern of rising annual expenditure in a social insurance pension scheme, the PAYG cost rate is low at the inception of the scheme and increases each year until the scheme is mature. Figure 5.1 at the beginning of the chapter shows the evolution of the PAYG rate for a typical public pension scheme.

Box 5.1[3] Basic formulae on financing

(A) Financial equilibrium

The basic equations for the financial equilibrium of a pension scheme can be derived as follows:

Let:

- $V(t)$ = Reserve at the end of year t
- $R(t)$ = Annual total income in year t (including interest income)
- $C(t)$ = Annual contribution income in year t (excluding interest income)
- $I(t)$ = Annual interest income in year t
- $B(t)$ = Annual expenditure in year t
- $S(t)$ = Total insurable earnings in year t
- $CR(t)$ = Contribution rate in year t
- $i(t)$ = Interest rate in year t

Then, the following accounting identities hold:

Formula 5.1
$$R(t) = C(t) + I(t)$$

Formula 5.2
$$I(t) = [\sqrt{1+i(t)} - 1] * [C(t) - B(t)] + i(t) * V(t-1)$$

Formula 5.3
$$\Delta V(t) = V(t) - V(t-1) = R(t) - B(t)$$

Formula 5.4
$$C(t) = CR(t) * S(t)$$

By using the above formulae, the fund operation is simulated on a yearly basis. From these equations, it follows that:

Formula 5.5
$$V(t) = [1 + i(t)] * V(t-1) + \sqrt{1+i(t)} * [CR(t) * S(t) - B(t)]$$

or:

Formula 5.6
$$v(t) * V(t) = V(t-1) + v(t)^{\frac{1}{2}} * [CR(t) * S(t) - B(t)]$$

where:
$$v(t) = (1 + i(t))^{-1}$$

This is a recursion formula with respect to $\{V(t)\}$; it describes the evolution of the fund in each year. The solution is as follows:

Formula 5.7

$$U(t)V(t) = U(n-1) * V(n-1) + CR(t) * [\overline{S(t)} - \overline{S(n-1)}] - [\overline{B(t)} - \overline{B(n-1)}]$$

where:

$$\overline{S(t)} = \sum_{k=1}^{t} S(k) * W(k) \qquad \overline{B(t)} = \sum_{k=1}^{t} B(k) * W(k)$$

$$U(t) = \prod_{k=1}^{t} v(k) \qquad W(t) = U(t-1) * v(t)^{\frac{1}{2}}$$

(B) Major financial systems

PAYG

The PAYG contribution rate is given by:

Formula 5.8

$$PAYG_t = \frac{B(t)}{S(t)}$$

This contribution rate can be expressed as a product of two factors:

Formula 5.9

$$PAYG_t = d(t) * r(t)$$

where, $d(t)$ is called the "system demographic dependency ratio" and $r(t)$ the "system replacement ratio", such that:

$d(t)$ = (number of pensioners in year t) ÷ (number of active contributors in year t)

$r(t)$ = (average pension in year t) ÷ (average insurable earnings in year t)

Level contribution rate

The level contribution rate (or discounted average premium) for the period $[n,m]$ is given by:

Formula 5.10

$$CR_{[n,m]}^{level} = \frac{\overline{B(m)} - \overline{B(n-1)} - V(n-1)}{\overline{S(m)} - \overline{S(n-1)}}$$

By tending m to infinity, the GAP can be obtained.

Contribution rate keeping target reserve ratio

Let $\kappa = V(t-1) \div B(t)$ be called "the reserve ratio", which measures the reserve in terms of annual expenditure. Suppose the target value of the reserve ratio is given by κ_0, the contribution rate under which the reserve ratio attains the target value at the end of the period [n,m] is given by:

Formula 5.11

$$CR(\kappa = \kappa_0; n, m)$$
$$= \frac{\kappa_0 * U(m-1) * B(m) - U(n-1) * V(n-1) + [\overline{B(m-1)} - \overline{B(n-1)}]}{\overline{S(m-1)} - \overline{S(n-1)}}$$

If we substitute $\kappa_0 = 0$ in the above equation, we obtain the formula of the level premium over the period [n,m-1].

Contribution rate keeping target balance ratio

Let $\lambda_t = [B(t) - C(t)] \div I(t)$ be called "the balance ratio", which indicates the income/expenditure situation. Suppose the target value of the balance ratio is given λ_0, the contribution rate under which the balance ratio attains the target value at the end of the period [n,m] is given:

Formula 5.12

$$CR(\lambda = \lambda_0; n, m) =$$
$$\frac{[1+\lambda_0*[v(m)^{-1/2}-1]]*U(m)*B(m)+\lambda_0*[1-v(m)]*[\overline{B(m-1)}-\overline{B(n-1)}-U(n-1)*V(n-1)]}{[1+\lambda_0*[v(m)^{-1/2}-1]]*U(m)*S(m)+\lambda_0*[1-v(m)]*[\overline{S(m-1)}-\overline{S(n-1)}]}$$

If we substitute $\lambda_0 = 1$ in the above equation, we obtain the formula of the scaled premium, which enables the fund to be stable (i.e. the balance is 0) at the end of the period.

Theoretically, when the scheme is mature and the demographic structure of the insured population and pensioners is stable, the PAYG cost rate remains constant indefinitely. Despite the financial system being retained for a given scheme, the ultimate level of the PAYG rate is an element that should be known at the onset of a scheme. It is important for decision-makers to be aware of the ultimate cost of the benefit obligations so that the capacity of workers and employers to finance the scheme in the long term can be estimated.

5.4.2 Full funding

Full funding is not a very common financial system in social security schemes. One example of the application of this system is the actuarial valuation performed periodically for the Kuwait Public Institution for Social Security.

Box 5.2 Actuarial balance sheet of the Kuwait Public Institution for Social Security as of 30 June 1995

Assets (in $)		Liabilities (in $)	
Reserve fund	2 356 054	PV of future payments to existing pensioners and survivors	3 762 431
PV of future contributions with respect to active insured persons	1 190 350	PV of future pensions and benefits with respect to active insured persons	7 062 251
PV of contributions from the Treasury	3 396 514		
Actuarial deficit	3 881 764		
Total	10 824 682	Total	10 824 682

Note: PV = present values.

Under the financial system adopted for Kuwait, an actuarial balance sheet is established with the following components: the present value of payments to existing pensioners, plus the present value of future pensions and benefits to active insured persons, is compared with the value of the reserve on the valuation date, plus the present value of future contributions on behalf of active insured persons based on the legislated contribution rate. From this equation, an actuarial surplus or deficit emerges. Any deficit is then amortized either by way of an increase in the legislated contribution rate or by a decrease in benefit expenditure. The duration of the amortization period for the deficit (by way of an increase in contributions) normally depends on the nature of the deficit (experience deficit, modifications to the law, etc.). The actuarial balance sheet defined here follows the principles of the aggregate cost methods used for the valuation of certain private pension schemes.

The Kuwaiti valuation presents the actuarial balance sheet on two bases: the closed-group and the open-group approach. Under the closed-group approach, only those insured persons that are present on the valuation date are considered in the present value of contributions and benefits. Present values are computed over the total expected lifetime of the closed group of contributors and pensioners. Under the open-group approach, present values also consider new cohorts of participants entering the scheme after the valuation date. Deciding on the number of cohorts to consider in the present value calculations is important when using the open-group approach.

5.4.3 Partial funding

Between these two opposing financing methods – PAYG and full funding – there is a wide range of partial funding approaches. The system chosen by the

Figure 5.3 Contribution rates under the scaled premium system

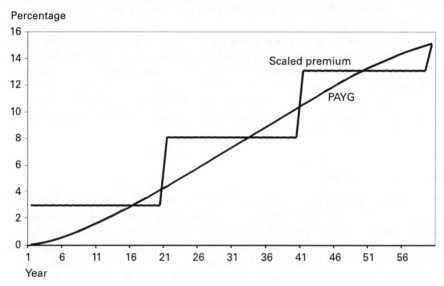

actuary depends on a variety of factors, such as the history of the scheme's financing, the state of the scheme's maturity and the capacity of the stakeholders to absorb a given level of contributions.

Classical scaled premium

One system based on partial funding is the scaled premium system, which was initially formulated by Valentin Zelenka (then Chief of Social Security at the ILO) in 1958 and was widely used by the ILO between 1960 and 1980 in the valuation of social security schemes in developing countries. The concept was generalized by Thullen[4] to indicate a system characterized by steadily increasing level contribution rates in successive control periods, with a non-decreasing reserve fund.

According to this system, the contribution rate is established so that, over a determined period of equilibrium, say 15 or 20 years, contribution and investment income will be sufficient to meet benefits and administrative expenses, with the constraint that the reserve does not decrease. This condition allows reserve funds accumulated over previous periods to be sunk into long-term investments.

The scaled premium method makes it possible for a new scheme to charge an initial contribution rate lower than under the GAP system (described below), and the level of contribution can be more easily absorbed by workers and employers. Another advantage of the scaled premium is that it makes it possible to maintain stable contribution rates for relatively long periods of time. For political reasons, adjusting the contribution rate every three years may prove difficult. The scaled premium assures the stability of the contribution rate for an extended period and gives the government time to plan for the next increase.

In practice, the setting of the premium in a way that takes into account the capacity of the economy to absorb investable funds has not been successfully applied. Furthermore, the rule for raising the contribution rate for a subsequent period of equilibrium has very often been ignored by governments. So the theoretically satisfying scaled premium system has not really been much of a success.

Reserve ratio system

The financial system may stipulate that, over a given period, the projected reserve should never be lower than a certain reserve ratio. The latter is the ratio of the reserve at the end of a given year divided by the annual expenditure of the scheme for that year. The target reserve ratio should vary according to the degree of maturity of the scheme. In the early years of a pension scheme's existence, the reserve ratio is normally high, since the number of pensioners is very low in comparison with the number of contributors and the contribution rate is more than sufficient to meet the annual expenditure on benefits. On the other hand, when the scheme is mature, the ratio of pensioners to contributors stabilizes and there is no more need to maintain important reserves. The contribution rate then approaches the PAYG cost for the scheme.

The ideal level of reserve ratio is not given by any mathematical formula but it is normally based on the following considerations:

- the level of maturity of the scheme;
- the ultimate PAYG cost of the scheme;
- the expected smoothness of contribution rate increases;
- the timing of actuarial reviews and consequent contribution rate increases.

When determining the reserve ratio, the actuary also needs to take into account other considerations. The contribution rate should not exceed the capacity of insured persons, employers and the economy in general to support it. The reserves generated should not exceed the capacity of the country to absorb the investments profitably. Depending on the capacity of the government to amend the law governing social security regularly, it may be desirable that the contribution rate remains stable for sufficiently long periods of time. After considering all these factors, the actuary may recommend a schedule of reserve ratios to be reached at specific points in time. The contribution rates will result directly from the application of the target reserve ratios to the financial projections of the scheme.

Financial systems

Box 5.3 Application of the reserve ratio system to the Demoland case

The social security scheme of Demoland has been in operation for some 30 years. The present contribution rate is 8.3 per cent and the long-term PAYG cost is projected to stabilize at around 27 per cent after 2040. The current reserve ratio of the scheme is equal to four times the annual expenditure and, if the contribution rate remains unchanged, it is projected that the reserve will be completely exhausted 17 years from now.

In the actuarial valuation of 31 December 1998, it was decided to apply the reserve ratio system, given the following constraints:

- The contribution rate would increase every three years in order to coincide with the timing of periodic actuarial reviews;
- Each contribution rate increase would be approximately of the same magnitude;
- The ultimate reserve ratio would be 2;
- The ultimate reserve ratio would be met 40 years after the valuation date (70 years after the start of the scheme).

According to these constraints, the actuary specifies the reserve ratio objectives as follows. The contribution rate of the pension branch is established such that the reserve ratio of the branch is equal to 4 in 2010, 2.5 in 2030, and 2 after 2040. A recommendation is made for the financing rule to be included in the law governing social security. Figure 5.4 shows the contribution rates that result from the application of that rule. Reserve ratios resulting from the application of these contribution rates are illustrated in figure 5.5.

Figure 5.4 Contribution rates for Demoland (actual versus recommended)

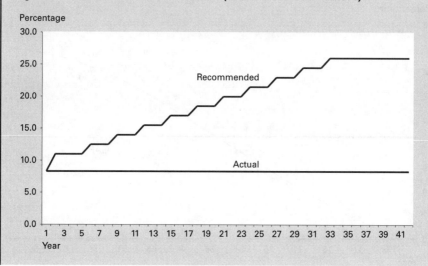

Actuarial practice in social security

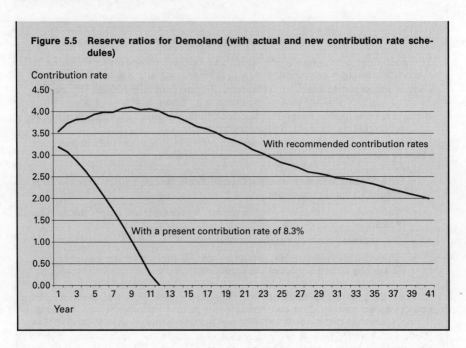

Figure 5.5 Reserve ratios for Demoland (with actual and new contribution rate schedules)

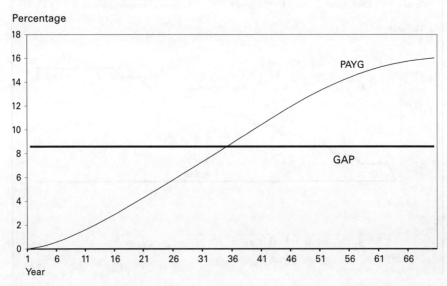

Figure 5.6 Contribution rate under the GAP system

Box 5.4[6] Financial systems in selected countries

This box illustrates the application of financial systems in various existing social security pension schemes. For this purpose, three Organisation for Economic Co-operation and Development (OECD) countries have been selected, namely Canada, Japan and the United States.

Canada

In the 15th actuarial valuation of the Canada Pension Plan,[7] the so-called "15-year formula" is applied to determine the contribution rates for the period after 2016.[8] This formula is described as follows:

1. The contribution rate is raised every year at a constant rate.
2. The annual rate of increase of the contribution rate is revised every five years.
3. The rate of increase is determined as the lowest rate of increase such that, if it were applied for the next 15 years, the expected reserves at the end of this period would be at least equal to twice the expenditure in the subsequent year.

From condition 1, the formula for the contribution rates after 2016 is:

Formula 5.13

$$CR(t) = CR(i) + \Delta CR(I) * (t - t_i)$$
(for $t = t_i + 1, ..., t_i + 5$; $t_i = t_0 + 5i$, $i = 0, 1, 2...$)

where:

t_i = Years of i-th contribution review after 2016 (recurring every five years)
$CR_{(t_i)}$ = Contribution rate in year t_i
$\Delta CR_{(t_i)}$ = Annual rate of increase in the contribution rate for $t_i + 1 \leq t \leq t_i + 5$

For each year of contribution review t_i, the rate of increase applied for the next five years, $\Delta CR(t_i)$, is determined in accordance with condition 3, i.e. $\kappa_{ti} + 15 \geq 2$.[9] To estimate $\kappa_{ti} + 15$, it has been assumed that the contribution rate is raised continuously at the constant annual rate $\Delta CR(t_i)$ until $t = t_i + 15$.

The provision explained above concerning the schedule of future contribution rates was changed in subsequent amendments of the Act. According to the reports of 16th and 17th actuarial valuations,[10] the following methods have been applied to set the long-term contribution rates.[11]

1. The schedule of increase in contribution rates until 2002 is prescribed and no subsequent increase is scheduled.
2. For the period in and after 2003, a level contribution rate, called the "steady-state contribution rate", is applied.
3. The "steady-state contribution rate" is determined as the lowest constant rate, which will enable the reserve ratio to remain generally constant.

In condition 3, the interpretation of the requirement of "generally constant" reserve ratio is left to the judgement of actuaries and may be reviewed for each valuation. In practice, the comparison of the reserve ratios in 2030 and 2100 was adopted (i.e. $\kappa_{2030} = \kappa_{2100}$) in the 16th valuation. In the 17th valuation, however, the reserve ratios in 2010 and 2060 were chosen for this purpose (i.e. $\kappa_{2010} = \kappa_{2060}$. The projection results show that $\kappa_{2010} = 4.12$ and $\kappa_{2060} = 5.38$ under the standard set of assumptions.).

Japan

According to the 1994 actuarial valuation of the Employee's Pension Insurance of Japan,[12] the future contribution rate is determined by the following conditions:

1. The contribution rate is raised every five years[13] at a constant rate.
2. A level contribution rate, called the "ultimate contribution rate", is applied after the increase in costs becomes stationary.
3. The balance is maintained positive every year.
4. A certain amount of reserve is set up for unforeseen economic changes (reserve ratio at least equal to 1).

Conditions 1 and 2 lead to the following formula for the future contribution rate:

Formula 5.14

$$CR(t) = CR(t_0) + \Delta CR^* ([(t - t_0) \div 5] + 1) \text{ (for } t_0 \leq t \leq T - 1) =$$
$$= CR_{max} \text{ (for } t \geq T)$$

where:

t_0	=	Base year of the valuation
$CR(t_0)$	=	Contribution rate in the base year
CR_{max}	=	Ultimate contribution rate
ΔCR	=	Step of increase in the contribution rate for every five years
T	=	Target year of the ultimate contribution rate (assumed to be 2025)
$[x]$	=	The integer part of x

United States

The social security system of the United States defines a test of financing adequacy in reference to the scheme's actuarial balance over a period of 75 years:

- *income rates*, determined as the ratio of contribution income to insurable earnings, are calculated for each projection year;
- *cost rates*, defined as the ratio of total expenditures to insurable earnings, are calculated for each projection year.

> The series of income rates are summarized by calculating the ratio of the present value of contribution income for the period to the present value of insurable earnings for the same period. A similar exercise is performed on the series of cost rates. The difference between the summarized income rate and summarized cost rate determines the actuarial balance. A positive actuarial balance is then interpreted as a surplus position of the scheme over the contemplated period, whereas if the actuarial balance is in deficit, the size of the deficit may be interpreted as that rate which, if added to the combined employee-employer contribution rate for each of the next 75 years, would bring the scheme into exact actuarial balance.
>
> The scheme is said to be in *close actuarial balance* for the long-range projection period (75 years) if the income rate is between 95 and 105 per cent of the cost rate for the period. In addition, under the OASDI, benefits are adjusted according to changes in the consumer price index (CPI). However, there is a provision[14] which states that if the reserve ratio, named the "OASDI trust fund ratio", is less than 20 per cent at the beginning of the year, then the cost-of-living adjustment in benefits in that year will be limited to the CPI increase or the wage increase, whichever is the lower.[15]
>
> The OASDI Board of Trustees has also adopted a short-range test of financing adequacy, which requires that the "OASDI trust fund ratio" be at least equal to 1 throughout the next ten years.

The ultimate reserve ratio may be determined at a very low level, such as one or two years of expenditure, just to cover any unexpected economic downturn, which could affect contributions or benefits, and to give the government enough time to adjust the contribution rate. It may also be set in order to obtain a stability of the contribution rate over a long period of time. This was the approach taken by the Canada Pension Plan in 1997, when it was decided to establish the reserve ratio at five times the annual expenditure[5] to be able to maintain a contribution rate under 10 per cent indefinitely, even if the PAYG rate of the scheme is expected to exceed 12 per cent in the long term. Investment earnings are expected to fill the gap.

Usually, this method of determining the contribution rate is applied once a scheme has been in operation for a certain period of time, since fixing a reserve ratio at 40 or 50 times annual expenditure in the early years of a scheme is not justified. What is often the case is that the initial contribution rate was determined some 20 to 30 years earlier and the rate has gone on unrevised because of good reserve accumulations. The reserve ratio system is then adopted so that the ultimate cost of the scheme can be reached in an orderly manner.

The general average premium (GAP)

The GAP represents the *constant* contribution rate that would be adequate to meet the disbursements of the scheme over a specified period. It is calculated by (1) equating the present value of projected future benefits and administrative expenses for existing and future insured persons and beneficiaries minus the value of the existing reserve at valuation date to (2) a factor multiplied by the present value of projected future insurable earnings of insured persons (present contributors and new entrants).

(PV of future expenditure) - (Initial reserve) = Factor x (PV future insurable earnings)

Solving the equation for the "factor" in the right portion of the equation provides the estimated annual contribution rate as a proportion of insured earnings, which would, in theory, be adequate to meet disbursements of the scheme over the determined period. If the length of the period is long enough (between 50 and 75 years depending on the scheme's maturity), the GAP then represents the constant contribution rate, which could be immediately enforced and maintained unchanged in order to ensure the permanent financing balance of the scheme.

In the early years following the implementation of a pension scheme, the GAP exceeds the PAYG cost rate. Consequently, if the GAP was used in practice, it would mean that the annual revenue of the scheme (contributions plus investment income) during the period just following inception would exceed its annual expenditures. This would lead to the accumulation of a technical reserve. This accumulated reserve would eventually be necessary to meet the growing benefit expenditure of the maturing scheme.

The GAP is a theoretical financial system rarely used in practice for the financing of public pension schemes. It is, nevertheless, still calculated and presented in the actuarial report. Its key advantage is that it is possible to compare the costs of different benefit packages or alternative assumption scenarios by using a single value instead of a stream of contribution rates varying over time.

For example, if the authorities want to know the consequences of different retirement ages, or of different eligibility criteria, the actuary can easily calculate the GAP for the various options. This allows the authorities to make their decision based on the relative financial weight of alternative solutions.

Notes

[1] Taken from American Academy of Actuaries: *Actuarial standard of practice No. 32: Social insurance*, Committee on Social Insurance, adopted by the Actuarial Standards Board, Doc. No. 062, Jan. 1998 (Washington, DC).

[2] The term "pay-as-you-go" is sometimes misleadingly used by international advisers to encompass all schemes other than individual capitalization schemes.

[3] This box provides only a short summary of the actuarial equations used in a standard model, taken from ILO: *ILO-PENS: The ILO pension model* (Geneva, 1997), which cannot replace a full explanation of the mathematical theory in actuarial science. All relevant theoretical bases for social security actuaries can be found in the second book of this series: S. Iyer: *Actuarial mathematics of social security pensions* (Geneva, ILO/ISSA, 1999).

[4] See P. Thullen: *Techniques actuarielles de la sécurité sociale* (Geneva, ILO, 1973).

Financial systems

⁵ Under the Canada Pension Plan, a reserve ratio of five times the annual expenditure represents an approximate funding level of 20 per cent. With this objective of reserve ratio at five, the reserve will always represent 20 per cent of the accrued liability under the scheme.

⁶ This box is taken from: K. Hirose: "Topics in quantitative analysis of social protection systems", in: *Issues in social protection*, Discussion Paper (Geneva, ILO, 1999).

⁷ *Canada Pension Plan 15th Actuarial Report as at 31 December 1993*, prepared by the Office of the Superintendent of Financial Institutions, pursuant to paragraph 115(3) of the Canada Pension Plan Act.

⁸ In the 15th actuarial report, the annual rates of increase in the contribution rate from 1992 to 2015 were set as follows: 0.2 per cent for 1992–96, 0.25 per cent for 1997–2006, 0.2 per cent for 200–716. This contribution schedule was called the "25-year schedule" and was assumed to be revised every five years.

⁹ In our notation, the definition of the reserve ratio should be modified as: $(t = V(t)(B(t+1))$.

¹⁰ *Canada Pension Plan 16th Actuarial Report as at September 1997; Canada Pension Plan 17th Actuarial Report as at 31 December 1997*, prepared by the Office of the Superintendent of Financial Institutions, pursuant to paragraph 115(3) of the Canada Pension Plan Act.

¹¹ It is said that this amendment of the contribution schedule is aimed at averting the continuous increase in contribution rates over a long period and achieving a more equal cost-sharing among different generations.

¹² Report of the 1999 actuarial revaluation of the Employee's Pension Insurance and National Pension, prepared by the Actuarial Affairs Division of the Pension Bureau, Ministry of Health and Welfare of Japan.

¹³ The Employee's Pension Insurance Act provides that the contribution rate must be re-evaluated when the actuarial valuation is carried out every five years (paragraph 84(iv)).

¹⁴ Social Security Act, paragraph 215(i).

¹⁵ In this case, when the "OASDI fund ratio" improves to more than 32 per cent, benefits will be retroactively increased to the level calculated without applying the provision. However, the provision has not come into effect since its introduction in 1983, and is not expected to be implemented for the next several years.

ACTUARIAL MODELLING FOR PUBLIC PENSIONS 6

6.1 DEFINITION OF THE ACTUARIAL MODEL

The social security actuary must deal with uncertain future events and with complex interrelated systems. To be able to project a possible future scenario for these events, the actuary uses a simplified representation of this reality, which is called a model. Actuarial models are:

- ... constructed to aid in the assessment of the financial and economic consequences associated with phenomena that are subject to uncertainty with respect to occurrence, timing, or severity. This requires:
- understanding the conditions and processes under which past observations were obtained;
- anticipating changes in those conditions that will affect future experience;
- evaluating the quality of the available data;
- bringing judgement to bear on the modelling process;
- validating the work as it progresses;
- estimating the uncertainty inherent in the modelling process itself.[1]

The model is a simplification and does not take into account the totality of factors that could affect the results. The person using the model should bear this constantly in mind, for it means that the model will change over time, as the user discovers new variables or interactions between variables that explain the reality under study better. So how should a model be built?

An actuarial model can be constructed using data from prior experiments, data from related phenomena, or judgement. Such a model can be validated by comparing its results to the actual outcomes of the phenomena being modelled. [2]

Inputs to a social security actuarial model comprise statistical data and assumptions on the future behaviour of critical variables. Outputs of the model include revenue and expenditure of the scheme and tools to set the financing strategy. For the social security actuary, the data may come from the scheme itself or from external sources. The data from the scheme may not be statistically credible to explain a phenomenon correctly. For example, in the case of a new scheme, the mortality or disability experiences may include an insufficient number of observations. In such a case, the actuary will need to rely on general population data or on the experiences of a similar pension scheme. In other situations, the data simply may not exist, such as when a new type of risk is to be covered. Then, the judgement of the actuary will be necessary.

In practice, the level of sophistication required to perform projections depends on different factors. The purpose of the modelling exercise should indicate whether it calls for accurate results or whether the aim is simply to obtain a general overview of tendencies. For example, the supplementary study to a basic actuarial valuation may only require a simplified modelling approach, whereas the study of various reform proposals on benefit provisions or investment strategies may require a more advanced approach. Another factor that determines the level of sophistication is the statistical information available. It could be misleading to use a very sophisticated model when most of the input data and assumptions are unavailable and must be based on the judgement of the user. The model-builder must also consider the available tools to collect the data and run the applications; the model may be built on a simple spreadsheet or may involve sophisticated computer techniques. The actuary must also consider the timing constraints and the resources available.

6.2 DETERMINISTIC VERSUS STOCHASTIC MODELS

Models are of two main types: stochastic and deterministic. A stochastic model is a mathematical model in which the representation of a given phenomenon is expressed in terms of probabilities. The stochastic model is used to derive an estimate of the expected value of a random variable and a confidence interval for this variable. The output of a stochastic model thus includes a wide range of possible results, each of which is associated with a probability of occurrence. The deterministic model, on the other hand, is based on one given set of data and assumptions, and produces one set of outputs:

Actuarial practice in social security

A deterministic model is a simplification of a stochastic model in which the proportion of occurrences of a given event estimated by the stochastic model is assumed to occur with probability one. [3]

In a deterministic model, the input consists of using a predetermined set of assumptions. In the context of social security projections, this means that the deterministic model applies one series of decrements and economic variables (which may, however, change over time) to a starting population to bring the population forward in time and to obtain one pattern of service, salaries and reserve accumulation. The output includes a single set of values for each projec-

---

Box 6.1   An example of the stochastic approach to project the rate of return

It is possible to produce actuarial projections combining stochastic and deterministic modelling. The basic valuation may be based on a deterministic model, and the stochastic approach may be applied to some economic assumptions with a high degree of uncertainty.

The stochastic approach can be used, for example, to project the rate of return on a scheme's assets. The assumption will take the form of an average rate of return of, say, 7 per cent, with a standard variation of 5 per cent, assuming a normal distribution of the rate of return. These parameters are determined using the data of previous years. The model-builder then generates a series of random numbers between 0 and 1 and converts them into rates of return in accordance with the assumed distribution.

Random number	Associated point of the standard normal Distribution	Converted return (as a %)
.2660	−0.625	3.9
.7881	0.800	11.0
.5793	0.200	8.0
.8413	1.000	12.0
.6915	0.500	9.5
.1587	−1.000	2.0

By performing a sufficiently high number of experiments, it is then possible to define intervals with their associated probabilities. In this case, the result of the simulation could be expressed as follows: *There is a 50 per cent probability that the rate of return falls between 4 per cent and 10 per cent.*

Following that assessment, the actuarial projections of the deterministic model are performed twice, using the rates of return of both limits of the interval (4 per cent and 10 per cent), and the final result of the valuation will be presented as: *The contribution rate necessary to finance expenditures over the next 20 years, given a specified reserve ratio, will be between 12 per cent and 14 per cent with a probability of 50 per cent.*

tion year. In order to estimate the variability of results in this type of model, the model-builder must perform sensitivity tests by modifying one or more input variables or assumptions and measuring the effect on the results.

In a stochastic model, assumptions are expressed in terms of random variables. Probability distributions are assigned to each input variable. In mathematical theory, it would be possible to calculate the probability distribution for key model outputs, such as PAYG contribution rates, directly. However, this implies complex calculations on the joint distribution of different input variables, and on the assumptions on stochastic dependence and independence, etc.

In practice, stochastic models generally operate using the Monte-Carlo method, which assumes probability distributions for key random variables and uses a random number generator. Distributions of output variables are then established by undertaking a series of simulations, often as many as 1,000. For each simulation, the random number generator "picks" a set of random numbers for all the input distributions. On the basis of that set of random numbers for the input variables, one output result is calculated (for example, a PAYG contribution rate). The combination of all the results then produces a discrete approximation of a continuous probability distribution for the result variables.

In practice, stochastic modelling is usually reserved for important specific studies; the modelling work is often simply too heavy. Also, communicating the results is more difficult, since they must be presented as a range of possible results, each with its own probability, while users of the actuarial report generally prefer straightforward and single answers. In general, the use of sensitivity testing through scenario analyses under a deterministic model is a sufficient substitute for stochastic modelling.

6.3 MODELLING SOCIAL SECURITY PENSIONS: THE OBJECTIVES

In the context of social security pensions, the purpose of the pension model is twofold:

- Firstly, it is used to assess the financial viability of the long-term benefits branch. This refers to the measure of the long-term actuarial balance between the revenue and expenditure of the scheme. When an imbalance occurs, it is recommended that the contribution rate or the benefit structure be revised.
- Secondly, the model may be used to examine the financial impact of different reform options, thus assisting policy-makers in the design of benefit and financing provisions.

The actuarial valuation presents the projection of revenue (contribution, investment income and other sources of income) and expenditure (benefits

Actuarial practice in social security

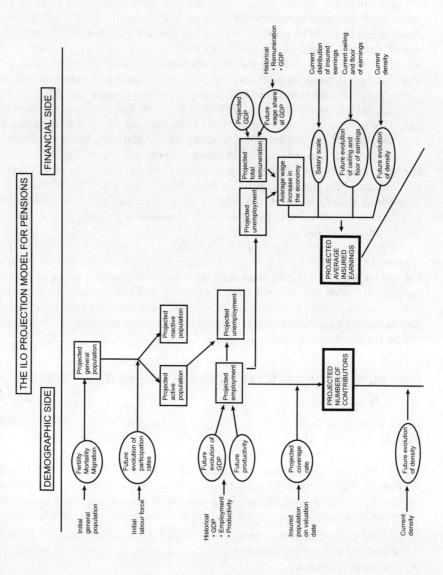

Figure 6.1 The ILO projection model for pensions

Actuarial modelling for public pensions

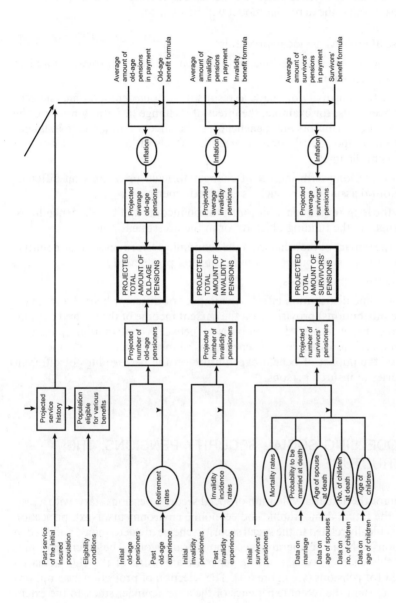

and administrative expenditure). With the choice of an appropriate rate of return, it is then possible to calculate the reserve for each year of projection. From these results, the actuarial model will be used to:

- analyse alternative financing methods;
- determine the effect of various modifications to benefit provisions and/or financing provisions;
- measure the sensitivity of financial results to various demographic and economic scenarios, for example, the effect of a change in fertility rates on the number of contributors and beneficiaries, the effect of an increase in unemployment on the contribution income, the effects of lower interest rates on investment income;
- measure the long-term impact of changes to legal provisions on different behavioural assumptions, such as early retirement;
- assess the long-term impact on contribution income and benefit expenditure of changes in the funding objective or in the investment policy;
- assess the impact of the scheme on the economic performance of the country, notably on the state budget, labour costs and productivity;
- analyse structural reforms;
- analyse some distribution effects: the impact of different benefit and financing (contributions) provisions on the current income of the insured population and beneficiaries; the comparison between contributions paid and benefits received by successive generations of insured persons; the measurement of the impact of benefit expenditure on the net earnings of different categories of insured persons.

6.4 MODELLING SOCIAL SECURITY PENSIONS: THE STRUCTURE

Modelling for the actuarial valuation of social security pensions starts with a projection of the future demographic and economic environments. Next, projection factors specifically related to the social security scheme are determined and used in combination with the demographic/economic framework. The description presented in this chapter focuses on the general framework of the ILO actuarial model used for pensions (see figure 6.1). The selection of projection assumptions takes into account the recent experience of the scheme under study to the extent that this information is available. It should be remembered, however, that the assumptions are generally selected to reflect long-term trends rather than giving undue weight to recent experience.

6.4.1 The demographic environment

The general population is projected starting with most current data and then applying appropriate mortality, fertility and migration assumptions. The detailed methodology for demographic projections is presented in Chapter 9.

6.4.2 The economic environment

The projection of the labour force, that is, the number of people available for work, is obtained by applying assumed labour force participation rates to the projected number of people in the general population. The labour force is then separated into two components: the employed population and the unemployed population. Rates of economic growth and labour productivity increases must also be projected.

The number of workers covered by the social security scheme is obtained by applying assumed coverage rates to the projected employed population.

Regarding the payment of contributions to the scheme, the individual pattern of insured persons is determined, over time, by using an annual density factor. This assumption is needed to assess the future eligibility for pensions of different groups of insured persons.

It is possible, and sometimes necessary, to assume movement of participants between the groups of active and inactive insured persons. Some people may be unemployed at the time of the valuation, or may be out of the labour force, but still have past accrued rights under the scheme. In the future, these people may reintegrate the active insured status and recover their right to a pension. They thus represent a potential liability to the scheme. If it is considered that these people represent an important part of the insured population, then a provision should be made for their possible re-entry into the scheme.

Once the population of workers is projected, it is then necessary to project the earnings on which they will contribute and from which benefits will be calculated. In addition to the projection of average earnings, distribution assumptions may also be useful to simulate the impact of minimum and maximum pension provisions. A detailed methodology for projecting the economic environment is presented in Chapter 9.

6.4.3 The future development of the scheme

In addition to the demographic and macroeconomic frame already described, pension projections require a set of assumptions specific to the social insurance scheme. The database as of the valuation date includes the current insured population according to the insured status (active and inactive), the distribution of insurable wages among contributors, the distribution of past credited service and pensions in payment.

Actuarial practice in social security

> **Box 6.2[4]   The mathematics of a typical social security pension model**
>
> This section explains the mathematical structure of a standard actuarial pension model, which the ILO pension model (ILO-PENS) follows. The mathematical structure assumes that environmental inputs, such as exogenous economic and demographic variables, have already been determined. Estimations and assumptions referring to these inputs will be explained in later chapters. Generally, the actuarial calculations are undertaken in two steps. The first step is to estimate the future expenditure and contribution base; the second is, based on the results obtained in the first step, to establish the future contribution rate on the basis of the financial system adopted by the scheme.
>
> *(a) General*
>
> The yearly simulation method is generally used to estimate future costs. For each generation, the transition of status of a person (active person, inactive person, pensioner) is mapped onto the next year's status by using actuarially assumed transition probabilities (mortality rate, retirement rate) and applying eligibility conditions and the pension formula. This cycle is iterated until the end of the projection period.
>
> The basic calculation structure is as follows:
>
> On the income side, the contribution base is calculated by multiplying the assumed contributors and assumed average insurable earnings (and collection factor):
>
> **Formula 6.1**
>
> $$\textit{Contribution base} = (\textit{contributors}) \times (\textit{average insurable earnings}) \times (\textit{collection factor})$$
>
> The three terms on the right-hand side of the above formula are regarded here as exogenous.
>
> On the expenditure side, the benefit expenditure is calculated by applying the survival factors and the adjustment factors to the previous year's expenditure and by adding the newly awarded pensions:
>
> **Formula 6.2**
>
> $$\textit{Expenditure} = (\textit{previous year's expenditure}) \times (\textit{survival rate}) \times (\textit{adjustment factor}) + (\textit{newly awarded pensions})$$
>
> The previous year's expenditure is known; the survival rate and adjustment factor are to be assumed. The newly awarded pensions are derived as a result of projections. The following sections provide more details on the different components of the two basic formulae.
>
> *(b) Estimating the covered population*
>
> *Definitions*
>
> $Reg(x,t)$:

Registered population in year t is defined as those people who are registered in the scheme and have made contributions during at least one contribution period (usually, one month) until that year. Those who have already died or become pensioners should be excluded.

Ac(x,t):

Active population in year t is defined as those people who have made at least one contribution during that year.

Inac(x,t):

Inactive population in year t is defined as those people who are registered in the scheme but have made no contribution during year t.

From this, it follows that the sum of active population and inactive population is the registered population:

Formula 6.3

$$Reg(x,t) = Ac(x,t) + Inac(x,t)$$

Cont(x,t):

Contributors in year t is defined as the average of those people who made the contributions of each contribution period during year t.

Generally, the number of contributors is not more than that of the active population, because not all workers work on a full-time basis and without any cessation of employment. In other words, the difference between these two numbers indicates the degree of completion of the covered employment. Thus, we define the "density factor" as the percentage of the contributors to the active population.

Formula 6.4

$$Dens(x,t) = Cont(x,t) \div Ac(x,t)$$

Nent(x,t):

New entrants in year t is defined as those people who are newly registered during year t and have made at least one contribution.

Rent(x,t):

Re-entrants in year t is defined as those people who belonged to the inactive population in year t-1 but belonged to the active population in year t.

Estimation

The number of the active population is estimated by applying the coverage rate to the projected base population by age and sex. The coverage rates are assumed by taking into account the forecast of the labour force participation rate, unemployment rate and observed past experiences. The base population can be national population, labour force population, or employed population.

Formula 6.5

$$Ac(x,t) = Covrate(x,t) * Pop(x,t)$$

where:

$Pop(x,t)$ = Base population in year t

$Covrate(x,t)$ = Coverage rate in year t

Let $S[Ac(x,t)]$ be the members of $Ac(x,t)$ who remain in active population in year $t+1$ (how $S[Ac(x,t)]$ is calculated will be explained below). Then, consider the difference $D(x+1,t+1) = Ac(x+1,t+1) - S[Ac(x,t)]$. The following two cases may occur:

(i) $D(x+1,t+1) > 0$

Usually, this occurs at a younger age. In this case, the gap is to be made up either by new entrants or re-entrants. We introduce an exogenous variable $NR(x,t)$, the ratio of new entrants to re-entrants ($NR(x,t) = 1$ at younger age, $= 0$ at older age).

The new and re-entrants are estimated as:

Formula 6.6

$$Nent(x+1,t+1) = NR(x+1,t+1)^*D(x+1,t+1)$$

Formula 6.7

$$Rent(x+1,t+1) = [1 - NR(x+1,t+1)]^*D(x+1,t+1)$$

In case there are not enough inactive persons to become re-entrants, i.e. $S[Inac(x,t)] < Rent(x+1,t+1)$, then $Ac(x+1,t+1)$ would need to be adjusted (reduced) so that it allows for the maximum possible number of re-entrants. At the same time, the $\{Ac(k,t+1); k < x+1\}$ would need to be readjusted so that the total number of active population remains the same as assumed.

(ii) $D(x+1,t+1) < 0$

Usually, this occurs in older age. In this case, $D(x+1,t+1)$ should be classified as the inactive population. Thus, we arrive at the number of the active population, new entrants and re-entrants of the next year. The registered population, inactive population and contributors are estimated as follows:

Formula 6.8

$$Reg(x+1,t+1) = S[Reg(x,t)] + Nent(x+1,t+1)$$

Formula 6.9

$$Inac(x+1,t+1) = Reg(x+1,t+1) - Ac(x+1,t+1)$$

Formula 6.10

$Cont(x+1,t+1) = Ac(x+1,t+1) * Dens(x+1,t+1)$

(c) Transition from active status to pensioners (demographic part)

The transition from active (or inactive) status to pensioners is simulated by using transition probabilities:

Formula 6.11 $VAC = Ac(x,t) * Invrate(x,t)$

Formula 6.12 $DAC = Ac(x,t) * Mort(x,t)$

Formula 6.13 $RAC = Ac(x,t) * Retrate(x,t)$

Formula 6.14 $ZAC = S[Ac(x,t)] = Ac(x,t) - VAC - DAC - RAC$

From these, the number of new pensioners is calculated:

Formula 6.15 $NINV(x+1, t+1) = VAC$

where:
  NINV = Number of invalidity pensioners

Formula 6.16 $NRET(x+1, t+1) = RAC$

where:
  NRET = Number of old-age pensioners

Formula 6.17 $NSURV(s(x), t+1)$ is calculated by a subroutine (note, that there can be survivors on the death of pensioners).

where:
  NSURV = Number of beneficiaries of survivors' pensions

(d) Transition from active status to pensioners (financial part)

The new pensioners' pensions are calculated by using the assumed acquired credit and assumed past salary.

The active population, as well as the inactive population, are classified by their acquired past credits and by income level. In the simulation, the credit distribution is constructed by taking account of an influx of contributions paid in that year and an outflow of contributions withdrawn in that year.

The pensions of newly awarded pensioners can be estimated by applying the eligibility conditions for pensions and the pension formula to all subgroups of the population by credit and salary (and their correlation).

$NINV\$(x+1, t+1)$
$NRET\$(x+1, t+1)$

At the same time, the credit that turned into benefits should be deducted from the active person's cumulated past credits.

(e) Transition from active to active

If an active worker stays active one year, then the credit will increase by the contributed period.

Formula 6.18 $Cred(x+1, t+1) = Cred(x,t) + Dens(x,t)$

Formula 6.19 $Bal(x+1, t+1) = Bal(x,t) * [1 + Int(t)] + CR(t) * Sal(x,t) * Dens(x,t) * i(t) \div 2$

> where:
> - $Cred(x,t)$ = Average acquired credit
> - $Bal(x,t)$ = Average balance of individual savings accounts (this is used for the valuation of DC schemes)
> - $i(t)$ = Interest rate in year t
> - $CR(t)$ = Contribution rate in year t
> - $Sal(x,t)$ = Average insurable salary at age x, in year t
>
> **(f) Transition from pensioner to pensioner**
>
> This transition can be simulated as follows:
>
> **Formula 6.20** $Pens\#(x+1,t+1) = Pens\#(x,t)*[1-q(x,t)] + NPens\#(x+1, t+1)$
>
> **Formula 6.21** $Pens\$(x+1,t+1) = Pens\$(x,t)*[1-q(x,t)]*[1+adj(t)] + NPens\$(x+1,t+1)$
>
> where:
> - $Pens\#(x,t)$ = Number of pensioners
> - $Pens\$(x,t)$ = Amount of pension benefits

Scheme-specific assumptions, such as disability incidence rates and the distribution of retirement by age, are determined by referring to the scheme's provisions and its historical experience. The projection of the annual investment income requires information on the existing assets on the valuation date. An interest-rate assumption is formulated on the basis of the nature of the scheme's assets, the past performance of the fund, the scheme's investment policy and assumptions on future economic growth. Each of these assumptions is presented in more detail in Chapter 10.

Under the methodology described in box 6.2, pension projections are performed following a yearly cohort methodology, having as its starting point the initial insured population and current pensioners on the valuation date. The existing insured population is aged and gradually replaced by the successive cohorts of participants on an annual basis according to the assumptions on coverage and demographic decrements.

Notes

[1] Society of Actuaries and Casualty Actuarial Society: *General principles of actuarial science*, Discussion draft (Schaumburg, Illinois, 15 Aug. 1998).

[2] ibid.

[3] ibid.

[4] This box is based on the methodology section of ILO: *ILO-PENS: The ILO pension model* (Geneva, 1997). The ILO pension model is available free of charge to the ILO constituents from ILO FACTS.

THE DATA AND INFORMATION BASE FOR THE VALUATION 7

Behind every sound actuarial valuation is a solid database. The building of the statistical base must be in line with the methodology of the model that the actuary intends to use. The sources of information need to be well known in order to put a critical view on the extent and quality of the data, and the actuary needs to determine a process whereby the sufficiency and reliability of the database can be checked. In some cases, when the information is incomplete or contains a high degree of uncertainty, sound judgement on the part of the actuary will be needed.

Modelling the future financial status of a social insurance scheme requires a set of information describing model variables and the scheme's rules. They typically include:

- the general demographic and economic environments;
- the legal provisions of the social security scheme under review, including the definition of the covered population, insurable earnings, eligibility conditions, benefit formulae, etc.;
- the characteristics, on the valuation date, of contributors (number, earnings, past contribution credits), beneficiaries (number, average pension) and dependants of insured persons; the profile of new entrants to the insured population and the pattern of exits and re-entries into the group of insured persons;
- past experience appertaining to retirement behaviour, invalidity incidence and mortality rates.

7.1 SOURCES OF STATISTICAL INFORMATION

This section summarizes the typical sources of information used for the valuation of a public pension scheme and comments on their usefulness and limitations in the context of the actuarial valuation. The detailed compilation of

> **Box 7.1 Sources of information for the actuarial valuation of a social insurance pension scheme**
>
> *I General population projections and vital statistics*
>
> Sources of information
>
> - National demographic projections;
> - *World Population Prospects*, prepared by the United Nations Population Council;
> - Other demographic studies performed by regional or international development institutions.
>
> Comments
>
> (a) Population forecasts produced at the national level can, for a variety of reasons, be biased (for example, when they are used to allocate public funds to different geographical areas of a country). The actuary should enquire about the methodology used for national population projections. Where a national committee made up of representative groups of interest is taking part in the process, then the reliability and accuracy of the projections can normally be accepted.
>
> (b) The characteristics of the general population concerning mortality rates may not be directly applicable to the insured population of a scheme. In many developing countries, the social security system only covers the segment of the workforce in salaried employment, which typically enjoys better living conditions than the rest of the population.
>
> *II Economic and labour market statistics*
>
> Sources of information
>
> - National economic development plans providing key information for the short and medium-term macroeconomic frame as developed by the ministries responsible for planning and finances, by international financial institutions, such as the International Monetary Fund (IMF), and by other bodies, such as the Economist Intelligence Unit;
> - Labour force statistics compiled from labour market surveys put together by the national statistical office;
> - Wage statistics compiled from labour market surveys, the ministry responsible for finances and the central bank's information base; also from organizations, such as chambers of commerce and trade organizations;
> - Household surveys[1] providing information on income distribution of the population.
>
> Comments
>
> (a) A thorough knowledge of the definitions used in the compilation of employment statistics is vital; it may be necessary to adjust the gross data to fit the way insured persons are considered to be active and paying contributions to the scheme.

The data and information base for the valuation

(b) Although national economic development plans provide useful information, they are usually limited to the very short term; the actuary must prepare extensions of these projections and validate them with the competent bodies.

(c) The use of alternative sources of information other than government institutions should be made with caution.

III Scheme-specific information

Sources of information

- A computer system containing the database on registered employers, individual insured persons and beneficiaries;
- A department in charge of planning and technical studies, which provides projections and actuarial estimates to management;
- A legal department responsible for the application of the law and regulations on social security;
- An accounting and finance department in charge of preparing financial statements and typically involved in the valuation of assets of the social security scheme;
- An investment department;
- A department responsible for the collection of contributions (notably concerning the compliance issue);
- An inspection department;
- Taxation authorities, for information on the fiscal treatment of contributions and benefits and on compliance issues;
- A department responsible for the delivery of benefits (application of eligibility conditions and benefit delivery process);
- A decentralized social security offices in charge of contribution collection and benefit delivery;
- Alternative delivery systems, such as post offices and banks, collecting contributions and paying benefits.

Comments

(a) The actuary must become familiar with the computer system containing the database.

(b) The actuary must be acquainted with the entire reporting process, from the time an employer files regular information and remits contributions to the social security organization to the moment the information is compiled at the central level and reported to management. In particular, close consultation with regional and other decentralized offices of the social security system is necessary. Where there are problems of communication in a complex administrative organization, the actuary should take the initiative by consulting decentralized offices and working at reconciling the information with other general data provided by headquarters. The actuary can then play an advisory role in improving the flow of information, the statistical reporting and the monitoring system.

statistics required for the actuarial valuation is provided in subsequent sections. Technical Brief I at the end of this book reproduces blueprints of tables that are typically used for the compilation of data.

The reliability of the information provided at the national level must be assessed by carefully reviewing the data collection process. External factors may affect the information, particularly surveys. One must also look at the applicability of national statistics to the specifics of the social security system. There may be differences in the definition of the data collected, for example, the number of children per person should only refer to "dependent" children under the social security scheme. The actuary is advised to develop a procedure for cross-checking the information.

The collection of data needs to be compatible with the methodology of the model used. For example, a choice must be made between using the data on a specific date or using annual averages. Annual averages are sometimes preferable in countries where there is much volatility in inflation and where the inflation and wage growth assumptions reflect annual "average" rates of change.

7.2 LEGAL PROVISIONS OF THE SCHEME

The actuarial model must be adapted to the law and regulations on social security for the purpose of projecting future demographic and financial outcomes. The actuary must, therefore, be familiar with legal provisions and their actual interpretation in the daily operations of the scheme. This includes having a understanding of: social insurance coverage, definitions of contingencies for which protection is provided, the eligibility conditions for benefits, the calculation of benefit amounts, the sources of financing (mainly in relation to contributions), the definition of insurable earnings, the rules governing the

---

Box 7.2   Particular issues related to legal provisions

Two problems are often encountered regarding the legal provisions of a social security scheme, especially in developing countries:

(a) Unclear provisions

Although the social security laws of some countries are quite explicit, many contain only minimal information. Laws are normally complemented by regulations that are regularly updated. When the laws and regulations are too vague or silent, the actuary must analyse the actual operation of the scheme, that is, the interpretation by the personnel responsible for the collection and recording of contributions and for the processing of claims. Some schemes may have been put in place with a minimal set of provisions, with the management benefiting from a highly flexible interpretation of the law. Over time, this may lead to an irregular treatment of cases. All key issues in the form of amendments to the law or regulations in such systems should be clarified.

The data and information base for the valuation

> **(b) Ineffective provisions**
>
> The actuary is in a key position to point out to management discrepancies between the intention of the law and its actual application. Potential loopholes in the law influencing the behaviour of contributors and beneficiaries should be identified. This is particularly relevant to provisions regarding the number of years that are required for a person to become entitled to a pension and to the method used to calculate final average pensionable earnings on the basis of a limited number of years of past contributions, prior to retirement. The actuary should advise on ways to remedy ineffective benefit provisions.

determination of the contribution rate, if any, and the rules governing investments. This analysis of legal documents, together with a consultation on their practical application, serves to guide the collection of data by the actuary and to adjust and refine the actuarial model to fit the particular case of the scheme under study.

All planned changes in the legislation concerning financing and benefit provisions need to be reflected in the assumptions and the design of the actuarial model.

7.2.1 Coverage

There are various ways of categorizing the registered insured population contributing to the scheme and thus accumulating pension credits. Typical categories of workers that can potentially be covered under a social insurance scheme are presented in box 7.3.

7.2.2 Contingencies covered

The contingencies covered by public pension systems are normally those of retirement, disability and death. For each of these risks, benefits may take the form of pensions or lump sums (grants). Benefits may also be extended to the dependants of insured persons in case of disability and death.

The actuary must understand the scope of protection offered by the system and the way in which it is related to other available sources of insurance protection.

The definition of retirement usually refers to the insured person leaving gainful employment. In countries where pension benefits are too low, retired people often continue some form of activity in order to earn additional income. Sometimes, insured persons may be allowed to enter retirement gradually, by continuing to work on a part-time basis while collecting a reduced pension. In these cases, the actuary must study how the contributions will continue to be paid and the way in which additional periods of partial employment may induce an adjustment of benefits over time.

> **Box 7.3 Typical categories of insured persons under a social insurance pension scheme**
>
> *Wage employees*
>
> Although the usual aim of a social security system is to cover the entire working population, many countries have systems that cover only a portion of the labour force. This is often due to the existence of a separate scheme covering public-sector workers, which may have been put in place prior to the existence of the social security system and kept separate when the social security system was introduced. Other countries provide social security through a number of schemes set up according to the occupational groups covered.[2] Wage employees are found in private-sector and public-sector enterprises.
>
> *Self-employed workers*
>
> Even if the law requires that the self-employed be covered, enforcing their participation is often difficult. In some cases, the self-employed are covered on a voluntarily basis, which may present adverse selection issues. There are also cases where the self-employed can be covered conditionally to their previous attachment to the scheme as wage employees.
>
> *Rural and informal-sector workers*
>
> Rural workers and informal-sector workers are rarely covered by social security schemes. Some countries, such as Turkey and Bulgaria, where an extensive infrastructure of agriculture cooperatives exist, provide coverage for agricultural workers on the basis of their income collected from the sale of their products through cooperatives. Contributions can take the form of a direct *ad valorem* tax on the proceeds of their sales. Compliance is, of course, an issue; most of these workers earn very low wages and prefer to retain all their immediate income rather than pay any contributions. Where rural and informal-sector workers are covered, the basis for collecting contributions and calculating earnings-related benefits is usually set in reference to their gains and profits or to a flat amount, such as the minimum wage.

The other key concern for the actuary is the definition of disability (permanent or temporary, total or partial). These different definitions have a significant impact on the incidence of new invalidity cases. The actuary must carefully address the different levels of the administration to understand how the legal provisions are interpreted and applied in practice. The role of physicians in the assessment and re-evaluation of invalidity cases must also be investigated.

7.2.3 Covered earnings

The definition of insurable earnings establishes the basis on which contributions are levied and benefits are calculated. It indicates which components of remuneration are included: salary, bonus and other specific compensation supplements. Insurable earnings usually refer to gross earnings. The actuary is advised to consult with taxation authorities and government officials responsible for wage setting and reporting. This should allow the actuary to give an accurate assessment of the contribution base providing the main source of income to the scheme. It is also important to note whether contributions and benefits are based on the same remuneration basis. In some cases, the remuneration for contribution purposes excludes some additional emoluments received by the salaried, while benefits are based on the total remuneration received by the person.

In most cases, a maximum amount is set on individual earnings subject to the payment of social security contributions. The earnings ceiling may be explicitly set in the law as a nominal amount, or it may be expressed as a multiple of a readily available statistical indicator, such as the national average wage. The ceiling is mostly found in countries where there are other mechanisms available for providing income replacement after retirement – the social insurance system being referred as the first tier of some multi-pillar systems for providing income replacement to the elderly. Where the ceiling is set at a nominal amount, the actuary must carefully study the past adjustments that should have been applied to such a ceiling in the light of wage developments in the economy.

Reference to national statistics may be inadequate if these statistics do not reflect the situation under the social security system. For example, the national average wage in many countries is set in accordance with wage levels found in the public sector only, since this is often the only reliable source of information on wages in the economy. The actuary should be aware that sometimes wage data collected by the social security system are more accurate and complete than national wage data. It is possible to develop ways of forcing employers and insured persons to report the total amount of earnings, even if earnings used for the scheme's purposes are limited to a ceiling.

7.2.4 Eligibility conditions

Eligibility conditions for entitlements to benefits are usually expressed in terms of a contribution or service requirement as well as an age criterion for retirement pensions and survivors' pensions. A maximum age may also apply to determine when a benefit stops in the case of invalidity and survivors' pensions. Many schemes turn the invalidity pension into an old-age pension once an insured person reaches pensionable age.

7.2.5 Amount of benefit

The pension formula

The pension formula determines the level of the pension at the time of benefit entitlement. In most schemes, the formula is earnings-related, that is, the pension represents a percentage of an earnings base. The percentage may be uni-

> **Box 7.4 Typical pension formulae**
>
> **Proportional earnings-related pension formula**
>
> $$2\% \times \text{Number of years of contribution} \times \text{Reference earnings}$$
>
> **Non-proportional earnings-related formula**
>
> $$\left(20\% + \left(1.5\% \times \text{Number of years of contribution in excess of 15}\right)\right) \times \text{Reference earnings}$$
>
> **Formula with earnings-related and flat components**
>
> $$\text{Flat amount} + \left(1\% \times \text{Number of years of contribution in excess of 15}\right) \times \text{Reference earnings}$$

form for everyone but usually it is proportional to the length of participation of the new pensioner. Some formulae include a flat-rate component.

Reference earnings

Reference earnings used in the pension formula are usually expressed in terms of the average insurable earnings over a given period preceding retirement and may include a formula to ensure pre-retirement indexing. They are implicitly capped by the ceiling on contributory earnings, if applicable.

Reference earnings are highly dependent on the provision for pre-retirement indexing, which ensures that the real value of earnings at the time contributions were paid is maintained to calculate pensions. If no provision exists, then an analysis of the past development of insurable earnings in relation to key economic variables, such as the national average wage or the minimum wage, is recommended. This should indicate to what extent wages in the economy are covered by the scheme.

A study of possible loopholes must be undertaken, since they could alter the data collected. The actuary should be in a position to estimate the extent of the under-declaration of earnings. For example, if the definition of reference earnings takes into account only a limited number of highest insurable earnings over the period just before benefit entitlement, then it is possible that some employers and employees might collude to declare a lower level of earnings in the earlier years of their careers, which would make it possible for employers and employees to pay lower amounts of contributions without the level of the pension being negatively affected.

The data and information base for the valuation

> **Box 7.5 Typical formulae for the determination of reference earnings**
>
> **I. Final earnings**
>
> Ref. earnings $= Sal(y-1) = Sal(x) \times (1+g)^{(y-1)-x}$
>
> **II. Final three-year average**
>
> Ref. earnings $= \frac{1}{3} \times [Sal(y-3) + Sal(y-2) + Sal(y-1)]$
> $\qquad\qquad\quad = \frac{1}{3} \times Sal(x) \times [(1+g)^{(y-3)-x} + (1+g)^{(y-2)-x} + (1+g)^{(y-1)-x}]$
>
> **III. Career-average**
>
> Ref. earnings $= 1/(y-ea) \times [Sal(ea) + \ldots + Sal(x) + \ldots + Sal(y-1)]$
> $\qquad\qquad\quad = 1/(y-ea) \times Sal(x) \times [(1+g)^{ea-x} + \ldots + 1 + \ldots + (1+g)^{(y-1)-x}]$
>
> | | |
> |---|---|
> | Ref. earnings | = Reference earnings |
> | $Sal(x)$ | = Average salary earned at age x |
> | g | = Assumed average wage growth rate (constant for all years) |
> | x | = Age at valuation date; $x<y$ |
> | y | = Age at time of retirement (legal normal retirement age) |
> | ea | = Entry age into the scheme |

Redistribution

The redistribution function of a social insurance pension scheme is mainly achieved through its pension formula. Where the provision of a flat benefit in nominal terms is given to all pensioners, the extent of redistribution depends on the level of the flat benefit and how its real value is maintained over time. Also, the provision for a fixed percentage replacement rate of insurable earnings for anyone having met the minimum contributory requirements allows for redistribution, mainly to workers who have been unemployed for relatively long periods during the course of their careers. The minimum pension is another redistribution mechanism, which mainly goes to lower-income earners.

Maximum pension

A maximum ceiling is usually placed on the amount of the monthly pension. This may also be done indirectly through the application of the earnings ceiling. In addition, a maximum is often imposed on the total combined old-age and survivor's pensions a person may receive.

Minimum pension

Minimum benefit guarantees are usually provided either as a fixed amount (which is revised on an ad hoc basis or through automatic adjustments) or in terms of a multiple applied to the legal minimum wage or to the national average wage.

The study of the minimum pension in relation to average insurable earnings (or to other key economic variables, such as the national average wage, the minimum wage or the minimum subsistence level) gives a perspective on the degree of benefit protection provided. The past adjustment of the minimum pension in relation to price and wage developments is important in order to build projection assumptions on indexing.

Grants

A grant is often paid in lieu of a pension to insured persons not fulfilling the minimum contributory or service requirement concerning pension eligibility. The requirements may vary greatly from one country to another. The ILO's Conventions concerning minimum standards for social security provide a useful reference for determining the adequacy and fairness of provisions for ineligible people: a person with 15 years of pension credits should be entitled to at least some form of pro rata lifetime pension.

Indexing provisions

Inflation has a direct impact on minimum benefits, fixed-cash benefits, pensions in payment and the ceiling on insurable earnings. These parameters should be adjusted to maintain their real value over time, otherwise the intent and relevance of the social security system is affected. This is done either by way of an automatic mechanism set in the law or on an ad hoc basis.

Various considerations are taken into account to determine an indexation adjustment for the scheme's parameters. Box 7.6 presents those that commonly apply.

Adequacy of benefits

The actuary's analysis of the pension formula prior to undertaking the actuarial projections helps to assess the level of protection offered and the significance of the scheme. The following procedure may be used:

- A table of the percentage replacement rates for all lengths of contribution or service periods; this should indicate whether the system has a bias towards longer or shorter careers;
- For a system providing reduced pension benefits to people not fulfilling the minimum eligibility criteria: the actual degree of reduction should be compared with the actuarial equivalence to determine whether there might be some cross-subsidization for early retirements ("early" not only in the sense of retiring at an age earlier than the normal retirement age but also

The data and information base for the valuation

Box 7.6 Considerations for defining the basis for indexing social security benefits

1. Reference statistics: changes in price inflation or wage developments.
2. Frequency of adjustments in line with the administrative capacity of the scheme and the time lags for reporting the reference statistics.
3. The period over which changes in the reference statistics are observed, perhaps in relation to past changes over a specific period or to projected changes in the future.
4. The calculation basis including the minimum degree of change in the reference statistics that provoke adjustments, the proportion of the change in the reference statistics that is taken into account and the maximum inflation adjustment. For example, benefits are adjusted if the annual rate of increase of the national average wage is above 3 per cent, and then only 80 per cent of the change is taken into account up to a maximum inflation adjustment of 8 per cent.

---

in the case of a person retiring at an age above the insurable age with a record of contributions below the minimum); and

- A study of the maximum pension in relation to average insurable earnings and to other key economic variables, such as the national average wage, the minimum wage or the minimum subsistence level; this should give a perspective on the degree of protection provided.

The actuary should communicate a quantitative analysis of the scheme's benefit provisions to management to document the policy analysis. In some situations, parameters of the scheme have not been adjusted for extended periods of time to reflect price or wage increases and benefits have gradually lost their significance. The actuary has the responsibility to raise these types of issues.

The ILO Social Security (Minimum Standards) Convention, 1952 (No. 102) provides useful guidelines for setting the minimum a scheme should offer. For example, these standards state that the normal retirement age should not be set at an age later than 65. In addition, a lifetime pension of at least 40 to 50 per cent of the total career earnings for someone with a 30-year contributory/service record should be provided. A benefit must be provided if the person has at least a 15-year contributory record. A brief overview of ILO Convention No. 102 is provided in Technical Brief II.

7.2.6 Financing provisions

The law usually determines the basis upon which contributions are calculated, including the definition of insurable earnings and the level of contribution rates. In a number of cases, the law only stipulates that contribution rates must be

Actuarial practice in social security

fixed according to the recommendations of an actuary and that it must be reviewed at least every three to five years. In some countries, scheduled increases in contribution rates are stipulated in the law.

7.3 GENERAL DEMOGRAPHIC AND ECONOMIC DATA

The macroeconomic and population projections provide the general framework for the actuarial valuation. The actuary must carefully assess the environment in which the scheme is likely to evolve in the future, and the actuarial valuation parameters and assumptions should be consistent with the general environment.

Box 7.7   Checklist of the data to be collected for building the demographic and macroeconomic frames for an actuarial valuation

General population data
- Population by sex and age group (historical and future)
- Fertility rates and sex ratio of newborns (historical and future)
- Mortality rates (historical and future)
- Immigration and emigration (historical and future)
- Marriage rate by sex and age group (historical and future)

Labour force, employment and unemployment
- Labour force participation rates (historical and future)
- Employment, average number of people (historical and future)
- Self-employment, average number of persons (historical and future)
- Unemployment, average number of persons (historical and future)
- Unemployment rates (historical and future)

Wages, interest rates, inflation, GDP
- Total compensation in nominal values (historical)
- Wage share of GDP (historical)
- Average wages for the economy and by sectors
- GDP by economic sectors
- GDP deflators by sector
- GDP by expenditure components
- GDP expenditure deflators
- Primary factor income distribution
- Inflation and interest rates
- Exchange rate
- National budget

This is even more important for schemes providing a quasi-universal coverage of the population and where a majority of the old-age population relies on social security benefits.

Improved life expectancy, decreasing fertility rates, changes in employment forecasts and variations in real wage are all factors that can have a strong impact on the future of a scheme, and need to be reflected in the projection assumptions.

Box 7.7 provides a checklist of key information to be collected for building the demographic and macroeconomic frames.

It is often useful to study past developments as far back as possible to assess whether there have been any significant variations over time. In countries where the economy has been unstable, either for a long time or at different recurrences, the more recent period (if there are signs of stability) is more relevant. However, although it might seem logical to do this in order to make projections of 50 to 100 years into the future, there is much debate about the appropriateness of relying on past experience to do so. A time series study could reveal particular behaviour and trends that may be accounted for in the development of actuarial assumptions.[3]

7.4 SCHEME-SPECIFIC DATA

7.4.1 Appraisal of the institution's data maintenance system

It is essential to investigate the social security administrative process concerning every stage of an individual's participation. These stages include the following: the worker is registered under the system, the employer reports insurable earnings, the employer pays contributions, the insured claims a benefit, the insured dies, survivors claim benefits and the last survivor dies. An analysis of these processes will normally reveal the existence of inadequate procedures, unnecessary delays, etc.

The record maintenance system needs to be studied to determine which statistical extractions can be performed directly from the scheme's data. This will be an opportunity to recommend possible improvements to the recording system, which should have a positive effect on the database available for future actuarial reviews.

The determination of actuarial assumptions should pay consideration to the administrative function of the social security institution, notably:

- the need for records on individual insured persons and employers;
- the nature of social insurance records, record-keeping obligations to the scheme;
- records relating to employers: classification of employers, structure and logic of the registration system, non-compliance records, etc.;

Actuarial practice in social security

- records relating to insured persons: classification and link to the employer and other classes, individual contribution records (number of pension credits), insurable earnings, personal data, family data, etc.;
- records relating to beneficiaries;
- enforcement: benefits managed with sufficient rigour, in particular for continuing to pay invalidity benefits, collection of contribution arrears, etc.;
- different structures of data maintenance systems: centralized/decentralized records, system of control.

7.4.2 Database on the insured population

For an ongoing system, the historical data on the number of active contributors and inactive insured persons are normally available. These populations should be compared with the potential insured population (according to the law) and used for the calculation of historical coverage rates. For a newly introduced scheme, the potential insured population may be calculated from the legal provisions of the scheme and global data on employment, but a realistic assumption on actual coverage should take into account other factors, notably the administrative structure in place and planned improvements in coverage.

The actuary must determine the main characteristics of the insured groups (age, sex, employed versus self-employed). The valuation is usually undertaken using a certain number of groups with similar characteristics. Separate groups are normally used, at least for men and women. If the data are avail-

---

Box 7.8   Breakdown of insured persons under a pension scheme

(a) Initial (at beginning of year) active insured persons contributing to the scheme and continuing as active contributors throughout the year;

(b) Initial (at beginning of year) active insured persons who stop contributing to the scheme during the year while retaining entitlement to benefits in the future;

(c) New entrants to the group of active insured persons contributing to the scheme and continuing as active contributors throughout the year;

(d) New entrants to the group of active insured persons contributing to the scheme but leaving the groups of active contributors at some point during the year;

(e) Initial (at beginning of year) inactive insured persons with pension entitlements who will re-enter the group of active contributors during the year (similar to c);

(f) Initial (at beginning of year) inactive insured persons with pension entitlements, who remain inactive throughout the year while retaining entitlements to benefits in future.

able, it is also useful to segregate between employees of the public sector, private-sector employees and the self-employed. The actuary must be aware of the individual characteristics that may be lost by grouping the data, notably with respect to the distribution of insurable earnings and the annual pattern of employment, which could affect the records of years of contribution. The use of data by individual age around the retirement age allows a more precise assessment of the incidence of new old-age pensions.

Typically, the groups of insured persons are divided as shown in box 7.8.

The collection of data should be sufficiently detailed for the actuary to determine the variability of data around the average. Where dispersion is important, the actuary may decide to allow for additional sub-groups of insured persons. This is relevant, for example, where insurable earnings and records of past contributory/service credits vary greatly. Strictly using averages may lead to truncated projections in the case of a model that determines the eligibility for benefits by considering only the average number of years of credits. If the average falls above the minimum requirement for entitlement to a pension, then the entire cohort entering into retirement will be projected to receive a pension, while in reality a proportion of them may not be entitled to receive a pension because of an insufficient record of pension credits.

Number of insured persons at the valuation date

The insured population includes present contributors and inactive insured persons registered in the past but not having contributed during the last financial year. Inactive insured persons have an impact on the scheme's financial situation because they have acquired rights to benefits from past contributions and they are potential beneficiaries, even if they pay no more contributions. They could also re-enter the scheme as active contributors and accumulate further credits.

The age and sex distribution of active and inactive insured persons is necessary to project future new beneficiaries. Although individual-age data offer the most accurate picture, it is possible to rely on provided data that have been divided into five-year age groupings.

The age-distribution of the insured population normally follows the ageing process observed in the general population. This implies that the average age of insured persons may be increasing over time, which may imply higher average wages and thus higher pensions in the long term.

The actuary must be aware of the following issues when collecting and analysing the past data on insured persons:

- the need for consistency between the historical development of the insured population, the labour force and the employed population;
- the need for a suitable basis to determine the age of an insured person: age nearest birthday, average age, etc.;

- possible data problems due to the computer system of the social security organization as well as alternative methods to estimate the necessary information where no accurate data are available;
- the danger of using grouped data that require interpolation, with the possibility that important information on the characteristics of the insured population will be lost.

New entrants and re-entrants to the insured population

New entrants in a particular year are those newly registered insured persons who have never contributed to the scheme. Re-entrants in a particular year are those who have been registered in previous years and have already contributed to the scheme but not during the last year. A time series on new entrants and re-entrants may indicate specific patterns that can be compared with employment patterns to develop scheme-specific assumptions in projecting the group of contributors for each future year.

Although information on insured persons may be available, it is more difficult to collect reliable information on annual flows of new entrants and re-entrants as this requires the analysis of individual records. The actuary may have to make an educated guess as to the pattern of new entries and re-entries, notably on their age distribution and the economic sectors where it is expected to occur in the future.

Level of earnings

Insurable earnings are those earnings that are subject to the payment of contributions. On an annual basis, two elements differentiate the rate of salary for an individual from the actual earnings on which contributions are paid:

- the presence of an earnings ceiling and/or an exemption limit;
- the density of contribution, which takes into account the fact that the average worker does not have a full year of presence in the labour market over a year.

For valuation purposes, earnings data should be collected on two bases: firstly, total earnings, not including the ceiling and the exemption, and secondly, earnings subject to contributions and thus taking into account any ceiling or exemption. The reason to obtain earnings on these two bases is that the earnings of the insured population and the ceiling may evolve differently. If, for example, the ceiling is not adjusted every year to reflect the general increase in earnings, contributory earnings will represent, over time, a gradually decreasing proportion of total earnings. In addition, an end product of the actuarial valuation may consist of estimating the effect, for example, of raising the earnings ceiling or extending coverage to new sectors of the labour force. A complete data set on total earnings is essential for that purpose. Information on total (unlimited) earnings is also crucial in assessing the earnings coverage rate by social security (the catchment factor). It enables the actuary to calculate a time series of the ceiling as a multiple of average earnings in the economy. This serves to indicate whether the coverage of earnings by the social insurance scheme has remained constant or whether it has been eroded by inflation in the past. If the ceiling has not been adjusted over the years to reflect the general rise in wages in the economy, then the insurable earnings have gradually decreased in proportion to wages in the economy.

When an exemption is present, the scheme may exclude earnings below a certain level for the purpose of calculating contributions but may also take into account those earnings in the computation of benefits. As a consequence, some workers with total earnings below the exemption limit (mostly part-time workers) are excluded from participating in the scheme, which decreases the total number of insured persons and increases the average earnings of the covered population. In the Canada Pension Plan, for example, the first C$3,500 of annual earnings is not subject to contributions, but those earnings are nevertheless used in the computation of benefits.

In building the database for an actuarial valuation, the actuary should try to obtain total earnings for the various components of the workforce and, from there, obtain the subset of those total earnings corresponding to the covered earnings of the insured population. Table 7.1 presents average insurable earnings for Demoland under two bases, one limited to the ceiling, the other unlimited.

In order to reflect the impact of lower and upper limits on the revenue and expenditure of the scheme adequately, it is also necessary to obtain the distribution of total unlimited earnings according to earnings classes.

The projection of insurable earnings for the first few years following the valuation date are largely influenced by the data collected on the population

Table 7.1 Average earnings of active contributors (the Demoland case)

Age	Average monthly insurable earnings in $ (including the effect of the earnings ceiling)		Average monthly salary rate in $ (not limited to the scheme's ceiling)	
	Males	Females	Males	Females
17	4 725	4 511	8 977	7 849
22	8 755	7 814	16 634	13 596
27	12 675	9 602	24 083	16 707
32	14 794	10 116	28 109	17 602
37	16 234	11 972	30 845	20 831
42	21 465	15 037	40 784	26 164
47	21 532	14 451	40 911	25 145
52	22 043	16 527	41 882	28 757
57	23 146	18 697	43 977	32 533
Total	20 077	14 236	29 294	19 469

of active contributors for the period just preceding the valuation date. These data are very important for the short-term credibility of the valuation. The actuary must carefully study the data provided and the basis under which they were collected. If they have been extracted from administrative files, insurable earnings will normally reflect the amount on which contributions were calculated. They are then limited to the earnings ceiling and (when looked at on an annual basis) will reflect the fact that the insured persons may have been unemployed for part of the year. In that case, earnings should be recorded for a short period (such as monthly), usually corresponding to the frequency of the collection of contributions. Then, later in the treatment of earnings, a density factor, corresponding to the proportion of the year worked by the average worker, will allow the step between the monthly rate of earnings and the annual earnings subject to contributions to be made.

But these data are not sufficient to measure the impact of, for example, increasing the earnings ceiling. Therefore, if at all possible, it is important to obtain the data on total earnings not limited to any ceiling.

The computation of insurable earnings must be consistent with the approach used to determine the number of contributors over a given year. For example, an insured person is defined here as a person who has contributed at least once during the year. Using the monthly rate of earnings times 12, multiplied by the density factor produces the annual insurable earnings corresponding to that population. If another basis is used for the determination of the insured population, the definition of insurable earnings must be adjusted accordingly.

The actuary should collect the data on aggregate contribution income and insurable earnings base and perform reconciliation adjustments on individual records where necessary. This reconciliation of total contribution income may be based on the comparison of the social security institution's financial statements and individual computer records. An exemption limit may be specified to allow low-income earners to be exempt from contribution payments. Some schemes, however, do not require the reporting of such earnings below the floor level, which implies they are excluded from participating in the scheme. Ultimately, this means that the total number of insured persons is lower than it should be and the scheme's average earnings are higher than they should be.

Past accumulated credits

Past credits are used in the actuarial valuation for two purposes:

- When a covered contingency occurs, such as retirement, invalidity or death, past credits act as the benchmark for assessing the eligibility of the insured person for a lifetime pension or other benefits, such as grants. Entitlement is usually expressed in terms of a required minimum number of units of paid contributions or credited service, along with an age criterion for old-age benefits.

- The computation of a pension or grant is usually based on past accumulated credits and insurable earnings.

Past credits may be calculated as the accumulated number of contributions made on behalf of an individual or as the number of years of past service. In the first instance, which is the most frequent, any contribution deducted by the employer and not remitted to the social security authority goes unrecorded and penalizes the participant at the time a benefit entitlement has to be assessed. In the second case, where insurance credits are equal to actual years of service, the entitlement and amount of pensions are not affected by the employer's compliance. This second method is usually found in schemes for civil servants. In any case, insurance credits are affected by the density of contribution payments and hence by any period of unemployment. Initial insurance credits form an important part of the profile of an insured person under the system, since they reflect accrued rights of the initial insured population as of the valuation date. The scheme is committed to honour such rights in the future by way of providing a lifetime pension when eligibility requirements have been satisfied.

The age and sex distribution of pasts credits among active contributors and inactive insured persons is required for a more accurate assessment of the accrued rights of the existing insured population as of the valuation date and to project future benefits.

Where the scheme covers almost 100 per cent of the labour force, another method to estimate past credits can be used. In such a case, past general economic data of the country can be assumed to reproduce the employment behaviour of the scheme's insured population. For an age-sex cohort, the probability of being employed during a year (the ratio of employed people to the total active population) may be assumed to represent the amount of credit that this age-sex cohort accumulates during that year. Thus the accumulated past service of each cohort can be assumed to be equal to the sum of annual employment rates from the first age at which a person can become eligible in the scheme.

Density of contribution payments

Time series on the average number of paid contributions or credited service are used to calculate the density of contribution payments, which reflects the average proportion of a year for which the contributions were paid by active contributors in that year.[4] Alternatively, density factors may be defined as the ratio of the average number of contributors during the year to the total number of insured persons who paid at least one contribution or credited service during the year.

The computation of density factors is usually performed from the age and sex distribution of the number of people who contributed for different periods during a given year. Using this distribution, an average number of months of contributions paid or service is calculated. Such an average is then divided by

> **Box 7.9 Past service of the insured population (the Demoland case)**
>
> The data on the accrued past service of the active and the inactive insured population were available in the administrative file of the National Insurance Scheme (NIS). For each age and sex group, the average number of years of past insurance credits has been distributed over a given span of years in order to reflect more accurately the effect of eligibility conditions on the number of new emerging pensions. A normal distribution is used, with a standard deviation of the number of years equal to one-third of the average.
>
> Average past credits of the inactive insured persons were assumed equal to the ones used for active persons.
>
> **Assumed average past credits of active and inactive insured persons**
>
> | Age | Average number of weeks of past contributions | |
> |---|---|---|
> | | Males | Females |
> | 15–19 | 38 | 30 |
> | 20–24 | 161 | 143 |
> | 25–29 | 254 | 219 |
> | 30–34 | 389 | 349 |
> | 35–39 | 615 | 492 |
> | 40–44 | 723 | 603 |
> | 45–49 | 862 | 671 |
> | 50–54 | 842 | 719 |
> | 55–59 | 838 | 819 |

the number of time units in the year (12, if using monthly contributions) to obtain density factors.

7.4.3 Database on beneficiaries

Number of pensioners

The sex and age distribution of pensioners receiving a pension as of the valuation date must be collected for each type of benefit. Where there are subcategories of benefit types, detailed data must be gathered, for example, on partial and total disability pensions.

The actuary should aim to collect disaggregated data on the number of new cases and pensioners in payment, including information on the distribution of amounts by age and sex as of the valuation date. Special attention should be paid to pensioners who receive more than one type of pension. The actuary should develop a checking procedure for the reliability of the data collected and the observed information that may have been collected at random in, for example, regional offices. In any case, a preliminary assessment of the reliability of the institution's records is needed.

Cohort tables should be built according to the year of birth of pensioners. They will be useful in building assumptions on the incidence of the various pensions. Such cohort tables will be used for the determination of invalidity, mortality and rehabilitation rates, etc. The actuary should analyse past patterns of newly awarded benefits in relation to the insured population.

Amount of pensions

The database on pensioners must also include their average pension amounts. The actuary should collect information and perform preliminary analysis on:

- the total benefit expenditure by year;
- the reconciliation of total benefit expenditure between individual records obtained from the information system and the financial statements;
- average pensions and average replacement rates;
- the historical development of average pensions by age and by number of years since inception; this should reflect the effect of inflation in the event that no protection is offered against inflation and whether pensions have developed in line with insurable earnings;
- the historical development of minimum benefits in relation to inflation and wage developments in the economy.

This information is of particular use in analysing the adequacy of income protection provided by pensions.

Notes

[1] It is important to stress the differences between 'enterprise' and 'household' surveys. Enterprise surveys usually gather more accurate information on wages, since they relate to clear-cut situations, such as how many employees worked more than x-number of hours over the given period (e.g. one month). Household surveys are more complex in their way of addressing the issue of employment (how many hours worked last month in any form of gainful employment). The information compiled through household surveys is often incompatible with the requirements for the macroeconomic projections of employment and difficult to check for accuracy. This is especially relevant in countries with a significant proportion of workers engaged in informal gainful activities.

[2] This was the case in certain Latin American countries, such as Chile, Colombia and Peru, where major differences in the level of benefit protection developed over time because of different political situations, which, of course, caused inequitable treatment. The actuary may be asked to do a comparative study to compare benefit protection according to different provisions (cf. section 7.2.5 on the collection of data on the benefit formula and section 12.1.3 on the modelling of alternative benefit provisions).

[3] For further information on macroeconomic data, see W. Scholz, K. Hagemejer and M. Cichon: *Social budgeting* (Geneva, ILO/ISSA, 2000).

[4] Contributors of a particular year being defined as the group of insured persons having paid at least one unit of contributions in that given year.

THE ANALYSIS OF PAST EXPERIENCE   8

Before examining the projection of the pension scheme's future development, it is first necessary to look at past experience and trend patterns. To undertake this type of analysis, the actuary primarily uses the information contained in the financial statements of the social security institution, but other sources of information include specific reports on the collection of contributions, benefits, administrative expenses and investments. A careful analysis of the past reinforces the basis for determining certain assumptions on the future development of the scheme.

8.1 FINANCIAL STATEMENTS

Every enterprise – public or private – produces annual financial statements. For private enterprises, they represent the set of information that provides a picture of the value of the company and of the evolution of its activities over time. They are also used for calculating the company's tax liabilities. For public bodies, financial statements represent the main tools by which the board of directors, government officials, politicians and financiers of these institutions can monitor the financial development of a scheme and evaluate the quality of management.

A balance sheet is a statement of what an entity owns and what it owes at a particular point in time. It shows the assets and how the assets are financed. Liabilities indicate what sums of money have been made available to finance the assets. Total assets always equal total liabilities.

The balance sheet needs to be supported by an income and expenditure statement, which complements the balance sheet by showing revenue and expenditure of the entity over the last financial period and, consequently, the surplus or deficit generated during that period.

8.1.1 Cash versus accrual basis

Financial statements can be presented on a cash or accrual basis.[1] The cash basis records receipts and disbursements at the time they are received or disbursed. The accrual basis allocates, as precisely as possible, the revenue and expenditure to the financial period to which they refer, even if the actual receipt or disbursement of money occurred in a different period. For example, the collection of contributions may take some time between the payroll deduction made by the employer and the deposit of money to the social security institution. Under the accrual basis of accounting, contribution income should be allocated to the year in which the payroll deduction occurred. Another example refers to the initial payment of an invalidity pension. Because of the medical evaluation necessary to establish eligibility for an invalidity pension, a period of several weeks normally elapses between the date of the claim and the date of emission of the first pension payment. In this case, the first pension payment usually includes a retroactive adjustment. Under the accrual basis of accounting, if the period of medical evaluation by the institution overlaps the end of the financial period, the retroactive payment should be split between the two periods.

8.1.2 Financial reporting

Periodically, an institution must report on its financial position as of a given date and on the results of its operations over the past year. These reports exist for internal monitoring as well as for external purposes (for example, the legal submission of budget statements). Other financial reports are made available to the general public but they are more of a statistical rather than financial reporting nature. The form and content of external reports are sometimes prescribed by the government, mainly in order to be compatible with other government accounts. Ideally, such statements should be audited by qualified external firms or by agencies that specialize in government work.

In general terms, financial reporting should provide information that will help the general public understand the system. Therefore, it should be comprehensible to people with only a basic knowledge of financial issues. The primary purpose of financial reporting is to give an accurate measure of a scheme's performance.

In addition to the balance sheet and income and expenditure statement of the scheme, a certain number of financial reports can be of use to the actuarial valuation. The investment report gives information on the structure of the investment portfolio and on past investment income for each type of investment. This will be important to the actuary for the analysis of the investment performance, the establishment of an investment policy and the determination of assumptions on the future rate of return on the scheme's reserve.

An analysis of the financial statements may show cross-subsidization between the different benefit branches. In such a situation, and to respect the

Actuarial practice in social security

financial system recommended for each branch, the actuary normally recommends that the branches be separated for accounting and financing purposes. If the accounting of the different benefit branches is not clearly separated, the short-term benefit branches then usually attract all the revenue they need for their PAYG financing, and the pension branch is credited only with the residual revenue. If this is done systematically over long periods, the financing of the pension branch may be compromised.

The actuary should reconcile the information contained in the financial statements with the information collected from the individual records of the institution, particularly on contributions collected and on benefits paid

---

Box 8.1   Typical balance sheet of a social security institution

Assets		Liabilities	
Cash	95	Payables	675
Receivables	512	Bank borrowing	987
Investments	23 465		
Fixed assets	1 456	Reserves	23 866
Total assets	**25 528**	**Total liabilities**	**25 528**

Box 8.2   Typical income statement of a social security scheme

Income	
Contributions	
Employees	5 000
Employers	5 000
Government subsidy	1 000
Investment earnings	1 000
Other income	50
Total income	12 050
Expenditure	
Benefits	10 000
Administrative expenses	1 000
Total expenditure	11 000
Excess of income over expenditures	1 050
Reserve at the beginning of the year	15 000
Reserve at the end of the year	16 050

during a given period. This check may reveal a particular accounting practice used by the institution and may also help the actuary fix the basis for projections (cash versus accrued basis) more accurately. In this case, the actuary needs to determine on which basis the projection results will be presented – adjustment factors may be necessary to present the results in a familiar way to the readers of the report. Special attention should be paid to the consistency of the assets valuation, including notes to the financial statements, to assess whether an adjustment might be needed in case of non-performing investments that might be written off in the short term.

8.2 EXPERIENCE ANALYSIS AND KEY INDICATORS

The actuarial valuation of a social insurance scheme usually starts with the analysis of past experience in order to see trends and to help in determining assumptions[2] on the future development of the scheme, at least for the short term. The first step is thus a look at the global items of revenue and expenditure appearing in the financial statements of the scheme and an analysis of explanations for differences between the reality and the projections of the last actuarial valuation. In the valuation process of occupational pension schemes, this exercise is called the "gain and loss analysis". However, the process is different in public pension schemes, since here we are dealing with flows of funds in an open-group environment, rather than present values for a closed group.

The experience analysis then takes, separately, each item of revenue and expenditure and their evolution since the last valuation. Differences between previous projections and actual results need to be separated into their various components:

- In the case of contributions, differences may arise because of rises in salary higher or lower than projected, the annual adjustment of the earnings ceiling, or differences between the recommended contribution rates and those actually enacted. In addition, the performance of the institution in collecting contributions can also have a significant impact on the actual amount of contributions collected. General economic conditions also affect the contribution income. An increase in unemployment normally has a negative effect on the number of contributors, which directly reduces the contribution income.
- The investment income is the result of the portfolio composition combined with the rate of return in each investment sector. The general level of interest rates, as well as, in certain cases, the evolution of the markets (when part of the portfolio is invested in equity) affects the global investment return. Differences between projections and actual results may also come from a change

in the portfolio composition that was not expected at the time of the last valuation.
- The comparison of actual versus expected benefit expenditures is normally made separately for each type of benefit. Firstly, regarding the number of retirement pensions, one should look at the retirement behaviour of the insured population. The economic environment, any legal change or the entry into force of another separate programme encouraging retirement may affect the retirement rate and generate a greater number of new retirees compared with the projections. The invalidity incidence, a variable that may vary greatly over very short periods, can explain some other variations in results. For example, the adoption of a new administrative procedure to study invalidity claims may affect the number of new beneficiaries. Experience is generally more stable on survivors' pensions, but it is necessary to examine the differences between the number of new survivors' pensions and the number of funeral grants in order to ascertain whether the assumption on the proportion of insured persons who have a spouse was correctly estimated. As to the amount of pensions, differences usually result from the gap between the actual rate of indexation of benefits and the evolution of the index assumed in the last valuation (CPI, increase in national wage, etc.). Any ad hoc revaluation of pensions in payment occurring between two valuation dates can also create discrepancies.

The analysis of past financial operations may also be done using various indicators. Some indicators presented here concerning the past evolution of the scheme are also used to describe the future evolution of the scheme (see Chapter 11). Determining past periods helps ensure continuity between past experience and projections.

- The PAYG cost rate represents the ratio of annual expenditures over total insurable earnings. It reveals what should be the contribution rate in the absence of any reserve, just to support the current expenditures of the scheme. This ratio may be calculated for each expenditure component. A comparison of the PAYG rate with the actual contribution rate of the scheme may quickly show the need for a rapid increase in the contribution rate.
- The reserve ratio is calculated as the ratio of the reserve at year-end over the annual expenditures of the scheme. This ratio can be interpreted as the length of the period (in years) over which the present reserve may support a scheme's expenditures in the absence of contributions and investment income. Historical reserve ratios must be analysed with a view to the maturing process of the scheme. Large reserve ratios in a new scheme, for example, are not necessarily a sign of a good financial situation; they simply show that the annual expen-

diture is very low. It is also important to separate the reserve by benefit branch in order to identify correctly the amount of reserve allocated to pensions, this reserve having a different role than the one played by the reserves of the short-term branches. The reserve ratio observed over recent years should be compared with the evolution of the ratio projected in the last valuation in order to measure the correct application of the financial system and the attainment of the funding objectives established for the scheme.

- Past demographic ratios may be calculated for each year as the number of pensioners over the number of contributors. The past evolution of the ratio should be analysed separately for each type of benefit.
- Average replacement rates are calculated as the ratio of average pensions over the average insurable earnings of active contributors, and can be compared with the theoretical replacement rate according to the scheme's provisions. The actuary is then in a position to give an opinion on the attainment of the earnings replacement objectives of the scheme.

8.3 THE ANALYSIS OF ADMINISTRATIVE EXPENSES

The actuarial report does not need to go through a detailed analysis of administrative expenses of the institution, since this falls within the management consultant's brief. However, the actuary should be aware of the weight of administrative expenses in the total expenditure of the scheme as well as know how the evolution of administrative expenses can affect future contribution rates.

The main administrative functions of a social security institution are:

- the registration of workers and employers;
- the collection of contributions;
- the maintenance of records on contributions and insured earnings;

Box 8.3 Typical administrative expenses of a social security institution

1. Salaries
2. Transportation
3. Communication
4. Professional fees
5. Rent
6. Maintenance
7. Office supplies
8. Material and equipment
9. The amortization of buildings and equipment

- the reception and assessment of benefit claims;
- the calculation and payment of benefits.

An analysis of administrative expenses should ideally be made separately by function in order to identify strengths and weaknesses and to recommend appropriate action to reduce the costs of the scheme. To perform the analysis, it is common to express administrative expenses as a percentage of contributions or benefits, or as a percentage of total insured earnings. For example, expenses related to the collection of contributions are better analysed when expressed in terms of contributions or insured earnings. The expenses of processing benefit claims are better analysed when related to total benefit expenditure.

Caution is, however, necessary when expressing administrative expenses as a percentage of contributions, since the contribution rate of the scheme may be gradually rising and the ratio of administrative expenses may be decreasing, simply because of the increase in the denominator (contributions). The ratios of administrative expenses may be compared with similar schemes to highlight possible problems, but such a comparison must always be taken with caution because of differences in the risk covered, the size of the schemes and their age. For example, a new scheme normally incurs high administrative costs at its inception as a percentage of benefits paid. Or the social security institution may have recently changed its computer system, which will affect the level of its expenses for a certain number of years. In such a situation, it may be worthwhile to isolate these ad hoc expenses before calculating the ratios.

The value of the analysis of administrative expenses resides mainly in the fact that it makes a regular follow-up necessary. An evaluation of administrative expenses at regular intervals allows trends to be studied and is a way of recommending appropriate action for future reductions in expenses.

8.4 THE ANALYSIS OF INVESTMENT PERFORMANCE

There are a number of different ways of measuring the investment return of a pension fund. Box 8.4 presents the internal rate of return, the time-weighted rate of return and the average portfolio methods.

It is the net rate of return that is useful for evaluating the financial status of the scheme. To judge its adequacy for the scheme, the observed investment return should be compared with market indices, with the inflation rate and/or with the rates offered on specific government securities, the choice of indices depending on the composition of the portfolio. It is possible to compare the return of each type of asset (bonds, shares, mortgages, real estate) with a general index related to each type of asset (for example, the S&P 500 index in the United States). The choice of index, in this case, is critical to the analysis. This kind of comparison should be made over sufficiently long periods to avoid opinions based on short-term observed data that might be biased

Box 8.4   Calculation of the rate of return of a pension fund

(a) Dollar-weighted rate of return (internal rate of return)

The rate of return that makes the accumulated value of the initial reserve, plus the accumulated value of cash flows during the period, equals the reserve at the end of the period.

This method depicts the actual return and is dependent on the particular cash flows of that fund. The timing of cash flows in or out of a fund can have a profound influence on the investment return achieved by it.

Example : Suppose $A(t)$ and $B(t)$ are respectively the value of the fund at the beginning and at the end of the year, and $CF(a)$ and $CF(b)$ are the net cash flows respectively six and nine months after the beginning of the year.

Formula 8.1

$$A(t) * [1 + i(t)] + CF(a) * [1 + i(t)]^{\frac{1}{2}} + CF(b) * [1 + i(t)]^{\frac{1}{4}} = B(t)$$

(b) Time-weighted rate of return

This method is useful when comparing the returns of different asset managers. A lump-sum investment is invested at the beginning of a period and the resultant value at the end of the period is calculated, assuming that there is no cash flow in or out of the portfolio during that time. The global time-weighted rate of return for the period is then calculated as the compound rate of the individual subperiods.

This method avoids the distortion created by specific cash flows.

Example: Suppose the following rates of return for each quarter, corresponding to the frequency of cash flows into a fund:

1st quarter	4 per cent
2nd quarter	6 per cent
3rd quarter	9 per cent
4th quarter	2 per cent

The time-weighted rate of return is the geometric average of these rates of return, thus ignoring the effect of cash flows into the fund.

Formula 8.2

$$\text{Time-weighted rate of return} = ((1.04)^{\frac{1}{4}} * (1.06)^{\frac{1}{4}} * (1.09)^{\frac{1}{4}} * (1.02)^{\frac{1}{4}})$$
$$- 1.00 = 5.218\%$$

(c) Average rate of return

The average rate of return is calculated from four basic figures:

- $A(t)$ is the reserve at the beginning of the period for which the interest rate is calculated;

- B(t) is the reserve at the end of the period for which the interest rate is calculated;
- I(t) is the investment income during the period;
- CF(t) is the cash flow during the period, excluding the investment income.

The general equation to generate $B(t)$ from $A(t)$ is the following:

Formula 8.3

$$B(t) = A(t) + CF(t) + I(t)$$

In order to calculate the average rate of return, here called $i(t)$, resulting from the investment, the following equation applies:

Formula 8.4

$$I(t) = [A(t) * i(t)] + [CF(t) * i(t) \div 2]$$

This equation assumes that $CF(t)$ is received by the fund on average at the middle of period t. Combining formulae 8.3 and 8.4 generates:

Formula 8.5

$$i(t) = 2 * I(t) \div [A(t) + B(t) - I(t)]$$

owing to a particular economic environment at the moment of the assessment. Special treatment may be necessary when evaluating the return on foreign investments, for example in the choice of comparison indices.

The observed return should also be compared with the rate of return expected from the application of the investment policy of the scheme. Any important differences should be explained and, if the return of the scheme is systematically lower than expectations, a review of the investment policy itself should be envisaged. It may be necessary to review the expected return considering recent performance, or the exercise may call for a review of the portfolio composition in order to reach the level of return used in actuarial projections. In some countries, investment opportunities are very limited and a change in the investment policy can only be envisaged for the long term. It must be recalled that the investment policy should be in line with the rate of return assumed by the actuary under the financial system.

The analysis of investment return must take into account investment expenses. It should be noted that, very often, investment earnings are reported net of expenses in the financial statements of the social security institution. Then, the actuary has to use other specific reports to enquire about the level of these expenses and how they affect the effective rate of return.

8.5 DETERMINING THE VALUE OF THE RESERVE

Recommendations regarding the future financing and funding objectives of a social security scheme use as a starting point the value of the reserve as of the valuation date. Determining this value is, therefore, extremely important. Financial statements are the main source of information. The actuary should, however, be warned that a figure directly extracted from the financial statements may not be adequate enough to reflect the value of the reserve in a long-term perspective. It is, therefore, necessary to choose an appropriate basis for the valuation of investments; smoothing techniques may be needed to avoid unwarranted variations in the market value of investments; some other adjustments may also be advisable.

8.5.1 Value of investments

The principal instruments used for the investment of social security reserves are:

Fixed-income securities:

- government securities
- securities issued by statutory corporations or other bodies that are guaranteed by a government

---

Box 8.5 A smoothing technique to estimate the value of a social security reserve[3]

Consider the following information concerning the assets of a pension scheme and its investment earnings over the period 1985 to 1988:

Time k	Investment earnings for previous year (A_k)	Value of the reserve at time k (M_k)	$P_k = P_{k-1}(1 + A_k \div M_{k-1})$
31 December 1985	–	150 000	1.000000
31 December 1986	2 000	196 500	1.013333
31 December 1987	3 000	238 000	1.028804
31 December 1988	–50 500	228 000	0.810507
Average			0.963161

P_k represents the value of a unit in the fund at time k.
If N_k represents the number of units into the fund, then, on 31 December 1988:

$N_k = M_k \div P_k = 228{,}000 \div 0.810507 = 281{,}305$

The actuarial value of the reserve (V_t) may be calculated as the market value of the reserve at time k, multiplied by the average value of the unit over the past four years:

$V_t = 0.963161\,(281{,}305) = 270{,}942$

- corporate bonds
- mortgages
- bank deposits

Equities:
- shares
- real estate

When an active market exists for a security, it should normally be measured at market value. But the value put on each instrument depends on its nature. Loans may be valued at cost, at the lesser of their cost price and market value, or at an amortized value, taking into account the future flow of income to be received from that investment. If it is expected that these investments will be held until maturity, there is no need to use the market value. In the case of shares, market value generally represents the best basis of valuation. For real estate, the value at cost less depreciation is generally used.

A portion of the scheme's assets often includes the scheme's premises, office furniture and equipment. Their value should be determined using an appropriate depreciation schedule.

8.5.2 Smoothing techniques

If the market value is used to estimate a large portion of the investment portfolio, it may be preferable to avoid temporary fluctuations and to try to obtain a value closer to the intrinsic long-term value of the security. One can calculate an actuarial value of investments that smoothes the value observed over a certain period, hence avoiding the undesirable effects of overestimating or underestimating the reserve value because of the particular conjuncture at the time of the valuation. Various methods exist to perform this operation. Box 8.5 presents one such technique.

8.5.3 Adjustment of particular items

If the actuarial projections present revenue and expenditure on an accrual basis, it may be necessary to adjust the gross reserve figure to take into account contributions or benefits that relate to past years but that will be received or paid during the next financial year. For example, because of the delay in collecting contributions, part of the contributions due at the end of 1999 will, in fact, be received by the social security institution only in 2000. The value of the reserve should then be increased to account for those receivables. The same applies (but conversely) to benefit payments incurred but not yet reported.

This kind of adjustment is unnecessary when the actuarial projections present financial figures on a cash basis.

> **Box 8.6 Example: Adjusted reserve as of 31 December 1999**
>
> Reserve before adjustment　　　　　　　　　　　　　　　　14 424
>
> Plus:
> - Contributions due for 1999 but received in 2000　　　　　256
> - Interest due for 1999 but received in 2000　　　　　　　　93
>
> Minus
> - Benefits due for 1999 but paid in 2000　　　　　　　　　　30
> - Accounting adjustment for a decrease in the value of buildings　118
> - Reserve after adjustment　　　　　　　　　　　　　　　　14 625

Notes

[1] The accrual basis is more generally used and meets accounting standards.

[2] The main assumptions used for an actuarial valuation are discussed in Chapters 9 and 10.

[3] Adapted from: A.W. Anderson: *Pension mathematics for actuaries* (Wellesley, Pennsylvania, The Windsor Press, 1990).

DEMOGRAPHIC AND MACROECONOMIC FRAMES FOR PROJECTIONS 9

The evolution of the general population and the economic and labour market environments of a country directly influence the financial development of a social security scheme. On the demographic side, the age structure of the population dictates the potential number of contributors and beneficiaries to the scheme. On the economic side, the evolution of GDP (its primary factor income distribution), labour productivity, employment and unemployment, wages, inflation and interest rates all have direct and indirect impacts on the projected revenue and expenditure of a scheme.

9.1 PROJECTION OF THE GENERAL POPULATION

The projected population is the figure arrived at based on various assumptions on mortality, fertility and migration applied to a distribution of the population at a given date. In section 9.1.4, figure 9.1 illustrates the way a population is projected from one year to the next.

The demographic frame for the valuation should ideally start from national projections. National statistical offices are usually competent to perform population projections. In addition, the use of just one source for both national projections and the actuarial valuation facilitates communications between the actuary and the national counterparts and avoids unnecessary discussions about assumptions. However, national forecasts often do not extend for more than 15 to 20 years, which is insufficient for the purposes of an actuarial valuation, which requires projections of at least 50 years into the future. Hence, the actuary should extend national projections, when available, in order to satisfy the required length of time covered by an actuarial valuation.

9.1.1 Fertility

Assumptions regarding fertility are usually expressed in terms of fertility rates. The fertility rate for a given age group is the number of births during a year attributable to women in the specific age group divided by the number of women in the group. The total fertility rate is the ratio of total births during a year divided by the total female population at reproductive age (generally 15 to 49). The total fertility rate is the sum of age-specific fertility rates. Projection models generally use the evolution of the total fertility rate as the base assumption and then, in a second step, explode the total fertility rate for each future year into age-specific fertility rates. Depending on the level of development of a country, it can be assumed, for example, that the birth pattern will change to a later average child-bearing age, in line with higher education levels and improved family planning.

Since the 1970s there has been a general trend towards decreasing fertility rates in developed countries, a decline that has generally coincided with the increase in the participation rate of women in the labour force and is being observed in most countries. During the 1970s and the 1980s many actuarial valuations projected that the ultimate total fertility rate would drop to 2.1 (the population replacement rate) in the long term, expecting that measures would be taken to prevent fertility rates dropping below that level. However, fertility rates in most developed countries have continued to decline, falling below the population replacement rate. So, when projecting fertility rates, if the rate is already under 2.1, it is often assumed to remain constant in the future. Sometimes, a link is made with the assumptions on migration in order to reach a plausible rate of growth of the total population. In developing countries, where fertility rates are still at extremely high levels, it is often assumed that the rate will gradually fall to around 2.1 after a certain period. Population projections of the United Nations provide indications on possible scenarios on the evolution of fertility.

9.1.2 Mortality

When the model allows it, mortality assumptions should be dynamic, including a provision for future improvements in life expectancy. This is particularly important in the case of social security projections that are performed for periods of 50 years or more. Sophisticated methods exist to project improvements in life expectancy. The actuaries of the OASDI in the United States, for example, project life expectancy improvements for each separate cause of mortality and later combine them to obtain a global life expectancy improvement for all causes. The United Nations methodology, on the other hand, is based on a projection of life expectancy at birth and on a set of model life tables (see box 9.1).

Box 9.1 The United Nations methodology for mortality projections[1]

The mortality assumptions used in United Nations projections are given in the form of life expectancies at birth and age and sex patterns of the probabilities of surviving, corresponding to different levels of life expectancy at birth. The assumed schedule of age and sex-specific survival rates is obtained from model life tables or, when reliable data are available, from national life tables. There are nine model life tables: the West, North, South and East models of the regional model life tables and the General, Latin American, Chilean, Far Eastern and South Asian models of the United Nations model life tables.

Working models for improvements in life expectancy have been developed for the preparation of population projection assumptions. The model postulates that the higher the initial life expectancy, the slower the velocity of improvements.

Working model for improvements in life expectancy, quinquennial gains (in years) in life expectancy at birth, according to initial level of mortality

Initial life expectancy at birth	Fast		Middle		Slow	
	Males	Females	Males	Females	Males	Females
55.0–57.5	2.5	2.5	2.5	2.5	2.0	2.0
57.5–60.0	2.5	2.5	2.5	2.5	2.0	2.0
60.0–62.5	2.5	2.5	2.3	2.5	2.0	2.0
62.5–65.0	2.3	2.5	2.0	2.5	2.0	2.0
65.0–67.5	2.0	2.5	1.5	2.3	1.5	2.0
67.5–70.0	1.5	2.3	1.2	2.0	1.0	1.5
70.0–72.5	1.2	2.0	1.0	1.5	0.8	1.2
72.5–75.0	1.0	1.5	0.8	1.2	0.5	1.0
75.0–77.5	0.8	1.2	0.5	1.0	0.3	0.8
77.5–80.0	0.5	1.0	0.4	0.8	0.3	0.5
80.0–82.5	0.5	0.8	0.4	0.5	0.3	0.3
82.5–85.0	–	0.5	–	0.4	–	0.3
85.0–87.5	–	0.5	–	0.4	–	0.3

In certain countries, it may be necessary to make specific provisions for the mortality rates because of the large number of premature deaths from acquired immune deficiency syndrome (AIDS), since these deaths may greatly affect the population of potential contributors and could eventually affect the dependency ratio.

9.1.3 Migration

Migration is a volatile factor in the evolution of most populations. A migration assumption should start with a careful analysis of past migration data in order to identify trends. In some countries, migration may be the result of political turmoil, and in these cases, in order to project long-term assumptions on migration, it will be necessary to identify the general underlying pattern to avoid these peaks in migration being reproduced in the actuarial projections. Migration may also be the result of government policies allowing the entry of a certain number of immigrants per year, policies that can be used as a way of setting short-term assumptions on migration. In the very long term, owing to the volatility of this factor and the fact that very little information is generally available to perform a robust projection, migration is often assumed to be zero.

9.1.4 A standard population projection model[2]

Population projections generally adopt the *cohort component method*, which can be sketched out as follows:

- The total population of the base year is disaggregated into cohorts according to single age and sex;
- A yearly "ageing" of each cohort takes into account death and migration (in the case of national population projections);
- The number of newborns is calculated by applying fertility rates to the female population in fertile age groups.

The method consists of the following equations:

Formula 9.1

$$L_{s,x+1}(t) = L_{s,x}(t) * p_{s,x+\frac{1}{2}}(t+\tfrac{1}{2}) + N_{s,x+1}(t)$$

(for $x = 0, 1, 2... 99$; $t = 0, 1, 2...$; s = male, female)

where:
- $L_{s,x}(t)$ = Population of sex s and curtate age x at the middle of year t[3]
- $p_{s,x+\frac{1}{2}}(t+\tfrac{1}{2})$ = Rate of survival from exact age $(x+\tfrac{1}{2})$ at the middle of year t to exact age $(x+1+\tfrac{1}{2})$ at the middle of year $t+1$
- $N_{s,x}(t)$ = Net migration (i.e. immigrants minus emigrants) from the middle of year t to the middle of year $t+1$, in the curtate age x at the middle of year $t+1$

We use this equation to estimate the *population* on the left-hand side of the formula, provided that all the values on the right-hand side are known.

Let us define mortality rates in the life table in year t as follows:

$q_{s,x}(t)$ = Mortality rates in a year of those with the exact age x (= integer) at the beginning of year t

Then *rates of survival* $p_{s,x+\frac{1}{2}}(t+\tfrac{1}{2})$ are calculated as follows:[4]

Actuarial practice in social security

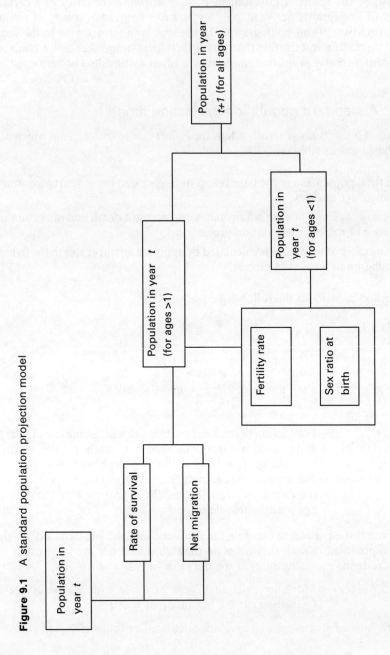

Figure 9.1 A standard population projection model

Formula 9.2

$$p_{s,x+\frac{1}{2}}(t+\tfrac{1}{2}) = [1 - q_{s,x}(t)] \div [1 - \tfrac{1}{2} * q_{s,x}(t)] * [1 - \tfrac{1}{2} * q_{s,x+1}(t+1)]$$

The *number of newborns* is estimated by applying fertility rates to the female population in fertile ages (let us assume, ages 15–49):

Formula 9.3

$$NB(t) = \sum_{x-15}^{49} f_x(t) * L_{female,x}(t)$$

where:

$f_x(t)$ = Age-specific fertility rates applicable to the period from the middle of year t to the middle of year $t+1$

Subsequently, the population of the group aged 0 is calculated as follows:

Formula 9.4

$$L_{s,0}(t+1) = k * NB(t) * [1 - \tfrac{1}{2} * q_{s,0}(t)] + N_{s,0}(t)$$
$$(k = sr \div [sr + 1] \text{ if } s = male; k = 1 \div [sr + 1] \text{ if } s = female)$$

where:

sr = Sex ratio of newborns (i.e. newborn males divided by newborn females)

We assume here that the mortality rates $q_{s,x}(t)$ and fertility rates $f_x(t)$ are given. If this is not the case, then mortality and fertility patterns must be assumed using standards patterns, such as those published by the Population Division of the Department for Economic and Social Information and Policy Analysis of the United Nations.[5]

9.2 THE MACROECONOMIC FRAME[6]

The financial projections of a social security scheme depend on:

- the number of people who will pay contributions to the scheme;
- the average earnings of these contributors;
- the number of people who will receive benefits;
- the amount of benefits that will be paid, related to past earnings and possibly indexed;
- the investment earnings on the reserve.

All these factors depend on the economic environment in which the scheme will evolve. In order to develop robust assumptions on the future economic environment, it is first necessary to analyse past trends. The core conclusions drawn from these observations are then used as a basis for the development

> **Box 9.2 Basic macroeconomic relationships for the determination of actuarial assumptions on employment, wages and interest rates**
>
> *(a) Employment and unemployment*
>
> - Start with historical values of real GDP for the country;
> - Calculate historical values of labour productivity (average productivity per worker) as follows:
>
> **Formula 9.5**
>
> Productivity per worker = Real GDP divided by Number of employed persons
>
> - Assume a rate of future real GDP growth and obtain GDP for all future years;
> - Assume a future growth of the productivity per employed person;
> - Multiply average productivity per employed person by the assumed productivity growth factor;
> - Then apply for each future year:
>
> **Formula 9.6**
>
> Number of employed persons = Real GDP divided by Productivity per worker
>
> - Calculate (dependent) employees as a constant or varying share of the total number of employed, the starting value to be estimated from past observations, and apply that share to the projected number of total employed persons to obtain the figures for dependent employment for each future year.
>
> **Formula 9.7**
>
> Number of unemployed persons = (Total labour force) minus (Number of employed persons)
>
> - This process can be refined further by calculating GDP and productivity for each sector of the economy, then using appropriate weights for each sector and adding the results to obtain total employment values.
>
> *(b) Annual increase in average wage*
>
> - Calculate the share of wages in nominal GDP:
>
> **Formula 9.8**
>
> Share of wages in GDP = Total sum of workers' remuneration divided by Nominal GDP

Demographic and macroeconomic frames for projections

- Assume a future evolution of the share of wages in nominal GDP;
- Then apply for each future year:

Formula 9.9

Total wages = Nominal GDP * (share of wages in nominal GDP)

Formula 9.10

Average wage = Total sum of wages divided by Number of employed persons (from (a) above)

- The annual increase in wages is then calculated as the ratio of these projected average wage values.

(c) Interest rates

The interest rate may be seen as the ratio of the annual profit component within overall remuneration of capital over the annual investment in the capital stock. Thus, project GDP and separate it into its two components – workers' remuneration and capital remuneration – using the share of wages in GDP to project the workers' remuneration component. Estimate the profit share within capital income. Then, project nominal GDP by its demand components, using plausible assumptions on the future shares of private and government consumption, private and government investments, exports and imports.

Formula 9.11

Remuneration of capital (proj.) = GDP (proj.) minus Total workers' remuneration (proj.)

Formula 9.12

Profits = Percentage of remuneration of capital (starting percentage to be estimated from past observations)

Formula 9.13

Interest rate = Profits (proj.) divided by Nominal investments of the private sector

Use "interest rate" – as calculated – as a dummy variable to be correlated with the future development of a long-term financial markets interest rate.

of consistent long-term economic and labour market projections serving as a basis for the actuarial valuation of the scheme.

The economic variables necessary to develop a suitable macroeconomic frame include:

- economic growth
- the separation of GDP between remuneration of workers and, broadly, remuneration of capital
- labour force, employment and unemployment
- wages
- inflation
- interest rates

Economic assumptions generally have to be discussed with national experts in ministries of planning, of economy and of finance. The actuary may suggest and analyse alternative long-term assumptions. However, it is not the objective of the actuarial valuation to run an economic model and to take the place of economic projections performed at the national level.

Various approaches exist to project economic variables over time. This section describes one methodology that ensures consistency between the most important economic variables. Real rates of economic growth, labour productivity increases and inflation rates are exogenous inputs to the economic model presented here.

9.2.1 Economic growth

The annual increase in GDP results from the increase in the number of workers, together with the increase in productivity per worker. A choice must be made as to how each of these two factors will affect the global GDP growth rate. As regards a social security scheme, a larger increase in the number of workers affects the number of people who contribute to the scheme. In the long run, the increase in productivity normally affects the level of wages and the payroll covered by the scheme. Hence, the assumption on GDP growth has a direct impact on the revenue of the scheme.

For the short term, the annual GDP growth rate may be based on the estimates published by organizations specialized in economic projections. For the long term, an ultimate growth rate is generally established by the actuary as an exogenous assumption. The short-term and ultimate rates are then linked together, based on an interpolation technique. Nominal GDP is calculated by multiplying real GDP for each and every year by the GDP deflator. The GDP deflator is ex post, calculated by dividing nominal GDP by real GDP. Its future evolution is usually based on exogenous assumptions on future GDP inflation rates.

Future nominal GDP development is combined with an assumption on the evolution of the share of wages in nominal GDP to obtain the part of GDP that represents the remuneration of workers. Total workers' remuneration is used

Demographic and macroeconomic frames for projections

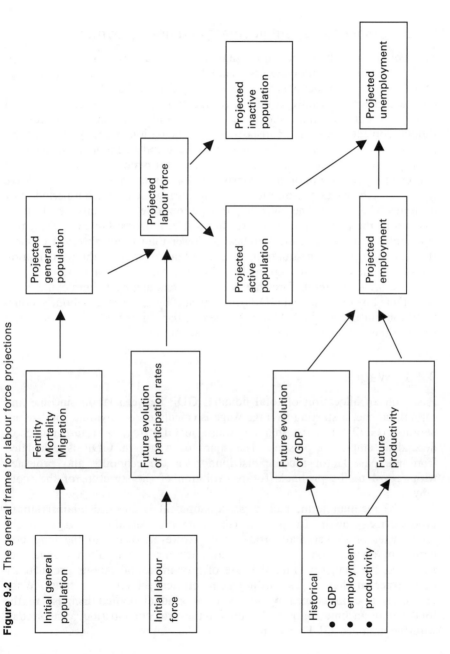

Figure 9.2 The general frame for labour force projections

later, in combination with dependent employment, to determine the average wage.

9.2.2 Labour force, employment and unemployment

The projection of the labour force, that is, the number of people available for work, is obtained by applying assumed labour force participation rates to the projected number of people in the general population. The data on the labour force are generally readily available, by age and sex, from national statistical offices. Recent past data should be sought, and if available, the actuary should consider national forecasts on participation rates performed by these offices. The same applies for employment and unemployment data.[7]

To project the evolution of participation rates is no easy task. Data and national projections are often non-existent. One common approach is to leave the age-specific participation rates constant during the projection period. Any projected changes in the overall participation rate then only result from changes in the population structure. In most economies, however, the participation rates of women are significantly lower than those observed of men. It is common in such a situation to assume that, over time, the participation rates of women will catch up, at least in part, with those of men.

Once the total labour force has been projected, aggregate employment can be obtained by dividing real GDP (total output) by the average labour productivity (output per worker). Unemployment is then measured as the difference between the projected labour force and total employment.

9.2.3 Wages

Based on an allocation of total nominal GDP between labour income and capital income, a starting average wage is calculated by dividing total remuneration (GDP times the share of wages in GDP) by the total number of dependent employed persons. The share of wages in GDP is calculated from the past factor income distribution in the economy and projected with regard to the probable future evolution of the structure of the economy.

In the medium term, real wage development is checked against labour productivity growth. In specific labour market situations, wages might grow faster or slower than productivity. However, owing to the long-term nature of an actuarial study, the real wage increase is often assumed to merge, in the long run, into the rate of growth in real labour productivity (it is expected that wages will adjust to efficiency levels over time). Wage growth is also influenced by an assumed gradual annual increase in the total labour income share of GDP over the projection period, concomitant with the assumed GDP growth.

Demographic and macroeconomic frames for projections

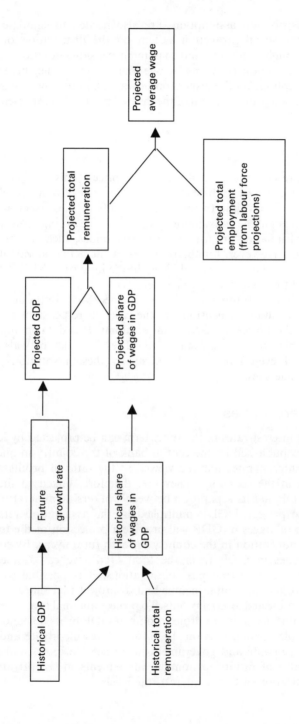

Figure 9.3 Determination of the average wage in the economy

Wage distribution assumptions are also needed to simulate the possible impact of the social protection system on the distribution of income, for example, through minimum and maximum pension provisions. Assumptions on the differentiation of wages by age and sex must then be established, as well as assumptions on the dispersion of wages between income groups. A discussion of the wage distribution of the insured population is presented in section 10.2.

9.2.4 Inflation

Inflation represents the general increase in prices. This general rise is usually associated with an average basket of goods, the price of which is followed at regular intervals. From time to time, the contents of the basket are changed to adapt to changes in the consumption patterns of the average consumer. Various definitions of inflation are used in most economies, such as, for example, the GDP deflator. However, for the purposes of the actuarial valuation, the CPI is most often used as a statistical basis. In the long run, the GDP deflator and the CPI might be assumed to converge.

Assumptions on future inflation rates are necessary for the actuarial study to project the evolution of pensions, in the case where pensions are periodically adjusted to reflect price increases in the economy. Past data on inflation are generally available from national statistical offices. The data may also be available on short and even long-term forecasts by these institutions or by other government agencies.

9.2.5 Interest rates

The level of interest rates in the short term can be projected by looking at the level of rates published by the central bank of the country in question. In the long term, interest rates may be viewed as the ratio of profits over nominal investments in the economy. They are, therefore, linked to the assumption made for GDP and its separation between workers' remuneration and capital income. The projected GDP multiplied by the assumption retained for the future share of wages in GDP will provide a projection of the total projected workers' remuneration in the country for each future year. By subtracting the share of wages in GDP from the total GDP, we can isolate the capital income component. From past observations, it is possible to estimate the share of "profits" in capital income and to project that share in the future to determine a projected level of profits. To project nominal investments in the private sector, it is necessary to project nominal GDP by its demand components, using plausible assumptions on the future shares of private and government assumptions, private and government investments, exports and imports. The projected ratio of profits to nominal investments in the private sector thus gives an indication of future interest-rate levels.

Demographic and macroeconomic frames for projections

For determining the specific assumption regarding the investment return on a scheme's reserve, appropriate adjustments to the theoretical interest rates have to take into account the composition of the portfolio of the scheme and its projected evolution.

Another consideration is the size of the social security reserves compared with the total savings in the country. In some small countries, social security reserves have a great influence on the level of interest rates. In that case, at least for the short to medium term, the actuary will determine the interest-rate assumption for the scheme by referring directly to its investment policy.

9.2.6 Other considerations

Generally, national statistical offices provide their own projections of the economically active population, employment and unemployment levels, and GDP. In addition, ministries of finance usually make short-term forecasts, for budgetary purposes, on the levels of employment, inflation and interest rates. These sources of information should be considered by the actuary, particularly when performing short-term actuarial projections. Governments often want to relate their budget assumptions or their mid-term financial plans to the actuarial projections. It is thus imperative that at least one of the scenarios in the actuarial report reflects the economic assumptions of the government.

Notes

[1] From United Nations: "Mortality Assumptions" in: *World Population Prospects: The 1988 revision*, Chapter I, section E (New York, 1989).

[2] Extracts from ILO: *The ILO population projection model: A technical guide*, draft (Geneva, 1997).

[3] People with curtate age x ($=$ integer number) are aged between x and $x+1$ (x inclusive and $x+1$ not inclusive). Note that the average age of this population at mid-year is equal to $x+\frac{1}{2}$.

[4] The derivation of formula 9.2: Suppose that the deaths at any age are spread uniformly over a year. Then, for the time length of h less than y year ($0 < h < 1$), we have:

$$_hq_{s,x}(t) = h \cdot q_{s,x}(t)$$

$$_hp_{s,x}(t) = 1 - h \cdot q_{s,x}(t)$$

$$_{(1-h)}q_{s,x+h}(t+h) = (1-h) \cdot q_{s,x}(t) \div [1 - h \cdot q_{s,x}(t)]$$

$$_{(1-h)}p_{s,x+h}(t+h) = [1 - q_{s,x}(t+h)] \div ([1 - h \cdot q_{s,x}(t)])$$

Thus, we have the following:

$$p_{s,x+\frac{1}{2}}(t+\tfrac{1}{2}) = \tfrac{1}{2}p_{s,x+\frac{1}{2}}(t+\tfrac{1}{2}) \cdot \tfrac{1}{2}p_{s,x+1}(t+1) = [1 - q_{s,x}(t)] \div [1 - \tfrac{1}{2} \cdot q_{s,x}(t)] \cdot [1 - \tfrac{1}{2} \cdot q_{x+1}(t+1)]$$

[5] For example, see United Nations: *Unabridged model life tables corresponding to the new United Nations model life tables for developing countries* (New York, 1982).

[6] This section contains extracts from ILO: *The ILO social budget model* (Geneva, 1996) and W. Scholz, K. Hagemejer and M. Cichon: *Social budgeting* (Geneva, ILO/ISSA, 2000).

[7] Caution is necessary regarding unemployment data. According to the ILO, an unemployed person is defined as an individual without work, seeking work in a recent past period, and currently available for work. But the definition of unemployment can vary from one country to another, in particular, the definition of job search can be very elastic. In some cases, unemployment data

Actuarial practice in social security

may refer only to people receiving unemployment benefit from the public unemployment insurance programme. In other cases, unemployment is defined independently from the insurance programme and thus better reflects the generally accepted definition.

SCHEME-SPECIFIC ASSUMPTIONS 10

Once the demographic and macroeconomic frames have been established, the next step consists of analysing the scheme itself and determining a possible path for its future evolution. This chapter presents the set of assumptions that are directly related to the insured population and its characteristics of age, sex and earnings, and on specific probabilities that will be applied to that population in order to project future emerging pensions and the survival rate of pensioners. One important point to remember throughout is that consistency between the various assumptions is paramount at all times.

In setting actuarial assumptions for the purpose of valuating a social security scheme, the actuary usually uses *best-estimate assumptions,* in contrast to, for example, the process of life insurance rating in which the actuary often uses a certain margin of conservatism, especially in pricing new products. The social security actuary must remember that the cost of a scheme is supported by workers, employers and, sometimes, the government. Any overstatement of the recommended contribution rate may have a direct effect on the economy.

10.1 DEVELOPMENT OF THE INSURED POPULATION

10.1.1 Coverage rate

In general, a social security scheme covers a substantial part of the labour force. In practice, however, the coverage is often lower than intended owing to legal and administrative factors.

On the legal side, the definition of covered workers may specifically exclude certain groups such as, for example, the self-employed or agriculture workers. Other groups, such as voluntary contributors, may be outside the labour force but may actually be contributing. In other situations, the scheme may have been set up to cover only public-sector employees. In practice, time-series data of coverage rates are calculated by comparing the actual number of insured contributors (the active insured population) with the legally covered population. Such coverage rates often show anomalies because of data discrepancies and differing definitions of statistics (the definition of an employed person versus the definition of an insured contributor in a given year). The actuary needs to obtain precise data on the characteristics (number, earnings) of the various subsets of the labour force, which will enable the actuary to compute the theoretical coverage rate that would result from the direct application of the legal provisions.

On the administrative side, a number of factors can contribute to reducing the coverage rate yet further. Some workers and/or employers try to evade paying contributions, and the compliance system in place may not be able to enforce participation in the scheme. The actuary should, therefore, identify any discrepancies in coverage related to evasion on the part of employers and workers, as well as making a note of deficient supervisory and compliance monitoring systems on the part of the social security institution. The extent of evasion will depend on the types of controls applied, and may also result from the interaction between the taxation and the social security systems. Using the financial statements, the actuary has to compare the actual contribution income with the income that would result from the direct application of the legal provisions.

This issue of coverage is particularly delicate when extending coverage to new sectors of the labour force, for example, the self-employed, is being considered. If a good control system is in place, which can identify these people and the level of their earnings, then it is easier to determine the possible implications of extending coverage to a specific group on a mandatory or voluntary basis. The actuary should also analyse the possible cross-subsidies between various groups of the insured. A study of the benefit/contribution ratios for each of these groups may show little incentive for a part of the labour force to contribute. Such discrepancies in benefit/contribution ratios may also be observed between age groups. For example, the benefit formula may discourage compliance during the early years of a career.

Once the current coverage situation has been documented, the actuary must determine its future evolution. Projected social insurance coverage rates are determined from the study of patterns of past coverage rates, along with other external factors, such as, for example, the implementation by the social security institution of a programme to enforce coverage compliance.

The different approaches for calculating the effective coverage rate are shown in box 10.1.

Scheme-specific assumptions

Box 10.1   Illustrative methods to calculate effective coverage rates

$$\text{Specific coverage rate } (z, x, t) = \frac{\text{Number of contributors } (z, x, t)}{\text{Number of workers in the economy } (z, x, t)}$$

$$\textit{Global coverage rate}(t) = \frac{\sum_{z=1}^{n} \sum_{x=\text{minimum age}}^{\text{maximum age}} \text{Number of contributors } (z, x, t)}{\sum_{z=1}^{n} \sum_{x=\text{minimum age}}^{\text{maximum age}} \text{Number of workers in the economy } (z, x, t)}$$

where:
- z = Category of insured persons
- x = Age
- t = Year

Notes

- The global coverage rate in a given year refers to the overall coverage of the social security scheme.
- The specific coverage rate is calculated for a given category of insured persons or age group. It is an indirect measure of the efficiency of the administration, notably in its enforcement function. The actuary must develop an assumption on the projected future effective coverage rate, particularly if additional resources at the institutional level are invested into improving the means of inspecting workplaces and their social insurance records. The actuary must consult with management and quantify expectations. There is no direct rule other than good judgement.

10.1.2   Components of the insured population

The insured population is classified as a subset of the labour force, which is itself a subset of the general population. It is easy to determine, at any one point in time, the various components of the population and the percentage that actually contributes to the scheme. However, the population of active contributors is not static; there are movements between workers and the unemployed, and even between the economically active and the inactive population (see figure 10.1).

For a given year, insured persons can be separated into two groups:

- active contributors who have paid contributions at a certain point during the year;[1]

Actuarial practice in social security

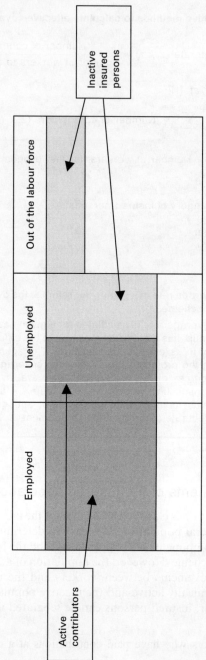

Figure 10.1 Classification of insured persons in the total population

- inactive insured persons who are registered under the scheme, have paid contributions to the scheme at some point in the past (but not during the year under consideration) and have accrued rights under the system.

During the course of their careers, some insured persons[2] may experience periods of unemployment or may leave the labour force. Nevertheless, their insurance record will remain valid under the social security scheme. They may keep their eligibility for certain benefits during their periods of inactivity and their past service will be taken into account when they re-enter the labour force and eventually claim their old-age pensions. The actuarial model should be able to simulate the movements between active and inactive insured persons.

Different methods exist to project the number of insured persons. Under the cohort method, annual decrements by age and sex are applied to the existing group of active contributors, reflecting all possible causes of termination (retirement, invalidity, death, termination of employment, etc.). Each year, the age-sex category is increased by an assumed number of new entrants. The assumed total number of new entrants is determined on the basis of the assumptions on overall employment growth and coverage rates. Under the aggregate basis, the actuary starts by projecting the employed population by age and sex and applies to this projected working population an appropriate coverage rate for each age and each sex. This latter method ensures consistency over the long term between the macroeconomic frame and actuarial projections on the number of insured. However, various adjustments may be needed to reflect adequately the retirement behaviour and movements between active and inactive insured persons.

10.1.3 New entrants and re-entrants

The valuation of a social security scheme is usually made using the open-group method, which means that each year a number of new people enter the labour force and participate in the scheme. In addition to these new entrants (who generally enter the scheme at younger ages), some former contributors who left the scheme re-enter the workforce and become contributors again. The treatment of these populations and the assumptions regarding their movements depend on the general approach used (cohort or aggregate approach, see section 10.1.2 above). The total number of new entrants and re-entrants in a year should be consistent with what the actuary projected to be the rate of increase of the employed population.

Under the cohort approach, assumptions are established on the age-sex distribution of entries and re-entries, and these distributions should reflect the projected evolution of the age and sex structure of the employed population. The classical approach is for the total number of new entrants to be estimated on the basis of the projected increase in the total insured population; they are then distributed by age and sex on the basis of the observed scheme's past experience and the expected evolution over time.

Under the aggregate approach, the number of new entrants and re-entrants is arrived at by comparing the number of contributors at age x and time t with the number of contributors at age $x+1$ and time $t+1$, after taking into account every possible way of leaving the contributors' status between t and $t+1$ for this cohort, so that their number is more of a result than an assumption. A mathematical example (box 10.2) describes this approach.

Under the aggregate approach, particular difficulties may be encountered when the number of people who leave the labour force is being reconciled with the number of new retirees. A series of adjustments may be necessary at this point in order to build a consistent model and for the actuarial valuation to produce appropriate results, especially with regard to short-term projections.

Box 10.2 Mathematical example of the treatment of new entrants and re-entrants

If we recall box 6.2 describing the aggregate approach, *Ac(x,t)* represented the number of active insured persons aged *x* in year *t* who have made at least one contribution during that year, while *S[Ac(x,t)]* represented the part of *Ac(x,t)* who are still in the active insured population one year later, meaning that neither did they become invalids nor did they die during the past year. This population can be designated mathematically as:

Formula 10.1

$$S[Ac(x,t)] = Ac(x,t) - VAC(x,t) - DAC(x,t)$$

where *VAC(x,t)* designates those actives who became disabled and *DAC(x,t)* those who died during the past year.

Then consider the following situations:

- If *S[Ac(x,t)]* is greater than *Ac(x+1,t+1)*, then the population of the age-sex category has decreased during the year, which may be because of people retiring or because of people moving from an active to an inactive status. In this scenario, an assumption needs to be made on the proportion of the decrease that is due to retirement and the proportion that results from the move to an inactive status. The provisions of the scheme usually provide clues for this distribution.
- If *S[Ac(x,t)]* is lower than *Ac(x+1,t+1)*, then the population of the age-sex category has increased, which may be due to the arrival of new entrants or re-entrants into the scheme. In this scenario, an assumption should be made on the proportion of new entrants and the proportion of re-entrants. This distribution will usually be based on age, since new entrants are generally young people and re-entrants older people. Past experience of the scheme helps specify this distribution.

Box 10.3 Definition of a salary scale[3]

For the projection year t = 0, the salary scale is deduced from the single-age salary values specified as inputs. The values of the salary scale are standardized salary values, which are obtained by specifying an average value of 1,000 to the 20–24 age group.

For the other projection years, the salary structure can be perpetuated by using the same salary scale. Alternatively, it can be modified for the following reasons:

- to obtain values of salary scale more in line with those of other countries or schemes;
- to anticipate labour market changes that could imply, for instance, a reduction in the importance of age as a determinant of working conditions or, alternatively, a desire to prevent the early withdrawal of older workers from the labour market;
- to test the sensitivity of the results.

Changes to the salary structure are made effective by assigning a value different from 1 to the adjustment factor. The values of the salary scale are then recalculated as shown in formula 10.2, and assuming an average value of 1,000 for the 20–24 age group:

Formula 10.2

$$SS(x,t) = SS(x-1,t) * \left[\frac{SS(x,0)}{SS(x-1,0)}\right]^{ADJ(t)}$$

where:

$SS(x,t)$ = Salary scale value of active people aged x in year t
$ADJ(t)$ = Adjustment factor for year t

A value of the adjustment factor greater (or smaller) than 1 implies a widening (or narrowing) of the salary scale. The values will be the same for all ages if the adjustment factor is set equal to 0.

Total earnings are allocated to each age in proportion of the number of employed persons and the values of the salary scale. In other words, the salary scale corresponds to the effective distribution of salary by age for all the projection years. The details of calculation are shown in formula 10.3:

Formula 10.3

$$Sal(x,t) = SS(x,t) * [1 + g(t)]$$
$$* \left[\frac{\sum_{x=15}^{69} Sal(x,t-1) * Ac(x,t-1) \Big/ \sum_{x=15}^{69} Ac(x,t-1)}{\sum_{x=15}^{69} SS(x,t) * Ac(x,t) \Big/ \sum_{x=15}^{69} Ac(x,t)}\right]$$

> where:
>
> $Ac(x,t)$ = Active population in year t and defined as those people who have made at least one contribution during that year
> $Sal(x,t)$ = Average insurable salary of active people aged x in year t
> $g(t)$ = Salary increase assumption for year t
>
> A modification of the salary scale has no impact on the annual rate of increase of average earnings, which is specified as an exogenous assumption. However, a modification of the salary scale generates different rates of salary rises for different cohorts. For instance, a narrowing of the salary scale will imply a lower salary increase for younger people, who normally experience a sharp progression in earnings. This will result in larger salary increases for older groups, assuming there is a fixed rate of increase of average earnings.
>
> The salary scale assumption needs to be specified with care to avoid any awkward progression of salaries for some cohorts. It can be checked by looking at the effective rates of salary rises for different age groups.

10.2 PROJECTION OF INSURABLE EARNINGS

The projection of insurable earnings requires assumptions to be made on the annual growth and distribution of earnings, the evolution of the earnings ceiling and the density of contributions.

10.2.1 Earnings growth

The evolution of earnings is usually considered to include two components:

- an *individual* component reflecting the increasing experience of the worker, promotions, merit, etc. This component is reflected in the use of a salary scale, which is usually built on the basis of the age of the worker, and varies also by sex. It is, however, possible to build a salary scale on the basis of seniority (number of years of service) if it is considered that this gives a better reflection of the individual component of earnings evolution;
- a *collective* component that takes into account the general increase in wages observed in the economy. This component represents productivity gains that are eventually reflected (at least in the long run) in general wage levels (see section 9.2.3 for a methodology on projecting general wage increases).

In modelling salary projections, it is important to ensure that, after taking into account the individual component (the salary scale), the resulting general wage increase is consistent with the economic framework established for the projection. A way of achieving this goal is first to determine the future

Scheme-specific assumptions

Box 10.4 Simple methods for constructing a salary scale

In an occupational scheme, the salary scale is used to add a merit component to the general wage increase, which already includes inflation and productivity components. There is no need for an enterprise's wage increase to match the general wage increase in the economy. In a social insurance scheme, which generally covers most of the labour force in a country, the total salary increase in the scheme's insured persons must be consistent with the general wage increase in the country. Thus the merit component measured by the salary scale is not added to the general wage increase. The unique role of the salary scale is to work out an age distribution (for the various cohorts of contributors) of the general wage increase.

Sources of data

- Basic data generally come from the scheme under study;
- If available, general salary data on the total labour force, especially if the scheme covers a large part of the total employed population of a country;
- A longitudinal study would be ideal, that is, follow the salary of a group of workers of different ages during a sufficiently long period;
- In practice, data are often available only on the salary distribution as of a given date. In this case, one must assume that this distribution reflects the evolution of salaries over different age groups for a given cohort of contributors.

Construction methods

The salary scale can be based on age or seniority, although age is usually used for social security schemes.

The static method

If the data are available for a single date:

- Put an arbitrary value on the lowest age of the table. For example, a value of 1,000 is placed at age 18. Then S_{18} equals 1,000.
- Compute the ratio of the salary at a given age to the salary at age 18 and multiply this ratio by 1,000 to obtain the value of the salary scale value at that age. For example, a value of 1,210 is calculated for age 35. Then S_{35} equals 1,210.
- In the actuarial model, the salary of a new entrant aged 18, will be equal, 17 years later, to:

$$Sal(35) = Sal(18) \,^*[SS(35) \div SS(18)] = Sal(18) \,^* 1.210$$
$$Sal_{35} = Salary_{18} \,^*[S_{35} \div S_{18}] = Salary_{18} \,^* 1.210$$

> *The cohort method*
>
> If the data are available for several dates of observation:
>
> - Compute for each individual the ratio of the salary in year t $S(t)$ to the salary in year $t-1$ $S(t-1)$.
> - Group the data in five-yearly intervals. In each age group, compute an average annual increase in salary for the group.
> - Graduate the ratios.
> - Interpolate to derive individual-age ratios $S(t+1) \div S(t)$.
>
> *Adjustments*
>
> - The salary scale's appropriateness should be measured with regard to the provisions of the scheme (for example, pension calculation using the past five years). For example, if the slope of the salary scale decreases as the retirement age approaches, it may be more appropriate to assume a flattening of the salary scale as people get older.
> - A realistic beginning and end of scale are needed. If the exercise was based on the data at a single date, the actuary may need to produce a more realistic curve at the extremities of the scale.
> - Gross results may need to be smoothed to avoid unnecessary fluctuations from one age to the next. Any of the usual graduation methods can be used.
> - The effect of the scale on valuation results should be measured.

annual average earnings for the entire insured population and then to distribute it by age in accordance with the salary scale assumption.

If participation is limited to a sector of the economy benefiting from more generous salary rises than the rest of the workers, it may be appropriate, at least in the short run, to have a salary increase assumption for the scheme that differs from the general salary increase in the country.

The actuary needs to be aware of the importance of this assumption. For example, if it is assumed that insured persons have an annual rate of increase of salary one percentage point higher than the rate assumed for the national average wage, their salaries at the end of a 20-year period will then be 22 per cent higher than the average national wage.

10.2.2 Earnings distribution[4]

An assumption of salary distribution within each cohort of participants has to be specified when the level of benefit or the contribution rate is a function of the salary. In the case of pension schemes, it usually takes the form of an earnings ceiling or a minimum pension.

Scheme-specific assumptions

The assumption that earnings at a particular age are log-normally distributed is widely accepted. It can also be used to describe the distribution of total income, although the number of people with high incomes can possibly be under-estimated, considering the high concentration of wealth. The log-normal distribution of probabilities has the following characteristics:

- a range of values from 0 to infinity;
- a non-symmetrical distribution around the average;
- a wider range of values for the upper tail of the distribution (high-income group).

Because of the non-symmetrical distribution around the average, the average level of earnings (average) is greater than the earnings of the average worker (median), and the proportion of people who earn less than the average earnings is greater than 50 per cent.

The exact shape of the log-normal distribution depends on the specification of two parameters: the average value and the parameter of dispersion. The latter can be measured either in absolute terms (standard deviation) or as a percentage of the average (the coefficient of variation):

Formula 10.4

$$Coefficient\ of\ variation = \frac{Standard\ deviation}{Average}$$

The average is deduced from the assumption of salary scale and salary inflation, and the coefficient of variation is estimated based on the earnings data available. An estimation will usually be carried out using quinquennial age group data, followed by the application of an interpolation technique to obtain the data for individual ages. The parameters of the distribution can also be estimated empirically, since the natural logarithm of the log-normal random variable X follows a normal distribution:

Formula 10.5

$$\ln(X) = N(\mu, \sigma)$$

It is possible to estimate the values of μ and σ on the basis of the data (X_i) available:

Formula 10.6

$$\mu = \frac{\sum_{i=1}^{n} \ln(X_i)}{n}$$

> **Box 10.5 Parametric or non-parametric distributions?**
>
> Income distributions can be defined either by specifying a parameter of the coefficient of variation (parametric distribution) or by using discrete data on income distribution at a particular date as the assumption of income distribution (non-parametric distribution). The ILO wage distribution model was developed as a parametric model because:
>
> - using a coefficient of variation provides a simple indicator of income distribution, which makes it possible to "get a feeling" of the level of the dispersion of income;
> - it is easier to compare the wage distributions of different populations and to test the sensitivity of results with alternative assumptions;
> - it makes the specification of an assumption of income distribution when limited data are available easier;
> - it is possible to vary the assumption of income distribution over time by changing the coefficient of variation.

Formula 10.7

$$\sigma = \sqrt{\frac{\sum_{i=1}^{n}(\ln(X_i) - \mu)^2}{n}}$$

and then estimate the parameters of the log-normal distribution from the following equations:

Formula 10.8

$$E[X] = \exp^{\mu + \frac{\sigma^2}{2}}$$

Formula 10.9

$$V[X] = \left[\exp^{2\cdot\mu+\sigma^2}\right] * \left[\exp^{\sigma^2} - 1\right]$$

The salary distribution of the whole population is a function of the salary scale, the salary distribution and the age distribution of the population.

Each single age is assumed to follow a log-normal distribution, but it does not necessarily mean that the income distribution for the population as a whole is log-normally distributed.

10.2.3 Total versus insurable earnings

Once total earnings have been distributed and those distributed earnings have been projected, it is then possible to project insurable earnings taking into account the scheme's parameters that limit earnings covered by the scheme. If, for example, it is assumed that earnings are distributed according to a lognormal distribution, the coverage of earnings by the scheme can be illustrated, as in figure 10.2.

Figure 10.2 Effect of a ceiling on insurable earnings

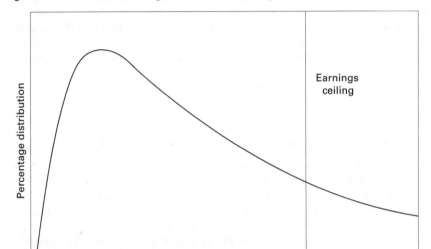

10.2.4 Density of contributions

Once the salary levels have been projected, the actuary then computes the amount of earnings on which contributions will actually be paid, because some workers may be out of employment for a part of the year, which will cause a reduction in the actual earnings on which they contribute. The density of contributions represents the factor that is applied to the annual rate of salary in order to determine the amount of salary on which contributions are calculated. The density of contributions normally varies by age and sex.

The density of contributions can be defined as the proportion of the financial year during which the average active insured person has made contributions to a scheme. It may also be defined as the ratio of the average number of contributors during the year to the total number of insured persons who made at least one contribution during the year. To compute density factors, the data are usually obtained on the number of months (or another period if more appropriate) of contributions, by age of the active insured persons. Past density factors are calculated for each age as the average number of months of contribution divided by 12.

Legal provisions are not very precise when it comes to determining insurable earnings for the self-employed, who can thus manipulate the level of their earnings. Density factors for this group must, therefore, take this reality into account.

The projection of density factors usually starts with the observed past pattern of density factors. From that point, it can be assumed that density factors will evolve each year in relation to changes in employment rates (since the latter is the main factor affecting density). Any projected increase in the scheme's compliance rate (the proportion of those who have the legal obligation to contribute that actually pays contributions) should also be taken into account.

10.3 ACCUMULATION OF INSURANCE CREDITS

Insurance credits are used for two purposes. Firstly, when a risk covered by the scheme (retirement, death or disability) occurs, they are used to establish the eligibility of the insured person for the benefit. Eligibility requirements are generally expressed in terms of months or years of past coverage. The scheme may also offer a grant instead of a pension if the length of coverage is less than a specified period. Secondly, past credits are used for computing the amount of benefit to be awarded. The pension formula generally uses the number of months or years of service as a parameter.

The ideal way of treating past service in the valuation is first to obtain a distribution within age and sex groups of the number of years of past service of the insured population as of the valuation date. For example, 4 per cent of male insured persons aged 45 have five years of service, 5 per cent have six years of service, etc., for a total of 100 per cent for the cohort.

On the basis of the initial stock of insurance credits accrued to the existing insured population, an assumption must be made relating to the continuing accumulation of insurance credits after the valuation date. This assumption should be closely linked to the assumption on the density of contribution payments. Past credits are then added to new credits that emerge each year as a result of contributions paid by insured persons. From the accumulation of new service generated by the actuarial model, the length of service is gradually increased over the years for the corresponding age-sex category, and the distributed length of service is used for that cohort when eligibility or benefits have to be measured at a later date. It is necessary to obtain this distribution of insurance credits for both active and inactive insured populations.

Scheme-specific assumptions

The actuary must also make assumptions on possible provisions allowing additional credits for special situations, such as periods of disability before the retirement age has been reached.

10.4 MORTALITY RATES

Ideally, the mortality table should be built from the scheme's past experience. If the data are unavailable, are not statistically credible, or if the scheme covers a large proportion of the total population of the country under study, it is then appropriate to use the mortality rates of the general population.

The actuary should consider using a different mortality table for pensioners than the one used for the general population. Often, the general population shows a more stable pattern of mortality rates, but life expectancy is generally higher among the insured population. The only reliable set of mortality rates that can normally be developed from a social security scheme's statistics relates to pensioners. Usually, a complete track record is kept of this group (as opposed to the insured population for whom no survival record is kept because many leave the scheme temporarily or permanently). Hence, the actuary could apply a series of graduated factors to the general population mortality rates on the basis of a study of mortality among pensioners, and using pensioners' cohort tables. To analyse the appropriateness of using a specific mortality table for each type of pensioner, past data on mortality rates must be obtained with a sufficient degree of disaggregation by sex and age. If detailed data are unavailable, a loading factor can be applied to the mortality table of the general population.

The actuary must also build an assumption on mortality rates that may differ by category of beneficiaries. For example, old-age pensioners usually live longer than elderly people drawing invalidity pensions.

In some countries, it is necessary to adjust the mortality rates to take into account the large number of premature deaths occurring because of AIDS. This generally takes the form of an extra mortality rate attributable to AIDS, calculated from the projected ratios of the additional number of deaths due to AIDS over the population at each age. In such an exercise, the general population mortality rates used as a base should not already include deaths from AIDS. Care must also be taken in countries where AIDS is the main cause of premature death in the adult population (this is currently the case in some African countries).

10.5 RETIREMENT BEHAVIOUR

To set assumptions on future retirement patterns, the data need to be collected on past retirement experience under the scheme, for which the data on new retirement pensions awarded, by age at retirement and by sex, are necessary. The calculation of retirement rates must be consistent with the rule applicable to testing the eligibility of insured persons for the retirement pension (for example, by referring to contribution credits). If the retirement age has recently been changed, experience data may need adjusting before they are used to calculate retirement rates, taking into account possible time lags between the scheme's modification and the time the modifications appear in the statistics.

The mode of calculating retirement rates depends on the way they are used in the actuarial model. Some models use pure rates, defined, in the same way as mortality rates, as the probability of a person aged x retiring between age x and age $x+1$. Other models use "take-up rates", representing the proportion of the total population of a cohort of individuals that will retire at a specific age, the total of all take-up rates of a cohort equalling 100 per cent. These two types of measuring retirement patterns can be determined from the scheme's past experiences on retirement and the appropriate population likely to retire at each age.

Models that use the aggregate approach[5] define new retirements as the residual element of a comparison between the number of active insured persons aged x in a given year and the number of active insured persons one year later at age $x+1$. These models make the link between the evolution of the total employed population in a country and the number of persons actively contributing to the social security scheme. The number of new retirees is calculated by comparing the number of active contributors for two successive years at ages at which retirement is possible. The difficulty with this kind of model is ensuring consistency between the general economic data on employment and the scheme's statistics on retirement.

There is generally a link between retirement behaviour and a country's economic conditions. Retirement rates can be influenced by a recession (rising unemployment forces some older workers to retire). Also, in the case where benefits are not automatically indexed, high levels of inflation may induce some people to delay retirement in order to avoid their pension amount being frozen and thereby suffering a rapid loss of purchasing power.

10.6 INVALIDITY INCIDENCE AND TERMINATION

Two aspects of disability experience need to be studied: disability incidence and disability termination.

The number of new cases of disability pensions during recent past years are normally used to estimate future disability incidence rates. To estimate the incidence rate, the data on new cases should be collected by age and sex, and be related to the corresponding eligible population. The invalidity incidence rate represents the probability that an insured person will become an invalid during the coming year in accordance with the definition of invalidity of the scheme under analysis. There is a great diversity of definitions of invalidity in the various public pension schemes, in addition to a great diversity of administrative practices among social security institutions. Therefore, it is important to use the specific experience of the scheme as a basis for the determination of this

Scheme-specific assumptions

Box 10.6   Determination of retirement take-up rates

Retirement take-up rates represent the distribution of retirements by age for a cohort of insured persons. They can be calculated by constructing a multiple-decrement table taking into account mortality, invalidity and retirement for the cohort.

Age (x)	1_x	d_x	I_x	R_x
59	1000	20	25	–
60	955	19	24	200
61	712	14	18	150
62	530	11	13	150
63	356	7	9	100
64	240	5	6	100
65	129	3	4	122
66	0			
Total				822

where:
- l_x = Population at exact age x
- d_x = Number of deaths between x and $x+1$
- I_x = Number of new invalidity pensioners between x and $x+1$
- R_x = Number of new old-age pensioners between x and $x+1$

Take-up rates are calculated as the distribution of R_x for the cohort. They can be used to determine the number of new old-age pensioners in a pension scheme in which the valuation model provides, in a previous step, the ultimate number of retirees for the cohort.

Age	Retirement take-up rates (as a %)
60	24.4
61	18.2
62	18.2
63	12.2
64	12.2
65	14.8
Total	**100.0**

assumption, in order to generate the correct number of new annual invalidity pensioners in the valuation. The invalidity incidence rate should be determined according to age and sex. The problem with a large number of schemes is that the experience is not statistically credible because the observed number of invalids is very low at certain ages or because the experience data do not cover a sufficiently long period. In such situations, it is possible to use the age-sex pattern of an existing standard table and to weight that table in order to reproduce the adequate number of new annual pensioners. It should be remembered that the annual number of new invalidity pensioners (for a given age-sex category) is arrived at by taking three factors into consideration:

1. the insured population;
2. the invalidity incidence rate;
3. the probability that the person meets the eligibility criteria (based on past insurance credits).

In determining the assumption on the incidence rate, the actuary must not forget item 3 above when comparing the annual number of new beneficiaries generated by the model with the actual number observed in the scheme.

A disability pension can be terminated by the death or recovery of the pension holder. A full table of disability termination rates will thus need the data by age, sex and cause of termination. It should be noted that most social security schemes do not have readily available data on disability termination. One good example of an invalidity termination table is the one built by the Office of the Chief Actuary of the Social Security Administration in the United States.[6] Many schemes also do not have a sufficient number of past disability cases to justify the construction of a scheme-specific invalidity termination table. In this case, global data must be used to build loading factors that will be applied to a standard table used for similar schemes. In some cases, it may be suitable to use, as a basis for the termination rates of invalidity pensioners, the mortality table of the insured population by applying to it a loading factor at the earliest age of eligibility for the invalidity pension, and to reduce gradually that factor with increasing age in order to use the same mortality rates for invalids and for other pensioners after the normal retirement age. For example, one can use mortality rates for invalidity pensioners equal to five times the mortality rates of the active insured population at age 20, decreasing the factor linearly to 1 at age 60.

The disability termination table is sometimes select and ultimate, reflecting the fact that mortality and recovery rates are higher during the years immediately following the inception of invalidity. In this case, the data on terminated pensions must also be collected according to the duration of disability. Actuaries of the OASDI in the United States compute such a table for invalidity pensioners.

10.7 ENTITLEMENT TO SURVIVORS' BENEFITS

Information on the family structure of the insured persons is necessary to project survivors' benefits. Assumptions need to be established on the probability of having a spouse at time of death, on the age difference between the spouses, on

Scheme-specific assumptions

Box 10.7 Determination of invalidity incidence rates with limited experience data

Suppose you are working on the actuarial valuation of a small social security scheme and the number of new annual cases of invalidity is not sufficient to determine specific invalidity incidence rates by age and sex. A way of establishing incidence rates in this case is to use the age-sex pattern of a well-known table and to weight it in order to reproduce the number of new annual invalidity pensioners observed in the scheme under study. The actuary must first study the definition of disability under the reference scheme to be sure that it is in line with the definition applied in the scheme under study. We assume here that invalidity incidence rates of the US social security scheme for the year 1998 are appropriate to reflect the age-sex pattern of our scheme. It must be noted that a person is considered an invalid under the US scheme if that person is unable to engage in any gainful activity and the condition is expected to last at least 12 months. Rates from the US table are as follows:[7]

Incidence rates per thousand exposed
under the US social security scheme, 1998

Age group	Males	Females
15–19	0.40	0.24
20–24	1.06	0.78
25–29	1.41	1.23
30–34	1.99	1.97
35–39	2.74	2.93
40–44	3.76	4.06
45–49	5.11	5.46
50–54	8.33	8.67
55–59	14.45	13.42
60–64	17.24	13.49

The next step is to compute for each age group, under our scheme, the number of people exposed to the risk of invalidity. This is calculated as the number of insured persons who meet the eligibility criteria for the invalidity pension (for example, the number of insured persons who have at least five years of contribution history and who have paid contributions during six months over the past year).

Suppose that the application of the US rates to the eligible population under our scheme generates 1,000 new pensioners. On the other hand, the experience under the scheme over the past three years shows a constant number of new beneficiaries of around 700 per year. We can thus use 70 per cent of the rates of the US table as a good estimate of the incidence rates applicable to our scheme.

the average number of children gaining the right to an orphan's pension and on the average age of those children.

10.7.1 Probability of having a spouse at time of death

On the question of the probability of having a spouse at time of death, the definition of spouse contained in the law must be carefully studied. Survivors' pensions may be limited to married people only, or may be extended to common-law partners. Ideally, statistics from the scheme should be used to establish the assumption on the probability of having a spouse at time of death. One should compare the actual number of deaths among the insured population with the actual number of survivors' pensions generated. When no data are available from the scheme, using population vital statistics is permissible. But in this case, adjustments will usually be necessary to reproduce the scheme's definition. In addition, vital statistics often do not present a precise picture of common-law unions, and very rough assumptions must be made in the absence of data from the scheme.

In some countries, the tradition of polygamy exists. Its effect on the assumption of the probability of having a spouse at time of death will depend on the provisions of the law regarding the payment of the survivors' pensions. If the pension is shared between all the existing spouses of an insured person, then the probability will be the same had the insured person had only one spouse. Attention must then be devoted to the assumption on the average age of the spouse (see next section). In the case where the death of the insured person may generate more than one survivor's pension, then the probability of having a spouse may be greater than 1 at certain ages.

10.7.2 Average age of spouse

Ideally, this assumption should be built from the scheme's statistics by constructing tables from the population of new widows' (widowers') pensions and relating the ages of both spouses. However, if the data are unavailable and the scheme covers a substantial proportion of the population, the actuary can use population vital statistics as a base.

In the case of polygamy, the actuary must look carefully at the provisions of the scheme. If, for example, the total widow's pension is shared among all the existing spouses, then the age of the youngest spouse should be taken as an approximation for the average age of the spouse, since the pension will be payable until the death of the last surviving spouse.

10.7.3 Number and age of children

A series of assumptions is necessary to assess the number of children and the average age of the children at the time of death of a contributor. Those

Scheme-specific assumptions

assumptions allow for the calculation of the number of orphans' pensions generated by that death and for the duration of payment of those pensions. In addition, a survival table (in the status of orphan) must be built, mainly to take into account the age at which the orphan's pension will cease (for example, at age 18), and the possibility of the orphan continuing to receive the pension while still in education after that age.

10.8 RATE OF PENSION INDEXING

Pensions are normally adjusted at regular intervals. The adjustment can be automatic or ad hoc and is normally linked to the variation of a price or wage index. It is also usually applied to the amount of the minimum pension, the earnings ceiling and all flat-rate benefits provided by the scheme.

The assumption on the rate of indexing is based on the general set of assumptions composing the economic framework of the valuation, mainly the inflation rate and the general wage increase. The actuary must be aware of the periodicity of the adjustments and any limit imposed by the law on the annual percentage increase.

Even if the law is silent on the annual adjustment of pensions and other parameters of the scheme, projections are generally made under the assumption that these parameters will be adjusted continuously during the course of the scheme. In practice, even when there is no legal obligation to index pensions, ad hoc adjustments are adopted on an ad hoc basis. The actuary should consider that, even in the absence of a legal requirement to index pensions regularly, pension projections cover several decades in the future and the scheme would

---

Box 10.8   Biometric data for survivors' benefit calculations (the Demoland case)

Age	Probability of being married at death	Average age of spouse	Average number of children	Average age of children
22	0.02	20	1.5	1
27	0.10	24	2.0	2
32	0.20	29	2.5	4
37	0.70	34	3.0	7
42	0.70	39	3.0	10
47	0.80	44	3.0	13
52	0.80	49	3.0	16
57	0.80	54	2.0	17
62	0.80	59	1.0	18
67	0.70	64	–	–
72	0.60	69	–	–
77	0.55	74	–	–
82	0.50	80	–	–
87	0.45	85	–	–

quickly lose its significance if its parameters and pensions in payments were not adjusted from time to time in line with the economy.

10.9 INVESTMENT RETURN

The investment policy of the scheme should be established with due regard to the rate of return assumed by the actuary in previous actuarial reviews. On the other hand, the actuary consults investment managers about their practices and short- to medium-term plans for the portfolio composition before setting the assumptions, which illustrates just how closely linked the determination of the assumption on the rate of return and the establishment of the investment policy for the scheme are.

The assumption on the investment return acquires more importance as the level of funding of the scheme increases. If the scheme operates under a financing system that does operate important reserves, investment earnings do not represent an important revenue item. On the other hand, large reserves generate important amounts of investment earnings and, in this case, even a small change in the rate of return assumption can have a significant impact on the financial projections of the scheme.

It is common for a social security institution administering different schemes (pensions, short-term benefits, employment injury benefits, etc.) to apply a pooled-fund approach, mixing the technical reserves of the long-term benefits with the contingency reserves of the short-term benefits. In setting the assumption on the future investment return, the actuary should, at the very least, look at the projected weight of each type of reserve in the total funds held and should take into account the projected composition of the portfolio. It may also be advisable, for investment purposes, to recommend a clear separation of reserves (technical versus contingency) for each benefit branch. It then becomes easier to identify the contingency reserves that should be invested in short-term, liquid investments and the technical reserves that should be invested in long-term, higher-yielding investments.

10.9.1 General level of interest rates

Before going into the specific rate of return of the social security fund, the actuary should have an idea of the general evolution of interest rates for the period of projection. The general level of interest rates can be projected on the basis of the rate of growth assumed in the economic framework established for the valuation (see section 9.2.5).

Scheme-specific assumptions

Box 10.9 Setting assumptions on future investment return

(a) The building block approach[8]

Investment return includes the following components:

- inflation
- real risk-free return
- risk premium
- lack of liquidity or marketability

Real return is equal to the sum of all components excluding inflation. Then:

- Find the real return for each type of investment. An analysis of past observed returns on various types of investments over sufficiently long periods of time permits an assessment of the real rate of return on each type of investment.
- Compute a weighted real rate of return by the proportion of the portfolio invested in each type.
- Add the assumed inflation rate.

Illustration:

Type of investment	Proportion of the portfolio (as a %)	Real return (as a %)
Corporate stocks	40	5
Mortgages	20	3
Bonds	30	2
Cash	10	0

The combined real return is then calculated as:

$(5\% * 0.4) + (3\% * 0.2) + (2\% * 0.3) + (0\% * 0.1) = 3.2\%$

and the total nominal return, assuming an inflation rate of 4.5 per cent, is then 7.7 per cent.

The shortcomings of the approach are that:

- the composition of the portfolio may change over time. This should be taken into account in the projection of the rate of return assumption;
- adding inflation to the real rate is a simplification of reality. High inflation may result in a low rate of return on some types of investments;
- the quality of the investment management strategy may not be measured by this method, since the return is affected by the timing of investments.

(b) The new-money rate approach

This method is more refined and reflects the yield on current assets, assuming an evolution in the composition of the portfolio over time. The steps to be taken are as follows:

- Current fixed-income securities: calculate the future cash flows from existing coupon rates and expected maturities.
- Current equity investments: assume an inflation rate, a real return, and a rate of turnover of the portfolio.
- Assume a distribution of future investments by category (investment policy).
- Assume a future new money interest rate for a risk-free security, and a consistent new money rate for each other type of security.
- Distribute future positive cash flows under the scheme, including income from the existing portfolio, according to each category of investments.

10.9.2 Return by type of investment

Once the basic interest rate in the economy has been assumed, it is possible to determine the particular interest rates of various types of fixed-income securities by adding an appropriate risk premium. This is the case with government securities, corporate bonds, mortgages, etc. Historical data of rate differentials by type of investment may be useful at this stage.

The rate of return on equity investment (common and preferred stocks, real estate, etc.) is usually based on the assumption of a risk premium added to the risk-free interest rate. Again, historical average net returns observed on generally recognized common stock indices over sufficiently long periods may indicate a risk premium appropriate for equity investments.

Once a rate of return has been assumed concerning each type of investment, the actuary may use a weighted average rate of return based on the projected percentage of the portfolio represented by each type of investment for the projections.

10.10 CONTRIBUTION COLLECTION RATE

The direct application of the contribution rate to total contributory earnings calculated from the data extracted from the scheme's administrative files may result in a theoretical amount of contributions that differs from the amount in the scheme's financial statements. One reason for this is that part of the contributions collected during a financial year relates to previous financial years, because of the usual delays in collecting contributions. Another reason might be that the social security institution is unable to apply the law fully and to enforce the payment of all contributions due to the scheme. The contribution collection rate is the ratio of the actual amount of contributions collected to the theoretical amount that would result from the correct application of the law.

Scheme-specific assumptions

Box 10.10   Social security investments in the Caribbean

Most Caribbean schemes are unable to invest abroad, a limitation that is either dictated by the schemes' Act and Regulations, by foreign exchange controls or simply by the will of the government of the day. Capital markets in these countries are also limited. Social security schemes, therefore, are restricted to fixed-income securities, government paper (both short and long term), commercial bank deposits and loans to government corporations/statutory bodies. Most schemes currently invest heavily (40 per cent or more) in government bonds, debentures and treasury bills.

Most of the fixed-income securities have returns that are fixed at issue. Others have returns tied to the prime rate. Interest rates, however, tend to be rather static, not fluctuating as economic conditions might suggest they should in a more efficient economy.

Some schemes hold shares in recently privatized utilities. The availability of equities is limited, not only because only a few publicly traded companies exist but because many of the shareholders see their common shares as assets to be passed on to heirs, not as investments that can realized for profit. However, with the recent privatization of utilities and other formerly government-run institutions, and the increased awareness of companies of the benefit of going public, the Caribbean should see an increase in available equity investment opportunities in the near future.

The schemes are generally not very active fund managers. Often, fixed-income investments are bought and held to maturity, and equities are held indefinitely. There is little buying and selling of securities, when price changes could enable schemes to realize profits or obtain securities at "cheap" rates.

Returns on the portfolio tend not to be volatile as most of the assets are in fixed-income securities in an environment where prevailing rates fluctuate little. Therefore, investment income only includes interest and dividends, thus adding to the stability of the declared rate of return.

Monitoring investment performance can sometimes become a subjective exercise. The returns earned by privately managed pension funds are usually not public information and there are no indices that track performance, other than for equities. Because the investment portfolio of the social security scheme is usually the largest single pool of funds, and the investment objectives differ from those of private funds, it may not be fair to compare the return with that of privately managed funds.

At the asset class level, however, comparisons are a little easier. Equity performance in those countries with stock markets (Jamaica, Trinidad and Tobago, and Barbados) can be compared with the stock market's index or local mutual fund performance. Returns on fixed deposits, which have maturities of up to a year, can be compared with prevailing rates. But comparing the yield on long-term bonds, government or otherwise, that have fixed coupon rates, with prevailing long-term rates, may not be advisable.

Finally, the return on social investments is expected to be low, or in some cases zero. On these assets, the financial return may be low, but the social return, which usually is unmeasurable, can be significant.

In setting the long-term interest rate for an actuarial projection, consideration must be given to:

> - the current distribution of assets;
> - past returns on investments;
> - inflation expectations;
> - expected changes in asset distribution;
> - expected returns on each asset class;
> - future liquidity needs.
>
> Given the size of the schemes, the types of investments and the nature of the economy, simplified assumptions on expected future investment returns are usually used. This may take the form of either a level expected return or a select and ultimate assumption, where the ultimate long-term rate is lower than the rates in the early years of the scheme.
>
> Only a few Caribbean schemes currently have international (US) investments, although many schemes are, however, now considering investing abroad. Initially, the proportion of assets that may be placed outside the region will be small, but this may increase over time, given the limited opportunities within the region. Investing overseas should enable schemes to earn higher yields over the long term, but they may encounter increased volatility, especially if they invest heavily in equity-type investments.
>
> Most of the schemes are still many years away from having to liquidate assets to meet benefit and administrative expenditures. Long-term projections of interest rates, therefore, may not have to consider the possibility of having to liquidate investments at depressed prices.

The calculation of the contribution income in the actuarial valuation thus needs an adjustment factor. The data must be obtained on the timing of contribution collection to estimate the first factor. The scheme's provisions are also necessary to understand the phenomenon fully. In particular, the presence of an earnings ceiling, the modification of the contribution rate and the legal requirements on the delay for employers to remit contributions to the social security institution are elements that explain this discrepancy.

The actuary must also make an assumption on the future evolution of that factor, in particular the way the administration of the institution's contribution collection process will evolve. If plans are already in place to improve the collection of contributions, the actuarial valuation may take them into account.

10.11 FUTURE LEVEL OF ADMINISTRATIVE EXPENSES

Box 8.3 of Chapter 8 presented the typical administrative expenses incurred by a social security institution. In order to set an assumption on the future level of administrative expenses, it is necessary to analyse the nature of the current

Scheme-specific assumptions

Box 10.11 An example of a contribution collection pattern

When one compares the amount of contributions actually collected during a financial year with the theoretical amount calculated by multiplying the contribution rate by the total insurable earnings (on an accrued basis), there is normally a difference that can be explained by the contribution collection pattern.

The legal requirement and the actual pattern of contribution payment

As a general rule, employers deduct contributions for social security from the salaries of their employees and are required to send these employees' contributions, along with employer contributions, to the social security institution (or to any other designated collecting agent). There is usually a period of time which is specified for the payment of these contributions by the employer, varying from one to three months. However, the actual delay is, for a number of reasons, often over the legal requirement.

Development of a contribution payment factor

Useful information for the reconciliation of contributions on an accrued basis is the proportion of contributions received during a year and attributable to past contribution years. Suppose, for example, the following pattern of contribution collection, assuming a 25 per cent annual increase in the contributions due and a constant pattern of collection.

Scheme's financial year	1995	1996	1997	Total paid
Paid in 1995	600 000			
Paid in 1996	300 000	750 000		
Paid in 1997	100 000	375 000	937 500	1 412 500
Paid in 1998		125 000	468 750	
Paid in 1999			156 250	
Total due	1 000 000	1 250 000	1 562 500	

Contributions due for the financial year 1997 are 1,562,500, but the amount of contributions actually collected is only 1,412,500, due to the fact that 33.6 per cent of contributions paid in 1997 related to previous financial years. Contributions increase each year due to one or more of the following factors:

- an increase in the general average earnings;
- an increase in the level of the ceiling on covered earnings;
- an increase in the contribution rate.

In addition to these factors, the social security institution may improve its efficiency and reduce contribution payment evasion, thereby also increasing the contribution income.

expenses, to determine an economic indicator that will better reflect the evolution of the expenses over time and then project the changing weight of each type of expense in total expenses.

For example, it might be expected that the staff of the institution will double over the next decade, considering the efforts that will be made into collecting contributions, or considering a foreseen increase in the number of claims to be handled owing to the arrival at retirement age of a large generation of contributors. Then, the weight of salaries in the total administrative expenses would be expected to increase. It may be assumed, for example, that the expenses related to staff salaries will follow the evolution of the average national wage over time, while other expenses will follow price inflation. A weighted-average of the two rates will determine the rate of growth of administrative expenses for the scheme.

Administrative expenses can also be projected to represent a fixed percentage of insurable earnings, contributions or benefits. They can also be expressed as a percentage of a measure combining contributions and benefits. This approach is legitimate, since administrative expenses are incurred specifically to collect contributions and pay benefits. However, these gross estimates should be used with caution when projected over long periods because of the existence of fixed costs that are not reflected in such a formula. In addition, expressing administrative expenses as a percentage of contributions can lead to extraordinary high growth rates of expenses during a period of increasing contribution rates.

Notes

[1] It should be noted here that the number of active contributors for a year differs from the average number of contributors over each month of the year. In the model described here, a person is considered a contributor as long as one contribution for one month has been collected (if the month is the frequency of contribution collection). The density factor (described later) will be used to reflect the part of the year during which the person contributed and thus the total amount of contributions to the scheme.

[2] It may be useful to recall the specific terms employed throughout this module to identify various subsets of the population:

- *Insured persons*: Those people who are registered under the scheme and who have made contributions during at least one contribution period before the valuation date, excluding those who have died and those who are receiving long-term benefits.
- *Active insured persons*: Those people on whose behalf a contribution has been paid under the scheme during the last financial year.
- *Inactive insured persons*: Those people on behalf of whom no contributions have been paid during the last financial year.
- *New entrants*: Those people who were first registered as insured persons within the last financial year.
- *Re-entrants*: Insured persons who moved from an inactive to an active insured status during the last financial year.

[3] This box is taken from ILO: *ILO-DIST: The ILO wage distribution model* (Geneva, 1998).

[4] The formulae of this section have been taken from ILO: *ILO-DIST: The ILO wage distribution model* (Geneva, 1998).

[5] See section 10.1.3.
[6] See Social Security Administration: "Social security disability insurance program workers' experience", in: *Actuarial Study No. 114* (Baltimore, 1999).
[7] ibid.
[8] S. Itelson: *Selection of interest assumptions for pension plan valuation*, in: *Study Notes No. 462-23-91* (Schaumburg, Illinois, Society of Actuaries, 1991).

RESULTS AND SENSITIVITY ANALYSIS   11

The purpose of the actuarial valuation is to describe the future financial status of a social security scheme. Various indicators exist to illustrate the reality of the scheme in brief; the most commonly used indicators are presented in this chapter.

Once a base scenario has been developed, sensitivity analysis is a way of informing the users of an actuarial report of the fact that actuarial projections performed over several decades in the future cannot, of course, be 100 per cent accurate. The actuarial report usually provides information on the potential variability of the results by comparing results under alternative sets of assumptions.

The actuarial report of Demoland, presented in Chapter 21, shows one typical way of presenting the results of the actuarial valuation of a social security scheme. The actuary may choose to put more emphasis on certain results, which will depend on, among other factors, the objective of the valuation, the size of the scheme and the available database.

11.1 VALUATION RESULTS

An actuarial valuation can be separated into demographic and financial results. Demographic projections provide information on the relationship between the number of people who pay contributions and those who receive benefits, which is a good indicator of the general trend in costs that will have to be supported by contributors, especially in the context of an ageing population. Financial projections include, in addition to the demographic effect, the impact of all economic variables that influence the monetary values of a scheme. They show the earnings base on which contributions are based, the benefit expenditure of the scheme and the resulting reserve levels.

Results and sensitivity analysis

Box 11.1 Valuation results under status quo projections (the Demoland case)

Demographic projections

Year	Contributors			Pensioners								Ratio of pensioners to contributors (as a %)
	M	F	Total	Old age		Invalidity		Widows	Orphans	Total		
				M	F	M	F					
1999	79 916	56 631	136 547	16 142	4 549	1 467	462	6 723	1 544	30 887		23
2000	80 725	57 624	138 349	15 911	4 597	1 624	507	7 239	2 622	32 500		23
2001	81 619	58 684	140 303	15 705	4 648	1 784	554	7 712	3 530	33 933		24
2002	82 616	59 827	142 442	15 547	4 718	1 947	603	8 142	4 297	35 254		25
2003	83 714	61 058	144 772	15 460	4 825	2 112	654	8 533	4 939	36 523		25
2004	84 870	62 380	147 251	15 482	4 975	2 280	708	8 889	5 460	37 794		26
2005	86 119	63 800	149 919	15 610	5 171	2 451	765	9 212	5 878	39 087		26
2010	93 324	72 161	165 485	17 513	6 849	3 358	1 087	10 490	6 817	46 114		28
2020	102 648	85 294	187 942	25 114	14 074	5 324	1 930	12 663	5 645	64 750		34
2030	106 012	96 594	202 606	31 217	23 633	6 969	2 851	15 126	4 532	84 328		42
2040	109 758	109 144	218 902	34 344	30 696	7 966	3 527	16 558	3 978	97 069		44

(continued)

Box 11.1 (continued)

Financial projections

Year	Revenue (in million $)			Total expenditure	Reserve (end of year)	Reserve ratio	PAYG rate (as a %)
	Contributions	Investment	Total				
1999	3 071	772	3 843	2 735	11 296	4.1	7.4
2000	3 848	904	4 752	3 826	12 222	3.2	8.3
2001	4 147	923	5 070	4 247	13 045	3.1	8.5
2002	4 434	873	5 306	4 740	13 612	2.9	8.9
2003	4 756	958	5 714	5 316	14 010	2.6	9.3
2004	5 088	976	6 064	5 990	14 084	2.4	9.8
2005	5 444	970	6 414	6 721	13 776	2.1	10.2
2010	7 629	371	8 000	11 891	2 944	0.3	12.9
2020	14 180	–	14 180	33 791	–	–	19.8
2030	24 910	–	24 910	75 302	–	–	25.1
2040	42 933	–	42 933	141 280	–	–	27.3

The following results and descriptors represent the standard outputs of the actuarial valuation:

1. The demographic projections of the number of active insured persons and beneficiaries including the corresponding relative demographic ratios;
2. The financial projections of total insurable earnings and benefit expenditure, both in current and constant monetary terms;
3. The projected average insurable earnings and average benefits including the corresponding average replacement ratios;
4. The projected PAYG cost rates;
5. The projected total expenditure expressed as a percentage of GDP, including its breakdown by benefit branch;
6. The GAP for the full projection period;
7. The projected levels of the reserve according to the present legal levels of the contribution rate and according to the recommended levels;
8. The projected reserve ratios that reflect the level of reserve in terms of annual benefit expenditure;
9. The projected levels of the reserve and contribution rates on the basis of an alternative financing method;
10. The capitalization (or full-funding) ratio which reflects the level of the actual reserve in relation to the amount of reserves that would be necessary to fund all benefits in payment and the accrued benefits of the insured population;

11. The required government subsidies (other than for the payment of its contribution to the scheme as an employer) in absolute terms and as a ratio to total expenditure and/or total insurable earnings.

11.2 CALCULATION OF INDICATORS

The outputs of the social security model enable various indictors to be computed for the analysis of the scheme's future evolution. These indicators usually help in the setting of recommendations on the financing, coverage or benefit levels. The choice of indicators for the purpose of the analysis depends on:

- the degree of maturity of the scheme;
- the financial system in place;
- the projected demographic environment; and
- the size of the scheme.

Some of the indicators presented below follow the basic equation expressing the PAYG cost of a pension scheme as the product of the demographic dependency ratio and the financial ratio (average replacement rate).

Formula 11.1

$$\begin{aligned}\text{PAYG} &= \text{Demographic ratio} \times \text{Financial ratio} \\ &= \frac{\text{Number of pensioners}}{\text{Number of contributors}} \times \frac{\text{Average pension}}{\text{Average earnings of contributors}}\end{aligned}$$

A disaggregation of the PAYG cost into its components is part of the validation process. For example, the demographic ratio can be calculated separately for each type of pension, showing the evolution of the weight of the different types of benefits in the global cost of the scheme.

Calculating the financial ratios for the various types of pensions makes it possible to validate the financial results by enabling a comparison to be made with the legal provisions of the scheme. For example, taking into consideration the average age at entry, the normal retirement age and the pension formula, the actuary can compare the financial ratio for the old-age pension with the replacement rate according to the provisions of the law.

11.2.1 Demographic indicators

The actuary should provide detailed information on the following indicators, with comments on their appropriateness as to general demographic developments.

Demographic ratio

The demographic ratio for the scheme is defined as the number of pensioners to the number of active contributors. This ratio can be compared with the dependency ratio of the general population of the country, calculated using the age at entry into the pension scheme and the usual retirement age.

Coverage rate

The effective coverage rate of the scheme can be compared with the legal coverage rate, that is, by comparing the number of insured persons (active and inactive) with the potential number of people who should be covered according to the legal provisions.

Contributors' ratio

This is defined as the number of active insured persons to the total number of insured persons (active and inactive), and gives an idea of the potential weight of inactive insured persons in the total liability of the scheme.

11.2.2 Financial indicators

Financial indicators provide information on the future evolution of costs and on the capacity of the scheme to support them in the long term. A brief list of the key financial indicators follows.

PAYG rate

This represents the ratio of total expenditure of the scheme (benefits and administrative expenses) in a given year to the total insurable earnings for the same year. It translates the annual total cost of benefits and other expenses or components thereof into percentages of insurable earnings. This indicator describes which contribution rate would have to be charged if the expenditure of the scheme were financed with a contribution rate specifically levied for that purpose. The ultimate level of the PAYG rate is compared with the present contribution rate to give some early assessment of the future increases in the contribution rate that will later be necessary. It is also possible to compute an *adjusted PAYG cost rate* representing the rate to be charged to contributors (workers and employers) to cover only the expenditure of a given year that is not already covered by the interest on the reserve or by other income (for example, government subsidy).

GAP

This is calculated by equating the present value of future projected contributions of insured persons (present contributors and new entrants), plus the value of existing reserves, to the present value of projected future benefits and administration expenses for existing and future insured persons and beneficiaries. This does not mean that the scheme will be in perfect balance each year, but that the scheme will arrive at the end of the chosen period with a zero balance. Technically, this premium can be interpreted as the long-term average adjusted PAYG premium.

Total expenditure as a percentage of GDP

This indicator provides an additional perspective on the expenditure of the scheme in relation to the total value of goods and services produced in the country. It may provide insight as to the capacity of the economy to support the scheme in the long term. The scheme's expenditure as a percentage of GDP illustrates the place and weight of the social security scheme in the economy.

Actuarial balance

This represents the difference between an income rate and a cost rate computed over various periods, in a currency unit and as a percentage of insured earnings. This indicator is used by the US social security system (see Box 5.4 for more details).

Reserve ratio

This represents the ratio of the reserve to the annual expenditure of the scheme. This relative measure of the reserve gives a rough indication of how long the scheme would be able to operate in the event of it suddenly no longer receiving contributions and investment earnings.

Funding ratio

This indicator expresses the amount of current reserves as a percentage of the total amount of liabilities of the scheme. The amount of liabilities represents the present value of future benefits to current pensioners and the total accrued rights of the insured population.

Average pension replacement rate

This is calculated as the average pension divided by the average insurable earnings, and shows how the scheme meets, over time, its earnings replacement objective.

Catchment ratio

This ratio reflects the effect of a ceiling and/or of an exemption limit on the total payroll covered by the scheme. It is calculated as the amount of earnings subject to the payment of contributions (insurable earnings) to the total amount of earnings received by insured persons from employment.

Year of reserve exhaustion

In the case of a contribution rate specified in the law, with no systematic financial system, this indicator presents the number of years the scheme may continue to operate without any changes being made to the legislated contribution rate.

11.3 SENSITIVITY ANALYSIS

The actuarial valuation of a social security scheme cannot, of course, pretend to project the future with perfect accuracy. Projections are based on imperfect models and assumptions, and the variables used in the models may react to unpredictable factors.

When using a deterministic model, sensitivity analysis is the only way of showing the potential variability of results. It can be performed on assumptions that have the most impact on future costs or, alternatively, on those assumptions that present a lower level of credibility because of a lack of data. In the actuarial valuation process, the actuary may face a situation where the database is not as complete as it should be to build strong enough assumptions on the future development of some aspects of the scheme. If this is the case, sensitivity analysis can inform the readers of the report of the extent of the eventual gaps that will occur between what has been projected and the reality. For example, the economic environment may have been unstable for some time before the valuation date, and the level of employment may be difficult to project even for the coming year. In such a situation, it is necessary to present sensitivity tests on key assumptions concerning the future evolution of the labour market. On the other hand, certain long-term assumptions, such as migration levels, can depend on political priorities that change over time. This is the case, for example, with the number of migrants a given country will receive each year. As regards the fertility rate, even if one can assume that its level in a developing country will eventually drop to the level currently observed in most developed economies, the pace at which this decline will take place is open to many possibilities.

Critical variables on which sensitivity tests are usually performed are:

- fertility rates
- future improvements in life expectancy
- migration

Results and sensitivity analysis

Box 11.2 Summary of factors influencing the financial equilibrium of a pension scheme[1]

	Impact on income	Impact on expenditure
Economic factors		
(1) growth	increase in insured persons and wages	increase in entitlements and beneficiaries
(2) employment growth – likely to depend on (1)	increase in insured persons	increase in beneficiaries
(3) wage share and wages increase – might depend on (1)	increase in insurable earnings	increase in benefit amounts
(4) wage increase/inflation	increase in insurable earnings	increase in benefit amounts
(5) interest rate increase	increase in investment income	
Demographic factors		
(1) initial population age structure	relationship of actives to beneficiaries	increase in benefit amounts
(2) improvements in life expectancy		increase in the number of beneficiaries and longer service of benefits
(3) fertility increase	increase in the number of contributors (long run) if economic development permits	increase in the number of beneficiaries (long run)
Governance factors		
(1) design	contribution provisions	pension formula and entitlement conditions determining the number and amounts of benefits
(2) maintenance (adjustment)	ceiling on insurable earnings	benefit levels
(3) administrative efficiency		
(4) administration cost decrease	increase in income	decrease of expenditure on administration
(5) increase registration compliance	short-term direct increase in insurable earnings	direct long-term increase in beneficiaries
(6) increase wage compliance	short-term direct increase in insurable earnings	long-term increase in benefits

Box 11.3 Sensitivity tests performed in the 1997 report of the Quebec pension plan[2]

	Test 1	Base case	Test 2
Demography			
Fertility rate	1.3 (2002 and after)	1.75 (2007 and after)	2.1 (2012 and after)
Net migration (as a %)	0.15 (1998 and after)	0.30 (2012 and after)	0.4 (2012 and after)
Life expectancy (in years)	1998: Males: 75.1 Females: 81.6	1998: Males: 75.1 Females: 81.6	1998: Males: 74.9 Females: 81.5
	2050: Males: 81.4 Females: 86.4	2050: Males: 79.4 Females: 84.8	2050: Males: 74.9 Females: 81.5
Economy			
Participation rate (as a %)	5 (in 2050)	60 (in 2050)	62 (1998 and after)
Unemployment rate (as a %)	10 (until 2020)	7.0 (in 2030)	6.0 (in 2010)
Inflation (as a %)	2.0 (2001 and after)	3.0 (2015 and after)	4.0 (2020 and after)
Real wage growth (as a %)	0.8 (2015 and after)	1.2 (2016 and after)	1.5 (2019 and after)
Real interest rate, 2020 and after (as a %)	3.0	4.1	5.0

- economic growth
- employment level
- price increases
- real wage growth
- rate of return on investments
- effective age at which people retire (given that the scheme allows flexibility)
- disability incidence rates

Decision-makers and users of actuarial valuations are likely to enquire about the practical impact of a gap between what the actuary has projected and what will be observed. What if salary increases are lower than projected? What if employment shrinks? These sort of questions can be answered by conducting sensitivity analysis.

Macroeconomic frames developed by public administrations are usually limited to very short periods. Considering that actuarial valuations are conducted to extend projections to as far as 50 years into the future, the actuary needs to extend the assumptions concerning the economy, taking into account the perceptions of the government representatives of a country. There are a number of exogenous assumptions that must be determined on the basis of discussions with economists and other experts, who will normally include experts and academics working closely with the social security system and the specialists of the ministries responsible for labour, finance, health and welfare and economic planning. This may, however, lead to diverging views on the long-term macroeconomic development of a country. The actuary should then perform sensitivity analysis to indicate the various outcomes of different macroeconomic scenarios.

Sensitivity tests may be done in two ways. The first is to perform a series of individual assumptions, showing in each case the impact on the PAYG rate or on the GAP. The other method is to combine assumptions under a number of different scenarios. The actuary may define a base scenario, including the most

---

Box 11.4 Reconciliation between two valuations (the Demoland case)

Two factors explain the differences between the results of the fourth and fifth actuarial valuations:

1. In the 1993 valuation, the rate of growth of the active insured population had been assumed constant at 1 per cent per year. In the 1998 valuation, the rate of growth of this population had been projected to be higher during the first 20 years of the projection – at 1.4 per cent from 1999 to 2010 and 1.3 per cent from 2011 to 2020.
2. The 1993 valuation used a rate for the indexing of benefits equal to the rate of increase of wages. Considering the legislative provisions and current practice, it has been assumed in the present valuation that pensions will continue to be indexed on the basis of price increases.

These two factors led to the cost of the scheme in the 1998 valuation being lower than in the 1993 valuation. This is firstly because the amount of benefits, once in payment, evolve less rapidly because of the lower indexation factor, and secondly because the relatively larger number of contributors per pensioner results in a lower cost as a percentage of payroll. The following table presents a comparison of PAYG rates and dependency ratios under the two valuations.

Comparison of results of the 1993 and 1998 valuations

Year	PAYG cost rate (as a %)		Ratio of pensioners to contributors (as a %)	
	1993 valuation	1998 valuation	1993 valuation	1998 valuation
1999	9.8	7.4	26	23
2009	14.9	12.3	34	28
2019	23.9	19.1	45	34

probable assumptions on the future development of the scheme. Some assumptions contained in the base scenario are then modified to create an optimistic and a pessimistic scenario.[3] Although sensitivity analysis can be broken down in a meticulous manner to reflect the impact of every possible change in assumptions, the actuary should still provide the results in as concise a manner as possible by presenting alternative projections for a limited number only of scenarios.

11.4 RECONCILIATION OF RESULTS WITH THE PREVIOUS VALUATION

It is often useful to include in the actuarial report a reconciliation of the long-term costs of two successive valuations. The exercise can consist of a reconciliation of the long-term PAYG rate or the GAP of the two valuations in order to identify the causes that may emerge from different factors. A comparison between two successive actuarial valuations may also be done by identifying the year in which the reserve is due to be exhausted (the period of equilibrium).

The causes of differences in the projections of two successive valuations can be explained as follows.

Differences between assumptions and the reality since the last valuation

Since the last valuation, some people may, for example, have retired at different ages than those projected, leading to a different distribution of starting pensioners for the new valuation. Inflation may have been higher than projected, thereby increasing the average starting pension. The minimum pension and the earnings ceiling may also have evolved differently than projected. The scheme's reserve on the valuation date of the new valuation will be affected by such differences.

Changes to the legal provisions of the scheme between two valuations

Modifications to the scheme may have affected the level of benefits or the eligibility conditions. The legal contribution rate or the rule for determining the earnings ceiling may have been modified, directly affecting the basis on which the actuarial valuation lies.

Modifications to the future development of the scheme

The environment may have changed significantly since the last valuation, forcing a revision of critical assumptions on the scheme's future development.

These modifications may affect demographic assumptions (mortality, fertility, migration levels), general economic assumptions (future employment, real wage increases, inflation, interest rates), or the scheme's parameters (coverage rate, retirement age, disability incidence). One way of following the experiences

Results and sensitivity analysis

of the scheme between successive actuarial valuations is to reconcile the long-term PAYG rate of the present valuation with the PAYG rate of the previous valuation. Alternatively, a similar exercise can be conducted using the GAP or the scaled premium for two successive actuarial valuations.

Notes

[1] Taken from M. Cichon and K. Pal: *Reflections on lessons learned: Financing old-age, invalidity and survivors' benefits in Anglophone Africa* (Geneva, ILO, 1997).

[2] Régie des rentes du Québec: *Analyse actuarielle du régime de rentes du Québec au 31 décembre 1997* (Quebec, 1998).

[3] The Trustees Report of the OASDI in the United States presents actuarial valuation results on this basis.

THE VALUATION OF MODIFICATIONS TO A SCHEME   12

A social security scheme has a life of its own, evolving over time and adapting to changes in the environment. The actuarial report usually contains recommendations for adjusting certain benefits or for restoring the long-term financial viability of the scheme. This chapter presents the most commonly encountered adjustments to public pension schemes and advises the actuary how to handle them in order to measure their impact on the financial evolution of the scheme. Modifications may require making alterations to assumptions or changes to the financing approach.

This chapter deals with adjustments to ongoing schemes, and it is assumed that the nature of the scheme is not undergoing major reforms. Structural reforms (for example, changing from a DB to a DC scheme) are looked at in Chapter 13.

Because of the demographic prospects in most countries (an ageing population) and the fiscal situation of many governments, the revision of a social security scheme often translates into downsizing benefits. Modifications are also adopted to correct design or management errors. On the financing side, corrective action can take the form of adjustments being made to the contribution rate, usually on a gradual basis, or extending the salary base used for computing contributions. Some of the more frequent types of adjustments and their actuarial treatment are listed below.

12.1 MODIFICATIONS TO BENEFITS

12.1.1 Eligibility conditions (contribution requirements)

Eligibility conditions for pensions are usually expressed in terms of a certain minimum number of weeks, months or years of past contributions. A modification to the scheme may call for an increase in the number of years of past contributions required for contributors to be eligible for an old-age pension, from ten to 15 years, for example.

To estimate the impact of such a modification can be as simple as changing the line in the computer program of the model specifying the required number of years of service. This will be the case if the input data on the population of registered participants on the valuation date include a distribution of past service, and not only an average past service by age and sex. In addition, it is important that each year the model takes into account the increase in accumulated service of the active insured population according to the actual service credited, also taking into consideration participants' actual working patterns. Depending on the precision of the model mechanics, any alterations to eligibility conditions can be difficult to estimate or, in the worst-case scenario of a model using only average values, the model may not react to the modification. In this case, specific estimates may be carried out on the basis of the distribution of past service of several cohorts of new pensioners (in the past five or ten years, for example), on condition that the scheme has been in operation for a sufficient number of years.

Ideally, the model should be able to take into account the fact that a modification to the eligibility conditions for the old-age pension will affect the retirement behaviour of the insured population. More stringent conditions, for example, will delay the average retirement age. If the model does not react automatically to the impact of a modification to the eligibility conditions on retirement behaviour, the actuary must make specific adjustments to the retirement rates.

12.1.2 Retirement age

In addition to rationalizing the pension entitlement provisions, gradual increases in the retirement age provide additional cost-containment or cost-reduction elements of a pension reform. Early retirement reduction factors can also be introduced under the pension reform package of the existing scheme, as well as incentives for deferred retirement.

It is generally difficult to assess the impact of changing the retirement age on the behaviour of the insured population. The retirement rates have to be adjusted using the actuary's judgement. If possible, the data from the occupational schemes can be used as an indication of the possible reaction of the insured population to a change in the retirement age.

When modelling the impact of an increase in the retirement age, it is particularly important to ensure that there is consistency between the retirement behaviour and the structure of the labour force. Projecting that people will start receiving their retirement pension at a later age, for example, may mean that they will be part of the labour force for an additional number of years. In such a case, under the assumption that the number of total workers in the economy is unchanged, the result will be higher unemployment levels for younger workers. Given the differences in average earnings of the various age groups, the rise in the retirement age will affect not only the timing of pension payments but also the amount of contributions paid to the scheme. On the other

---

Box 12.1 Increasing the retirement age (the Demoland case)

The ultimate contribution rate of the pension branch (26 per cent) would seem to be high, considering the future capacity of the scheme's financiers to support it. At the same time, the current retirement age of the scheme (60) is relatively low in comparison with international standards. And this does not take into consideration the fact that life expectancy is projected to increase significantly during the next 50 years. From age 60, life expectancy, being the average duration a person is expected to live as a pensioner under the scheme, is currently 15.9 years for men and 18.8 for women, and these figures are projected to increase to 19.4 and 22.3 respectively by 2050. This is an important factor that is contributing to the increase in the PAYG cost of the scheme over the years. It would thus be logic to integrate into the scheme's design an element of dynamics by linking the retirement age to the expected length of time a person is expected to live, on average, from the time that person retires.

The ILO Social Security (Minimum Standards) Convention, 1952 (No. 102) requires that an old-age pension be provided no later than the age of 65. There is thus a possibility for the NIS to look at gradually increasing its retirement age. As an illustration of the possible financial impact of such a measure, we have simulated the effect of gradually increasing the retirement age from 60 to 65 between the years 2005 and 2015. This would bring a reduction in the ultimate contribution rate of the Pension branch from 26 per cent to 21 per cent. There are a large number of scenarios for increasing the retirement age, according to:

- the timing of the first increase;
- the length of the period for the transition between the current retirement age and the ultimate one;
- ultimate retirement age to be reached.

The above example is just one of many and represents a range of possible savings that could be made if one of these alternative scenarios was adopted.

The increase in the retirement age should be considered in parallel with the national employment policy. Requiring older workers to stay on in the labour force for a certain number of additional years means that employment opportunities should be available to them. Currently, an increase in the retirement age would not be compatible with the high level of unemployment in Demoland. Obliging older workers to stay in the labour market would just mean that fewer jobs would be available to young people entering the workforce. In the medium term, however, a careful follow-up of the evolution of the labour force and the timely introduction of retirement age increases could be beneficial to the scheme and to the economy as a whole.

The valuation of modifications to a scheme

hand, people retiring later may be unable to hold on to their jobs, particularly those engaged in seasonal employment or in certain industrial sectors. In this case, the macroeconomic frame of the valuation will not be affected by a change in the normal retirement age, and the measure aiming at increasing the retirement age will just translate into delayed pension payments, having no impact on the contribution side.

In some instances, a scheme increasing its normal retirement age allows people to continue to retire at the same age as before, but with a reduction in their pensions. Depending on the extent of this reduction (actuarial equivalent basis or not), the impact on the labour force could be minimal, the sole impact being on the amount of emerging pensions.

12.1.3 The pension formula

Annual accrual rate

Pension formulae in social security DB pension schemes are generally expressed as a percentage accrual per year of credited service, multiplied by an earnings base calculated as the average earnings over a given period preceding the starting date of the pension. Modifications to be made may relate to the annual percentage accrual or to the period over which the final earnings base is calculated.

It is generally agreed that a proportionate link between contributions and benefits is desirable. For existing schemes with a skewed pension formula that allocate a higher unit of benefit entitlement in the earlier years of participation (a device justified at the inception of a scheme to facilitate pension entitlement to people of middle or advanced age), a transitional adjustment providing a uniform factor may be contemplated. It is often argued that such a measure reduces contribution evasion. The new pension formula should be geared to providing targeted replacement rates in accordance with the pension reform package.

In the case of a change to the accrual rate, benefit reductions usually relate only to future benefit accruals, for obvious political reasons. A simple change to the computer program determining future pension amounts would then fully reflect the impact of the modification.

Reference earnings

The reference period for calculating final earnings is sometimes extended, and has the effect of reducing the replacement rate because of the progression of the salary. An evaluation of the salary curve on a segmented basis, a task that involves additional statistical and actuarial work, provides further insight into the earnings progression by age. The salary curve varies greatly according to the sector of the economy:

- In the public sector and the structured or formal private sector of the economy, the salary usually increases steadily with age.

- In the case of temporary or seasonal workers, or those engaged in occupational activities in the primary sector of the economy, the earnings peak is usually reached between the ages of 45 and 50, followed by a period of stable earnings and an eventual decline just prior to retirement. Hence, modelling the insurable earnings for that sector might provide actuarial insights into the effect of an indexed career average pension formula rather than a final average pension formula. This may necessitate a reformulation of the projection model.

A modification to the earnings base used in the pension calculation may have a retroactive impact on current contributors. For example, a calculation of the average final earnings over a ten-year period preceding retirement instead of a five-year average may have a direct impact on the pension of a person retiring the next year. Depending on the shape of the salary scale, the change to the earnings base may be difficult to assess. For example, when the salary scale shows an average salary levelling off after the age of 50, a calculation of the average earnings over five or ten years (with a retirement age at 60) will show the same result. The salary scale may then require an adjustment to avoid inconsistent results.

A modification that may be more difficult to evaluate is the change from a final-average to a career-average formula. In a large number of social security institutions, earnings data are not available for the whole career of individual participants. The final-average formula was often a convenient way of avoiding having to keep records of all the past earnings of insured persons. In such a case, the impact of a new formula using career-average earnings cannot be measured directly from the scheme's data and a rough estimate must be done on the basis of the salary scale used for the valuation.

12.1.4 Adjustments to pensions in payment

The provisions governing cost-of-living adjustments (COLA) to avoid the erosion of pensions can be modified by introducing a minimum threshold that will trigger an adjustment, under either ad hoc or automatic pension adjustment methods. In addition, the actuary should assess the tax provisions applicable to earnings prior, and pensions after, retirement to assess the effect of COLA adjustments on net pensions, in comparison with the net salary, after deducting taxes. This exercise could also be applied to the pension formula and to targeted real replacement ratios. An adjustment to the minimum pension only, a device that is rather common in Latin America, can lead over time to flat-benefit pensions, regardless of the level of earnings prior to retirement. An adjustment based on the evolution of prices protects the standard of living of pensioners but can also cause a financial burden if real wages are decreasing. Wage indexation implies higher long-term actuarial costs, under the expectation that wages tend to increase faster than inflation. Utilizing the lower of either wage or price inflation is another possible basis for indexing pensions.

The scheme may move from ad hoc to automatic indexing. It is, therefore, common in the projections to use an assumption of regular increases or to assume that cumulative adjustments will be made at regular intervals (say, every five years) to catch up with past price increases. In this case, the valuation under reform will not show any financial projections that differ significantly from the base scenario.

12.1.5 Level of minimum and maximum pensions

Provisions regarding maximum and minimum pensions are commonly used as redistribution devices. Capping maximum pensions or insurable earnings at a level much lower than effective salaries encourages evasion and the underreporting of income. The minimum pension is usually based on the floor of protection principle of a national pension system but, as stated before, it should be correlated with the needs of an earnings-related scheme or with a flat-benefit formula.

The valuation of these modifications requires a distribution of the earnings of the insured population in order to estimate the number of insured persons who will be affected by the new minimum and maximum pensions (see section 10.2.2 on earnings distribution).

12.1.6 Earnings test at retirement

Often, social security pension schemes do not require that people actually retire from the labour force in order to be eligible for their old-age pensions, which means that they can combine a pension income with a working income. To reduce costs and also to target social security benefits to people in need of income because they have taken full retirement, it may be necessary to reduce the periodic amount of the old-age pension by a certain percentage of the working income received by the pensioners.

Under such a modification, financial projections are affected in two ways:

- Some people will retire later in order to avoid a reduction in their pension.
- Those who do not retire later but who have a working income incur a reduction in their pension amount.

It should be kept in mind that the work activity itself may depend on the provision of the social security scheme; some people stop working at a certain age just because the social security scheme pays a pension. Another problem is the way the earnings from work received at retirement are declared by the individual and controlled by the social security institution. In the case of a direct link between the income-tax authority and the social insurance scheme, all the information should be available, although this is rarely the case. Even when the link exists, there may be long delays between the time the income is earned and the time the social security institution is informed. If the controls are inefficient, the actuary must be more conservative in the valuation of the modification, assuming, for example, that no change will occur in the retirement behaviour and that no cost savings will be observed, at least in the short term. On the other hand, if it can be assumed that all earnings from work will be declared, then specific data and assumptions will enable an evaluation of the reducing impact on the scheme's costs. The actuary will base the valuation on the following data and assumptions:

- The earnings test should affect the behaviour as regards the effective retirement age. The data on retirement behaviour in general are, therefore, needed, not just from the social security scheme. Retirement rates under private schemes and for employees of the public sector generally represent useful data.
- Once the retirement pattern has been stated, the actuary must estimate the extent to which the amount of the average old-age pension will be reduced for those who will combine a pension and a working income. To measure the effect of such a modification, the actuary needs to obtain the data by age on the earnings from work. A survey on the economic activity of the retired population might provide some insight in this respect.

12.1.7 A more stringent definition of invalidity

It is quite frequent in social security schemes that, after a period of time, people become more aware of their right to an invalidity pension and the medical criteria used by the institution become more liberal. Consequently, the cost of the disability pension becomes more difficult to monitor. Measures are then taken to reinforce administrative controls or to change the legal definition of disability recognized by the scheme. Such a modification is not easy to evaluate because, most of the time, experience data are unavailable. In some cases, it is possible to use the data from other schemes or from private invalidity insurance programmes to estimate the impact of these new administrative procedures on the incidence of invalidity in the scheme under study.

As an example, in developing economies, the global rate of invalidity incidence can fluctuate between 1 per cent and 4.5 per cent of the insured population. The highest level indicates an environment where liberal criteria are being used by medical advisers and accepted by the scheme. These figures show that a complete reformulation of the invalidity evaluation process could have a significant impact on the cost of a scheme.

12.1.8 Survivors' benefits

Rationalizing a scheme may also apply to survivors' benefits. Here are some modifications that are commonly applied in practice:

- It may be decided to change the age criteria concerning eligibility for a pension, stating, for example, that the survivor's pension will be paid only to people aged 45 and over at the time of death of the insured person. The assumption on the age difference between spouses then becomes crucial for evaluating the incidence of this modification.
- The pension formula itself may be changed in order to target those people presumably more in need. A direct reduction in the replacement rate or the introduction of a pension composed of a flat amount plus a percentage of earnings (to target beneficiaries with low earnings) can usually be done by a simple change being made to the computer program.
- A limit may be imposed on the combined amount of old-age and survivors' pensions. In this case, it is necessary to obtain a distribution of old-age pensions for each level of survivors' pensions. This cannot be done solely from average pension amounts. In this type of modification, even if we have the actual distribution of pension amounts, complications can arise from the need to determine the distribution of earnings that will apply in the future, especially when it is projected that women will have higher relative earnings (compared with men) and higher labour force participation rates in the future.
- It is common for schemes gradually to remove discriminatory provisions. A frequent modification is the extension of survivors' pensions to widowers. This modification usually involves simple programming adjustments in the actuarial model in order to include male beneficiaries.
- Many schemes provide survivors' benefits to parents or to sisters/brothers when there is no principal beneficiary. These pensions are paid on the criteria that the parent or sibling is financially dependent on the insured. The analysis of past experience regarding these "second-degree" beneficiaries provides the actuary with indications as to the future costs of these benefits, their incidence and the possible need to amend these provisions according to the social and family evolution in the country.

12.2 MODIFICATIONS TO CONTRIBUTIONS

Possible changes to the financial system of a DB scheme can involve a pure PAYG system (financed by bipartite contributions or a payroll tax), a partial capitalization or scaled premium system, or, in rare instances, a full capitalization system. The degree of demographic and financial maturity of the scheme can influence the selection of the financial system. In very new schemes accumulating large reserves, it might be undesirable or unfeasible to recommend a full capitalization financial system. Conversely, in very mature schemes, pension expenditure might be rather close to its ultimate level. As a by-product of the valuation, the actuary should provide an insight into the economic or financial feasibility of a recommended financing mechanism, with regard also to the political sensitivity of the issue. This could involve an input in the fiscal implications of the financial system and the situation of public finance, the potential erosion of the real value of the reserves under significant inflationary conditions, and the assessment of the situation and/or potential of the financial market.

12.2.1 Modifications to the contribution rate

Gradual increases in the contribution rates are generally easy to include in the actuarial model. A modification to the financial system might require further important modifications. For example, modifying the financial system might require programming the mathematical formulae of the scaled premium system or creating a link between revenue, expenditure and reserve levels in order to apply the reserve ratio system. The guidelines set out in Chapter 5 may be of use to the actuary when adjusting the model.

Most national schemes provide for a uniform contribution rate for people of all ages and earnings levels. However, when the actuary is confronted with assessing variable contribution rates according to age or earnings, appropriate adjustments in the financing methodology must be introduced.

12.2.2 Extensions of the salary base

To measure the impact of an extension of the salary base, it is necessary to obtain the data on the total earnings of insured persons (not limited to the earnings ceiling) and also on the distribution of active insured persons by class of earnings.

Any recommendations on the part of the actuary concerning the extension of the salary base should be evaluated in conjunction with the provisions regarding maximum pensions and the redistribution effect that is sought. For example, in the early years of the operation of a pension scheme financed under the PAYG system, the contribution rate is usually very low compared with the true long-term cost of the scheme. A high (or no) ceiling generates high pensions for people with high earnings, although these people pay only a fraction of the real cost of the scheme. This, therefore, generates a regressive redistribution of income from people with low earnings to people with high earnings and from future generations of contributors to the present generation.

12.3 OTHER CONSIDERATIONS

Projections performed in the context of reform scenarios should be undertaken in a manner consistent with the status quo projections. Results under the reform package should be analysed using the same indicators as those used for the analysis under status quo, so as to provide a common basis for comparison.

Although the actuary provides projections in a manner consistent with the status quo projections and using the same indicators, under certain situations the reform extends coverage beyond the traditional scope of the existing scheme. Simulations are then required to illustrate the cost progression with an expanded population base and, as a limit, to provide pure PAYG cost projections under the generalized formula:

Formula 12.1

$$CR = r(t) x D$$

where CR is the contribution rate, $r(t)$ the replacement ratio and D the dependency rate of the labour force.

The same would apply to a partial funding financial system.

Should the national pension scheme operate under a fragmented structure with a scheme for civil servants segregated from the national scheme covering the private sector, sometimes with differing benefit provisions or financial systems, then actuarial projections in the context of a reform might require modifications being made to the actuarial assumptions. In particular, the density of contributions in the public sector is higher than in the private sector. The actuary may decide to carry out separate projections for each different group and then combine the different projections in a global result.

Concerning the revision of financing rules, the scheme's administrators often push for a rapid increase in the contribution rate in order to improve the financial situation of the scheme. On the other hand, the government may be in a difficult budgetary position and may want to delay a contribution rate increase. Contributors, that is, workers and employers, are often more confident in a scheme in which contribution rate increases are planned, but they generally prefer gradual increases. The actuary must give due consideration to the political feasibility of recommended changes to restore the financial equilibrium of a scheme by way of contribution rate increases or reductions in future benefit protection.

12.4 PRESENTING THE EFFECT OF MODIFICATIONS

One way of presenting the effect of modifications that have been analysed is to reproduce a table of yearly financial projections showing the revenue, expenditure and reserve levels of the scheme. However, this kind of presentation involves a multitude of figures that most non-actuarial users will find difficult

> **Box 12.2 The effect of a modification to the minimum pension (the Demoland case)**
>
> The modification that has been analysed is a gradual increase in the minimum pension from its present level of 50 per cent of the minimum wage to 100 per cent of the minimum wage over a period of five years. It should be observed that:
>
> - the minimum number of years of contributions necessary to be eligible for the old-age pension is 15;
> - the salary scale used for projections shows a fast progression of contributory earnings during the contributor's career.
>
> Consequently, the modification to the minimum pension does not significantly affect the amount of new old-age pensions awarded after the valuation date. It does, however, affect the amount of old-age pensions in payment on the valuation date (assuming here that pensions in payment would be adjusted to the new minimum pension) and the amount of invalidity pensions. The long-term effect of this modification is small because the average length of service of people reaching the age of eligibility for the old-age pension increases over time, with the resulting effect on the average pension of future new beneficiaries.
>
> The following table presents the effect of this modification on the GAP. It can be observed that the effect is more important in the short term, since it generates an increase in the pensions in payment, mostly during the next five years. The effect of the modification decreases over time, in relative terms, because of an increase in the average length of service of future pensioners and the higher average earnings on which the new pensions will be calculated.
>
> **Effect on the GAP of increasing the minimum pension**
>
> | Period (in years) | GAP (as a %) | |
> | --- | --- | --- |
> | | Status quo | Increase in the minimum pension |
> | 10 | 9.6 | 10.2 |
> | 20 | 12.5 | 13.1 |
> | 30 | 15.6 | 16.1 |
> | 40 | 18.2 | 18.6 |

to interpret. Therefore, the actuary may prefer to present a schedule of contribution rates for each scenario, an approach that is suitable when the modification to the scheme has, as a principal objective, the requirement to reduce the contribution rate burden for employers and workers. Another approach is to compute the GAP of the scheme under the various reform scenarios and to compare it with the GAP under status quo conditions. This has the advantage of replacing a stream of contribution rates by a single figure that facilitates communications with national counterparts (see box 12.2).

In a scheme functioning under the reserve ratio system, it may be appropriate to present the effect of modifications in terms of the year in which the reserve reaches a certain proportion of the annual expenditure of the scheme.

STRUCTURAL REFORM CONSIDERATIONS   13

The preceding chapter considered adjustments to ongoing schemes. In some countries, however, the changes being introduced can be more radical, altering the very nature of the scheme. Under such structural reforms, it is much more difficult to define a general approach that can be applied by actuaries in every single type of case. Each reform has its own characteristic, and actuaries must use their ingenuity to solve any newly emerging actuarial issues.

This chapter focuses on some recent examples of structural reform and illustrates the new kinds of actuarial problems that actuaries are now having to face.

13.1 CONVERTING A DB SCHEME INTO A DC SCHEME

An important change may consist of gradually replacing the DB scheme with a mandatory DC scheme. Such a structural reform took place in Chile beginning in 1981. Details on the salient characteristics of a DC scheme are provided in Technical Brief III at the end of this book.

Totally replacing a DB scheme requires a valuation to be undertaken of the accumulated liabilities under the scheme, taking into consideration pensions already in payment and the value of the accumulated rights of the current insured population. This type of calculation is rarely relevant to social insurance pension schemes unless a reform is envisaged to go from a DB to a DC pension scheme. Under such a reform, the government needs to know the magnitude of its financial obligations under the former DB pension scheme. The valuation of accrued liabilities shows the real cost of the promised benefits that will have to be borne by present and future contributors, or by taxpayers, if the government guarantees the payment of these pensions.

Structural reform considerations

> **Box 13.1 The Chilean pension reform**[1]
>
> Under the Chilean reform, the existing public PAYG DB pension scheme was replaced by a mandatory retirement savings scheme of the DC type.
>
> - The system was launched in May 1981.
> - It is a DC scheme (10 per cent of wage, up to a certain cap) with individual capitalization accounts, which is mandatory for employees and optional for the self-employed.
> - It includes insurance against death and disability through private insurance companies.
> - The system is administered by private pension fund management companies (AFPs).
> - AFP duties: to collect mandatory and voluntary contributions; credit them to the corresponding individual capitalization accounts; invest those resources in financial instruments; obtain death and disability insurance coverage; provide fund members with benefits.
> - A number of investment rules *apply* to AFPs concerning diversification, valuation, transaction and disclosure.
> - Types of pension benefits at retirement: a pension in the form of a programmed withdrawal from the capitalization account (managed by an AFP); an annuity contracted from an insurance company; or a combination of the two.
> - Fund members can choose to change their AFP, to define the amount of contribution above the minimum and to decide on the timing of retirement once certain minimum conditions have been fulfilled.
>
> All new workers must participate in the new DC scheme. There was a transition period during which participants of the old system over a certain age could choose to continue participating in the former DB scheme. Those contributors who decided or were forced to transfer to the new DC scheme were issued a recognition bond representing the value of their rights in the old system. The value of that bond is, from then on, considered an asset, earning interest until retirement, and it will be converted into a pension at retirement like the rest of the individual's account balance. In addition, the government guarantees a minimum pension for those contributors who have been participating for at least 20 years.

One task of the actuary when converting a DB into a DC scheme is to estimate the value of this liability and to recommend a way of financing it. However, such a reform usually provides that people insured under the former scheme may continue participating in the old system, if they so wish.

In estimating the future revenue and expenditure of the former DB scheme, the actuary needs to modify some of the demographic and financial bases. For example:

- The old scheme will usually not accept new entrants, so it will become a closed-group valuation, with a gradual decrease in the insured population, and eventually a closed group of pensioners.
- Earnings used to calculate pensions may be frozen at their value at the time of the scheme's conversion, thus reducing (in real terms) the amount of new emerging pensions.
- The new scheme may guarantee a minimum pension that will have to be taken into account in the valuation of the old scheme.

Another crucial task is to assess the level of contributions required under the new scheme in order to achieve a targeted replacement rate or, conversely, to assess the ultimate replacement rate that will be obtained, given a specific level of contributions into the individual account.

13.1.1 Valuation of a scheme's liability at conversion

Components of the actuarial liability

The concept of actuarial liability at conversion should not be confused with the notion of the implicit debt of an ongoing scheme. Box 13.2 presents the implicit debt concept as described by the World Bank.

Components of the actuarial liability at conversion represent commitments of the scheme on the conversion date, for:

- current pensioners; and
- the accrued rights of current contributors.

Box 13.2   Two World Bank concepts: the implicit pension debt and the pension debt overhang

The *implicit pension debt concept* was formulated by World Bank specialists in the 1990s.[2] "The concept of the implicit pension debt recognizes that workers and pensioners have claims on current and future governments that are not unlike those of government bondholders." Hence, a comparison is made between a country's external debt and its implicit pension debt.

Following this idea, the concept of the *pension debt overhang* makes an analogy between the servicing of external debt and the cost rate of a pension scheme calculated as the ratio of the present value of pension expenditure to the portion of the wage bill covered by the pension system. The cost rate is the ratio of pension expenditure to the portion of the wage bill covered by the pension system. A cost rate above the statutory contribution rate would indicate that pension expenses could not be met by contributions alone and, therefore, would require transfers from general revenue, a higher contribution rate, or a lower pension benefit.[3]

Structural reform considerations

Another component may arise owing to the guarantee of a minimum pension, which is often granted when the accumulated capital at retirement under the new scheme is insufficient to purchase a minimum annuity. This minimum guarantee may also be offered through the introduction of a formal non-contributory assistance scheme.

The actuarial valuation of the actuarial liability at conversion is based on the standard methodology applied to the assessment of the unfunded liability on a plan termination or curtailment basis, as described later in this section.

Apportionment of credits

The valuation of the actuarial liability at conversion from a DB to a DC scheme requires the actuary to attribute benefits to periods of service under a plan's benefit formula. If the pension formula is a static factor per year (say, 1.5 per cent per annum), attribution is directly related to periods of service. On the other hand, under a skewed pension formula placing greater weight on the earlier years of contributions than on later years, the actuary should assess the actuarial liability by reconverting the total expected benefit at retirement into a unit average credit per year. Otherwise, the liability at conversion might be overstated.

Specific assumptions

The valuation should quantify the actuarial liabilities of a social security scheme that is converted from a DB into a DC system, assessing separately the present value of:

- pensions in the course of payment;

Box 13.3 An example of apportionment of credits

A social security scheme provides a pension formula of 40 per cent for the first ten years of contributions (that is, 4 per cent per year) and 1 per cent per year after ten years, with a 60 per cent maximum. For an employee with ten years' service, the attribution for past services should be based on the expected relative pension at retirement, divided by the ratio of the number of years of present service to the total number of years at retirement. If the expected pension service at retirement is 60 per cent with 40 years' service (1.5 per cent per year), then with ten years the attribution factor should be 15 per cent rather than 40 per cent; with 20 years it should be 30 per cent rather than 50 per cent, and so on.

- vested DB pensions earned to date by the active insured but payable at retirement; and
- the non-vested portion on behalf of active members to be transferred to the new DC scheme.

Since future compensation levels cease to be an obligation of the third component, their effect should be valued as an accumulated benefit obligation (ABO), based on current compensation levels. If vested active members maintain a right to an earnings-related pension at retirement, the liabilities at conversion should be valued on a going-concern or projected-benefit basis (PBO), based on pensionable compensation at retirement, assuming the plan's pension formula is based on average final earnings.

If the vested active staff eligible for a DB contingent pension are also entitled to invalidity or death benefits while in service, this additional liability should also be computed. However, this is not necessary in the case of non-vested employees being transferred to a DC scheme contracting these benefits with an insurance company.

Some considerations regarding the valuation methods and assumptions used in such a context are listed below.

Assets	The plan's assets should be measured at their fair value. Fair value should be measured, when possible, by the market price, if an active market exists for the investments. Otherwise, cash-flow valuation methods might be helpful, provided the discount factor is commensurate with the risk involved. Fixed assets should be measured at cost, less accumulated depreciation.
Discount rate	The discount rate reflects the time value of money but not the actuarial or investment risk. The rate used to discount annuities or pensions, actual or deferred, should be determined by referring to market yields at the conversion date. The discount rate should be consistent or mutually compatible with the rates used for the actuarial projections.
Incidence of pension payments contracted outside the scheme	If, at conversion, pensions in payments or deferred pensions are contracted with insurance carriers, the actuary should adjust the valuation basis by referring to the annuity contract (mortality discount factor, including the incidence of administrative expenditure, etc.).
Unfunded liability	The unfunded liability would then be equivalent to the difference between the actuarial obligations and the fair value of assets. This provides a quantitative

approach on behalf of the first two components of the scheme's total liabilities: pensioners and earned benefits of active insured persons. The valuation of the potential liabilities arising from the state guarantee of a minimum pension should be derived indirectly, as a by-product of the actuarial projection, as well as the liability arising from non-contributory or assistance pensions.

Ancillary benefits

Under a DB scheme, ancillary benefits, such as invalidity and survivors' benefits, on the death of an active insured person, are usually costed as an integral element of the PAYG or scaled premium system of financing. The introduction of a DC substitutive or complementary scheme implies that the PAYG system will be replaced with a system of terminal reserve or with an assessment of constituent capital. Hence, the actuary should determine whether any liability should be computed for these risks. If the DC scheme contemplates contracting out those risks, which would be the most common arrangement, a premium surcharge should be computed by the actuary to underwrite emerging invalidity, permanent disability and death among active insured persons, after assessing the local insurance market, the cost of annuities for such contingencies and the provisions regarding benefits. The supplementary premium is expected to be ceded to the insurance carrier who accepts and can also reinsure the risks.

Determination of the unfunded liability

Once assumptions have been set in the specific context of the reform, the actuarial liability at conversion can be calculated as follows:

- The present value of pensions in payment (including survivors' pensions)
  plus
- the present value of projected or accumulated vested benefits on behalf of active participants (PBO or ABO)
  plus
- the present value of accumulated benefits of non-vested participants (ABO)
  plus
- the present value of ancillary benefits of active vested participants (if applicable)
  plus
- the present value of derivative costs due to a minimum pension guarantee or a newly introduced assistance pension
  minus
- the fair value of assets.

13.1.2 Specific considerations in the context of a reform

The social security scheme may be part of a global pension package offered to the population that may also include occupational pension schemes and DC instruments. If this is the case, the actuary should consider:

- the level of income replacement offered by the social security DB pension scheme as part of the global income replacement offered by the total system; and
- the impact of a modification to the DB scheme contribution rate on the overall cost to employers, workers and the government.

The effectiveness of a conversion from a DB to a DC scheme should also be assessed in the actuarial projections in terms of comparative replacement rates. In this context, the actuary should evaluate the past performance of the financial sector and, in particular, past experience regarding real rates of return. Regardless of the financing bases set forth by other professionals involved in the technical design or policy-making process, the actuary needs to show good judgement in formulating actuarial forecasts. In particular, under a DC model, alternative replacement ratios under a variant of density and real rates of return are essential for assessing the potential reform's effectiveness. These alternative projections are required for a proper appraisal of the pension model adapted to the particular situation of a country.

Furthermore, the actuary should point out that the actuarial projection scenarios might be altered by exogenous factors that are not an integral element of the projections, in particular, the growth rates of the economy. Economic stagnation could seriously reduce employment rates and undermine the individual savings principle underlying the DC scheme. Hence, the actuary can introduce, in the long-term quantitative assessment of the efficiency of a DC model vis-a-vis a DB scheme or two-tier model, additional parameters dealing with growth, productivity, sectoral employment patterns and other economic elements.

Administrative expenditure, which is rather high in some DC schemes, should take into consideration the system of pension administration to be set up (one entity, such as in Singapore, two entities, as in Bolivia, or an open market of AFPs, as in Chile).

13.2 THE SWEDISH PENSION REFORM[4]

13.2.1 Description of the new scheme

On 1 January 1999, a new pension system was introduced in Sweden. The first year in which new pensions will be partly calculated under the new scheme will be 2001, and it will not be before 2015 that new pensions (for a person born in

Structural reform considerations

1954 and drawing a pension at the age of 61) will be calculated entirely under the new provisions.

The new system is compulsory, contains an earnings-related element and offers, in addition, a minimum pension to those with only a low earnings-related pension.

The earnings-related scheme consists of two parts: a PAYG scheme and a fully funded scheme. The total contribution rate to the scheme is 18.5 per cent, from which 2.5 per cent goes to the fully funded part and 16.0 per cent to the PAYG scheme.

The main features of the new PAYG scheme are as follows:

- The benefit formula is based on all the earnings over an individual's career. Hence, there is a close link between benefits and contributions on an individual basis. The contribution rate is meant to remain unchanged indefinitely and, therefore, all contributions paid throughout a career will give rise to the same amount of pension credits. Pension rights are indexed according to average wages and accumulated during the entire course of a career.
- Certain periods with social security benefits or without earnings give rise to pension rights, financed partly by the state and partly by the individual.
- The retirement age is flexible from the age of 61.
- The pension of the first year is obtained by dividing the accumulated pension rights by an annuity factor. Benefits are made dependent on life expectancy, the result being that a benefit drawn at a certain age by an individual belonging to one cohort will be lower than for preceding cohorts if life expectancy has increased.
- Indexation rules are linked to wage growth in order to make pensions reflect the development of the contribution base. Pension benefits are indexed with the CPI, plus the growth in the average wage minus 1.6 per cent.
- A reserve fund functions as a buffer for fluctuations in the age distribution of the population.
- The whole system is designed to be financially in permanent balance in order to make it possible to have the same contribution rate indefinitely. Hence, the balancing item of the system is not the contribution rate (as is usual in PAYG systems) but the amount of the retirement pension.

13.2.2 The intervention of the actuary

The annuity factor for the PAYG scheme

A first domain in which the actuary may be involved in the application of such a reform is in calculating the annuity factor. To determine the initial pension of an individual reaching retirement age, the accumulated pension rights at retirement are divided by an annuity factor. Three elements are considered in determining the annuity factor:

- A "norm" real rate of return. The norm is 1.6 per cent and represents the assumed increase in average real wages. It should be remembered that pensions, in addition to being indexed with the CPI, also receive an adjustment in relation to growth in the average wage minus 1.6 per cent.
- Life expectancy at the age of 65 for a birth-year cohort.
- Age at retirement.

Determining the annuity factor clearly falls under the field of expertise of the actuary. In particular, it requires analysing mortality trends and following up economic parameters such as inflation and wage growth.

Transitional pensions

The reform is due to be introduced gradually. Pension promises under the former system are essentially to be fulfilled. People born before 1954 will be entitled to at least the pension they have earned, up to and including 1994, under the old rules. This potential liability related to the former scheme has to be estimated and the cost of its amortization has to be taken into account in the financing of the global pension system.

Minimum guaranteed pension

The cost of the guaranteed minimum pension is to be financed by the state budget. The government needs a projection of the expenditure related to this minimum pension in order to plan its financing. Actuarial calculations are needed to project the distribution of future earnings-related pension entitlements in order to assess the number of individuals that will be eligible for the supplement and also to estimate the gap between the earnings-related element earned by those individuals and the minimum guaranteed pension.

Cost of special credits

There will be pension rights in the earnings-related scheme not attributable to any earnings (child birth, periods of study) or to earnings for which contributions have not been paid (sickness, invalidity, unemployment). The state will finance separately all or part of the contributions needed to finance pension rights arising from these events. A valuation of the cost of these benefits needs to be carried out regularly.

Financial monitoring of the PAYG scheme

The key objective for establishing the annuity factor and the indexation rules of the PAYG scheme is that pension payments should be linked to the system's ability to meet its obligations at a stable contribution rate. The sustainability

Structural reform considerations

of the scheme will ultimately depend on how it supports the elderly and how big a share of GDP is spent on it. The way in which pension rights are established and pensions are calculated and indexed is intended to keep the development of public pension costs in line with economic growth, that is, the pension share at GDP should, on average, remain approximately constant in the long run. The problem with this type of general objective is that it is not possible to measure the effects of the scheme on the living standards of retired people under different demographic developments and economic growth scenarios, on the division of GDP between labour costs and gross profits, on the development of non-wage labour costs, and on inflation rates.

The financial base for minimum pensions is general revenue. The financial burden on the state budget will depend on how average real wages develop. The financial base for the earnings-related scheme are contributions based on the sum of wages and certain other earnings. How this financial base is linked to the overall economy depends on the division of GDP between different types of income.

The strain on the finances of the PAYG earnings-related scheme comes primarily from weaknesses existing in the balancing system, that is, in the combination of calculation rules, indexation mechanisms and size of reserves. Actuaries and economists are, therefore, invaluable for stimulating future pension disbursements and trends in wages in order to measure the impact of the new system on the income of the retired and on the state budget.

13.3 CONVERTING A PROVIDENT FUND INTO A DB SCHEME[5]

The change from a provident fund to a pension scheme has been a topic at a number of ISSA meetings, so in this book only the financial and actuarial aspects of such a conversion are considered. The difficult issue of whether or not to make this change, which involves questions of a socio-political-economic, and even a psychological, nature, has no place in this volume. The decision to make the conversion should be made with the benefit of financial and actuarial advice, but in the end it is a policy decision and not a technical matter. Therefore, it is assumed in this volume that the decision to move from a provident fund to a social insurance pension scheme has been taken, and the question to be answered is how to accomplish this satisfactorily for the existing provident fund members.

13.3.1 General considerations

Replacing a provident fund with a social insurance pension scheme inevitably focuses the members', and consequently the administrators', attention on what is going to happen to their balances in the fund: whether they will be "better off" (that is, get their balances back in periodic payments). Much attention is paid to the transitional measures, and unless a long-range perspective is applied, the design of the new pension scheme can easily be dictated by the need to convince the provident fund members that they should support the social insurance pension scheme. This approach, while understandable, fails to take into account the fact that current provident fund members will be contributors and beneficiaries of the pension scheme for around two generations, while the social insurance scheme will last indefinitely. A generous pension scheme that may appeal to provident fund members may turn into a future burden. Since it is extremely difficult to make substantial alterations to benefits in a social security scheme once they have been established, the pension scheme should be designed to meet the needs of current and future participants, taking into account socio-economic conditions and the capacity of the national economy to support the scheme. The conversion provisions are transitional measures, and they are a subsidiary consideration.

Suitable conversion provisions depend, to some extent, on the age of the provident fund. If a provident fund has been operating for only a few years, relatively straightforward conversion provisions may be possible. However, for a fund that has been operating for a considerably longer period, the conversion provisions required could be extremely complicated.

In general, provident funds have higher contribution rates than funded social insurance pension schemes, which means that if the provident fund contribution rate is retained for the pension scheme, under the usual systems of financing social insurance pension schemes, relatively high pensions can be provided. Since these systems of financing require increases in the contribution rate from time to time, this means that from an already high contribution rate, even higher rates will be required in the future. (This is an example of designing the pension scheme with overdue regard to the existing provident fund.) Rather, a more modest and sustainable level of pensions, along with other social insurance benefits (such as sickness and maternity cash benefits) and perhaps even a small lump-sum payment could be introduced. In fact, countries with provident funds generally do not have other contributory social insurance benefits, simply because, in order to produce reasonable lump-sum benefits at retirement, a provident fund requires such a high contribution rate that there is no possibility of obtaining contributions for other benefits.

13.3.2 Differences between provident funds and pension schemes

The usual benefits of provident funds and pension schemes are payable in the event of old-age (retirement) or invalidity and to survivors of the contributor.

Structural reform considerations

Certain differences between the two types of scheme can affect possible arrangements for the move from a provident fund to a pension scheme. The more important features, which have financial and actuarial implications for the changeover, are summarized in the following paragraphs.

Individual savings/pooling of risks

Provident funds are individual savings schemes, and are similar to savings accounts at a bank. Social insurance pension schemes involve a pooling of risk, and are founded on the basis of collective solidarity. In a provident fund, a member has, at any time, a specific well-defined balance in his or her favour. In a social insurance pension scheme, the participant has an acquired right to a benefit payable in the future according to a specified formula; the participant's equity in the fund at any time is not known. The individual savings approach of a provident fund means there is no subsidy from one member to another or from one generation to another.

Systems of finance

The systems of financing provident funds and social insurance pension schemes are entirely different. Provident funds can be considered to be fully funded on an individual basis, while social insurance pension schemes are partially funded or, in many industrialized countries, financed on a PAYG basis. The partial funding of the latter means that, in the future, contribution rates are expected to rise and that there will be a subsidy from successive generations. Under a partial funding financial system, the contribution rate can be set so that reserve funds are accumulated at a rate commensurate with the expectation of investing them productively.

Lump-sum benefit/periodic payments

The benefit in a provident fund is a lump-sum equal to the balance in favour of the member. This balance is the amount of a member's contributions and of the employer's contributions on the employee's behalf, accumulated with interest. In a pension scheme, the total of the periodic payments in respect of an individual participant depends on how long the participant and the surviving beneficiaries live after pension payments have commenced. Hence, the total payments do not bear any direct relationship to the accumulated contributions made in respect of an individual participant.

A typical earnings-related social insurance pension scheme has the following retirement pension formula:

$$\text{Annual pension} = \text{Final average earnings} \times \text{Years of contributory service} \times \text{Percentage}$$

where:

- *Final average earnings* is the average annual earnings of the participant near the time the retirement pension becomes payable;
- *Years of contributory service* is the number of years during which the participant has contributed or has received contribution credits;
- *Percentage* is the annual accrual rate for the retirement pension.

To illustrate, if the percentage is 1.5 per cent and the years of contributory service 40, the retirement pension would be 60 per cent of a participant's final average earnings. Pensions in the event of invalidity or death are usually based on the retirement pension formula with additional provisions. Other retirement pension formulae can be devised, such as a flat-rate pension, which, with an earnings-related supplement, is quite common.

Government guarantee or subsidies

Both provident funds and social insurance pension schemes invest in securities guaranteed by the government. Otherwise, a provident fund requires no subsidy or guarantee from the government. Pension schemes do not require a subsidy, but usually there is a guarantee from the government that promised benefits will be paid, which reassures participants. In practice, however, it is not required, since financing problems in a pension scheme are not usually unexpected. They can usually be anticipated, and corrective measures, such as increasing the contribution rate and/or changing benefit levels, can be taken before the situation deteriorates to the extent that the government is called upon to honour its guarantee.

Investment risk

In a provident fund, the investment risk (that is, the possibility that the provident fund rate of interest paid on members' balances will be lower than the rate of inflation) is borne entirely by individual members. In a social insurance pension scheme, the investment risk (that is, the possibility that the net rate of investment income on the assets of the scheme will be lower than the rate of inflation) is borne by the scheme, that is, it is shared collectively by the participants. The implication of this is that if a benefit becomes payable during a period when there have been several years of negative real rates of return (that is, years when the rate of inflation has exceeded the rate of interest), new pension scheme benefits will continue to be awarded in accordance with the formula. However, provident fund lump-sum payments will reflect the loss in real value of members' balances.

After a provident fund benefit has been paid or pension payments have commenced, the same assumption of the investment risk applies. Whether the beneficiary of a provident fund lump sum applies his lump sum so as to retain its real value depends entirely on the beneficiary. Periodic pension payments are generally adjusted to take into account inflation; hence, the social insurance pension scheme bears this risk.

Anticipation of benefits/retirement age

In a provident fund, it is of little importance when a member receives his or her benefit from the point of view of the solvency of the fund. If the member takes an advance or a loan that is not repaid, the balance in the member's own account is reduced. In a social insurance pension scheme, loans to participants are made from the collective fund, and must be repaid, otherwise the solvency of the fund can be threatened. Similarly, retirement age has no effect on the solvency of a provident fund. It is, however, a crucial issue in a pension scheme. Provident funds often have retirement ages of 55 or lower. In many countries with these funds, this is too low a retirement age for a viable and supportable pension scheme, taking into account the life expectancy of the population that would be covered by the scheme.

Records

The requirements of provident funds and pension schemes to record the data differ. In a provident fund, the basic requirement is that the balance in a member's account be known. Probably because of ancillary benefits, such as an insurance death benefit, which has a contribution requirement, a member's contributions history over the past year will be available. Beyond then, it is unlikely that a provident fund will be able to provide or reconstruct a member's contributions history. The fund simply does not need this information for its operations. A pension scheme, on the other hand, normally requires information on the total number of monthly contributions, not the amount. Information on actual earnings is needed only for the period used to calculate final average earnings. This period is usually no longer than five years, hence a pension scheme usually keeps records of actual contributory earnings for the most recent period corresponding to the earnings averaging period for calculating pensions.

13.3.3 Alternatives to moving from a provident fund to a pension scheme

Alternative A

Paying out the provident fund balances

All members are paid their provident fund balances at the time the pension scheme commences its operations. This would be inflationary and it would require the liquidation of investments, which cannot be realized in practice. So, this is not a viable alternative.

Alternative B

Freezing provident fund balances

Contributions to the provident fund cease and are directed to the pension scheme. Provident fund balances at the time of the changeover continue to receive interest and are paid out whenever they become payable under the provident fund regulations. This alternative would avoid the sudden liquidation of investments required under alternative A.

The major drawback of alternative B (as well as A) is that the pension scheme would have to start again from the very beginning, with participants having no credit for prior service. Under typical pension formulae and qualification requirements, it would take a considerable number of years before pensions would become payable, and longer yet before the pensions became a significant proportion of final average earnings. When a new pension scheme is set up, special transitional provisions are usually made so as to reduce the period until which the scheme is providing pensions and providing them at adequate levels. These transitional arrangements, which imply a subsidy from later contributors, would be inappropriate, since the participants who would be subsidized already have frozen provident fund balances.

Alternative C

Purchase of annuities with provident fund balances

Instead of paying a lump sum from the provident fund, the lump sum is converted into periodic annuity payments. This is an option in some provident funds. The amount of periodic payments depends on the amount of the lump sum. Hence, it might bear little relationship to a member's final average earnings. Anticipation of the lump-sum payment through advances or loans that have not been repaid is reflected in a reduced amount of periodic payments. It would be possible to calculate the periodic payments so they could be increased to take into account anticipated future increases in the cost of living. However, this would significantly reduce the initial periodic payments. The periodic payments would normally be calculated using actuarial annuity factors, and a separate fund would be set up into which the lump sums would be paid and from which annuity payments would be made. This is an insurance system, and the insurance and mortality risks associated with the annuities would be assumed by the fund.

A modification of this system is calculating annuities using factors more favourable than actuarial annuity factors, which can encourage members to opt for periodic payments. Presumably, the larger their balances and the more favourable the annuity factors, the more members would exercise this option. The real cost of the periodic payments that are awarded is the actuarial cost, and the difference between this and the lump-sums, which are applied at a favourable rate to calculate the annuity, must ultimately be met by the provident fund from a separate fund set up to meet the difference or from other sources.

Alternative D

Converting provident fund balances into pension credits

The problems and drawbacks associated with the above alternatives for moving from a provident fund to a pension scheme lead to the conclusion that it would be more desirable to devise a system whereby a social insurance pension scheme takes into account:

- prior contributions (that is, service) in the provident fund, so that the pension scheme can be fully operational from its inception and adequate pensions are payable;
- the concern of provident fund members over their individual accounts, particularly those members who are near retirement age and who have made plans for using their lump sums;
- the records that are likely to be available in the provident fund, which can be used to approximate periods of prior service for the pension scheme; and
- the need to adopt a simple system for conversion, so that members of the provident fund understand the system (especially if there are options) and the social security institution is able to cope with the administration of the conversion system.

The following method of converting a member's provident fund balance into periods of service in the pension scheme is based on the assumption that the annual rate of increase of wages is approximately equal to the rate of interest credited to provident fund balances. The approximate conversion calculation is the following:

Formula 13.1

$$\text{Years of service} = \frac{\text{Provident fund balance}}{\text{Final average earnings} \times \text{Provident fund contribution rate}}$$

This calculation cannot be applied directly to any provident fund being converted into a social insurance pension scheme; it needs to be modified to take into account the conditions applicable to a particular scheme. Whether the calculation gives reasonable estimates of members' years of contributory service depends on the validity of the assumption that rates of wage increases are approximately equal to rates of interest on the provident fund balances. This must be tested over periods of years in a particular country. The method provides a simple means of determining years of service to be credited to the pension scheme, taking into account the data that a provident fund should have available. It need not be applied until a benefit under the pension scheme becomes payable, so final average earnings data should also be available.

Members of a provident fund being converted into a pension scheme in this manner can be given the option of converting all or part of their provident fund balances into pensions at the time they (or their survivors) qualify for pensions. In order to qualify for a pension, it may be necessary for a portion of the provident fund balance to be converted into years of service in the pension scheme. A member with a significant balance would be able to decide the portion of his or her balance that is to be converted, and the remainder would be paid to the member in a lump sum. With this conversion procedure, the pension scheme administration would need to advise potential pensioners on their options. The procedure is, in fact, a "mixed system", providing both a pension and possibly a lump sum at the discretion of the beneficiary.

The social security institution would have to maintain separate accounts for the pension fund and the frozen provident fund balances until a member decides how his or her balance is to be applied. Once a provident fund balance has been converted, the amount converted becomes part of the pension fund reserve. Eventually, the provident fund accounts will all have been converted or paid out.

13.3.4 Countries that have changed from provident funds to pension schemes

Provident funds in Dominica, Grenada, Iraq, Saint Lucia, Saint Kitts and Nevis, Saint Vincent and the Grenadines, and the Seychelles have all been converted into pension schemes. In Iraq, the periods of provident fund contributions were taken fully into account by the pension scheme. In Dominica and Grenada, the accumulated individual balances were converted into periods of contributions to the pension scheme according to a formula, and in Saint Kitts and Nevis, and Saint Vincent and the Grenadines, the provident fund balances were frozen.

An ISSA report[6] has described two of these provident funds that were replaced with pension schemes. The Saint Lucia provident fund, which started operations in October 1970, was converted into a pension scheme in April 1979. At the time of the changeover, the fund had 26,000 active members. The Saint Lucia pension scheme has earnings-related benefits. Provident fund members had all their contributions transferred to the pension fund, and received credit towards pension benefits for their actual periods of contribution to the provident fund.

In the Seychelles, the provident fund commenced operations in June 1971 and a universal pension scheme came into effect in March 1979. The Seychelles pension scheme has a flat-rate retirement pension payable from the age of 65,

Structural reform considerations

subject only to residence and retirement conditions. In January 1979, provident fund balances were frozen. They continue to receive interest, however, and are paid to members when the latter become entitled to a lump sum under the rules of the provident fund.

Notes

[1] See J. Ariztia: *AFP: A three-letter revolution* (Santiago, Corporación de Investigación, Estudio y Desarrollo de la Seguridad Social, 1998).

[2] See C. Kane and R. Palacios: "The implicit pension debt", in: *Finance and Development* (The World Bank, Washington, DC, June, 1996), p. 37.

[3] Contribution rates under a pension scheme operating under the PAYG system are expected to increase periodically. Hence, the assessment of the implicit debt based on the current contribution rate results in an overstatement of the implicit debt. The calculation of the implicit debt should be carried out assuming periodic increases in contributions, as planned under the retained financial system. Anticipating a partial compensation of future net liabilities by future increased contributions provides a more accurate picture of the financial needs and degree of solvency of the scheme.

[4] See K.G. Scherman: "The Swedish pension reform", in: *Issues in social protection*, Discussion Paper (ILO, Geneva, 1999).

[5] Taken from W.R. McGillivray: "Actuarial aspects of converting provident funds into social insurance schemes", in: *Reports and summaries of discussions of the twelfth meeting of the Committee on Provident Funds* (Geneva, ISSA, 1992).

[6] K. Thompson: "Experiences gained in the conversion of provident funds into pension schemes", in: *Reports and summaries of discussions of the fourth meeting of the Committee on Provident Funds* (Geneva, ISSA, 1980).

PART III

THE VALUATION OF EMPLOYMENT INJURY BENEFITS

FINANCIAL AND RATING SYSTEMS 14

The financing and rating systems for employment injury and occupational diseases (EIOD) schemes reflect each jurisdiction's historical, institutional, cultural and financial circumstances. In this particular area of social security, it seems that the same questions relating to the cost-effectiveness of financing models can be answered in many different ways. Indeed, there are a large number of financial systems, from the PAYG to the full-funding systems and a wide range of set-ups in-between the two. Rating programmes aimed at pricing employers more or less according to their risks are also highly diversified. The spectrum of possibilities goes from the purely collective approach (one single rate for all employers) to the purely individual liability model under which some employers (large enterprises) may be charged the full cost of their workers' injuries.

Obviously, the correlation between the administrative capacity of the institution managing the scheme and the sophistication of the financial arrangements is significant. However, the social security institutions with limited capacities at some point are often in a good position to plan the refinements that become possible through technological improvements. They can then progressively develop the conditions allowing them to support more information-demanding financial systems. In all countries, the growth of the economy and the shift of emphasis from compensation to prevention may create demand from the stakeholders for the system to respond better financially to employers' injury experience.

Legislation in occupational health and safety was, for many countries, the beginning of government intervention in social insurance matters. Legislation regarding compensation of employment injury and insurance coverage for workers has been in force in all industrialized countries for many decades now. This does not necessarily mean that the insurance element of a scheme is administered by a public institution. In some jurisdictions, the role of the private sector in insurance coverage is highly important, as it is in the United States. In this type of environment, private insurance companies have to comply with laws and regulations that dictate their financing arrangements and actuarial practices. Some actuarial practices, which are justifiable and generally accepted in the social security environment, may not be compatible with the private sector, where short-term solvency concerns are of prime importance. This book is not intended to cover specific actuarial practices or standards applying to the private sector. Nevertheless, given that public bodies may adopt financial mechanisms similar to those of the private sector, some practices generally considered more typical of the private sector are covered here.

The first section of this chapter deals with financial systems and the second describes the key elements of rating systems. The latter are one aspect of financial systems and deal with the issue of spreading the cost among the stakeholders identified to pay for the social security plan. Financial systems are concerned with the questions: "Who pays?" and "How much has to be paid in a specific time period?" Or, in accounting terms, "What cost accrual technique is used?"

14.1 FINANCIAL SYSTEMS

14.1.1 Sources of funds

Most social employment injury schemes result from an explicit or implicit historical trade-off between employers and workers. Workers are compensated for damages resulting from employment injuries without having the burden of demonstrating the negligence of employers, and the employers' liabilities are limited to the premium they pay to the insurance scheme. Employers are protected from excessive damages that can result from tort systems. In some countries, however, employees can have access to the tort system for compensation, but this is limited to specific circumstances. Where this possibility exists, the public system generally provides for reduced compensation, taking into account the amount of the damages paid. In such a case, the employers' liability insurance is provided through private carriers (so its actuarial aspects are not considered here).

Determining the source of funds for the social security scheme is not an actuarial decision as such. Political, social, economic and institutional considerations are put together to determine the proper source of funds. The design of the plan may also have to be considered, since the plans that are strongly integrated with other parts of the social security scheme may not give much room for specific rules of financing the employment injury schemes. Potential sources of funds are employers, workers and the government.

The cost of the protection offered to workers is considered part of the cost of producing goods and services. This economic rationale would suggest including this cost in their commodity price, which is why 100 per cent financing by employers is fairly common. Different circumstances may lead to another reasoning and may suggest sharing the financing between employers and workers, or even general government revenues.

When part of the cost of the system is supported by workers or the government, this may have to be justified on cost considerations, and the actuary does have to play a role in quantifying the elements that need to be considered. For example, if some form of out-of-work protection is granted, then workers may contribute to this part of the system, and the actuary has to quantify the costs associated with this aspect. The actuary will then need to ensure that the database and the actuarial methods and assumptions are adequate enough to perform the relevant actuarial analysis.

14.1.2 Basic concepts

Basic concepts and definitions regarding the financing of other social security domains are valuable references in discussing the financing of EIOD schemes. It is worth recalling a few definitions already discussed in some of the preceding chapters.

The *financial system* is a systematic way of raising resources in order to meet the projected expenditures of a scheme. It will determine the contribution rate and the level of assets that will accumulate under the scheme.

The *financial equilibrium* states that the present value of future income (plus any existing reserves) equals the present value of future expenditures of the scheme. The financial system determines the pace at which contributions will be collected, so that the equilibrium is preserved.

The following characteristics of EIOD schemes should be considered when selecting the financing arrangements:

1. The annual benefit payments of a typical mature employment injury scheme are generally a small percentage of the covered earnings[1] (between 1 per cent and 2 per cent).
2. Compensation provisions of EIOD schemes are usually a blend of short-term and long-term benefits.
3. The intergenerational equity concept applies to employers. The life span of an enterprise varies significantly by economic sector and is usually much lower than that of human beings.

The maturing of the expenditure pattern depends on the particular mix of benefits. Typically, many injuries will incur a small amount of losses, while a small percentage of injuries will be very severe and costly. Costly benefits do not necessarily mean long-term benefits. For example, lump-sum benefits paid to survivors or the permanently disabled are costly but they are paid a few years after the accident has occurred. However, this is not typical of the majority of schemes (nor is it consistent with ILO Conventions recommending pensions rather than lump-sum payments).

Actuarial practice in social security

Figure 14.1 Benefit payments of an injury year[4] (no indexing of benefit payments)

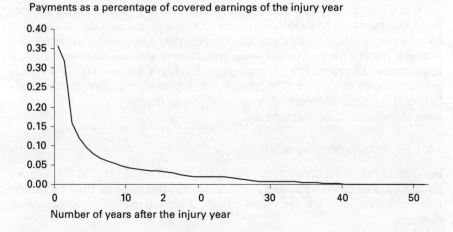

Figure 14.1 shows the typical expenditure pattern for a cohort of accidents occurring in a year and of diseases reported in the same year, expressed in terms of the covered earnings in the year of the accident.[2] No inflation is

Figure 14.2 Benefit payments related to all injury years (as a percentage of covered earnings in the current year) (system starts at year 0)

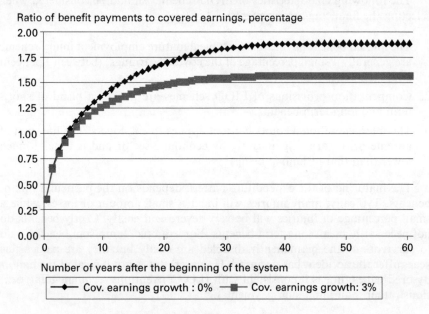

Financial and rating systems

> **Box 14.1 Example of a constant EIOD record**
>
> An EIOD experience is held constant when the number of new injuries each year varies according to the workforce variation, and the average cost per claim varies according to variations in the average assessable salary. The cost of an injury is defined as the present value of all payments made for the injury. The table below is an example of an EIOD-considered constant. The annual increases in demographic and economic variables are set at 1 per cent and 2 per cent respectively. The frequency of injuries is set at 4 per cent of the covered population and the severity at 50 per cent of the average salary.
>
> | Element | Time | | | |
> |---|---|---|---|---|
> | | Year 0 | Year 5 | Year 10 | Year 20 |
> | Covered workers | 1 000 000 | 1 051 010 | 1 104 622 | 1 220 190 |
> | Average wage per worker | 20 000 | 22 082 | 24 380 | 29 719 |
> | Number of injuries | 40 000 | 42 040 | 44 185 | 48 808 |
> | Average cost of an injury | 10 000 | 11 041 | 12 190 | 14 859 |
> | Total cost of injuries | 400 000 000 | 464 160 008 | 538 611 283 | 725 255 285 |
> | Cost of injuries/total earnings (as a %) | 2.00 | 2.00 | 2.00 | 2.00 |

assumed, the payments thus being expressed in monetary units of the injury year. In this example, benefit payments are over 0.30 per cent of covered earnings in the injury year, decreasing to 0.16 per cent in the third year[3] and below 0.10 per cent in the fifth year. They fall below 0.01 per cent in the 35th year.

In a relatively stable environment characterized by moderate growth of the workforce and salaries, total compensation payments grow substantially within a few years and rapidly reach a significant percentage of their ultimate level. Figure 14.2 shows the ratio of compensation expenditures to covered earnings[5] under two scenarios starting at time 0. In this example, it is assumed that the pattern of new accidents year after year is stable, the EIOD experience being held constant (see box 14.1). Under the first scenario, the covered earnings are constant (no growth). Under the second scenario, it is assumed that the covered earnings grow by 3 per cent each year. The growth can be the result of any combination of an increase in the number of workers and in their average salary, resulting in a 3 per cent growth of the exposure at risk. There is no indexing of benefits after they start being paid under both scenarios.

The ratio of benefits to covered earnings is smaller in the 3 per cent growth scenario because the increase in benefit payments lags behind the increase in covered earnings in each year. However, nominal amounts of benefits under the 3 per cent growth scenario are significantly higher than under the no-growth scenario. This analysis is interesting but is not fully realistic because the basic assumption of no indexing of benefits under the growth scenario after they have started to be paid may not be acceptable. For example, a worker earning the average annual salary of 20,000 who becomes totally disabled because of an accident in year 1 would be awarded a replacement income of 15,000, assuming a 75 per cent replacement rate of gross earnings. Another worker earning the average wage and becoming disabled in year 20 would be awarded a 22,289 income replacement indemnity. Part of the average annual 2 per cent salary increase is related to inflation, and under normal conditions, the 15,000 benefit would be indexed in the 20-year period and would probably be between 15,000 and 22,289.

Although the no-indexing scenario *per se* is unrealistic, the phenomenon illustrated here regarding the relationship between benefit payments and covered earnings is typical because the indexing of benefits is generally less important than the increase in the average salary.

14.1.3 PAYG method of financing

Under the PAYG system of financing, the EIOD scheme benefits are paid out of current premiums, and no significant fund is set aside in advance. Current premiums also cover administration expenses and include a provision to allow the contingency reserve to maintain its appropriate level. The size of the contingency reserve is determined in terms of months of benefit expenditure. Under a typical plan providing health care, rehabilitation benefits and income replacement indemnities, the contribution rate would grow fairly rapidly in the first ten years and would slowly tend to its ultimate level (see figure 14.2). The formula used by the actuary to estimate the premiums necessary for covering financial needs for any year is the following:

Formula 14.1

$$CR * S = B + A + Cc - I$$

where:

CR = Contribution rate
S = Covered earnings
B = Estimated benefit payments in the period
A = Budgeted administration expenditures in the period
Cc = Contribution to contingency reserve in the period (can be positive, zero or negative)
I = Investment income and other income

In the example of figure 14.2, the contribution rate would start at 0.36 per cent of covered earnings and reach an ultimate level of 1.88 per cent (0 per cent growth) or 1.57 per cent (3 per cent growth), depending on the assumption of their increase (Cc and I are set at 0).

14.1.4 Full funding

The full-funding method consists of levying each year the sums required for expected benefit payments regarding the accidents occurring in that year and the occupational diseases reported in that year. When deficits occur, they are amortized over a short period by supplemental contributions. Inversely, when surpluses occur, they can be used to reduce future premiums. This method implies that a portion of the sums levied is invested and the interest income will be used to pay future benefits. This system is called full funding because it accumulates a reserve that equals the value of accrued benefits. Should the plan terminate, there would be enough reserve to pay the benefits for all the injuries that occurred until the termination date as well as the management costs associated with them. The components of the formula are provided below:

Formula 14.2

$$CR * S = PVB + PVA + SD$$

where:

CR = Contribution rate
S = Covered earnings
PVB = Present value of benefits to be paid for injuries occurring in the year and occupational diseases reported in the year
PVA = Present value of expenses related to the administration of benefits considered under PVB^6, plus other current expenses not directly related to the administration of benefits

---

Box 14.2 Full funding versus terminal funding

It is interesting to compare the full-funding method with the terminal funding[7] method, which is also known as "assessment of capital constituents". In the actuarial literature, the system of capital constituents is generally associated with the funding of pensions at the time of the award, while the definition of full funding stated above implies the funding of all benefits related to the injuries of a given year. For example, an injury that occurred in the workplace may initially lead to a short-term incapacity allowance, say, for one year. At the end of the one-year period, the incapacity allowance is replaced by a long-term pension. The full-funding approach includes both the short-term and the long-term components in its present value calculation relative to the injury year, while the terminal funding approach would consider only the long-term pension and only at the time that the long-term pension starts.

> SD = Sums required to fund previous deficits or credits resulting from past surpluses used to reduce the premium (can be positive, zero or negative)

The rationale for the full-funding method deserves explanation. The financing of employment injury compensation programmes is more cost-effective if short periods of injury occurrences are successively considered for the rate setting, which then responds to changes in the experience. Under a yearly approach, contribution rates quickly reflect the benefits of prevention measures or the deterioration of the workplace environment. This approach adequately supports the ultimate, but probably unrealistic, target of completely eliminating injuries and diseases related to work. Also, given that benefit recipients tend to have a longer life than companies or even industries, the funding of benefits at the time an accident occurs protects the worker against any slowdown in the industry and employers against the burden of increasing costs.

The cost accrual differs for accidents and occupational diseases. An accident is an objective event that is easy to identify and there is generally unanimity about its time of occurrence, which is not the case for diseases. When does a disease first manifest itself? At the time of the first exposure to the damaging substance? After the appearance of the first symptoms? At the time of a doctor's diagnosis? For financing purposes, the most practical compromise is generally considered to be informing the EIOD institution of the reporting date. This approach is not totally consistent with the idea of full funding for diseases with a long latency period. More refinement should be possible, but a fair degree of arbitrariness concerning the build-up of liabilities as well as their financing makes the construction of reliable models difficult. Although an interesting issue, it is considered beyond the scope of this book.

Another issue of debate is the question of considering future administration costs in the model. In the social security area, it may be difficult to carry out a proper functional expense analysis of expenditures that would adequately support the modelling. The concept of the present value of administration costs may be difficult to explain to decision-makers in the area of operational expenses. Consequently, the PAYG approach for administration expenditures is often combined with the full funding of benefits.

It is interesting to compare the constant contribution rates under the full-funding system (which is 1.53 per cent of covered earnings for both scenarios illustrated in figure 14.3) with the ultimate ones under the PAYG approach.[8] Under the no-growth of covered earnings scenario in the PAYG approach, the ultimate contribution rate is 1.88 per cent, which is significantly higher than the full-funding rate. Under the full-funding approach, income on investments is available as revenues because premium incomes of 1.53 per cent exceed benefit payments in the injury year and thereafter, and can be invested (very little investment income is available in the PAYG approach).

Figure 14.3[11] Reserve as a percentage of covered earnings

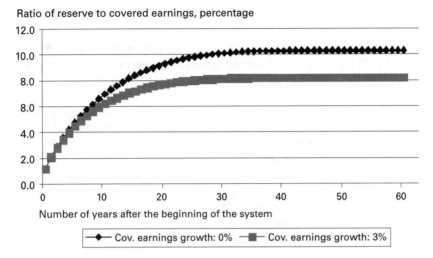

Under the 3 per cent growth of covered earnings scenario in the PAYG approach, the ultimate contribution rate is 1.57 per cent, which is very close to the full-funding rate. The reason is that the growth of ultimate benefit payments under the 3 per cent growth scenario is lower than the growth of covered earnings to which they are related.[9]

Figure 14.3 shows the size of the reserve for the benefits, which correspond to the example of figure 14.2, under the full-funding approach. In figure 14.3, the ultimate size of the reserve lies between 8 per cent and 10 per cent of covered earnings, depending on the growth of the exposure (covered earnings).[10] The ratios would be higher under the growth scenario if benefits were indexed.

14.1.5 Mixed systems

In theory, there is an infinite number of intermediate financial systems between the PAYG and the full-funding systems. One of the most popular consists of using the PAYG approach for the financing of temporary incapacity benefits, medical expenses reimbursement and the annual cost of rehabilitation programmes, and the full funding for permanent incapacity and survivors' pensions. The terminal funding financial system is normally used to finance these pensions.

The formula is as follows:

Formula 14.3

$$CR * S = BST + PVBLT + PVALT + CST + SDLT$$

Actuarial practice in social security

where:

CR	=	Contribution rate
S	=	Covered earnings
BST	=	Estimated short-term benefit payments in the period
$PVBLT$	=	Estimated present value of long-term benefits awarded during the year
$PVALT$	=	Present value of expenses related to the administration of benefits considered under $PVBLT$, plus administration expenses related to the administration of the institution for the fiscal year, excluding the portion related to the management of long-term claims
CST	=	Contribution to contingency reserve related to short-term benefits in the period (can be positive, zero or negative)
$SDLT$	=	Sums required to fund previous deficits or credits resulting from past surpluses used to reduce the premium related to long-term benefits

The short-term benefit element of the formula is exactly the same as under the PAYG approach, but the long-term benefit element is not the same as the full-funding one because of the rule governing the timing of the capitalization of long-term benefits. Under the mixed system, the pension is capitalized in the year that it starts to be paid, while under the full-funding system, an estimation is made in the year of injury of the present value of all the pensions that will be awarded for those injuries.

Figure 14.4 Comparison of reserve levels under the full-funding and mixed systems

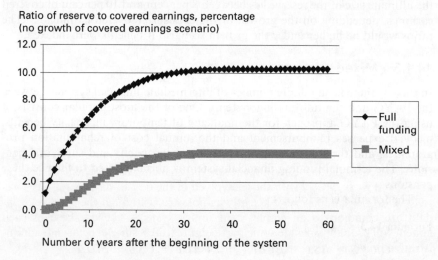

The premium rate will be between the PAYG one that increases rapidly to its ultimate level and the uniform rate of the full-funding system. The reserve accumulates to cover the future payments related to pensions that are capitalized.

Figure 14.4 shows the relationship between the size of the reserve under the full-funding and mixed systems described above. This relationship depends on the mixture of benefits in each plan. In this particular example, the reserve of the mixed system will eventually reach less than 50 per cent of the full-funding reserve. One of the perceived advantages of this mixed system is its greater simplicity; there is no need to calculate benefit liabilities for short-term benefits and potential increases in awards to existing long-term benefit recipients.

Most of the financial systems that apply to retirement pensions, such as the GAP and the scaled premium, can also apply to schemes in the employment injury area. Because the contribution rates that are determined under these systems are generally not very responsive to short-term variations in the injury record, they do not tend to support adequately the incentive for prevention and for an early return to work of injured workers.

14.1.6 The actuary and the financial system

The selection of a financial system among the possibilities described above is the first step in designing the financial arrangements of the scheme.

Although selecting a financing method is not an actuarial decision, the actuary is generally the best person to explain the consequences of the decisions taken on the plan's financial monitoring, including the accounting procedures that are most suitable. The financial statements should be designed so that the financial position can be clearly comprehended. Accountants need to understand actuarial concepts and actuaries must be sensitive to accounting standards. Close collaboration between the two is important, because experience data used by the actuary should be reconciled with past income and expenditures in the financial statements, and the actuary's projections will eventually be compared with the corresponding observed results in the financial statements. Accounting data have to be rearranged, sometimes in order to be in the format that is necessary for the actuarial analysis. The actuarial analysis should also be understood by the accountants. For that reason, the actuary is usually involved in the design of the accounting system. Accounting procedures need to be adapted to the selected funding system.

The actuary also needs to be familiar with all the procedures and administrative practices that have an influence on the financing of the scheme. The actuary should work closely with those involved in the day-to-day operations so as to develop the database as efficiently as possible. Although the most relevant data are common to all employment injury systems, the database of each system will probably include some particular features, since benefits and administrative practices are never exactly the same.

14.2 RATING SYSTEMS

The risk of occupational injury varies widely among different economic activities. Miners, for example, are exposed to a greater risk of employment injury than primary-school teachers. Moreover, the exposure to risk within the same economic activity can differ between enterprises because of different standards of safety conditions. Prevention activities and the commitment of employers and workers to the early return to work of injured workers will also have an impact on the experience of individual employers. The rating system can be designed to be more or less responsive to the risk. The assessment rate can be uniform or it may vary by economic activity.

The elements to be considered for the selection of the rating system are:

- the degree of integration of the employment injury scheme with other parts of the social security system;
- the desire to avoid cross-subsidization among industries;
- the need to promote prevention; and
- the administrative capacities of the institution.

In theory, the more refined a system is, the better will be the incentives for prevention and the return to work of injured workers, although the costs of administering the system will be higher. However, higher administrative costs can be more than offset by a reduction in the total cost of injuries, and the system can then be considered more efficient. This trade-off is not automatic and in order to achieve the desired result, the rating system needs to be carefully designed.

Each actuary should be aware of the requirements of more refined systems in terms of data availability as well as aware of the daily operations of the staff involved in the allocation of injury costs by employer, even though the current environment does not require the use of sophisticated actuarial techniques.

Rating systems can be grouped under three headings. The following subsections describe the most relevant actuarial considerations associated with each of them. In theory, each of the three approaches can be used with any financing method. In practice, there may be a correlation between the rating formula and the financing method. More risk responsive systems can be considered more appropriate for full-funding financial systems. Under the PAYG system, intergenerational equity between employers is generally low. The weight of the experience related to more recent injuries has to be significant when determining differential rates to make them risk responsive. This condition may be more difficult to meet in a PAYG system, given that the benefit payments related to accidents that have occurred a long time ago still have to be funded.

14.2.1 Uniform rates

Under the 100 per cent collective liability approach, the assessment rate is uniform among employers. It is determined according to the following formula for a given year:

Formula 14.4

$$R = expected\ cost\ /\ covered\ earnings$$

The expected cost can be determined according to any of the financing methods described in the preceding section (however, the full-funding financing method and the uniform rate approach would be a strange combination, and the authors are not aware of any application of this combination). The costs includes all financial needs: compensation costs, administration expenditures and any other provision required by the financial system. The value R can be determined every year or remain constant over a certain period.

The greatest advantage of this system is its simplicity. The collection of premiums can be combined with other social security branches and the sums pertaining to the employment injury scheme can be determined on an aggregate basis. Under normal circumstances, the rate would not vary significantly from year to year and would be, for that reason, readily predictable to all employers. The disadvantage of this approach is that it provides little incentive to individual employers to introduce safety measures or to implement rapid return-to-work strategies. It also introduces cross-subsidization among industries, which may not be economically efficient.

This system may be appropriate when the integration of the employment injury system with other parts of the social security is significant and the benefits paid under the employment injury scheme represent a relatively small part of the total benefits. It may also be the only feasible alternative at the onset of a system when no database exists to support a more refined system.

14.2.2 Differential rates

Given that the employment injury risk varies by economic activity, employers may be grouped or classified according to their risk characteristics for the purpose of rate assessment. Specific rates are set for each class of employers. Such a rating system requires a classification system and an actuarial method for calculating the appropriate rates of each class.

Basic formulae

The general formula for the calculation of the rate of each group can be expressed as follows:

> **Box 14.3 Illustration of formula 14.5**
>
> An example will clarify the meaning of formula 14.5. We need to determine the rate R_i for unit i. Assume the following data:
>
> (Risk relativity)$_i$ = 1.2
> Compensation cost = 300,000
> Covered earnings = 20,000,000
> L = 1.25
> F = 0.001 x covered earnings
>
> Then:
>
> $$R_i = [1.2 \times (300,000/20,000,000) \times 1.25 + 0.001] = 2.35\%$$
>
> while the uniform rate R would be:
>
> $$R = [(300,000/20,000,000) \times 1.25 + 0.001] = 1.975\%$$

Formula 14.5

$$R_i = L * [(\text{Risk relativity})_i * (\text{Compensation cost}/\text{covered earnings})] + (F/\text{Covered earnings})$$

where:

R_i	=	Rate for classification group i
(Risk relativity)$_i$	=	Relation between the risk of the unit and the average risk of all employers
Compensation cost	=	Estimated cost of compensation programmes in the assessment year
Covered earnings	=	Estimated assessable earnings in the assessment year
L	=	Loading factor for administration expenses and any provisions related to the financing method that are proportional to risk
F	=	Administration expenses and any provisions related to the financing method that are not proportional to risk (may be set at 0)

It is important to determine the spread of administration expenditures between those that are proportional to risk and those that are considered independent of the injury experience. Usually, all expenditures associated with claims management and financial charges related to the injury experience are financed according to risk. Expenses that are charged through a uniform rate of covered earnings should include specific services that are considered proportional to the size of employers, irrespective of their risk situation. For example, large employers may benefit from more customized services, and the expenditures linked to these services could be assessed by a uniform rate applicable to all employers, irrespective of their risk category.

Design of the classification structure

Differential rates can be used in any financial system. The design of a classification structure is generally the result of an interdisciplinary process. The actuary has an important role to play in assessing the efficiency of the rating system. People with an in-depth knowledge of the industries in the country must also be involved. There is no single profession that combines all the requirements; economists, engineers, specialists in industrial relations can all be of use. Employers, and possibly workers, should also be involved through the appropriate consulting process.

The question as to how many groups should make up the classification structure is a complex one. The objective of the rating system is to calculate a specific assessment rate for each group of employers that exhibit similar risk characteristics. Fairness suggests that one should define as many groups as necessary to charge the proper cost to each employer. In practice, however, the number of groups has to be limited because the injury experience of many groups would not be statistically credible and the administration of the system would be difficult. The workload related to classifying and the risk of making a mistake in classification increases with the number of rate pools. It is generally recognized that a classification structure must meet the following criteria:

Homogeneity: risks within a group should exhibit similar characteristics.
Credibility: the experience must be large enough to be statistically credible.
Neutrality: definitions of each class should be precise enough to avoid the possibility that two similar risks be classified differently by different people.
Cost efficient: the system should not create an undue burden to employers and to the institution administering it.

Industry classification systems used for the reporting of economic statistics on national economies may not be fully appropriate for the purpose of an employment injury system. Those systems are based on economic activities and may group together operations that have different risk characteristics, even though they pertain to the same economic sector. Industry classification systems are generally used as a starting point, but they may have to be adjusted to respond to the needs of the rating system. A classification structure should be dynamic and has to be periodically adapted to the changing environment. New risks and safer methods of operations must be recognized properly to ensure equity and acceptance of the system by employers. A permanent updating process must be put in place.

There is no actuarial formula to determine the optimal number of groups in a particular environment. Undue complexity is costly and not necessarily a guarantee of success. Over-simplicity is not desirable because this may generate a significant degree of inequity. Refined classification systems may comprise a few hundred rate units. This is usually not possible nor even necessary in all jurisdictions. Generally, the diversity of operations requires defining several units for each of the main economic sectors. The actuary must ensure that the collection of data can support the actuarial analysis for the calculation of rate groups. Economic sectors can be expressed more or less as follows:

- agricultural and fishing
- forestry
- mining
- construction
- manufacturing (light)
- manufacturing (heavy)
- transportation
- wholesale and retail
- government and public entities
- services

The number of risk pools within each sector depends on the diversity of the economy of each country. Subsectors may be absent in some and predominant in others. However, it is clear that several units may be necessary in groups that encompass a large number of activities with strongly varying risks. The manufacturing sector is generally significant and diversified in all countries; making furniture is different from making plastics. In the construction industry, the erection of metal structures does not imply the same risk as building residential houses, and so on. The basic classification structure should properly reflect the mix of activities of the particular country and consider the provisions of the system regarding the coverage. Should a complete sector be excluded from coverage, it would not be necessary to consider it in the design of the structure. In many situations, using more than 50 rate units may not be practical.

The number of rate units for classification purposes does not mean that specific rates have to be set for each of them. Whenever two units in two different economic sectors present similar risk characteristics in terms of frequency and severity of injuries, their experience can be pooled together and one single rate can be calculated for both classification units. In theory, a classification structure of 100 units may end with 100 rates or one dozen rates, but the latter alternative should not be the ultimate target. The grouping of risks within rating categories has to be carefully monitored. Risks may migrate from one class to another because of new trends in the experience resulting from a structural change in their operations. Technical Brief IV presents notes regarding the methodology for calculating rates by pools of risk.

14.3 EXPERIENCE-RATING SYSTEMS

Experience rating generally shifts a greater degree of the responsibility for workers' compensation costs from the industry rate group as a whole to the particular employers actually incurring the injury costs. The rate of assessment payable by an employer may vary above or below the standard rate applicable to the rate group or subclass. Experience-rating programmes modify an individual employer's assessments by comparing the firm's claims cost with the average experience for the class in which the employer falls or by comparing the firm's claims cost experience with the firm's assessments.

14.3.1 Nature of experience rating

Experience rating is intended to serve as an incentive for employers to reduce both the number of workers injured and the length of lost time by encouraging the employer to establish and maintain safety and prevention programmes and to assist the worker to return to work as soon as possible. Employers can accomplish these goals by preventing injuries from happening in the first place, by effectively tracking the progress of claims and by rehabilitating and re-hiring injured workers.

Experience-rating programmes make a firm responsible for its injury costs to varying degrees. Employers with claims costs above the industry average must pay a surcharge or an increase in their assessment rate. Firms with costs below the industry average receive rebates or refunds or a lower assessment rate. The adjustment to the employer's rate is based on the employer's past claims experience. Adjustments can be made retrospectively or prospectively to the rate of assessment.

With retrospective adjustments, the employer starts each year by paying the basic assessment rate for the industry; once the year is over, retrospective refunds or surcharges are made to reflect the employer's actual experience. Prospective programmes, on the other hand, adjust future assessments through discounts or surcharges based on the experience of past years. Prospective programmes are generally compulsory. Retrospective programmes are available for large employers and can be compulsory or optional. Experience-rating programmes can be limited to specific sectors of activities or can apply to all employers. When the programme applies only to certain categories and meets its objectives, the demand for extension will naturally come from other employers.

Supporters of experience rating maintain that experience-rated assessments provide a more equitable distribution of injury costs among employers, an incentive for prevention programmes, and a stimulus for claims management programmes. Opponents argue that experience rating compromises the collective liability principle, encourages employers to control costs after an injury has occurred through under-reporting, diverts attention away from accident prevention to claims cost control and increases litigation.

Experience-rating systems require reliable databases pertaining to each employer and more sophisticated tools for the billing of individual employers. They also generate the need for more or better-trained staff, which means higher administrative costs. However, the increase in administration expenditures is generally more than offset by the decrease in the cost of compensation programmes resulting from improvements in the experience. This assertion is difficult to demonstrate in jurisdictions in which programmes have been in force for a long time: the impact is easier to track during the years immediately following the implementation of a programme.

Legislative authority in instituting experience-rating programmes is normally conferred in the jurisdiction's Act. The decision to implement an experience-rating programme is a political one. The success of the programme is related to its acceptance by all the stakeholders, employers as well as workers. It is generally the actuary who designs the provisions of the programme and who should ensure that all the parties fully understand the provisions by going through the appropriate consultation process.

14.3.2 Prospective programmes

The rationale behind prospective experience rating programmes is that past experience will affect future rates. The past experience of the employer is compared with the past experience of the group in which the employer is classified. The nature of the process is similar to the one used for calculating unit rates, but the technique must be adapted to consider the smaller volume of experience data available for each employer and its vulnerability to fluctuations. Employers' premiums must be responsive to experience, but rebates and surcharges must bear a reasonable relationship to employers' experience variations, taking into consideration their size. Insurance principles dictate that it would not be appropriate to charge a small employer the full cost of claims.

The design of prospective programmes is influenced by the minimum size of employers that are eligible. For very small employers, the merits or demerits have to be related to a very simple indicator of the experience, such as the number of injured workers in a specified period. For this purpose, an employer is considered small according to criteria that have to be defined objectively. For example, the criterium could be the following one: employers whose probability of having at least one injured worker in one year is not greater than 50 per cent. More detailed considerations regarding this topic are presented in Technical Brief IV.

14.3.3 Retrospective programmes

Under the retrospective approach, the prospectively rated premium of the employer is adjusted after a certain period following the end of the injury year. The actual claims cost of the employer for the injury year is then compared with the premium that has been assessed at the onset of the year, and if the actual cost is less than the premium, the difference is reimbursed to the employer (if the actual cost is larger, the difference is charged to the employer). In order to avoid excessive differences between the original premium and the final charges, an appropriate insurance mechanism must be included in the design of the rating system. Retrospective plans are intended to promote prevention and early return to work because employers benefit directly from their good experience or are penalized if their injury record deteriorates. This approach requires particular administration facilities in order to keep track of the development of the experience of each employer and of their reimbursements and charges.

Retrospective plans are usually accessible to large employers whose experience is highly credible. In theory, they can apply to any employer whose experience has a minimum of credibility, but the adjustments will be proportional to the credibility, and the cost/benefit relationship may not justify application of this rating system to small-sized employers. Moreover, the adjustments usually occur several years after the end of the injury year and a large proportion of small employers may no longer exist after this period. Provisions dealing with the closure of enterprises before the date of adjustment can handle these situations, but the frequency of their utilization should be minimized, given the intricacies of the law and judicial practices regarding the establishment and closure of enterprises.

Participating in the retrospective rating system can be compulsory or optional. Compulsory participation ensures that all large employers are assessed using the same technique and that the particular administrative costs of the plan are spread over a sufficient number of employers. An optional plan may open the door to anti-selection and may require a more sophisticated actuarial device in order to ensure equity among the employers participating in the plan as well as between the group of employers participating and other employers.

Other aspects of the design of retrospective plans are presented in Technical Brief IV.

ANNEX 14A DEMONSTRATION OF THE PRINCIPLE THAT THE CONTRIBUTION RATE UNDER A FULLY FUNDED SYSTEM AND THE ULTIMATE PAYG COST RATE CAN BE EQUAL

Assertion:

The contribution rate under a fully funded system and the ultimate PAYG cost rate are equal if the growth of covered earnings under the PAYG system is the same as the rate of interest under the fully funded system.

Actuarial practice in social security

Assumptions:

1. The experience of the system is constant and fully mature. The number of years during which benefits are paid to a cohort of injured workers (m) is smaller that the number of years that the plan has been in force (n). $m < n$.
2. The vector of benefit payments in each year after the injury related to the year of injury k ($k > m$) is represented by B_s, before any indexing; values of s run from 0 to $m - 1$.
3. f is the rate of indexing of benefits and indexing occurs at each anniversary of the injury.
4. The covered earnings in year k are E.
5. Injuries are assumed to occur in the middle of the year and payments are assumed to be made in the middle of each year.
6. The parameter g expresses a variable that is related to the financial system:
    - Under the PAYG system, g represents the average growth between each payment made in year k corresponding to the sth preceding injury year and the corresponding payment B_s that will be made to injured workers of year k (g corresponds to the growth of covered earnings because of assumption 1). The growth of covered earnings has three components: growth of the workforce, of productivity and of inflation (the indexing of benefits is assumed to correspond to inflation).
    - In the fully funded system, the parameter g represents the nominal rate of return.

The following formula presents the rate of contribution in year k. It applies to both the fully funded and the PAYG systems.

Formula 14A.1

$$\frac{\sum_{s=0}^{m-1} B_s \times (1+f)^s \times (1+g)^{-s}}{E}$$

Under the PAYG system, the formula represents benefit payments made in year k (the financial year) for the current injury year and the past $m - 1$ ones. Under the fully funded system, the formula represents the present value of benefits to be paid in the injury year and each of the following $m - 1$ ones for the injuries that occurred in year k (injury year).

If benefits are not indexed ($f = 0$), the formula shows that rates of contribution are the same if the growth of covered earnings (number of workers multiplied by their average earnings) is the same as the nominal rate of interest. If benefits are indexed, it shows that rates of contribution are the same if the

Financial and rating systems

growth of the workforce and the growth of productivity are equal to the real rate of interest. These conditions can be considered difficult to meet on a sustainable basis in any environment. Generally, the economic parameters associated with the full-funded formula are higher than those of the PAYG formula, which produces a lower employment injury premium.

Notes

[1] In this chapter, the expression "covered earnings" refers to salaries and earnings of independent workers that are assessable. The amounts considered for compensation purposes may differ because of the provisions regarding the maximum and minimum.

[2] Let $b(t)$ denote the benefit payments t years after the injury year and $S(0)$ the covered earnings in the injury year. Then figure 14.1 shows the ratio $b(t)/S(0)$.

[3] The third year in figure 14.1 refers to $t = 2$.

[4] In this example, permanent incapacity benefits terminate at the age of 65. For this reason and because of relatively liberal provisions regarding rehabilitation, the curve of the benefit payments over five years after the injury year can probably be considered steeper than that of many other plans.

[5] Let $B(t)$ denote the benefit payments in year t for all injury years from 0 to t and $S(t)$ denote the covered earnings in year t. Then figure 14.2 shows the ratio $B(t)/S(t)$.

[6] The claims management costs for a cohort of injuries occurring in one particular year are incurred during that year and over many years, that is, as long as benefits are paid.

[7] Terminal funding refers to the idea of funding the accrued pension when the worker comes to the end of his or her working life and retires. In matters relating to employment injury, the use of the wording terminal funding does not refer to a corresponding event in the life of the worker.

[8] The cost is constant under both scenarios because the assumption of a constant injury record is assumed.

[9] This illustrates the following principle. The contribution rate under a fully funded system and the ultimate PAYG cost rate are equal if the growth of covered earnings under the PAYG system is the same as the rate of interest under the fully funded system. See Annex 14A for a demonstration. In a rapidly developing economy, it may be anticipated that the growth of covered earnings will exceed the rate of interest. However, history indicates that this relationship cannot be maintained indefinitely and that the reverse holds in environments considered economically more mature.

[10] Let $R(t)$ denote the reserve at the end of year t and $S(t)$ denote the covered earnings during year t. Then figure 14.3 shows the ratio $R(t)/S(t)$.

[11] Note that the nominal amounts of the reserve would be much higher under the 3 per cent growth scenario than under the constant wage assumption. For example, in year 20, they would respectively be 6,215,629 (no growth) and 9,353,702 (3 per cent growth).

TEMPORARY INCAPACITY CASH BENEFITS 15

The first section of this chapter on temporary incapacity cash benefits discusses the main provisions related to incapacity benefits that are considered in the cost analysis. The second and third sections, respectively, present the methods and assumptions used in the valuation of temporary incapacity cash benefits. The fourth section illustrates experience analysis. The main aspects of statistical data reports for actuarial valuations are covered in Technical Brief IV.

15.1 LEGISLATIVE PROVISIONS

Most employment injury social security systems pay cash benefits to injured workers until the latter return to work or have reached maximum medical recovery. Temporary incapacity also includes periods of absence from work because of rehabilitation programmes aimed at minimizing the permanent loss of earning capacity. Benefits are said to be temporary because they are provided during the period immediately following the injury and cease to be awarded when medical recovery has reached a plateau and stabilized, or when the rehabilitation process has ended. The termination date of temporary incapacity cash benefits can be referred to as the medical consolidation date. As of this date, an evaluation of the permanent loss of earning capacity is made for severe injuries, and the right to permanent incapacity cash benefits is acquired more or less permanently. Permanent payments start immediately after the cessation of temporary incapacity benefits. These types of benefits will be considered in Chapter 16.

In practice, the distinction between temporary and permanent incapacity is not significant in terms of the benefits formula. The distinction is, however, useful from the actuarial point of view, because it generally allows easier modelling of the costs of the scheme. Administratively, the distinction is significant, because rules concerning the follow-up of the recipients of these benefits are totally different.

Temporary incapacity cash benefits

The cost of temporary incapacity benefits will vary according to the plan's provisions. The main provisions are related to the duration of payments (waiting period and time limits) and the level of benefits. Most systems have no waiting period, but when there is one, it is generally short (three days or so). Usually, the benefits stop when the injured worker is no longer disabled or becomes eligible for a permanent incapacity benefit. Plans may limit the duration of the short-term benefit to a specified period, such as 52 weeks or more. If the physical condition of the injured worker has not stabilized, the payment of the benefit will generally continue, thanks to a temporary extension, until the permanent loss of earning capacity can be assessed.

Benefits are generally based on an individual's earnings at the time of the accident or, in some circumstances, on the average of the worker's earnings for a short period before the accident, not more than one year. Benefits may also take into consideration the number of dependants. Flat benefits not related to earnings are an exception. The replacement rate is set according to the earnings base (gross or net), and the tax situation of the benefit (taxable or not). The replacement rate may vary during the disability period, either increasing or decreasing after a specified period. Gross earnings are considered up to the maximum insurable wage and minimum benefits are sometimes provided. Provisions of employment injury are generally stable over time. Actuaries permanently employed by an institution will generally devote most of their time to analysing the experience as it emerges, to producing periodic projections, as well as to valuating liabilities if the funding system so requires.

15.2 METHODOLOGY FOR FINANCIAL PROJECTIONS

The nature of the financial projections depends on the financial system. The PAYG system requires only cash-flow projections, while other systems may require the discounting of these cash flows. The projection of expected benefit expenditures over future financial years is a step of the actuarial valuation that is common to all financial systems. Discounting can be processed at a second stage.

The mathematical formulae used for financial projections are fairly simple, but the selection of appropriate assumptions is a complex issue. The experience of employment injury is volatile. The appropriateness of past experience in projecting the future must always be questioned, and the costing of proposed changes to legislation or administrative practices may require data that are not readily available.

There are a number of reasonable approaches to projecting benefits payments in a financial year. The formulae discussed in Chapter 17 dealing with medical benefits can also, for example, apply to short-term incapacity. However, in this chapter, only the formulae that can be considered unique to temporary incapacity benefits are presented. The basic components for the projection of temporary cash benefits are generally considered to be the following ones. Formula 15.1 expresses the projected benefit expenditure t years after the valuation date:

Formula 15.1

$$B(t) = N(t) * M(t) * K(t)$$

where:

$N(t)$ = Number of people cashing benefits in year t
$M(t)$ = Average number of days per benefit recipient in year t
$K(t)$ = Average daily benefit in year t

The number $N(t)$ can be expressed as the product of an exposure $E(t)$ and a frequency rate $F(t)$. This may not be practical because the exposure is often not available. Most of the time, the individual registration of workers is not required for the administration of the EIOD scheme. The total assessable payroll of each employer is sufficient for the purpose of rate assessment. This is an important operational characteristic that differentiates EIOD systems from pension plans.

The actuary has to select a method for the projection of N, M and K in year t. It is not generally convenient to forecast over time those variables as a mere function of the most recent observations at the valuation date. For example, regressing over observed values of N, M or K in the years preceding the valuation date and projecting according to the trend may be misleading because significant changes may have occurred, and a regression formula can only capture them at best very vaguely, and often not at all.

In order to obtain a satisfactory estimate of the number of people cashing benefits (N), the projection process is generally broken down into two main components: the number of workers whose injury occurred before the projection period and the number of workers corresponding to injuries occurring during the projection period. The number of days (M) and the average daily benefits (K) must then be modelled accordingly.

15.2.1 Benefits related to injuries that occurred before the valuation date

In order to simplify the formulae, we will make the arbitrary assumption that temporary incapacity benefit payments are paid over a maximum of ten years (this could be parameterized to any value n). Benefits payments for injuries that occurred in the ten years ending with the valuation date can be expressed as follows. It is assumed that the valuation year is year 0 and the first projection year is year 1. Let d denote the difference between the valuation year and the injury year and t the difference between the year of projection and the valuation year.

Formula 15.2

$$B(t) = \sum_{d=0}^{9-t} N_d(0) \times P(d,t) \times M(d+t) \times K(0) \times f(t)$$

where:

$N_d(0)$ = Number of benefit recipients in the year of valuation whose injury occurred d years before the year of valuation, $0 \leq d \leq 9$.
$P(d,t)$ = Proportion of benefit recipients in year d after their injury year who are recipients in year $d + t$, $P(d,t) = 0$ for $d + t \leq 10$
$M(d + t)$ = Average number of days per benefit recipient $d + t$ years after the injury year
$K(0)$ = Average daily benefit in the valuation year
$f(t)$ = Indexing factor of the average benefit per recipient over t years

N and K are statistical values available at the valuation date. P and M are assumptions that are set by the actuary after a proper analysis of the past experience.

It is assumed that K is independent of the injury year and duration and that benefits are adjusted annually, irrespective of the injury year. This is a simplistic assumption, given that the average daily benefit generally depends on the duration (the variables d and t). The distribution of terminations is never exactly proportional to the number of workers grouped by size of average daily benefit.

A possible variation of formula 15.2 would be to use the number of benefit recipients on the day of the valuation date instead of in the year ending at the valuation date. Under this alternative, N, P and K would have to be redefined as follows:

$N_d(0)$ = Number of benefit recipients at the valuation date whose injury occurred d years before the valuation date, $0 \leq d \leq 9$.
$P(d,t)$ = Proportion of benefit recipients at the valuation date whose injury occurred d years before the valuation date who are recipients in year $d + t$, $P(d,t) = 0$ for $d + t \geq 10$
$K(0)$ = Average daily benefit at the valuation date

In theory, this approach should produce better results because the number of recipients at the valuation date is a more accurate starting point for the projection period. However, the calculation of P values that are consistent with this approach is more complex, and requires more than just making a link between the number of recipients in successive years after the injury year. Indeed, the probability of being a recipient in any particular year is linked to the fact of being a recipient at a particular date. It is interesting to observe that all

$P(d,1)$ are equal to 1 or close to 1 because all benefit recipients at the valuation date should receive a benefit in the following year for at least one day.

It is possible to refine this formula yet further in order to make it work for an individual projection of benefits paid to each benefit recipient at the valuation date. The probability of being a recipient at any time after the valuation date would be determined according to the duration of incapacity of recipients at the valuation date. This would require more computer capacity.

When the volume of data is small, it may be difficult to estimate separately the number of benefit recipients in each year after the injury year and their average number of compensated days. They may be combined, and then a distribution of the number of days paid for each injury by year after the injury (including the year of injury) is used for the projection. The formula would then be the following for $1 < t < 9$.

Formula 15.3

$$B(t) = \sum_{d=0}^{9-t} I_d \times D(d+t) \times K(0) \times f(t),$$

where:

I_d = Number of new injuries that occurred d years before the valuation date, $0 \leq d \leq 9$

$D(d+t)$ = Number of days paid in year $d+t$ after the injury year per worker injured

Discounting the cash flows of the expected benefit expenditures related to injuries that occurred prior to the valuation date produces the actuarial liabilities related to those injuries. The formula is as follows, under the simplistic assumption of uniform distribution of payments during the year.

Formula 15.4

$$AL(0) = \sum_t B(t)/(1+i)^{t-\frac{1}{2}}$$

where:

$AL(0)$ = Actuarial liabilities in year t
i = Nominal rate of interest

15.2.2 Benefits related to injuries occurring after the valuation date

When injuries occurring in the projection period must be considered, an assumption needs to be set regarding the number of new injuries in each year. Each new cohort of injuries in the projection period is projected according to the method used for injuries having occurred before the valuation date. Let j denote the difference between the injury year and the valuation year.

Formula 15.5

$$B(t) = \sum_{j=\max(1,t-9)}^{t} I_j \times D(t-j) \times K(j) \times f(t-j)$$

where:

I_j = Number of new injuries occurring j years after the valuation date

$K(j)$ = Average daily benefit at onset of incapacity of new injured in year j

The value of I_j depends on the assumption regarding the variation of the workforce covered and the rate of injury. One reasonable formula is the following:

Formula 15.6

$$I_j = W(0) \times (1+g)^j \times F(0) \times (1+v)^j$$

where:

$W(0)$ = Number of people covered in the year preceding the projection period

g = Rate of growth of the population covered

$F(0)$ = Rate of injury frequency in the first year preceding the projection period

v = Annual rate of variation in injury frequency

W is a statistical data, while the other variables are assumptions. The selection of assumptions g and F can generally be supported by past statistical data and forecasts of the appropriate indicators of the economy. The assumption related to the rate of variation in the injury frequency (v) is a complex issue. Expected changes to the mix of activities and the potential impact of occupational health and safety measures on the occurrence of injuries have to be considered. $K(j)$ would be related to $K(0)$ and to the general increase in salaries from year 0 to year j and to the impact of the change to the expected mix of activities in that period on the frequency of injuries by sector.

15.3 ASSUMPTIONS

According to the formulae shown in the preceding section, assumptions need to be set regarding the following variables: duration of benefits, the amount of the basic benefit and the number of new injuries (the latter not being necessary for

Table 15.1 Form of experience data

Duration = year of payment minus year of injury	A Days paid in 1998 for injuries in	B Number of injured workers in	C Number of days compensated per 1 000 injured
0	1998	1998	A ÷ B x 1 000
1	1997	1997	A ÷ B x 1 000
2	1996	1996	A ÷ B x 1 000
3	1995	1995	A ÷ B x 1 000
4	1994	1994	A ÷ B x 1 000
5	1993	1993	A ÷ B x 1 000
etc.	etc.	etc.	etc.

the valuation of liabilities). Each of these items will be discussed, but particular emphasis is given to the duration of incapacity.

15.3.1 Duration of incapacity

The formulae of the preceding section use two techniques for modelling duration. The simplest one is a distribution of the number of days paid in each year after the injury for a given number of newly injured people (see variable D in formula 15.3). Such a distribution can be based on the most recently observed data. Table 15.1 illustrates the process.

Suppose that we are in the year 2000 and that the experience data of the financial year 1998 are available. Here is how to construct a table that is based only on this observation year.

Column A is the set of data representing the most recent information related to the number of temporary incapacity benefits for each past injury year. Column B presents for each injury year the number of injured workers who have received temporary incapacity benefits at any time since the injury year. These data are necessary to relate the data of column A to a volume of injured worker. Column C shows the data that are needed to project the future benefits, that is, the assumption regarding duration.

The process can be refined and the observation of more than one year be used. For example, if observations of the years 1996 to 1998 are used, the required assumption would be obtained through an average of the numbers of column C.

Table 15.2 is a numerical example, where it is assumed that the benefits are paid for a maximum of five years after the injury. The first part of the table presents the total number of days paid per injury year for each duration. The duration is the difference between the year of payment and the year of injury. For example, the number of days paid to workers injured in 1994 at duration 3 (in 1997) is 120,532. The second part of the table shows the average number

Temporary incapacity cash benefits

Table 15.2 Illustration of formula 15.3

Injury year	Number of injured	Total number of days paid by duration*					
		0	1	2	3	4	5
1991	20 051						35 930
1992	19 267					129 615	44 523
1993	19 431				156 455	100 700	28 966
1994	19 570			237 421	120 532	107 014	
1995	19 655		458 070	235 499	144 534		
1996	20 386	427 650	400 496	204 421			
1997	20 092	509 327	438 984				
1998	20 535	479 970					
		Average number of days paid by duration					
1991	20 051						1.79
1992	19 267					6.73	2.31
1993	19 431				8.05	5.18	1.49
1994	19 570			12.13	6.16	5.47	
1995	19 655		23.31	11.98	7.35		
1996	20 386	20.98	19.65	10.03			
1997	20 092	25.35	21.85				
1998	20 535	23.37					
Average by duration		23.23	21.60	11.38	7.19	5.79	1.86

*Duration = year of payment minus year of injury

of days paid. The average number of days paid per worker injured in 1994 at duration 3 is 6.16 (120,532/19,570).

The last row of the second part of the table shows the three-year average number of days paid per duration. This set of numbers constitutes the assumption for the expected future number of days. For example, an actuarial valuation that uses this assumption would assume that the average number of days paid in the first year after the injury year is 21.60. It is interesting to note that the sum of the average numbers of days for all years of payment (0 to 5) is 71.05. This figure represents the expected average number of compensated days for a new cohort of injured people that would experience the average duration observed during the years 1996 to 1998.

Technically speaking, calculating the average number of days per worker is not an essential step. Indeed, the distribution of the number of days in each year for a cohort of a given number of injured workers, for example 20,000, could be calculated by adjusting the total number of days in the first part of the table by the ratio of 20,000 to the number of injured workers for each injury year. Of course, formula 15.3 should be adjusted accordingly.[1]

Actuarial practice in social security

Table 15.3 Illustration of formula 15.2

Injury year	Number of injured	Number of benefit recipients in the year of payment					
		0	1	2	3	4	5
1991	20 051						256
1992	19 267					456	294
1993	19 431				523	324	234
1994	19 570			743	637	432	
1995	19 655		7 724	753	632		
1996	20 386	20 386	8 431	876			
1997	20 092	20 092	7 943				
1998	20 535	20 535					

	Ratio of the number of benefit recipients in each financial year to the number of injured					
1991						0.0128
1992					0.0237	0.0153
1993				0.0269	0.0167	0.0120
1994			0.0380	0.0325	0.0221	
1995		0.3930	0.0383	0.0322		
1996	1.0	0.4136	0.0430			
1997	1.0	0.3953				
1998	1.0					
Average	1.0	0.4006	0.0397	0.0305	0.0208	0.0134

	Average number of days paid by recipient in each financial year					
1991						140.4
1992					284.2	151.4
1993				299.1	310.8	123.8
1994			319.5	189.2	247.7	
1995		59.3	312.7	228.7		
1996	21.0	47.5	233.4			
1997	25.3	55.3				
1998	23.4					
Average	23.2	54.0	288.5	239.0	280.9	138.5

15.3.2 Evolution of the number of benefit recipients

Formula 15.2 uses another technique for modelling the projection of benefit payments. Both the development of the number of injured people and the number of average days paid in each financial year are considered. Table 15.3 shows the process using the same total number of days as table 15.2. The table assumes that the data are available on an incurred basis. This means that benefits are allocated to the year in which the benefits are incurred, not

Table 15.4 Probability of a benefit recipient in the valuation year being a benefit recipient in year t after the valuation year

Valuation year − injury year	Projection year − valuation year				
	1	2	3	4	5
0	0.4006	0.0397	0.0305	0.0208	0.0134
1	0.0991	0.0761	0.0519	0.0334	
2	0.7679	0.5237	0.3370		
3	0.6820	0.4389			
4	0.6435				

the one when they are paid. Let the financial year be the number of years after the injury year. By definition, the financial year 0 corresponds to the injury year.

In this example, the number of workers whose injury occurred in 1996 (20,386) who were benefit recipients in 1998 (1996 + 2) is 876, the ratio being 0.043 (876/20,386). The average number of compensated days of these 876 benefit recipients was 233.4 in 1998 (204,421/876).

It is interesting to note the following from table 15.3:

1. The average number of days grows substantially at duration 2. Recipients reaching that duration are generally severely injured and a large proportion is indemnified during the whole year.
2. The last row of the second and third parts of table 15.3 are the assumptions corresponding to the experience in the years 1996 to 1998, and using the experience of injury years 1991 to 1998.
3. The reader will be interested to verify that according to the assumptions of table 15.3, the average number of days paid per newly injured worker is 71.27.[2]

The Ps in formula 15.2 can be derived from the last row of the second part of table 15.3, and are shown in table 15.4.

15.3.3 The continuation table

A continuation table shows, for an arbitrary number of newly injured people (the radix of the table), the number of people that will be compensated for one day, two days and so on, until the last day that compensation can be paid. It is similar to a life survival table, and is a refinement of the model shown in the preceding section. Table 15.5 shows an example of such a table at specific points. A complete table would comprise a much larger range of values.

Given that the number of benefit recipients varies significantly at the beginning of the table, values would normally be calculated exactly at each

Table 15.5 Continuation table for temporary incapacity benefits

Days after the injury	Number of benefit recipients
1	100 000
3	80 000
15	40 000
30	30 000
91	10 000
182	7 000
365	4 000
730	3 000
1 095	2 000
1 460	1 000
1 825	0 000
Average duration	70.00 days

daily duration. When the rate of the decrease in recipients stabilizes, values can be determined at longer intervals, such as 30 days. Separate tables should be constructed to consider the variables that affect the duration. Appropriate analysis should be conducted to identify the most significant variables affecting duration such as: accidents or disease, sex, age, industry. Using more than one or two variables is often impractical, since a huge volume of data will then be required.

A continuation table allows for a more precise calculation of the future benefits to each individual, since the individual's past duration is considered more exactly. It is also an essential tool for costing changes to benefit formulae. For example, if the introduction of a waiting period is considered, the existing continuation table is the best starting point, but care must be taken when considering the elasticity factor. The elasticity factor is the ratio of the variation of the duration to the variation of the benefit. An elasticity factor of 20 per cent would signify that a 10 per cent rate of increase in the replacement rate would generate a 2 per cent rate of increase in the average duration. Indeed, experience shows that the waiting period has an impact on the utilization of temporary incapacity benefits. A proportion of slightly injured people with a short expected duration may remain at work in order to avoid losing the earnings of the waiting period. In the example above, the introduction of a two-day waiting period would normally modify the experience in such a manner that the number of recipients per 100,000 newly injured people would be fewer than 80,000.

Empirical studies show that the duration tends to increase when the earnings replacement rate increases and, conversely, the duration tends to decline when the earnings replacement rate decreases. Unfortunately, there is no actuarial model for suggesting the appropriate elasticity factor for each circumstance. Actuaries need to rely on published empirical studies and good judgement in order to adapt their conclusions to the specific situation that is being considered.

15.3.4 Basic amount of benefits

The basic amount of benefits is the amount of money that is paid for the smallest interval of time considered in the formula for the projection of temporary benefits. Generally, it is a daily or a weekly amount. The formulae presented in this chapter assume that this variable depends on the valuation year and the year of payment for the sake of simplicity. The injury year and the number of years spent between the injury year and the year of payment are variables that may be significant enough to be considered.

When the actuarial analysis consists of projecting payments related to accidents that have occurred up until the projection date, then the assumption that needs to be set is the one concerning the evolution of the basic amount of benefits that is paid during the valuation year. If the actuarial analysis deals with a projection that includes injuries occurring in the future, an assumption has to be made with respect to the evolution of the basic benefit for new injuries between the more recent injury years preceding the valuation date and each future injury year.

Evolution of the basic amount between the injury year and the year of payment

The basic amount related to benefit recipients in the valuation year or at the valuation date is a statistical datum. For an individual worker, the evolution of the basic amount depends solely on the plan's provisions. The replacement ratio may change or, if there is a partial return to work, the benefit may be reduced by earnings.

If there is indexing (total, partial or ad hoc), then this has to be considered. The general considerations discussed in Part II of the book regarding the economic assumptions will then apply.

The average amount of benefits is subject to variation in the duration of incapacity by earnings level. For example, it is possible that the basic amount varies because low- or high-wage earners return to work at different durations. The analysis of past experience in a particular environment should support the setting of assumptions.

Evolution of the basic amount between injury years

The basic amount of benefits for new injuries occurring in the future depends mainly on the demographic change of the covered population, the growth of the average salary, the change in the industry mix and the impact of prevention activities. Moreover, improvements in the workplace environment may affect various classes of workers differently and will influence the average basic amount paid to newly injured workers.

Demographic changes to the covered population alter the distribution of the injured by sex and age, which should be reflected in the average benefit.

The growth of the average salary depends on the economic assumptions regarding productivity and inflation. Salaries usually vary according to industry. Assumptions regarding the industry mix should be supported by recent trends and the experience observed in other countries.

The impact of prevention activities can differ among workers by age, sex and industry group. It is generally not possible to set assumptions on the basis of experience. By definition, prevention activities aim to change the workplace or the behaviour of workers, and the success of campaigns cannot be known in advance. The experience of other countries can help the actuary, but the user of the report should be informed of the degree of arbitrariness of these assumptions.

15.3.5 Number of new injuries

The number of new injuries is linked to the evolution of the active workforce, changes in the mix of industries and the assumption regarding changes in the workplace environment. Assumptions related to a few years following the valuation date can be articulated around the analysis of the recent short-term trends. Long-term assumptions can be inspired by the experience of other countries at corresponding stages of evolution. When there is no solid argument to justify an assumption other than a stable number of annual new injuries, it is more appropriate to assume either a stability in future incidence or a continuation of past trends for a certain period followed by a stable annual incidence.

The relationship between economic cycles and the frequency of injury is an issue that has been intensively analysed. Many studies support the conventional wisdom that the number of claims increases as people lose their jobs in an economic downturn and remaining employees file claims for conditions that previously may have gone unreported. Studies also demonstrate that higher disability costs also occur in a strong economy. The volume of claims rises

Table 15.6 Projection of benefit days

Injury year	Number of benefit days projected in:				
	1999	2000	2001	2002	2003
1994	38 502				
1995	121 075	38 418			
1996	160 771	128 866	40 887		
1997	227 093	144 466	115 799	36 744	
1998	444 221	235 197	149 690	119 980	38 111
Total	991 662	546 947	306 376	156 724	38 111
Cash flow					
All injury years	51 566 405	29 57 888	17 231 535	9 167 233	2 318 387

when employment levels increase and the average number of hours on the job increases, probably because of employee fatigue and a workforce that is less experienced and probably more injury-prone. When econometric models are used to project injury frequency, careful disclosure of the uncertainty related to the basic assumptions should be made to users of the actuary's work.

The duration is sensitive to changes in the composition of injured by sex and age. Changes to this distribution can be observed on a long-term basis only in order to make it consistent with the assumed population of newly injured workers.

15.4 ANALYSIS OF EXPERIENCE DEVIATIONS

This section gives a brief outline of an experience analysis. In order to do so, the projection of payments will be completed using formula 15.2 and the assumptions developed in tables 15.3 and 15.4. It may not be possible to reproduce all the figures exactly in the tables of this section because of rounding.

15.4.1 Projection

The number of benefit days projected in each of the five financial years following the valuation year is shown in table 15.6. The cash flow is illustrated in the last row of the table, assuming that the average daily benefit is 50 in the valuation year and that inflation is constant over the period, at 4 per cent per year. The indexing of benefits is assumed to occur at the anniversary of the injury. The cash flow is shown for all injury years combined, but it should be available to the actuary for each injury year.

It is interesting to calculate the benefits liabilities at the valuation date, which is 31 December 1998 for this illustration, and at the end of each subsequent financial year. A constant discount rate of 7.5 per cent is used and it is assumed that payments are made at mid-year.

Table 15.7 shows the liability at the valuation date and the estimated liability at the end of each subsequent year if all the assumptions are realized in the future. Note that this estimated liability does not consider the injuries that will occur beyond the valuation date, thus giving an incomplete picture of

Table 15.7 Projected actuarial liability for the injury years up to 1998

Financial year	Liability at 31 December
1998	99,446,118
1999	53,439,390
2000	26,779,300
2001	10,921,712
2002	2,236,051

> **Box 15.1 Numerical example**
>
> The liabilities in table 15.7 are calculated as follows:
>
> 1998: 51,566,405÷1.075^0.5 + 29,578,888÷1.075^1.5 + 17,231,535÷1.075^2.5 + 9,167,237 ÷1.075^3.5 + 2,318,387÷1.075^4.5
> 1999: 29,578,888÷1.075^0.5 + 17,231,535÷1.075^1.5 + 9,167,237÷1.075^2.5 + 2,318,387 ÷1.075^3.5
> and so on.
>
> The expected investment income is calculated as follows:
>
> 99,446,118*0.075 − 51,566,405*(1.075^0.5 − 1) = 5,559,677

what the total actuarial liabilities will be at each future valuation date. For example, the liabilities for new injuries occurring in 1999 should be added to the liabilities shown at 31 December 1999 in table 15.7 in order to obtain the scheme's total liabilities. This amount will depend on the projected number of newly injured workers in 1999. This information is not needed for the purposes of the following example, which is limited to past injury years.

Under the fully funded system, the expected benefits expenses in the 1999 financial statements is the sum of the payments (51,566,405) and of the variation in liabilities (53,439,390 − 99,446,118 = −46,006,728), which is 5,559,677 (51,566,405 − 46,006,728). An investment income of 5,559,677 is expected, so that the revenue and expenditure statement should show no gain or loss if all the assumptions are realized.

The difference between the income and the expenditures will differ from 0 if either the income or the expenditures or both are not exactly what has been projected. The purpose of the experience analysis is to explain the sources of differences between the projections and the reality.

15.4.2 Sources of deviations

We will concentrate our experience analysis on the expenditures. Under all financial systems, it is necessary to explain any differences between the projected payments and the actual ones. It is useful to understand the theory behind this. In order to do so, formula 15.2 is used to express the projected payments in 1999, from which formula 15.7 is obtained.

Formula 15.7

$$B(1) = \sum_{d=0}^{8} N_d(0) \times P(d,1) \times M(d+1) \times K(0) \times f(1)$$

Similarly, the actual benefits expenditures can be expressed with:

Formula 15.8

$$B'(1) = \sum_{d=0}^{8} N_d(0) \times P'(d,1) \times M'(d+1) \times K'(0) \times f'(1)$$

where P', M' and f' express the observed variables.

Note that the value of N is a starting value and that there is no deviation associated with it. It was mentioned earlier that K is subject to experience deviations related to factors other than inflation, which is the uneven distribution of terminations by size of average daily benefits.

There will be a loss if the actual payments are larger than the projected ones. This may occur if at least one of the following circumstances occurs:

- The number of benefit recipients is larger than expected.
- The average number of compensated days is larger than expected.
- Inflation is larger than expected.
- The rate of termination of benefit recipients with a daily benefit above the average daily benefit is smaller than the one of benefit recipients under the average.

Of course, there will a gain if the situation is reversed.

In the case of inflation, the experience analysis should consider any potential offset resulting from any deviation between the economic assumptions and the results. Under the fully funded system, higher investment returns may compensate higher inflation, but this offset may not be fully reflected in a single financial year but over a certain period. We will concentrate our attention on the variables related to the compensation of injured workers. Table 15.8 summarizes the experience analysis that the actuary should be in a position to conduct regarding those elements. We know that the total payments are 53,218,135. This amount is larger than the expected one by 1,651,730 (see table 15.6).

For the sake of simplicity, it is assumed that there is no gain or loss from inflation and that the terminations are spread evenly by size of average daily benefit. This means that the average amount paid in 1999 is 52, that is, the basic amount for 1998 (50), indexed by 4 per cent. The two potential sources of gains and losses are then related to the number of recipients and the average number of days. Table 15.8 shows that the number of recipients was higher than expected, but that the number of average days paid per benefit recipient was lower than expected. The total amounts paid were higher than the expected ones, but this is the result of two deviations between the assumptions and the reality that tend to offset each other. The analysis of components is more revealing of trends affecting major cost drivers, and may be of interest to management.

Actuarial practice in social security

Table 15.8 Example of an experience analysis

Injury year	Number of recipients in 1998	Expected			Observed			
		Probability of being a recipient in 1999	Number of recipients in 1999	Average days paid per recipient	Total days	Probability of being a recipient in 1999	Number of recipients in 1999	Average days paid per recipient	Total days
1998	20 535	0.4006	8 226	54.0	444 221	0.4305	8,840	59	521 579
1997	7 943	0.0991	787	288.5	227 093	0.0856	680	245	166 581
1996	876	0.7679	673	239.0	160 771	0.7980	699	254	177 558
1995	632	0.6820	431	280.9	121 075	0.5600	354	263	93 081
1994	432	0.6435	278	138.5	38 502	0.6800	294	220	64 627
All years			10 395	95.4	991 662		10 867	94.2	1 023 426
						Ratio (observed / expected)			
			1.0453				0.9872		1.0320

Table 15.9 Sources of surpluses and deficits

Nature of source	Observed less expected	Impact on payments
Number of recipients in 1999	(10 867 − 10 395) = 472	(472*52*95.4) = 2 340 405
Average number of days paid	(94.2 − 95.4) = −1.2	(−1.2*10 395*52) = −658 775
Sum of components		1 681 630
Observed deviation		1 651 730

Table 15.10 Revised projections at 31 December 1999

| Injury year | Number of days projected in | | | |
	2000	2001	2002	2003
1995	31 543			
1996	133 919	42 493		
1997	124 785	100 021	31 735	
1998	252 748	160 787	128 880	40 894
Total	542 995	303 302	160 615	40 894
Cash flow				
All injury years	29 365 151	17 058 654	9 394 864	2 487 716

It may be interesting to show the contribution of each source of deviation to the total loss in monetary units. Table 15.9 illustrates one way of doing this. Firstly, the differences in experience are calculated for each variable by assuming that all other variables experience their expected value. The sum of these components will be different from the total gain or loss because of their combined impact. The difference may be spread proportionally to each source or disclosed as such. Another way of presenting the experience analysis would be to determine the marginal impact of each variable by gradually replacing the expected values of each variable by the observed ones.

Under the fully funded system, the difference between the expected liability at the end of the year and the actual one is also a source of surplus or deficit. Assume that the actuary updates the present value of the liabilities at the end of 1999 by considering the number of benefit recipients in 1999. For the sake of simplicity, it is assumed that the table of probabilities of being a recipient of benefit is not updated to consider the experience of 1999. Table 15.10 shows the revised projections of the number of days to be paid.

In order to determine the surplus or deficit in the 1999 fiscal year, we need to calculate the liability at the end of 1999. Moreover, the projection for future years has changed. Table 15.11 presents the revised figures at the end of all future years.

The projected liabilities are now smaller than those initially estimated with the data at 31 December 1998. At that date, the difference between the observed liability and the estimated one is −39,811 (53,399,579–53,439,390). This is a sur-

Table 15.11 Revised projected actuarial liability for the injury years up to 1998

Financial year	Liability at 31 December
1999	53 399 579
2000	25 077 313
2001	9 772 357
2002	1 931 395

plus, because the variation between the liabilities at the beginning of the year and those at the end is −46,046,538 rather than −46,006,728.[3] This surplus is related to the number of benefit recipients during 1999 and should be added to the amount that is declared as a deficit related to the number of benefit recipients related to payments in 1999. This contributes to decreasing the deficit related to this element.

It may seem strange that the deviation related to the number of benefit recipients generates a deficit for the payments and a surplus for the liabilities. This is related to the combination by injury year of the deviations regarding the number of benefit recipients. In order to understand this phenomenon, one has to compare Tables 15.6 and 15.10. The number of days to be paid in the future is smaller in Table 15.10 for the years 2000 and 2001. This is mainly related to the injury year 1997, for which the number of benefit recipients was 13.6 per cent lower than estimated in 1999. This has a proportional impact on the estimation of the payments that will be made to recipients of this injury year during the next three years. On the other hand, the experience of injury year 1998 contributed strongly to the deficit related to payments in 1999, because the number of benefit recipients is 7.5 per cent higher than expected, and this deviation applies to a large number of recipients that generate about 45 per cent of the total number of days paid in 1999. When the liabilities are calculated again at the end of 1999, the major impact of the 7.5 per cent deviation on the number of benefit recipients for the year 1998 has already been taken into account and its impact over the next four years does not offset totally the favourable deviation of injury year 1997.

It is important to remember that the revised calculation of the liabilities at 31 December 1999 would be different if the assumptions regarding the probabilities of being a recipient and the average number of days to be paid were modified to integrate the experience of 1999. The updating of assumptions in periodic actuarial valuations is a major actuarial issue. There is no general rule that applies to all circumstances, but the actuary should adopt a consistent approach. The policy regarding the updating of assumptions should be disclosed to the users of the report. The actuary may choose to maintain the same assumptions year after year and change them only when there is substantial evidence that the experience differs from the past. With this approach, the differences in experience are identified in relation to the same reference every year, and when the assumptions are changed, the impact of the change is specifically disclosed and identified as a surplus or deficit.

On the other hand, when the assumptions are consistently updated every year, the estimate of the future experience changes, which is a source of surplus or deficit *per se*. Under this approach, the surplus or deficit arising from the change to the assumption is part of the process and does not have to be reported separately. If the experience is erratic and randomly fluctuates around its mean, this approach does not generate a significant gain in precision. However, when new trends are emerging, it smoothly integrates the appropriate new information in the projection of the estimates.

Another important decision that has to be made is related to the opportunity to project trends or to rely exclusively on past experience to set the assumptions. Under the first approach described above, where the actuary is expected to change the assumptions after new trends are identified and maintain them for a while, past experience provides an objective ground to set the assumptions, and the need to anticipate future changes should be limited. Slight adjustments to observed data are generally appropriate to reflect the most reasonable future expectations. Under the second approach, where assumptions are regularly updated, it is generally preferable to use the experience as such, unless there is a clear indication that it would be completely inappropriate.

The approach does not have to be the same for the valuation of all benefits. For example, the contingencies for which short-term experience is highly credible because large volumes of data are generated in short periods can be handled under the second approach. This is probably often the case for most variables regarding temporary incapacity benefits. The reverse is true for contingencies generating small volumes of data, which generally apply to many variables used in the valuation of long-term incapacity benefits.

The above remarks regarding the updating of assumptions apply when actuarial valuations are made at frequent and periodic intervals. In all other circumstances, the actuary generally selects the assumptions that best correspond to his or her expectations and performs sensitivity analysis to demonstrate the potential range of results to the users of the report.

ANNEX 15A

Table 15 A.1 Illustration of formula 15.3

Injury year	Number of injured	Total number of days paid by duration					
		0	1	2	3	4	5
1991	20 051						35 930
1992	19 267					129 615	44 523
1993	19 431				156 455	100 700	28 966
1994	19 570			237 421	92 567	107 014	
1995	19 655		458 070	235 499	144 534		
1996	20 386	427 650	400 496	204 421			
1997	20 092	509 327	438 984				
1998	20 535	479 970					

	Total number of days paid by duration per 20 000 injured					
1991						35 765
1992					127 161	43 680
1993				159 201	102 468	29 474
1994			242 638	94 601	109 365	
1995		471 484	242 395	148 766		
1996	443 920	415 733	212 198			
1997	508 032	437 867				
1998	483 305					
Average	478 419	441 695	232 410	134 189	112 998	36 306

Notes

[1] See Annex 15A.
[2] $71.27 = 23.2 + 0.4006 * 54.0 + 0.0397 * 288.5 + 0.0305 * 239.0 + 0.0208 * 280.9 + 0.0134 * 138.5$.
[3] This is surplus because the observed amount of expense is smaller than the expected one.

PERMANENT INCAPACITY AND SURVIVORSHIP BENEFITS   16

This chapter deals with permanent incapacity and survivorship cash benefits related to injuries that occur in the workplace. Given that both benefits are generally paid out over a long period of time, the methodology required for their actuarial valuation is quite similar. The first section of the chapter discusses the main features of these benefits that need to be considered for the actuarial valuations. The second section presents the formulae used for the financial projections and the third discusses all other items relevant to actuarial valuations, such as the selection of assumptions and the experience analysis.

16.1 LEGISLATIVE PROVISIONS

The common characteristic of permanent incapacity and survivorship benefits is the long period over which these benefits are expected to be paid in many schemes. This is a general rule, but a significant percentage of plans also provide lump sums, which are generally paid within a few years following the injury. This chapter focuses on the actuarial methodology related to periodic payments. The actuarial techniques regarding lump-sum benefits can be considered a particular case, since they consist of one single payment; a few remarks on this type of benefit are included when necessary to avoid any ambiguity.

16.1.1 Permanent incapacity benefits

Permanent incapacity benefits are paid after the medical condition of the injured person has stabilized and the worker has gone through vocational rehabilitation programmes, whenever these are available. There are different rationales leading to the determination of permanent incapacity benefits. Some are linked to the degree of impairment (the degree to which a person is less than a whole person, irrespective of the loss of earning capacity, also called loss of bodily functions) and others are related to the loss of earning capacity, either actual or presumed. When the disability is total, the replacement ratio is generally the same as for temporary incapacity benefits. The systems that are designed according to the loss of earnings approach also pay a lump-sum benefit for permanent impairment, which is often not earnings-related but age-related. The rationale behind the compensation of permanent incapacity does not influence the actuarial techniques that are used. However, the costing of a change of system, switching, for example, from an impairment approach to an earning-capacity approach, is a complex issue, because past experience is no longer directly usable. The information required to adjust the statistical data to the new provisions may not be readily available.

When the disability is partial, the options for determining benefits are more complex and varied. Benefits are expressed as a percentage of the benefits paid for total incapacity or are defined as the presumed or actual earnings loss. The administration is generally more costly under the loss of earnings approach because determining the loss of earning capacity requires medical and occupational expertise and because the periodic re-examination of the injured worker may be necessary to ensure that benefits match the loss. The adjustments of benefits to changes in the earnings situation of the injured may be designed to give workers an incentive to return to their previous earnings situation. The provisions dealing with this issue will directly influence the experience of the plan regarding the level of benefits or even the need to compensate at all when the injured worker subsequently returns to work with no wage loss.

Benefits for total disability are generally paid for life, a specified duration or until a presumed retirement age at which a retirement benefit starts to be paid. The plan's provisions dictate if the pension paid after the retirement age should be charged totally or partially to the EIOD system. Provisions regarding the duration of benefits for partial incapacity may differ from those provisions of total disability. Given this and other diverging features, the actuarial techniques used for total and partial incapacity may have to be different.

An important characteristic of permanent disability benefits is whether or not they are indexed. As is the case for any pension system, the cost of this provision is high and its assessment requires the use of consistent economic assumptions over a long-term period.

The management philosophy and the economic conditions may significantly influence the experience of permanent incapacity. Familiarity with the medical procedures and the claims management practices, including their past evolution, is essential for a correct assessment. Comparison between schemes of neighbouring countries is becoming more frequent and, indeed, unavoidable, with the globalization of the economy. Two apparently similar plans in countries with few differences in their industry mix may show significantly different costs because of diverging emphases on facilities regarding the return to work.

16.1.2 Survivorship benefits

When a worker dies due to a work-related accident or disease, benefits are paid to the survivors; the surviving spouse and children are always considered. If there are no survivors or if they are not dependent on the deceased, other relatives, such as the parents or siblings, may be considered. Benefits may take the form of a pension or a lump sum. In either case, the benefits may or may not be earnings-related. In the latter case, they may be limited to a minimum or maximum amount. The duration of the benefit to the spouse may be payable for life or terminate under certain circumstances. The limitation may be based on duration, attainment of a specified age, remarriage or the presence of dependent children. Benefits to children terminate at a specified age or can be maintained after its attainment under school attendance conditions or indefinitely in case of severe disability. As is the case for permanent incapacity benefits, benefits may or may not be indexed. The definition of spouse can vary broadly among countries. For example, spouses of the same sex are now accepted in some countries and the marital status of an injured worker may include obligations towards ex-spouses or more than one spouse, which creates the need to set rules concerning the rights of each of them.

Most plans also pay the deceased's funeral expenses, up to a specified amount. The valuation of these benefits requires less complex actuarial techniques because of the small size of the amounts and their payment soon after death. Techniques related to this type of benefit will be mainly covered in the next chapter, which deals with the payments of services.

From an actuarial point of view, work-related deaths are characterized by low frequency and the high amounts involved, which makes the experience subject to volatility. Deaths are generally concentrated in high-risk industries, such as mining, construction and the transport sectors. Substantial changes in the mix of these industries or targeted intensive prevention campaigns may significantly influence the incidence of survivorship benefits.

16.2 METHODOLOGY FOR FINANCIAL PROJECTIONS

The nature of financial projections requested from the actuary depends on the financial system. In fully funded and mixed systems, the calculation of liabilities related to pensions in payment at the valuation date has to be performed at the end of each financial year. The calculation of these liabilities is relatively simple in terms of actuarial modelling and the selection of assumptions. Some financial systems require the projection of the value of new pension awards to set rates.

Actuarial practice in social security

Fully funded systems require the calculation of liabilities for pensions in payment at the valuation date and for those to be awarded to workers whose injuries occurred before the valuation date (and are probably cashing temporary incapacity benefits at the date of valuation). Finally, projections regarding injuries that will occur in the future and the pensions they will generate are also needed for general budgeting and social policy planning.

This chapter has been organized so that the basic formulae are presented first, with successive ones referring back to these basic formulae. For example, the projection of the cash flow related to the new awards of pensions can be obtained through using the formulae developed for the projection of pensions in payment. Most formulae apply to permanent incapacity and survivorship benefits. Major differences will be mentioned when it is considered necessary to avoid any ambiguity.

16.2.1 Pensions in payment at the valuation date

The cash flow associated with the projection of pensions paid at the valuation date is obtained through the application of formulae that are of the same nature as those that apply to pensioners of other parts of the social security scheme, such as old-age and invalidity.

For a pension of amount $K(0)$ in payment at the valuation date, the expected amount to be paid in year t after the valuation can be expressed as in formula 16.1 below $(B_{[x+u]}(t))$. It is assumed that:

- pension payments are due at the beginning of each month;
- the age of the benefit recipient was x at the onset of the pension;
- the pension has been paid for u years at the date of the valuation;
- the cash-flow projection is made the day before the next pension payment is due.

Formula 16.1 is fairly refined because it considers the time elapsed since the award of the pension in the setting of termination assumptions. This refinement is rarely used in the projection of survivors' benefits and applies mainly to recovery assumptions of permanent incapacity benefits.

Formula 16.1

$$B_{[x+u]}(t) = 12\,K(t) \times {}_{t-1}p_{[x+u]} \times (1 - {}^{11}/_{24}\,q_{[x+u]+t-1})$$

where:

$K(t)$ = Monthly pension in year t after the valuation date
${}_{t-1}p_{[x+u]}$ = Probability that the pension is still in payment at the end of year $t-1$

Permanent incapacity and survivorship benefits

$q_{[x+u]+t-1}$ = Probability that the pension terminates during year t

t = Number of years between the year of payment and the year of valuation; $t = 1, 2, 3\ldots$ (it is implicitly assumed that the date of valuation is the last day of a financial year, which is why t is assumed to start at 1)

The value of the pension $K(t)$ is related to the value at the date of valuation and an inflation factor. $K(t)$ is a value that is unique to each benefit recipient and it may be practical to add up all the monthly benefits paid to all recipients of the same age and the same duration. $K(t)$ can be expressed in terms of the pension paid at the date of valuation and an inflation factor $f(t)$ in such a manner that $K(t) = K(0) \times f(t)$ – see formula 16.1. For permanent partial incapacity benefits, it might be appropriate to add another source of variation, which would represent the partial recoveries. If the provisions of the plan include reviews of pensions after they have been awarded, then $K(t)$ could be expressed in terms of the indexing factor and the percentage of the full pension that is paid. Algebraically, we have $K(t) = K(0) \times f(t) \times g(u+t)$, where $g()$ is the set of values indicating the relation between the percentage of the pension paid in year $u+t$ years after the onset of disability. This total duration is generally more significant than the duration since the valuation date.

The formula assumes that terminations are distributed uniformly during each financial year. When there is more than one cause of decrement, then the probability $q_{[x+u]+t-1}$ is the sum of all the decrements. The probability $_{t-1}p_{[x+u]}$ is the cumulative product of annual probabilities for a pensioner at the valuation date to remain a benefit recipient until the end of year $t-1$. This can be expressed as follows:

Formula 16.2

$$_{t-1}p_{[x+u]} = \prod_{j=0}^{t-2}(1 - {_1q^{(1)}_{[x+u]+j}} - {_1q^{(2)}_{[x+u]+j}} - \ldots - {_1q^{(n)}_{[x+u]+j}}) \text{ for } t > 1$$

and $_0p_{[x+u]} = 1$

where:

$_1q^{(i)}_{[x+u]+j}$ = Probability that a pension in payment at the end of year j after the valuation date ceases to be in payment during the year for reason i.

At a valuation date, the liabilities for all pensions in payment are obtained by discounting the cash flow that is projected for each benefit recipient according to the following formula:

Actuarial practice in social security

Formula 16.3

$$PV_{[x+u]}(0) = \sum_{t=1}^{\omega-x-u} B_{[x+u]}(t) \div (1+i)^{t-\frac{1}{2}}$$

where:

ω = Last age for which the probability of survival is greater than 0

When there is a full indexing of benefits, the relevant assumption is the real rate of interest. This real rate can be used as such in formula 16.3 as long as the indexing factor for the pension in formula 16.1 is set at 0.

When cash flows are unnecessary, it may be practical to make tables showing the present value applying to a monthly pension of one monetary unit. This is an annuity factor and it can be calculated for each age x through the application of formula 16.3, where the value 1 must be assigned to $K(0)$. However, functions $f()$ and $g()$ applying to the amount of pension must remain built-in in formula 16.1 in order to reflect what they are intended to model (indexing and partial incapacity variation) correctly. In fact, many valuation systems are now designed in such a manner that the calculation of liabilities is made through the application of these factors to the total benefit payments by individual age (and not using the duration since the onset of benefits) at the valuation date. The advantages of designing a model that projects cash flows rather than using present value factors only are that it makes the experience analysis easier and the sensitivity testing more flexible.

16.2.2 Present value of new awards at date of award

The present value of a new award is determined through the use of formulae similar to those presented in the preceding section. The formulae are similar, but the meaning of some factors may differ. However, if a pension is awarded exactly on the date of valuation with the first payment due the following day, then the present value of the award of a pension $K(0)$ to a person age x (NA_x) can be calculated by using formula 16.3, u being set at 0.

Formula 16.4

$$NA_x = PV_{[x]}$$

Formula 16.1 can be redesigned slightly in order to express the present value of a pension of 1 payable monthly. New symbols are used for terms with a different meaning:

Formula 16.5

$$NAA_x = 12 \sum_{tt=1}^{\omega-x} {}_{tt-1}p_x \times (1 - {}^{11}\!/_{24}\, q_{x+tt-1}) \times f(tt-1) \div (1+i)^{tt-\frac{1}{2}}$$

where:

$_{tt-1}p_x$ = Probability that a pension awarded to a person age x is still in payment at age $x + tt - 1$ (tt does not refer to a financial year but to the duration in terms of years since the onset of the pension)

q_{x+tt-1} = Probability that the pension terminates while the pensioner is age $x + tt - 1$

$f(tt-1)$ = Indexing factor of the pension until the $tt - 1$ year following the award (set to 1 if no indexing at all)

$tt - 1$ = Number of years after the award, where $tt > 1$

One might be interested to project, by financial year, the cash flow associated with a new award by combining formulae 16.1 and 16.5. This is discussed in Annex 16A.

16.2.3 Future awards for past injuries

Some actuarial analysis may require a projection of the new awards expected to be made after a valuation date resulting from all the injuries that have occurred before and on the valuation date. In order to do so, the number of new awards in each year after the valuation date has to be estimated. The techniques used to project this number generally refer to the concept of injury year.

There are many ways of expressing relations between variables. The following formula illustrates one such approach. It refers to awards made to benefit recipients of age x in the projection year t, and represents their value in the year t after the valuation.

Formula 16.6

$$PINA_x(t) = \sum_{d=0}^{m-t} I_d \times LT_x(d+t) \times K_x(0) \times f(t) \times NAA_x \text{ (for } t \leq m\text{)},$$

$$PINA_x(t) = 0 \text{ (for } t > m\text{)}$$

where:

$PINA_x(t)$ = Total value of awards to recipients of age x that start to be compensated in year t for injuries that occurred before the valuation date

Actuarial practice in social security

I_d	=	Number of new injuries that occurred d years before valuation year, $0 \leq d \leq m$
$LT_x(d+t)$	=	Factor applicable to I_d in projecting the number of new awards of pensions to people of age x in year $d+t$ after the injury year
$K_x(0)$	=	Monthly pension to benefit recipients of age x in the year of valuation
$f(t)$	=	Indexing factor of the pension between the year of valuation and the financial year t, $t = 1, 2, 3 \ldots$
NAA_x	=	Present value of a monthly benefit pension of 1 paid to an injured worker of age x (formula 16.6)
d	=	Difference between the year of valuation and the year of injury, $0 \leq d \leq m$
t	=	Number of years between the year of award and the year of valuation; $t = 1, 2, 3 \ldots m$ (it is implicitly assumed that the date of valuation is the last day of a financial year, which is why t is assumed to start at 1)
m	=	Maximum value of u for which $LT_x(u)$ is larger than 0

The factor $LT_x(d+t)$ can be related to the total number of new injuries during a year or to any other exposure indicator that would be considered more relevant. Techniques for determining the number of new cases vary significantly between incapacity and survivorship benefits. The formula should then be adjusted accordingly; the product $I \times LT$ should be replaced by the appropriate term. More will be said in the following section on assumptions. The basic amount of pension $K_x(0)$ is the one applicable in the year of valuation.

The cash flow corresponding to pension payments can be obtained by appropriately developing NAA_x. Note that formula 16.6 projects the present value of new awards in each of the financial years following the valuation year. If the present value is wished-for at the valuation date, each of these values must be discounted by the appropriate factor, that is $(1+I)^{t-\frac{1}{2}}$. These actuarial liabilities are sometimes called outstanding claims, which indicate that the liabilities apply to past injuries but that a final decision regarding the permanent incapacity has not yet been made.

16.2.4 Future awards for future injuries

The actuary may be asked to make projections that include the financial outcomes of injuries occurring in the projection period. The approach for doing so is the same as the one presented in the preceding subsection, except that the number of new injuries that is used for the projection of new awards is related to injury years after the date of valuation rather than those before it.

Permanent incapacity and survivorship benefits

The following expresses the value of new awards made to people of age x in year t.

Formula 16.7

$$FINA_x(t) = \sum_{j=\max(1,t-m)}^{t} I_j \times LT_x(t-j) \times K_x(j) \times f(t-j) \times NAA_x$$

where:

$FINA_x(t)$ = Total value of awards to recipients of age x that start to be compensated in year t for injuries that occurred after the valuation date

I_j = Number of new injuries occurring j years after the valuation date

$K_x(j)$ = Monthly pension to new benefit recipients of age x in injury year j

$f(t-j)$ = The indexing factor of the pension between the year of injury and the financial year t, which is the year of the award

This formula assumes that the value of the monthly benefit is available for the year of injury. This value is usually determined from the corresponding values in the year of valuation and the assumptions regarding the increase in salaries between the valuation year and the year of injury. The factor $f(t-j)$ would normally be related to the index base of pensions.

16.2.5 Successive liabilities

For the purposes of the experience analysis, it is necessary to express the liabilities at the end of the financial year in terms of the liabilities at the beginning of the year and the elements that contribute to their variations during the year. If we consider formula 16.3, then the liabilities at the end of the first year after the valuation date can be expressed as follows:

Formula 16.8

$$PV_{[x+u]}(1) = PV_{[x+u]}(0) \times (1+i) - B_{[x+u]}(1) \times (1+i)^{\frac{1}{2}}$$

This formula can be generalized and we may define the actuarial liabilities at the end of any year n after the valuation date as follows:

Formula 16.9

$$PV_{[x+u]}(n) = \left(\sum_{t=n+1}^{\omega-x-u} B_{[x+u]}(t) \div (1+i)^{t-n-\frac{1}{2}} \right)$$

Formula 16.8 can also be expressed as follows:

Formula 16.10

$$PV_{[x+u]}(n) = PV_{[x+u]}(n-1) + I - B_{[x+u]}(n)$$

$$I = PV_{[x+u]}(n-1) \times i - B_{[x+u]}(n) \times ((1+i)^{\frac{1}{2}} - 1)$$

The liabilities at the end of any year are equal to those at the end of the preceding year, plus the interest earned on the fund, minus the payments made during the year. Of course, this happens in real life if all assumptions are perfectly realized, which is never the case, and this is why there are gains and losses. It is interesting to present formula 16.10 in an accounting perspective (see 16.11): on the left we have the expected income and on the right the expected expenses, which are the sum of the variation in liabilities and the payments. This former term is generally negative in the case of pension annuities but it can be positive when the probabilities of termination are high in the current year.

Formula 16.11

$$I = (PV_{[x+u]}(n) - PV_{[x+u]}(n-1)) + B_{[x+u]}(n)$$

16.3 ASSUMPTIONS

The formulae presented in the preceding section require the setting of assumptions according to variables that can be classified under three headings:

- terminations of pensions in payment;
- the number and demographic profile of recipients of pensions expected to be awarded after the valuation date;
- the amount of benefits related to pensions awarded after the valuation date.

The above classification applies to both permanent incapacity and survivorship pensions. The methods required for the analysis of statistical data are similar for both types of pensions, but the specific contingencies to be measured or their relative importance do differ. For example, the number of new permanent incapacity awards related to past injuries at a specific valuation date is generally significant, while the corresponding number of survivorship awards is fairly small.

As for pension benefits, the development of the experience is sometimes spread over many years, in contrast to temporary incapacity benefits. The actuary may be faced with a total lack of experience data from the country for a while and will then have to rely on outside sources and sound judgement. The monitoring of the emerging experience is especially important in these circumstances and the actuary has to adjust the assumptions gradually in order to integrate the information. Disclosing any element of uncertainty to the management of the institution is a major ethical issue.

16.3.1 Terminations of pensions in payment

Termination assumptions can be divided into three headings: mortality (which is a necessary assumption for both permanent incapacity and survivorship pensions); causes other than death for permanent incapacity; and causes other than death for survivorship benefits.

Mortality

The methodology and principles regarding the construction of a mortality table with the experience data of a retirement system also apply to employment injury schemes. Specific additional considerations regarding EIOD schemes are discussed below.

Permanent incapacity

After a pension has been in force for several years, death generally becomes the major source of termination of a permanent incapacity pension. In the early years after the award, however, recovery may be more significant. Mortality rates vary by sex. The mortality rates of pensioners generally vary according to the nature of the injury (accident or disease) and the degree of impairment. The mortality rates of pensioners suffering specific degenerative diseases, such as silicosis or asbestosis, are higher than those of pensioners whose impairment is due to an accident or injuries classified as a disease but that does not really affect vital parts of the body (such as tendinitis or bursitis).

The mortality of pensioners suffering a severe impairment is generally worse than that of the total population. However, those with a slighter degree of impairment experience lower mortality rates than those of the total population. The explanation for this is that workers are generally in better physical condition than the subset of the population that is not in the workforce because of the selection process made by employers; working requires one to be healthy and a slight impairment does not necessarily change the basic health status of

Table 16.1 Illustration of an adjustment to a population mortality table

Degree of impairment (as a %)	Accidents and diseases other than lung diseases		Lung diseases	
	a	b	a	b
1–10	0.85	0.0025	1.05	0.007
11–25	0.98	0.0010	1.65	−0.006
26–50	1.09	0.0022	1.44	0.011
51–100	1.39	0.0018	2.03	0.021

injured workers. A large volume of data is needed to construct a mortality table that correctly reflects the specific experience of a scheme. When experience data start to be available, a comparison of observed deaths to expected deaths according to the general population table can indicate the general level of mortality of pensioners and suggest appropriate modifications.

When the volume of experience data is sufficient, it is possible to construct mortality tables through a technique that reproduces the observed number of deaths and their average age at death (see Annex 16B). The mortality rates for the EIOD scheme can be calculated through formula 16.12.

Formula 16.12

$$q_x^1 = a \times q_x + b$$

where:

q^1 = Mortality rate according to the nature and degree of impairment

q = Mortality rate according to the population table

Parameters a and b should be calculated by using the most recent experience. They apply uniformly over all ages of the basic mortality table. Illustrative values of these parameters are shown in table 16.1. However, as parameters a and b are based on a particular experience, they will vary according to the case under study.

When the mortality rates of the reference mortality table are projected into the future in order to reflect the potential improvements in life expectancy, the actuary must determine if it is appropriate to use the projected rates for the mortality rates of permanent incapacity pensioners. It is reasonable to assume that the improvement rate of the mortality of permanent incapacity pensioners may differ from that of the general population, but the volume of data is rarely sufficient to conduct a study that stands on its own and would support the assumption. Assuming no improvement at all is unrealistic and may underestimate the liabilities.

Survivorship

Assumptions regarding the mortality of dependants are generally based on the mortality of the total population. The mortality rates of the spouses of workers may be appropriately estimated by the mortality of the general population. Whenever the mortality of spouses of deceased workers is different, it may tend to be lower than that of the general population. Improvements in the life expectancy of the population apply to the spouses.

The mortality of the general population also applies to other types of dependants, such as children, parents or other relatives. The mortality rates of children are often set at 0 for the sake of simplicity. Rates are very low at ages over 0 and the relatively small volume of benefits paid to children does not justify the carrying out of elaborate analyses in order to set the appropriate bases.

Recovery of permanent incapacity pensioners

Total incapacity

Rates of recovery depend on the design of the system and the administrative policies regarding the verification of the pensioner's situation, when such provisions exist. In many situations, the recovery rates of totally disabled pensioners can be set at 0. In situations where the possibility of recovery exists, such recovery happens in the first few years after the onset of the pension. The experience then develops relatively rapidly so that appropriate data can become available to assess the recovery rates quite early at short durations. Recovery rates are generally small and volatile. Consistency from valuation to valuation is desirable and the actuary should avoid changing the assumptions in the absence of any clear evidence of modifications to the trend. The most significant variable for the application of recovery assumptions is the duration since the onset of the disability. Other variables, such as age and the nature of the injury, may also be relevant.

Partial incapacity

The recovery of partially permanent incapacity pensioners can be a more difficult issue, especially when compensation is based on the loss of earning capacity rather than the degree of impairment. Full recovery has to be distinguished from partial recovery. Full recovery takes place when the pension terminates. Partial recovery occurs when the pension decreases because of changes in the earnings situation of the benefit recipient. Some systems also include the possibility of increases in pensions because of a further deterioration in the worker's condition. This can be considered as a negative termination, which needs to be carefully measured in order to avoid any confusion with the indexing of benefits.

An illustration of an analysis of the termination experience related to partial incapacity is presented below. At the time the analysis was made, the plan had been in force for 12 years. The experience of the five most recent financial years was analysed. Thus, there is no experience available for pensions that have been

Table 16.2 Terminations of partial incapacity pensions

	Experience of the fourth year preceding the valuation year			Experience of the year ending on the valuation date		
(1) Duration	(2) Exposure	(3) Termination	(4) Rate	(5) Exposure	(6) Termination	(7) Rate
0	66 270 657	9 570 070	0.1444	64 276 757	6 829 791	0.1063
1	119 726 372	9 222 252	0.0770	146 538 018	8 724 738	0.0595
2	71 262 781	3 115 024	0.0437	149 791 338	3 534 850	0.0236
3	48 475 946	1 858 670	0.0383	159 581 424	7 743 697	0.0485
4	36 734 581	1 418 883	0.0386	137 641 887	10 056 528	0.0731
5	23 203 564	824 827	0.0355	108 007 369	1 334 995	0.0124
6	12 239 038	334 364	0.0273	62 243 690	479 544	0.0077
7	4 367 238	27 328	0.0063	41 415 266	591 614	0.0143
8	448 648	0	0.0000	32 201 547	1 420 711	0.0441
9	n.a.	n.a.	n.a.	19 626 450	1 468 028	0.0748
10	n.a.	n.a.	n.a.	9 566 597	546 246	0.0571
11	n.a.	n.a.	n.a.	3 473 990	108 541	0.0312
12	n.a.	n.a.	n.a.	266 614	−21 474	−0.0805
Total	**382 728 825**	**26 371 418**	**0.0689**	**934 630 947**	**42 817 809**	**0.0458**

n.a. = not applicable.

paid for more than 12 years and the experience is fairly limited at durations 7 and over. Table 16.2 includes only parts of the data. The complete set of data is shown in Annex 16C.

The period of exposure runs from the beginning of a financial year to its end, for example, from 1 January to 31 December. The valuation date is 31 December. The duration in column (1) is the number of years since the award of the pension at the beginning of the financial year rounded to the nearest integer. For example, the numbers reported for duration 0 refer to pensions awarded in the last half of the year immediately preceding the start of the exposure period; numbers reported for duration 1 refer to pensions awarded in the first half of the year immediately preceding the start of the exposure period and the last half of the year before the year preceding the exposure period, and so on. The exposure is the amount of pension liabilities at the beginning of the exposure period reduced by a proportion of the liabilities of terminations for death or any reason that is not recovery. The proportion is the fraction of the year remaining after their termination. Amounts shown under terminations are the pension liabilities related to the part of the pension that is terminated. The rate is the ratio of terminations to the exposure. In this particular case, the liabilities were chosen as the exposure unit in order to reflect the financial impact of terminations on liabilities. Younger pensioners and those with large pensions are implicitly given more weight.

The exposure in the year ending at the valuation date is much more important than the one of the fourth year preceding it. This is due to the maturing pro-

Figure 16.1 Observed recovery rates

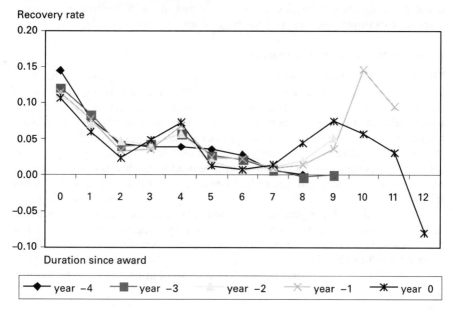

cess of the system. As time passes, the number of new awards increases in each financial year for a certain number of years. For example, there were five injury years potentially contributing to the exposure at duration 2 in the fourth year before the valuation year and there are nine in the year ending at the valuation date. It is impossible to have an exposure at duration 9 and over for the oldest year. The experience emerges very slowly at those durations. For example, the exposure at duration 10 (9,566,597) of the most recent year corresponds to the cohort of pensions in payment at duration 6 (12,239,038) four years earlier.

Rates vary by duration, and the pattern of increases that is observed reflects the provisions that stipulate reviews of the earning capacity at specific intervals after the award. Figure 16.1 shows the curve of the observed rates for each of the years ending with the valuation year (year −4 to year 0). Extreme values have been omitted.

In order to obtain the best estimation of the experience, the terminations at each duration are added together over the five financial years and the ratio is made against the corresponding sum of the exposure. The experience can be used with great confidence for durations 0 to 8, but for higher durations the experience data are of little help. It is clear that the actuary has to rely on judgement and outside sources to set the assumptions for the remaining durations.

Additional analysis should be performed in order to ensure that the duration is the most significant variable to be considered in the modelling of recovery rates. For example, age, sex and the type of injury should also be tested.

Terminations of survivorship pensions

The sole reason for the termination of pensions awarded to spouses (other than death) is remarriage. The incidence of remarriage varies according to the age of the spouse and is related to the social and cultural practices of a community, which are likely to change over time. Given that the number of spouses receiving benefits is generally not high enough to provide statistically credible experience for all ages, the review of this assumption can only be made at intervals of a few years. The experience of the scheme should be used as much as possible and completed when necessary with the experience of other comparable social security schemes.

Terminations of benefits to dependent children are generally related to school attendance. The terminations are generally concentrated around a few ages following attainment of majority, so that the experience can generally be assessed confidently with the data of the plan. In the absence of these data at onset, statistics of the general population on school attendance can be helpful.

16.3.2 Future awards

This section deals with the determination of the factors $LT_x(d+t)$ that appear in formulae 16.6 and 16.7. These factors apply to the number of injured workers (or any other relevant exposure) of the injury year j that have reached age x in the year t (which is called the "duration after injury") when the permanent (incapacity or survivorship) benefit starts to be paid to them. The award of permanent incapacity benefits generally extends over many years after the injury year because the stabilization period of the medical condition and of the rehabilitation of injured workers varies according to the nature of the traumas suffered. Relapses occurring many years after the injury may also give rise to awards of new long-term benefits, which must be linked for proper analysis and costing to the year of the injury. The awards of survivor benefits generated by workers suffering an accident is generally concentrated in the injury year and the year immediately following, but those resulting from disease are generally spread over many years after the disease has been first reported. In Chapter 14, it was mentioned that the injury year associated with disease is the year when it is reported to the scheme.

Age is an important characteristic of the recipients because it determines the cost of the pension. A life pension awarded to a 60-year-old worker is less costly than the same pension awarded to a 20-year-old worker. Basically, there are two ways of considering the age of benefit recipients. The simpler way is to determine the average age of benefit recipients, which may be convenient in some cir-

Permanent incapacity and survivorship benefits

Table 16.3 Example: New awards of permanent incapacity benefits per 100,000 injuries

Number of years after the injury year	Age at the time of injury						Cumulative distribution
	−34	35–44	45–54	55–59	60+	Total	
0	0	0	0	3	10	13	0.0151
1	3	0	3	24	89	119	0.1486
2	3	3	11	37	54	108	0.2691
3	4	7	19	36	19	85	0.3645
4	4	11	21	26	13	75	0.4480
5	4	12	24	17	0	57	0.5116
6	5	12	22	11	0	50	0.5672
7	5	12	20	6	0	43	0.6154
8	5	13	17	4	0	39	0.6591
9	5	12	15	3	0	35	0.6993
10	5	12	13	0	0	30	0.7327
11	5	11	10	0	0	26	0.7623
12	5	10	8	0	0	23	0.7876
13	5	8	6	0	0	19	0.8089
14	5	7	5	0	0	17	0.8271
15	5	6	4	0	0	15	0.8431
16	4	5	4	0	0	13	0.8580
17	4	5	3	0	0	12	0.8725
18	4	5	0	0	0	9	0.8829
19	4	5	0	0	0	9	0.8932
20	4	5	0	0	0	9	0.9034
21	4	5	0	0	0	9	0.9133
22	4	4	0	0	0	8	0.9227
23	4	4	0	0	0	8	0.9314
24	4	3	0	0	0	7	0.9394
25	4	2	0	0	0	6	0.9466
26	4	2	0	0	0	6	0.9530
27	4	1	0	0	0	5	0.9592
28	4	0	0	0	0	4	0.9637
29	4	0	0	0	0	4	0.9682
30	4	0	0	0	0	4	0.9726
31	4	0	0	0	0	4	0.9769
32	4	0	0	0	0	4	0.9809
33	3	0	0	0	0	3	0.9885
35	3	0	0	0	0	3	0.9919
36	3	0	0	0	0	3	0.9949
37	2	0	0	0	0	2	0.9977
38	2	0	0	0	0	2	1.0000
Total	152	182	205	167	186	891	–

Note: if in one particular year t, the number of new injuries is 125,000, then the expected number of injured workers in the age group 35–44 in the year of injury who will be awarded a pension $t + 10$ years later is 37.5 ((125,000 * 30) / 100,000).

cumstances, especially when the benefit is paid as a lump sum (or as a temporary pension over a short period) and there is no need to follow-up any cash flow over a long period. At the other extreme, the most sophisticated method consists of modelling a distribution by individual ages to reflect, as accurately as possible, the number of new awards by attained age. Such a distribution can be cum-

> **Box 16.1   Alternative estimation of new awards**
>
> In table 16.3, the number of future awards is linked to the number of injured workers in the injury years. For a particular injury year, the number of future awards is independent of the number already awarded. The number of future new awards could be estimated in relation to the total number of past awards for each injury year. Then, the cumulative distribution (last column of the table) would be used for calculating the total number of new awards.
>
> Assume that, for a particular injury year, the total number of injuries is 100,000 and that the number of permanent incapacity awards is 350 at the end of the fourth year after the injury year. The expected number of new awards according to the table is 400. At that duration, the ratio of past awards to total awards is 0.4480 according to the table. If the distribution of new awards over time is considered more reliable than the numbers of new awards at each duration, then the expected number of new awards for years 5 and over is obtained through the following calculation 350 * (1 / 0.448−1).
>
> The alternative approach consists of modifying at each valuation the estimation of the ultimate number of awards for a particular injury year according to the development of the experience. The approach described in the text maintains at each valuation date the estimation of the remaining future new awards without taking into consideration the past development of each injury year.

bersome to manage because a distribution for each year after the injury year is required. This may be difficult to build because the volume of data is generally not sufficient to support such refined modelling. The usual compromise consists of working with age-grouping techniques for the setting of assumptions.

Table 16.3 shows the number of new awards related to permanent incapacity per 100,000 new injuries with at least one day of time lost in a year. This table is shown for illustrative purposes only, and cannot be considered typical of the experience of new permanent incapacity awards. Such experience is highly dependent on the industry mix, the design of benefits and the disability management practices. Under an earnings loss system, there would be two tables, one for total loss of earning capacity and another one for the new awards to workers suffering a partial loss of capacity. Such a table is generally built by using the experience of many years in order to obtain a sufficient volume of data.

Each number in the table indicates the expected number of new awards in the corresponding year after the injury year. The age grouping refers to the age in the year of injury, and the actual age of workers in the year of the award is equal to the age at injury, plus the number of years that have elapsed since the injury year. The central age of each age group can be used as an indication of the average age in the year of injury, or an exact age at the time of injury can be calculated.

The table shows that the total number of permanent incapacity awards is 891 per 100,000 newly injured workers in one year. In this example, the number of new awards is spread over 39 years, but the majority of new awards occur a few years after the injury year. New awards made many years after the injury are usually the result of relapses and aggravations (partial loss of earning capacity becoming total). When the system is newer and the emerging experience indicates that the number of awards will extend over many years into the future, the actuary needs to rely on judgement to shape the tail of the curve of the number of new awards. The estimates must then be supported by an in-depth understanding of claims management practices and by the appropriate sensitivity analysis.

16.3.3 Basic amount of benefits related to new awards

This section deals with the assumption regarding K and $f(\ )$ in formulae 16.6 and 16.7. The factor K represents the yearly amount of benefit that is awarded to the injured in monetary units of the valuation year. This amount varies by age and is set by considering two components: the insured earnings of injured workers and their loss of earning capacity or degree of impairment. The factor $f(\ )$ considers the impact of economic factors, such as the increase in wages or inflation after the award, depending on the provisions of the scheme.

The assumptions regarding the basic amount of benefit are generally determined separately for the injured workers who are paid a full indemnity and for those who are paid a partial indemnity. It is practical to express the basic amount of benefits for permanent incapacity in terms of the corresponding basic amount for temporary incapacity. This latter amount is a statistical data that matures rapidly, and the observed correlation between both types of benefits can be used to set the assumptions regarding the amounts related to future awards of permanent incapacity benefits. For totally disabled workers, this ratio turns around 100 per cent, but it may be different because, within each age group, the earnings profile of the subset of injured workers who become totally disabled tends to differ from that of temporary incapacity benefits recipients.

Note

[1] At the valuation date, the present value of $PINA_x(t)$ is $PINA_x(t) \div (1+i)^{t-0.5}$.

Actuarial practice in social security

ANNEX 16A CASH FLOW OF NEW AWARDS IN TERMS OF FINANCIAL YEARS

A new award can be made at any time during a financial year. For that reason, payments in the year of the award do not cover the whole year and some projections may require cash flows by the financial year. The purpose of this annex is to rearrange formula 16.6 in terms of financial years instead of years of payment of the pension.

We have to make an assumption regarding the date of the award. The simplest one is used. The onset is at mid-year and six monthly payments will be made during this first year.

Formula 16A.1

$$NAA_x \approx 6(1 - {}^5\!/_{24} q_x) \div (1+i)^{\frac{1}{4}} + 12 \sum_{t=1}^{\omega-x} {}_{t-\frac{1}{2}}p_x \times (1 - {}^{11}\!/_{24}\, q_{x+t-\frac{1}{2}})$$
$$\times f(t) \div (1+i)^t$$

The differences between formulae 16A.1 and 16.5 are related to:

- the probabilities of survival and decrements, which are at fractional ages in one and at integers in the other;
- the interest discounting factors that apply in the middle of each individual period considered in the projection.

ANNEX 16B TECHNICAL NOTE ON MORTALITY TABLES BY DEGREE OF IMPAIRMENT

DEFINITION OF VARIABLES

$E(x)$ = Exposure at exact age x
$q(x)$ = Mortality rate indicated in the reference table
$\emptyset(x)$ = Number of registered deaths
$D(x)$ = Number of expected deaths according to the reference table $q(x)$
$D'(x)$ = Number of expected deaths according to the new table $q'(x)$
$q'(x)$ = $a \times q(x) + b$
$D(x)$ = $E(x) \times q(x)$
$D'(x)$ = $E(x) \times q'(x)$

CORRECTION FACTORS

Correction factors a and b are set in such a way that:

$q'(x) = a \times q(x) + b$

Permanent incapacity and survivorship benefits

and that the sum of registered deaths is equal to the sum of deaths according to the new table, and that the average age at death of registered deaths is the same as the average age of death according to the new table.

The following equations are set at:

1. $\sum_x D'(x) = \sum_x \emptyset(x)$

2. $\sum_x x D'(x) = \sum_x x \emptyset(x)$

We know that $D'(x) = E(x) \times q'(x)$
$ = a \times E(x) \times q(x) + b \times E(x)$
$ = a \times D(x) + b \times E(x)$

Both conditions can be rewritten as follows:

1. $a \sum_x D(x) + b \sum_x E(x) = \sum_x \emptyset(x)$

2. $a \sum_x x D(x) + b \sum_x x E(x) = \sum_x x \emptyset(x)$

from where unique values of a and b can be obtained.

ANNEX 16C

Table 16C. 1 Partial permanent incapacity terminations

Duration	4 years before valuation year			3 years before valuation year			2 year before valuation year		
	Exposure	Terminations	Rates (as a %)	Exposure	Terminations	Rates (as a %)	Exposure	Terminations	Rates (as a %)
0	32 591 633	−112 769	−0.35	38 127 625	27 968	0.07	36 750 247	356 748	0.97
1	69 828 333	371 840	0.53	68 649 977	889 340	1.30	88 578 408	825 218	0.93
2	87 354 212	22 754	0.03	61 260 701	431 171	0.70	60 046 429	147 858	0.25
3	74 118 646	138 839	0.19	73 629 123	−105 237	−0.14	53 892 905	437 154	0.81
4	40 160 768	−674	0.00	61 652 627	−203 631	−0.33	62 989 368	−12 886	−0.02
5	15 549 060	−14 599	−0.09	33 047 122	67 792	0.21	52 484 710	394 562	0.75
6	6 062 095	4 840	0.08	12 008 549	−45 667	0.38	27 093 820	196 294	0.72
7	420 499	−10	0.00	4 734 958	−14 302	−0.30	9 707 560	51 907	0.53
8	153 739	0	0.00	231 684	−14	0.01	3 769 118	14	0.00
9	0	0	0	132 055	0	0.00	568 313	0	0.00
10	0	0	0	0	0	0	114 606	0	0.00
11	0	0	0	0	0	0	0	0	0
12	0	0	0	0	0	0	0	0	0
Total	326 238 985	410 221	0.13	353 474 421	1 047 420	0.30	395 995 484	2 396 869	0.61

Table 16C. 1 (Continued)

Duration	1 year before valuation year			Valuation year			5 years combined		
	Exposure	Terminations	Rates (as a %)	Exposure	Terminations	Rates (as a %)	Exposure	Terminations	Rates (as a %)
0	30 007 708	464 576	1.55	78 873 582	1 204 858	1.53	216 350 795	1 941 381	0.90
1	78 268 145	595 917	0.76	94 703 852	1 857 387	1.96	400 028 715	4 539 702	1.13
2	80 300 470	−5 180	0.01	70 370 545	−377 762	−0.54	359 332 266	218 841	0.06
3	53 348 620	17 126	0.03	72 882 554	428 897	0.59	327 871 848	916 779	0.28
4	46 269 516	390 647	0.84	47 029 533	245 601	0.52	258 101 812	419 057	0.16
5	53 686 640	−20 153	−0.04	39 904 567	4 192	0.01	194 672 099	431 794	0.22
6	44 954 375	−151 693	−0.34	46 231 622	214 666	0.46	136 350 461	218 440	0.16
7	22 755 617	−120 745	−0.53	39 526 973	−186	0.00	77 145 607	−83 336	−0.11
8	8 018 815	41 357	0.52	18 669 390	73 737	0.39	30 842 746	115 094	0.37
9	2 897 522	337	0.01	6 549 466	−25 296	−0.39	10 147 356	−24 959	−0.25
10	533 589	8 393	1.57	2 339 919	188	0.01	2 988 114	8 581	0.29
11	96 413	0	0.00	23 941	0	0.00	120 354	0	0.00
12	0	0	0.00	75 320	0	0.00	75 320	0	0.00
Total	421 137 430	1 220 582	0.29	517 181 173	3 626 282	0.70	2 014 027 493	8 701 374	0.43

MEDICAL EXPENSES AND REHABILITATION BENEFITS 17

The first section of this chapter on medical expenses and rehabilitation benefits discusses the main features of the benefits that will have to be considered for the actuarial valuation. The second section illustrates some aspects of statistical data reports for actuarial purposes. The third section presents the formulae used for financial projections and the fourth discusses all other items relevant to actuarial valuations, such as the selection of assumptions and the experience analysis.

17.1 LEGISLATIVE PROVISIONS

Medical expenses and rehabilitation benefits can be provided under the workers' compensation legislation or under general programmes not limited to work injuries and diseases. In the latter case, the workers' compensation system may have to reimburse the costs related to the treatment of injured workers to the general system. The valuation techniques discussed in this chapter apply to all the cases in which the workers' compensation scheme pays for the cost of those benefits serviced through its own system or through a general one. However, the valuation techniques are not intended to apply to systems where the care is provided by the scheme's own facilities, such as hospitals or rehabilitation centres operated by the system. In the latter case, budgeting techniques based on cost accounting are generally more suitable than the actuarial methods addressed in this chapter. Nevertheless, these budgeting techniques may use analytical tools that are similar to those discussed here, which means that the reader can probably adapt the approaches described below to many other situations.

17.1.1 Medical expenses

Medical expenses generally cover the cost of hospitalization (including all services available at a hospital, such as X-rays and laboratory tests), physicians, dentists, nurses, drugs and prosthesis. The injured worker is generally entitled to receive the medical attention necessary for a full recovery, but limitations on the duration of time during which benefits are covered or maximum amounts may limit the patient's access to services. The conditions under which services are made available may also affect the rate of their utilization. It is important that the actuary becomes familiar with the medical and administrative practices and the rules governing the authorization of benefits. For the same injury, the medical treatment under two different schemes can vary according to factors such as the supply of services, the degree of sophistication of facilities, the differences between fees for services to injured workers and services to the general population.

The prices of services are generally set in regulations or administrative agreements resulting from negotiations between parties, the board and the service providers. The actuary may be asked to cost the impact of various changes to the services covered, such as an increase in fees, the inclusion of new treatment or modifications introduced in the administrative procedure for the authorization of benefits or for the control of services. This type of valuation requires a detailed analysis of the relationship between all the parties involved in the administration of medical care to injured workers, the board's medical staff, the claims manager and the service providers. For example, changes in the structure of physicians' fees may generate modifications to the pattern of medical treatment, and the actuary will need a certain degree of knowledge of medical procedures to assess such potential effects.

There is increasing pressure in some countries to cover the services of health professionals involved in alternative medicine or para-medical practices, such as chiropractors, acupuncturists, homeopaths, naturopaths, and so on. When these services are available to the injured workers, limits are set on the number of visits or the total costs by type of service. Costing the introduction of these benefits is generally performed through the use of external data. Groups urging for the inclusion of these benefits may argue that these benefits are, overall, cost neutral, firstly because they are used instead of traditional medical services and secondly because of the ensuing reduction in income disability costs, owing to the reduction in duration resulting from the improved health of the injured worker. There is still little empirical evidence to support the actuarial work in these circumstances.

Travel and lodging costs incurred while receiving medical care may also be covered, and they are included in the package of medical care as a specific item.

17.1.2 Rehabilitation

The rehabilitation benefits considered in this chapter include the expenses incurred for the services that are needed to return workers to their work and day-to-day living. The cost of physiotherapy and ergonomics can be considered as medical rehabilitation. The issue of considering these two services as rehabilitation or medical care is not that important, although there is an interest for cost analysis purposes in maintaining the costs of the two separately. Vocational rehabilitation includes all the costs that are incurred to support the worker returning to work, such as counselling and retraining, adapting the workplace for the worker left with functional limitations, or subsidies to help the worker start a business. Other expenses may also be incurred to support injured workers in their day-to-day living, including the services of psychologists and, for severe injuries, the carrying out of modifications to the worker's home and vehicle as well as the services of any personnel that might be needed for maintaining the home.

The actuary may be asked to measure the expected reduction in the cost of disability benefits resulting from additional money spent in rehabilitation services. There is no direct mathematical answer to this question, and the cost estimates have to rely on a thorough analysis of the particular circumstances.

17.2 DATABASE AND STATISTICAL REPORTS FOR ACTUARIAL VALUATIONS

The information regarding the identification of the injured worker and the circumstances of the accident are described in Technical Brief IV, and should be made available to anyone receiving medical expenses and rehabilitation benefits, except for slight injuries that do not lead to any time being lost in the workplace. Indeed, there are a certain number of injuries requiring medical treatment that do not generate temporary incapacity costs. For those injuries, it may not be worth capturing and maintaining detailed information on the circumstances of the accident. Achieving a proper balance between the exhaustiveness of the database and the cost of its maintenance depends largely on the resources and circumstances of each system.

17.2.1 Description of the database

Keeping a detailed database of medical and rehabilitation information may lead to a huge volume of data, since the number of services used by injured can be significant. A detailed database would keep track of the following types of information for each service made available to an injured worker:

- the nature of the service (hospital stay, physicians' fees, etc.);
- the date of service;
- the amount of payment.

The list of services should be detailed enough to make the analysis of experience for each type of service possible. The following list is given as a guideline. It shows the main items and, for each of them, a detailed list of components. This list is based on the nature of services.

Health professionals	General practitioners, specialists, dentists, optometrists, medical assessments
Hospitals	Hospitalization, external services
Pharmacy	Drugs, other pharmaceutical products
Prosthesis and orthesis	Ocular devices, hearing aids, dental, thorax-limbs, others
Other health practitioners	Acupuncturists, audiologists, psychologists, physiotherapists, chiropractors, occupational therapists, podiatrists
Technical aids	Locomotive aids, communication aids, therapeutic aids, aids for daily living, other technical aids
Travel and living expenses	Travel, lodging, meals, parking, expenses for accompanying people, expert witnesses
Vocational rehabilitation	Retraining programmes, vocational training programmes, external professional services, learning aids, adaptation of the work-site, planning and implementation, occupational mobility, consulting services
Social rehabilitation	Professional services of social workers, adaptation of the home, adaptation of the car, personal home help, day care, home maintenance expenses
Other	Translation expenses, damages to clothing, other expenses

This level of detail is probably not practical for systems with scarce resources. When this is the case, the detailed information by service should be grouped by financial year only, that is, the year when the payment for the service is issued by the system. The information in the database would then be the following:

- the number of services by type and year of injury of the recipient;
- the number of recipients by type of service and year of injury of the recipient;
- the amount of payment by nature of service and financial year of payment.

Organizing the data according to the year of payment rather than to the year the service is given represents a compromise with respect to the precise timing of events. This practice is generally acceptable for accounting and actuarial purposes, although the database will then be less useful for statistical analysis, when the time between the date of a service and its reimbursement is significant.

It is well known that the prices of medical services vary year after year according to a pattern that differs from general prices. This issue is critical when it comes to costing these benefits. In order to maintain the proper historical information related to the benefits covered by the workers' compensation, the actuary needs to keep a record of the agreements with the service providers. This information is essential for understanding the experience. Sudden changes in payments may result from a sudden increases in fees. The format of the database regarding this information depends on the circumstances of the case. When prices are set by regulations, the actuary can generally rely on the archives of the institution and then may not have to design a special database.

17.2.2 Statistical reporting

The remarks made in Technical Brief IV on the reconciliation of actuarial data with those of other sources also apply to medical and rehabilitation benefits. The statistical reporting of medical expenses and rehabilitation benefits has its own distinctive features. Indeed, some services (such as medical care by physicians) are characterized by high frequency and low severity, while the opposite is the case for other services (such as home maintenance). For actuarial valuation purposes, it may be more practical to combine all the benefits together (or in a few categories) in order to obtain a volume of data that is sufficiently stable year after year. In these circumstances, the statistical reports supporting the actuarial valuation are simple; they merely consist of the distribution of amounts paid by injury year and year of payment. Table TBIV.6 of Technical Brief IV is the basic format to be used, and one that can also be appropriate for a more detailed analysis. Each of the cost components, that is, the number of services and the average amount paid by recipient, is presented by the injury year and financial year of payment.

17.3 METHODOLOGY FOR FINANCIAL PROJECTIONS

Section 17.3.1 focuses on the development of payments regarding injuries that have already occurred at the date of projection, while section 17.3.2 looks at the injuries occurring during the projection period. The development of components section illustrates how the formulae of Chapter 15 regarding temporary incapacity benefits can also be adapted for the financial projection of medical expenses and rehabilitation benefits. These formulae develop the number of recipients and the average amount of benefit separately. In the section entitled, The development of payments, more general formulae based on the development of benefits paid are discussed.

Many social security schemes have only a few employment injury cases. In addition, the data situation does not often allow the backtracking of the expenditure history of a specific payment case. In this instance, the number of cases of medical expenses/rehabilitation benefits should be split between the cases of medical cost compensation and short-term benefit cases. The expected benefit

Medical expenses and rehabilitation benefits

payment should then be projected on the basis of the standard insurance cost estimation technique.[1]

Formula 17.1

$$B(t) = \sum_{w} CH(w,t) \times MR(w,0) \times f(t) \times d(w,t)$$

where:

$CH(w,t)$ = Number of health care cases in category w of benefit in year t
$MR(w,0)$ = Average cost per case in category w in valuation year
$f(t)$ = General inflation from the valuation year to year t
$d(w,t)$ = Deviation of medical inflation from general inflation

$$d(w,n) = \frac{MR(w,n)}{MR(w,n-1)} \div \frac{f(n)}{f(n-1)}$$

The number of cases per category can be estimated as a multiplier of the number of benefit recipients in a specific category (e.g. long-term disability benefits). The estimate of the number of benefit recipients has already been explained in previous chapters.

The following sections describe a fully hedged cost assessment method for countries with a comprehensive data set. It is described here for the principal purpose of demonstrating that the calculation of health care costs under employment injury schemes ideally relates expenses to a specific group of events (such as an injury in a certain year of a certain population group). If expenses cannot be clearly associated with groups and years, risk and experience rating procedures would not be possible.

17.3.1 Benefits related to injuries that occurred before the valuation date

The development of components

A certain number of methods can be used to perform the financial projections of medical expenses and rehabilitation benefits. The formulae shown in Chapter 15 on temporary incapacity benefits can easily be adapted for these purposes, since they project separately the number of service recipients and the average amount paid for each recipient in each financial year. For example, formula 17.1 could become the following (formula 17.2) after being properly adapted. The reader should be aware that the simplistic assumption that was made regarding the number of years after the injury year during which payments are assumed to be made, that is, nine years, is rarely applicable in the case of medical expenses and rehabilitation benefits; the number of years for a cohort of injured people is

Actuarial practice in social security

much more than nine. However, this has been maintained in formula 17.2 to facilitate comparisons with the general discussion in Chapter 15.

Formula 17.2

$$B(t) = \sum_{d=0}^{9-t} N_d(0) \times P(d,t) \times L(d+t) \times f(t)$$

where:

$N_d(0)$ = Number of benefit recipients in the year of valuation whose injury occurred d years before the year of valuation, $0 \leq d \leq 9$

$P(d,t)$ = Proportion of benefit recipients in year d after their injury year who are recipients in year $d+t$, $P(d,t) = 0$ for $d+t \geq 10$

$L(d+t)$ = Average amount per benefit recipient $d+t$ years after the injury year in monetary units of the valuation year

$f(t)$ = Indexing factor of the average benefit per recipient over t years

The average amount per benefit recipient includes all medical and rehabilitation services, and is not the cost per service but the total cost of all services paid during the year by the recipient. Of course, this figure is made up of a large number of combinations of services. Some injured workers may visit just one physician, while others may use many services. In some circumstances, it may be necessary to split the average amount per benefit recipient into its two components, that is, the number of services (possibly by class of service) during the year per benefit recipient (utilization) and the average cost per service. This kind of analysis must be performed when there is a need to project the cost of specific benefits resulting from changes in legislation. For regular periodic actuarial valuations, it is generally not convenient to refine the formulae to express $L(d+t)$ in terms of these two components, because the volume of data may be small. The variable $L(d+t)$ is expressed in terms of monetary units of the valuation year, and expresses the development of payments for an injury year in constant monetary units.

The inflation factor in formula 17.1 should be related to the inflation in the cost of services that are considered in the formula. This assumption is often expressed in terms of the general price factor, to which a value is added to reflect that the inflation of medical services is higher than the inflation of general prices, mostly because of continuous improvements being made in medical technology.[2]

Medical expenses and rehabilitation benefits

The development of payments

The technique that we refer to consists of estimating future payments through applying factors to the benefits paid before the valuation date. These factors are based on past experience and express the relationship between the payments that will be made in the future to those that have been made in the past. The pattern of this relationship may change over time for a variety of reasons, and the factors have to be updated regularly to reflect the most recent trends but still encompass enough experience to capture cycles. This technique can be applied according to the two different approaches described in the next two subsections.

The development of annual payments

Formula 17.3 shows the projected value of the benefit expenditures t years after the valuation date for past injury years.

Formula 17.3

$$B(t) = \sum_{d=0}^{m-t} D_d(0) \times F(d,t) \times f(t)$$

where:

$D_d(u)$ = Total amount of benefits paid u years before valuation for injuries that occurred d years before the year of valuation.

$F(d,t)$ = Relationship between the amounts paid $d+t$ years after the injury year to those paid d years after the injury years not considering changes in prices of services over time

m = First value of $d+t$ for which $F(d,t)$ is equal to 0.

The first factor of the formula $D_d(0)$ is the starting point of the projection. It is defined as the total amount of payments in the valuation year corresponding to a specific injury year. For large values of d, these amounts can be small and fluctuate widely year after year. It may be preferable to introduce a mechanism to eliminate undue volatility in the projection of future costs. This can be achieved by using the payments made during a certain number of financial years ending with the valuation year adjusted by the appropriate development and inflation factors so as to reproduce the expected payments in the valuation year for each injury year. For example, if the benefits paid in the last three years are used, then the adjusted value of the starting payments in the valuation year can be defined, as shown by formula 17.4 in box 17.1.

The second factor of formula 17.3 is the development factor, which expresses for any injury year the relationship between the payments made in

> **Box 17.1 Averaging of observed past payments**
>
> The easiest way to illustrate this adjustment is by way of an example. Assume that a valuation is performed in the year 2000 and (1) the payments made for the accident year 1970 are 500 monetary units and (2) the expected amount paid in 2001 for this accident year will be 450. The actual amount paid under some circumstances could be significantly higher if there were relapses or aggravations. This might create instability in the projection of future payments, which would happen if a new valuation were performed at the end of 2001 and the starting payments in that year were, for example, over 600 (instead of a number close to 450). The amount of 600 may be more or less representative of those paid in the future and the payments of more than one year may be a better indication of the future. According to formula 17.4, payments made in the years 1998 to 2000 for the accident year 1970 would be used. Those made in the years 1998 and 1999 would be projected to the year 2000 with the same factors (F) as those used after the valuation date. The appropriate inflation factor between the years 1998 and 1999 are used in order to have the payments expressed in the monetary values of 2000.
>
> **Formula 17.4**
>
> $$DA_d(0) = \left(\sum_{u=0}^{2} (D_d(u) \times F(d-u, u) \times pf(u)) \right) \div 3$$
>
> where:
>
> $DA_d(0)$ = Adjusted amount of benefits paid in the year of valuation for injuries that occurred d years before the valuation date
>
> $pf(u)$ = Indexing factor of the average benefit per recipient over u years before the valuation date

the future to those made in a preceding duration. In practice, this factor is always the product of t terms, each expressing the relationship between payments made in a given year to those made in the preceding year. For example, if R_u is the ratio of payments u years after the injury year to those of the preceding year, then the factor $F(d,t)$ can be expressed as follows:

Formula 17.5

$$F(d, t) = \prod_{u=d+1}^{t} R_u \quad \text{(by definition, } F(d, 0) = 1\text{)}$$

The factors F depend on the provisions of each system, except for long durations, where they tend to reflect the combined rate of mortality of injured work-

Medical expenses and rehabilitation benefits

ers. Indeed, the type and quantity of services to injured workers stabilize at longer durations.

The development of cumulative payments

The second approach is similar to the preceding one. The formula has the same pattern, but its terms have a different meaning. Instead of using the payments in the year of the valuation date, this technique relies on the cumulative payments of each injury year expressed in the monetary units of the valuation year. Thus we have the following formula:

Formula 17.6

$$B(t) = \sum_{d=0}^{m-t} DC_d(0) \times FC(d,t) \times f(t)$$

where:

$DC_d(0)$ = Total amount of benefits paid up to the year of valuation for injuries that occurred d years before the year of valuation, indexed to monetary values of the valuation year.

$FC(d,t)$ = Relationship between the amounts paid $d+t$ years after the injury year to those paid during the first d years after the injury year adjusted to monetary values of the year of valuation

The first term of the formula can be expressed as follows in terms of payments made before the valuation date.

Formula 17.7

$$DC_d(0) = \sum_{u=0}^{d} D_d(u) \times pf(u)$$

Formula 17.7 is the sum of payments adjusted for inflation between the year each payment is made to the year of valuation. It is important to be aware of the difference between formula 17.4, which uses the annual payment in the valuation year, and formula 17.7, which uses cumulative payments until the valuation year. Similarly, if we return to the second term of formula 17.6, FC is a development factor expressing the size of the expected payment in the year t. Given that FC applies to cumulative payments at the valuation date, its size will be much smaller than the corresponding one in formula 17.3, which is $F()$.

The total liabilities regarding medical expenses and rehabilitation benefits at the valuation date can be obtained by discounting the values obtained by formula 17.3 or formula 17.6 for all the financial years (all t) after the valuation date.

Formula 17.8

$$AL(t) = \sum_{t} B(t) \div (1+i)^{t-\frac{1}{2}}$$

17.3.2 Benefits related to injuries occurring after the valuation date

For the estimation of the cost of services related to injury years following the valuation date, payments in any year t are expressed in terms of the value of the payments projected in the year of injury, that is, $D_k(k)$, where k ($0 < k < t$) is the injury year after the valuation date. The value of $D_k(k)$ is generally expressed in terms of $D_0(0)$, that is, the amount of payments made in the year of injury corresponding to the year of valuation. The projection factor will consider the change in the exposure and the frequency of injuries from year 0 to year k and the inflation of the costs of benefits. Formula 17.9 shows the payments resulting from the injuries occurring after the valuation date determined according to the first approach.

Formula 17.9

$$B(t) = \sum_{j=\max(1,t-m)}^{t} D_0(0) \times IK_j \times F(0, t-j) \times f(t)$$

where:

IK_j = Factor that considers the change in the frequency of injuries between the year of valuation and year j after the valuation date

The factor IK is intended to reflect the variations in the number of injured workers after the valuation date and any other phenomenon that has an impact on the cost of medical expenses and rehabilitation benefits, except variations in prices of services. For example, the rate of utilization could vary to take into consideration changes due to the nature of injuries resulting from changes in the industry mix. Factors $F(\ )$ are assumed to be constant over the projection period. This is a practical assumption, although it may not be considered realistic in some circumstances. However, it is very difficult to project changes in the pattern of development factors.

The cost of the benefits for one injury year can be obtained by discounting the payments for all years regarding the particular injury year. For example, the cost of the medical expense benefits related to injuries occurring in year j measured at 1 July of that year can be expressed by formula 17.10.

Formula 17.10

$$CO_j = \sum_{t=j}^{j+m-1} [D_0(0) \times IK_j \times F(0, t-j) \times f(t)] \div (1+i)^{t-j}$$

where:

CO_j = Cost of medical expenses and rehabilitation benefits for injuries occurring in year – following the valuation date valued at mid-year of the injury year

17.4 ASSUMPTIONS

In this section, we show how development factors should be set. These factors are needed for working out the development of cumulative payments, described in the subsection on the development of annual payments.

17.4.1 Raw data

Table 17.1 shows the basic data used. They are the payments made in the 11 most recent financial years broken down by injury year. This particular plan was in force for 60 years at the time that the development factors were set, which is why payments for 60 injury years are shown. The first column refers to the difference between the financial year and the year of injury. For example, in the column for 1995, the payments in row four are related to the injury year 1991. For the 11 most recent injury years (1989 to 1999), the table shows all the amounts paid up to the valuation date. For the other injury years, the method uses the payments made during the last 11 financial years. The payments of injury years 1989, 1979, 1969, 1959 and 1949 are shaded in each column. The data are representative of the employment injury scheme in the province of Quebec, Canada.

Before making the development factors, the actuary must analyse the raw data and determine if there are any apparent abnormalities that would require further investigation and adjustments. We assume (more or less arbitrarily) that the data do not show any obviously strange phenomenon. However, it seems apparent that the first year of payments has increased more than the total payments from 1991 to 1992. This is not a strange phenomenon but an important characteristic of the database. The actuary must look out for any changes in the administrative procedures that might explain this and be careful when setting the development factor from duration 0 to 1, that is, R_1.

Actuarial practice in social security

Table 17.1 Example: Payments in current monetary values

Duration	Calendar year the payments are made										
	1989	1990	1991	1992	1993	1994	1995	1996	1997	1998	1999
0	36 101	42 697	60 110	64 641	68 626	69 232	76 890	87 928	83 415	79 121	83 853
1	27 495	32 802	38 758	37 461	33 344	38 537	46 966	60 743	62 106	50 791	52 303
2	9 857	10 590	9 943	12 094	11 161	11 008	14 387	19 495	24 142	19 698	14 941
3	6 293	6 762	5 329	5 926	8 033	8 534	8 722	13 743	19 723	14 399	11 132
4	3 856	5 227	3 755	3 488	3 791	5 552	6 972	7 403	11 624	8 633	10 458
5	2 575	3 367	3 365	2 984	2 619	3 210	4 533	6 120	6 589	6 170	6 844
6	2 002	2 090	2 522	2 625	2 168	2 055	3 062	4 542	5 578	4 774	5 004
7	1 462	1 882	1 794	1 959	2 212	1 642	2 060	2 821	4 323	4 421	3 929
8	1 241	1 560	1 590	1 439	1 575	1 683	1 678	2 142	2 262	3 154	3 510
9	1 226	1 093	1 251	1 341	1 129	1 573	1 899	1 718	2 062	2 029	2 596
10	1 012	1 285	1 083	1 309	1 199	1 200	1 550	1 871	1 883	1 548	1 960
11	812	1 067	1 284	903	1 144	1 188	1 310	1 608	1 707	1 452	1 328
12	692	881	935	1 245	815	1 135	1 359	1 570	1 750	1 724	1 292
13	586	700	700	915	1 095	770	1 160	1 213	1 598	1 291	1 701
14	486	527	612	843	777	1 019	850	1 281	1 316	1 392	1 207
15	480	493	601	808	643	805	1 188	941	1 296	1 182	1 343
16	338	518	560	581	593	694	750	1 239	1 050	1 306	1 007
17	598	411	528	541	457	583	744	1 039	1 086	907	1 135
18	600	819	381	514	530	438	725	781	890	1 104	848
19	501	685	596	356	523	521	515	774	775	948	1 046
20	438	579	594	611	366	504	516	558	664	582	738
21	178	418	455	457	527	385	588	481	573	676	612
22	279	214	485	513	448	530	395	651	587	556	555
23	162	318	208	376	480	480	630	420	647	516	558
24	112	129	262	223	324	474	505	535	415	542	618
25	215	112	201	151	222	312	491	465	568	332	526
26	79	189	157	168	214	215	369	505	436	463	311
27	208	78	122	159	165	204	182	438	510	453	614
28	101	206	98	98	137	188	215	206	481	528	357
29	49	106	183	106	105	125	168	199	166	297	507
30	107	38	94	190	79	95	118	211	172	171	341
31	142	81	142	89	176	106	132	102	210	141	182

Medical expenses and rehabilitation benefits

32	100	161	106	66	86	208	92	118	108	168	160
33	48	95	162	105	94	93	151	89	118	122	141
34	106	38	93	147	69	60	94	239	80	92	117
35	32	192	56	106	127	69	64	95	205	90	111
36	153	53	96	99	92	125	46	57	100	178	76
37	100	218	40	107	50	106	136	54	51	72	202
38	26	173	101	42	78	44	108	118	50	94	74
39	17	29	57	82	30	82	37	158	111	63	41
40	55	17	22	67	57	32	94	44	136	93	45
41	48	101	14	16	68	68	44	116	46	184	90
42	86	79	28	19	14	55	99	32	98	46	107
43	22	92	102	56	19	13	47	133	33	112	49
44	5	15	59	68	50	55	12	44	72	26	100
45	1	1	11	38	43	32	26	12	36	66	31
46	15	14	12	15	31	77	30	29	17	33	64
47	5	8	0	7	15	27	57	41	16	13	43
48	6	0	10	1	6	14	18	20	31	20	12
49	0	0	7	11	0	4	14	50	14	28	26
50	4	3	3	6	16	0	11	17	21	14	27
51	4	0	0	3	8	4	0	6	43	20	31
52	0	0	3	0	3	9	3	0	7	38	22
53	0	0	5	2	0	5	6	1	0	5	28
54	0	0	1	6	1	0	4	5	3	0	3
55	0	0	0	1	4	3	0	4	11	3	0
56	0	0	0	0	0	0	3	0	0	8	3
57	0	0	0	0	0	0	0	0	4	4	8
58	0	0	0	0	0	0	1	1	0	0	4
59	0	0	0	0	0	0	0	0	2	0	0
60	0	0	0	0	0	0	0	0	0	0	0
Total	101 116	119 214	139 686	146 184	146 638	156 182	182 825	225 226	242 017	212 893	214 971

Table 17.2 Example: Variations in general prices

Period	1989–90	1990–91	1991–92	1992–93	1993–94	1994–95	1995–96	1996–97	1997–98	1998–99
Factor	1.044	1.040	1.041	1.044	1.041	1.048	1.048	1.058	1.018	1.019
Period	1989–99	1990–99	1991–99	1992–99	1993–99	1994–99	1995–99	1996–99	1997–99	1998–99
Factor	1.481	1.418	1.364	1.310	1.255	1.205	1.150	1.098	1.037	1.019

17.4.2 Observed development factors

The second step of the process consists of calculating the development factors, which are, for a given injury year, the ratio of the payments at a given duration to the payments at the preceding duration (in constant monetary units). In principle, the calculation of constant monetary units should rely on an index of prices for medical expenses and rehabilitation benefits. In practice, this kind of information is not always available, and an index of general prices may be used instead. When this happens, the development factor between each duration implicitly includes any differences between the variations in prices of medical expenses and rehabilitation benefits and the variations in general prices. For the projection of payments after the valuation date, the inflation factor must reflect the expected variation in general prices only. Indeed, the utilization of the development factors for the projection of benefits after the valuation date implies that the difference between the two indices is assumed to be the same in the projection period as it was in the period covered by the data used for calculating the development factor. This method will be used in the example under study.

Table 17.2 shows the ratio of general prices between successive years as well as its cumulative value, which expresses the payments of each financial year in the constant monetary value of the valuation year.

The next step is to calculate the individual development factors, which are presented in table 17.3. What follows is an illustration of the calculation for a factor expressing the development between durations 4 and 5, which would be the factor R_5 according to formula 17.5, which is observed for 1997.

$$R_5^{1997} = \frac{6,589}{7,403 \times 1.058} = 0.841$$

For illustrative purposes, only three decimals are kept in the table, but a minimum of six decimals should remain in the calculation at this stage.

If the increase in the prices of medical expenses and rehabilitation benefits were known, it would be used instead of the increase in general prices (that is, 1.058). For example, assuming that the increase in medical and rehabilitation benefits is 1.07, then the development factor calculated in formula 17.10 would be 0.832, which is smaller than the one obtained (0.841). If this information is

Medical expenses and rehabilitation benefits

Table 17.3 Example: Observed development factors

Duration	1989–90	1990–91	1991–92	1992–93	1993–94	1994–95	1995–96	1996–97	1997–98	1998–99
1	0.870	0.873	0.599	0.494	0.539	0.647	0.754	0.668	0.598	0.649
2	0.369	0.291	0.300	0.285	0.317	0.356	0.396	0.376	0.312	0.289
3	0.657	0.484	0.573	0.636	0.735	0.756	0.911	0.956	0.586	0.555
4	0.796	0.534	0.629	0.613	0.664	0.780	0.810	0.799	0.430	0.713
5	0.836	0.619	0.763	0.719	0.813	0.779	0.838	0.841	0.521	0.778
6	0.777	0.720	0.749	0.696	0.754	0.910	0.956	0.861	0.712	0.796
7	0.900	0.825	0.746	0.807	0.728	0.957	0.879	0.900	0.779	0.808
8	1.022	0.812	0.771	0.770	0.731	0.975	0.992	0.758	0.717	0.779
9	0.844	0.771	0.810	0.752	0.959	1.077	0.977	0.910	0.881	0.808
10	1.004	0.953	1.005	0.856	1.021	0.940	0.940	1.036	0.737	0.948
11	0.870	0.873	0.599	0.494	0.539	0.647	0.754	0.668	0.598	0.649
12	0.369	0.291	0.300	0.285	0.317	0.356	0.396	0.376	0.312	0.289
13	0.657	0.484	0.573	0.636	0.735	0.756	0.911	0.956	0.586	0.555
14	0.796	0.534	0.629	0.613	0.664	0.780	0.810	0.799	0.430	0.713
15	0.836	0.619	0.763	0.719	0.813	0.779	0.838	0.841	0.521	0.778
16	0.777	0.720	0.749	0.696	0.754	0.910	0.956	0.861	0.712	0.796
17	0.900	0.825	0.746	0.807	0.728	0.957	0.879	0.900	0.779	0.808
18	1.022	0.812	0.771	0.770	0.731	0.975	0.992	0.758	0.717	0.779
19	0.844	0.771	0.810	0.752	0.959	1.077	0.977	0.910	0.881	0.808
20	1.004	0.953	1.005	0.856	1.021	0.940	0.940	1.036	0.737	0.948
21	0.914	0.756	0.739	0.826	1.010	1.113	0.889	0.971	1.000	1.032
22	1.152	1.116	1.083	0.939	0.966	0.979	1.056	1.153	0.953	0.806
23	1.092	0.935	0.745	0.896	1.029	1.134	1.015	0.939	0.864	0.985
24	0.763	0.792	1.030	0.825	0.949	1.004	0.810	0.934	0.823	1.175
25	0.958	1.498	0.554	0.954	0.925	0.988	0.879	1.003	0.786	0.952
26	0.842	1.348	0.803	1.357	0.930	1.129	0.981	0.886	0.801	0.919
27	0.946	0.621	0.973	0.941	0.916	0.808	1.133	0.955	1.021	1.301
28	0.949	1.208	0.772	0.825	1.095	1.006	1.080	1.038	1.017	0.773
29	1.005	0.854	1.039	1.026	0.876	0.853	0.883	0.762	0.607	0.942
30	0.743	0.853	0.997	0.714	0.869	0.901	1.198	0.817	1.012	1.127
31	0.725	3.593	0.910	0.887	1.289	1.326	0.825	0.941	0.805	1.044
32	1.086	1.258	0.446	0.926	1.135	0.828	0.853	1.001	0.786	1.114
33	0.910	0.968	0.952	1.364	1.039	0.693	0.923	0.945	1.110	0.824
34	0.758	0.941	0.872	0.629	0.613	0.964	1.510	0.850	0.766	0.941
35	1.735	1.417	1.095	0.828	0.961	1.018	0.964	0.811	1.105	1.184
36	1.586	0.481	1.698	0.831	0.945	0.636	0.850	0.995	0.853	0.829
37	1.365	0.726	1.071	0.484	1.107	1.038	1.120	0.846	0.707	1.114
38	1.657	0.445	1.009	0.698	0.845	0.972	0.828	0.875	1.811	1.009
39	1.068	0.317	0.780	0.684	1.010	0.802	1.396	0.889	1.238	0.428
40	0.958	0.729	1.129	0.666	1.025	1.094	1.135	0.814	0.823	0.701
41	1.759	0.792	0.699	0.972	1.146	1.312	1.178	0.988	1.329	0.950
42	1.576	0.267	1.304	0.838	0.777	1.389	0.694	0.799	0.982	0.571
43	1.025	1.241	1.921	0.958	0.892	0.815	1.282	0.975	1.123	1.045
44	0.653	0.617	0.640	0.855	2.781	0.881	0.893	0.512	0.774	0.876
45	0.192	0.705	0.619	0.606	0.615	0.451	0.954	0.773	0.900	1.170
46	0.958	11.538	1.310	0.781	1.720	0.895	1.064	1.339	0.900	0.952
47	0.894	0.000	0.560	0.958	0.837	0.706	1.304	0.521	0.751	1.279
48	1.533	0.687		0.821	0.897	0.636	0.335	0.715	1.228	0.906
49	0.000	0.841	1.057	0.000	0.640	0.954	2.651	0.662	0.887	1.276
50			0.823	1.393		2.624	1.159	0.397	0.982	0.946
51	0.718		0.961	1.277	0.240		0.520	2.391	0.936	2.173
52	0.000	0.962		0.958	1.081	0.716		1.103	0.868	1.079

Table 17.3 (continued)

Duration	1989–90	1990–91	1991–92	1992–93	1993–94	1994–95	1995–96	1996–97	1997–98	1998–99
53			0.640		1.601	0.636	0.318		0.702	0.723
54			1.153	0.479		0.763	0.795	2.836		0.589
55			0.961	0.639	0.000		0.954	2.079	0.982	
56				0.000	0.720			0.945	0.714	0.981
57						0.318			0.982	0.981
58							0.954			0.981
59							0.000	1.890		
60								0.000		

available and the development factors are calculated accordingly, the inflation factor for the projection of benefits after the valuation date must take into consideration the specific increase in the prices of medical expenses and rehabilitation benefits.

At every step of the process, the actuary must look closely at the results and assess the need to adjust the data. Graphics are often useful for identifying values that are out of range. In table 17.3, it seems that there is at least one number that differs markedly from expectations. This is the development factor at duration 46 in the second column (1990–91), that is, 11.538. The reliability of raw data should be investigated. When the actuary is satisfied that there are no errors, then a decision has to be made regarding the opportunity to adjust the data. In this particular example, the data are valid and the actuary may wish to make an adjustment at this stage or later on in the process. (The factor 11.538 will not be used in the next stages to avoid undue distortion in the results.) No factor is shown in the cells where the denominator is 0 and the numerator is positive or 0.

Outlying values of development factors are possible in the area of the benefits considered in this chapter. The payments of a cohort may fluctuate because of relapses or aggravations that generate awards of benefits to a few injured workers. Similarly, large amounts of benefits may be made to a few injured workers less frequently than every year, causing peaks when they occur. This can be the case for the replacement of prostheses or when costly surgery is needed for the elderly. The example is worked out without making any adjustments to the data of table 17.2 at this stage.

The next step is to calculate the average development factors at each duration. A first decision regarding the maximum number of experience years was made when the actuary processed data of 11 years. The main advantage of considering a large volume of experience is that it lends credibility to the data and helps minimize fluctuations. However, trends may change in the experience period, and the more recent experience may be more representative of future experience. Credibility is not just a matter of volume but also of relevancy. Table 17.4 shows the geometrical average factors made with the complete

Table 17.4 Example: Average development factors

Duration	Ten years	Five years	Duration	Ten years	Five years
1	0.658	0.661	31	1.089	0.971
2	0.327	0.343	32	0.912	0.908
3	0.670	0.735	33	0.959	0.888
4	0.665	0.688	34	0.857	0.977
5	0.743	0.741	35	1.083	1.008
6	0.789	0.843	36	0.909	0.824
7	0.830	0.862	37	0.921	0.950
8	0.826	0.836	38	0.945	1.052
9	0.874	0.926	39	0.791	0.880
10	0.940	0.915	40	0.890	0.898
11	0.901	0.893	41	1.076	1.140
12	0.971	1.022	42	0.829	0.845
13	0.886	0.891	43	1.096	1.036
14	0.941	0.978	44	0.836	0.771
15	0.992	0.987	45	0.637	0.811
16	0.949	0.950	46	1.070	1.018
17	0.952	0.959	47	0.781	0.857
18	0.982	0.975	48	0.798	0.701
19	0.959	1.008	49	0.897	1.136
20	0.905	0.851	50	1.037	1.023
21	0.917	0.998	51	0.925	1.261
22	1.015	0.983	52	0.846	0.927
23	0.957	0.983	53	0.687	0.566
24	0.902	0.940	54	0.908	1.003
25	0.925	0.918	55	0.936	1.249
26	0.982	0.937	56	0.672	0.872
27	0.945	1.030	57	0.674	0.674
28	0.966	0.976	58	0.968	0.968
29	0.875	0.800	59	0.945	0.945
30	0.911	1.001	60	0.000	0.000

experience and those made with the most recent experience from 1994 to 1999 (an average of five factors). At long durations, where some individual factors are 0, the arithmetical mean is substituted for the geometrical one.

The curve of the development factors has the following characteristics. The smallest factor is at duration 2. Then the factors increase steadily and tend to stabilize around 0.95. At longer durations, they become more volatile and fluctuate around 1. The volatility is partly related to the fact that fewer factors were used in computing the average factor. The irregular pattern at long durations because of a small volume of data must be managed with care, and judgement is then an important factor in the setting of the assumptions.

Understanding past experience and new trends is essential for feeding the actuary's judgement for the selection of the experience period to be considered. A graph of the two curves may help assess any differences.

Figure 17.1 shows the ratios of the average five more recent development factors over those of the average of the ten most recent development factors. Ratios are generally slightly higher than 1. Fluctuations around unity increase

Figure 17.1 Ratio of development factors (DF 5 years of experience ÷ DF 10 years of experience)

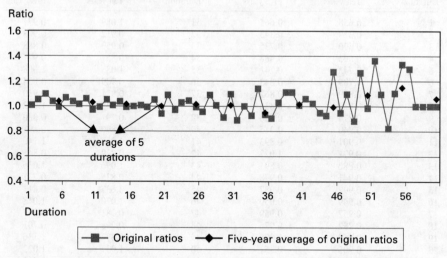

sharply with duration. The difference between the ten-year experience and the five-year experience is not very large. This shows that the experience has been fairly stable, at least for the first 25 durations, where the volume of data is probably significant enough to minimize random fluctuations. The actuary should be particularly careful when setting the experience at short durations, since they have a strong influence on the estimation of payments at longer durations.

Because the observed development factors are volatile by duration, significant differences between the projected and observed payments should be expected for each cell of injury year and financial year. However, the differences may tend to offset each other, and those of a financial year or of an injury year (if a cohort is considered) should be within a reasonable range.

We continue the example with the ten-year development factors because they are more stable by duration. This will facilitate the last step of the process, which is to build a smooth table that represents the most probable expected experience.

17.4.3 Graduated development factors

Table 17.5 presents the factors that have been set after the raw data have been graduated. The factor at duration 1 is the only one that is the same as the raw data. Development factors for durations 2 to 60 are obtained by applying a smoothing formula to the raw data, and factors at duration 61 are set to 0. Figure 17.2 indicates the impact of the graduation process.

Table 17.5 Graduated development factors

Duration	Factor	Duration	Factor	Duration	Factor
1	0.6612	21	0.9569	41	0.9109
2	0.3433	22	0.9542	42	0.9063
3	0.6618	23	0.9514	43	0.9013
4	0.7026	24	0.9488	44	0.8960
5	0.7413	25	0.9464	45	0.8903
6	0.7776	26	0.9443	46	0.8843
7	0.8112	27	0.9424	47	0.8780
8	0.8417	28	0.9409	48	0.8714
9	0.8688	29	0.9395	49	0.8645
10	0.8923	30	0.9383	50	0.8573
11	0.9121	31	0.9370	51	0.8498
12	0.9282	32	0.9357	52	0.8421
13	0.9408	33	0.9343	53	0.8340
14	0.9502	34	0.9326	54	0.8256
15	0.9566	35	0.9306	55	0.8169
16	0.9605	36	0.9282	56	0.8079
17	0.9624	37	0.9255	57	0.7986
18	0.9625	38	0.9224	58	0.7890
19	0.9614	39	0.9190	59	0.7791
20	0.9594	40	0.9151	60	0.7689

Figure 17.2 Development factors

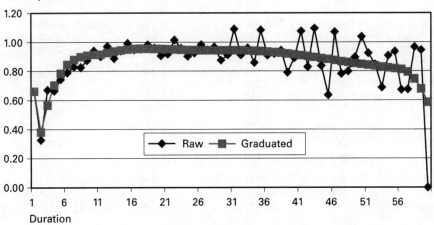

Actuarial practice in social security

The graduation has been performed with a Whittaker-Henderson type formula weighted by the amounts of payments at each duration by using the data from durations 3 to 60. Duration 61 is the first where the factor is 0. The transition between the factor at duration 60 and duration 61 is fairly abrupt, and an actuary might prefer to make an adjustment to shorten the stage. For example, one might prefer to be prudent and set a duration where the development factor is 0 at an age higher than 60. In theory, the longest duration could be the difference between the ultimate age of the mortality table and the youngest age at which a worker can be injured. The development factor table probably slightly underestimates the potential payments to be made at long durations, but sensitivity tests would indicate that this is not really material in the present circumstances.

17.4.4 Tests

The factors are now ready to be tested with real data. The tests consist of projecting the payments in the next financial years and calculating the cost of an injury year and the liabilities. Table 17.6 shows the estimated payments in the

Table 17.6 Development factors

Duration	Amounts paid in 1999	Projected amounts in 2000	Adjusted amounts in 1999	Projected amounts in 2000
0	83 853		83 853	
1	52 303	57 107	52 806	57 107
2	14 941	18 494	17 450	18 672
3	11 132	10 185	13 018	11 895
4	10 458	8 056	10 804	9 421
5	6 844	7 985	8 007	8 249
6	5 004	5 482	5 615	6 413
7	3 929	4 181	4 062	4 691
8	3 510	3 406	3 751	3 522
9	2 596	3 141	2 889	3 357
10	1 960	2 386	1 875	2 655
11	1 328	1 841	1 503	1 761
12	1 292	1 270	1 440	1 436
13	1 701	1 252	1 633	1 395
14	1 207	1 665	1 360	1 599
15	1 343	1 189	1 402	1 340
16	1 007	1 329	1 139	1 387
17	1 135	998	1 220	1 129
18	848	1 125	916	1 209
19	1 046	840	1 057	907
20	738	1 034	839	1 044
21	612	727	639	827
22	555	601	614	628
23	558	544	546	601
24	618	545	556	533

Medical expenses and rehabilitation benefits

Table 17.6 (continued)

Duration	Amounts paid in 1999	Projected amounts in 2000	Adjusted amounts in 1999	Projected amounts in 2000
25	526	602	550	542
26	311	512	338	535
27	614	302	528	328
28	357	595	397	511
29	507	345	493	385
30	341	490	355	477
31	182	329	166	343
32	160	175	150	160
33	141	154	164	145
34	117	135	110	157
35	111	112	101	106
36	76	106	78	97
37	202	72	184	74
38	74	192	77	175
39	41	70	58	73
40	45	39	49	55
41	90	42	91	46
42	107	84	131	85
43	49	99	43	122
44	100	45	95	40
45	31	92	27	87
46	64	28	61	25
47	43	58	34	55
48	12	39	12	30
49	26	11	19	11
50	27	23	25	17
51	31	24	18	22
52	22	27	18	16
53	28	19	31	16
54	3	24	4	26
55	0	3	0	3
56	3	0	3	0
57	8	2	7	2
58	4	7	3	6
59	0	3	0	3
60	0	0	0	0
Total	**214 971**	**140 243**	**223 414**	**146 553**

year following the valuation year according to two sets of reference payments in the valuation year: the reference payments are those of the valuation year or a weighted average of the last three years (except for durations 0 and 1). In the latter case, the adjusted payments are calculated with formula 17.4 and the inflation factors of table 17.2. The inflation between the valuation year and the next year is assumed to be 3 per cent.

The ratio of adjusted reference amounts to non-adjusted reference amounts is 103.9 per cent, while the ratio of projected payments is 104.5 per cent. The adjustment payments are higher than those observed of the valuation years, except at long durations. This means that the experience has been improving at short durations, and that the reverse is true at long durations. A 4 per cent difference in the projected payments is a material one, which stresses the importance for the actuary to analyse past trends in order to understand the origin of the difference and to assess the most probable evolution in the future. In the end, the actuary must judge which approach is the most appropriate in each particular circumstance. Sensitivity analyses are useful for illustrating to the users of the actuarial reports the range of results that appear reasonable.

The costing of changes to the benefits provided by the scheme requires that the actuary make a thorough analysis of the experience in order to assess the impact of changes on the development factors. This can generally be achieved by simulating the new provisions on the amounts paid in the past and by calculating the development factors with this modified database.

Notes

[1] Cf. M. Cichon et al.: *Modelling in health care finance: A compendium of quantitative techniques for health care financing* (Geneva, ILO/ISSA, 1999), p. 132.

[2] ibid.

PART IV

THE VALUATION OF SHORT-TERM CASH BENEFITS

SICKNESS AND MATERNITY BENEFITS

18

From the point of view of cost determination, sickness cash benefits and maternity allowances have similar characteristics and appeal to the same general methodology, which is why they are examined together in this chapter. Where appropriate, though, differences in the characteristics of these two types of benefits, which may require a different costing approach or particular actuarial considerations, will be addressed.

18.1 THE FINANCIAL SYSTEM

Short-term benefits, which are payable for a limited period (generally not more than one year), are characterized by an annual expenditure that is more stable than the expenditure of a pension scheme, where the maturing process results in rising costs, at least for some decades.

The PAYG finance system usually determines the contribution rate for short-term benefits. Under this system, current contributions are estimated to meet current expenditures on benefits and administration. In order to maintain stable contribution rates, a small margin is added to the contribution rate, and the funds arising from this margin are held in a contingency reserve.

There are no hard and fast rules for determining the ideal level of contingency reserve to maintain in short-term benefits. The objective of the reserve is to support the scheme during a period of exceptionally high expenditure or at times when there is a reduction in the earnings base for contributions, without having to rely on external sources of funds to maintain the scheme.

The level of the contingency reserve should be related to the scheme's capacity to react rapidly to adverse experience and, in particular, to the period necessary to adjust the contribution rate. For example, the legislative and political environments may allow for a rapid modification of the law to raise the contribution rate in the case of adverse experience. Then, the contingency reserve could be very low, representing only a few months' expenditure. On the other hand, it may have been decided that any contribution rate revision should take place at the same frequency as the actuarial reviews of the scheme (every three years, for example), in which case a higher contingency reserve, as high as one year's expenditure, might be justified.

The level of the reserve may also be determined on the basis of risk theory, calculated according to the observed variability of the historical expenditure pattern. For example, the level of reserves might be larger in countries exposed to frequent epidemics or natural catastrophes. On that basis, the contingency reserve could be fixed at a number of standard deviations of the benefit expenditure observed over an appropriately chosen period.

18.2 DATA REQUIREMENTS

18.2.1 For sickness cash benefits

Legal provisions pertinent to cost projections include coverage rules, eligibility conditions, waiting periods, methods for determining benefits, duration of payment and rules of coordination with the long-term invalidity pension, if applicable.

Concerning data requirements for the valuation of an existing scheme, the actuary should first obtain a complete history of the income and expenditure under the scheme in order to analyse general trends in expenditure and coverage. Then, for a more refined analysis, the following data must be obtained:

- the historical sex and age distribution of the number of new benefit awards;
- the historical sex and age distribution of the average duration of payment for terminated cases;
- the historical sex and age distribution of average individual amounts of benefits;
- the starting and ending dates of each individual temporary cash benefit (for the eventual construction of a continuation table).

For a new scheme, it may be necessary to rely on external data; statistics on absenteeism and sick leave in the general labour market then become useful guides. It may also be useful to obtain sickness benefits data from other comparable countries. It is also necessary to be aware of the interaction between short-term cash benefits and other forms of social protection. For example, claimants could be expected to make greater use of those benefits that offer the higher benefit rate.

18.2.2 For maternity allowances

As for sickness benefits, the valuation of maternity benefits requires data on the applicable legal provisions: coverage rules, eligibility conditions, waiting periods, methods for determining benefits and duration of payment. Coordina-

Sickness and maternity benefits

tion rules with unemployment and sickness benefits may also be necessary. In addition, provisions concerning the various types of beneficiaries are essential. For example, benefits may be payable to either parent. The duration of payment to the father may be different than the one applicable to the mother. Benefits may be shared between the two parents according to their wishes. The scheme may also cover adoption under special rules.

Concerning statistical data, in addition to the global income and expenditure trends over past years, the actuary should obtain information on the following:

- the proportion of women in the insured population;
- the historical number of births per insured woman;
- the historical number of new benefit awards, by age;
- the historical average duration of payment (not necessarily the maximum legal duration), by age (calculated on the basis of terminated cases);
- the average relative wage of women relative to men;
- the starting and ending dates of each individual temporary cash benefit in order to build a continuation table.

In addition to these data specific to the scheme, the data and projection of the general population, available from national statistical offices or from the demographic frame used for pension projections, will give more information on future costs trends. The observed and projected fertility rates of the general population can be used as a guide. At the same time, a comparison must be made between the fertility rate of the general population and the particular rate for women covered under the scheme who may have a lower fertility rate as a result of being part of the labour force. The economic framework established for the purpose of the pension projections is also useful for assessing the future evolution of the proportion of women in the total and insured population, with its consequences on the cost of maternity benefits.

18.3 COST PROJECTIONS[1]

18.3.1 The general formula

The method presented here is based on the prospective approach. The contribution rate is fixed, in advance, according to the actuarial estimates, which used, as a basis, the previous experience of the scheme or the experience drawn from other schemes. The contribution rate thus arrived at should include a margin of safety, allowing for a contingency reserve to be set up to absorb non-foreseeable variations and occasional fluctuations in expenditure. It is important that the contribution rate is fixed in such a way that it can be kept stable for as long a period as possible.

It is extremely important that the financial regulations of the scheme contain precise provisions for fixing the contribution rate. They should also prescribe, in detail, how to determine the best time to modify the contribution rate.

The basic formula for the financial equilibrium of a social security scheme is written as:

Probable receipts = Probable expenditure

where Probable expenditure includes benefit expenditure and administrative expenditure.

The objective of actuarial estimates is, therefore, to establish the probable annual benefit expenditure. This may be done either by estimating the global amount or, when the contribution rates are fixed as a percentage of wages, the estimates often aim at establishing the relative cost, which is the annual benefit expenditure related to the total annual amount of wages in which contributions are assessed.

Box 18.1   Cost calculation for short-term benefits

Probable receipts = Contribution rate
×
Total covered insured earnings
= Contribution rate
×
Number of insured persons
×
Average insured earnings

Probable expenditure = Probable benefit expenditure
+
Probable administrative expenditure
= (Number of people exposed to risk (insured persons)
×
Frequency of occurrence of the risk
×
Average number of days per case
×
Average cost per day)
+
Estimated administrative expenditure

In this context, the insured population must be well defined. The population will normally vary according to the risk covered. For example, the self-employed are often excluded from the coverage of sickness benefits.

18.3.2 Special considerations for sickness benefits

New scheme

Depending on the reliability of the statistical basis used for the calculations, it may be necessary to add a safety margin in order to absorb unforeseen variations in the various elements that have entered into the formula or to build up the minimum contingency reserve required by the definition of the actuarial equilibrium. If the scheme is new, which means that the elements are not drawn from the experience of the scheme, one has to be particularly prudent. Firstly, if the estimates have been based on statistics available on absenteeism in establishments, these statistics will be influenced by a series of factors that do not apply to a new scheme, so that it cannot be assumed that the data represent the morbidity (that is, disability) rate that a social security scheme will have to face. These factors include, for example, the level of benefits for temporary incapacity granted by the establishment compared with the level provided by the social security scheme, the attitude of individuals towards the benefits, the control of temporary incapacity, etc. All such factors have to be taken into account when assessing the basic data for actuarial estimates.

What is also important is the fact that experience shows that the morbidity rate is low during the first years of a new scheme before the insured persons have become fully aware of their rights. The morbidity rate will, therefore, increase gradually over a rather long period. Consequently, the experience of a scheme in its first years cannot be taken as representative for the future operation of the scheme, and this is particularly the case if the scheme is being introduced in stages, by geographical region, by industry, or by size of establishment. Under some schemes, the fact that the benefit expenditure has proved to be substantially lower than the estimates during the first years has led some authorities to raise the benefits. Later, when the scheme has been in operation for a sufficiently long period, the receipts may no longer be sufficient to cover the expenditure and it will be necessary to have recourse to an increase in contributions, to subsidies from public funds, or to a reduction in benefits.

Recent changes

The scheme may have been modified over recent years. If the calculations are based on past experience, the actuary may have to adjust the frequency, average duration or benefit amounts to estimate the real future costs.

Actuarial practice in social security

Seasonal employment

Seasonal employment brings particular problems for the application of a sickness benefit scheme. The eligibility conditions for sickness benefits are often expressed in terms of a number of weeks of contribution during a recent period (for example, 13 weeks of contribution over the past six months). In this case, seasonal workers gradually lose their right to a benefit as time passes, even if they are regularly employed on a seasonal basis. The actuary is often asked to review the eligibility conditions for sickness benefits in order to improve the coverage of seasonal workers. This may be done, for example, by extending the period over which the eligibility test is performed (the scheme could use a period of observation of 12 instead of six months). Alternatively, the actuary could propose proportional benefits to seasonal workers, based on the fact that they do not pay contributions for the whole year. The recommendation of the actuary should take into account the profile of seasonal employment in the country and the weight that seasonal workers represent in the total labour force.

If it is observed that most sickness benefits are paid to seasonal workers, this may be a sign that sickness benefits are being used to replace UI. On the other hand, if almost no benefits go to seasonal workers, this may be the result of too stringent eligibility conditions.

Average earnings

The earnings profile of insured persons who claim benefits should be compared with the average earnings of the total population of contributors to the scheme. It may happen that claimants in certain sectors of the economy have particular earnings characteristics, which may have an important effect on costs.

18.3.3 Special considerations for maternity benefits

Fertility rate of women in the labour force

There is almost certainly a significant difference between the fertility of women in the labour force and that of women outside the labour force, with working women having a lower fertility rate. However, fertility statistics are usually available only for the general population, so the actuary may need to carry out special investigations or surveys, especially to do the costing of a new plan. In such a situation, age-specific fertility rates will have to be matched with the distribution of insured women by age, paying attention to the proportion of married women within each age group. For an existing plan, the scheme's previous experience can be compared with general demographic data to detect any trends and reflect them in the cost projections.

Duration of benefit

Attention must be given to the level of the maternity benefit in proportion to wages. A low benefit level may force women to return to work before the maximum number of weeks of benefit is up. Therefore, it is not certain that all beneficiaries will stay on benefit for the maximum duration allowed by the scheme.

Another factor that will influence the duration of benefits is whether the national labour law protects a woman's job while she is absent from work to care for a newborn child, and for how long this protection is guaranteed.

Benefit recipient

Some schemes allow either parent to receive the "maternity" benefit, although the initial portion (say, for the first three or four months) is normally reserved for the mother. This flexibility might increase the average duration of benefits slightly or it might mean somewhat higher costs if some of the benefits are paid to a parent (usually the father) with higher earnings. However, the experience in a number of countries (such as Sweden and Canada) has shown that the take-up of parental benefits by fathers is normally very low, with well over 90 per cent of such benefits being paid to mothers.

Adoption

Benefits are sometimes paid on the adoption of a child, which means that the database should also include adoption data. While this is generally not an important cost element, the actuary should consider all possible cases, of which adoption is one.

18.3.4 Possible refinements

Refinements in the basic formula can be introduced by subdividing the insured population into sub-groups, for example by age, sex, geographical region, occupation, etc. Insured earnings and benefit expenditure are then divided according to the chosen categories, separate costs are determined for each one, and a global contribution rate may be calculated by applying the appropriate weights.

Another refinement consists of building a continuation table showing, for a given number of new cases, the number of cases still on benefit at specific durations. With the continuation table, the average duration is replaced by a table showing, for an initial number of new benefit cases, the number of people still receiving benefits after a certain number of days, weeks or months. This type of table enables, for example, an estimation to be made of the effect of extending the waiting period, or the effect of limiting the maximum benefit duration. The reader can refer to section 15.3.3, which discusses the construction of a continuation table for temporary incapacity cash benefits in the work injury context. The same methodology applies to sickness and maternity benefits.

Notes

[1] This section contains extensive extracts from ILO: *Social security financing* (Geneva, 1997).

UNEMPLOYMENT INSURANCE 19

19.1. INTRODUCTION

19.1.1 UI and the insurance concepts

In the particular field of UI, actuaries can draw on their knowledge of the design and operation of insurance plans, while nevertheless making allowances for the fact that a UI scheme is more akin to the group form of private insurance than to the individual form. UI also comprises social and welfare characteristics, which are irrelevant to private insurance, thus earning it the designation of social insurance.

Most of the traditional insurance concepts still apply to UI, such as the following factors:

- there is an insurable risk (that of unemployment), which is outside the control of the insured; its occurrence, timing and severity is uncertain but predictable according to the law of large numbers; the fact that the risk has occurred must be objectively verifiable;
- there is an insurable interest, something of value to lose by the occurrence of the risk, namely the earnings from the employment that would otherwise have continued;
- there is a specified benefit;
- there is a deductible, in the form of an initial waiting period before benefits are paid;
- there is a co-insurance, since earnings are only partially replaced;
- it avoids moral hazard, for example, by at least partially denying or delaying benefits to people leaving employment voluntarily;
- it pays out benefits as a matter of right without any means, needs or income tests; and
- it pools risks.

Among the group insurance characteristics of UI are:

- uniform premiums;
- mandatory coverage in lieu of an individual selection and assessment of risks;
- a uniform benefit rate, as opposed to individually chosen levels of coverage;
- the sharing of costs between employees and employers; and
- the participation of employers in premium collection and in claims administration.

Social or welfare characteristics would be, for example:

- the extension of coverage to seasonal workers;
- higher rates of benefit for people with dependants, and
- a longer allowed duration of benefits in areas of high unemployment.

It would not be appropriate to ascribe such objectives as income redistribution, income maintenance or support, maintaining of purchasing power, or improvements in the national income as a UI programme's primary goals; some of these may flow from the natural operation of a UI programme. But it is important to maintain clear objectives in the design of UI – or else the plan will lose its focus and become ineffective. UI, like any insurance plan, should serve to protect people against an unpredictable loss that would be too onerous to bear in the absence of insurance. In the case of UI, it is the loss of earnings caused by unemployment that is insured through a partial replacement of those earnings. By its very nature, such a scheme will obviously lead to a redistribution of income from the employed to the unemployed – in the same way that any insurance plan leads to a redistribution "in favour" of those who suffer a contingency. But such redistribution is a result and not an objective, and should not be taken as one. In a broad sense, it is correct to say that the goal of a UI plan, indeed of many insurance plans, is the prevention of poverty. However, this should not lead to benefits being targeted mainly or only on those already at or near poverty levels, since that would imply that it was not an insurance undertaking. If such targeting is indeed intended, then the scheme should be one of unemployment assistance, with means and needs tests, attendant rules and general revenue financing.

19.1.2 Expertise and background required of a UI actuary

The UI actuary should have a large enough knowledge of economics to understand the context within which the insurance scheme will operate, as well as an understanding of applicable labour legislation and legal principles. The accounting and financial framework for public institutions should also be understood. The actuary should be acquainted, too, with the other public and private schemes alongside which UI has to operate and which interact with it: welfare, workmen's compensation, short- and long-term disability insurance, public and private pensions, severance laws and indemnities, and any other source of income available to individuals who lose their jobs.

In order to develop and apply sound methodology when establishing projected costs and revenue for UI, the actuary needs a solid background in such issues as business cycles, economic forecasts, inflation and labour market trends. The actuary would not usually be responsible for making economic forecasts but should be in a position to understand them and eventually to make informed choices when faced with different opinions or when having to provide a range of high and low projections.

In addition to the above, the UI actuary should be fully acquainted with the design of the legislation under review as well as with its policies and field operations. These policies and operations may evolve in a way that will have a significant result on financial outcomes, sometimes as significant as the formal legislative rules adopted by legislators. Actuaries should, therefore, not confine themselves to the role of technical expert but should view their role as encompassing a working knowledge of all related fields, notably accounting, legal and financial matters, statistical reporting and computer systems.

A good knowledge of Conventions and Recommendations of the ILO that relate to employment and unemployment is also necessary. The ILO Employment Promotion and Protection against Unemployment Convention, 1988 (No. 168) sets an international standard for protection against unemployment, expanding the previous Social Security (Minimum Standards) Convention, 1952 (No. 102), which still applies to developing countries. The accompanying Employment Promotion and Protection against Unemployment Recommendation, 1988 (No. 176) intends to orient national policies. As noted in Article 2 of Convention No. 168, it is important to coordinate the system of protection against unemployment and employment policy. In particular, the parameters of a UI programme should not be "such as to discourage employers from offering and workers from seeking productive employment". The Convention also encourages the active promotion of employment opportunities through training and special measures for disadvantaged people, whether "women, young workers, disabled persons, older workers, the long-term unemployed, migrant workers lawfully resident in the country and workers affected by structural change".

In providing advice on any aspect of a UI programme, the actuary should constantly have these objectives in mind, along with the insurance principles quoted above. Any proposal that runs counter to them would be of little worth.

19.2 UI PROJECTIONS IN GENERAL

What is needed in respect of each relevant factor is a historical perspective on how each factor behaved or would have behaved under a UI programme, which can then be linked to economic and labour force forecasts for the ensuing period.

All projections are predicated on the availability of adequate statistics for the required assumptions. The statistical systems of countries differ widely, so it is up to the actuary to assess the available sources of information and to make any essential adjustments. If it becomes necessary to supplement national data, the expertise and data of other countries can be of help to the actuary.[1]

19.2.1 Data sources

Within a country, there may be a variety of statistical data sources available. They can be broken down into four main categories:

1. Census data: for the general population and for each type of worker (employed or self-employed), their labour force activity at the time of the census and/or during the last year, their occupations, age and sex, their annual income by source, and frequently other types of information, all of which can be cross-tabulated in various ways.
2. Survey data: monthly labour force estimates (employment by industry/occupation/education, unemployment, previous activity, all by age, sex), estimates of average wages by industry, estimates of total wages, CPI, etc.
3. Operational and financial data: from the UI system itself for payouts and revenues (the latter from tax departments if they collect revenues on behalf of the UI programme), from tax departments for total declared income and deductions from revenue, potentially broken down by age, sex, sources of income, dependency status, etc.
4. Economic data: changes in GDP by component, usually published quarterly.

Each source has its own particular features. *Census data* will be quite complete and exhaustive but will generally not be available until at least a few years after each census has been conducted. Timeliness is thus an issue, especially concerning labour force data. *Survey data* will normally be the most current and thus a crucial source of information but they must be viewed with some caution because of potential sampling variability or errors. In addition, survey methodologies may at times be updated and historical continuity may not always be assured. Reliable and timely *operational and financial data* on the operations of the UI programme is vital, and should provide extensive information on the benefits paid, on beneficiaries, on contributors (employers and employees) and on the overall financial status of the UI programme. *Economic data* will provide an overall summary of the economy's behaviour and direction, with its components derived either from general or special surveys or from the aggregation of a wide variety of data from commercial firms, public administrations, financial institutions and other sources.

A thorough understanding of all of these sources is needed, of the concepts and definitions underlying each of them, of the methods used to collect and compile the statistics, of their limitations, of the degree of accuracy required by each agency and of the completeness with which they are reported, of their legislative setting and of any other relevant factors. In other words, it can never be assumed that statistical data have a particular meaning until they have been investigated in full. Unemployment, UI beneficiaries, average or total wages, to name just a few, can have different meanings in different settings or to different people: it is important to see which apply in the particular situation under study.

19.3 BUSINESS CYCLES AND STABILITY

19.3.1 The desirability of premium financing for UI (for macroeconomic stabilization)

A UI programme should be financed in such a way as to contribute to a counter-cyclical stabilization of the economy.[2] Namely, its revenue requirements should remain as stable as possible over time and especially not be increased with the onset of a recession, as this would only make the recession worse. Clearly, this implies the need for some form of dedicated financing that can be used to establish and maintain rainy day reserves. Such reserves are, in one sense, of the same type that exist for life insurance policies in that they are established to stabilize premiums against a contingency that occurs with very volatile probabilities. For life insurance, the variation is generally one of a steady growth in the probability of dying (though not necessarily so, if one considers the sharp rise in mortality rates for youths around the age of 20). For UI, the variation is one of successive ups and downs in the probability of becoming unemployed, following economic cycles.

19.3.2 A discussion of business cycles

The projection period should, therefore, be long enough to cover a business cycle. This would be true even without a dedicated form of financing, to allow the UI plan's sponsors and the general public to get a realistic perspective of the potential costs under varying economic conditions. There has been speculation, especially in North America, that economic activity may be getting less volatile and business cycles getting longer. Some of the factors invoked in those arguments are: the rise of the service and government sectors (which are less cyclical than the primary and secondary sectors), the use of automatic stabilizers (for example, the progressive income tax system and UI), various financial reforms, or changes in inventory behaviour and increased globalization.

Business cycles[3] are a recurring and widespread pattern of economic recession and expansion. Most countries are usually synchronized in their business cycles, although this is not necessarily the case if one looks at the situation in developing and industrial countries since the late 1980s. A model of short, steep recession followed by longer, slower expansion is common, as noted in an IMF working paper.[4] Similarly, the National Bureau of Economic Research (NBER) in the United States has measured the nine post-war cycles in the United States as lasting 5.1 years on average, with only 11 months of recession and 4.2 years of expansion. Such a model generally implies a rapid erosion of UI reserves at the recession's onset, followed by a slow period of rebuilding as the economy stabilizes and then regains its lost momentum.

However, there are no hard and fast rules as to the length or amplitude of business cycles. Furthermore, economic forecasters generally do not anticipate points of turnaround in business cycles, and some studies have indicated that the probability of recession has no relationship with the duration of an ongoing expansion. Business cycles have been observed to last anywhere from between a single year to up to eight or ten years, and their length can vary per country. A recent study found an average business cycle of 4.8 years in 13 industrialized countries since the Second World War.[5] The averages varied between 3.6 and 5.8 years, showing similarity among those countries.

What to do? The appropriate course would be to cover at least two significant cycles of expansion and recession, which would probably mean making projections for a period of about ten to 15 years (though one country[6] has been seen to have business cycles lasting an average of 15 years). However, given the poor economic forecasts of the past, it would be wise to make a set of projections that cover a multitude of scenarios as to the shape of future business cycles. This would provide a range of potential outcomes for UI benefit payouts and for the revenues needed to pay for them on which one could build short- and medium-term proposals for policy and revenue schedules.

By making such predictions, it should be possible to provide a range for the reserves needed to offset the additional benefits to be paid during recessionary periods. Barring the accumulation of adequate reserves, a modest increase in premium revenues could be implemented at some time after the peak of a recession, although it should be kept to a minimum. A reasonable degree of deficit financing might even be envisaged as an alternative, though this could run the risk of eroding confidence in the management of the UI programme and could provoke demands for benefit reductions through legislation.

Should financial pressures mount, benefit reductions of a temporary nature could be adopted until things improve. This assumes a broad consensus within society as to the continuing design of the UI scheme itself, but there will be calls for a permanent reduction in benefits. This debate is inevitable but should not take place in the midst of a recession and of fiscal constraints that render the discussion biased by current events[7] rather than on its merits and long-term strategic planning.

19.4 THE PROJECTION OF BENEFITS

The first task is the projection of benefit payouts. Conceptually, the annual cost of a UI programme is equal to the insured population, multiplied by the annual incidence of unemployment among that population, times the rate at which the unemployed meet eligibility requirements, times the average duration of claim, times the average periodical benefit while on claim.

The basic formula for projecting annual UI benefit costs is as follows:

Formula 19.1

$$\text{ANN\_UI\_COSTS} = \text{POP} * \text{ANN\_UN\_INC(INS)} * \text{QUAL\_RATE} * \text{AV\_DURN(CLM)} * \text{AV\_BEN}$$

where:

ANN_UI_COSTS	= Annual UI benefit costs
POP	= Insured population
ANN_UN_INC(INS)	= Annual unemployment incidence (in the insured population)
QUAL_RATE	= Rate at which the insured unemployed are eligible
AV_DURN(CLM)	= Average duration on claim in a year, expressed in weeks
AV_BEN	= Average weekly benefit paid to claimants

We shall consider each of these five factors in turn. The *insured population* depends on the specific terms of the enabling legislation, and will most frequently be limited to paid employees, paid hourly or salaried. The ILO's Convention No. 168 proposes that at least 85 per cent of paid employees be covered. This excludes self-employed workers, for whom the Convention recommends special provisions, as well as certain uninsured new jobseekers. Regular UI coverage cannot be extended to the self-employed because of their control over most aspects of their work (level and timing of reported earnings, extent and timing of employment or unemployment). There might be exclusions for certain industries or types of employment, but in modern economies the risk of unemployment has become a concern for most workers and broad coverage is thus generally preferable. It might have been appropriate in the past to exclude certain categories of stable or high-wage workers on the grounds that they had too small a risk of becoming unemployed, but this seems less valid today.

Unemployment insurance

The *incidence of insured unemployment* comes next in the equation. Unfortunately, historical data are seldom available. What is usually available, though, is the rate of *total* (not insured) unemployment, and it is possible to derive the incidence from that rate, as follows:

1. The incidence of total unemployment applied to the annual labour force would produce the number of people becoming unemployed in a year.
2. Multiplying this number by the average duration of unemployment would produce the total weeks of unemployment in a year.
3. The total weeks of unemployment can be found by multiplying the annual unemployment rate by the average labour force times the number of weeks in a year (52).
4. The annual labour force times the average number of weeks worked is equal to the average labour force times 52.

By substitution and rearrangement, the incidence of total unemployment can be found by multiplying the average annual rate of unemployment by the average number of weeks worked and dividing the result by the average duration of unemployment. The average duration used here would be for people being unemployed for a certain duration of the year, calculated from the time spent unemployed since the beginning of their current spell, even if it began in a previous year. Although this differs from the average that would be obtained for people becoming unemployed during the year, such a duration should be a reasonable proxy in most circumstances. One method of finding the average number of weeks worked in a year, if it is not available from published statistics, would be to divide the average earnings of paid workers (say, from taxation statistics) by their average weekly earnings, the latter usually being produced on a survey basis, after making any necessary definitional adjustments to each of these measures to ensure their consistency.

The formula for determining the incidence of insured unemployment is as follows:

Formula 19.2

$$UN\_INC(INS) \approx UN\_INC(TOT) = UN\_RATE * [AWW(LF) \div AV\_DURN(UN)]$$

from:

Formula 19.3

$$UN\_INC(TOT) * LF(ANN) = UN(ANN)$$

Formula 19.4

$$UN(ANN) * AV\_DURN(UN) = TOT\_WKS(UN)$$

Actuarial practice in social security

Formula 19.5

$$TOT\_WKS(UN) = UN\_RATE * LF(AV) * 52$$

Formula 19.6

$$LF(ANN) * AWW(LF) = LF(AV) * 52$$

where:

UN_INC(INS)	=	Unemployment incidence, insured
UN_INC(TOT)	=	Unemployment incidence, total
UN(ANN)	=	Annual number of people with some unemployment
UN_RATE	=	Unemployment rate, as generally published by statistical agencies
AWW(LF)	=	Average weeks worked in the total labour force (can be derived from total wages divided by average weekly earnings)
AV_DURN(UN)	=	Average duration of an unemployment spell within a year
TOT_WKS(UN)	=	Total weeks of unemployment within a year
LF(ANN)	=	Labour force, annual count
LF(AV)	=	Labour force, average during a year

The attentive reader will have seen that it is necessary to pay close attention to definitions and to the differences between annual counts and annual averages. It is important to understand fully all of the concepts involved and to work carefully through the formulae in order to be able to assess and work with their results.

As noted, the resulting incidence is for *total* unemployment and not for insured unemployment. If the insured population is a very high proportion of the total worker population, the actuary can consider this incidence as a reasonable proxy. Even if the proportion of insured to total labour force is less than, say, 80 per cent, the proxy should still be reasonably acceptable – unless it is known or believed that the insured population differs strikingly from the overall labour force in this regard. If so, some adjustment based on judgement should be made and the fact noted for future reviews based on eventual experience.

It should be noted that the risk being considered here is unemployment. By international standards, an unemployed person is one who is without work, is currently available for work and seeking work. People temporarily laid off with an expectation of recall as well as those waiting for a job to start soon will normally also be considered unemployed, again subject to their being available for work. That definition however may not always coincide exactly with the conditions under which unemployment benefits are paid. For example, people who have resigned without reason or have been fired due to misconduct are often considered ineligible for a period of time, even while they are legitimately seeking employment. Conversely, it may happen at times that out-of-work people receive unemployment benefit, even though they are not looking for work, perhaps because of a temporary lack of jobs in their area at that particular time of year. Such unemployment beneficiaries would usually not be included in the official count of the unemployed, yet they could be legitimate recipients of benefit. Official statistics and definitions need to be verified for their applicability in the operational setting and adjusted as necessary.

The *rate of eligibility* defines the proportion of the insured unemployed who qualify for benefits. This is the proportion of those former workers who had recently worked long enough (or had enough earnings, depending on legislative requirements) to be entitled to benefits. If the UI programme is to fulfil its role, by and large, most workers who lose their jobs involuntarily should qualify for benefit. ILO Convention No. 168 refers to a qualifying period that is long enough to prevent abuse, which should be adapted to the circumstances of seasonal workers. It is normal practice to impose a dual requirement of recency and sufficiency of insured employment to prove that the insured person has a material interest and to inhibit people from seeking employment for easy (benefit) money. These conditions are similar to a probation period in disability insurance, and seek to ensure that insurance is incidental to employment and not the main reason for obtaining it.

This rate of eligibility should not be based on the work experience of the entire insured population, since the out-of-work segment should have less labour force attachment (and lower earnings). However, to introduce a margin of conservatism in the projections, the experience of the whole of the insured population could be considered as an upper limit on expected outcomes.

Under commercial insurance, there are no premiums charged during such a probation period, because the insurance is not yet in force: any premiums would be refunded if benefit eligibility were not attained. Under UI, however, premiums would normally be payable during the initial period while eligibility was being built up. This is a characteristic of social insurance; the rationale behind it is that individuals gradually earn their right to benefit.

The *average duration of a claim* depends on the initial waiting period, on the duration of the unemployment period and on the rules setting out what period will be covered by the UI programme. It is usual practice to set out an initial waiting period during which no benefits are paid out. The length of the waiting period is usually at least one week, with the ILO Convention No. 168 recommending seven days but no more than ten days, subject to adjustments for seasonal workers.

There are a number of reasons for having a waiting period: (1) similar to the deductible in private insurance, a waiting period eliminates claims which individuals should be able to cover on their own; (2) it reduces benefit costs; (3) it eliminates administration costs for numerous small claims, which could otherwise be disproportionately high; (4) it provides the administrative apparatus with the time to set up the claim; (5) it allows for the efficient verification of claims, as it could otherwise be very difficult to establish whether people had really become unemployed or were just absent for a few days; and (6) many short absences are, in any case, covered by holiday or severance pay or other monies. If one's circumstances are such that even a short waiting period imposes an excessive financial strain, then general welfare should provide appropriate relief.

Once the waiting period has been served, the duration of benefits depends on how long a person will stay unemployed and on the maximum period of benefits that are allowed by legislation. Such a maximum period will frequently be related to the length of time worked (or to the amount of earnings) during the previous employment period. It could also be related to economic conditions, being somewhat longer if the rate of unemployment is higher. It will be necessary to obtain the data on the distribution of unemployment spells, and of insured unemployment periods in particular, in order to assess the expected duration of benefits. One should be careful when interpreting these data, since statistical agencies normally consider that a spell of unemployment has been interrupted or completed by any period of work or withdrawal from the labour force. Yet the application of the maximum UI duration would usually stipulate that the maximum number of benefit weeks could be spread over a longer period of time, for example, a maximum of 26 weeks within a 52-week window. This is to encourage unemployed claimants to take up any suitable job that may become available while on claim, which they could do without jeopardizing their UI entitlement. ILO Convention No. 168 requires a minimum duration of 26 weeks for each spell of unemployment, and of 39 weeks over 24 months.

The *rate of benefits* is the last component in the benefit formula. It will normally be set as a proportion of the average employment earnings over the recent period, with a minimum rate of 50 per cent being set out in ILO Convention No. 168. The formula for determining average earnings is critical. That average could vary significantly, depending on whether or not it includes weeks of low earnings and, in particular, the weeks of often reduced earnings just before job loss, when the worker's employment activities are gradually being wound down.

It would not be appropriate to use the average earnings of all workers as a proxy for those of job losers, because the incidence of unemployment is normally greater among workers with lower education and skills and among younger workers. It might be possible to consider the variation in earnings by age or educational status if it is available, or by occupation or industry for those most affected by unemployment. As for the rate of eligibility, the experience of all insured workers could at least be useful as a conservative upper limit.

Unemployment insurance

It should be borne in mind that the composition of unemployed workers may vary over the different phases of a business cycle. The onset of a recession could first bring layoffs among low-paid workers, in lower paid sectors or with lower seniority, but soon lead to the loss of better paying jobs and to a consequential rise in the average benefits paid. Depending on the nature of each recession, the affected industries could vary, and this too could affect the payout.

An alternative approach for the projection of UI benefits

With an understanding of the factors that underlie a benefit projection, an alternative methodology can – and probably should – be used once a UI programme has developed a base of experience. This starts from the simplest of equations, under which the annual cost of UI benefits equals the number of benefit weeks paid multiplied by the average benefit per week. The task is then to project both these components based on their expected rate of change from year to year.

An alternative costing formula for an ongoing UI programme is as follows:

Formula 19.7

$$\text{ANN\_UI\_COSTS}^Z = \text{ANN\_UI\_COSTS}^{Z-1} * [\text{LF(AV)}^Z \div \text{LF(AV)}^{Z-1}] \\ * [\text{UN\_RATE}^Z \div \text{UN\_RATE}^{Z-1}] \\ * [\text{BU\_RATIO}^Z \div \text{BU\_RATIO}^{Z-1}] \\ * [\text{AV\_BEN}^Z \div \text{AV\_BEN}^{Z-1}]$$

from:

Formula 19.8

$$\text{ANN\_UI\_COSTS} = \text{BEN\_WKS} * \text{AV\_BEN}$$

Formula 19.9

$$\text{BEN\_WKS} = \text{LF(AV)} * \text{UN\_RATE} * \text{BU\_RATIO} * 52$$

Formula 19.10

$$\text{BU\_RATIO} = \text{BEN} \div \text{UN(AV)}$$

where: Superscripted indices refer to the year under consideration (Z) or the previous year ($Z-1$).

ANN_UI_COSTS =	Annual UI benefit costs
LF(AV) =	Average labour force during a year
UN_RATE =	Unemployment rate of the total labour force
BU_RATIO =	Ratio of beneficiaries to unemployed

AV_BEN = Average weekly benefits paid to claimants
BEN_WKS = Total benefit weeks paid in a year
BEN = Average number of beneficiaries for a year
UN(AV) = Average number of unemployed (total) for a year

The costing formula shown above should be seen to derive directly from the fact that the annual benefit weeks equal the labour force multiplied by the unemployment rate times the ratio of beneficiaries to unemployed times 52. The number of benefit weeks for a year (or any period of time) must equal the average number of benefit recipients (also referred to as beneficiaries) over that period multiplied by its length, which is given. So, it is the number of beneficiaries that has to be projected. It is common to do this by considering the *ratio of beneficiaries to unemployed*, on the basis that a UI programme usually covers a large share or at least a fairly constant share of the labour force. Thus, barring important changes in legislation or in the work histories of the unemployed, this ratio should be fairly predictable. The number of beneficiaries could be tabulated once a month, for example, in the same week as the carrying out of the labour force survey. Alternatively, the number of benefit weeks paid in a month could be divided by the number of weeks in that month.

Historical trends in the ratio can be observed and related to factors such as the proportion of the labour force that is covered by the UI programme and the proportion of the unemployed who have been out of work for longer than the maximum benefit period. In addition, the ratio of beneficiaries to unemployed tends to fluctuate during a business cycle. For example, the ratio would be expected to rise in the early stages of a recession, since, after a period of economic prosperity, most job losers would have sufficient past work and earnings to qualify for benefits. Thereafter, the ratio could fall to below its pre-recession level, as persisting recession caused many UI claimants to exhaust their benefits while still unemployed. Then, as the economic recovery took hold and unemployment levels subsided, the ratio could move back up towards its long-term trend level.

The above behaviour of the ratio of beneficiaries to unemployed is only an illustration of possible outcomes, because the interplay of the economy and the labour market is vastly more complex than any simple description. Depending on institutional factors as well as on the occupations or skills that are in demand, the composition of the unemployed may evolve over time and may vary significantly between countries. One study, for example, comparing the unemployment rates for Portugal and for the United States from 1983 to 1997, found a similar rate of 6.5 per cent in both countries but much lower unemployment flows and much higher unemployment duration in Portugal than in the United States.[8]

To use the ratio of beneficiaries to unemployed as a projection tool, one needs labour force and unemployment projections. When the valuation of unemployment benefits is part of the actuarial review of the whole social security system, then the number of unemployed people may be extracted from the general macroeconomic framework established as a basis of the valuation. Otherwise, labour force projections are normally available from economic forecasters, whether from within the country or from international bodies such as the IMF or the OECD. In using such forecasts, the actuary needs to be mindful of the need for safety margins and should evaluate the effects of different economic scenarios.

The second component of the benefit projection, under the alternative methodology, is the *average benefit per week*. In addition to past history, the design of the benefit formula will indicate how responsive it will be to normal wage or price growth. If benefits are related to salaries – as is most likely – and there is a maximum level of protection, average payments will grow in line with increasing wages but subject to periodic adjustments in the maximum covered wage. Even if such adjustments would occur only infrequently, perhaps subject to legislative review and decision, it might still be best to assume periodic updates. Otherwise, the effective levels of benefit protection would be implicitly assumed to erode over time and real programme costs would be assumed to fall constantly. Assuming that there are adjustments to protect the real value of benefits, the ratio of the average weekly benefit to average weekly wages should remain relatively constant over time.

The brief outline presented above on the concepts and methodology that can be applied in the field of UI should be taken as an attempt to indicate the sort of thinking that has to go into these projections. It is, however, very likely that some, if not most, of these concepts will have to be adapted significantly in the context of each individual UI programme.

Projecting administration costs

The costs of administering a UI programme are significant, particularly in regard to the administration of benefits. The collection of premiums should be susceptible to integration with the collection of other revenues for other programmes, perhaps even with general tax revenues, and should thus be relatively less onerous. It may be quite difficult to establish in advance the level of all of these costs, since the level will depend critically on the parameters of the UI programme, on the existing structures of public administration, on the capacity and likely participation of employers in the various functions (mainly, delivering accurate and timely records of earnings, properly reporting the causes of job losses, collecting and remitting premiums) and on the cooperation of the workers themselves (mostly those who lose their jobs).

In respect of benefits, the bulk of administration relates to the setting up of claims, which requires collecting the necessary information on earnings and job losses from employers, and receiving and processing applications for benefits from claimants. Applications will be fairly lengthy and complex documents, containing the claimants' characteristics, including their occupation, statement of suitable job, whether or not they expect to be recalled to work by the same employer, etc. In cases where benefits could be denied, say, where the claimant left a good job without any valid reason or was fired for misconduct, an appeal could be lodged resulting in an administrative and judicial review, which could be quite costly. There is, therefore, a need for clear rules that should be understood and acceptable to most claimants so as to minimize the number of dubious cases and equally to allow for a clear and consistent disposition of all benefit claims.

Once a claim has been established, there is a need for a continuous verification of the eligibility of claimants by ensuring that they are available for work and substantially looking for a suitable job at all times. It is also necessary to verify that they have not in fact returned to work, and to cease payments if they have. Two approaches are possible: stringent tests and investigations up front to minimize the possibility of abuse or misuse of the UI programme; or a basic reliance on the declarations made by claimants, under threat of subsequent review and a significant penalty if need be. As the latter approach is one of deterrence rather than of prevention, it would be less costly to implement, less offensive to most people and probably just as effective as the first approach.

On the premium collection side of things, it is necessary to ensure that the right amount of premiums is paid in respect of all insured persons, their insurability status being sometimes in doubt and needing verification (for example, for workers for whom the border between employment and self-employment is tenuous and uncertain).

Apart from these costs for claims and premiums, there are the overhead costs of running a UI programme, securing office space and equipment, implementing operational and computer systems, human resource management, financial administration, statistical production, etc.

As a first estimate, a loading of 5 per cent of the projected benefits may be reasonable, plus 1 per cent of premiums. Assuming premiums are in balance with costs, the result could be a rough estimate of 6 per cent of benefit costs. This is suggested only as a first approximation, since the particulars of each UI programme will be different, as will be the particulars of each country in which each plan operates.

19.5 FINANCING

19.5.1 The desirability of premium financing, and some characteristics

The actuary will not only need to make a projection of the expected payouts under a UI scheme, but also a projection of revenues if there is to be some form of autonomous financing, as opposed to state financing from general funds. Such dedicated or earmarked financing is the preferable approach to financing UI, though it may be supplemented by state financing. Not only can premium financing contribute to macroeconomic stabilization, it reinforces the insurance character of UI and helps to mitigate the feeling of stigma that often accompanies the loss of a job and the need to rely on public assistance. In addition, premium financing may serve as a partial safeguard both against undue pressures to liberalize benefits and against those to cut them back to inadequate levels. And since premiums should be seen as belonging to contributors, this mode of financing should limit the capacity of public administrations to divert UI funds towards other purposes.

Dedicated premium revenues are consistent with the insurance character of UI and would also be most likely to sustain a UI programme on its own merits, when decisions have to be taken concerning its design and financing. In that regard, it might be preferable for the finances of the UI programme to be operated at arm's length from the State's budgetary results, in order that UI funds remain fully committed to the programme. In particular, the accounting set-up should be such that the annual balance of financial results, whether positive or negative, would not affect the budgetary results of the government under which the UI programme operates. If not, there could be strong incentives for the government to intervene in the affairs of the UI system, for reasons having little or nothing to do with its proper administration and continuance.

Full or partial financing by the State will frequently occur but this, too, might run the risk of fiscal pressures on the UI system, perhaps when the economy is falling into a recession, which is when UI benefits are most needed by individuals and the State's macrostabilization role is most crucial. This risk may, however, be lessened if there is sufficient public and institutional support for public financing.

The actuary's task in regard to projecting premium revenues should be simpler than for benefits, assuming relatively stable employment and wage levels – and omitting for now the possibility of experience rating for employer premiums. Contrary to benefits, which vary significantly over the business cycle, premium revenues only vary in proportion to the employment rate (which is the complement of the unemployment rate). Irrespective of the sharing of premiums between employers and workers,[9] it would be usual to base premiums on the wages of workers with some maximum limit. In line with insurance principles, this maximum limit should be the same as the one used for benefit purposes. A lower limit would make the financial system more regressive for workers and disadvantage small employers who pay low wages by forcing them to bear a larger portion of the total costs.

An additional question for premiums is whether they should be subject to a weekly or an annual maximum. The first approach would be more consistent with the basis for paying benefits and with insurance principles. The second approach would levy higher premiums, mainly on high-wage seasonal workers, while most other workers (and their employers) would pay about the same premiums under both systems. Since most UI programmes will almost inevitably subsidize seasonal employment, the annual contributory maximum may be preferred in order to reduce the financial transfers to this group of workers.

19.5.2 Projecting revenues

The actuarial methodology for projecting premium revenues should be straightforward: annual premiums equal the number of contributors times their average contributory earnings multiplied by the rate of premium. However, one could equally work from an annual or from an average count of contributors. In the first case, the actual average earnings would enter the equation (reflecting periods off work owing to unemployment, illness, etc.), whereas the second approach would imply the use of annualized insured earnings, equivalent to average weekly insured earnings multiplied by 52. The reasons for these differences should be obvious, and are related to whether the off-periods have been accounted for in the count of contributors or in the determination of average earnings. The choice of either approach could depend on the availability of statistics as well as on whether the contribution formula operates on a weekly or an annual basis. Average contributory earnings are, in either case, the earnings of contributors up to the maximum contribution limit. When working from published statistics on the total wages paid in the national economy and on wage distributions, the actuary should be careful to note whether special forms of compensation are subject to premiums or not, for example, severance pay, vacation pay or various forms of taxable benefits.

The formula for projecting revenues is as follows:

Formula 19.11

$$ANN\_REV = CONT * AV\_CONT\_EARN * PREM\_RATE$$

from:

Formula 19.12

First form:

$$ANN\_REV = CONT(ANN)*AV\_CONT\_EARN(ANN)*PREM\_RATE$$

Second form:

$$ANN\_REV = CONT(AV) *AV\_CONT\_EARN(AV) * PREM\_RATE$$

where:

ANN_REV	= Annual premium revenues
CONT	= Contributors, generally
CONT(ANN)	= Contributors, annual count

CONT(AV) = Contributors, average
AV_CONT_EARN = Average contributory earnings, generally
AV_CONT_EARN(ANN) = Average contributory earnings, annual count
AV_CONT_EARN(AV) = Average contributory earnings, average
PREM_RATE = Premium rate (combined, employees' and employer's)

Note:

Formula 19.13

CONT(ANN) * AWW(INS) = CONT(AV) * 52

Formula 19.14

AV_CONT_EARN(ANN) ÷ AWW(INS) = AWE(INS) = AV_CONT_EARN(AV) ÷ 52

where:

AWW(INS) = Average weeks worked by the insured population

AWE(INS) = Average weekly earnings but limited to insured earnings

Although the revenue projection shown above is not expressed as a function of the previous year's results, this is an easy transformation to do (see section 19.4 on the projection of costs). Also, it is assumed in the above that employee and employer premiums are levied on the same insured earnings base. If this is not the case, adjustments will need to be made to reflect the applicable base in each circumstance. There may also be a need to adjust the above gross premium revenues to account for potential refunds to employees who hold more than one job during a year, perhaps simultaneously, and thus contribute to more than the annual maximum. It would be unusual to provide similar refunds to their employers, since: (i) the annual maximum should never be exceeded by any employer for a given employee; (ii) determining the employer "share" of the above-noted employee premium refunds would require treating separate employments together; and (iii) extending such refunds would implicitly or explicitly inform employers of other jobs held during a year by their current or former employees, a likely breach of privacy.

19.5.3 Projecting reserves and recommending premium rates

The financial system used for UI could be defined as the PAYG system with a horizon of several years. Having produced revenue estimates at different rates of premium, accounting for any state contribution, the actuary is left with the task of establishing the desirable rates of premium over future years. At that point, the task is simply to compare two revenue streams on a what-if basis

(What if premium rates were higher or lower?), accounting also for interest on reserves. In principle, one would like to have rates of premium that remain fairly stable over time. However, it is unlikely that perfect stability will be attained and occasional adjustments will probably be needed, not only on account of imperfect projections for any given unemployment rate but also, and most especially, owing to unexpected fluctuations in unemployment levels.

Economic studies have shown that abrupt changes in premium rates are detrimental to job creation and maintenance, and so should be avoided during a recession. This leads to the necessity of establishing sufficient rainy day reserves to allow premium rates to remain level when economic downturns occur. However, the size of such reserves can become very contentious. Groups who would want to liberalize benefits may see large reserves as a justification for pressing their demands, while some public authorities may see large UI reserves as a convenient source of funds for other projects. In both cases, there would be the risk of depleting reserves below safe levels.

The fact that the timing, amplitude and duration of business cycles are all quite unpredictable compounds the difficulty of establishing adequate yet non-redundant reserves. Overall, the actuary should look to recent business cycles when making projections of needed reserves and should seek to avoid both excessive optimism as well as undue caution.

19.5.4 Some thoughts on experience rating

The possible experience rating of employer premiums was mentioned above. Such a practice is currently applied in only one country, namely in the individual state programmes of the United States. Economic theory would seem to favour such an approach, yet studies have not shown convincing results in favour of experience rating, as acknowledged by many American authors. A number of factors need to be considered. In favour of experience rating, there would be the notion of financial equity and the consequential responsibility that it should place on employers to stabilize their employment[10] and to assist in policing the UI system. Employers should thus also become more reluctant to "assist" workers to gain just enough work to qualify for benefits.

On the negative side is the fact that experience rating imposes extensive administrative and regulatory burdens on employers and on the UI administration. It can also cause some employers to dispute unfairly the benefit claims made by their former workers, leading to excessive litigation, difficult employer-employee relations and significant additional administration costs.

Should this debate be raised, it would seem appropriate to point out both the advantages and pitfalls of experience rating so that any decisions are taken in full knowledge of the potential consequences. A further perspective on this issue may be whether the prevailing collective view tends towards a philosophy of collective responsibility vis-à-vis unemployment or towards one of market-orientation and individual responsibility at the employer level. This again points out the significant role that the actuary can play in a social insurance environment, namely of a professional taking into consideration theoretical, practical and perhaps even societal implications.

19.6 VALIDATION OF RESULTS

It is not enough just to produce results that appear reasonable. There should be a full validation of the results by checking consistency and ensuring that various relationships are maintained. For example, total insured earnings should maintain a relatively stable relationship with total wage earnings. The ratio of the average weekly benefit to average insured earnings should remain fairly constant. A simple but powerful check is to set all critical assumptions constant, both for the costing of benefits and for the projection of insured earnings, and then divide the resulting yearly costs by yearly insured earnings. This should produce a constant cost ratio over time and, if it does not, it is very likely that the projection model has some internal bias. If there is a good reason for a changing ratio, for example, owing to a particular design characteristic of the UI plan, of which the importance will grow over time, the actuary should note this fact for the attention of those who will receive and consider the report.

19.7 CONCLUSION

This chapter has attempted to outline some of the more important methodological and practical issues that a UI actuary has to face. The domain of UI has not always been seen as one of prime concern to actuaries, yet it is one where actuarial training and insurance principles find full application. Perhaps one of the more important challenges to the actuary, in this and other areas, is to find the proper balance between professional and general expertise. Yet, if the actuary establishes credibility by providing a cogent and thorough analysis while drawing on the lessons learned by insurance institutions over time, he or she will soon find that their advice is sought after and appreciated in the various facets of a UI programme.

Notes

[1] The ILO has an online database that offers various labour statistics, although the data on developing countries are limited.

[2] The main contribution of UI to macroeconomic stabilization is undoubtedly due to the provision of benefits to the unemployed during a recession, and thus to the maintenance of their purchasing power. However, UI financing can and should also contribute to macroeconomic stabilization. See *Canada's unemployment insurance program as an economic stabilizer* and *The UI system as an automatic stabilizer in Canada*, both available online (**www.hrdc.gc.ca**) from Human Resources Development Canada, Ottawa, Canada, May 1995.

[3] See Chapter III of the IMF's 1998 *World Economic Outlook* for a review of the main features of business cycles and theories of the business cycle.

[4] *Concordance in business cycles*, IMF Working Paper WP/00/37 (Washington, DC, March 2000).

[5] U.M. Bergman, M.D. Bordo and L. Jonung: *Historical evidence on business cycles: The international experience* (Stockholm School of Economics, Sept. 1998).

[6] In *How long is the long run? A dynamic analysis of the Spanish business cycle*, IMF Working Paper WP/97/74 (Washington, DC, June 1997).

[7] The ILO reported, for example, in its *World Labour Report 2000: Income security and social protection in a changing world*, that "almost all OECD countries in the 1990s reduced the protection provided by their unemployment benefit systems as a result of increasing financial strains [and] the publication of various studies [...] which linked the unemployment rate to unemployment benefit variables". Such links may at times be exaggerated.

[8] O. Blanchard and P. Portugal: *What hides behind an unemployment rate?: Comparing Portuguese and U.S. unemployment*, Working Paper No. W6636 (Cambridge, Massachusetts, NBER, 1 June 1998).

[9] The consensus of economic studies seems to indicate that premiums levied on employers are eventually passed on to workers through lower wages.

[10] However, one author concluded that a UI system with greater experience rating might lead to smaller fluctuations in employment over the business cycle but to lower levels of average employment than a system with less experience rating and greater variance in employment. See C.J. O'Leary and S.A. Wandner (eds.): *Unemployment insurance in the United States: Analysis of policy issues* (Kalamazoo, Michigan, W.E. Upjohn Institute for Employment Research, 1997).

PART V

THE ACTUARIAL REPORT

PRESENTATION OF THE METHODOLOGY AND RESULTS[1] 20

The actuarial report is the tool by which the methodology and results of the actuarial valuation are presented. Its principal purpose is to show how the cost of a given scheme will evolve. However, it also has the objective of presenting a summary of the methods used so that another actuary will be able to understand the bases of the valuation, enabling the report to be reconciled to the next actuarial review. The actuarial report is also important in that it presents complementary information on benefit levels, administration, statistics and investments that are hard to find in other documents on social security schemes.

20.1 STANDARD STRUCTURE OF THE ACTUARIAL REPORT

A standard actuarial report should contain the five main components that are given in table 20.1. Chapter headings are listed so as to provide a checklist of topics that should be addressed in the report. The exact structure of the report will vary according to the objective of the valuation and the emphasis that the actuary wishes to give to certain aspects of the valuation. However, all these topics should be covered in one way or another.

20.1.1 Executive summary

This section should summarize the findings and recommendations of the valuation. It should be borne in mind that most national decision-makers will read this section only. Therefore, it needs to be as concise and comprehensible as possible in its policy suggestions.

20.1.2 Economic, demographic and governance context

This section should describe the context in which the scheme operates. Relevant aspects include:

Table 20.1   Standard content of an actuarial report

1.	Executive summary
2.	Economic, demographic and governance context
3.	Analysis of the present situation and performance – Description of legal provisions – The present financial status – Benefit experience
4.	Actuarial projections – Methodology – Database and assumptions – Results of status quo projections – Sensitivity testing of status quo results – Results of projections under alternative legal provisions and reform proposals (if applicable)
5.	Conclusions and recommendations
Annexes	
I.	Main legal provisions and observations in respect of ILO legal instruments
II.	Financial statements (detailed)
III.	The database
IV.	Methodology (detailed)

- the current macroeconomic performance, such as inflation and increasing unemployment, which both have an impact on the scheme, and expected future economic developments;
- the present situation and performance of relevant economic and financial institutions, such as the status of government finances, the efficiency of tax collection mechanisms, the performance of capital markets, commercial banks and investment funds, etc.;
- the recent and expected future development of general demographic trends, including the development of levels of fertility, migration, mortality and life expectancy as well as changes in the labour force;
- the development of social security at the national level and its possible development in view of longer term social policy trends;
- the governance of the social security system.

The main body of the report might simply summarize the main findings of the actuarial valuation, with specific detailed observations placed in an annex.

20.1.3   Analysis of the present situation and performance

Description of legal provisions

This section describes the main features of the scheme with respect to the legal provisions governing coverage, benefits and financing and, in particular, its sources and the pension financing method. Amendments to the legal provisions that have been enacted since the previous actuarial valuation must be identified. Their detailed description should be attached to the actuarial report in the form of an annex.

The actuarial valuation should contain observations as to the level of benefits compared with the levels prescribed in the ILO Social Security (Minimum Standards) Convention, 1952 (No. 102), or other relevant ILO standards.

This section could be complemented by an annex providing the list of ILO social security Conventions that have been ratified by the concerned country, and it should include comments on the compliance of the legal benefit provisions in relation to ILO Conventions on social security. The main ones include Convention No. 102 and the Invalidity, Old-Age and Survivors' Benefits Convention, 1967 (No. 128). Other ILO Conventions on social security include Conventions No. 3, 12, 17, 18, 19, 23, 24, 25, 35, 36, 37, 38, 39, 40, 42, 44, 48, 67, 68, 69, 95, 103, 118, 121, 130, 131, 134, 157, 167, 168 and 176. Even in the case of a country that has not ratified any of the ILO Conventions, comments would be due on the relationship between the benefits level provided and the minimum level prescribed by the "base" Convention No. 102.

The present financial status and the analysis of benefit experience

This section should contain a detailed analysis of the recent past experience of the social security scheme (preferably up to the ten years immediately preceding the valuation, but no less than three to five years). In particular, the analysis should cover the annual financial statements on revenue and expenditure (by benefit type), the balance sheets, and past investment performance, along with comments on the adequacy of the investment policy. Relevant material (such as a summary of the statement of revenue and expenditure and the balance sheets) could be placed in an annex. This section should also contain a description of the financial developments since the last valuation. Explanations should be provided on any differences between the projected developments and the actual developments since the last valuation (after appropriate corrections to the initial database).

The analysis of benefit experience should describe the past development of key performance indicators relevant to the insured population and to the different benefit branches of the scheme, such as:

- the social insurance coverage ratio;
- the catchment ratio;
- the demographic ratio; and
- the average benefit replacement ratio.

Analysing these indicators should take into account the stage of the scheme's maturity. Inter alia, observations should be made on the *de facto* observed average retirement age, the level of the ceiling on insurable earnings (if applicable), the relationship between the *de jure* level of the replacement rate and the *de facto* level of the replacement rate for old-age pensions, along with explanations on possible discrepancies that may be linked to the way the benefits in payment have been adjusted in the past.

If marked differences between the observed demographic ratios and financial ratios versus their projected values as per any prior actuarial valuation have been observed, then specific technical comments on these discrepancies will be needed.

20.1.4 Actuarial projections

Methodology

This section should briefly describe, in non-technical terms, the main procedures used to project the revenue and expenditure components of a social security scheme. It should set out, as a basic principle, that the methodology used to analyse and simulate the national social security system may only be undertaken with a view to the development of the country as a whole, that is, its population and economy. Regardless of the model used, reference should be made to a source of information that provides a full description of the model.

Database and assumptions

This section should summarize the content, quality and origin of the statistical data as well as the determination basis for demographic and economic assumptions used for the projections. The main elements of the database should be documented in the form of a statistical annex to the actuarial report. In particular, the actuarial projections need to be placed methodologically within the context of:

- the general demographic development;
- the macroeconomic environment;
- the parameters describing the scheme's present and likely future governance; and
- scheme-specific data describing the financial situation and system-demographics of the scheme in the past and at a given valuation date.

Only a brief summary of the essential data need be described in the main body of the actuarial report. The origins of the statistical data used may require additional comments, focusing on its quality and reliability, in particular on estimates or assumptions used in lieu of statistical data when the latter are unavailable.

Key assumptions determining the demographic and financial projection of the scheme must be clearly stated and their potential impact discussed. Such key assumptions should refer to the future demographic development of the scheme, the future development of economic determinants and the future development of critical scheme governance parameters (such as the catchment factor, the coverage rate and the contribution collection rate).

Results of status quo projections

Status quo projection results are central to the actuarial analysis. They usually display a series of descriptors for the demographic and financial development of a scheme (see section 11.1).

Sensitivity testing of status quo results

The reliability of models used to produce demographic and financial projections is always limited. Sensitivity testing should be used to assess the reliability of the modelling results and it should be applied to the status quo projections. It should not extend to modelling alternative legal provisions, which are covered in the next section, as this would only lead to a multiplication of test runs that would add very little to the overall quality of the analyses.

Sensitivity tests should, therefore, be employed to alert the user of the report to the relative importance of different determinants for the future financial development of their social security scheme. The most critical parameters, and in many ways the most uncertain, are usually economic growth and governance or compliance. At the very least, alternative economic growth paths and more optimistic and pessimistic compliance parameters should be tested by scenario analyses.

This section can be completed with the projected long-term development of the PAYG premium or the GAP of the present valuation being reconciled to the results of the last valuation.

The valuation of modified legal provisions and reform proposals

The modelling of alternative legal provisions requires modifications being made to the mathematical mapping of the status quo provisions. These modifications also usually include changes being made to governance parameters and behaviour assumptions, such as the pattern of entry into retirement. These adjustments to the modelling assumptions need to be explained in detail.

The modelling results based on a *ceteris paribus* set of assumptions should be compared with the corresponding status quo scenario results using some of the key indicators used in the report. The status quo scenario should serve as the benchmark for assessing the impact of proposed modifications and reforms. The impact of reforms should, therefore, be measured by the relative deviation of the financial development of a scheme caused by potential reforms or minor modifications from an expected "normal" (that is, status quo) development.

20.1.5 Conclusions and recommendations

This section should put forward a number of measures of action to preserve or establish the future financial equilibrium of the scheme. The emphasis should be placed on explaining and discussing the pros and cons of specific recommendations, since the executive summary only lists these recommendations. This section should also provide comments on the reliability of the quantitative results and the underlying database, and should alert the reader to any follow-up action that needs to be taken, such as the need to improve the statistical database, to modify the accounting frame and/or investment management, etc.

The recommendations should, if necessary, contain observations as to how the benefit levels of the scheme compare with ILO Conventions and Recommendations and should – if applicable – advise on how these levels can be reached.

From the analysis of the valuation's results, the actuary should be able to put forward a set of recommendations for correcting, if necessary, the financial situation of the scheme or for adjusting benefit levels or entitlements in order to meet the scheme's income replacement objectives. They may include:

- checking the adequacy of financing provisions to cover the scheme's accrued financial obligations and for future obligations under status quo provisions;
- checking the adequacy of the funding objective of the scheme;
- setting possible schedules of contribution rates and reserves according to alternative funding methods;
- measures to restore the financial equilibrium of the scheme in the event of a projected financial imbalance (in relation to the funding objective of the scheme) or to reduce the ultimate cost of the scheme, such as:
  - modifications to benefit provisions;
  - modifications to financing provisions, notably increases in the contribution rate;
  - correcting the redistribution effect of different benefit provisions on an individual and aggregate basis;
  - reducing the impact of ageing on the scheme's financial position;
  - adapting the investment policy to the national economic development objectives (for example, the issue of investments to promote employment creation);
  - limiting the level of administrative expenses.

In addition, the actuary is usually required to provide professional advice on the projected impact of the ceiling on insurable earnings and the projected level of the effective average pension replacement rate compared with the replacement rate as intended in the country's social security law. The actuary is often asked to tackle the deficiencies of the system by recommending regular adjustments of its financial parameters in line with price and wage developments in the economy.

20.2 COMMUNICATING THE RESULTS

The actuarial report should provide a clear picture of the financial situation and future direction of the scheme, allowing another actuary to be able to make an appraisal of the valuation.

The actuarial report is a relatively complex technical document. However, it needs to be understood by those people who will be in a position to act on the future evolution of the scheme. Otherwise, there is a risk that the recommendations contained in the report will not be considered. If a report is clearly written, the board and management of the scheme are more likely to use it to attract the attention of the social partners on financing issues and possible solutions.

The general public is increasingly focusing its attention on the financial situation of social security schemes, which implies that more and more people will wish to gain access to the actuarial report. Its content must, therefore, be well prepared in order to avoid misinterpretations being made.

Notes

[1] This chapter contains extracts from ILO: *Internal guidelines for the analysis of a national social security pension scheme* (Geneva, 1998).

A PRACTICAL EXERCISE: THE DEMOLAND CASE

21

This chapter presents the actuarial valuation report of the NIS of Demoland as of 31 December 1998. The case of a small country with a limited database was chosen to provide a simple demonstration of the concepts described in this book, in order to emphasize the general methodology of the actuarial valuation with the basic information that is usually available to the actuary in that process.

21.1 INTRODUCING DEMOLAND

Demoland[1] is a small Caribbean country with 766,000 inhabitants. The population is still relatively young, with only 10 per cent over the age of 60. Demoland's economy is mostly concentrated on mining and agriculture. Real GDP growth averaged 7 per cent per year over the period 1993–98, with the average inflation rate around 10 per cent. Participation rates in the labour force are currently 75 per cent for men and 40 per cent for women. The unemployment rate is 14 per cent. Wages are low, particularly in the public sector, which represents one-third of the total payroll covered by the country's social security scheme.

The NIS of Demoland covers the employed and self-employed. Active insured persons represent 50 per cent of the total employed population. The scheme is financed by contributions on earnings at a rate of 12 per cent (4.8 per cent by employees and 7.2 per cent by employers) of which 8.3 per cent goes to pensions, 1.5 per cent to employment injury benefits and 2.2 per cent to short-term benefits.

The normal retirement age is currently 60. The replacement rate of the old-age pension varies between 40 per cent and 60 per cent of the reference earnings,

---

[1] The reader may recognize this country as Guyana.

depending on the length of participation above 15 years. However, owing to low average service, low wages and inflation in the past 90 per cent of old-age pensioners are entitled to the minimum pension. Pensions are generally indexed on an annual basis but only after a discretionary decision of the National Insurance Board (NIB).

Social security reserves are substantial and are almost exclusively invested in Treasury bills.

21.2 THE DEMOLAND VALUATION REPORT

The rest of the chapter is made up of Demoland's actuarial report. (All cross-references in this chapter refer to the actuarial report.)

ACTUARIAL REVIEW OF THE NIS
AS OF 31 DECEMBER 1998

Table of contents

Page

Executive summary 322

1 Analysis of the present situation and performance 325
   1.1 Recent experience in revenue and expenditure 325
   1.2 Analysis of administrative expenses 325
   1.3 Analysis of investment results 327

2 Methodology of the actuarial valuation 328
   2.1 Modelling the demographic and economic developments 329
   2.2 Projection of income and expenditure of the NIS 330
   2.3 Financial systems 331

3 The general demographic and macroeconomic frame 332
   3.1 General population 332
   3.2 Economic and labour market projections 335

4 The database and assumptions specific to the scheme 339
   4.1 Insured population 339
   4.2 Insurable earnings 341
   4.3 Density of contributions 342
   4.4 Accrued past credits 342
   4.5 Pensions in payment on the valuation date 343
   4.6 Demographic assumptions related to the scheme 343

5 Cost projections under the present legal provisions 345
   5.1 Short-term benefits 346
   5.2 Employment injury benefits 347
   5.3 Pensions 349

A practical exercise: The Demoland case

6 Comparison with the previous valuation and sensitivity tests 353
   6.1   Comparison with the previous valuation 353
   6.2   Sensitivity tests 354

7 Financing strategy 356
   7.1   Reallocation of the reserves 356
   7.2   Recommended contribution rates 357

8 The effect of modifications to the scheme 359
   8.1   Increase in the minimum pension 359
   8.2   Extension of survivors' pensions to widowers 360
   8.3   Increase in the retirement age 361
   8.4   Qualifying conditions for sickness benefits 362

9 Other issues 363
   9.1   Investment policy 363
   9.2   Coverage of the self-employed 365
   9.3   Indexation of pensions 366
   9.4   Differentiation of pensions 366
   9.5   Maintenance of statistics 367

Conclusion 368

Annex 1 Overview of the legal provisions of the NIS of Demoland 368

Annex 2 Pensions in payment in December 1998 368

Annex 3 Operation of the technical reserve for the employment injury branch 371

EXECUTIVE SUMMARY

1 Future evolution of costs

Over the next few decades, Demoland will see an ageing of its population. In addition, the NIS will continue to mature so that the number of people eligible for pensions in proportion to the total population of the country will rise. These two factors will result in an increase in the ratio of pensioners to contributors in the scheme.

On the pensions side, the reserve ratio, which represents the reserve at the end of a given year divided by the annual expenditure of the scheme for that year, is currently equal to 4.1. If the scheme's provisions remain unchanged and the contribution rate is kept at its present level, the reserve will be exhausted in 13 years' time. The PAYG rate for pensions will increase from 7.4 per cent in 1999 to 27.3 per cent by 2040. This shows that the present contribution rate devoted to pensions (8.3 per cent) is just sufficient, in 1999, to cover the expenditure of the scheme. However, it also reveals that this contribution rate will have to increase significantly over the next three decades in order to reach a level of around 26 per cent. While there is no imminent financial crisis, action will be needed.

2 Financial autonomy of the three branches

It is recommended that each branch (short-term benefits, employment injury and pensions) be financially autonomous, instead of continuing to allocate total income and expenditure to the various branches according to arbitrary percentages. This separation would avoid any cross-financing taking place between the different benefit branches and would allow for a better follow-up of the reserves and contribution rates of each branch.

3 Reallocation of reserves

Because of the arbitrary allocation among the three branches of some items of income and expenditure, the reserves of the short-term and employment injury branches have accrued to unnecessarily high levels, in strong contrast to the funding objectives recommended in this report. Hence, a sum of $796 million could thus be transferred from the short-term benefits branch to the pension branch. In addition, an amount of $1,575 million could be transferred from the employment injury benefits branch to the pension branch.

4 Recommended contribution rates

The contribution rate recommended for the short-term benefits branch is 2.2 per cent and that for the employment injury benefits branch 1.5 per cent. These contribution rates should remain constant at their 1999 levels until the next actuarial review.

As for the pension branch, considering the anticipated rise in costs, there is a need to specify a rule for the determination of the actuarial equilibrium of the

Period	Contribution rates (as a %)			
	Pensions	Short-term benefits	Employment injury benefits	Total
1999	8.3	2.2	1.5	12.0
2000–03	11.0	2.2	1.5	14.7
2004–06	12.5	2.2	1.5	16.2
2007–09	14.0	2.2	1.5	17.7
2010–12	15.5	2.2	1.5	19.2
2013–15	17.0	2.2	1.5	20.7
2016–18	18.5	2.2	1.5	22.2
2019–21	20.0	2.2	1.5	23.7
2022–24	21.5	2.2	1.5	25.2
2025–27	23.0	2.2	1.5	26.7
2028–30	24.5	2.2	1.5	28.2
2031+	26.0	2.2	1.5	29.7

scheme in order to guide future contribution rate increases. It is recommended to establish funding objectives for the pension branch expressed in terms of reserve ratios. Taking into account the actual stage of maturity of the scheme and the projected cost increases, it is recommended to define a rule for the future determination of the contribution rates and to stipulate that rule into the law governing the NIS as follows: The contribution rate of the pension branch will be established such that the reserve ratio of the branch is equal to 4 in 2010, 2.5 in 2030 and 2 after 2040. The application of that rule would result in the contribution rates for the next three decades shown in the table above.

5 Effect of modifications to the scheme

As requested in the terms of reference, the report presents the financial impact of various modifications to the benefit provisions of the scheme.

Increase in the minimum pension

The modification that has been analysed consists of a gradual increase in the minimum pension from its present level of 50 per cent of the minimum wage to 100 per cent of the minimum wage over a period of five years. This modification has an important short-term impact, considering that it would apply to all pensions currently in payment.

Payment of windowers' pensions

The modification under study aims at providing the same conditions for widowers' pensions as those applicable to widows' pensions. This modification would increase the GAP of the scheme (calculated over 40 years) from 18.2 per cent to 18.7 per cent. This could be translated into a 0.5 per cent addition to the recommended contribution rates.

Qualifying conditions for sickness benefits

Concern has been expressed about the current eligibility conditions for sickness benefits for seasonal workers in the rice and sugar industries. To give these people proper coverage for sickness benefits and at the same time target the real seasonal workers who come back to work on a periodical basis, it would seem feasible to redefine the third condition for eligibility for sickness benefits as follows:

> ... had been employed in, and paid contributions for, insurable employment during at least eight contribution weeks in the period of 13 contribution weeks immediately preceding the contribution week in which the first day of the continuous period of incapacity for work occurred, or during at least 20 of the last 50 contribution weeks preceding incapacity.

Owing to the lack of data, the cost of this modification cannot be precisely estimated. However, the modification could be adopted with an unchanged contribution rate, which would be revalued at the next actuarial review on the basis of recent experience.

6 Investment policy

A portfolio diversification should be contemplated. A shift towards equity investments would normally increase the long-term return. However, such a modification to the investment strategy should be gradual and would need to take into account the opportunities existing in Demoland for investments that show a good balance between safety and return. The National Insurance Fund (NIF) could prudently increase the share of foreign investments in its portfolio if opportunities do not exist in Demoland.

It is also recommended that an investment unit in the NIS be set up, considering the fact that reserves of the pension branch will increase significantly in the future and that the institution will need to rely on a team of skilled investment managers.

7 Adjustment of pensions

The report recommends that the current practice of granting annual adjustments to pensions based on the increase in the CPI to ensure that pensions will keep their purchasing power over time be legalized. In the context of the increase in the minimum pension announced in October 1999, this CPI increase should be granted at the end of 1999 to those pensioners whose pensions are higher than the minimum.

8 Level of administrative expenses

The NIB should, as a target, maintain its administrative expenses below 1.5 per cent of insurable earnings over the next five years.

CHAPTER 1
ANALYSIS OF THE PRESENT SITUATION AND PERFORMANCE

1.1 Recent experience in revenue and expenditure

Table 1 presents income and expenditure and the evolution of the reserves for all three benefit branches for the years 1996, 1997 and 1998. It can be seen that all three branches are in surplus and that their reserves are increasing. Benefit expenditure of the short-term and employment injury benefits branches are steadily increasing owing to salary rises and the resulting effect on the average benefit. In addition, the benefit expenditure of the pension branch is increasing because the scheme is still not mature and the number of beneficiaries is continuing to rise each year. This is why this branch needs to maintain a larger reserve in order to amortize the expected increase in future expenditure.

1.2 Analysis of administrative expenses

Over the past three years, administrative expenditure has represented, on average, 14.4 per cent of contribution income, 26.5 per cent of benefit expenditure and 1.73 per cent of insurable earnings (see table 2).

These levels of administrative expenses appear high, especially considering that 25 cents of each dollar of benefit must be paid in administrative costs. Some benefits are more expensive to administer than others, such as invalidity benefits, which require closer intervention on the part of the administrative body to analyse the medical condition of the claimant. During certain periods, the collection of contributions may also cause significant increases in the level of administrative expenditure if the institution is working to improve its collection rate and is taking the necessary steps in that direction. In recent years, the NIS has embarked on a process of computerization, which, despite its high initial investment, should bring administrative cost savings in future years. Hence, the level of current administrative costs, while appearing high, should gradually decrease as a percentage of the total payroll as the benefits from recent investments in equipment and procedures materialize.

In the short run, it may be difficult to specify a target level of administrative expenses expressed in terms of contribution income or total insurable earnings, since these two figures will rise dramatically over the next two years, following the announced increase in the earnings ceiling that will take place in 1999 and

Table 1 Income, expenditure and evolution of the reserves of the NIS for 1996, 1997 and 1998 (in million $)

	1996			1997			1998[1]		
	Pension branch	Short-term benefits branch	Employment injury benefits branch	Pension branch	Short-term benefits branch	Employment injury benefits branch	Pension branch	Short-term benefits branch	Employment injury benefits branch
Reserve on 1 January	3 547	320	1 060	4 600	567	1 442	6 046	753	1 828
Income									
Contributions	1 786	573	381	2 360	532	354	2 573	580	386
Investment earnings	539	70	114	646	122	171	1 076	429	490
Other income	3	3	3	5	5	5	21	21	21
Total	2 328	646	498	3 011	659	530	3 670	1 030	897
Expenditure									
Benefits									
Pensions	989			1 256			1 533		
Short-term benefits		317			385			514	
Employment injury benefits			75			96			109
Administrative expenses	286	82	41	309	88	48	96	104	52
Total	1 275	399	116	1 565	473	144	144	618	161
Reserve on 31 December	4 600	567	1 442	6 046	753	1 828	7 817	1 165	2 564

[1] Unaudited.

Table 2 Level of administrative expenses in 1996, 1997 and 1998

Year	Total administrative expenses of the scheme (in millions $)	Administrative expenses (as a %)		
		Contribution income	Benefit expenditures	Total insurable earnings
1996	409	14.9	29.6	1.79
1997	445	13.7	25.6	1.64
1998	522	14.7	24.2	1.76

2000, as well as the increase in the contribution rate proposed in this report. However, the NIS should try to maintain its administrative expenses below 1.5 per cent of total insurable earnings.

1.3 Analysis of investment results

The interest rate credited to the NIF during the past three years is presented in table 3. It is compared with the rate of inflation. During the period 1996 to 1998, the NIS realized a rate of return on average 11 per cent in excess of the inflation rate. This is considered a good return, especially considering the high level of security associated with the type of investment in which these funds are invested. The present investment policy devoting most of the investments to Treasury bills has been advantageous to the scheme during the past few years. But this type of investment is not considered suitable for the investment of reserves supporting pension liabilities, which are usually linked to salaries increases. Also, the exclusive investment of social security funds in government papers may lead to an ever-increasing government liability for interest payment. Chapter 7 deals specifically with the investment policy of the NIS.

The allocation of investment earnings between the three benefit branches is currently made on the basis of arbitrary factors instead of reflecting the level of reserve and the evolution of funds in each branch. This has the effect of overestimating the investment earnings allocated to the short-term and employment

Table 3 Rate of return of the NIF (as a %)

Year	Average return of the NIF[1]	Inflation rate	Real rate of return
1996	13.4	7.1	6.3
1997	13.1	3.6	9.5
1998	21.9	4.6	17.3

[1] Calculated globally for all three benefit funds as equal to $2I \div ((A+B-I))$ where:
    A = Fund at the beginning of the year.
    B = Fund at the end of the year.
    I = Investment earnings during the year.

injury benefits branches. Following the previous recommendation in favour of making each branch financially autonomous and separating the operations of each branch as regards all items of income and expenditure, the investment portfolio of each branch should be clearly identified. This would make the computation of the investment income of each branch a straightforward exercise.

If, in the short term, it is not possible to separate investments clearly among the three branches, the share of total investment earnings allocated to each branch should be determined as follows. Let:

R_{lt} = Reserve of the pension branch at the beginning of the year
R_{total} = Total reserves of the three benefit branches at the beginning of the year
C_{lt} = Contributions of pension branch
C_{total} = Total contributions of the three benefit branches
B_{lt} = Benefits of the pension branch
B_{total} = Total benefits of the three benefit branches

In the example, investment earnings attributed to the pension branch would be equal to the total investment earnings of the scheme, multiplied by the following factor:

$$\frac{(R_{lt} + \frac{1}{2}(C_{lt} - B_{lt}))}{(R_{total} + \frac{1}{2}(C_{total} - B_{total}))}$$

CHAPTER 2
METHODOLOGY OF THE ACTUARIAL VALUATION

This actuarial review makes use of the new comprehensive methodology developed by ILO FACTS for reviewing the long-term actuarial and financial status of national pension schemes. In this review the generic version of the ILO modelling tools has been modified in order to fit the situation of Demoland and of the NIS in particular. These modelling tools include a population model, an economic model, a labour force model, a wage model, a pension model and a short-term benefits model.

The actuarial valuation starts with a projection of the future demographic and economic environment of Demoland. Next, projection factors specifically related to the NIS are determined and used in combination with the demographic/economic framework.

2.1 Modelling the demographic and economic developments

The use of the ILO actuarial projection model requires the development of demographic and economic assumptions related to the general population, economic growth, the labour market and the increase and distribution of wages. Other economic assumptions relate to the future rate of return on investments, the indexation of benefits and the adjustment of the earnings ceiling.

The selection of projection assumptions takes into account the recent experience of Demoland to the extent that this information is available. The assumptions are selected to reflect long-term trends rather than giving undue weight to recent experience. Additional details on key demographic and economic assumptions are provided in Chapter 3.

2.1.1 General population

The general population is projected starting with the most current data, and applying appropriate mortality, fertility and migration assumptions.

2.1.2 Economic growth and inflation

Real rates of economic growth and inflation rates are exogenous inputs to the economic model.

2.1.3 Labour force, employment and insured population

The projection of the labour force, that is, the number of people available for work, is obtained by applying assumed labour force participation rates to the projected number of people in the general population. Unemployment is calculated by applying unemployment rates (an exogenous assumption) to the labour force. Employment is then measured as the difference between the projected labour force and unemployment. The model assumes movement of participants between the groups of active and inactive insured persons.

2.1.4 Wages

Real wage increase is assumed equal to the increase in real labour productivity. It is expected that wages will adjust to efficiency levels over time. Wage distribution assumptions are also needed to simulate the possible impact of the social protection system on the distribution of income, for example, through minimum and maximum pension provisions. Assumptions on the differentiation of wages by age and sex, as well as assumptions on the dispersion of wages between income groups are established. Average career wages, which are used in the computation of benefits, are also projected.

2.2 Projection of income and expenditure of the NIS

This actuarial review addresses all revenue and expenditure items of the NIS. For short-term benefits, income and expenditures are projected using simple projection methods based on recent experience. Projections for pensions are done collectively for all groups of insured, hence without separating workers of the private sector, the public sector, the self-employed and voluntarily insured persons.

2.2.1 The purpose of pension projections

The purpose of the pension model is twofold. Firstly, it is used to assess the financial viability of the pension branch. This refers to the measure of the long-term balance between income and expenditure of the scheme. In case of imbalance, recommendations on the revision of the contribution rate or the benefit structure are recommended. Secondly, the model may be used to examine the financial impact of different reform options, thus assisting policy-makers in the design of benefit and financing provisions. More specifically, the pension model is used to develop long-term projections of expenditure and insurable earnings under the scheme, for the purpose of:

- assessing the options to build up a contingency or a technical reserve;
- proposing schedules of contribution rates consistent with the funding objective; and
- testing how the system reacts to changing economic and demographic conditions.

2.2.2 Pension data and assumptions

Pension projections require the demographic and macroeconomic frame already described and, in addition, a set of assumptions specific to the NIS.

As of the valuation date the database includes the insured population by active and inactive status, the distribution of insurable wages among contributors, the distribution of past credited service and pensions in payment. The data are disaggregated by age and sex.

Scheme-specific assumptions, such as disability incidence rates and the distribution of retirement by age, are determined with reference to the scheme provisions and the historical experience of the scheme.

The projection of the annual investment income requires information on the existing assets on the valuation date. An interest-rate assumption is formulated on the basis of the nature of the scheme's assets, the past performance of the fund, the scheme's investment policy and assumptions on future economic growth and wage development.

Details on scheme-specific data and assumptions are provided in Chapter 4.

2.2.3 The pension projection approach

Pension projections are performed following a year-by-year cohort methodology. The existing population is aged and gradually replaced by successive cohorts of participants on an annual basis according to the demographic and coverage assumptions. The projections of insurable earnings and benefit expenditures are then performed according to the economic assumptions and the scheme's provisions.

Pensions are long-term benefits. Hence, the financial obligations that a society accepts when adopting financing provisions and benefit provisions for them are also of a long-term nature: participation in a pension scheme extends over a person's whole adult life, either as a contributor or as a beneficiary, that is, up to 70 years for someone entering the scheme at the age of 16, retiring at the age of 65 and dying some 20 or so years later. During their working years, contributors gradually build up their entitlements to pensions that will even be paid, after their death, to their survivors. The objective of pension projections is not to forecast the exact development of income and expenditures of the scheme but to check the scheme's financial viability. This entails evaluating the scheme with regard to the relative balance between future income and expenditures. This type of evaluation is crucial, especially in the case of the scheme in Demoland, which has not yet reached maturity.

2.3 Financial systems

2.3.1 Short-term benefits

The contribution rate for the short-term benefits branch is determined under the PAYG financial system. Therefore, current contributions are estimated to meet current expenditures on benefits and administrative expenses, and to provide a margin for the build-up of a contingency reserve to deal with unfavourable fluctuations. The level of the contingency reserve is set at six months of expenditure. If the actual cost of the branch consistently exceeds or falls below the expected levels, an adjustment to the contribution rate will then be necessary. Excess contingency reserves arising from favourable experience can be transferred to the pension branch. Either of these steps is taken on the basis of recommendations arising from an actuarial review.

2.3.2 Employment injury benefits

The employment injury benefits branch operates under a combination of the PAYG system for short-term benefits and an "assessment of constituent capitals" system for long-term benefits. Under the assessment of constituent capitals system, the annual cost is determined from the present value of all future payments relative to disablement and survivors' pensions awarded during the year. This amount is transferred to a technical reserve, which is credited annually with interest and debited with pension payments made during the year. Annex 3 of this report presents the methodology for the annual computation of the technical reserves associated with the long-term benefits of the employment injury branch, including the actuarial factors for the calculation of present values.

2.3.3 Pensions

For pensions, future contribution rates are determined on the basis of funding objectives expressed in terms of reserve ratios to be reached at specific points in the future. The reserve ratio represents the amount of reserve of the pension branch at the end of a year divided by the amount of expenditure of the scheme in that year. Then after considering:

- the level of maturity of the scheme,
- the timing of actuarial reviews,
- the ultimate PAYG cost of the scheme and
- the expected smoothness of contribution rate increases,

the actuary may recommend reserve ratios to be reached at specific points in time. The contribution rate schedule results directly from the financial projections of the scheme.

CHAPTER 3
THE GENERAL DEMOGRAPHIC AND MACROECONOMIC FRAME

3.1 General population

The data on the current population were obtained from the projections made by the National Statistical Office of Demoland based on the 1990-91 census. The population in 1998 came to 766,023 inhabitants.

The main determinants for the future development of the population are fertility, mortality and migration rates.

3.1.1 Fertility

The recent data on the total fertility rate are presented in table 4.

Table 4 Total fertility rates in Demoland, 1993–97

Year	Total fertility rate
1993	2.3
1994	2.5
1995	2.5
1996	2.5
1997	2.7

For the present valuation, a total fertility rate of 2.4 has been assumed for the first year of projection and this rate is assumed to decrease gradually to 2.1 by 2008 and to remain constant thereafter.

3.1.2 Mortality

The mortality rates for the population projection have been determined with the methodology used for the development of the United Nations model life tables, which uses, as a base, life expectancy at birth. The complete mortality table is constructed using the formula developed by Heligman and Pollard. For the starting year, life expectancies at birth are established at 63.1 years for men and 69.4 years for women, based on the levels published by the United Nations. It is assumed that these values of life expectancy will increase gradually to reach 74 years for men and 78.9 years for women by 2050. Sample mortality rates are presented in table 5.

Table 5 Sample mortality rates for the general population

Age	Male			Female		
	1998	2025	2050	1998	2025	2050
17	.00140	.00066	.00040	.00074	.00034	.00033
22	.00195	.00091	.00056	.00109	.00048	.00041
27	.00237	.00111	.00068	.00140	.00060	.00048
32	.00286	.00139	.00087	.00171	.00079	.00060
37	.00369	.00190	.00123	.00220	.00113	.00091
42	.00515	.00282	.00190	.00304	.00170	.00137
47	.00752	.00439	.00307	.00447	.00269	.00220
52	.01128	.00698	.00506	.00685	.00429	.00339
57	.01707	.01117	.00840	.01069	.00690	.00511
62	.02587	.01791	.01395	.01679	.01124	.00812
67	.03912	.02864	.02312	.02640	.01844	.01334
72	.05880	.04551	.03809	.04133	.03068	.02395
77	.08749	.07159	.06214	.06418	.05079	.04389
82	.12830	.11090	.09982	.09841	.08499	.08277

3.1.3 Migration

The National Statistical Office estimates the net migration balance for the years 1995 to 1998 to be as follows:

Table 6 Net migration, Demoland, 1995–98

Year	Net migration
1995	−6 510
1996	−12 967
1997	−13 765
1998	−16 781

Owing to the high volatility of this factor, it is assumed that, in the long term, net migration will be 0. But for the first ten years of projections, net migration is assumed to decrease linearly from 10,000 people in 1999 to 0 by 2009. The number of migrants is projected to be equal for both sexes.

3.1.4 Projection of the general population

According to the above assumptions, the general population is projected to increase from 766,023 in 1998 to 956,782 by 2025 and to 1,078,647 by 2050. This represents an average annual population growth of 0.8 per cent from 1998 to 2025 and 0.5 per cent for the following period of 25 years.

Population projections also illustrate the ageing process. The ageing of the population is the result of lower future fertility rates compared with historical ones, and of the projected increase in life expectancy. The old-age dependency ratio, defined here as the number of people aged 60 and over divided by the number of people aged 15 to 59, is projected to increase from its current level of 10.0 per cent in 1998 to 39.2 per cent by 2050. This ratio shows that, in 1998, there are approximately ten people in the working-age group for each person over the age of 65, while this number will decrease to 2.5 people by 2050. But this trend in the dependency ratio increase is projected to start only after 2010. The long-term trend illustrates the effect of the ageing of the population on the cost of pensions, which have to be supported by the working-age population.

At the same time, increasing old-age burdens will be counterbalanced to some extent by a decrease in the children and youth dependency ratio, that is, the ratio of those between 0 and 14 to those aged 15 to 59. In 1998, it was 47.4 per cent and it is projected to drop to 35.4 per cent by 2050. As a result, the total dependency ratio will increase from 57.3 per cent in 1998 to 74.6 per cent by 2050 (table 7).

Table 7 Demographic ratios, 1998-2050 (as a %)

Year	Old-age dependency[1]	Children and youth dependency[2]	Total dependency[3]
1998	10.0	47.4	57.3
2010	12.7	37.7	50.4
2025	24.3	35.5	59.8
2050	39.2	35.4	74.6

[1] Ratio of people aged 60 and over to those between 15 and 59.
[2] Ratio of people aged 0 to 14 to those between 15 and 59.
[3] Ratio of people aged 0 to14, plus those aged 60 and over to those between 15 and 59.

It should be noted that the main counterbalancing effect of the decreasing children and youth dependency ratio will take place over the next decade. From then onwards, it will be more stable and the total dependency ratio will be mostly affected by the rise in the elderly population.

3.2 Economic and labour market projections

The general economic development and the labour market directly influence the financial development of the NIS. The development of consistent long-term economic and labour market projections serves as a basis for the actuarial valuation of the NIS. The evolution of GDP (its primary factor income distribution), labour productivity, employment and unemployment, wages, inflation and interest rates all have direct and indirect impacts on the projected revenues and expenditures of the scheme. These factors should be analysed extensively in order to build a credible economic framework.

During the collection of data, the actuary of this report was unable to obtain recent and complete data on the labour force; the most recent date back to 1992. Hence, it was not possible to make an analysis of the past productivity of labour or a precise estimation of the wage share of GDP, two elements which are essential for assessing the most probable future economic environment.

However, given the objective of the actuarial valuation, it was considered useful to develop a hypothetical future economic framework based on consistent assumptions in order to give an indication of the future growth of the insured population, the evolution of salaries, inflation and interest rates. In that context, the sensitivity tests presented in Chapter 6 become an integral part of the projection process by giving an idea of the possible variability of results according to various economic assumptions.

The general methodology to establish this economic frame was firstly to project the labour force by applying participation rates to the total population. An exogenous assumption on the future evolution of the unemployment rate then led, by subtraction, to the resulting employed population.

Table 8 Assumed participation rates by age and sex for 1998 and 2050 (as a %)

Age	Males		Females	
	1998	2050	1998	2050
17	59.0	59.0	29.4	47.2
22	81.6	81.6	43.6	65.2
27	80.8	80.8	42.3	64.4
32	81.4	81.4	47.4	65.0
37	86.8	86.8	51.8	69.7
42	100.0	100.0	50.6	80.0
47	83.0	83.0	42.0	66.5
52	85.5	85.5	41.4	69.2
57	74.4	74.4	36.7	58.8
62	67.8	67.8	28.7	54.7
67	7.0	7.0	2.2	1.1
Total	**75.5**	**65.4**	**39.7**	**50.1**

In order to project wages, the first step was to project the GDP growth exogenously. Real GDP growth was then divided into its two components: the rate of growth of the employed population (taken from labour force projections) and productivity growth (the residual item). Real wage growth was assumed equal to productivity growth. Based on an implicit assumption that the wage share of GDP is constant and consequently that capital stock grows at the same rate as GDP, the real interest rate was assumed to converge to the real GDP growth. Finally, an exogenous assumption on the inflation rate allowed the establishment of nominal rates of wage increases and interest rates.

3.2.1 Labour force, employment and unemployment

Labour force participation rates by age obtained from the 1992 survey were assumed constant for males over the whole projection period. For females, it was assumed that the participation rates for each age would increase gradually to reach 80 per cent of the rates for males by 2050. Projected participation rates are presented in table 8.

The 1992 labour force survey revealed a total unemployment rate of 8.4 per cent for males and 18.1 per cent for females. Due to indications that employment contraction occurred in 1999, unemployment rates assumed for 1999 are 11 per cent for males and 19 per cent for females. These unemployment rates are assumed to decrease linearly to 7.0 per cent for both sexes by 2050. The employed population is then obtained by subtracting the number of unemployed from the total labour force figures.

Table 9 presents the resulting labour force balance for the initial projection year, for 2025 and for 2050. Active insured persons expressed as a percentage of total employment are assumed constant for each age-sex category. We can

Table 9 Demoland's labour market balance, 1999, 2025 and 2050

	1999	2025	2050	Increase from 1999 to 2050	
				(in number)	(as a %)
Population	**766 903**	**954 782**	**1 078 646**	**311 743**	**41**
of which: Male	376 780	461 557	518 701	141 921	38
Female	390 123	493 226	559 945	169 822	44
Population aged 15 and over	**538 214**	**742 804**	**859 874**	**321 660**	**60**
of which: Male	261 989	357 111	411 358	149 369	57
Female	276 225	385 693	448 516	172 291	62
Labour force	**308 687**	**430 409**	**493 793**	**185 106**	**60**
of which: Male	198 023	255 802	269 097	71 074	36
Female	110 663	174 607	224 696	114 033	103
Employed persons	**265 878**	**388 121**	**459 228**	**193 350**	**73**
of which: Male	176 241	233 455	250 260	74 019	42
Female	89 637	154 666	208 967	119 330	133
Active insured persons	**136 547**	**195 564**	**232 824**	**96 277**	**71**
(as a % of employed population)	51	50	51		
Non-insured employed persons	**129 331**	**192 557**	**226 404**	**97 073**	**75**
(as a % of employed population)	49	50	49		
Unemployed persons	**42 809**	**42 287**	**34 566**		
of which: Male	21 783	22 347	18 837		
Female	21 026	19 940	15 729		
Unemployment rate (as a %)	**14**	**10**	**7**		
of which: Male	11	9	7		
Female	19	11	7		

observe from the table that, based on the assumed framework, the female labour force will increase significantly faster than the male labour force. Variations in the total coverage rate over the projection period result from modifications in the age-sex composition of the employed population.

3.2.2 GDP growth and inflation

Real GDP growth and inflation represent exogenous assumptions. These variables were projected using initially the joint economic forecasts of the Ministry of Finance of Demoland and the IMF. These forecasts appear in table 10. In the

Table 10 GDP growth and inflation projections (as a %)

Year	Real annual GDP growth	Consumer price increase
1999	1.8*	5.5*
2000	3.0*	4.8*
2001	3.5*	3.9*
2002	3.4*	3.2*
2003	4.0*	3.0*
2004–2010	4.0	3.0
2011–2020	3.5	3.0
2021–2030	3.0	3.0
2031+	2.5	3.0*

*Sources: Ministry of Finance of Demoland and IMF estimates.

long term, real GDP is assumed to grow at the rates shown in table 10 with an ultimate growth rate of 2.5 per cent after 2030.

The inflation rate is assumed constant at 3.0 per cent after 2003.

3.2.3 Wages

As mentioned earlier, real wage increases were assumed equal to real GDP growth. Concerning the years 1999 and 2000, in the context of negotiations

Table 11 Assumed wage increases (as a %)

Year	Real wage increase	Nominal wage increase (annual average)
1999	11.0	16.5
2000	10.6	15.4
2001–2009	2.1	5.2
2010–2019	2.1	5.1
2020–2029	2.2	5.2
2030–2039	2.0	5.0
2040–2049	1.9	4.9

Table 12 Interest rates (as a %)

Year	Projected nominal interest rate
1999	7.3
2000	7.8
2001	7.4
2002	6.6
2003–10	7.0
2011–20	6.5
2011–30	6.0
2031+	5.5

A practical exercise: The Demoland case

on pay increases between the government and public servants, the Arbitration Tribunal awarded an increase of 31.6 per cent for 1999 and a further increase of 26.6 per cent for 2000. An adjustment was thus made in the wage increases for 1999 and 2000 based on the assumption that the remuneration of public servants represented 33 per cent of the total remuneration covered by the scheme. The assumed wage growth for various periods appears in table 11.

3.2.4 Interest rates

Nominal interest rates are assumed equal to real GDP growth, plus the inflation rate. This estimation of future interest rate levels is based on the assumption of a constant wage share of GDP, leading to a constant capital share of GDP. The interest rate being viewed as the remuneration for capital, the rate of growth of GDP determines the rate of growth of capital and consequently equals the interest rate. The rates projected for this valuation are presented in table 12.

CHAPTER 4
THE DATABASE AND ASSUMPTIONS SPECIFIC TO THE SCHEME

In addition to the demographic and economic assumptions presented in the previous chapter, the projection of the future financial development of the NIS requires a database specific to the scheme (on its assets, characteristics of insured persons and pensions in payment) and some particular actuarial assumptions.

For the present valuation, base data and assumptions have been divided according to the sex of the insured persons.

The model makes separate projections for the two groups. The model also needs to be adapted to the specific provisions of the law governing the NIS. The main provisions are summarized in Annex 1 of this report.

4.1 Insured population

The data on the insured population were obtained from the NIS. The database presents a population of 139,785 active insured persons having contributed in 1998. The distribution of this population by age and sex is presented in table 13.

In addition to those people who contributed in 1998, the scheme covers others who contributed to the scheme in the past, but not in 1998. The data indi-

Actuarial practice in social security

Table 13 Active insured persons under the NIS, 1998

Age group	Active insured persons		
	Males	Females	Total
15–19	5 760	3 134	8 894
20–24	13 385	9 830	23 215
25–29	12 177	10 055	22 232
30–34	10 731	8 977	19 708
35–39	10 673	8 320	18 993
40–44	9 991	7 145	17 136
45–49	8 751	5 076	13 827
50–54	6 212	3 319	9 531
55–59	4 486	1 763	6 249
Total	**82 166**	**57 619**	**139 785**

cate that 386,813 people are present in the administrative files of the NIS but interrupted their insurance coverage before 1998. Part of this population has retired, others have left Demoland, and some others, for various reasons, may never return as contributors to the scheme. After an analysis of the annual number of new beneficiaries under the scheme, it became apparent that some of the new beneficiaries were former contributors. Consequently, a population of inactive insured persons has been considered in this valuation to take into account those people who contributed to the scheme in the past, are not current contributors but may re-enter the scheme in the future. Their characteristics are presented in table 14.

It is assumed that the future evolution of the number of active insured persons will follow the evolution of the employed population determined in Chapter 3. An age-specific coverage rate (number of insured persons at each age as a percentage of the total employed population at the same age) is determined as of

Table 14 Inactive insured persons under the NIS, 1998

Age group	Inactive insured persons		
	Males	Females	Total
15–19	548	161	709
20–24	1 884	371	2 255
25–29	3 505	583	4 088
30–34	4 540	722	5 262
35–39	5 255	824	6 079
40–44	4 981	851	5 832
45–49	4 220	718	4 938
50–54	2 871	457	3 328
55–59	2 196	313	2 509
Total	**30 000**	**5 000**	**35 000**

Table 15 Rate of increase of the active insured population (as a %)

Period	Rate of increase of the active insured population
1999–2010	1.4
2011–20	1.3
2021–30	0.8
2031–40	0.8
2041–50	0.6

the valuation date. In this valuation, it is assumed that these age-specific coverage rates will remain constant for the whole projection period. In effect, the global coverage rate of the scheme increases over time because of the increase in the average age of the employed population. Table 15 presents the average rate of increase of the active insured population for different periods.

4.2 Insurable earnings

The data on insurable earnings were not available directly from the contributors' administrative system, since the information on contributions is not yet computerized. A survey was conducted by the NIB on the annual earnings of active insured persons in 1998. However, it was not possible to reconcile the total amount of insurable earnings resulting from the survey data to the amount of contributions appearing in the financial statements of the scheme. An adjustment was thus made to the collected data in order to estimate the salary rate, that is, the level of salary measured at one point in time, not taking into account the period of unemployment during the year, and not

Table 16 Average earnings of active contributors, 1998

Age	Survey data on average monthly insurable earnings on which contributions have been paid (including the effect of density and earnings ceiling)		Estimated monthly salary rate (not limited to the scheme's ceiling)	
	Males (in $)	Females (in $)	Males (in $)	Females (in $)
17	4 725	4 511	8 977	7 849
22	8 755	7 814	16 634	13 596
27	12 675	9 602	24 083	16 707
32	14 794	10 116	28 109	17 602
37	16 234	11 972	30 845	20 831
42	21 465	15 037	40 784	26 164
47	21 532	14 451	40 911	25 145
52	22 043	16 527	41 882	28 757
57	23 146	18 697	43 977	32 533
Total	20 077	14 236	29 294	19 469

taking into account the earnings ceiling applicable under the scheme. Table 16 presents salaries on these two bases.

In order to measure the effects of the minimum and maximum pensions and the effect of the earnings ceiling more accurately, the actuarial model used for the projections translates average earnings into a complete distribution for each age and year of projection.

The upper limit on insurable earnings was $46,000 per month in 1998. This ceiling is assumed constant for 1999 and increases thereafter in line with the general wage increase assumption.

4.3 Density of contributions

The density of contributions represents the average proportion of the year during which an active insured person actually contributes to the scheme. This variable is applied to the annual rate of salary (12 times the monthly salary rate presented in section 4.2) in order to obtain the actual earnings on which contributions have been paid, taking into account periods of absence of earnings during a given year. The density of contributions is assumed constant over the whole projection period.

4.4 Accrued past credits

The data on the accrued past service of the active and the inactive insured population were available in the administrative files of the NIS. These data appeared to understate the actual past service of people reaching retirement, taking into consideration the percentage of people reaching age 60 and eligible for a pension and the average amount of new pensions granted. A simulation was performed with the level of past service used in the last actuarial report. The number and amount of new pensions, as well as the number of grants, appeared realistic when using the results of the earlier survey. It was, therefore, decided to use the same average past service as in the previous valuation. The data are presented in table 18. For each age and sex group, the average number of years

Table 17 Density of contributions (as a %)

Age group	Males	Females
15–19	53	45
20–24	71	61
25–29	78	71
30–34	80	69
35–39	78	71
40–44	80	68
45–49	88	76
50–54	78	69
55–59	78	68

Table 18 Assumed average past credits of active and inactive insured persons

Age	Average number of weeks of past contributions	
	Males	Females
15–19	38	30
20–24	161	143
25–29	254	219
30–34	389	349
35–39	615	492
40–44	723	603
45–49	862	671
50–54	842	719
55–59	838	819

of past insurance credits has been distributed over a given span of years in order to reflect more accurately the effect of eligibility conditions on the number of new emerging pensions. This normal distribution uses a standard deviation of the number of years equal to one-third of the average. Average past credits of the inactive insured persons were assumed equal to the ones used for active persons.

4.5 Pensions in payment on the valuation date

The number and average amounts of pensions in payment on the valuation date are presented in Annex 2 of this report.

4.6 Demographic assumptions related to the scheme

4.6.1 The mortality rates of insured persons

The mortality rates for the insured population have been assumed equal to the mortality rates of the general population (see Chapter 3). This mortality pattern is also used to project survivors' benefits payable on the death of insured persons or pensioners. As described earlier, mortality rates are assumed to decline continuously during the projection period.

The mortality rates of invalidity pensioners are assumed equal to those of the other groups of insured persons.

4.6.2. Invalidity incidence

The rates of entry into invalidity have been calculated from the scheme's experience over recent years. Invalidity incidence rates are kept constant for the whole projection period. The rates are presented in table 19.

Actuarial practice in social security

Table 19 Rates of entry into invalidity

Age	Males	Females
17	–	–
22	–	–
27	.000164	–
32	.000280	.000111
37	.000656	.000240
42	.001702	.000560
47	.003085	.000788
52	.007727	.003616
57	.016050	.013613

4.6.3 Retirement

The actuarial model used for this actuarial review takes retirement to be the residual element of a series of factors. The macroeconomic frame described in Chapter 3 provides the number of people employed each year. For a given age (at which retirement is possible under the NIS), the difference between the number of insured persons in two consecutive years is considered to be the new retirees. Consistency checks are performed to reproduce the retirement pattern observed under the scheme. Considering the scheme's provisions and the experience over recent years, retirement was assumed to occur at age 60 for all insured persons.

Table 20 Assumptions on family structure (for widows' pensions)

Age of the insured	Probability of being married at time of death	Average age of spouse	Average number of children	Average age of children
22	0.02	20	1.5	1
27	0.1	24	2	2
32	0.2	29	2.5	4
37	0.35	34	3	7
42	0.45	39	3	10
47	0.5	44	3	13
52	0.5	49	3	16
57	0.5	54	2	17
62	0.5	59	1	18
67	0.5	64	–	–
72	0.5	69	–	–
77	0.5	74	–	–
82	0.5	80	–	–
87	0.45	85	–	–

A practical exercise: The Demoland case

4.6.4 Family structure

Information on the family structure of the insured is necessary for the projection of survivors' benefits. For benefits payable on the death of an insured person, assumptions have to be established on the probability of being married, on the age difference between spouses, on the average number of children being eligible for a child supplement and on the average age of those children. The probability of being married at the time of death may appear low when compared with the vital statistics of the general population, but it has been set in order to reproduce the number of new survivors' pensions awarded annually by the scheme. Because widowers' pensions are paid out only in exceptional cases, projections only take into consideration the occurrence of widows' pensions.

The factors used in the current valuation are presented in table 20.

CHAPTER 5
COST PROJECTIONS UNDER THE PRESENT LEGAL PROVISIONS

The financial projections presented in this chapter take into account the public announcements made in October 1999 concerning the level of the minimum pension and the increase in the insurable earnings ceiling.[2] In this chapter, benefits have been grouped as follows:

Short-term benefits

Sickness benefit

Medical care (sickness)

Maternity allowance and grant

Employment injury benefits

Injury benefit

---

[2] A public announcement was made relative to the increase in the minimum pension from $5,700 to $7,500 per month effective as of 1 October 1999 and from $7,500 to $9,500 per month effective as of 1 January 2000. Announcements were also made relative to the increase in the monthly insurable earnings ceiling from $46,000 to $60,000 per month effective as of 1 October 1999 and from $60,000 to $76,000 per month effective as of 1 January 2000.

Table 21 Experience in sickness benefit

Year	Number of benefit cases per insured	Average number of days per case	Average cost per benefit day (in $)	Total cost (as a % of insurable earnings)
1996	0.1174	9.3	584	0.37
1997	0.0917	9.3	891	0.38
1998	0.1086	10.0	894	0.46

Disablement benefit
Death benefit
Medical care (employment injury benefits)

Pensions
Old-age pension and grant
Invalidity pension and grant
Survivors' pension and grant
Funeral benefit

5.1 Short-term benefits

5.1.1 Sickness benefit

The experience in sickness benefit has not been regular over the past three years. While the average number of days of benefit is stable around ten, the average amount of benefit per day increased substantially in 1997 (more than what could have been expected from the increase in the general wage levels) and remained stable in 1998, despite the important increase in the level of salaries between these two years. The frequency of sickness cases varied from 9 per cent to 12 per cent of the insured population. For cost projection purposes, the cost of the sickness benefit is assumed equal to 0.50 per cent of insurable earnings.

5.1.2 Medical care (sickness)

For people receiving sickness benefits, the cost of medical care may be reimbursed up to a maximum of $450,000. The cost of this benefit expressed as a per-

Table 22 Experience in medical care (sickness), 1996-98

Year	Cost of medical care (sickness) (as a % of total insurable earnings)
1996	0.76
1997	0.80
1998	1.01

Table 23 Experience in maternity allowance, 1996–98

Year	Number of benefit cases per insured	Average number of days per case	Average cost per benefit day (in $)	Total cost (as a % of insurable earnings)
1996	0.0201	52	424	0.26
1997	0.0144	66	503	0.24
1998	0.0181	51	632	0.28

centage of insurable earnings is presented in table 22. It varied from 0.76 per cent in 1996 to 1.01 per cent in 1998. For costing purposes, the cost of this benefit is established at 1.00 per cent of insurable earnings.

5.1.3 Maternity allowance and grant

The cost of the maternity allowance has been relatively stable over recent years. Variations observed in the frequency of cases over the years 1996 to 1998 have been compensated by changes regarding the average duration of payment. It should be noted that the maximum duration of payment of the allowance is 13 weeks (or 78 days) and that the average observed duration of payment of the allowance varies between 51 to 66 days. The total cost of maternity benefits (allowance and grant) is assumed equal to 0.30 per cent of insurable earnings.

5.1.4 Summary of costs of short-term benefits

The costs of short-term benefits are summarized in table 24.

5.2 Employment injury benefits

5.2.1 Injury benefit

The cost of the injury benefit expressed as a percentage of insurable earnings can be summarized as follows. The future cost of the injury benefit is assumed equal to 0.20 per cent of insurable earnings.

Table 24 Costs of short-term benefits

Type of benefit	Cost (as a % of total insurable earnings)
Sickness benefit	0.50
Medical care (sickness)	1.00
Maternity allowance and grant	0.30
Administrative expenses	0.40
Total	**2.20**

Table 25 Cost of the injury benefit, 1996–98

Year	Cost of the injury benefit (as a % of insurable earnings)
1996	0.17
1997	0.18
1998	0.13

5.2.2 Disablement benefit

The cost of disablement pensions has been calculated on the basis of the following assumptions. The cost is established at 0.75 per cent of insurable earnings.

Average disablement rate (as a %)	50
Average age at disablement	45
Present value of future pension payments (as a % of insurable earnings)	0.75

5.2.3 Death benefit

The cost of death benefits has been calculated on the basis of the following assumptions:

Average annual number of deaths	20
Average age of the widow	30
Average number of orphans	2.5
Present value of widows' pensions (as a % of insurable earnings)	0.15
Present value of orphans' pensions (as a % of insurable earnings)	0.05
Present value of parents' pensions (as a % of insurable earnings)	0.05

5.2.4 Medical care (employment injury benefits)

During the past three years the cost of medical care (employment injury benefits) has been as follows, when expressed as a percentage of insurable earnings.

Table 26 Cost of medical care, 1996–98

Year	Cost of the injury benefit (as a % of insurable earnings)
1996	0.06
1997	0.06
1998	0.08

Table 27 Costs of employment injury benefits

Type of benefit	Cost (as a % of total insurable earnings)
Injury benefit	0.20
Death benefit	0.25
Disablement benefit	0.75
Medical care (employment injury)	0.10
Constant attendance allowance	–
Administrative expenses	0.20
Total	**1.50**

The future cost of the injury benefit is assumed equal to 0.10 per cent of insurable earnings.

5.2.5 Summary of costs of employment injury benefits

The costs of employment injury benefits are summarized in table 27.

5.3 Pensions

5.3.1 Demographic projections

As illustrated in section 3.1.4, Demoland will see an ageing of its population over the next few decades. In addition, the NIS will continue to mature by which the number of people eligible for pensions in proportion to the total population of Demoland will increase. These two factors will result in an increase in the ratio of pensioners to contributors, as illustrated in the last column of table 28.

During the next 40 years, the number of male old-age pensioners will more than double and the number of female old-age pensioners will multiply by more than six. At the same time, under the macroeconomic frame used for the projection, the number of contributors will not follow this accelerating trend, leading to greater pressure on this population for the financing of pensions. Hence, the ratio of pensioners to contributors increases from 23 per cent in 1999 to 44 per cent by 2040.

5.3.2 Financial projections

Table 29 presents the financial ratios of the various pensions. These ratios represent the average pension of each type expressed as a percentage of the average earnings of the contributors to the scheme. The important increase observed in 2000 is the result of the increase in the minimum pension. All ratios rise over time, resulting from the projected increase in the average length of service of contributors. It should be noted that even if the scheme had reached a stage where present contributors could have

Table 28 Demographic projections for pensions

Year	Contributors			Pensioners							Ratio of pensioners to contributors (as a %)
	M	F	Total	Old age		Invalidity		Widows	Orphans	Total	
				M	F	M	F				
1999	79 916	5 631	136 547	16 142	4 549	1 467	462	6 723	1 544	30 887	23
2000	80 725	57 624	138 349	15 911	4 597	1 624	507	7 239	2 622	32 500	23
2001	81 619	58 684	140 303	15 705	4 648	1 784	554	7 712	3 530	33 933	24
2002	82 616	59 827	142 442	15 547	4 718	1 947	603	8 142	4 297	35 254	25
2003	83 714	61 058	144 772	15 460	4 825	2 112	654	8 533	4 939	36 523	25
2004	84 870	62 380	147 251	15 482	4 975	2 280	708	8 889	5 460	37 794	26
2005	86 119	63 800	149 919	15 610	5 171	2 451	765	9 212	5 878	39 087	26
2010	93 324	72 161	165 485	17 513	6 849	3 358	1 087	10 490	6 817	46 114	28
2020	102 648	85 294	187 942	25 114	14 074	5 324	1 930	12 663	5 645	64 750	34
2030	106 012	96 594	202 606	31 217	23 633	6 969	2 851	15 126	4 532	84 328	42
2040	109 758	109 144	218 902	34 344	30 696	7 966	3 527	16 558	3 978	97 069	44

Table 29 Financial ratios (average pension as a % of the average salary of contributors)

Year	Retirement pension		Invalidity pension		Widows' pension
	Males	Females	Males	Females	
1999	27	32	31	36	14
2000	33	39	34	39	12
2001	35	40	35	40	12
2002	36	42	37	42	13
2003	38	45	39	44	13
2004	41	48	41	46	14
2005	43	50	43	48	14
2010	54	62	49	55	16
2020	63	72	52	60	20
2030	63	73	51	61	23
2040	64	73	52	62	24

been covered by the scheme during their whole career (the scheme started in 1969), we observe that the average duration of the insurance coverage is relatively low, being just over 15 years for people reaching the retirement age of 60, whereas the potential contributory period may extend from age 16 to age 60. In this valuation, it is projected that the average past service of people reaching retirement age will increase significantly in the future.

Table 30 presents total income and expenditures of the scheme over the next 40-year period under the scheme's present provisions and using the current contribution rate allocated to pensions (8.3 per cent). It also presents the evolution of the reserve. The reserve ratio, which represents the ratio of the reserve at the end of a given year to the annual expenditures of the scheme in that year, is

Table 30 Financial projections for the pension branch under status quo conditions

Year	Income (in million $)			Total expenditures (in million $)	Reserve, end of period (in million $)	Reserve ratio (as a %)	PAYG rate (as a %)
	Contributions	Investment	Total				
1999	3 071	772	3 843	2 735	11 296	4.1	7.4
2000	3 848	904	4 752	3 826	12 222	3.2	8.3
2001	4 147	923	5 070	4 247	13 045	3.1	8.5
2002	4 434	873	5 306	4 740	13 612	2.9	8.9
2003	4 756	958	5 714	5 316	14 010	2.6	9.3
2004	5 088	976	6 064	5 990	14 084	2.4	9.8
2005	5 444	970	6 414	6 721	13 776	2.1	10.2
2010	7 629	371	8 000	11 891	2 944	0.3	12.9
2020	14 180	–	14 180	33 791	–	–	19.8
2030	24 910	–	24 910	75 302	–	–	25.1
2040	42 933	–	42 933	141 280	–	–	27.3

Table 31 The GAP for various periods (as a %)

Period (in years)	GAP
10	9.6
20	12.5
30	15.6
40	18.2

equal to 4.1 at the end of 1999, and this ratio will gradually decrease to 0 by 2011 if the contribution rate is not modified. If the scheme's provisions remain unchanged and the contribution rate is kept constant at 8.3 per cent, the reserve will be exhausted in 13 years' time.

The PAYG rate represents the contribution rate which would be just sufficient to pay the expenditures of the scheme for the current year. Therefore, over time it follows the demographic and financial evolution of the scheme. In the case of the NIS of Demoland, the PAYG rate increases from 7.4 per cent in 1999 to 27.3 per cent by 2040, showing that the present contribution rate devoted to pensions (8.3 per cent) is just sufficient, in 1999, to cover the expenditure of the scheme. However, it also shows that this contribution rate will have to increase significantly over the next three decades in order to reach eventually a level of around 26 per cent.

Another useful measure of the cost of a scheme is the GAP, which represents the constant contribution rate, applied over a specified period, necessary to fund fully the benefits paid during that period. For example, if calculated over the next 40-year period, the GAP for the NIS is 18.2 per cent, which means that, in order to keep the contribution rate constant for the next 40 years, it would be necessary to increase it immediately to 18.2 per cent. In practice, however, there is little interest to do this, since such an approach would generate a dramatic increase in the reserve, the totality of which could hardly be invested with the prospect of a good return. But the GAP is a good indicator of the long-term cost of the scheme and can be useful when comparing different scenarios on the future development of the scheme or to analyse the effect of various modifications.

A practical exercise: The Demoland case

CHAPTER 6
COMPARISON WITH THE PREVIOUS VALUATION AND SENSITIVITY TESTS

6.1 Comparison with the previous valuation

Two factors explain the main differences between the results of the fourth and fifth actuarial valuations:

1. In the 1993 valuation, the rate of growth of the active insured population was assumed constant at 1 per cent per year. In the 1998 valuation, the rate of growth of this population was higher during the first 20 years of the projection. The average rate of growth was 1.4 per cent from 1999 to 2010 and 1.3 per cent from 2011 to 2020.
2. The 1993 valuation used a rate of indexation of benefits equal to the rate of increase of wages. Considering the legislative provisions and current practice, it has been assumed in this valuation that pensions will continue to be indexed on the basis of price increases.

These two factors led the cost of the scheme in the 1998 valuation to be lower than in the 1993 valuation. Firstly, the amount of benefits, once in payment, evolves less rapidly because of the lower indexation factor. Secondly, there are relatively more contributors per pensioner, resulting in a lower cost as a percentage of payroll. Table 32 presents a comparison of PAYG rates and dependency ratios under the two valuations.

Table 32 Comparison of the results of the 1993 and 1998 valuations (as a %)

Year	PAYG cost rate		Ratio of pensioners to contributors	
	1993 valuation	1998 valuation	1993 valuation	1998 valuation
1999	9.8	7.4	26	23
2009	14.9	12.3	34	28
2019	23.9	19.1	45	34

6.2 Sensitivity tests

As mentioned in section 3.2, the macroeconomic frame used in this valuation, while based on a consistent set of assumptions, was not able to use recent labour force data. In addition, the current economic context of Demoland is unstable and the wage situation in particular may take a great number of directions. This section is, therefore, necessary to give some idea of the possible variability of the results presented in the report. A series of tests have thus been performed on some key economic assumptions to present a range of possible costs of the scheme in the long term.

6.2.1 The unemployment rate

In the first test, it is assumed that the unemployment rate will remain at its 1999 level (11 per cent for males and 19 per cent for females) instead of gradually decreasing to 7 per cent for both sexes by 2050. This results in a lower rate of increase in the active insured population, as illustrated in table 33.

This lower increase in the population of contributors results in an increase in the dependency ratio (ratio of pensioners to contributors) and consequently of the PAYG rate.

Table 33 Sensitivity test on the rate of increase of the active insured population (comparison of assumptions)

Period	Rate of increase of the active insured population (as a %)	
	Base run	Sensitivity test
1999–2010	1.4	1.2
2011–20	1.3	1.0
2021–30	0.8	0.5
2031–40	0.8	0.6
2041–50	0.6	0.5

Table 34 Sensitivity test on the rate of increase of the active insured population (results)

Year	Ratio of pensioners to contributors (as a %)		PAYG cost rate (as a %)	
	Base run	Test	Base run	Test
1999	23	23	7.4	7.4
2010	28	29	12.9	13.1
2020	34	36	19.8	20.3
2030	42	45	25.1	26.0
2040	44	48	27.3	28.3

6.2.2 Rate of increase of wages

In the second test, it is assumed that the rate of increase of wages will be lower than in the base run. Instead of an average rate of growth of real wage of 2.0 per cent per year assumed in the base run, it has been assumed in the sensitivity test that real wages would grow at 1.0 per cent per year. The principal effect of this change in assumptions is a lower growth of the salary base used for the computation of contributions to the scheme and, consequently, an increase in the PAYG cost rate.

Under this scenario, the PAYG rate increases by approximately 2 per cent (from 19.8 per cent to 21.7 per cent) by 2020 and 3 per cent (from 27.5 per cent to 30.7 per cent) by 2040. This can be translated into a GAP (calculated over 50 years) equal to 20.9 per cent under the sensitivity test instead of 20.1 per cent calculated for the base run, which means that under these conditions the scheme would need, during the next five decades, a constant increase of 0.8 per cent of its contribution rate on top of what is presented in section 7.2.

Table 35 Sensitivity test on the rate of increase of wages (comparison of assumptions)

Year	Assumed real wage increase (as a %)	
	Base run (annual average)	Sensitivity test
1999	11.0	11.0
2000	10.6	10.6
2001–09	2.1	1.0
2010–19	2.1	1.0
2020–29	2.2	1.0
2030–39	2.0	1.0
2040–49	1.9	1.0

Table 36 Sensitivity test on the rate of increase of wages (results)

Year	PAYG cost rate (as a %)	
	Base run	Test
1999	7.4	7.4
2010	12.9	13.6
2020	19.8	21.7
2030	25.1	28.1
2040	27.3	30.5

CHAPTER 7
FINANCING STRATEGY

7.1 Reallocation of reserves

The allocation of reserves to the three benefit branches as of 31 December 1998 is the result of a series of historical allocations of contribution income, investment income and administrative expenses, based on percentage distributions recommended in previous actuarial reports. As shown in Chapter 1, this arbitrary allocation led to undesirable results in terms of the rate of return by benefit branch and in terms of the level of reserves allocated to each branch. The establishment of a financing strategy for the scheme should thus start with a reallocation of reserves based on precise funding objectives appropriate to each branch.

The objective of the reserve for short-term benefits is to absorb any unfavourable benefit experience and should be in the order of magnitude of six months of benefits. As the total cost of this branch is estimated at 2.2 per cent of insurable earnings, a reserve equal to $369 million would be sufficient for this purpose. At the end of 1998, the reserve of the short-term branch was $1,165 million. An amount of $796 million could thus be transferred from the short-term branch to the pension branch.

Concerning employment injury benefits, the objective of the reserve differs according to the type of benefit. For benefits of a short-term nature (injury benefit and medical care), the reserve can be set at six months of benefits as in the short-term branch. This six-month contingency reserve would represent $50 million as of 31 December 1998. For disablement and death benefits, the reserve should represent the present value of future payments of pensions to present beneficiaries. This present value is equal to $939 million as of 31

Table 37 Reallocation of reserves as of 31 December 1998

Branch	Amount of reserves (in million $)
Pensions	10 188
Short-term benefits	369
Employment injury benefits	989
Total	**11 546**

A practical exercise: The Demoland case

December 1998. At the end of 1998, the reserve of the employment injury benefits branch is $2,564 million. An amount of $1,575 could thus be transferred from this branch to the pension branch.

As a result, the following allocation of reserves will be used for the financial projections presented in this chapter.

7.2 Recommended contribution rates

7.2.1 Contribution rates by branch for 1999

The combined contribution rate currently paid by employees and their employers is 12.0 percent. In Chapter 5, we estimated that the contribution rate recommended for the short-term branch should be 2.2 per cent and the rate for the employment injury benefits branch 1.5 percent. The contribution rate available for the pension branch is thus 8.3 per cent if we consider the total contribution rate of 12 per cent presently applied. Table 38 presents the recommended contribution rates for each branch and each category of insured persons for 1999.

7.2.2 Long-term contribution rate schedule

For the short-term and employment injury benefits branches, it is recommended that the contribution rates remain constant at their 1999 levels until the next actuarial review.

For the pension branch, considering the future increase in costs illustrated in Chapter 5, there is a need to specify a rule for determining the actuarial equilibrium of the scheme that will guide future contribution rate increases. It is recommended that the funding objectives for the pension branch be expressed in terms of reserve ratios. The reserve ratio is the ratio of the reserve at the end of a given year divided by the annual expenditures of the scheme. The target reserve ratio varies according to the degree of maturity of the scheme. In the early years of existence of a pension scheme, the reserve ratio is normally high, since the number of pensioners is very low compared with the number of contributors and the contribution rate is more than sufficient to pay annual expenditures on benefits. However, when the scheme is mature, the ratio of pen-

Table 38 Contribution rates for each category of contributors in 1999

Category of contributors	Contribution rate (as a %)	Branches covered
Salaried	12.0	All branches
Self-employed	10.5	Short-term benefits and pensions
Voluntary contributors	8.3	Pensions only
Employed persons below age 16 or over age 60	1.5	Employment injury benefits only

[1] For salaried employees, 40 per cent is paid by the employee and 60 percent by the employer.

sioners to contributors stabilizes; there is no need to maintain important reserve funds and the contribution rate approaches the PAYG cost of the scheme.

Even though it has been in operation since 1969, the NIS of Demoland has still not reached maturity. The ratio of pensioners to contributors will increase from 23 per cent in 1999 to 44 per cent by 2040 and, consequently, the PAYG cost will rise from 7.4 per cent in 1999 to 27.3 per cent by 2040. It is thus necessary to plan for these future cost increases. The reserve ratio of the scheme is equal to 4.1 at the end of 1999, which means that the current reserve can support four years of expenditure of the scheme. If the contribution rate is not raised, this reserve ratio will decrease to 0 by 2011.

Taking into account the actual stage of maturity of the scheme and the projected cost increases, it is recommended to define the rule for the future determination of the contribution rates as follows and to stipulate that rule into the law governing the NIS:

> The contribution rate of the pension branch will be established such that the reserve ratio of the branch is equal to 4.0 in 2010, 2.5 in 2030, and 2.0 after 2040.

Table 39 presents a contribution rate schedule that meets this rule. This schedule retains (after 2003) a revision of the contribution rate every three years, in accordance with the frequency of the actuarial reviews of the scheme. It will then be possible for each future actuarial review to give a timely recommendation as to the adequacy of the recommended schedule and to recommend adjustments, if necessary, on the basis of recent financial results and the future development of the scheme.

Table 39 Recommended contribution rate schedule for pensions under status quo provisions

Period	Contribution rates (as a %)			
	Pensions	Short-term benefits	Employment injury benefits	Total
1999	8.3	2.2	1.5	12.0
2000–03	11.0	2.2	1.5	14.7
2004–06	12.5	2.2	1.5	16.2
2007–09	14.0	2.2	1.5	17.7
2010–12	15.5	2.2	1.5	19.2
2013–15	17.0	2.2	1.5	20.7
2016–18	18.5	2.2	1.5	22.2
2019–21	20.0	2.2	1.5	23.7
2022–24	21.5	2.2	1.5	25.2
2025–27	23.0	2.2	1.5	26.7
2028–30	24.5	2.2	1.5	28.2
2031+	26.0	2.2	1.5	29.7

A practical exercise: The Demoland case

Table 40 Financial projections for the pension branch under status quo conditions with the recommended contribution rate schedule

Year	Income (in million $)			Total expenditures (in million $)	Reserve, end of period (in million $)	Reserve ratio (as a %)	PAYG rate (as a %)
	Contributions	Investment	Total				
1999	3 071	772	3 844	2 735	11 296	4.1	7.4
2000	5 099	952	6 051	3 826	13 521	3.5	8.3
2001	5 496	1 069	6 564	4 247	15 839	3.7	8.5
2002	5 876	1 104	6 980	4 740	18 079	3.8	8.9
2003	6 303	1 324	7 627	5 316	20 390	3.8	9.3
2004	7 663	1 511	9 174	5 990	23 574	3.9	9.8
2005	8 198	1 729	9 927	6 721	26 780	4.0	10.2
2010	14 248	3 117	17 365	11 891	48 285	4.1	12.9
2020	34 169	6 758	40 927	33 791	109 867	3.3	19.8
2030	73 529	10 708	84 237	75 302	186 424	2.5	25.1
2040	134 490	15 031	149 521	141 280	281 700	2.0	27.3

The application of this contribution rate schedule will generate significantly higher reserves and the investment earnings will become an important part of the financing of the scheme (see table 40). The investment policy, discussed in section 9.1 of this valuation, will have to take into account this trend in the evolution of reserves.

CHAPTER 8
THE EFFECT OF MODIFICATIONS TO THE SCHEME

8.1 Increase in the minimum pension

The modification that has been analysed is a gradual increase in the minimum pension from its current level of 50 per cent of the minimum wage to 100 per cent of the minimum wage over a period of five years. Owing to the fact that:

- the minimum number of years of contributions necessary to be eligible for the old-age pension is 15 years and
- the salary scale used for projections shows a fast progression of contributory earnings during the career,

Table 41 Effect on the GAP of increasing the minimum pension

Period (in years)	GAP (as a %)	
	Status quo	Increase in the minimum pension
10	9.6	10.2
20	12.5	13.1
30	15.6	16.1
40	18.2	18.6

this modification to the minimum pension does not significantly affect the amount of new old-age pensions awarded after the valuation date. It does, however, affect the amount of old-age pensions in payment on the valuation date (assuming here that pensions in payment would be adjusted to the new minimum pension) and the amount of invalidity pensions. The long-term effect of this modification is small, because the average length of service of people reaching the age of eligibility for the old-age pension increases over time, with the resulting effect on the average pension of future new beneficiaries.

Table 41 illustrates the effect of this modification on the GAP. It can be seen that the effect is more important in the short term, since it generates an increase in the pensions in payment during the next five years. The effect of the modification decreases over time, in relative terms, owing to an increase in the average length of service of future pensioners and the higher average earnings on which these new pensions will be calculated.

8.2 Extension of the survivors' pensions to widowers

Currently, survivors' pensions are payable to widowers only if, at the time of death of the insured person, the widower is at least 55 years of age, is incapable of working and this incapacity is likely to be permanent. In addition, he must have no income from any source other than under the Poor Relief Act and

Table 42 Effect on the GAP of extending the survivors' pensions to widowers

Period (in years)	GAP (as a %)	
	Status quo	Extension of survivors' pension to widowers
10	9.6	9.8
20	12.5	12.8
30	15.6	16.0
40	18.2	18.7

must have been married to the deceased for at least six months before her death. Because of these stringent conditions on 31 December 1998 only seven widowers' pensions were being paid out under the scheme.

The modification under study aims to provide the same conditions for widowers' pensions as those applicable to widows' pensions. This modification would increase the GAP of the scheme (calculated over 40 years) from 18.2 per cent to 18.7 per cent. This could be translated into a 0.5 per cent addition to the contribution rates recommended in section 7.2.2 of this valuation.

8.3 Increase in the retirement age

The ultimate contribution rate of the pension branch (26 per cent) may seem high considering the future capacity of the financiers of the scheme to support it. At the same time, the current retirement age of the scheme is relatively low in comparison with international standards. And this does not take into consideration the fact that life expectancy at retirement is projected to increase significantly during the next 50 years. From age 60, life expectancy being the average duration a person is expected to live as a pensioner under the scheme, is currently 15.9 years for men and 18.8 for women, and these figures are projected to increase to 19.4 and 22.3 respectively by 2050. This is an important factor, which is contributing to the increase in the PAYG cost of the scheme over the years. It would, therefore, be logical to integrate into the scheme's design an element of dynamics by linking the retirement age to the expected length of time a person is expected to live, on average, from the time that person retires.

The ILO Social Security (Minimum Standards) Convention, 1952 (No. 102) requires that an old-age pension be provided no later than the age of 65. There is thus a possibility for the NIS to consider gradually increasing its retirement age. As an illustration of the possible financial impact of such a measure, we have simulated the effect of gradually increasing the retirement age from 60 to 65 between the years 2005 and 2015. This would bring a reduction in the ultimate contribution rate of the pension branch from 26 per cent to 21 per cent. However, there are a large number of possible scenarios for increasing the retirement age, according to:

- the timing of the first increase;
- the length of the period for the transition between the current retirement age and the ultimate one;
- the ultimate retirement age to be reached.

The scenario presented above is just one of many and represents a range of possible savings that could be made if one of these alternative scenarios was adopted.

Raising the retirement age should be considered in parallel with Demoland's national employment policy. Requiring older workers to stay on in the labour force for a number of additional years means that employment opportunities should be available to them. Currently, the high level of unemployment in Demoland would not be compatible with a rise in the retirement age. Forcing older workers to stay on in the work force would mean that fewer jobs would be available to young people entering the labour market.

However, in the medium term, a careful follow-up of the evolution of the labour force and a timely introduction of retirement age increases could be beneficial to the scheme and to the economy as a whole.

8.4 Qualifying conditions for sickness benefits

Concern has been expressed on the current eligibility conditions for sickness benefits for seasonal workers in the rice and sugar industries.

The present conditions for eligibility are that the insured person:

- was engaged in insurable employment immediately prior to the day the incapacity commenced;
- has paid not less than 50 weekly contributions since his or her entry into insurance;
- has been employed in, and paid contributions for, insurable employment during at least eight contribution weeks in the period of 13 contribution weeks immediately preceding the contribution week in which the first day of the continuous period of incapacity for work occurred.

The above conditions ensure that the following requirements are met: being in insurable employment at the time the incapacity commenced, having a regular attachment to the labour force and having a recent history of contributing to the scheme. In the case of seasonal workers, who periodically leave and re-enter the labour force, it may be difficult to meet the third condition (eight weeks in the last 13) during the initial period of their re-entry into employment at the beginning of the season. On average, they are covered for sickness benefits during only half of their period of employment.

To give these people proper coverage for sickness benefits and at the same time target the real seasonal workers who come back to work on a periodical basis, the third condition could be redefined as follows:

> . . . had been employed in, and paid contributions for, insurable employment during at least eight contribution weeks in the period of 13 contribution weeks immediately preceding the contribution week in which the first day of the continuous period of incapacity for work occurred, or during at least 20 of the last 50 contribution weeks preceding incapacity.

Since no data on seasonal employment and on the specific contribution history of these workers were available to the actuary of this valuation, the cost of such a modification to the eligibility conditions cannot be estimated very precisely. However, it can be assumed that the average earnings of seasonal workers are lower than those of the rest of the workforce (we may expect a lower average benefit for seasonal workers) and that seasonal workers represent a small percentage of the total covered employment in Demoland.[3] In that context, and considering the margin already included in the contribution rate for short-term benefits, the modification could be adopted without having to change the contribution rate, which would be revalued at the next actuarial review on the basis of recent experience.

Finally, the question of the medical follow-up by the NIB of sickness beneficiaries coming from seasonal workers is very important, since these people may have little incentive to declare their recovery once the crop season is over.

CHAPTER 9
OTHER ISSUES

9.1 Investment policy

According to the financial projections contained in this report, the reserves of the NIS will grow significantly in the next few decades. The question of the investment of these sums is thus of crucial importance. As of 31 December 1997, assets of an equity nature (land, building, equities) represented only 14 per cent of the total assets of the NIF.

Out of the investment portfolio itself, fixed-income securities with short-term maturities (fixed deposits and Treasury bills) represented 78 per cent of the total. This is particularly high considering that the main purpose of maintaining social security reserves is to support future obligations of a long-term nature. Most of the investments included in the portfolio are secure and have attracted high returns in the past, but it cannot be expected that this situation will continue indefinitely. A diversification of the portfolio should, therefore, be contemplated. A shift towards equity investments would normally increase

---

[3]From J. Loxley and V. Jamal: *Structural adjustment and agriculture in Guyana: From crisis to recovery*, ILO Working Paper, SAP 2.84/WP143, 1999. Agriculture employs 27 per cent of the labour force, out of which 38 per cent are salaried and 11 per cent casual workers. Salaries in agriculture are equal to 67 per cent of those paid to salaried employees in urban areas.

Table 43 Distribution of the assets of the NIF as of 31 December 1997

Type of asset	Amount (in million $)	Percentage of total assets
Fixed assets (land, building, equipment)	237	3
Investment portfolio		
Equities	977	11
Debentures	509	6
Fixed deposits	3 336	38
Treasury bills	2 765	32
Other investments	200	2
Receivables	140	2
Other assets	539	6
Total	**8 703**	**100**

the long-term return. Such a modification to the investment strategy should be gradual and should take into account the opportunities existing in Demoland for investments ensuring a good balance between safety and return.

The NIB could prudently increase the share of foreign investments in its portfolio if opportunities do not exist in Demoland. Overseas investments should include only high-security investments offering a stable and reliable return, which can be readily liquidated. The policy of investing abroad should be based on a careful selection of countries in which these investments are made and a restriction as to the number of these countries.

Concerning the social and economic roles to be played by social security reserves, it should be remembered that social security reserves must first be used to generate investment earnings to complement the contribution income coming from employers and workers. Insured persons will demand that an adequate return be earned on the contributions they put into the scheme. The rate of return on these funds is thus of primary importance. Once there is sufficient assurance that this return can be achieved, then the scheme may consider that its reserves can play a role in the economic development of the country.

The NIB should review the responsibilities of its Investment Committee. The primary role of this committee is to establish the investment policy and to provide the general guidelines for investment. It should not be involved in all single decisions concerning the choice of specific securities. Currently, all decisions other than day-to-day Treasury bill transactions are taken by the Investment Committee. Considering the projected increase in the reserves of the NIS, the increasing workload that will be associated with this function and the appropriate skills required for the management of investments, it is recommended that an investment unit inside the NIS be set up.

A practical exercise: The Demoland case

9.2 Coverage of the self-employed

Concerns have been expressed on the possible advantage self-employed participants have in the NIS compared with salaried employees, in terms of the relation between the benefits they will eventually receive from the scheme and the contributions they pay during their working life.

Despite the scarcity of data according to the type of employment (salaried versus self-employed), we have calculated benefit/contribution ratios from the data available on levels of salaries by type of employment and from assumptions on the average length of service of each group.

From data presented in the NIS 1999 budget, the average insurable earnings are $21,229 for salaried employees and $14,435 for the self-employed. The average earnings of the self-employed are thus just over the level of the minimum wage of the public sector and, consequently, it may be assumed that most of them will receive the minimum pension at retirement. There are no data on the average length of service of each group separately, but taking into account that the old-age pension is payable after a minimum of 15 years of contribution, we present in tables 44 and 45 the benefit/contribution ratio for two cases: for a period of service of 15 years (which represents the average past service of present contributors reaching retirement age) and for a period of service of 25 years (which may be assumed to apply in the long term). One must remember that the old-age pension formula is weighted in favour of participants with low earnings (the presence of the minimum pension) and with short periods of service (40 per cent for the first 15 years and 1 per cent for each additional year).

The benefit/contribution ratio represents the present value of the old-age pension divided by the present value of contributions paid during the whole career. For the sake of simplicity, other benefits have been ignored.

Table 44 Benefit/contribution ratios, employed versus the self-employed (status quo provisions)

Length of service (in years)	Employed	Self-employed
15	3.5	4.0
25	2.4	2.9

Table 45 Benefit/contribution ratios, employed versus the self-employed (increase in the minimum pension, from 50 per cent to 100 per cent)

Length of service (in years)	Employed	Self-employed
15	4.9	7.4
25	3.2	4.5

It can be seen from tables 44 and 45 that under the scheme's current provisions, the self-employed do appear to have an advantage because of the level of their average earnings, but the difference is more important between two participants with different lengths of service. If it can be demonstrated that self-employed people have significantly lower average lengths of service than the employed, then their benefit/contribution advantage would become obvious. Further analysis of the actual situation as regards the career pattern of the self-employed is, therefore, recommended, so as to compare the two groups of insured persons more accurately.

In the second scenario, assuming an increase in the minimum pension (table 45), it becomes evident that, owing to their lower average earnings, most of the self-employed would benefit from the minimum pension and we can see their ratios almost doubling. The control over earnings declarations by the self-employed is thus an element to consider before adopting a higher minimum pension.

9.3 Indexation of pensions

At present, there is no legal requirement to adjust pensions periodically to reflect the evolution of prices or wages in the economy of Demoland. However, in practice, every year the NIB grants an adjustment to pensions in payment equal to the minimum between the inflation rate and 10 per cent.

In the financial projections contained in Chapter 5, the assumption was made that pensions in payment would periodically be adjusted to reflect the increase in the CPI in Demoland. There is thus no additional cost to consider if it is the intention of the board to turn this rule into a legal requirement. It is strongly recommended that this practice be legalized in order to ensure that pensions keep their purchasing power over time. The index chosen to adjust benefits should be the official national CPI as published by the Bureau of Statistics.

9.4 Differentiation of pensions

Because of economic factors and the historical development of the scheme, it appears that as much as 90 per cent of old-age pensioners receive the same amount of pension, the minimum pension. This results from the fact that the average past service of people reaching retirement age is short (probably because of high historical unemployment levels) and because the population of pensioners includes a greater proportion of former public-sector employees, whose salaries are generally lower than private-sector workers.

This non-differentiation of pension amounts may act as a disincentive, at least for self-employed people with high earnings, to pay contributions to the scheme and thus contributes to maintaining a low global coverage rate. But this situation should be regarded as temporary. The parameters used in the computation of new pensions lead to a differentiation of amounts, since the pension formula is based on the level of past earnings and the number of years of service. According to the assumptions used in the actuarial valuation, the average service of the insured population will gradually increase over the years, and wages will follow, in the future, a regular increasing pattern (after the adjustments granted to civil servants in 1999 and 2000). These two factors should lead to a gradual reduction in the proportion of pensioners receiving the minimum pension.

9.5 Maintenance of statistics

During the process of the actuarial valuation, and as mentioned from time to time in this report, the actuary sometimes had to use approximations because of the incomplete database. The statistical base for the actuarial valuation will need to be improved for the next actuarial reviews if a more precise assessment of the future evolution of the cost of the scheme is to be obtained. This comment mainly refers to data on the labour force for which the last survey goes back to 1992. It is hoped that, in future, the Bureau of Statistics will carry out more regular surveys.

The data specific to the NIS should also be improved:

- Concerning the earnings of contributors, it would be useful to maintain the data both on total earnings not limited to the earnings ceiling and on actual recorded insurable earnings. The data on average earnings are presently obtained from a survey. The computerization of the administrative system should enable the provision of the necessary data for the next actuarial review.
- The amount of widows' pensions appearing in the administrative files includes the supplement payable on behalf of dependent children. It is recommended that separate statistics on widows and children be maintained, even if the child supplement is paid as part of the widow's pension.
- The data on the past service history of contributors need to be confronted with the data used in the computation of new pensions to ensure consistency. It would be necessary to calculate separately the number of weeks of past service for active insured persons and for inactive insured persons.
- It will be necessary to analyse the composition of the inactive insured population. It is probable that a large proportion of the inactive insured population (people registered with the scheme but not currently contributing) will not become active again. For the next review, it will be important to validate the number of 35,000 estimated in the present valuation as those inactive insured persons who will eventually claim a benefit under the scheme.

Conclusion

The financial situation of the NIS is actuarially sound. After recommending a reallocation of the reserves of the various branches, it is shown that the costs of the short-term and employment injury branches have been stable over recent years and that the current contribution rates for these two branches are appropriate. However, the current report also reveals that the cost of the pension branch is projected to increase gradually over the next few decades, which calls for an increase in the contribution rate for that branch. An action plan to adjust the contribution rate gradually to this increasing cost pattern would allow the financial equilibrium of the scheme to be maintained and would help avoid sharp increases in the contribution rate at times when the economy may not be in a position to support such a rise. The report suggests implementing a rule for determining a funding objective and for guiding the contribution rate increases.

ANNEX I OVERVIEW OF THE LEGAL PROVISIONS OF THE NIS OF DEMOLAND

The general headings under which the provisions of the social security scheme are usually presented are as follows:

1.1 Coverage
1.2 Financing
1.3 Pensions
    1.3.1 Old age
    1.3.2 Invalidity
    1.3.3 Survivors
    1.3.4 Funeral grant
1.4 Short-term benefits
    1.4.1 Sickness
    1.4.2 Maternity
1.5 Employment injury benefits
    1.5.1 Injury benefit
    1.5.2 Disablement benefit
    1.5.3 Death benefit
    1.5.4 Medical care

ANNEX II PENSIONS IN PAYMENT IN DECEMBER 1998

II.1 Pension branch

A practical exercise: The Demoland case

Old-age pensions

	Males		Females	
Age group	Number	Average monthly pension (in $)	Number	Average monthly pension (in $)
60–64	3 978	5 858	1 139	5 953
65–69	3 747	5 772	1 092	5 746
70–74	3 670	5 787	1 043	5 766
75–79	2 543	5 743	693	5 794
80 +	2 458	5 760	534	5 878
Total	**16 396**	**5 790**	**4 501**	**5 826**

Invalidity pensions

	Males	Females		
Age group	Number	Average monthly pension (in $)	Number	Average monthly pension (in $)
20–24	3	5 925	–	–
25–29	8	5 886	7	8 161
30–34	36	6 801	22	7 296
35–39	76	6 202	24	6 968
40–44	117	6 712	50	6 907
45–49	267	6 890	62	6 664
50–54	419	6 757	117	6 700
55–59	382	6 652	136	6 564
Total	**1 308**	**6 712**	**418**	**6 746**

Surviving spouses' pensions

	Males		Females	
Age group	Number	Average monthly pension (in $)	Number	Average monthly pension (in $)
15–19	–	–	3	3 749
20–24	–	–	17	3 426
25–29	–	–	43	3 175
30–34	–	–	118	3 260
35–39	–	–	175	3 461
40–44	–	–	239	3 540
45–49	–	–	490	3 361
50–54	–	–	579	3 466
55–59	1	2 862	782	3 145
60–64	–	–	844	3 030
65–69	1	3 876	872	2 862
70–74	3	4 650	788	2 890
75–79	1	3 814	952	2 880
80 +	1	2 862	257	3 816
Total	**7**	**3 909**	**6 159**	**3 119**

Orphans' pensions

Age group	Children of surviving spouses		Full orphans	
	Number	Average monthly pension (in $)	Number	Average monthly pension (in $)
0–4	36	1 176	1	1 908
5–9	57	1 131	12	2 101
10–14	14	1 199	14	2 156
15–19	34	1 244	7	2 071
20+	3	1 651	1	1 908
Total	**244**	**1 192**	**35**	**2 106**

II.2 Employment injury benefits branch

Disablement pensions

Age group	Males		Females	
	Number	Average monthly pension (in $)	Number	Average monthly pension (in $)
15–19	11	1 198	–	–
20–24	45	3 036	–	–
25–29	90	2 614	7	1 754
30–34	110	2 010	8	1 716
35–39	168	1 265	10	1 270
40–44	188	1 292	11	1 305
45–49	160	1 467	9	1 365
50–54	164	1 192	21	1 302
55–59	146	1 241	28	1 034
60+	283	1 191	63	1 194
Total	**1 365**	**1 473**	**157**	**1 254**

Widows' pensions

Age group	Number	Average monthly pension (in $)
15–19	1	4 347
20–24	3	4 209
25–29	2	4 256
30–34	3	4 238
35–39	20	3 821
40–44	34	3 890
45–49	33	3 941
50–54	55	4 090
55–59	52	3 953
60–64	45	4 699
65–69	39	4 142
70–74	20	3 671
75–79	40	4 013
80+	16	3 671
Total	**363**	**4 058**

Orphans' pensions

Age group	Number	Average monthly pension (in $)
0–4	–	–
5–9	2	1 908
10–14	9	1 945
15–19	7	2 049
Total	**18**	**1 981**

ANNEX III OPERATION OF THE TECHNICAL RESERVE FOR THE EMPLOYMENT INJURY BRANCH

Under the financial system proposed for the long-term benefits of the employment injury branch (assessment of constituent capitals), it is required that the actuarial present values of future payments of all pensions awarded during a financial year be charged to the operations of that year. The amount of the actuarial present values, which is set aside in a technical reserve, represents the liability of the scheme in respect of future payments to injured persons and survivors.

Every year, the technical reserve is increased by the amount of the actuarial present values of pensions awarded in that year and by the investment income on the reserve, and decreased by the pension payments made during the year. A description of the movement of the reserve is given below:

Reserve at the beginning of the year
Plus Actuarial present values of pensions awarded during the year (at the time of the award) for disablement pensions and survivors' pensions
Plus Investment income on technical reserve
Minus Current payments in respect of pensions for disablement pensions and survivors' pensions
Equals Reserve at the end of the year

The present values of pensions are calculated as the monthly rate of pensions times the multiplying factor provided in table AIII.1.

Example
Type of pension   Disablement
Monthly amount $6,000
Age of the beneficiary   35
Sex   Male
Amount of the reserve $6,000 × 333 = $1,998,000

Table AIII.1 Factors for the calculation of actuarial present values of pensions
(to be applied to the monthly amount of pension)

Age	Disablement pension		Widow(er)'s pension		Orphans
	Males	Females	Males	Females	
0	–	–	–	–	203
1	–	–	–	–	205
2	–	–	–	–	198
3	–	–	–	–	189
4					179
90	50	57	50	57	
91	48	54	48	54	
92	45	51	45	51	
93	43	48	43	48	
94	41	45	41	45	
95	38	42	38	42	
96	35	38	35	38	
97	32	34	32	34	
98	28	30	28	30	
99	23	23	23	23	

The amount of $1,998,000 will be charged against the year's income of the employment injury branch and transferred to the technical reserve. The present values for other benefits (widows, orphans) will be calculated according to the same schema, using the appropriate column of table AIII.1. Factors vary by sex for the disablement and widow's pensions and have been computed using the mortality, interest and indexation assumptions used for the pension branch.

The actuary should assess the sufficiency of the accumulated reserve at the valuation date by multiplying pensions in course of payment by the factors of table AIII.1. This might show a surplus or a deficit when compared with the actual reserve maintained for the long-term benefits of the branch. The difference is due to deviations between the assumed and actual decremental factors (for example, the mortality rates of disabled people) and assumed versus actual investment returns.

TECHNICAL BRIEF I

EXAMPLES OF TABLES USED FOR THE COLLECTION OF SOCIAL SECURITY DATA[1]

General notes for the collection of data

(a) The "Year of valuation" refers to the calendar year of the actuarial valuation.
(b) Figures for the "Official forecast for future years" should be provided only if available and details on the projection method used should be provided.
(c) If the data are not as of mid-year, then indicate the period as of which the data are relevant.
(d) If the data are unavailable on a single-age basis, then data by five-year age groups should be provided.

---

[1] This technical brief reproduces tables from ILO: *Social security data required for the valuation of a national social security scheme* (Geneva, 1999).

Actuarial practice in social security

Table TBI.1 General information

---

(1) Actuarial valuation date:

Note: The actuarial valuation date is mainly used to assess the starting point for the insured population, beneficiaries and the reserve fund of the social security system.

(2) Organization, charts of :
— Social security institution(s)
— National statistical organization
— Overall structure of government ministries and institutions responsible for social security and their relation to social security institution(s)

(3) Required documentation:
— National statistical yearbook
— Annual reports/publications of social security institutions, the central bank and relevant ministries
— National development/economic plan

Note: This refers to the government perspective and development objectives, usually for the key sectors of the economy and for its social programme, for the short to medium term.

Technical Brief I: Tables used for the collection of social security data

Table TBI.2 General population: Number of people at mid-year, historical and future

Males

Age	Historical Five years					Year of valuation	Official forecast for future years (if available)
0 to 100							
Total							

Females

Age	Historical Five years					Year of valuation	Official forecast for future years (if available)
0 to 100							
Total							

Total (males and females)

Age	Historical Five years					Year of valuation	Official forecast for future years (if available)
0 to 100							
Total							

Source of information:
Method of data collection:
Date of last census:

Note: If the data are not as of mid-year, then indicate the period as of which the data are relevant.

Actuarial practice in social security

Table TBI.3 General population: Fertility rates and sex ratio of newborns, historical and future

Age group	Historical						Year of valuation	Official forecast for future years (if available)
	1970	1975	1980	1985	1990	1995		
0–14								
15–19								
20–24								
25–29								
30–34								
35–39								
40–44								
45–49								
TFR (*total fertility rate*)								
Sex ratio of newborns								

Source of information:
Method of data collection:

Note: The sex ratio of newborns refers to the ratio of the number of male newborns to the number of female newborns.

Technical Brief I: Tables used for the collection of social security data

Table TBI.4 General population: Mortality rates, historical and future

Males

Age	Historical						Year of valuation	Official forecast for future years (if available)
	1970	1975	1980	1985	1990	1995		
0 to 100								

Females

Age	Historical						Year of valuation	Official forecast for future years (if available)
	1970	1975	1980	1985	1990	1995		
0 to 100								

Source of information:
Method of data collection:

Table TBI.5 General population: Net migration (net number of migrants), historical and future

Males

Age group	Historical						Year of valuation	Official forecast for future years (if available)
	1990	1991	1992	1993	1994	1995		
0–9								
10–19								
20–29								
30–39								
40–49								
50–59								
60–69								
70–79								
80–89								
90–99								
100 +								

Females

Age group	Historical						Year of valuation	Official forecast for future years (if available)
	1990	1991	1992	1993	1994	1995		
0–9								
10–19								
20–29								
30–39								
40–49								
50–59								
60–69								
70–79								
80–89								
90–99								
100 +								

Source of information:
Method of data collection:

Note: Number of net migrants = Number of immigrants minus Number of emigrants

Table TBI.6 General population: Marriage rate by sex and age group, historical and future

Males

Age group	Historical						Year of valuation	Official forecast for future years (if available)
	1990	1991	1992	1993	1994	1995		
0–9								
10–19								
20–29								
30–39								
40–49								
50–59								
60–69								
70–79								
80–89								
90–99								
100 +								

Females

Age group	Historical						Year of valuation	Official forecast for future years (if available)
	1990	1991	1992	1993	1994	1995		
0–9								
10–19								
20–29								
30–39								
40–49								
50–59								
60–69								
70–79								
80–89								
90–99								
100 +								

Source of information:
Method of data collection:

Actuarial practice in social security

Table TBI.7 Labour force: Average number of people, historical and future

Males

Age group	Historical Five years					Year of valuation	Official forecast for future years (if available)
15–19							
20–24							
25–29							
30–34							
35–39							
40–44							
45–49							
50–54							
55–59							
60–64							
65–69							
70–74							
75+							
Total							

Females

Age group	Historical Five years					Year of valuation	Official forecast for future years (if available)
15–19							
20–24							
25–29							
30–34							
35–39							
40–44							
45–49							
50–54							
55–59							
60–64							
65–69							
70–74							
75+							
Total							

Technical Brief I: Tables used for the collection of social security data

Total (males and females)

Age group	Historical Five years					Year of valuation	Official forecast for future years (if available)
15–19							
20–24							
25–29							
30–34							
35–39							
40–44							
45–49							
50–54							
55–59							
60–64							
65–69							
70–74							
75+							
Total							

Source of information:
Method of data collection:
Detailed definition of labour force:

Note: Labour force data should reflect the average number of people in a given calendar year. If otherwise, indicate the exact basis.

Actuarial practice in social security

Table TBI.8 Labour force: Labour force participation rates, historical and future

Males

Age group	Historical Five years						Year of valuation	Official forecast for future years (if available)
15–19								
20–24								
25–29								
30–34								
35–39								
40–44								
45–49								
50–54								
55–59								
60–64								
65–69								
70–74								
75+								
Total								

Females

Age group	Historical Five years						Year of valuation	Official forecast for future years (if available)
15–19								
20–24								
25–29								
30–34								
35–39								
40–44								
45–49								
50–54								
55–59								
60–64								
65–69								
70–74								
75+								
Total								

Source of information:
Method of data collection:

Note: Labour force data should reflect the average number of people in a given calendar year. If otherwise, indicate the exact basis.

Technical Brief I: Tables used for the collection of social security data

Table TBI.9 Total employment: Average number of people, historical and future

Males

Age group	Historical Five years					Year of valuation	Official forecast for future years (if available)
15–19							
20–24							
25–29							
30–34							
35–39							
40–44							
45–49							
50–54							
55–59							
60–64							
65–69							
70–74							
75+							
Total							

Females

Age group	Historical Five years					Year of valuation	Official forecast for future years (if available)
15–19							
20–24							
25–29							
30–34							
35–39							
40–44							
45–49							
50–54							
55–59							
60–64							
65–69							
70–74							
75+							
Total							

continued overleaf

Actuarial practice in social security

Table TB1.9 (*cont'd*)
Total (males and females)

Age group	Historical Five years						Year of valuation	Official forecast for future years (if available)
15–19								
20–24								
25–29								
30–34								
35–39								
40–44								
45–49								
50–54								
55–59								
60–64								
65–69								
70–74								
75+								
Total								

Source of information:
Method of data collection:
Detailed definition of employment:

Note: Employment data should reflect the average number of people in a given calendar year. If otherwise, indicate the exact basis.

Technical Brief I: Tables used for the collection of social security data

Table TBI.10 Employees: Average number of people, historical and future

Males

Age group	Historical Five years					Year of valuation	Official forecast for future years (if available)
15–19							
20–24							
25–29							
30–34							
35–39							
40–44							
45–49							
50–54							
55–59							
60–64							
65–69							
70–74							
75+							
Total							

Females

Age group	Historical Five years					Year of valuation	Official forecast for future years (if available)
15–19							
20–24							
25–29							
30–34							
35–39							
40–44							
45–49							
50–54							
55–59							
60–64							
65–69							
70–74							
75+							
Total							

continued overleaf

Actuarial practice in social security

Table TB1.10 (*cont'd*)
Total (males and females)

Age group	Historical Five years						Year of valuation	Official forecast for future years (if available)
15–19								
20–24								
25–29								
30–34								
35–39								
40–44								
45–49								
50–54								
55–59								
60–64								
65–69								
70–74								
75+								
Total								

Source of information:
Method of data collection:
Detailed definition of employment:

Note: Employment data should reflect the average number of people in a given calendar year. If otherwise, indicate the exact basis.

Technical Brief I: Tables used for the collection of social security data

Table TBI.11 Self-employment: Average number of people, historical and future

Males

Age group	Historical Five years						Year of valuation	Official forecast for future years (if available)
15–19								
20–24								
25–29								
30–34								
35–39								
40–44								
45–49								
50–54								
55–59								
60–64								
65–69								
70–74								
75+								
Total								

Females

Age group	Historical Five years						Year of valuation	Official forecast for future years (if available)
15–19								
20–24								
25–29								
30–34								
35–39								
40–44								
45–49								
50–54								
55–59								
60–64								
65–69								
70–74								
75+								
Total								

continued overleaf

Actuarial practice in social security

Table TB1.11 (*cont'd*)
Total (males and females)

Age group	Historical Five years						Year of valuation	Official forecast for future years (if available)
15–19								
20–24								
25–29								
30–34								
35–39								
40–44								
45–49								
50–54								
55–59								
60–64								
65–69								
70–74								
75+								
Total								

Source of information:
Method of data collection:
Detailed definition of self-employment:

Note: Self-employment data should reflect the average number of people in a given calendar year. If otherwise, indicate the exact basis.

Table TBI.12 Unemployment: Average number of people, historical and future

Males

Age group	Historical Five years					Year of valuation	Official forecast for future years (if available)
15–19							
20–24							
25–29							
30–34							
35–39							
40–44							
45–49							
50–54							
55–59							
60–64							
65–69							
70–74							
75+							
Total							

Females

Age group	Historical Five years					Year of valuation	Official forecast for future years (if available)
15–19							
20–24							
25–29							
30–34							
35–39							
40–44							
45–49							
50–54							
55–59							
60–64							
65–69							
70–74							
75+							
Total							

continued overleaf

Actuarial practice in social security

Table TB1.12 (*cont'd*)
Total (males and females)

Age group	Historical Five years					Year of valuation	Official forecast for future years (if available)
15–19							
20–24							
25–29							
30–34							
35–39							
40–44							
45–49							
50–54							
55–59							
60–64							
65–69							
70–74							
75+							
Total							

Source of information:
Method of data collection:
Detailed definition of unemployment (registered) and the reference group to which it is compared:

Note: Unemployment data should reflect the average number of people in a given calendar year. If otherwise, indicate the exact basis.

Technical Brief I: Tables used for the collection of social security data

Table TBI.13 Unemployment: Unemployment rates, historical and future

Males

Age group	Historical Five years					Year of valuation	Official forecast for future years (if available)
15–19							
20–24							
25–29							
30–34							
35–39							
40–44							
45–49							
50–54							
55–59							
60–64							
65–69							
70–74							
75+							
Total							

Females

Age group	Historical Five years					Year of valuation	Official forecast for future years (if available)
15–19							
20–24							
25–29							
30–34							
35–39							
40–44							
45–49							
50–54							
55–59							
60–64							
65–69							
70–74							
75+							
Total							

Source of information:
Method of data collection:

Note: Unemployment data should reflect the average in a given calendar year. If otherwise, indicate the exact basis.

Actuarial practice in social security

Table TBI.14 Wages: Total compensation of employees (current prices), historical

Year	Total (in the economy)	By economic sector				
1970 to Year of valuation						

Source of information:
Method of data collection:
Detailed definition of "total compensation" and the reference groups to which it relates:

Table TBI.15 Wages: Wage share of gross domestic product (GDP)

Year	Total (in the economy)	By economic sector				
1970 to Year of valuation						

Source of information:
Method of data collection:

Table TBI.16 Wages: Average wages for the economy and by sector

Year	National average wage	Average wage by economic sector				
1970 to Year of valuation						

Source of information:
Method of data collection:
Detailed definition of "national average wage", including the method of calculation:

Table TBI.17 Gross domestic product (GDP) by economic sector

Year	GDP in current prices by economic sector			GDP in constant prices by economic sector		
1970 to Year of valuation						

Source of information:
Method of data collection:
Detailed definition of GDP, including the method of calculation:

Technical Brief I: Tables used for the collection of social security data

Table TBI.18 Gross domestic product (GDP) sectoral deflators

Year	Sectoral GDP deflators						
1970 *to* *Year of valuation*							

Source of information:
Method of data collection:

Table TBI.19 Gross domestic product (GDP) by expenditure components

Year	GDP in current prices by expenditure components				GDP in constant prices by expenditure components			
1970 *to* *Year of valuation*								

Source of information:
Method of data collection:
Detailed definition of GDP, including the method of calculation:

Table TBI.20 Gross domestic product (GDP) expenditure deflators

Year	GDP expenditure deflators						
1970 *to* *Year of valuation*								

Source of information:
Method of data collection:

Actuarial practice in social security

Table TBI.21 Primary income distribution (current prices)

	1980 to Year of valuation
Operating surplus, gross	
Mixed income, gross	
Operating surplus, net	
Mixed income, net	
Property income	
Interest	
Distributed income of corporations	
Dividends	
Withdrawals from income of quasi-corporations	
Reinvested earnings on direct foreign investment	
Property income attributed to insurance policyholders	
Rent	
Entrepreneurial income, gross	
Entrepreneurial income, net	
Compensation of employees	
Wages and salaries	
Employers' social contributions	
Employers' actual social contributions	
Employers' imputed social contributions	
Taxes on production and imports	
Taxes on products	
Value added type taxes (VAT)	
Taxes and duties on imports excluding VAT	
– Import duties	
– Taxes on imports excluding VAT and duties	
Export taxes	
Taxes on products excluding VAT, import and export taxes	
Others taxes on production	
Subsidies	
Subsidies on products	
Import subsidies	
Export subsidies	
Others subsidies on products	
Other subsidies on production	

Source of information:
Method of data collection:

Technical Brief I: Tables used for the collection of social security data

Table TBI.22 Inflation and interest rates

Year	Inflation		Nominal interest rates	
	Consumer price index	Annual rate of increase	Central Bank	Commercial
1970 to Year of valuation				

Source of information:
Method of data collection:
Detailed definitions of technical terms, including their method of calculation and any reference basis:

Note: The data for the CPI should also be collected on a monthly basis for at least three observation years.

Table TBI.23 Exchange rates (annual average)

Year	versus US$	versus EURO	versus YEN
1970 to Year of valuation			

Source of information:
Method of data collection:

Note: The exchange rates should also be collected on a monthly basis for at least three observation years.

Actuarial practice in social security

Detailed information should be provided on public finance for the past five to ten years, including a short-term forecast, if available, in particular for the social security institutions or for the relevant government institutions responsible for the budgetary preparation of social security programmes.

It should also include the information relevant to the procedure for the preparation of institutional budgets.

The table below is an example. Actual classification may reflect national practice.

Table TBI.24 General government revenue and expenditure (central and local governments separately)

Item	National currency	
	Statistics	*Projections*
Revenues		
• **Received capital income**		
from enterprises		
from other government levels		
• **Received transfers**		
Received current transfers		
– Taxes:		
Indirect taxes		
Direct taxes		
– Imputed social security contributions		
– Other current transfers		
– Transfers received from other government levels		
Received transfers of wealth		
• **Other revenues**		
Expenditures		
• **Interest payments on public debt**		
Interest on national debt		
Interest on international debt		
• **Paid transfers**		
Paid current transfers		
– Subsidies		
– Social benefits		
– Other current transfers		
– Transfers paid to other government levels		
Paid transfers of wealth		
• **Government consumption**		
Net purchase of goods and services		
Gross wages and salaries		
Other consumption expenditures		
• **Gross investments**		
Balance (Net lending or net borrowing)		

Technical Brief I: Tables used for the collection of social security data

Table TBI.25 Social security legal provisions

---

(1) *Social security laws, regulations and amendments*
This should include the effective time of implementation of new legal provisions and possible modifications.

(2) *Summary of legal provisions by benefit branch*, i.e. those effectively implemented as of the valuation date, including:
– Definition of legal coverage
– Sources of financing (e.g. contributions, investment income, regulated Government contribution, etc.)
– Insured contingencies
– Eligibility conditions for entitlement to benefits, including provisions allowing for early and postponed retirement and the latest legal age for entering into retirement
– Benefit formulae
– Duration of benefit payments
– Definition of the financial objective, i.e. with respect to the reserve
– Possibility of receiving double pensions
– Etc.

(3) Indirect social security mechanisms

(4) *Health care protection*: details concerning its coverage, its financing and the level of benefits provided. This should include details on possible transfers of funds from the social security scheme(s).

Table TBI.26 Social security financial reporting

---

(1) *Institutional budget* (statement of income and expenditure) for the past five to ten years and the short-term budget forecast, including detailed income and expenditure items by benefit branch such as contribution revenues, investment income, regulated government payment transfers, arrears, benefit payments by benefit type, administrative expenses, equipment expenses, inspection expenses, etc.

(2) *Statement of assets and liabilities* for the past five to ten years

(3) *Cash flow statement* for the past five to ten years

(4) *Statement on investments* for the past five to ten years, including complete details on the investment policy

(5) *Reserve funds* for the past five to ten years, including the legal financial objective of the scheme by benefit branch

(6) *Administrative audits*, including any prior external studies relevant to the social security scheme(s).

Actuarial practice in social security

Table TBI.27 Insured population: Number of people, historical

Year	Total insured population		Active insured persons		Inactive insured persons		Insured dependants (if relevant)	
	Males	Females	Males	Females	Males	Females	Males	Females
1970 to Year of valuation								

Source of information:
Method of data collection:
Detailed definition of the insured population and its sub-components, including information on the potential group of insured persons:

Notes:
(a) In case of differently insured populations by benefit branch, a separate table should be provided for each branch.
(b) Disaggregated data should be provided if the insured population is broken down further and records are maintained, e.g. by economic sector, public versus private sectors.
(c) Active insured persons are usually defined as those who have contributed for at least one month (or on another basis) in the year prior to the valuation date.

Table TBI.28 Insured population: Age distribution at valuation date

Age group	Total insured population		Active insured persons		Inactive insured persons		Insured dependants (if relevant)	
	Males	Females	Males	Females	Males	Females	Males	Females
0–14								
15–19								
20–24								
25–29								
30–34								
35–39								
40–44								
45–49								
50–54								
55–59								
60–64								
65–69								
70–74								
75+								

Source of information:
Method of data collection:

Notes:
(a) In case of differently insured populations by benefit branch, a separate table should be provided for each branch.
(b) Disaggregated data should be provided if the insured population is broken down further and records are maintained, e.g. by economic sector, public versus private sectors.

Technical Brief I: Tables used for the collection of social security data

Table TBI.29 Insured population: Development of density factors (density for contribution payments)

Age	Number of active insured persons who contributed exactly for a given number of months in the year prior to the valuation date												Average no. months of paid contributions (c)	Density factors (d)
	1 mth	2 mths	3 mths	4 mths	5 mths	6 mths	7 mths	8 mths	9 mths	10 mths	11 mths	12 mths		
15 to 74														
Total or Average														

Notes:
(a) Table TBI.29 develops the density factor, although there may be other valid methods of arriving at the same result.
(b) Table TBI.29 should be determined also for additional years (three to five) prior to the valuation date in order to assess whether there may be a changing density pattern over time.
(c) The "average number of months of paid contributions" is determined on an annual basis and is equal to $A \div B$, where A and B are defined as follows:

A = [1 mth * No. of actives of age x who contributed exactly for 1 month]
   + [2 mths * No. of actives of age x who contributed exactly for 2 months]
   + [3 mths * No. of actives of age x who contributed exactly for 3 months] + ... + [12 mths * No. of actives of age x who contributed exactly for 12 months]

B = Total no. of actives of age x

(d) The "density factor" is determined on an annual basis and is equal to the "average number of months of paid contributions" divided by 12.

Actuarial practice in social security

Table TBI.30 Insured population: Insurable earnings and lower and upper limits, historical

Year	Average insurable earnings of Active insured persons		Lower limit on insurable earnings (floor) (if applicable)	Upper limit on insurable earnings (ceiling) (if applicable)
	Males	Females		
1970 to Year of valuation				

Source of information:
Method of data collection:
Basis and monetary unit (e.g. monthly insurable earnings in US$):
Detailed definition of insurable earnings:

Notes:
(a) Insurable earnings should reflect the "actual" earnings received in a month for which a contribution payment has been made, i.e. in the case of monthly insurable earnings, the annual amount of earnings should be divided by the number of months of paid contributions (hence, they should not be calculated as the annual earnings divided by 12).
(b) In case of differently insured populations by benefit branch, a separate table on insurable earnings should be provided for each branch.
(c) Disaggregated data on insurable earnings should be provided if the insured population is broken down further and records are maintained, e.g. by economic sector, public versus private sectors.
(d) Active insured persons are usually defined as those who have contributed for at least one month (or on another basis) in the year prior to the valuation date.

Table TBI.31 Insured population: Monthly insurable earnings in year of valuation

Age	Average monthly insurable earnings	
	Males	Females
15 to 74		

Source of information:
Method of data collection:
Basis and monetary unit (e.g. monthly insurable earnings in US$):

Notes:
(a) Monthly insurable earnings should be calculated as the average for the 12-month period prior to the valuation date. They should reflect actual earnings received in a month for which a contribution payment has been made, i.e. they should be equal to the average total amount of insurable earnings for the 12-month period divided by the average number of months of paid contributions.
(b) Earnings may be provided on another periodicity basis, e.g. weekly, quarterly, etc.
(c) In case of differently insured populations by benefit branch, a separate table on insurable earnings should be provided for each branch.
(d) Disaggregated data on insurable earnings should be provided if the insured population is broken down further and records are maintained, e.g. by economic sector, public versus private sectors.
(e) Active insured persons are usually defined as those who have contributed for at least one month (or on another basis) in the year prior to the valuation date.

Technical Brief I: Tables used for the collection of social security data

Table TBI.32 Insured population: Past insurable credits of active insured persons as of valuation date

Age	Number of actives who cumulated the given number of past insurable credits as of the valuation date					Average past insurable credits since entry into scheme
	0 to 1 year	1 to 2 years	...	54 to 55 years	55 + years	
15 to 74						
Total						

Source of information:
Method of data collection:
Reference basis (e.g. in reference to paid or declared contributions or to periods of rendered service):
Detailed definition of past insurable credits for active insured persons:

Notes:
(a) Active insured persons normally refer to registered insured persons who have paid at least one contribution payment in the year prior to the valuation date.
(b) Data provided in table TBI.32 should refer to the corresponding data on active insured persons of table TBI.28.

Table TBI.33 Insured population: Past insurable credits of inactive insured persons as of valuation date

Age	Average past insurable credits since entry into scheme of inactive insured persons	
	Males	Females
15 to 74		
Average		

Source of information:
Method of data collection:
Basis (e.g. monthly, weekly, annual):
Reference basis (e.g. in reference to paid or declared contributions or to periods of rendered service):
Detailed definition of past insurable credits for inactive insured persons:

Notes:
(a) Inactive insured persons normally refers to registered insured persons who have not paid any contribution in the year prior to the valuation date.
(b) Data provided in table TBI.33 should refer to the corresponding data on the inactive insured persons of table TBI.28.

Actuarial practice in social security

Table TBI.34 Insured population: New entrants, historical

Year	Total annual number of new entrants	
	Males	Females
1970 to Year of valuation		

Source of information:
Method of data collection:
Detailed definition of the new entrants:

Notes:
(a) In case of differently insured populations by benefit branch, a separate table should be provided for each branch.
(b) Disaggregated data should be provided if the insured population is broken down further and records are maintained, e.g. by economic sector, public versus private sectors.

Table TBI.35 Insured population: New entrants' age distribution in three years prior to valuation date

Age group	New entrants in year prior to valuation date		New entrants in second year prior to valuation date		New entrants in third year prior to valuation date	
	Males	Females	Males	Females	Males	Females
0–14						
15–19						
20–24						
25–29						
30–34						
35–39						
40–44						
45–49						
50–54						
55–59						
60–64						
65–69						
70–74						
75+						

Source of information:
Method of data collection:

Notes:
(a) In case of differently insured populations by benefit branch, a separate table should be provided for each branch.
(b) Disaggregated data should be provided if the insured population is broken down further and records are maintained, e.g. by economic sector, public versus private sectors.

Technical Brief I: Tables used for the collection of social security data

Table TBI.36 Long-term benefit branch: Historical number of beneficiaries and expenditure

Year	Old-age		Invalidity (non-work-related)		Survivorship (widows' and orphans' pensions separately)		Lump-sum payments (separately by benefit type)	
	Number	Expenditure	Number	Expenditure	Number	Expenditure	Number	Expenditure
1970 to *Year of valuation*								

Source of information:
Method of data collection:
Basis and monetary unit for benefit expenditure (e.g. monthly US$):
Detailed definition of pension benefits and lump-sum payments, including the description of other benefits not covered in this generic table:

Notes:
(a) The data should be provided for all benefit types including those that may not be included in table TBI.36. In particular, lump-sum payments should be provided separately for each type of benefit, e.g. lump-sum payments for insured persons not eligible for an old-age pension, lump-sum payments for insured persons not eligible for an invalidity pension, etc.
(b) Invalidity pensions are related to non-work-related invalidities. They should be disaggregated between full and partial invalidities, if applicable.
(c) Survivorship pensions should be provided separately for widows, widowers, orphans and other dependants.

Table TBI.37 Long-term benefit branch: Pensions in payment at valuation date (e.g. in month prior to the valuation date)

Table TBI.37a Old-age pensions in payment at valuation date

Age	Males		Females	
	Number	Expenditure	Number	Expenditure
15 to 100				
Total				

Note: The data should be collected from the youngest age at which it is possible to begin receiving an old-age pension.

Table TBI.37b Invalidity pensions in payment at valuation date (non-work-related) (full and partial invalidity pensions separately, if applicable)

Age	Males		Females	
	Number	Expenditure	Number	Expenditure
15 to 100				
Total				

Table TBI.37c Widow(er)s' pensions in payment at valuation date (non-work-related)

Age	Males		Females	
	Number	Expenditure	Number	Expenditure
15 to 100				
Total				

Technical Brief I: Tables used for the collection of social security data

Table TBI.37d Orphans' and other dependants' pensions in payment at valuation date (non-work-related)

Age	Males		Females	
	Number	Expenditure	Number	Expenditure
0 to 100				
Total				

Source of information:
Method of data collection:
Basis and monetary unit for benefit expenditure (e.g. monthly US$):
Are work injury pensions still payable after a person has reached the usual retirement age? Or does he/she then begin to receive an old-age pension?

Notes:
(a) The data should be provided for all benefit types including those that may not be included in table TBI.37.
(b) Invalidity pensions are related to non-work-related invalidities. They should be disaggregated between full and partial invalidities, if applicable.
(c) Survivorship pensions should be provided separately for widows, widowers, orphans and other dependants.

Actuarial practice in social security

Table TBI.38 Long-term benefit branch: New benefit cases in three years prior to valuation date

Table TBI.38a Male old-age pensions: New cases

Age	New cases in 1st year prior to valuation date			New cases in 2nd year prior to valuation date			New cases in 3rd year prior to valuation date		
	Number	Average pension	Average past insurable credits	Number	Average pension	Average past insurable credits	Number	Average pension	Average past insurable credits
15 to 100									
Total/ Average									

Table TBI.38b Female old-age pensions: New cases

Age	New cases in 1st year prior to valuation date			New cases in 2nd year prior to valuation date			New cases in 3rd year prior to valuation date		
	Number	Average pension	Average past insurable credits	Number	Average pension	Average past insurable credits	Number	Average pension	Average past insurable credits
15 to 100									
Total/ Average									

Technical Brief I: Tables used for the collection of social security data

Table TBI.38c Male invalidity pensions: New cases (non-work-related) (full and partial invalidity pension separately, if applicable)

Age	New cases in 1st year prior to valuation date			New cases in 2nd year prior to valuation date			New cases in 3rd year prior to valuation date		
	Number	Average pension	Average past insurable credits	Number	Average pension	Average past insurable credits	Number	Average pension	Average past insurable credits
15 to 100									
Total/ Average									

Table TBI.38d Female invalidity pensions: New cases (non-work-related) (full and partial invalidity pension separately, if applicable)

Age	New cases in 1st year prior to valuation date			New cases in 2nd year prior to valuation date			New cases in 3rd year prior to valuation date		
	Number	Average pension	Average past insurable credits	Number	Average pension	Average past insurable credits	Number	Average pension	Average past insurable credits
15 to 100									
Total/ Average									

Table TBI.38e Widows' pensions: New cases (Widowers' pensions should be provided separately if there is a significant number of them)

Age	New cases in 1st year prior to valuation date			New cases in 2nd year prior to valuation date			New cases in 3rd year prior to valuation date		
	Number	Average pension	Average past insurable credits	Number	Average pension	Average past insurable credits	Number	Average pension	Average past insurable credits
15									
to									
100									
Total/ Average									

Table TBI.38f Orphans' and other dependants' pensions: New cases

Age	New cases in 1st year prior to valuation date			New cases in 2nd year prior to valuation date			New cases in 3rd year prior to valuation date		
	Number	Average pension	Average past insurable credits	Number	Average pension	Average past insurable credits	Number	Average pension	Average past insurable credits
15									
to									
100									
Total/ Average									

Source of information:
Method of data collection:
Basis and monetary unit for average pensions and past insurable credits (e.g. monthly US$; and years of contributions):

Note: The data for old-age pensions should be collected from the youngest age at which it is possible to begin receiving the benefit.

Technical Brief I: Tables used for the collection of social security data

Table TBI.39 Long-term benefit branch: Pensioners' cohort tables

Table TBI.39a Male old-age pensioners' cohort table

Cohort year of birth	1985				1986					...	Year of valuation				
	No. pens. at start of year	New entries	Exits by death	Exits (others)	No. pens. at end of year	No. pens. at start of year	New entries	Exits by death	Exits (others)	No. pens. at end of year	...	No. pens. at start of year	New entries	Exits by death	Exits (others)	No. pens. at end of year
	$A(85)$	$+B(85)$	$-C(85)$	$-D(85)$	$=E(85)$	$A(86)$ $=E(85)$	$+B(86)$	$-C(86)$	$-D(86)$	$=E(86)$	...	$A(y)$ $=E(y-1)$	$+B(y)$	$-C(y)$	$-D(y)$	$=E(y)$
1895																
1896																
1897																
1898																
1900																
1901																
to																
x																

Notes:
(a) The pensioners' cohort tables are used for the development of assumptions.
(b) x is the last year of birth for which it is possible to begin receiving an old-age pension.

Actuarial practice in social security

Table TBI.39b Female old-age pensioners' cohort table

Cohort year of birth	1985					1986					...	Year of valuation				
	No. pens. at start of year	New entries	Exits by death	Exits (others)	No. pens. at end of year	No. pens. at start of year	New entries	Exits by death	Exits (others)	No. pens. at end of year	...	No. pens. at start of year	New entries	Exits by death	Exits (others)	No. pens. at end of year
	$A(85)$	$+B(85)$	$-C(85)$	$-D(85)$	$=E(85)$	$A(86)$ $=E(85)$	$+B(86)$	$-C(86)$	$-D(86)$	$=E(86)$	...	$A(y)$ $=E(y-1)$	$+B(y)$	$-C(y)$	$-D(y)$	$=E(y)$
1895																
1896																
1897																
1898																
1900																
1901																
to																
x																

Note: x is the last year of birth for which it is possible to begin receiving an old-age pension.

Technical Brief I: Tables used for the collection of social security data

Table TBI.39c Male invalidity (non-work-related) pensioners' cohort table

Cohort year of birth	1985					1986					...	Year of valuation				
	No. pens. at start of year	New entries	Exits by death	Exits (others)	No. pens. at end of year	No. pens. at start of year	New entries	Exits by death	Exits (others)	No. pens. at end of year	...	No. pens. at start of year	New entries	Exits by death	Exits (others)	No. pens. at end of year
	$A(85)$	$-B(85)$	$-C(85)$	$-D(85)$	$=E(85)$	$=A(86)$	$-B(86)$	$-C(86)$	$-D(86)$	$=E(86)$	...	$A(y)$ $=E(y-1)$	$+B(y)$	$-C(y)$	$-D(y)$	$=E(y)$
1895																
1896																
1897																
1898																
1900																
1901																
to																
Year of valuation																

Table TBI.39d Female invalidity (non-work-related) pensioners' cohort table

Cohort year of birth	1985					1986					...	Year of valuation				
	No. pens. at start of year	New entries	Exits by death	Exits (others)	No. pens. at end of year	No. pens. at start of year	New entries	Exits by death	Exits (others)	No. pens. at end of year	...	No. pens. at start of year	New entries	Exits by death	Exits (others)	No. pens. at end of year
1895	$A(85)$	$-B(85)$	$-C(85)$	$-D(85)$	$=E(85)$	$=A(86)$	$-B(86)$	$-C(86)$	$-D(86)$	$=E(86)$	....	$A(y)$ $=E(y-1)$	$+B(y)$	$-C(y)$	$-D(y)$	$=E(y)$
1896																
1897																
1898																
1900																
1901																
to																
Year of valuation																

Source of information:
Method of data collection:

Notes:
(a) The pensioners' cohort table is used to derive the mortality, invalidity and other incidence rates for future projections. However, a preliminary assessment of the observed past experience must determine if it is sufficiently reliable to serve as a basis for these future projections. Each cohort is represented by the same year of birth and the corresponding data must be filled for each of the observation years from 1985 up to the year of valuation, or the latest possible.
(b) $A(y)$ = Number of pensioners at the beginning of observation year y
 $B(y)$ = Number of entries during observation year y, i.e. number of new pensioners
 $C(y)$ = Number of exits as a result of death during observation year y, i.e. number of deceased pensioners
 $D(y)$ = Number of exits other than by death during observation year y, i.e. number of pensioners who stopped receiving benefits because of rehabilitation, etc.
 $E(y)$ = Number of pensioners at the end of observation year y, i.e. number of remaining pensioners in payment.
 $E(y) = A(y) + B(y) - C(y) - D(y)$
 $A(y+1) = E(y)$

TECHNICAL BRIEF II

ILO SOCIAL SECURITY CONVENTIONS AND RECOMMENDATIONS[1]

This paper was written to provide a short overview of the ILO's social security standards.[2] Although it deals with all the most significant aspects of these standards, it is not exhaustive, and for the precise terms of any matters dealt with here readers are referred to the wording of the Conventions and Recommendations themselves.

II.1 GENERAL REMARKS

From its outset, one of the core activities of the ILO has been the adoption of international labour standards, either in the form of Conventions or Recommendations. These standards fix minimum requirements which, in the case of a Convention, are legally binding for all member States having ratified it. In all other cases, the standards may provide useful guidance for the internal legislation.

Under the ILO Constitution, arrangements are made for the general supervision of standards. Within a specified period after their adoption, member States of the ILO have to submit Conventions and Recommendations to their national parliaments or other authorities competent in enacting legislation. Governments are requested to provide regular reports on the application of ratified Conventions and, on request, also on non-ratified Conventions or Recommendations. These reports are submitted for scrutiny to a committee of independent experts – the Committee of Experts on the Application of Conventions and Recommendations – and the most important cases are examined by a tripartite Committee of the International Labour Conference before which the governments concerned are invited to explain themselves.

II.2 SOCIAL SECURITY STANDARDS

The set of ILO instruments on social security adopted after the Second World War revises all the Conventions in this area which had been adopted before. They comprise lower, minimum standards contained in the Social Security (Minimum Standards) Convention, 1952 (No. 102), and superior, higher standards contained in Conventions Nos. 103, 121, 128, 130 and 168, which are complemented by Recommendations.

The ILO Conventions define nine branches of social security. These are:

(a) medical care

(b) sickness benefit

(c) unemployment benefit

(d) old-age benefit

(e) employment injury benefit

(f) family benefit

(g) maternity benefit

(h) invalidity benefit and

(i) survivors' benefit

All but the first of these benefits are paid in cash, but two of them – employment injury and maternity – also include an element of medical care. Family benefit may comprise a variety of components. In addition, the Maternity Protection Convention (Revised), 1952 (No. 103), provides for maternity leave, nursing breaks and protection against dismissal.[3]

Convention No. 102 covers all nine branches of social security. However, a ratifying State is not obliged to accept all parts of it and can confine ratification to merely three of the nine branches, including at least one of the following: unemployment, employment injury, old-age, invalidity or survivors' benefits.[4] The country is also required to meet defined standards for the minimum coverage of its population, minimum rates or amounts of benefit and minimum provision of medical care, where appropriate. The Convention requires, as a rule, equality of treatment for nationals and non-national residents; it sets out the circumstances in which a benefit may be suspended and requires that claimants and beneficiaries should have a right of appeal against the refusal of benefit. Other general provisions define the responsibility of the State and limit the extent to which employees (in an insurance-based scheme) or people of small means should be obliged to finance their benefits by direct contributions or special taxation. These matters are set out more fully below.

A State of which the economy and medical facilities are insufficiently developed may, when ratifying a Convention, claim as a temporary exception reduced requirements regarding the minimum coverage and the duration of benefits or, in the case of higher standards, also regarding the volume of medical care, the rate of unemployment benefit, the possibility to convert employment injury benefit into a lump-sum payment, etc.[5]

II.3 SOME CONTINGENCIES COVERED

The contingencies covered by the Conventions on social security correspond to the nine branches detailed above. The following observations explain further some of the important points:

As a general rule, the *pensionable age* shall be not more than 65 years.[6] It shall be lowered, under prescribed conditions, in respect of persons who have been engaged in occupations deemed to be arduous or unhealthy.[7] Moreover, a lower pensionable age is recommended for people:

- whose unfitness for work is established or presumed (the handicapped);
- who have been involuntarily unemployed for a prescribed period (e.g. one year); or
- for whom such a measure is justified on social grounds.

Wherever possible, provisions for a gradual transition from working life to retirement and flexibility of pensionable age subject, as the case may be, to increments or reductions are recommended as well.[8]

Whereas the Conventions themselves do not contain a definition of *industrial accident*,[9] the following definition can be found in Recommendation No. 121:[10]

- accidents, regardless of their cause, sustained during working hours at or near the place of work or at any place where the worker would not have been except for his employment;
- accidents sustained within reasonable periods before and after working hours in connection with transporting, cleaning, preparing, securing, conserving, storing and packing work tools or clothes;
- accidents sustained while on the direct way between the place of work and:
  - the employee's principal or secondary residence; or
  - the place where the employee usually takes his or her meals; or
  - the place where the employee usually receives his or her remuneration.

On *occupational diseases*, Convention No. 121[11] offers the choice of three definitions:

- by prescribing a list of diseases comprising at least those enumerated in Schedule I to the Convention (list system);
- by stipulating a general definition broad enough to cover at least the diseases enumerated in Schedule I to the Convention (global definition);

- by prescribing a list of diseases in conformity with Schedule I and to complement it by a general definition (mixed system).

Unless proof to the contrary is brought, it is recommended[12] that there is a presumption of the occupational origin of diseases known to arise out of the exposure to substances or dangerous conditions in processes, trades or occupations where the employee:

- was exposed for at least a specified period; and
- has developed symptoms of the disease within a specified period following termination of the last employment involving exposure.

Where national legislation contains a list establishing a presumption of occupational origin in respect of certain diseases, proof should be permitted of the occupational origin of diseases not so listed and of diseases listed when they manifest themselves under conditions different from those establishing a presumption of their occupational origin.

Survivors' benefits shall be paid at least in the case of the loss of support suffered by the widow or child as the result of the death of the breadwinner; in the case of a widow, the right to benefit may be made conditional on her being presumed to be incapable of self-support.[13] This may be the case, for instance, when the widow has attained a prescribed age, is an invalid or has to care for a dependent child of the deceased. A minimum duration of marriage may be required only in the case of a childless widow.[14]

It is recommended that an invalid and dependent widower shall enjoy the same entitlements to a survivor's benefit as a widow.[15]

Unemployment is defined as "the loss of earnings due to inability to obtain suitable employment in the case of a person capable of working available for work and actually seeking work".[16] Convention No. 168 extends unemployment protection to the contingencies of partial unemployment – that is, a temporary reduction in the normal or statutory hours of work – and of temporary suspension of work, without any break in the employment relationship on the one hand and to part-time workers actually seeking full-time work on the other.[17]

II.4 PERSONAL SCOPE OF PROTECTION

Contrary to previous Conventions, the Conventions adopted after the Second World War no longer define the categories of protected persons in purely juridical terms (that is, in terms of the type of the labour contract), but they fix percentages of the population. These percentages relate either to:

- all employed persons;
- the whole working population (including the self-employed); or
- all residents.

II.5 QUALIFYING PERIODS

A qualifying period may be a period of contribution, employment or residence preceding the contingency.[18] For medical care, sickness, unemployment and maternity benefits (short-term benefits) there may be imposed "such qualifying period as may be considered to preclude abuse"[19] or, in the wording of Convention No. 130, "the conditions governing the qualifying period shall be such as not to deprive of the right to benefit persons who normally belong to the categories of persons protected".[20] It is recommended, however, that the right to medical care should not be made subject to any qualifying period.[21]

For family benefit, there may be a qualifying period of no more than three months of contributions or employment, or of one year of residence.[22]

Standard rates of old-age benefit should be made available, subject to a qualifying period of no more than 30 years of contributions or employment, or 20 years of residence. A reduced rate should be secured, however, after at least 15 years of contributions or employment. Where a contributory scheme covers, in principle, all economically active persons, there is an alternative formula – a prescribed yearly average number of contributions over a prescribed period.[23]

Similarly, standard rates of invalidity or survivors' benefits should be available after not more than 15 years of contributions or employment, or ten years of residence. A reduced rate should be secured, however, after at least five years of contributions or employment. In the comprehensive contributory scheme, there is an alternative formula – a prescribed yearly average number of contributions over a period of three years.[24]

It is recommended to reduce even further or to eliminate completely qualifying periods for invalidity benefits in favour of young workers or where invalidity is due to an accident.[25]

Employment injury benefits are to be afforded without any qualifying period.[26]

II.6 MINIMUM STANDARDS FOR MEDICAL CARE

The minimum content of a medical care programme includes:

(a) general practitioner care, including home visits;
(b) specialist care in hospitals and similar institutions for in-patients and out-patients;

(c) "essential" pharmaceutical supplies;

(d) pre-natal, confinement and post-natal care by medical practitioners or qualified midwives; and

(e) hospitalization where necessary.[27]

Convention No. 130 includes in the list necessary pharmaceutical supplies, dental care, medical rehabilitation and the supply, maintenance and renewal of prosthetic and orthopaedic appliances.[28]

In the maternity benefit branch, the medical care element should include items (d) and (e) of this list.[29] Moreover, Convention No. 103 guarantees the freedom of choice of doctor and of the hospital.[30]

The standard minimum medical care element of employment injury benefit is more comprehensive, adding dental care, the provision of artificial limbs and other prostheses, the provision of eye-glasses and a wider range of specialist services.[31]

In the case of ordinary sickness (that is, not in case of employment injury and maternity), cost-sharing by the beneficiary is admitted, provided the rules are so designed as to avoid hardship and not to prejudice the effectiveness of medical and social protection.[32]

II.7 MINIMUM STANDARDS FOR DETERMINING RATES OF PERIODICAL CASH BENEFIT

The guidelines for determining the standard minimum rates of benefit are tied to a schedule of "standard beneficiaries" and "indicated percentages". The standard beneficiary is a family unit, the composition of which varies according to the contingency. The indicated percentages may relate either to the wage of a "skilled manual male employee" or to the wage of an "ordinary adult male labourer" according to the pension formula.

The following situations may arise:

1. Where the rate of benefit is calculated by reference to the previous earnings of the beneficiary or covered person, the rate of benefit payable to a standard beneficiary, together with any family allowance involved, should be not less than the indicated percentage of the previous earnings, plus family allowance. Formal rules should be described for the calculation of the previous earnings. An upper limit may be set to the rate of benefit, or to the level of reckonable earnings. This level should not be set below the earnings of a skilled manual male employee (the Conventions give an earnings level "equal to 125 per cent of the average earnings of all the persons protected" as one of the alternatives).[33]

2. Where benefits are at a flat rate, the rate of benefit payable to a standard beneficiary, together with any family allowance involved, should be not less than the indicated percentage of the wage, plus family allowance, of an ordinary adult male labourer. The latter is defined either as a person deemed typical of unskilled labour in the manufacture of machinery other than electrical machinery,[34] or as an unskilled labourer employed in the major group of economic activities with the largest workforce covered for the benefit.[35]

3. In a third situation, where all residents are covered, the rate of benefit may be determined by taking into account the means of the beneficiary and family, according to a prescribed scale. The prescribed rules should allow substantial amounts of the other means of the family to be disregarded before the scale rate of benefit is reduced. The total of benefit, and other means (if any) over and above the amount disregarded, should be comparable with benefit calculated elsewhere under the "flat-rate" formula.[36]

As to family benefits, a different formula is provided in Convention No. 102: Their total value shall represent either 3 per cent of the wage of an ordinary adult male labourer multiplied by the total number of children of people protected or 1.5 per cent of the said wage multiplied by the total number of children of all residents.[37]

II.8 ADJUSTMENT OF BENEFITS

The Conventions prescribe that the rates of current periodical payments in respect of old age, employment injury (except in the case of incapacity for work), invalidity and death of breadwinner (that is, all long-term benefits) shall be reviewed "following substantial changes in the general level of earnings where these result from substantial changes in the cost of living".[38]

II.9 FORM AND DURATION OF BENEFIT

In all contingencies, the cash benefit shall be a periodical payment.[39] In case of partial permanent incapacity due to employment injury, however, it may be commuted for a lump sum:

- where the degree of incapacity is slight (for example, less than 25 per cent);[40] or

- where the competent authority is satisfied that the lump sum will be properly used.[41]

Medical care and cash sickness benefit may be limited to 26 weeks on any one occasion, but medical care should, in any case, continue as long as sickness benefit remains in payment.[42] Under Convention No. 130, medical care shall be provided throughout the contingency, and the minimum duration of sickness benefit has been extended to 52 weeks.[43] Sickness benefit may be withheld for the first three (waiting) days.[44]

Maternity cash benefits may be limited to 12 weeks, unless a longer period of abstention from work is required or authorized by national laws – in which case, benefit shall continue throughout the period of abstention.[45]

Unemployment benefit may be limited, where classes of employees are covered, to 13 weeks in any 12 months; or where residents are covered subject to a means test, to 26 weeks in any 12 months.[46] This period has been extended to either 26 weeks in each spell of unemployment or to 39 weeks over any period of 24 months, respectively, by Convention No. 168.[47] Up to seven waiting days may be imposed.[48]

Family allowances or orphans' pensions may be paid until the child has reached school-leaving age or 15 years of age. Conventions Nos. 121 and 128 extend the payment period, as far as orphans' pensions are concerned, for children who are apprentices, students or suffering a chronic illness or infirmity disabling them from any gainful activity.[49]

Apart from these exceptions, the Conventions establish the principle that all benefits should be paid for the duration of the contingency.[50]

II.10 MISCELLANEOUS MATTERS

1. In general, non-national residents should have the same rights as national residents,[51] but Convention No. 102 accepts that:
   (a) where benefits are payable wholly or mainly from public funds, special qualifying rules apply to persons who were born outside the territory; and
   (b) where benefits are payable under a social insurance scheme, the rights of the nationals of another country be subjected to the terms of a reciprocal agreement between the countries concerned.[52]
2. Benefits under various branches may be suspended:
   (a) during absence abroad;
   (b) while a person is maintained at public expense in an institution;
   (c) if a person is simultaneously entitled to two forms of cash benefit – other than family benefits (the person should receive not less than the amount of the larger of the two conflicting benefits);
   (d) where the contingency was caused by wilful misconduct or criminal offence on the part of the claimant, or the claim was fraudulent;
   (e) where a person neglects to make use of medical or rehabilitation services, or fails to observe prescribed rules of behaviour during the contingency;

(f) in the case of unemployment benefit, where the claimant neglects to make use of the employment services, or lost his or her job as the result of a trade dispute, or left the job voluntarily without just cause; or

(g) in the case of survivors' benefit, where a widow is living with a man as his wife.

In the cases and within the limits prescribed, part of the benefit otherwise due shall be paid to the dependants of the person concerned.[53]

3. Claimants should have a right of appeal against the refusal of benefit, or in respect of its quality or quantity, but, where medical care services are provided by a government department, complaints in that respect are to be referred to the appropriate authority.[54]

4. The cost of benefits and administration is to be borne collectively in such a way that:

(a) hardship to people of small means is avoided;

(b) the economic situation of the country and of the classes of persons protected is taken into account; and

(c) in branches covered by social insurance arrangements (and excluding family benefit and, normally, employment injury), the total of the employees' contributions should not exceed 50 per cent of the total cost.[55]

5. The Conventions do not impose specific terms of administration but they oblige the State to accept general responsibility for the administration of social security and for securing and monitoring the financial soundness of social security funds, and they provide for associating representatives of the protected persons, and employers, with the management of social security institutions where appropriate.[56]

Notes

[1] This paper was prepared by A. Otting, Legal Specialist of the Planning, Development and Standards Branch of the ILO's Social Security Department, in 1992.

[2] It does not, however, deal with Conventions Nos. 19, 118 and 157 on equality of treatment and the maintenance of migrant workers' rights in social security.

[3] Convention 103, articles 3, 5 and 6.

[4] C.102, art.2.

[5] C.102, art.3; C.121, art.2; C.128, art.4; C.130, art.2; C.168, art.5.

[6] C.102, art.26.

[7] 7 C.128, art.15.

[8] Recommendation 131, paragraphs 6 and 7; R.162, chapter IV.

[9] C.121, art.7 only specifies that "commuting accidents" should be included under prescribed conditions.

[10] R.121, para.5.

[11] R.121, art.8.

[12] R.121, para.6 and 7.

[13] C.102, art.60; C.128, art.21.

[14] C.102, art.63(5); C.128, art.21(4).
[15] R.131, para.12.
[16] C.102, art.20; C.168, art.10(1). The concept of suitable employment is defined in C.128, art.21(2) and in R.176, para.14 and 15.
[17] C.168, art.10(2) and (3).
[18] C.102, art.1(1f); C.128, art.1(i); C.130, art.1(i).
[19] C.102, art.11, 17, 23, 51; C.168, art.17. Such a qualifying period may be, for instance, three months for medical care and cash sickness benefits and six months for maternity and unemployment benefits.
[20] C.130, art.15 and 25.
[21] R.134, para.4.
[22] C.102, art.43.
[23] C.102, art.29; C.128, art.18.
[24] C.102, art.57 and 63; C.128, art.11 and 24.
[25] R.131, para.14 and 15.
[26] C.102, art.37.
[27] C.102, art.10.
[28] C.130, art.13.
[29] C.102, art.49.
[30] C.103, art.4(3).
[31] C.102, art.34; C.121, art.10.
[32] C.102, art.10(2); C.130, art.17.
[33] C.102, art.65; C.121, art.19; C.128, art.26; C.130, art.22.
[34] Group 382 of the international standard industrial classification of all economic activities (revised 1968).
[35] C.102, art.66; C.128, art.28; C.130, art.24.
[36] C.102, art.67; C.128, art.28; C.130, art.24.
[37] C.102, art.44.
[38] C.102, art.65(10) and 66(8); C.121, art.21; C.128, art.29.
[39] C.102, art.16, 22, 28, 36, 42, 50, 56 and 62; C.121, art.13 and 14; C.128, art.10, 17 and 23; C.130, art.21; C.168, art.13.
[40] C.121, art.14 (4) and 15 in conjunction with R.121, para.10.
[41] C.102, art.36(3).
[42] C.102, art.12 and 18.
[43] C.130, art.26.
[44] C.102, art.18; C.130, art.26(3).
[45] C.102, art.52; C.103, art.3.
[46] C.102, art.24.
[47] C.168, art.19. Where the benefit based on insurance has expired, C.168, art.16 provides for the payment of a means-tested unemployment assistance benefit sufficient to guarantee healthy and reasonable living conditions.
[48] C.102, art.24(3); C.168, art.18.
[49] C.102, art.1(1e); C.121, art.1(e); C.128, art.1(h).
[50] C.102, art.30, 38, 58 and 64; C.128, art.12, 19 and 25.
[51] C.121, art.27; C.130, art.32; C.168, art.6.
[52] C.102, art.68.
[53] C.102, art.69; C.121, art.22; C.128, art.32; C.130, art.28; C.168, art.20.
[54] C.102, art.70; C.121, art.23; C.128, art.34; C.130, art.29; C.168, art.27.
[55] C.102, art.71(1) and (2).
[56] C.102, art.71(3) and 72; C.121, art.24 and 25; C.128, art.35 and 36; C.130, art.30 and 31; C.168, art.28 and 29.

TECHNICAL BRIEF III

THE MAIN CHARACTERISTICS OF DC SCHEMES

In a DC scheme, each worker/participant accumulates savings in an individual account. DC schemes are operated by the state (or a statutory body) or by private institutions subject to state regulation. At the time of retirement, the balance of the savings plus the interest in the participant's account is applied to purchase a pension, which depends on the amount of the balance.

Statutory public DC schemes are not a new development. The Employees Provident Fund of Malaysia and the Central Provident Fund of India commenced operations in the early 1950s, and later, in the Caribbean, in English-speaking countries in Africa and in a few countries elsewhere, provident funds were set up. In the Caribbean, these funds were converted to social insurance DB pension schemes and this process is now underway in provident funds in Africa. Starting in the 1980s, some DB schemes, notably in South and Central America and in countries in transition from command economies, were reformed to include a DC component. These DC schemes differ from national provident funds by the manner in which they are operated, administered and supervised.

III.1 RATIONALE FOR DC SCHEMES

An actuary dealing with these new DC schemes must understand the rationale for their introduction, and the expectations and risks of the government and participants. When a DC scheme with individual account managers is implemented, expectations of the new DC scheme usually include that it will:

- be cheaper than the DB scheme it replaces, thereby increasing the disposable income of participants;
- avoid the political risk that governments can repudiate promises as they can in DB schemes;

- deal effectively with demographic changes, that is, the projected increasing numbers of pensioners relative to active workers;
- increase domestic savings;
- promote economic growth; and
- result in higher rates of return on contributions than in the DB scheme.

The bibliography at the end of this book contains references to the extensive literature on these issues. The following paragraphs discuss issues of particular relevance to the transition from a DB to a DC scheme.

Pensions are transfers

All pensions are transfers of resources from active workers to inactive retired people. The amounts paid in pensions which pensioners then convert into goods and services that they consume are equivalent to consumption (and investment), which workers forego. Pensions can be financed following the PAYG system, whereby the transfer is made directly through taxes or contributions paid by workers, or they can be financed by pensioners accumulating assets that they liquidate by selling the assets to active workers. In both cases, workers' disposable income is reduced by the amount of the resources transferred to the retired.

Individual saving

In a microeconomic sense, individuals can save for their own retirement. However, since any national pension scheme implies a transfer of resources from active workers to retired people, societies – the collectivity of individuals – cannot.[1] A national pension scheme is not simply a large occupational pension plan, and principles that are relevant to occupational plans are apt to be irrelevant to a national scheme. Citing the fallacy of composition, Barr[2] disagrees that funded national pension schemes are inherently safer than PAYG schemes and states. "For *individuals* the economic function of a pension scheme is to transfer consumption over time. But (ruling out the case where current output is stored in holes in people's gardens), this is not possible for society as a whole; the consumption of pensioners as a group is produced by the next generation of workers. From an *aggregate* viewpoint, the economic function of pension schemes is to divide total production between workers and pensioners, that is, to reduce the consumption of workers so that sufficient output remains for pensioners. Once this point is understood it becomes clear why PAYG and funded schemes, which are both simply ways of dividing output between workers and pensioners, should not fare very differently in the face of demographic change."

Retirement burden

Reducing the burden of supporting retired people can only be accomplished through reductions in one or more of the following ratios:

- the *aggregate consumption ratio* (total consumption ÷ total output);
- the *retired person's dependency ratio* (retired persons ÷ total population), for example, by raising the retirement age;
- the *living standards ratio* (average consumption of retired persons ÷ average consumption of total population), for example, by reducing the average amount of pensions through measures such as lowering the benefit accrual rate or deferring the indexation of pensions.[3]

Both DB and DC schemes face a demographic risk, i.e. that the proportion of pensioners relative to active workers will increase. DB schemes depend on the performance of the economy and consequently face labour market risks. DC schemes depend on investment performance and thus capital market risks. In DB schemes, the risk is borne collectively, and ultimately by the government. In DC schemes, the risk is borne by the individual.

Economic growth

The support of increasing relative numbers of retired people is possible only if economic growth is sufficiently robust to generate the resources to be transferred to the retired without unduly depriving active workers. Increases in total output can reduce the aggregate consumption ratio, thereby facilitating the transfer.

Savings and investment

Savings (and the investment arising therefrom) are a prerequisite to economic growth. Demonstrating whether domestic saving can be increased through individuals' savings accumulated in a DC pension scheme confounds economists. Although their convictions sometimes lead to vigorous opinions, the dynamic interactions of numerous factors render a definitive conclusion elusive. Intuitively, funded schemes ought to increase domestic saving (or at least not reduce saving). DB (PAYG) schemes do not create saving. Advocates of funded DC schemes thus contend that (privately managed) DC schemes are preferable, since, on balance, there is a chance they will result in greater savings. In any event, there is general agreement that these schemes foster the development of domestic capital markets, which is an important development objective.

Rate of return

The individual approach to saving for retirement leads to assessments of the actuarial equivalence of contributions and pensions in DB schemes. Such assessments ignore the redistribution element present in most DB schemes, and are very sensitive to assumed interest and mortality rates. People who retire in the early years of a scheme inevitably experience high rates of return on their contributions, while returns to those retiring later when schemes are maturing are often inferior to returns that individuals might have achieved by prudently investing on their own account. While this rate of return analysis can be persuasive and is appropriate to personal savings schemes, it ignores the redistribution and income transfer features of public DB pension schemes.

III.2 RISKS OF DC SCHEMES

Public DB pension schemes are subject to political risk, since governments can repudiate benefit promises that have been made and on which workers and pensioners have been relying. In a DC scheme, participants trade this political risk, which is collectively borne in DB schemes, for the investment risk, which they bear individually in DC schemes. The risk of mismanagement of public DB schemes is traded for the regulatory risk in privately administered individual accounts DC schemes. Governments bear the risk that DC schemes will not perform as expected, and that they will be obliged to supplement pensioners' retirement income from general revenue (see section III.4).

III.2.1 Participants' risks during the accumulation period

The pension depends on the amount accumulated in the individual account (or accounts) of a retiring participant. The "accumulation risk", the risk that the amount in a participant's individual account will be insufficient to produce an adequate pension, is borne by the participant. The accumulation risk is based on:

- the participant's own work history (earnings pattern, continuity of employment and contributions); and
- the investment performance of the participant's individual account.

Continuity of employment and contributions risk

Continuity of employment refers to the portion of a participant's career when the participant is in employment covered by the scheme. When a participant is in uncovered employment, for example, during periods of unemployment or employment in the informal sector (or self-employment, where coverage is voluntary), there are no contributions to the participant's individual account. Young, low-paid, domestic, casual and part-time workers are apt to experience more periods of intermittent employment, leading to low balances in their accounts that can result in inadequate pensions.

Continuity of contributions also depends on participants' compliance with the contribution conditions of the scheme. It is expected that the close link between benefits and contributions in DC schemes would induce compliance with contribution obligations, since evasion directly results in lower pensions.[4] This rational response does not seem to be reflected by high levels of compliance in the DC schemes that have replaced DB schemes. Myopic behaviour (placing too low a value on future retirement consumption needs)[5] and current consumption predominate over prudent saving for retirement.

Investment risk

In most industrialized countries, security market indices over the last quarter of the twentieth century generally rose. In many developing countries, domestic capital markets developed, showing great promise, which made the DC approach attractive, both as a means of saving for retirement and supporting the development of domestic capital markets. However, markets do not rise indefinitely, and participants in DC schemes must be aware that over a working career spanning 40 years or so, continuous growth of their individual accounts will not occur. In addition, there is the individual risk that at the time a participant retires, the value of the assets in the participant's account will be depressed. In order to try to moderate this risk, a life-cycle approach to investing a participant's savings can be applied. During the first part of a participant's career, investments can focus on equities, and as the participant approaches retirement the portfolio is shifted to less volatile fixed-income securities.

The individual account approach with multiple alternative investment managers empowers a participant to select an investment management institution in which the participant has confidence and to redirect contributions if the participant chooses. Participants are provided with information (principally performance indicators) on which to base their decisions. Although some contributors may be able to draw appropriate conclusions and take sound decisions on the allocation of their contributions, the capacity of most participants to make informed decisions is limited. Their decisions to switch investment managers are generally induced by agents of the fund managers.

Investment managers seek to attract contributors on the basis of their performance, and performance indicators are regularly produced. This leads to a short-term approach to investment and encourages trading. Pension liabilities are, however, long term, and funded social security schemes can invest for long periods, notably in projects that develop national infrastructure and can increase productivity. Long-term investments that are not subject to a "herd behaviour" mentality can be a stabilizing influence on markets. The short-term approach can be detrimental to the national interest and to the interests of individual participants.

In a developing country, institutions investing social security funds often face the limited capacity of the domestic capital market. The lack of sufficient investments appropriate for social security funds leads to investments in projects and to calls for social security funds to be invested abroad. Project investments often carry a significant risk. Foreign investments would facilitate diversification but create an exchange rate risk. (However, developing countries often have weak currencies; to the extent that their investments are made in strong currencies, there is a potential exchange rate profit.) A country that is not running a trade surplus risks forcing down the value of its currency if it seeks to export capital. On the other hand, in some countries it is unlikely that a privatized DC scheme can function unless investments are made abroad; otherwise there would be an unacceptable concentration of capital in a limited number of domestic investments.

III.2.2 Risks of pensioners

Annuity risk

In DC schemes, participants at retirement must arrange to convert the balances in their accounts into periodic payments to sustain them during their retirement. A retiree may select a life annuity (or a joint life annuity with the retiree's spouse), an annuity certain or a "programmed withdrawal" over a period.

In the case of an annuity certain or a programmed withdrawal, a misunderstanding of life expectancy, a possibly mistaken perception of one's own state of health and the desire to receive the maximum amount of pension payments can lead individuals to seek to "front load" their pension payments. As a result, when a pensioner "draws down" the lump-sum balance over a specific period, the pensioner (and survivors) risks outliving the pension payments. A pensioner may, for example, choose the annuity period to match his or her life expectancy at retirement age.[6] This means that if the annuitant dies at any time up to the end of the period of life expectancy, there will be no "loss", since the payments will have been made either to the annuitant or to the annuitant's estate. However, a substantial number of annuitants will live longer than their life expectancies at retirement. This situation is inevitable when holders of individual accounts are determined that their balances shall be used by themselves and their successors alone, and not be pooled in any public or private insurance arrangement.

To restrict the right of individuals to proceed in this manner is criticized as paternalistic and an infringement of their liberty to freedom of choice. However, those people who outlive the pension payments they have elected may, thereafter, receive a guaranteed benefit or a tax-financed assistance benefit paid by active workers. In order to avoid the risk of this additional transfer, the State has a right, and perhaps an obligation, to restrict the payment arrangements a pensioner may elect.

An annuity payable for the life of the pensioner avoids the risk that the pensioner will outlive the pension payment period. Because of the cost of individual life annuities, the annuity market is sometimes considered to be imperfect. People who opt for life annuities perceive themselves to be in good health and consider their life expectancies to be longer than the average for people of their age, thus making the purchase of a life annuity an attractive proposition. Companies writing individual life annuities must cover their acquisition and administration expenses, and they must protect themselves against this selection against them. Consequently, the premium that they charge for an annuity takes the self-selection of annuitants into account. While the individual immediate annuity market can be very competitive, lower premiums are possible if the element of anti-selection is reduced or eliminated (for example, by mandating some form of life annuity purchase at retirement).

The cost of an annuity is very sensitive to the yield rate on investments at the time the annuity is purchased. Those retiring and purchasing annuities run the risk that interest rates will be low at the time of purchase.

Pension adjustment risk

A risk for all pensioners, and a problem for all pension schemes – public, private or personal; DB or DC; PAYG or funded – is the adjustment of pensions in payment to take into account wage or price inflation so as to maintain pensioners' standard of living. In DB PAYG schemes, pensions can be adjusted automatically or on an ad hoc basis. When adjustments are ad hoc, very often failure to make adjustments results in, after a few years, derisory pensions.

In funded schemes where an annuity of a fixed amount is purchased at retirement, traditional methods of adjustment involve the assumption of a lower-than-market interest rate to calculate the annuity premium and using this interest-rate margin, plus any additional interest earnings, to supplement annuity payments. An increasing annuity can also be calculated. These methods involve *a priori* arrangements that may or may not reflect actual future inflation. Although the correlation between market values and inflation is not perfect, variable annuities where the periodic payment depends on the market value of a portfolio of securities can provide inflation protection. Where indexed securities are available, these can provide a possible means of immunizing immediate annuities against inflation.

III.2.3 Regulation risk

Regulations that are needed to ensure fiduciary responsibility to protect the funds that participants have deposited in trust in privately managed individual accounts DC schemes have led to these schemes being described as "public schemes managed privately". Regulatory risk refers to the adequacy of the regulations that are enacted, and to the regulatory body's independence, authority, capacity and perseverance to enforce the regulations.

Regulation involves not only the pension scheme but the entire financial sector, including banking, insurance, the securities market and income tax. Regulations must require transparency and disclosure, and in countries with nascent financial infrastructures and unsophisticated investors, they must be rigorous and enforced. The supervisory authority must moderate and control competition among private managers administering mandatory individual accounts, in particular their marketing and operation expenses. While regulations regarding investments and investment yields on individual accounts can reassure contributors, they will inevitably constrain the independence of private investment managers and their ability to compete.

III.2.4 Government risk

A DC scheme with privately managed individual accounts may be considered to be insulated from government interference. However, governments must regulate private schemes. Inevitably, there will be participants who have insufficient accumulations in their individual accounts at retirement to provide adequate pensions. For these participants a minimum pension must be guaranteed by the State. If pensions are generally too low, governments will be called upon to supplement them, since it is socially and politically unacceptable for pensioners and their dependants to live in poverty. Thus, whether they wish to or not, governments play an important role in statutory pension systems. The social protection of retired people is simply too important for governments to leave pension arrangements solely to the vagaries of market forces and the prudential behaviour of individual participants.

III.3 DC SCHEME BENEFITS

III.3.1 Periodic payments

Fixed periodic payments

A *perpetuity* is an annuity that is payable indefinitely. The periodic payments consist of investment income earned by the original capital, which is not depleted to make the payments. The capital required to produce a perpetuity of a specific amount is the amount of the annual annuity divided by the assumed rate of interest. At usual interest rates, the capital required is so large as to render a perpetuity impractical.

An *annuity certain* is payable for a specified period. Payments consist of investment income and a portion of the original capital. At the end of the specified certain period, the capital is exhausted. As with all annuities with fixed payments, the higher the interest rate that is assumed, the greater is the periodic payment produced by a given amount of capital.

A *life annuity* is payable for the lifetime of the annuitant. Payments consist of investment income and a portion of the original capital according to the annuity mortality table, which is applied to a group of annuitants by the annuity underwriter. After the death of an annuitant, none of the original capital is available to the estate of the annuitant. Since none of the capital remains for distribution to heirs after the death of a life annuitant, a "straight" life annuity is unpopular. In the case of the premature death of an annuitant after only a few periodic payments have been received, the annuity underwriter is criticized for profiting unduly, despite the fact that other people in the pool of people for whom the underwriter has written life annuity contracts will live to advanced ages and receive payments exceeding the amount of their original capital. This is inevitable in a system of underwriting annuity contracts where risks are pooled and is, indeed, fundamental to the principles on which insurance and life annuity contracts are based.

In order to avoid this unsatisfactory feature of life annuities, underwriters offer a *life annuity with a guaranteed period*. This is a combination of an annuity certain for the guaranteed period and a life annuity thereafter. Variations include a *cash refund annuity*, which guarantees payments equal to the amount of the original capital.

In order to protect the survivors of the retired person, a *joint life annuity*, which is a life annuity payable to the last survivor of two or more people, can be selected. Typically, these annuities are written to cover spouses.

Variable periodic payments

Variable annuities (unit-linked annuities) provide periodic payments that are linked to the market value of a portfolio of securities in which the capital of the retiree is invested. In its simplest form, each periodic payment is equal to the number of annuity units attributed to the retiree at the time of retirement, multiplied by the market value of a unit at the time of payment. The number of units is determined by dividing the retiree's capital accumulation by an annuity factor equal to the present value of one annuity unit at the retiree's age. To the extent that the movement of the market value of the portfolio corresponds to the rate of inflation, a variable annuity can maintain the real value of the periodic payments. Historically, over long periods it has been demonstrated that judiciously selected portfolios can maintain their real value. Inevitably, there are intervals – sometimes long ones – when the rate of inflation and the change in the value of an annuity unit diverge.

Programmed (or phased) withdrawals allow a retiree to select the timing and the amounts of payments that will be drawn from the accumulated capital in the retiree's account. For example, a retiree may wish to receive a substantial sum at the time of retirement to meet associated expenses, or a retiree may wish to conserve resources to meet potential future expenses for long-term medical and custodial care. Tax considerations can also play a role in this decision. In order to curtail possible retiree myopia – the risk that retirees will exhaust the balances in their accounts and thereafter rely on a state guarantee or demand other support from the State – restrictions on programmed withdrawals are generally applied.

Drawdown arrangements may allow the retiree to determine how the capital value of the account balance at retirement will be invested. Risk-averse retirees focus on fixed-income investments. Since equity funds (mutual funds, unit trusts) have over long terms historically provided higher returns and may allow retirees to maintain the purchasing power of their assets much better, these funds (or a judicious combination of equity funds and fixed-income investments) may be selected. The problem is how, from the multitude of alternatives that may be available, a retiree can ascertain the optimum investment strategy and vehicle(s).

Selection of a system of periodic payments

Even if all these types of periodic payments are not available, in DC schemes retiring participants face a bewildering number of choices as to how to organize retirement income for themselves and their dependants. Confounding this situation is the fact that decisions on the method of periodic payment may be irrevocable.

Participants have been empowered to make their own choices, but they generally do not have the information necessary to make informed decisions. In their dilemma, there is no shortage of professional advisers and salespeople to provide advice. Added to this can be the needs of participants for funds for major expenditures in the period just after retirement and participants' often unrealistic understanding of life expectancy. An important factor that is difficult for a retiring participant to assess is the financial stability of an institution that the participant might trust to manage the accumulated capital. How carefully are these institutions regulated? Is there a system of solvency insurance?

The expectation of life is a useful index for comparing mortality tables. However, illustrations of pensions are often based on payments to an *average* pensioner, who is conventionally considered to be a person whose remaining lifetime after retirement is the expectation of life at the age of retirement. This use of life expectancy obscures the important fact that significant numbers of pensioners live beyond their life expectancy at retirement. For example, from English Life Table No. 15 (England and Wales population mortality for 1990-92), for males the (complete) expectation of life at age 65 is 14.3 years (that is, to age 79.3). But, according to the table, at age 84, one-quarter of the cohort is still alive, 10 per cent is still alive at age 89 and 5 per cent at age 92. Cox (1970, p. 26) admonishes: "Because of possible misunderstandings, use of the expression 'expectation of life'... is better avoided wherever possible."[7] Retirees who decide how to receive their periodic payments based on their life expectancy at retirement age incur a great risk of outliving their pensions.

III.3.2 Individual life annuities

The purchase of a life annuity avoids a pensioner outliving payments from the balance in the pensioner's DC account at retirement, but features common to annuity markets where annuities are underwritten by commercial enterprises (generally, insurance companies) can render the purchase of an annuity unattractive. The cost (that is, the components that produce the present value) of an immediate annuity is determined by assumptions on:

- the rate of interest, which will apply throughout the expected payment period;
- the mortality rates, which will apply to the cohort purchasing annuities; and
- marketing (advertizing and commission) and administration expenses.

Just as a person retiring runs an interest-rate risk that, at the time of the person's retirement, interest rates will be low, an annuity underwriter runs the risk as to whether he or she will be able to reinvest the balance of the funds that he or she has received for writing the annuity at a rate of interest at least equal to the rate assumed. The increasing longevity of annuitants increases the reinvestment risk. The nature of the annuity payment guarantee means that investments are normally made in fixed-income securities, but these may not be available with the wished-for maturities. A further consideration is whether the underwriter's investment income will be subject to different taxation over the period of the annuity contract. In nascent markets, sufficient and appropriate fixed-income securities with the wished-for maturities may not be available.

Increased life expectancy has increasingly become a concern of annuity underwriters. Past improvements and current short-term projections of increased life expectancy are well documented. It is speculated that by 2050 medical advances, including anticipated developments in human genetics, organ cloning and the biology of ageing, could lead to increases in life expectancy at birth in the order of 50 years. On the other hand, it may be that, in the long term, the increase in life expectancy will diminish. Scope for further improvement resulting from increased standards of public health is decreasing. Some causes of death have been eliminated only to be replaced by others (such as AIDS), and increases in longevity associated with fighting diseases are ever more costly. While the effect of a major increase in the longevity of pensioners would be long deferred, it is clear that annuity underwriters face great uncertainties (and thus risk) regarding the extent and pace of increased life expectancy. This risk is even greater in countries where there is insufficient experience in the mortality of annuitants. A further complication occurs when the same mortality assumptions (that is, a unisex table) must be applied to both males and females, despite the lower mortality rates generally experienced by women.

One reason why people seek other ways of receiving periodic payments during their retirement is that they consider themselves to be less healthy than their peers and choose not to run the risk of purchasing a life annuity from which they might receive few payments. Individual retirees who opt for life annuities perceive themselves to be in good health. To take into account this *adverse selection* (selection against the underwriter), annuity underwriters apply mortality tables, which take into account the favourable mortality rates that are anticipated by both the individual annuitants and the underwriter.

Marketing expenses are normally subject to constraints imposed by competition and, failing this, by regulation. The administration expenses of paying annuities should be negligible. In addition, statutory reserve requirements in some jurisdictions and prudence may require an underwriter of individual annuities to hold a solvency margin.

III.3.3 Compulsory annuities

Given the market risks, annuity underwriters often do not offer attractive individual annuity contracts. Retirees who want periodic payments over their future lifetimes often find that the difference between the amounts of periodic payments from individual life annuities and seemingly prudent alternative systems of receiving payments from the balances in their DC accounts is sufficient to lead them to opt for arrangements other than life annuities. In order to reduce the cost of life annuities, it is necessary to limit the risks that underwriters must take into account.

Adverse selection can be reduced by requiring all retirees to purchase life annuities (at least up to a certain minimum amount). In a competitive market, this would lead to underwriters seeking annuitants whose expectation of life is below average ("creaming" the market), and consequently might require regulations on an acceptable range of annuity purchase rates. With a single annuity underwriter (where all risks are pooled), this problem would not occur.

If the scheme has wide coverage, mandating the purchase of annuities would result in the mortality rates of annuitants approaching general population mortality rates. This does not, however, remove the mortality risk that actual mortality experience will be lighter than the assumed mortality rates.

III.3.4 Programmed withdrawals

Limits that are set on the amounts that a pensioner can withdraw from the balance in the pensioner's individual account are normally related to the life

Technical Brief III: The main characteristics of DC schemes

expectancy of the pensioner at the time of the withdrawal. Section III.3.1 makes it clear that this method can result in decreasing periodic payments and/or pensioners outliving their pensions.

III.3.5 Adjustment of annuities in payment[8]

Retirees must not only select a system of receiving periodic payments from their DC balances, they need also to seek an arrangement that maintains the real value of the payments. Maintenance of real value means that periodic payments are adjusted to reflect changes in prices or, if it is intended that retirees benefit from real growth (that is, productivity gains), changes in wages. In the case of programmed withdrawals, whether payments keep up with inflation depends on the drawdown arrangement selected. For variable annuities, the extent to which annuity values track inflation determines whether the payments change according to the rate of inflation.

The adjustment of individual annuities with periodic payments that are fixed at the time of purchase in exchange for a retiree's DC accumulation is not easily accomplished. An increasing annuity certain or life annuity, where the annuity payments increase throughout the payment period to take into account anticipated inflation, can be designed. However, for a given amount of capital, such an increasing annuity would be unattractive, since for many years the annual payments would be substantially lower than for an annuity with level payments.

In participating (with profit) individual annuity contracts, retirees receive dividends (bonuses) based on favourable investment, mortality and/or expense experience of the annuity underwriter (i.e. actual mortality and investment yields that are higher than assumed and/or expenses that are lower). To avoid reductions in future periodic payments, dividends are applied to raise all the remaining annuity payments. Since annuity reserves decline over time, so will the excess interest earnings component of dividends. Dividends can increase the periodic payments but their incidence is largely independent of the rate of inflation.

If bonds (normally issued by the State), with the principal and yield indexed to the rate of inflation are available, periodic payments can be adjusted to take inflation into account. These investment instruments would be available to finance annuity payments that are adjusted according to the rate of inflation taken into account in the indexed bonds. The real value of annuity reserves would be maintained and interest in excess of the assumed rate (the underlying rate on the bonds, which would normally be low) would be available to increase the periodic payments. Such an arrangement transfers the post-retirement inflation risk from retirees to the government.

III.3.6 Disability and survivors' benefits

Most DC schemes are for old-age pensions only. Disability and survivors' benefits are generally insured by separate DB arrangements, which are often bought from private insurance companies.

III.4 STATE GUARANTEES

Privatizing the management of social security pensions – trading the monopoly of a public pension scheme for a privately administered individual accounts DC scheme – does not relieve the government of income-support responsibilities for the retired. In DC schemes, individuals bear the risk that their benefits will be inadequate: neither the scheme (or individual account managers) nor the State is legally responsible for this result.

However, governments usually provide a basic "floor of protection" pension and social assistance from contributions or general tax revenues. Since DC schemes do not offer the possibility of redistribution to ensure that people who have low incomes and intermittent employment receive adequate pensions, support of these people will ultimately be the responsibility of the State (in the absence of uncertain charity or private-sector initiatives). The consequent recourse to general-revenue-financed pensions or pension supplements and political pressure from the retired make it inevitable that the State will be called upon to provide retirement-income support. If a significant proportion of retired people is receiving state-financed pensions, increasing numbers of pensioners and their political influence can lead to overwhelming pressure on governments to raise the levels of these pensions.

Minimum pensions

In some countries, members of DC individual accounts schemes are guaranteed general-revenue-financed minimum pensions by the government. Whenever necessary, pensions of participants who have contributed for a specified mini-

Table TBIII.1 Minimum pension provisions in selected countries

Country	Minimum contribution period (years)	Amount
Argentina*	30	discretionary
Chile	20	= 25% of average wage
Colombia*	22	one minimum wage = 60% of average wage
Mexico*	25	Mexico City minimum wage = 40% of average wage
Uruguay*	35	discretionary

* Applies to both public DB and private DC individual accounts schemes.
Source: Queisser (1998), pp. 67–68.

mum period are supplemented up to the level of a guaranteed minimum pension. Table TBIII.1 indicates the minimum pension provisions in a number of selected countries.

Government minimum pension guarantees can create a moral hazard for contributors who may decide to forego contributions in order to take advantage of the guarantee. Participants may decide to rely on the minimum pension (possibly along with other savings) to finance their retirement, or they may conclude that continuing to contribute is not going to produce a pension significantly higher than the minimum pension. Eliminating a guaranteed minimum pension would remove the potential moral hazard, but would not solve the problem of providing retirement income support for those whose pensions, for whatever reason, are low.

Clearly, DC-scheme minimum pension guarantees can create fiscal burdens for governments. Unlike a DB pension scheme, there is no pooled fund from which minimum pensions can be paid. Little experience of DC offering minimum pension guarantees exists; however, long-term projections of the take-up of guaranteed minimum pensions under alternative assumptions can illustrate possible future fiscal implications for governments.

III.5 ASSUMPTIONS

III.5.1 Accumulation period

The amount in a participant's individual account at retirement depends on:

- the investment income credited to the account; and
- the timing and amounts of net contributions to the account.

Investment income

Assumptions with respect to investment income in funded DB schemes (see section 10.9 of the main text) can be applied to a DC individual accounts scheme. However, a major objective of setting up DC schemes with competing individual account managers is to achieve higher investment returns through liberalized investment regulations and aggressive investment management. It is necessary to estimate the extent to which this objective of higher real returns can be achieved, given the permissible investments of the scheme and the investment environment, and it is necessary to take into account an accumulation period that can be as long as 40 years.

Past investment performance is an uncertain guide to the future, but estimates of future investment returns that individual account managers base on performance in the recent past can be very persuasive for participants, who can switch managers. Actuaries can temper these estimates, and establish realistic standards for estimates of long-term real returns on investments, thereby enabling participants to evaluate alternative investment managers on an independent and comparable basis.

Net contributions to the account

Net contributions refer to gross contributions (which are normally a percentage of covered earnings) minus a deduction for expenses and for financing disability and survivors' benefits.

Maximum expenses are generally limited by regulations. *Acquisition expenses* (commission and advertising) and future administration expenses in respect of a contribution are deducted from the gross contribution at the time the contribution is paid.

Premiums for disability and survivors' benefits provided through insurance contracts are deducted from gross contributions.

Insurable earnings on which contributions are paid are estimated in the same way as for a DB scheme (see section 10.2 of the main text). This estimate takes into account real earnings growth and participants' average continuity of service in employment (*density*), which is covered by the scheme.

Density of contributions is equally applicable to DB and DC schemes. Density can be taken into account by the ratio: period during which contributions are paid divided by the total potential period of contributions. This definition takes into account legitimate periods during which a participant is not liable to contribute, evasion by the participant's employer due to failure to register eligible workers and evasion by the participant. Different density assumptions can be made by sex and by type of employment. This definition does not take into account the under-reporting of earnings subject to contribution. An alternative density definition is an estimate of the annual earnings on which contributions are paid compared with the annual earnings on which contributions are payable by a full-year contributor. This definition incorporates periods when contributions are not paid and the under-reporting of contributory earnings.

Density is also affected by the level of *compliance* with the contribution conditions by a participant during periods when the participant is in covered employment. The effect of density in DB and DC schemes differs. In a DB scheme, a low density can result in lower replacement rates and/or a higher contribution rate than would otherwise be required to pay pensions. In DC schemes, individual participants bear the risk that their benefits will be inadequate, and low densities arising from periods of non-contributory employment or evasion of contribution obligations will result in lower account balances and consequently lower periodic payments during retirement.

In a DB scheme that uses a final average earnings benefit formula, it is important to be in contributory employment during the period near retirement so that the earnings applied are high. In a DC scheme, the operation of compound interest makes it important to commence contributions early.[9] Assumption of a uniform density over a potential contributory period does not take into account the incidence and duration of non-contributory periods (owing to unemployment, employment not covered by the scheme and/or evasion).

III.5.2 Payout period

At interest rates typically applied to calculate life annuities, a 1 per cent increase in the assumed rate of interest produces (very) approximately a 7 per cent to 8 per cent increase in the amount of periodic payments. Mortality and interest-rate assumptions are not made independently: a one-quarter per cent increase in the interest rate is capable of absorbing a reduction in mortality of 6 to 7 per cent.[10]

III.6 PROJECTIONS

III.6.1 Individual account balances

Estimates of DC scheme individual account balances are readily constructed and there are no generally accepted standards regarding the assumptions that must be made concerning interest rates and rates of wage growth during the active (contribution payment) period. Density is generally ignored (as is mortality) during the accumulation period. Projections may be made over an active period of 40 years (for example, age 20 to 60 or 25 to 65), but few participants will have a full 40 years of contributions. Even if projections over 40 years can be sufficiently robust for a group, they are unlikely to apply to any specific member of the group. Consequently, projected individual account balances at the end of the accumulation period can be deceptive.

Notes

[1] R.L. Brown: "Social security: Regressive or progressive", in: *North American Actuarial Journal*, Vol. 2, No. 2, 1998.

[2] N. Barr: *The economics of the welfare state* (Stanford, Stanford University Press, 1987).

[3] L. Thompson: "Principles of financing social security pensions", in: *International Social Security Review* (Geneva), Vol. 49, No. 3/96, 1996, pp. 47–48.

[4] See E. James: "The political economy of social security reform", in: *Annals of Public and Cooperative Economics*, Vol. 69, pp. 451–482, 1998.

[5] See L. Thompson: *Older and wiser: The economics of public pensions* (Washington, DC, The Urban Institute Press, 1998).

[6] Contrary to the popular perception that a life annuity at age x is equal to annuity certain for the (curtate) expectation of life at age x, the latter, in fact, exceeds the former (Jordan, 1967).

[7] P.R. Cox: *Demography* (Cambridge, Cambridge University Press, 4th edition, 1970).

[8] See W. Scholz and A. Drouin: "Regular adjustment of financial parameters of social protection systems in volatile inflationary environments", in: *International Social Security Review* (Geneva), Vol. 51, No. 4, 1998.

[9] For a mathematical treatment of density of DC scheme contributions, see Iyer (1999).

[10] D.M. McGill: *Life Insurance* (Homewood, Illinois, Irwin, 1967), p. 104.

TECHNICAL BRIEF IV

ADVANCED TOPICS ON THE VALUATION OF EMPLOYMENT INJURY BENEFITS

This Technical Brief elaborates more extensively certain topics that were outlined in Part III on employment injury schemes. It is composed of two main sections. The first relates to section 15.2 covering rating systems and the second deals with the data that are required for the actuarial valuations of benefits discussed in Chapters 16 and 17.

IV.1 RATING SYSTEMS

IV.1.1 Differential rates

This section presents the actuarial techniques that can be used for calculating rates by class of risks.

IV.1.1.1 Calculation of risk relativities

Rate relativities can be calculated each year or, if this is not feasible, not less frequently than every three years. The purpose of a differential rating system is to promote prevention and early return to work, which can be achieved only if the system responds quickly to change. However, such responsiveness can cause significant yearly fluctuations to the contribution rates, which should be avoided. Yearly calculations are efficient as long as the actuarial method ensures rate stability and eliminates undesirable fluctuations resulting from random variations in the experience. In order to obtain a sufficient volume of data for each rating group and to ensure their stability, a few years of experience (for example, three or five) will need to be used to compare the compensation cost of each rate unit with the average compensation cost of all employers. The determination of the proper experience to be used for this purpose is an important element of actuarial work.

Under the mixed financial system, the total premiums must be sufficient to cover the sum of benefit payments and awards of long-term benefits that are pro-

> **Box TBIV.1 Calculation of rate relativities**
>
> | Step | Nature of work | Potential outcomes |
> |---|---|---|
> | 1 | Calculate for each rate pool the ratio of observed benefit costs to covered earnings for as many years as possible in the past to the ratio of benefit costs of all employers to total covered earnings (this is the observed rate relativity). | Large fluctuations will probably be observed among all groups. This indicates that one-year experience is not a stable indicator of the expected experience. |
> | 2 | Calculate moving averages (three to five years) of the ratios calculated in step 1. Determine their predictive power of the rate relativities of the second subsequent year. | Fluctuations will be reduced, but will probably remain significant for a large number of rate groups. |
> | 3 | Process steps 1 and 2, limiting the experience considered through various techniques (see the discussion after the table). | There will probably be a combination of rate relativities showing sufficient stability. Process the appropriate combination through to step 5. If no combination is satisfactory, go to step 4. |
> | 4 | Process step 3 again using credibility factors. Fluctuations may be more important in the rate pools where the volume of data is smaller. Calculate adjusted rate relativities considering the degree of credibility of each pool (a discussion of credibility follows the table). | If this process does not produce acceptable rates, a particular environment may be the explanation. The rating process will need arbitrary adjustments if the system is to work properly. The actuary should disclose his or her findings and discuss the alternatives with management. |
> | 5 | Test the correlation between the rate relativities resulting from step 1 to those of step 2. | The results will be acceptable if there is no significant inconsistency between the two sets of ratios. For example, if rate relativities of five units are in the interval 0.7-0.9 under the no-limit database and they are in the interval 1.2-1.4 under the limited database, the method would not be acceptable. |
> | 6 | Analyse the need of limiting the year-to-year variations rate relativities by unit rate. This variation should be independent of the variation in the average rate for all employers. | This step should end the process. Reporting will be the next phase. |

jected for the assessment year and of other elements (for example, administrative expenses). Let us assume that the classification structure is made of 30 units. Box TBIV.1 illustrates the path of an actuarial analysis that can be processed to determine the method of calculation of rate relativities. This calculation only considers the experience related to the compensation cost. Expenses and other cost elements are considered through a coefficient that is applied to the premium, which is determined for the compensation cost, and through a fixed factor.

IV.1.1.2 Limit on large claims

Fluctuations in the yearly basic relativities may be due to large claims, since their occurrence is volatile. Tests should be conducted on the impact of limiting the amount of individual claims. This can be accomplished by setting a limit on the sum of benefits paid by benefit recipients in a particular year or, alternatively, by setting a limit by type of benefit of each recipient. For example, total payments made in a year to each benefit can be limited to two times the maximum earnings covered. The amount of death benefits may be uniform for all deaths, irrespective of the real amount paid (which can be determined on the basis of the observed average for all claimants).

The limit must be set low enough to eliminate the part of the experience that is volatile, but it must be high enough to avoid undue transfer of risk between units. The transfer of cost is unavoidable when data are limited because the distribution of claims by size differs by rate units. The method implicitly generates the pooling among all rate units of claims payments that exceed the per claim limit. For example, if the formula eliminates 10 per cent of total costs, all rate units according to their experience below the maximum considered implicitly share this part of the cost. Table TBIV.1 illustrates this phenomenon. The rates of each unit are determined by using formula 14.5 of Chapter 14. The estimated contribution rate for the compensation programmes is 1.5 per cent of covered earnings (300,000 ÷ 20,000,000). The factor applicable to this basic for claims management expenses is 1.25 and a fixed factor of 0.1 per cent of covered earnings is added to cover the cost of other administrative expenditures. The rate is 1.975 per cent of covered earnings (1.5 per cent × 1.25 + 0.1 per cent).

The risk relativity of each rate unit is the ratio of the amount of injury experience to the covered earnings to the corresponding ratio for the total.

Table TBIV.1 Illustration of rate calculation

	Rate unit			Total
	1	2	3	
Covered earnings	5 000 000	8 000 000	7 000 000	20 000 000
Gross injury experience				
Amounts	120 000	114 000	66 000	300 000
Risk relativities	1.6000	0.9500	0.6286	1.0000
Calculated rate (as a %)	3.100	1.881	1.279	1.975
Limited injury experience				
Amounts	102 000	108 300	65 340	275 640
Risk relativities	1.4802	0.9823	0.6773	1.0000
Calculated rate (as a %)	2.875	1.942	1.370	1.975
Transfer resulting from the pooling of large claims (as a %)	−0.225	0.060	0.091	—

For rate unit 1 under the "Gross injury experience" scenario, we have the following:

$$R_1 = \left(120{,}000 / 5{,}000{,}000\right) \div \left(300{,}000 / 20{,}000{,}000\right) = 1.6000$$

and the calculated rate is: $1.5\% \times 1.6000 \times 1.25 + 0.1\% = 3.100\%$.

It can be observed that rate unit 1 benefits from the pooling of large claims, with the two other rate units supporting this shift in cost. At the unit rate level, the cost transfer should be kept to a minimum. The objective of limiting the claims experience is not to shift the cost of large claims between units but to eliminate the part of the experience that is related to random fluctuations. In other words, if the stability of risk relativities is not sufficiently improved by limiting the amount of claim considered, for reasons of equity, it would seem best to use the highest per claim limit possible and to use a longer experience period to promote stability in risk relativities.

IV.1.1.3 Balance factor

Table TBIV.1 illustrated a major step in the determination of rate relativities that are intended to be used for the setting of future rates. One further step remains to be processed – making the link between the observed past experience, which has been used for the setting of rate relativities, and the estimated cost for the future. The determination of rate relativities and of the total estimated expenses in the assessment year are generally two distinct actuarial processes and a balance factor has to be used to establish the proper rates. Assume that

Table TBIV.2 Example of the balancing process

Estimated covered earnings			25 000 000
Estimated compensation cost			315 000
Administration expenses ($0.25 \times$ Compensation cost $+ .001 \times$ Covered earnings)			103 750
Total premium income needed			418 750
Average rate (total premium income needed (estimated covered earnings)) (as a %)			1.67
Balancing process			
	Unit 1	Unit 2	Unit 3
Projected earnings	5 750 000	9 500 000	9 750 000
Tentative rate (as a %)	2.431	1.647	1.167
Balanced rate (as a %)	2.484	1.682	1.191

rate relativities are those calculated in table TBIV.1 under the "limited injury experience" scenario and that the estimated parameters for the coming assessment year are those of table TBIV.2. An overall improvement to the injury record and a shift to the mix of activities are assumed in the estimation of future costs. The estimated contribution rate for the compensation programmes is now 1.26 per cent of covered earnings (315,000 ÷ 25,000,000), and we assume that the parameters for the administration expenses are the same.

The tentative rates for each rate unit are those obtained by applying the rate relativities to the part of the average rate that is risk related (1.575 per cent) and adding the uniform percentage of 0.1 per cent to the result. If these tentative rates were used, the total projected premium income would be less than what is required, that is, 385,025 instead of 393,750 (418,750 − 25,000). The balance factor will provide the adjustment to the rates. It is the ratio of the projected cost according to risk (393,750) to the estimated income according to risk (385,025), that is, 1.0227. After applying this factor, the desired financial equilibrium is reached. This process can be modelled with the following formula.

The effective rate for unit j, that is c_j, can be expressed as follows:

Formula 1

$$c_j = CR \times r_j \times \frac{\sum_j S_j}{\sum_j S_j r_j} + F$$

where:

CR = Average contribution rate according to risk
r_j = Risk relativity of class j
S_j = Estimated covered earnings for class j
F = Part of the rate that is uniform

IV.1.1.4 Credibility

Credibility can be defined as the degree of reliability associated with a set of data used to make an estimate. For a given application and model, when two sets of data are combined to make an estimate, this approach results in a set of relative weights, each one assigned to a given set of data. The estimate is obtained through the following formula:

Formula 2

$$E = D_1 \times Z + D_2 \times (1 - Z),$$

where $0 \leq Z \leq 1$, and D_1 and D_2 are the two sets of data and Z is the credibility associated with the set of data that is most closely associated with the phenomenon for which the estimate E is calculated. For calculating rate relativities, D_1 would be the experience data associated with the particular rate unit and D_2 would be determined according to the specific circumstances. It could be the particular rate unit experience outside the experience period considered for the set of data D_1 or another unit experience with presumed similar risk characteristics in question. The actuarial challenge is related to determining the proper values of Z. The description of the statistical theories behind the techniques used to calculate the values of Z is beyond the scope of this book, although it is important to present two families of formulae for the calculation of Z.

The oldest approach to credibility is probably the limited fluctuations approach. A credibility of 100 per cent is allocated to a volume of data through a statistical formula and the credibility for smaller volumes of data is calculated according to the following formula:

Formula 3

$$Z = \left(\frac{Data}{Credibility\ floor}\right)^N, N < 1$$

The credibility floor is the smallest volume of data for which full credibility is assumed. It would have to be determined empirically on the basis of the experience data. In its purest form, the formula refers to a number of claims and the exponent is 0.5. However, the data giving the number of claims may not as reliable as the amounts paid in some circumstances and using the amounts may become the only possible alternative.

The value of N must be determined through conducting tests on the overall experience. A typical resulting value would be between 0.5 and 0.7. Figure TBIV.1 indicates credibility curves for three values of N. The degree of credibility is always higher than the ratio of observed data to the credibility floor, because marginal credibility decreases as the credibility degree increases. The rate at which the credibility degree increases depends on the value of the exponent.

Another formula that is frequently used in the workers' compensation area has the following form and is known as the Bühlmann approach (see figure TBIV.2). The Bühlmann-Straub model is a generalization that is of major practical interest. The formula for Z is the following:

Formula 4

$$Z = \frac{n}{n+k}$$

where:

n = Number of exposure units

$k = \dfrac{\text{expected value of the process variance}}{\text{variance of the hypothetical means}}$

Figure TBIV.1 Credibility curve: Limited fluctuations approach (formula 3)

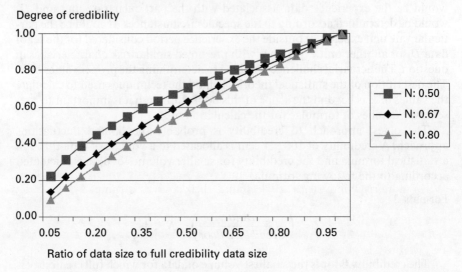

According to this formula, Z can never reach 1 in theory. The value of Z will depend on the relationship between the numerator and the denominator of k. The smaller the expected value of the process variance in relation to the variance of the hypothetical means, the larger the value of Z.

In our example, the expected value of the process variance is a measure of the variation in the claims experience of individual employers around the average experience observed in the exposure period. The process variance considers

Figure TBIV.2 Credibility curve: Bühlmann approach (formula 4)

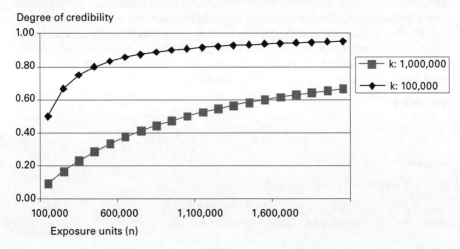

Technical Brief IV: Advanced topics on employment injury benefits

this measure for all employers. If the experience of the employers in their exposure period is very close to the average for the period, the numerator of k will tend to be small (and vice versa). The variance of the hypothetical means is a measure of the variance of the means of all units. If the distribution of the means around their average is wide, then the denominator of k will tend to be large (and vice versa). This model does not work properly in all circumstances because it is possible to obtain negative values of k in some circumstances, which is not appropriate. There is no way of correcting this result when it occurs, so the method should not be used.

IV.1.1.5 Database and responsiveness

The distribution of payments by injury year usually differs by group rates. When more risky industries are declining, their covered earnings will probably decrease more rapidly than benefit payments, which will generate increasing rate relativities. This can be justified by intergenerational equity considerations but may be difficult to apply in some circumstances. Due consideration should be given to the possibility of limiting the use of older injury years in order to meet the objective of risk responsiveness properly. Part of the experience related to older injury years could be pooled among all the units. The technique to be used would be the same as the one demonstrated in section IV.1.2.

In order to optimize the responsiveness objective, the database can be limited to the more recent injury years and the data can be grouped differently for the determination of rate relativities. Table TBIV.3 proposes a method that uses the data of the five most recent injury years. For each injury year, benefit payments in the reference period are added together. This method is suitable for all financial systems and is probably the one we would most recommend under the full-funding environment. It is assumed that rate relativities will be applicable for assessment year t, that the actuarial analysis is processed during yeat $t-1$ and that past data are available until year $t-2$.

Rate relativities could be calculated by injury year for years $t-7$ to $t-3$ or $t-2$, depending on the maturity of the experience that is considered acceptable.

Benefit payments should include the capitalization of permanent awards. The actuary should carefully verify that the pattern of capitalization in rating units is not biased. More risky industries can generate more severe accidents

Table TBIV.3 Database for the calculation of rate relativities of year t

Database	Injury year				
	$t-7$	$t-6$	$t-5$	$t-4$	$t-3$
Benefit payments in years	$t-7$ to $t-3$	$t-6$ to $t-3$	$t-5$ to $t-3$	$t-4$ to $t-3$	$t-3$
Covered earnings in years	$t-7$	$t-6$	$t-5$	$t-4$	$t-3$

and a longer medical consolidation or rehabilitation period may defer the determination of the permanent impairment. The full impact of bad record experience would, therefore, not be considered in the rate relativities.

Under a typical system, the benefit payments for year $t - 7$ would be much more significant than the payments of year $t - 3$. The rate relativity could be obtained through a simple arithmetic mean of the rate of each single injury year or by weighted average. Weights could consider the relative importance of the covered earnings in each injury year. Whenever appropriate, the experience of older injury years could be given more weight in order to take a larger volume of data into consideration. Any set of weights should be carefully designed to ensure consistency and equity.

IV.1.2 Prospective experience rating systems

This section shows some examples of the design of experience rating systems and illustrates how the actuarial techniques used for calculating rates by pool risks described in the preceding section can be used for calculating personalized rates.

IV.1.2.1 Small employers

The experience of small-size employers generally has the following characteristics: the majority of them have no claim in one year and the total cost related to small employers as a group is generated by those having one or more claims. If the occurrence of claims is the result of a full random process, then the group of employers having claims should differ from year to year. The experience rating programme can be designed by considering the appropriate relationship between the cost generated by the worst employers and the number of injuries occurring in their enterprises. Generally, the rebate is small but is applicable to a large proportion of employers. By contrast, surcharges should be significant and apply to a small proportion of employers, but they have to be limited in order to avoid burdening the employers too heavily.

Box TBIV.2 is an example of a plan designed specially for small employers, inspired by a plan in existence in the province of Ontario, Canada.

IV.1.2.2 Other employers

For employers that are not considered small, it is possible to compare the claims costs of employers to the claims costs of their industry group according to the same principles used for calculating industry rates by comparing industry experience with the overall experience. Formulae 1 to 4 can then be applied with the appropriate adjustments to the definition of parameters. However, techniques must be adapted to a smaller volume of data environment. In particular, the credibility given to each employer's experience requires careful

> **Box TBIV.2 Illustration of an experience-rating plan for small employers**
>
> The plan applies to employers who paid average premiums of between 2 per cent and 50 per cent of the maximum assessable earnings (MAE) for the most recent three-year period. An employer's performance is based on the number of new claims made during the three-year review period (excluding occupational disease claims), where the cost of each claim exceeds 0.05 per cent of the MAE. The following table shows the adjustments to the contribution rate of the employer for the group in which the employer is classified in year t, based on the injury experience of years $t-4$ to $t-2$.
>
> **Table TBIV.4 Table of adjustment to the basic rate (as a percentage)**
>
> | Average premiums (as a % of MAE) | Number of claims | | | | | | | |
> |---|---|---|---|---|---|---|---|---|
> | | 0 | 1 | 2 | 3 | 4 | 5 | 6 | 7 or more |
> | 2.0–3.0 | −5 | 0 | +5 | +20 | +40 | +50 | +50 | +50 |
> | 3.0–4.0 | −5 | 0 | +5 | +19 | +38 | +50 | +50 | +50 |
> | 4.0–6.0 | −5 | 0 | +5 | +17 | +34 | +50 | +50 | +50 |
> | 6.0–10.0 | −5 | 0 | +5 | +15 | +30 | +50 | +50 | +50 |
> | 10.0–20.0 | −6 | 0 | +5 | +13 | +26 | +44 | +50 | +50 |
> | 20.0–30.0 | −7 | 0 | +5 | +11 | +22 | +38 | +50 | +50 |
> | 30.0–40.0 | −8 | 0 | +5 | +8 | +16 | +30 | +46 | +50 |
> | 40.0–50.0 | −10 | −5 | 0 | +5 | +11 | +22 | +35 | +50 |
>
> Two more provisions are included in the programme. Employers with a fatality will receive an automatic premium increase of 25 per cent and there is an increase of 10 per cent for each claim with costs in excess of 10 per cent of the MAE. The maximum increase of 50 per cent applies to the combination of all provisions.
>
> About 70 per cent of employers are expected to receive the rebate and only a very small proportion will be charged the maximum surcharge of 50 per cent. Any actuaries wishing to implement a programme of this nature should carefully investigate the past experience of their jurisdiction in order to ensure that rebates and surcharges are actuarially sound. This means that the sum of rebates should be offset by the sum of surcharges.

testing of the rate variations. Pressure comes from employers to keep formulae simple. This can be achieved to a certain extent, although oversimplification may lead to inconsistent results.

The balance factor is generally significant and a decision has to be made regarding the method retained for its application. The balance can be made per rate unit or over all the units. For reasons of equity, it would be appropriate to make the balancing by rate unit. If the balance factors by rate units tend to be significantly different from 1 and fluctuate year after year, it may be preferable to balance over all the units. Table TBIV.5 shows an illustration of balancing according to both approaches.

Table TBIV. 5 Prospective rating and balancing

	Rate unit			
	1	2	3	Total
Payroll	5 750 000	9 500 000	9 750 000	25 000 000
Rates (as a %)	2.484	1.682	1.191	
Expected premiums	142 837	146 971	104 005	393 813
Premiums after exp. rating	140 000	152 000	99 875	391 875
Balancing factor	1.02027	0.96691	1.04135	1.00495
Final manual rate				
Balancing by unit (as a %)	2.534	1.626	1.240	—
Overall balancing (as a %)	2.496	1.690	1.197	—

Insurance mechanisms used for calculating rate relativities should be more important than the corresponding ones used for the calculation of the unit rates. For example, the per claim limit should be smaller than the one used for the calculation of unit rates. Of course, full credibility cannot be given to the experience of each employer and the balance between the employer's experience and its industry's group can be achieved through different approaches.

Box TBIV.3 is a presentation inspired by existing programmes in a few Canadian provinces.

IV.1.2.3 Prevention groups

Prospective experience rating based on claims cost can also be made available to small employers through a grouping system. Under such a system, individual employers may be thought of as a single employer for the purpose of determining their rates. Their experience will be pooled and their participation factor will be increased. These systems are made available to employers promoting prevention as well as the rehabilitation and return to work of injured workers. These arrangements are based on a contractual relationship between the institution and the group of employers.

Each year, the prevention group submits its membership, and the institution accepts or rejects the request depending on its eligibility. Eligibility conditions deal with the existence of prevention programmes, the collection record of employers and the composition of the group according to geographic or industry criteria. The pooling of the experience should be designed to avoid antiselection against the institution. This can be achieved through a number of different techniques. For example, when a new employer is admitted to a group, there must be a time lag before the employer's premium totally reflects the group's experience. The premium should be a mixture of the employer's premium as an individual employer and of the employer's premium as a member of

Box TBIV.3 Illustration of an experience-rating plan for middle-sized employers

The plan is based on an employer's claim cost experience compared with the industry average over a three-year period. If an employer has a lower than average claim cost experience, the employer can earn a discount of up to 40 per cent from their industry contribution rate. If an employer has a higher than average claim costs experience, the employer can receive a surcharge of up to 40 per cent.

The amount of discount or surcharge is based on three factors:

1. the claim costs experience of the individual employer (experience ratio);
2. the employer's three-year industry rate premium (participation factor);
3. the number of years the account has been open within the experience period (eligibility factor).

> **Experience ratio × Participation factor × Eligibility factor = Rate adjustment**

Experience ratio

The experience ratio is the comparison between the employer's accident experience and the average of the industry in which the employer is operating, and is determined by comparing an employer's claim costs with the industry's average claim costs. In this comparison, certain types of claims are excluded in the numerator as well as in the denominator. These are claims that cannot be charged to an employer's account, such as: claims transferred from an employer to another one, overpayment, claims suspended or denied, certain claims for occupational disease with a long latent period and claims resulting from a condition or injury occurring prior to the accident.

In doing so, claim costs are capped to provide appropriate insurance protection. The Maximum Per Claim Cost (MPCC) limits the amount that can be charged to an employer for a single claim. The MPCC is 10 per cent of the employer's industry rate premium for the experience period, up to the maximum annual insurable earnings. The MPCC emphasizes frequency of claims rather than severity to protect employers from shifts in their premium rates due to the random occurrence of a single expensive claim.

In addition, a Maximum Per Incident Cost (MPIC) limits the impact of rare cases, when a single incident results in multiple claims for an employer (for example, a car accident with several passengers). The MPIC is capped at twice the maximum insurable earnings amount to protect employers against random incidents where multiple claims occur. It is the employer's responsibility to identify MPIC claims and notify the institution of their occurrence. Only one-third of the difference between the experience ratio of the firm and the experience ratio of the industry group will be considered for the calculation of merit/demerit. This can be considered as a co-insurance device within the scheme.

Participation factor

The degree to which an employer participates in experience rating varies according to the size of the employer. Employer discounts and surcharges are limited by their participation factor. For every 10 per cent of the maximum earnings of industry rate premiums over the three-year experience period, an employer receives a 1 per cent participation factor (to a maximum of 50 per cent; the minimum participation factor for qualifying employers is 5 per cent). The participation factor protects employers from excessive changes in their premium rates and also ensures that rate adjustments are based on statistically credible information. This participation factor needs to be supported by adequate credibility principles.

Eligibility factor

The eligibility factor refers to the number of years the employer's account was open during the three-year experience period. Since one or two years of experience does not usually provide sufficient statistical information to adjust premium rates reliably, employers with less than three years experience are only partially eligible for experience rating adjustments.

Years of experience	Eligibility factor
1	$\frac{1}{3}$
2	$\frac{2}{3}$
3	1

Calculations

The method of calculating the merit/demerit is as follows:

1. Firm costs ÷ Firm payroll = Firm ratio
2. Subclass costs ÷ Subclass payroll = Subclass ratio
3. $\dfrac{\text{(Subclass ratio} - \text{Firm ratio)}}{\text{Subclass ratio}}$ 100% = % Variance
4. % Firm variance × Participation factor = % Merit/Demerit at full eligibility
5a. Merit/Demerit × $\frac{2}{3}$ = Final Merit/Demerit for 2 years of experience
5b. Merit/Demerit × $\frac{1}{3}$ = Final Merit/Demerit for 1 year of experience

The merit/demerit applies to the industry premium. After the rebates and surcharge have been calculated, the expected total premiums will differ from the corresponding premiums before the application of the experience-rating programme. If balancing is required, then all industry rates should be adjusted by the appropriate percentage.

the group. Similarly, when an employer leaves the group, the employer's premium continues to be influenced by the group experience for a certain number of years. These provisions are essential for maintaining equity between employers and ensuring the financial health of the system.

IV.1.3 Retrospective programmes

This last section on rating systems discusses the additional aspects of the design of retrospective rating programmes that are usually available to large employers only.

The effective date of calculation of the actual claims cost and the rules regarding this calculation are the two key elements of the design of a retrospective plan. The longer the period between the end of the injury year and the date of calculation of the cost, the more exact the calculation. However, employers are interested to know their finance record as soon as possible and to close their books within a reasonable time-frame. Preliminary calculations can be performed a few months or a year after the end of an injury year and the final calculation can be made several years later. Generally speaking, the final calculation for a particular injury year should not be performed before the ratio of the reserves for the benefits to be paid after the date of calculation to the payments made at the date of calculation is smaller than 1. Because uncertainty is unavoidable in the development of the future costs, the degree of equity of the system is generally perceived proportional to the ratio of payments to the total estimated cost. Moreover, the reserving system may generate some uncertainty because the condition of more severely injured workers may not have stabilized at the date of calculation. A few years must elapse between the end of the injury year and the date of calculation in order to satisfy these conditions.

In order to avoid litigation, the method used for setting the reserves must be known before the beginning of the year. All the parameters can be set in advance, in which case the gains and losses resulting from the application of the retrospective system are borne by the insuring institution or they can be set with the experience data available at the predetermined calculation date. In the latter case, the institution can balance the system, but the employers are left with an element of uncertainty.

Depending on the imputation policies of compensation costs to individual employers, certain claims should not be taken to be part of the employer's experience. For example, claims of injured workers with pre-existing conditions may be waived to individual employers. The cost of those claims should be financed through a charge to all employers who are eligible for the retrospective plan. This charge can be expressed in terms of the original premium or of the retrospective compensation cost.

The purpose of insurance mechanisms is to avoid excessive charges being made to the employers that would endanger their ability to pay the premium or even their overall solvency in case of a catastrophe. The most common device consists of setting a limit to the adjusted premium that the employer will pay. This limit is expressed as a percentage of the original premium. Another common technique consists of limiting the amount charged per claim. This limit can apply to the compensation cost of the claim or to the total of the compensation cost and the administrative costs of the claim. A charge for the insurance mechanism is made to the employer in the calculation of the adjusted premium. This charge is expressed in terms of the original premium paid. Risk aversion differs among employers and so flexibility in the selection of the insurance levels should be available to them. For example, employers could be given the option of an overall limit of their premium; potential limits could be 110 per cent, 125 per cent or 150 per cent of the original premium. The lower the limit, the higher will be the insurance charge.

The calculation of the adjusted premium must consider appropriately the time value of money. There are many ways of doing this and a proper balance between simplicity and precision has to be defined in order to keep the administration costs within reasonable limits.

The total adjusted premium of the employer may be seen as the sum of four components for each year:

- the cost of benefits (payments and reserves) for the injuries that occurred during the year and that are imputed to the employer's file;
- a charge for the cost of benefits for injuries that are not imputed to individual employers;
- a charge for the insurance (per claim limit and/or overall limit);
- administration costs.

The total amount obtained is first compared with the maximum amount that can be charged, and the smaller of both constitutes the retrospective premium. The difference between the original premium and the retrospective premium constitutes a refund or a charge to the employer for that particular injury year.

IV.2 DATABASE AND STATISTICAL REPORTS FOR ACTUARIAL VALUATIONS

This section is composed of two main parts. The first discusses the elements that should be included in the database and the second deals with the structuring of statistical reports. Basic concepts apply to all types of benefits, but details of application may differ by type of benefits. In order to make the features that are different by type of benefits, both sections have been broken down into subsections by type of benefits corresponding to Chapter 15 on temporary incapacity cash benefits and Chapter 16 on permanent incapacity and survivorship benefits. Specific issues on medical expenses and rehabilitation benefits have been dealt with in Chapter 17.

IV.2.1 Database considerations

The data requirements for the purpose of an actuarial analysis will generally be similar to those of other functions such as operational procedures for the payment of benefits, accounting, occupational health and safety activities, and so forth. Actuarial analysis may also require specific information, and the actuary should be able to demonstrate the marginal value of additional features of the database. The following discussion is intended to draw a picture of what is desirable and possible in moderately developed environments and identifies the essential elements of any employment injury database.

The actuary should be familiar with the entire structure of the data processing, starting with the capturing of data to the ultimate processing of aggregated statistics. It may be more efficient if the actuary has direct access to the basic file and can process the data independently from the computer personnel. The actuary acquires a better understanding of the data and, to the extent that he or she possesses basic knowledge in statistical data programming, the processing will be more efficient if the data crunching is done by the actuary. Time will not be lost explaining all the intricacies of the actuary's requirements. However, after the periodic basic reports that are needed have been designed, it may be advantageous to use specialist programming people to ensure the cost efficiency of computer time for large volume extracts. Given that the actuary remains the ultimate person responsible for the validity and reliability of the data used, the actuary has a duty to conduct appropriate checks of any data extracts, even for apparently fool-proof and time-tested extracts. Any apparent inconsistencies must be dealt with. The actuary should always be able to reconcile his or her findings to the results presented in the financial statements.

The elements of the base can be grouped under a few headings. The first two are common to all types of benefits.

IV.2.1.1 Identification of the injured worker

Only basic demographic data of the injured worker are considered. Personal data, such as the name and address of the worker, which are essential for the payments of benefits, are not used in the actuarial database.

- Injured person code;
- Sex;
- Date of birth;
- Profession (according to an appropriate coding system);

- Employer and the firm's corresponding data (made available through a link with the employer database);
- Place of residence at the time of the accident (according to an appropriate coding system).

The injured person code should be a unique number that corresponds to a single worker and remains the same throughout the worker's whole life. It is recommended that the date of birth of each worker be captured rather than the worker's age, because the former is more flexible for the purpose of data analysis. Date of birth is one of the most relevant datum (age being a cost driver) and appropriate consistency checks should be made (very low or old ages). Making a note of the profession (nurse, miner, electrician) is not essential for most actuarial valuations, although it is necessary for work-prevention activities and specialized actuarial analysis. The actuary should ensure that the codification is monitored. Proper identification of the employer means that it should be possible to track the characteristics of the employer (size, industry classification, rate assessment classification).

IV.2.1.2 Circumstances of the accident

The data are as follows:

- Claim number (must be unique for each injury);
- Date of accident or date of reporting of occupational disease;
- Date of relapse or aggravation (a variable number of entries is possible);
- Date of claim reporting;
- Identification of the work site where the injury occurred;
- Nature of injury (properly coded);
- Part of body affected by the injury (properly coded);
- Nature of event – the manner in which the injury was produced (properly coded);
- Source of injury, that is, the object, substance, bodily motion or work environment that directly produced the injury.

The claim number is the basic identifying code of each injury. A new code should be generated for each injury. If a worker has ten accidents in the course of his or her life, the worker should have one single injured person code but 10 claim numbers. Provisions regarding the re-occurrence of the temporary incapacity will govern the need to maintain additional statistical information on relapses. A relapse occurs when the physical condition of the worker related to the injury deteriorates after return to work. The worker

Technical Brief IV: Advanced topics on employment injury benefits

would normally be entitled to temporary cash benefits until his or her condition stabilizes. The waiting period, if any, may or may not apply again. This contingency should be related to the original injury because it is a consequence of its occurrence. For any rating system other than the uniform rate, equity normally requires this process, because the worker may have moved to another employer in the meantime. The cost of the relapse should be linked to the employer at the time of the original injury, not to the one the employee is working for when the relapse happens. The proper recording of this information becomes more important as the workforce ages, since the occurrence of relapses or aggravations normally increases.

For the purpose of periodical actuarial valuations, only the identification code of the injury and the date of accident are essential. The qualitative information on the circumstances of the accident is of prime importance for prevention activities and also very useful for the understanding of the cost of the employment injury scheme. It can be used in actuarial analysis regarding the impact of changes to the design of the plan or to the medical and administrative procedures. For example, back injuries may represent a significant cost, and specific analysis can be conducted to improve the rehabilitation of those injured workers.

IV.2.1.3 Temporary incapacity benefits

This section deals with temporary incapacity benefits.

Information on the level of benefits

The data are as follows:

- Gross earnings at time of injury;
- Gross earnings used for the determination of the benefit (and its nature if different from gross earnings at the time of the injury);
- Net earnings used for the determination of the benefit (if the benefits are based on net earnings);
- Nature of work contract (full-time, part-time, seasonal, occasional, self-employed, and so on);
- Family situation in terms of number of dependants (as long as it influences the amount of benefits);
- Amount of temporary benefit expressed in terms of the basic time interval for payment of benefits (daily, weekly, every two weeks).

The proper design of the database concerning the information on the earnings base for the determination of benefits requires an in-depth knowledge of the working conditions of the enterprise or industry. For most periodical actuarial analyses, the basic information on the amount of benefit may be sufficient (gross earnings and amount of benefit). However, the work environment is becoming more complex and the provisions determining the amount of benefits to injured workers who are not full-time regular employees may require specific analysis. More detailed information then becomes necessary.

The amount of temporary benefit should be expressed in terms of either the smallest time unit for which a payment can be made (generally one day or one week) or whatever constitutes the basic unit that is most usually referred to by the administration. This could be the annual benefit, but the formula used to determine the corresponding amount for smaller units of time must be applied uniformly and consistently. For example, if the annual benefit is 20,000 and the smaller time unit for the benefit payment is one day, then the one-day benefit can be expressed in different ways, such as: 1/365 times the yearly benefit, that is, 54.8 (when indemnity benefits are defined in terms of calendar days), 1/5 of 1/52 (1/260) times the yearly benefits, that is 76.9 (when benefit periods are defined in terms of days of work), etc. The definition of the basis does have an impact on the total benefits an injured worker cashes for a period of temporary incapacity. The database should be designed according to the particular circumstances. It is generally easier to handle the statistical data when the benefits are defined in terms of calendar days.

Information on the benefits paid

The data regarding the duration of benefits are considered. The design of this part of the database is strongly linked to administrative and accounting procedures. The spectrum of possibilities is large. The following information should be available for each injury:

- the starting date of temporary incapacity;
- the ending date of temporary incapacity;
- the total amount of benefits paid in each financial year.

The time lost should be measured inclusively from the day after the day of the injury, to the day prior to the day of return to work. If the relapse issue is significant, the above information should be available for each benefit period. The data should allow for the number of days of incapacity in each year for which a benefit has been paid to be determined. If this is not the case, additional information should be inserted in the database to make this possible. The indexing of temporary benefits is not usual but it must be considered in the database structure when it exists. This issue is considered in more depth in the permanent incapacity section that follows; these considerations are also applicable to temporary incapacity benefits.

Consistency checks between the amount of benefits paid and its components (basic benefit and duration) are of the utmost importance. The data on duration are the most relevant ones for actuarial valuations and their reliability should be given high priority.

IV.2.1.4 Permanent incapacity and survivorship benefits

The information regarding the identification of the injured worker and the circumstances of the accident that have been described in sections IV.2.1.1 and IV.2.1.2 of this brief should be available for each recipient of permanent incapacity benefits or any deceased worker whose survivors have been awarded a benefit. The identification of survivors is a specific topic that is covered separately.

In order to avoid potential ambiguities, we present the data elements separately for permanent incapacity and survivorship benefits, although many are common to both types of benefits. The next two subsections apply to permanent incapacity and the rest to survivorship benefits.

Information on the permanent incapacity and the level of benefits

The elements that were listed in the temporary incapacity section are also necessary for any actuarial analysis regarding permanent incapacity.

The following elements are specific to permanent incapacity. In order to cover a broad range of possibilities, we look at a system in which benefits for both loss of bodily functions and loss of earning capacity are paid out.

- the date of award of permanent incapacity benefits;
- the degree of impairment (medical condition);
- the type of loss of earnings capacity (total or partial);
- for partial incapacity only, information on the size of the loss at the onset of permanent incapacity and at the date of any subsequent change (see explanation below);
- the amount of permanent incapacity benefit expressed in terms of the basic time interval for benefit payments (generally monthly) at the onset and at any date of subsequent change.

The date of award of benefits refers to the date when a decision has been made regarding the permanent incapacity. This may or may not coincide with the date when the first payment is due for the pension benefit; it depends on the administrative procedures. The date of award of a lump-sum benefit differ from the date of award of periodic payments for the loss of earning capacity, and so should be recorded separately.

The degree of impairment is expressed as a percentage. Generally, it should not be higher than 100 per cent, but a few systems include the possibility of a worker being awarded a percentage higher than 100 per cent for lump-sum benefits. These data are related to the loss of bodily functions and will generally indicate the level of compensation related to it, as a lump sum or a pension, depending on the design of the plan.

A time tag is recommended to indicate whether the incapacity is total or partial. This will not be necessary if the type of incapacity can be deduced from the rest of the information.

The information on the size of the loss depends on the design of the system. If the benefit is expressed in terms of the benefit for total incapacity, then a percentage is used. When this percentage is 100 per cent, this indicates a total disability. If the benefit is related to an effective or presumed loss of earnings, then the most practical information is the salary that the injured earns or is deemed to be able to earn. It should be possible to calculate the benefit paid for partial incapacity by relating these earnings to those of the recipient at the time of the injury. Historical data regarding the level of compensation of benefit recipients should be kept for analysis. The same remark applies to the basic amount of benefits paid.

Information on the permanent incapacity benefits paid

Once pensions have started to be paid, the follow-up of payments is fairly simple: The following elements refer to periodic payments:

- the date when the first permanent incapacity payment is due;
- the total amount of benefits paid in each financial year;
- the date and reason of the termination of permanent incapacity payments.

Whenever a lump-sum payment is included in the benefit package, the following information should be made available:

- the amount and date of payment.

Information related to survivors

The information concerning the nature of the injury and the circumstance of the accident should be adapted to include the basic information related to the death of the worker, such as the date. For each survivor receiving a pension, the following information should be available:

- the relation to deceased worker;
- the date of birth;
- the sex;
- the proportion of basic pension due to the survivor;
- the basic amount of pension at onset of payments;
- the date of termination of payments if they are not payable for life.

This information should be kept permanently in the historical files for each death that occurs, and should be arranged so that making a link with the deceased worker is relatively straightforward. It is essential that the data processing system allow for the determination of the demographic profile of each deceased worker in terms of number and type of dependants at death. In some cases, the payment of benefits may be contingent on the particular situation of the survivor, for example, school attendance by children over a certain age. If the conditions giving right to the benefit are not multiple, it is not really essential to add an element of information indicating that the condition is fulfilled. This conclusion can be reached by the fact that the survivor is eligible for a pension.

Information on survivorship benefits paid

For each benefit recipient, the following information should be available:

- Date when the first payment is due;
- Total amount of benefits paid in each financial year;
- Date of the end of payments;
- Reason for the termination of payments.

IV.2.2 Statistical reporting

Statistical reporting depends on the availability of data and the needs of actuaries. Actuaries' needs may be the same or they may differ from other people involved in data processing, such as accountants, work-prevention statisticians or the stakeholders (employers, workers and the government). The actuary should always be in a position to explain apparent differences between the data being used and other official data published by the institution. Failure to do so may undermine the credibility of the actuarial valuation.

Basic concepts regarding the reporting and illustrations of data requests are discussed separately by type of benefit.

IV.2.2.1 Temporary incapacity benefits

Injury year and financial year

In employment injury matters, the reference period regarding the data included in statistical reports is defined in terms of injury year or financial year.

A report designed on an injury year basis considers injuries that have occurred in a predefined period of one year, which may start at any date, and presents the data related to those injuries. In many cases, an injury year means a calendar year (1 January to 31 December) but it could run from 1 July to 30 June or any other two consistent dates. Statistical data reported according to the injury year approach are subject to a development

Actuarial practice in social security

process and the date at which the data are compiled must be considered in the interpretation of data. Assume that the injury year runs from 1 January to 31 December 1996. The number of new injuries will differ in extracts made on 31 December 1996, 31 December 1997 and so on until the experience no longer matures. This is normal because of delays in administrative procedures regarding reporting and the handling of claims. In employment injury, the maturing process concerning the number of injuries is usually rapid.

A report designed on a financial year basis considers the data observed during a specified year corresponding to the one-year period of financial statements, irrespective of the year when the injury occurred. This is the usual approach used for statistics dealing with operations. The number of workers to whom a temporary incapacity cash benefit has been paid in a financial year is an example of this kind of reporting.

The modelling of employment injury costs is usually more efficient when the data can be grouped either by injury year or financial year and cross-references are possible. The process can be illustrated through a diagram that is comparable to the Lexis diagram in population projection.

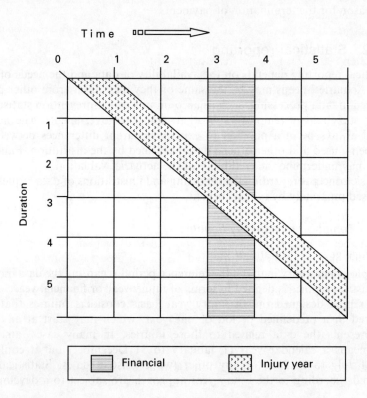

Table TBIV.6 Temporary incapacity benefit payments

Injury year	(Year of observation) − (Injury year) + 1					
	1	2	3	4	5	6
1994	xxxx	xxxx	xxxx	xxxx	xxxx	xxxx
1995	xxxx	xxxx	xxxx	xxxx	xxxx	
1996	xxxx	xxxx	xxxx	xxxx		
1997	xxxx	xxxx	xxxx			
1998	xxxx	xxxx				
1999	xxxx					

Diagonals starting in the year of the injury and developing over time can represent the payments made to a cohort of workers injured in a year. Each vertical layer (a column) would represent payments made in a financial year for all injuries that have occurred before and during that year. A horizontal slice would represent the development age of each injury year. Injury year reports would consider the information corresponding to payments between the two diagonals starting at the beginning and the end of an accident year. Financial year reports consider information between two vertical lines.

A statistical report classifying the data by injury year and financial year may have the following format (see table TBIV.6). The report is effective at 31 December 1999. We assume that the system started on 1 January 1994 and that there is a five-year time limit on temporary incapacity benefits. The injury year 1994 is fully developed and its experience is shown in the first line. The experience of the most recent financial year appears in the last diagonal. The cells with xxxx represent statistical data. The actuary's projections will fill the empty cells of each injury year in the rectangle.

Illustrations of reports for temporary incapacity benefits

Most of the reports presented below should be considered basic for actuarial valuation purposes.

- Number of new lost-time injuries in each year

The number of injuries occurring in one year and resulting in the payment of temporary incapacity benefits. Breakdowns according to the nature of injury (accident or disease), sex and age group at the time of injury and economic sectors or the classification units for rating will generally be required. Given the small volume of data, grouping by only one or two variables at a time is sufficient.

- Temporary cash benefits paid by year

This is the basic financial information. Basic actuarial analyses require a breakdown by injury year. Each monetary unit paid in a single year should be related to the year when the injury of the recipient occurred. Each monetary unit should also be related to the year in which the payment is incurred (retroactive payments covering periods in preceding years).

- Average earnings base and its distribution by size

The average earnings base of new lost-time injuries in each year. The same breakdowns as those mentioned under new injuries are possible. The distribution of earnings by layers is necessary for the analysis regarding the impact of the minimum and maximum on benefits paid. Interpretations of the statistics on the earnings base must be made carefully because the duration of benefits may vary with the size of earnings. A simple arithmetic mean of the earnings base of newly injured workers does not represent the average base for temporary benefits paid to those workers. Weight should be given to the duration of benefits payments for this purpose.

- Average amount of basic temporary benefit

The average amount paid according to the unit-time interval selected (day, week, month, year) for the new lost-time injury in each year.

The statistical reports on the duration of incapacity were discussed in Chapter 15.

IV.2.2.2 Permanent incapacity and survivorship benefits

The statistical reporting of permanent incapacity benefits has its own distinctive features and it is worth discussing again the question of injury year and financial year. Fully funded and mixed financial systems require the calculation of the present value of benefits for financial statement purposes. This, in turn, needs a specific set of information, which will be covered separately.

Injury year and financial year

The concept of injury year described in section IV.2.2.1, also applies to permanent incapacity and survivorship benefits, but care must be taken to define the concept of duration correctly. Under the injury year reporting approach, the duration would normally be defined as the number of years between the injury year and the year of award of the permanent incapacity or survivorship benefits. This concept is important for the assessment of the total cost of the EIOD related to injuries that occur in a specific year. Indeed, permanent incapacity benefits can be awarded many years after the injury has occurred. This issue is also relevant in the matter of survivorship benefits, because deaths resulting from diseases may occur many years after their onset.

Duration is a concept that is also used to express the number of years during which permanent incapacity benefits have been paid. It is necessary to consider the duration of a pension for the actuarial valuation when probabilities of terminating vary according to the number of years that have elapsed since the

Table TBIV.7 Permanent incapacity benefit awards

Injury year	(Year of award) − (Injury year) + 1					
	1	2	3	4	5	6
1994	xxxx	xxxx	xxxx	xxxx	xxxx	xxxx
1995	xxxx	xxxx	xxxx	xxxx	xxxx	
1996	xxxx	xxxx	xxxx	xxxx		
1997	xxxx	xxxx	xxxx			
1998	xxxx	xxxx				
1999	xxxx					

benefits started to be paid. For example, probabilities of recovery may be high during the years following the onset of partial incapacity benefits and then decrease rapidly.

Table TBIV.7 is arranged in a way that shows the number of awards of permanent incapacity benefits by year after the injury. For the sake of simplicity, it is assumed that the situation of the plan would be the same as in the Injury year and financial year section. The new awards of the most recent financial year appear in the last diagonal. In a typical plan, the number of awards at short durations would be small. This format applies as well to awards of lump sums. The first column indicates the number of awards made in the same year as the injury year, the second one the number of awards made in the year following the occurrence of the injury. By definition, there would be no new awards after duration 6. Statistical data regarding the level of benefits, for example, the total monthly benefit awarded corresponding to the number of new awards, should be available according to the same breakdown.

In order to analyse the continuation of pensions paid, it is often practical to consider their duration since the start of payments. The termination experience can be studied by financial year and duration. Then the data could be arranged as follows.

By relating the number of terminations in duration 1 to the number of new awards in duration 1, it is possible to calculate the probability of termination

Table TBIV.8 Permanent incapacity terminations

Financial year	(Financial year) − (Year of award) + 1					
	1	2	3	4	5	6
1994	xxxx					
1995	xxxx	xxxx				
1996	xxxx	xxxx	xxxx			
1997	xxxx	xxxx	xxxx	xxxx		
1998	xxxx	xxxx	xxxx	xxxx	xxxx	
1999	xxxx	xxxx	xxxx	xxxx	xxxx	xxxx

before the end of the year of the award. By relating the number of terminations in duration 2 to benefit recipients remaining at the end of the year of award, the probability of a termination during the second year is obtained, and so on. The last row shows the experience of terminations in the most recent financial year. It is important to note that this framework is of little use in analysing the terminations due to death. Death is age-related and the traditional methods used to analyse mortality by age are more suitable.

It is interesting to observe that the number of durations appearing in this table would increase by 1 every year until the plan is fully mature. Maturity is reached when the younger injured workers reach the ultimate age (that is, the maximum possible age a person can receive a pension), which is many years after the inception of a plan when pensions are paid for life.

Statistical reports of benefits in payment at the valuation date

The calculation of liabilities has to rely on the most accurate inventory of pensions in payment on the valuation date. For the calculations of liabilities, a relatively small volume of information is necessary for each benefit recipient in addition to the amount of the periodic payment. This information refers to the parameters that are used for the proper calculation of liabilities:

- the identification code of the recipient;
- the type of recipient (total or partial incapacity benefits/relation to the deceased for survivorship benefits);
- the amount of periodic payment on the valuation date;
- the date of birth of the recipient;
- the sex of the recipient;
- the degree of impairment (for permanent incapacity).

The identification code of the benefit enables a link to be made with other variables, such as the year of injury, nature of injury, and so on for any statistical or financial analysis regarding the liabilities. The date of birth of the recipient enables one to determine the age of the recipient at the valuation date according to any technique (nearest or last birthday, etc). Gender is not always used as a variable for the selection of assumptions. The degree of impairment or any other similar data are often used for the selection of mortality assumptions. It is not practical to make a list of variables that would cover all situations; it would be too long and many items would apply to very few circumstances. The above list is shown as a guide, which the actuary is advised to complete, according to the prevailing circumstances.

Although the proper identification of benefit recipients at a particular date may appear routine, the actuary often faces problems regarding the exhaustiveness and the reliability of the data. Cases may be pending on the valuation date because information regarding the right to receive benefits is missing (for example, proof of an orphan's school attendance) and a decision has to be made regarding the inclusion or exclusion of these pensions in the inventory. There is no single way to deal with these circumstances, but there are general principles that the actuary can rely on. Consistency in the processing of these cases from one valuation to the next is one of the most important principles. The actuary must avoid causing fluctuations in the amount of liabilities resulting from changes in the manner of treating those cases. The appropriate involvement of the actuary in the design of operational procedures is recommended. The actuary should keep the staff working in the operation services informed of the findings resulting from the tests that are made to assess the reliability of the data. For example, tests performed on the age of pensioners can be useful for verifying the potential under-reporting of deaths, if the number of people reaching extreme old age is high.

In the matter of the valuation of pension liabilities, it is relatively easy to carry out checks on the recipients at the valuation date by reconciling the data to those of the preceding valuation. There are many ways of doing so and they are mostly inspired by the following formula.

Formula 5

$$PR(t) = PR(t-1) + NA(t) - T(t)$$

where:

$PR(t)$ = Number of benefit recipients at the end of year t
$PR(t-1)$ = Number of benefit recipients at the end of year $t-1$
$NA(t)$ = Number of new awards of pension during year t
$T(t)$ = Number of pension terminations during year t

The check can also be processed on the amount of periodic payments paid by substituting in the above formula the amount of periodic payments to the number of recipients. If there is indexing during the year, the formula should then be adapted in order to consider it in the reconciliation process. The gain and loss analysis is another tool that can be used to identify anomalies in the basic data.

Statistical reports related to permanent incapacity benefits

The work of the actuary is not limited to the calculation of liabilities for pensions in payment at a specified date. Permanent incapacity benefits are costly and the experience is subject to changes in the work environment, in the medical and judicial practices as well as in the philosophy regarding the management of cases within the awarding institution. The actuary should carefully follow the experience and report regularly to the management of the institution. The following illustrations may help the actuary design the appropriate reports. These reports should be produced on an annual basis.

- Number of new awards of permanent incapacity benefits in each year

The number of new awards of permanent incapacity pensions (and the number of new awards of lump sums when the dual system exists). Breakdowns according to injury year, type of incapacity (total or partial), nature of injury (accident or disease), sex and age group at the time of injury, degree of medical impairment (by percentage distribution) and economic sectors or classification units for rating will generally be required. Given the small volume of data, grouping by only one or two variables at a time is very useful.

- Average amount of new periodic pensions awarded in each year

The average amount of periodic payments corresponding to new awards reported in the report mentioned above. Whenever possible, the pension benefit paid for partial incapacity should be related to the corresponding pensions that would be paid for permanent incapacity. This would be a proportion that is less than one.

- Terminations of pensions in each year

In order to follow each cohort of pension recipients, it is important to monitor the decrement rates of pensions according to the most significant variables. Pensions may terminate on the death, recovery or attainment of a specified age or duration of a person. Each of these decrements should be analysed separately. When the partial incapacity pensions are subject to changes related to modification of the benefit recipient earnings situation, rates of termination determined using the basic amount may differ substantially from rates calculated using the number of recipients. For lifetime pensions, death is the major source of decrement, and the general principles and techniques related to the construction of mortality tables apply. In the matter of EIOD, it is generally recognized that death rates vary according to the nature of the impairment (accident or disease) and its degree (severe, moderate or slight). The length of time since an injury is also a variable that may influence the level of mortality. It takes a lot of time before a system develops a credible volume of experience on termination, which is why it is so important to keep historical files so as to accumulate a sufficient volume of data.

- Permanent incapacity benefits paid by year

This is the basic financial information. Basic actuarial analyses require a breakdown by injury year. Each monetary unit paid in a single year should be related to the year when the injury of the recipient occurred. It should also be related to the year in which payment is incurred (retroactive payments covering periods in preceding years).

- Average earnings base and its distribution by size

The average earnings base at the time of an injury of new awards in each year. This should not be confused with the corresponding data for temporary incapacity. The distribution of new permanent incapacity awards by earnings groups will differ from temporary incapacity benefits because the frequency of permanent incapacity injuries differs by industry from the frequency of temporary incapacity injuries.

Statistical reports related to survivorship benefits

The frequency of fatal injuries at work is relatively low, but the cost of a claim is generally significant. The death of a worker greatly affects the life of the deceased's family and great attention is generally given to its occurrence in the management of an EIOD scheme. Investigations on the surrounding circumstances are generally conducted in order to ascertain whether the work environment conforms to safety regulations or guides. The actuary should give great attention to the proper capturing of data.

- Number of deaths

The number of deaths in each year and its distribution by injury year. Breakdowns by nature of injury (accident or disease), sex, age group, industry and some description of the accident or disease.

- Demographic characteristics of survivors with pension rights

Typical reports on deceased workers show, by age group of the deceased workers, the distribution of survivors by type (spouses, children and other relatives) and their average age at the death of the worker.

- Amount of pensions awarded

The average amount of pension awarded to each survivor according to the same format as the report mentioned above.

- Survivorship benefits paid by year

This is the basic financial information. It should be broken down by type of survivor and related to the year of injury of the worker.

- Terminations of pensions paid in each year

Terminations of survivors' pensions vary with the plan's provisions. Death is always a major cause of termination of pensions paid to spouses and parents of the deceased. Other possible causes are the remarriage of spouses, the attain-

Actuarial practice in social security

ment of a specified age by orphans or the end of their school attendance, and the attainment of a specific duration. Reports relating the number of terminations to the exposure by attained age enable the actuary to monitor the experience regarding these elements.

- Average earnings base and its distribution by size

The average earnings base of the deceased at the time of the injury. Consistency tests can be made by combining this information with the statistics on the average amount of pensions awarded by type of survivor.

LIST OF SYMBOLS

The following is a list of the special symbols that have been adopted for the purposes of this book, in the order in which they appear in each chapter.

Chapter 5

V(t)	Reserve at the end of year t
R(t)	Annual total income in year t (including interest income)
C(t)	Annual contribution income in year t (excluding interest income)
I(t)	Annual interest income in year t
B(t)	Annual expenditure in year t
S(t)	Total insurable earnings in year t
CR(t)	Contribution rate in year t
i(t)	Interest rate in year t
$PAYG_t$	Pay-as-you-go contribution rate
d(t)	System demographic dependency ratio
r(t)	System replacement ratio
CR[n,m]	Level contribution rate from year n to year m
κ	Reserve ratio
λ_t	Balance ratio
t_i	Years of i-th contribution review after 2016 (recurring every five years)
$CR(t_i)$	Contribution rate in year t_i
$\Delta CR(t_i)$	Annual rate of increase in the contribution rate for $t_i + 1 \leq t \leq t_i + 5$
t_0	Base year of the valuation

Symbols

$CR(t_0)$	Contribution rate in the base year
CR_{max}	Ultimate contribution rate
ΔCR	Step of increase in the contribution rate for every five years
T	Target year of the ultimate contribution rate (assumed to be 2025)

Chapter 6

$Reg(x,t)$	Registered population in year t is defined as those people who are registered in the scheme and have made contributions during at least one contribution period (usually, one month) until that year. Those who have already died or become pensioners should be excluded.
$Ac(x,t)$	Active population in year t is defined as those people who have made at least one contribution during that year
$Inac(x,t)$	Inactive population in year t is defined as those people who are registered in the scheme but have made no contribution throughout year t
$Cont(x,t)$	Contributors in year t is defined as the average of those people who made the contributions of each contribution period during year t
$Dens(x,t)$	Percentage of the contributors in the population
$Nent(x,t)$	New entrants in year t is defined as those people who are newly registered during year t and have made at least one contribution
$Rent(x,t)$	Re-entrants in year t is defined as those people who belonged to the inactive population in year $t-1$ but belonged to the active population in year t
$Pop(x,t)$	Base population in year t
$Covrate(x,t)$	Coverage rate in year t
$S[Ac(x,t)]$	Members of $Ac(x,t)$ who remain in active population in year $t+1$
$NR(x,t)$	Ratio of new entrants to re-entrants

Symbols

$D(x+1, t+1)$	Sum of new entrants and re-entrants of the past year
VAC(x,t)	Actives who became disabled during the past year
DAC(x,t)	Actives who died during the past year
RAC	Actives who retired during the past year
ZAC	Number of remaining population after deducting withdrawals on groups of death and entry into invalidity from the active insured population aged x in the year $(t-1)$
NINV	Number of invalidity pensions
NRET	Number of old-age pensions
NSURV	Number of beneficiaries of survivors' pensions
Cred(x,t)	Average acquired credit
Bal(x,t)	Average balance of individual savings accounts (this is used for the valuation of DC schemes)
$i(t)$	Interest rate in year t
CR(t)	Contribution rate in year t
Sal (x,t)	Average insurable salary at age x, in year t
Pens# (x,t)	Number of pensioners
Pens$(x,t)	Amount of pension benefits

Chapter 7

Sal(x)	Average salary earned at age x
g	Assumed average wage growth rate (constant for all years)
ea	Entry age into the scheme

Chapter 8

A(t)	Reserve at the beginning of the period for which the interest rate is calculated
B(t)	Reserve at the end of the period for which the interest rate is calculated

Symbols

I(t)	Investment income during the period
CF(t)	Cash flow during the period, excluding the investment income
i(t)	Average rate of return

Chapter 9

$L_{s,x}(t)$	Population of sex s and curtate age x at the middle of year t
$P_{s,x+\frac{1}{2}}(t+\frac{1}{2})$	Rate of survival from exact age $(x+\frac{1}{2})$ at the middle of year t to exact age $(x+1+\frac{1}{2})$ at the middle of year $t+1$
$N_{s,x}(t)$	Net migration (i.e. immigrants minus emigrants) from the middle of year t to the middle of year $t+1$, in the curtate age x at the middle of year $t+1$
$q_{s,x}(t)$	Mortality rates in a year of those with the exact age x ($=$ integer) at the beginning of year t
NB(t)	Number of newborns
$f_x(t)$	Age-specific fertility rates applicable to the period from the middle of year t to the middle of year $t+1$
sr	Sex ratio of newborns (i.e. newborn males divided by newborn females)

Chapter 10

Ac(x,t)	Active population in year t is defined as those people who have made at least one contribution during that year
S[Ac(x,t)]	Members of $Ac(x,t)$ who remain in active population in year $t+1$
VAC(x,t)	Actives who became disabled during the past year
DAC(x,t)	Actives who died during the past year
SS(x,t)	Salary scale value of active people aged x in year t
ADJ(t)	Adjustment factor for year t
Sal(x,t)	Average insurable salary at age x in year t
g(t)	Salary increase assumption for year t

Symbols

l_x	Population at exact age x
d_x	Number of deaths between x and $x+1$
I_x	Number of new invalidity pensioners between x and $x+1$
Rx	Number of new old-age pensioners between x and $x+1$

Chapter 12

CR	Contribution rate
r(t)	Replacement ratio
D	Dependency rate of the labour force

Chapter 14

CR	Contribution rate
S	Covered earnings
B	Estimated benefit payments in the period
A	Budgeted administration expenditures in the period
Cc	Contribution to contingency reserve in the period (can be positive, zero or negative)
I	Investment income and other income
PVB	Present value of benefits to be paid for injuries occurring in the year and occupational diseases reported in the year
PVA	Present value of expenses related to the administration of benefits considered under PVB, plus other current expenses not directly related to the administration of benefits
SD	Sums required to fund previous deficits or credits resulting from past surpluses used to reduce the premium (can be positive, zero or negative)
BST	Estimated short-term benefit payments in the period

Symbols

PVBLT	Estimated present value of long-term benefits awarded during the year
PVALT	Present value of expenses related to the administration of benefits considered under PVBLT, plus administration expenses related to the administration of the institution for the fiscal year, excluding the portion related to the management of long-term claims
CST	Contribution to contingency reserve related to short-term benefits in the period (can be positive, zero or negative)
SDLT	Sums required to fund previous deficits or credits resulting from past surpluses used to reduce the premium related to long-term benefits
R_i	Rate for classification group i
(Risk relativity)$_i$	Relation between the risk of the unit and the average risk of all employers
L	Factor for administration expenses and any provisions related to the financing method that are proportional to risk
F	Administration expenses and any provisions related to the financing method that are not proportional to risk (may be set at 0)

Chapter 15

N(t)	Number of persons cashing benefits in year t
M(t)	Average number of days per benefit recipient in year t
K(t)	Average daily benefit in year t
$N_d(0)$	Number of benefit recipients in the year of valuation whose injury occurred d years before the year of valuation, $0 \leq d \leq 9$
P(d,t)	Proportion of benefit recipients in year d after their injury year who are recipients in year $d+t$, $P(d,t) = 0$ for $d+t \geq 10$

Symbols

M(d+t)	Average number of days per benefit recipient $d+t$ years after the injury year
K(0)	Average daily benefit in the valuation year
f(t)	Indexing factor of the average benefit per recipient over t years
Id	Number of new injuries that occurred d years before the valuation date, $0 \leq d \leq 9$
D(d+t)	Number of days paid in year $d + t$ after the injury year per worker injured
AL(t)	Actuarial liabilities in year t
i	Nominal rate of interest
Ij	Number of new injuries occurring j years after the valuation date
K(j)	Average daily benefit at onset of incapacity of newly injured in year j
W(0)	Number of persons covered in the year preceding the projection period
G	Rate of growth of the population covered
F(0)	Rate of injury frequency in the first year preceding the projection period
v	Annual rate of variation in the injury frequency

Chapter 16

K(t)	Monthly pension in year t after the valuation date
$_{t-1}P_{[x+u]}$	Probability that the pension is still in payment at the end of year $t-1$
$q_{[x+u]+t-1}$	Probability that the pension terminates during year t
t	Number of years between the year of payment and the year of valuation; $t = 1, 2, 3\ldots$ (it is implicitly assumed that the date of valuation is the last day of a financial year, which is why t is assumed to start at 1)

Symbols

$_1q^{(i)}_{[x+u]+j}$	Probability that a pension in payment at the beginning of year j after the valuation date ceases to be in payment during the year for reason i
ω	Last age for which the probability of survival is greater than 0
NAA_x	Present value of a monthly benefit of 1 paid to an injured worker of age x
$_{tt-1}p_x$	Probability that a pension awarded to a person age x is still in payment at age $x + tt - 1$ years later (tt does not refer to a financial year but to the duration in terms of years since the onset of the pension)
q_{x+tt-1}	Probability that the pension terminates while the pensioner is age $x + tt - 1$
$f(tt-1)$	Indexing factor of the pension until the $tt - 1$ year following the award (set to 1 if no indexing at all)
$tt - 1$	Number of years after the award where $tt > 1$
$PINA_x(t)$	Total value of awards to recipients of age x that start to be compensated in year t for injuries that occurred before the valuation date
I_d	Number of new injuries that occurred d years before valuation year, $0 \leq d \leq m$
$LT_x(d+t)$	Factor applicable to I_d in projecting the number of new awards of pensions to people of age x in year $d + t$ after the injury year
$K_x(0)$	Monthly pension to benefit recipients of age x in the year of valuation
$f(t)$	Indexing factor of the pension between the year of valuation and the financial year $t, t = 1, 2, 3$
d	Difference between the year of valuation and the year of injury, $0 \leq d \leq m$
m	Maximum value of u for which $LTx(u)$ is larger than 0
$FINA_x(t)$	Total value of awards to recipients of age x that start to be compensated in year t for injuries that occurred after the valuation date

Symbols

I_j	Number of new injuries occurring j years after the valuation date
$K_x(j)$	Monthly pension to new benefit recipients of age x in injury year j
$f(t-j)$	Indexing factor of the pension between the year of injury and the financial year t, which is the year of award
q^1	Mortality rate according to the nature and degree of impairment
q	Mortality rate according to the population table
$E(x)$	Exposure at exact age x
$q(x)$	Mortality rate indicated in the reference table
$\emptyset(x)$	Number of registered deaths
$D(x)$	Number of expected deaths according to the reference table $q(x)$
$D'(x)$	Number of expected deaths according to the new table $q'(x)$

Chapter 17

$CH(w,t)$	Number of health care cases in category w of benefit in year t
$MR(w,0)$	Average cost per case in category w in valuation year
$f(t)$	General inflation from the valuation year to year t
$d(w,t)$	Deviation of medical inflation from general inflation
$N_d(0)$	Number of benefit recipients in the year of valuation whose injury occurred d years before the year of valuation, $0 \leq d \leq 9$
$P(d,t)$	Proportion of benefit recipients in year d after their injury year who are recipients in year $d+t$, $P(d,t) = 0$ for $d+t \geq 10$
$L(d+t)$	Average amount per benefit recipient $d+t$ years after the injury year in monetary units of the valuation year

Symbols

$f(t)$	Indexing factor of the average benefit per recipient over t years
$D_d(u)$	Total amount of benefits paid u years before valuation for injuries that occurred d years before year of valuation
$F(d,t)$	Relationship between the amounts paid $d+t$ years after the injury year to those paid d years after the injury years not considering changes in prices of services over time
m	First value of $d+t$ which $F(d,t)$ is equal to 0
$DA_d(0)$	Adjusted amount of benefits paid in the year of valuation for injuries that occurred d years before the valuation date
$pf(u)$	Indexing factor of the average benefit per recipient over u years before the valuation date
$DC_d(0)$	Total amount of benefits paid up to the year of valuation for injuries that occurred d years before the year of valuation, indexed to monetary values of the valuation year
$FC(d,t)$	Relationship between the amounts paid $d+t$ years after the injury year to those paid during the first d years after the injury year, adjusted to monetary values of the year of valuation
IK_j	Factor that considers the change in the frequency of injuries between the year of valuation and year j after the valuation date
CO_j	Cost of medical expenses and rehabilitation benefits for injuries occurring in the year following the valuation date valued at mid-year of the injury year

Chapter 19

ANN_UI_COSTS	Annual UI benefit costs
POP	Insured population
ANN_UN_INC(INS)	Annual unemployment incidence (in the insured population)
QUAL_RATE	Rate at which the insured unemployed are eligible

Symbols

AV_DURN(CLM)	Average duration on claim in a year, expressed in weeks
AV_BEN	Average weekly benefit paid to claimants
UN_INC(INS)	Unemployment incidence insured
UN_INC(TOT)	Unemployment incidence total
UN(ANN)	Annual number of persons with some unemployment
UN_RATE	Unemployment rate, as generally published by statistical agencies
AWW(LF)	Average weeks worked in the total labour force (can be derived from total wages divided by average weekly earnings)
AV_DURN(UN)	Average duration of an unemployment spell within a year
TOT_WKS(UN)	Total weeks of unemployment within a year
LF(ANN)	Labour force, annual count
LF(AV)	Labour force, average during a year
LF(AV)	Average labour force during a year
UN_RATE	Unemployment of the total labour force
BU_RATIO	Ratio of beneficiaries to unemployed
BEN_WKS	Total benefit weeks paid in a year
BEN	Average number of beneficiaries for a year
UN(AV)	Average number of unemployed (total) for a year
ANN_REV	Annual premium revenues
CONT	Contributors, generally
CONT(ANN)	Contributors, annual count
CONT(AV)	Contributors, average
AV_CONT_EARN	Average contributory earnings, generally
AV_CONT_EARN(ANN)	Average contributory earnings, annual count
AV_CONT_EARN(AV)	Average contributory earnings, average
PREM_RATE	Premium rate (combined, employees' and employers')

Symbols

AWW(INS)   Average weeks worked by the insured population

AWE(INS)   Average weekly earnings but limited to insured earnings

GLOSSARY OF TERMS

Active insured person An individual on whose behalf at least one contribution payment has been paid to the scheme during a given financial year.

Actuarial balance The difference between the present value of revenue and expenditure of a pension scheme over a given period. In the context of US social security, actuarial balance is defined with reference to an income rate (ratio of contribution income to insurable earnings) and a cost rate (ratio of total expenditure to insurable earnings). The actuarial balance is then defined by comparing the income rate with the cost rate over a specified period.

Actuarial liability The present value of benefit entitlements accumulated up to a given point in time by insured persons and actual pensioners.

Annuity An arrangement to provide an income for a specified number of years, or for the remaining lifetime of an individual, or the remaining lifetime of more than one individual.

Assessment of constituent capitals A financial system applied to employment injury benefits under which the annual cost of the scheme is determined as the present value of all future payments relative to pensions awarded during that year. Under that system, a reserve is continuously maintained equal to the present value of pensions in payment.

Catchment ratio The ratio of the total amount of earnings subject to the payment of contributions to the total amount of earnings received by insured persons from gainful employment. This ratio reflects the effects of the ceiling on insurable earnings or the effect of the exemption of some parts of the total earnings from the payment of contribution.

Cohort A collection of individuals born during the same period.

Compliance rate The ratio of the number of people on whose behalf contributions are actually paid to the scheme to the number of people who are legally covered by the scheme.

Glossary

Contribution rate A determined percentage of the covered insurable earnings that is to be collected for the financing of the scheme.

Contributors' ratio The ratio of the number of active insured persons (contributors) to the number of insured persons (active and inactive).

Cost rate The ratio of total expenditure of a scheme to total insurable earnings, for a given year.

Coverage rate The ratio of the number of active insured persons to the number of employed persons in the economy.

Defined-benefit scheme A scheme under which the benefit is a defined amount, which depends on the number of contribution or insurance years and on the amount of earnings.

Defined-contribution scheme A pension plan under which contributions are paid to an individual account for each participant. The retirement benefit is dependent on the account balance at retirement. The balance at retirement and consequently the benefits paid depend on amounts contributed and investment earnings.

Demographic ratio The ratio of the number of pensioners to the number of active insured persons.

Density of contributions The ratio of the average number of contributions actually paid during a financial year to the maximum potential number of contributions that can be paid during that financial year.

Deterministic model A simplification of a stochastic model in which the proportion of occurrences of a given event estimated by the stochastic model is assumed to occur with probability 1.

Economically active population (labour force) The economically active population comprises all people of either sex who furnish the supply of labour for the production of economic goods and services as defined by the United Nations systems of national accounts and balances during a specified time-reference period. According to these systems, the production of economic goods and services includes all production and processing of primary products whether for the market for barter or for own consumption, the production of all other goods and services for the market and, in the case of households that produce such goods and services for the market, the corresponding production for own consumption.

Glossary

Employed person The "employed" comprise all people above a specified age who, during a specified brief period, either one week or one day, were in the following categories:

- "paid employment";
- "at work": people who during the reference period performed some work for wage or salary, in cash or in kind; or
- "with a job but not at work": people who, having already worked in their present job, were temporarily not at work during the reference period and had a formal attachment to their job.

Financial system The systematic arrangement for raising the resources necessary to meet the financial obligations of a scheme. This is an expression often used to refer to the selected method of financing long-term pensions under a defined-benefit scheme (pay-as-you-go, partial funding or full funding). Such methods mainly differ through the timing of contribution payments for the purpose of financing present and/or future pension obligations.

Full funding A financial system under which the objective is to raise reserves equal to the total amount of accrued liabilities.

Funding ratio The ratio of the amount of reserves to the amount of actuarial liability under a scheme.

General average premium A financial system based on a theoretical constant contribution rate that can be applied indefinitely. It is calculated by equating the present value of projected future contributions of actual insured persons and all future new entrants plus the value of existing reserves, to the present value of projected future benefits and administration expenses, relative to existing and future insured persons and beneficiaries.

Gross domestic product The aggregate measure of the production of a country. It is equal to the sum of the gross values added of all resident institutional units engaged in production (plus any taxes and minus any subsidies on products not included in the value of their outputs).

Inactive insured person A person who is registered in the scheme but has made no contributions during the last financial year.

Income rate The ratio of contribution income to insurable earnings for a given year.

Insured person A person who is registered under the social security scheme.

Glossary

New entrant A person who was first registered with the scheme as an insured person within the last financial year.

Past insurance credits The total number of yearly/monthly/weekly contributions or periods of service which have been paid on behalf of an insured person or have been credited to the person from his/her entry into the scheme to the valuation date.

Pay-as-you-go rate (PAYG) The ratio of the total expenditure of a scheme to the sum of insurable earnings of that scheme.

Provident fund A fully funded, defined-contribution scheme in which funds are managed by the public sector.

Public pension scheme A pension scheme administered by a public entity.

Re-entrant A person paying contributions to a scheme after a break in contribution payments of at least one financial year.

Reference earnings The amount of earnings used in the pension formula. They usually refer to the average earnings over a specified period preceding the beginning of the pension.

Replacement rate The ratio of the amount of the pension benefit to the amount of the insurable earnings.

Reserve The net result of the accumulation of contributions, plus investment earnings, less benefit payments, less administrative expenses, under a scheme.

Reserve ratio The ratio of the reserve at a given date to the amount of expenditure of a scheme for the previous year.

Salary scale The table of factors showing the evolution, by age, of the salary of an individual over his/her career.

Scaled premium system A financial system for pensions under which contribution rates are increased throughout the life-cycle of a pension scheme on a step-by-step basis (where the duration of each individual "step" is called the period of equilibrium). In a more narrow definition (the *Thullen scaled premium*), the contribution rate is calculated for a defined period of years, that is, the period of equilibrium (which often ranges from ten to 25 years), with the objective of equating, at the end of the period of equilibrium, the income from contributions and the investment income to the expenditure on benefits and administration.

Social security All social transfers in kind and in cash that are organized by state or parastatal organizations or are agreed upon through collective bargaining processes. Benefits include cash transfers, such as pensions, employment injury benefits, short-term cash benefits (sickness and maternity benefits, unemployment benefits), as well as benefits in kind, such as health services.

Stochastic model A mathematical model in which the representation of a given phenomenon is expressed in terms of probabilities. The stochastic model is used to derive an estimate of the expected value of a random variable and a confidence interval for this variable.

Terminal funding A financial system under which a premium equal to the present value of a pension is paid at the time the pension starts. The premium is set aside as a reserve for the guarantee of future benefit payments.

Unemployed person The "unemployed" comprise all people above a specified age who, during the reference period, were:

- "without work", that is, were not in paid employment or self-employment;
- "currently available for work", that is, were available for paid employment or self-employment during the reference period; or
- "seeking work", that is, had taken specific steps in a specified recent period to seek paid employment or self-employment. The specific steps may include the person registering at a public or private employment exchange; sending applications to employers; checking at work-sites, farms, factory gates, markets or other assembly places; placing or answering newspaper advertisements; seeking the assistance of friends or relatives; looking for land, building, machinery or equipment to establish an enterprise; arranging for financial resources; applying for permits and licences, etc.

Unfunded liability Actuarial liability less the amount of the accumulated reserve.

Wage share at GDP The ratio of the total amount of "remuneration paid to employees by resident employers" (System of National Accounts definition) in a given year to the total amount of GDP. Remuneration includes wages, all types of non-wage cash benefits, as well as social security contributions.

BIBLIOGRAPHY

Aaron, H.J. 1982. *Economic effects of social security* (Studies of Government Finance, Washington, DC, The Brookings Institution).

—; Bosworth, B.P.; Burtless, G. 1989. *Can America afford to grow old? Paying for social security* (Washington, DC, The Brookings Institution).

American Academy of Actuaries. 1996. *Actuarial standard of practice No. 27 for selection of economic assumptions for measuring pension obligations*, No. 53, Pension Committee, Actuarial Standards Board (Washington, DC).

—. 1998. *Actuarial standard of practice No. 32: Social insurance*, Doc. No. 062, Committee on Social Insurance, Actuarial Standards Board (Washington, DC).

Anderson, A.W.1990. *Pension mathematics for actuaries* (Wellesley, Pennsylvania, The Windsor Press).

Ariztia, J. 1998. *AFP: A three-letter revolution*. (Santiago, Corporacion de Investigación, Estudio y Desarrollo de la Seguridad Social).

Association des commissions des accidents du travail du Canada. 1998. *Analyse comparative des prestations d'indemnisation– 1998* (Mississauga, Ontario).

Association internationale de la sécurité sociale (AISS). 1993. *Le rôle de la statistique des accidents pour la prévention des accidents*. Rapport V de la XXIVe assemblée générale, Acapulco, 1992 (Geneva).

Association of Workers' Compensation Boards of Canada. 1998. *Workers' compensation industry classifications, assessment rates, and experience rating programs in Canada–1998* (Mississauga, Ontario).

Barr, N. 1987. *The economics of the welfare state* (Stanford, Stanford University Press).

Beattie, R.; McGillivray, W. 1995. "A risky strategy: Reflections on the World Bank Report, Averting the Old Age Crisis", in: *International Social Security Review*, Vol. 48 (Geneva, ISSA).

Bergman, U.M.; Bordo, M.D.; Jonung, L. 1998. *Historical evidence on business cycles: The international experience* (Stockholm School of Economics).

Blanchard, O.; Portugal, P. 1998. *What hides behind an unemployment rate?: Comparing Portuguese and U.S. unemployment*, National Bureau of Economic Research Working Paper No. W6636, July (Cambridge, Massachusetts, NBER).

Blom, A.C. 1997. "The Netherlands recover from their illness", in: *The Geneva Papers on Risk and Insurance, Issues and Practice* (Geneva), No.84, July.

Board of Trustees of the Federal Old-Age and Survivors Insurance and Disability Insurance Trust Funds. 1998. *1998 Annual Report of the Board of Trustees of the Federal*

Bibliography

Old-Age and Survivors Insurance and Disability Insurance Trust Funds (Washington, DC, U.S. Government Printing Office).

Bodie, Z.; Mitchell, O.S.; Turner, J.A. 1996. *Securing employer-based pensions: An international perspective* (Philadelphia, Pension Research Council).

Bowers, N.L.; Gerber, H.U.; Hickman, J.C.; Jones, D.A.; Nesbitt, C.J. 1986 and 1997 (2nd ed.). *Actuarial mathematics* (Itasca, Illinois, Society of Actuaries).

Brown, J. 1998. *International benefit guidelines – 1998. A report on employee benefits in 60 countries around the word* (Leatherhead, Surrey, William M. Mercer, 21st ed.).

Brown, R.L. 1998. "Social security: Regressive or progressive", in: *North American Actuarial Journal*, Vol. 2, No.2 (Schaumburg, Illinois).

Butler, E. 1997. "Principles and economic effects of private and state systems", in: *The Geneva Papers on Risk and Insurance, Issues and Practice* (Geneva), No. 84, July.

Canadian Institute of Actuaries. 1994. *Standards of practice for valuation of pension plans*, Committee on Pension Plan Financial Reporting (Ottawa).

Castro Gutiérrez, A. 1997. *Diagnótico y modelamiento financiero-actuarial para el programa de riesgos del trabajo de las instituciones de seguridad social*. Paper presented at the Second Conference of the American Commission of Actuaries of the Inter-American Conference on Social Security (CISS) (Rio de Janeiro).

Casualty Actuarial Society. 1990. *Foundations of casualty actuarial science* (New York, 2nd ed.).

Chandhravitoon, N. 1998. *Financing of public service pensions (public servants)*.

Cichon, M.; Newbrander, W.; Yamabana, H.; Weber, A.; Normand C.; Dror, D.; Preker, A. 1999. *Modelling in health care finance: A compendium of quantitative techniques for health care financing*, Quantitative Methods in Social Protection Series (Geneva, ILO/ISSA).

Cichon, M.; Pal, K. 1997. *Reflections on lessons learned: Financing old-age, invalidity and survivors' benefits in Anglophone Africa* (Geneva, ILO).

Commission de la santé et de la sécurité du travail. 2000. *Tarification 1999* (Quebec).

—. 2000. *Evaluation du passif actuariel au 31 décembre 1999* (Quebec).

Conte-Grand, A. H.; Rodríguez, C.A. 1999. *Cobertura de los riesgos del trabajo. Manual con experiencias actuales y alternativas* (Geneva, ILO).

Coppini, M.A.; Laina, G. 1984. *Mieux connaître les transferts sociaux par l'utilisation des modèles économétriques* (Geneva, ILO).

Cox, P.R. 1970. *Demography* (Cambridge, Cambridge University Press, 4th ed.).

Daykin C. 1998. *"Una perspectiva actuarial de los régimenes de pensiones de cotizaciones definidas"*, Estudios de la seguridad social, No. 84 (Geneva, ISSA).

—. 1998. *Funding the future? Problems in pension reform* (London, Politeia).

—; Lewis, D. 1999. "A crisis of longer life: Reforming pension systems", in: *British Actuarial Journal*, Vol. 5, Part I.

Bibliography

Desseille, C. 1997. "Private versus state systems for industrial accident: The Belgian case", in: *The Geneva Papers on Risk and Insurance, Issues and Practice* (Geneva), No.84, July, pp. 314–326.

Garza-Zavaleta, P.A. 1997. "Elements of an effective worker's compensation system", in: *The Geneva Papers on Risk and Insurance, Issues and Practice* (Geneva), No. 84, July, pp. 327–335.

Gillion, C.; M Turner, J.; Bailey, C.; Latulippe, D. 2000. *Social security pensions: Development and reform* (Geneva, ILO).

Goovaerts, M. J.; Kaas, R., van Heerwaarden, A. E.; Bauwelinckx, T. 1990. *Effective actuarial methods*, Vol. 3, Insurance Series (Amsterdam, North-Holland/Elsevier Science Publishers).

Government Actuary Department, United Kingdom. 1990. *Report by the Government Actuary on the second quinquennial review under Section 137 of the Social Security Act* (London, National Institute Fund, Long Term Financial Estimates/HMSO).

Herzog, T. N. 1996. *Introduction to credibility theory* (Winsted, Connecticut, Actex Publications Inc., 2nd ed.).

Hickman, J.C. 1997. "Introduction to actuarial modeling", in: *North American Actuarial Journal*, Vol. 1, No. 3 (Schaumburg, Illinois).

Hirose, Kenichi. 1996. "A generalisation of the concept of the scaled premium", in: *Social security financing: Issues and perspectives* (Geneva, ISSA).

—. 1999. "Topics in quantitative analysis of social protection systems", in: *Issues in social protection*, Discussion Paper (Geneva, ILO).

Holzmann, R. 1991. *Adapting to economic change: Reconciling social protection with market economies*, Tripartite Symposium on the Future of Social Security in Industrialized Countries, CTASS/1991/6 (Geneva, ILO).

Human Resources Development Canada. 1995. *Canada's unemployment insurance program as an economic stabilizer* (Ottawa).

—. 1995. *The UI system as an automatic stabilizer in Canada* (Ottawa).

—. 1998. *Chief actuary's report on employment insurance premium rates for 1998* (Ottawa).

Imhoff, E. Van. 1992. "Demographic developments and social security expenditures", in: *Planning and financing in the nineties*, Proceedings of the Sixth Seminar for Actuaries in Social Security (Zoetermeer, The Netherlands, Social Security Council).

International Labour Office (ILO). 1984. *Introduction to social security* (Geneva, 3rd ed.).

—. 1985. *How to read a balance sheet– an ILO programmed book* (Geneva).

—. 1986. *Introduction à la sécurité sociale* (Geneva, 3rd ed.).

—. 1992. *Social Security Conventions and Recommendations* (Geneva).

—. 1996. *World Employment 1996/97 – National policies in a global context* (Geneva).

—. 1996. *The ILO social budget model* (Geneva).

—. 1997. *Pension schemes* (Geneva).

—. 1997. *The ILO population projection model: A technical guide* (draft) (Geneva).

—. 1997. *ILO-PENS: The ILO pension model* (Geneva); mimeo.

—. 1997. *Social security financing* (Geneva).

—. 1998. *ILO-DIST: The ILO wage distribution model* (Geneva); mimeo.

—. 1998. *Internal guidelines for the analysis of a national social security pension scheme* (Geneva).

—. 1998. "Una perspectiva actuarial de los régimenes de pensiones de cotizaciones definidas", in: *Estudios de la seguridad social*, No. 84.

—. 1999. *Guyana: Fifth actuarial review of the National Insurance Scheme as of 31 December 1998* (Geneva).

—. 1999. *Kuwait: The sixth actuarial valuation of the Kuwait Public Institution for Social Security* (Geneva).

—. 1999. *Social security data required for the valuation of national social security scheme* (Geneva).

—. 2000. *World Labour Report 2000: Income security and social protection in a changing world* (Geneva).

International Monetary Fund (IMF). 1997. *How long is the long run? A dynamic analysis of the Spanish business cycle*, IMF Working Paper WP/97/74 (Washington, DC).

—. 1998. *IMF's World Economic Outlook for 1998*, Chapter III (Washington, DC).

—. 2000. *Concordance in business cycles*, Working Paper WP/00/37 (Washington, DC).

International Social Security Association (ISSA). 1988. *Economic and social aspects of social security financing* (Geneva).

—. 1996. *Cost-effective financing of social risks: The model of employment accident and occupational disease insurance*, Report X of the XXVth General Assembly, Nusa Dua, Bali, 1995 (Geneva).

—. 1996. *The legal and organizational framework of co-ordination of occupational risk prevention and compensation schemes*, Report XI of the XXVth General Assembly, Nusa Dua, Bali, 1995 (Geneva).

Itelson, Steven. 1991. "Selection of interest assumptions for pension plan valuation", in: *Study Notes No. 462-23-91* (Schaumburg, Illinois, Society of Actuaries).

Iyer, S. 1999. *Actuarial mathematics of social security pensions,* Quantitative Methods in Social Protection Series (Geneva, ILO/ISSA).

James, E. 1998. "The political economy of social security reform", in: *Annals of Public and Cooperative Economics*, Vol. 69, pp. 451-482.

Jordan, C.W., Jr. 1967. *Society of Actuaries' textbook on life contingencies* (Chicago, Society of Actuaries, 2nd ed.).

Kahn, K. F. 1999. "Studies: Growing economy, employee shortage increases injuries", in: *Workers' Compensation Monitor, 12*(8), 2.

Kane, C.; Palacios, R. 1996. "The implicit pension debt", in: *Finance and Development*, June (Washington DC, World Bank).

Bibliography

Kohli, M.; Rein, M.; Guillemard, A.-M.; van Gunsteren H. 1991. *Time for retirement – Comparative studies of early exit from the labour force* (Cambridge University Press).

Kolnaar, A. 1992. "Economic aspects of social security", in: *Planning and financing in the nineties*, Proceedings of the Sixth Seminar for Actuaries in Social Security (The Netherlands, Social Security Council).

Lie, A. 1992. "Funding of the sickness and unemployment benefits Acts (The Netherlands)", in: *Planning and financing in the nineties,* Proceedings of the Sixth Seminar for Actuaries in Social Security (The Netherlands, Social Security Council).

Loxley, J.; Jamal, V. 1999. *Structural adjustment and agriculture in Guyana: From crisis to recovery*, ILO Working Paper, SAP 2.84/WP143 (Geneva, ILO).

MacDonald, J. Bruce. 1997. "Differences in valuation methods and assumptions between social insurance and occupational pension plans", in: *Study Notes No. 567-44-97* (Schaumburg, Illinois, Society of Actuaries).

McGill, D.M. 1967. *Life insurance* (Homewood, Illinois, Irwin).

—. et al. 1996. *Fundamentals of private pensions* (University of Pennsylvania Press, Philadelphia, 7th ed.).

McGillivray, W.R. 1992. "Actuarial aspects of converting provident funds into social insurance schemes", in: *Reports and summaries of discussions of the twelfth meeting of the Committee on Provident Funds* (Geneva, ISSA).

—. 1996. "Actuarial valuations of social security schemes: Necessity, utility and misconceptions" in: *Social security financing: Issues and perspectives* (Geneva, ISSA).

—. 1998. *Retirement system risks*, Paper presented to the Inter-American Conference on Social Security (Montevideo).

—. 1999. *Observations on annuitization*, Paper presented to the IVth International Conference of Actuaries of the Inter-American Conference on Social Security (Bogota).

—. 2000. *Contribution evasion: Implications for social security pension schemes*, Paper presented to the Third APEC Regional Forum on Pension Fund Reform (Bangkok).

Marples, W.F. 1962. "Salary scales", in: *Transactions of the Society of Actuaries*, Vol. XIV (Schaumburg, Illinois).

New Zealand's Accident Compensation Corporation. 1999. *Half year report – 1998/99* (Wellington).

Office of the Superintendent of Financial Institutions, Canada. 1993. *Canada Pension Plan 15th Actuarial Report as at 31 December 1993* (Ottawa).

—. 1997. *Canada Pension Plan 16th Actuarial Report as at September 1997* (Ottawa).

—. 1997. *Canada Pension Plan 17th Actuarial Report as at 31 December 1997* (Ottawa).

O'Leary, C.J.; Wandner, S.A. (eds.) 1997. *Unemployment insurance in the United States: Analysis of policy issues* (Kalamazoo, Michigan, W.E. Upjohn Institute for Employment Research).

Queisser, M. 1997. *Organization and management of pension schemes: optimizing services and results– Regulation, monitoring and control*, VIIth American Regional Conference of the ISSA, Montevideo (Geneva).

—. 1998. *The second-generation pension reforms in Latin America* (Paris, OECD).

Régie des rentes du Québec. 1995. *Analyse actuarielle du régime de rentes du Québec au 31 décembre 1997* (Quebec).

Scherman, K.G. 1999. "The Swedish pension reform", in: *Issues in social protection*, Discussion Paper (Geneva, ILO).

Scholz, W.; Drouin, A.. 1998. "Regular adjustment of financial parameters of social protection systems in volatile inflationary environments", in: *International Social Security Review*, Vol. 51, No. 4 (Geneva, ISSA).

Scholz, W.; Cichon, M.; Hagemejer, K. 2000. *Social budgeting,* Quantitative Methods in Social Protection Series (Geneva, ILO/ISSA).

Society of Actuaries and Casualty Actuarial Society. 1998. *General principles of actuarial science*, Discussion draft, 15 Aug. (Schaumburg, Illinois).

Sokoll, G. 1997. "Private versus public systems for industrial accidents and invalidity insurance – The German solution", in: *The Geneva Papers on Risk and Insurance, Issues and Practice* (Geneva), No. 84, July.

Sorensen, O.B. 1997. *Variability of retirement age practices: An appropriate response to the labour market developments?*, First Technical Conference: Social Benefits and Employment: Complementary Policies for More Effective Social Security, ISSA/TEC/CONF/1/C (Geneva, ISSA).

Thompson, K. 1980. "Experiences gained in the conversion of provident funds into pension schemes", in: *Reports and summaries of discussions of the fourth meeting of the Committee on Provident Funds* (Geneva, ISSA).

Thompson, L. 1996. "Principles of financing social security pensions", in: *International Social Security Review* (Geneva), Vol. 49, No. 3/96.

—. 1998. *Older and wiser: The economics of public pensions* (Washington, DC, The Urban Institute Press).

—. 1998. *The social security reform debate: In search of a new consensus – A summary* (Geneva, ISSA).

Thullen, P. 1964. "The scaled premium system for the financing of social insurance pension schemes: maximum periods of equilibrium", in: *International Review on Actuarial and Statistical Problems of Social Security*, No. 10 (Geneva, ISSA).

—. 1973. *Techniques actuarielles de la sécurité sociale* (Geneva, ILO).

United Nations. 1982. *Unabridged model life tables corresponding to the new United Nations model life tables for developing countries* (New York).

—. 1989. *Projection methods for integrating population variables into development planning*, Vol. I, Methods for comprehensive planning, Module One: Conceptual issues and methods for preparing demographic projections (New York).

—. 1989. *World Population Prospects: The 1988 revision* (New York).

Bibliography

United States General Accounting Office. 1998. *Social security financing, Implications of Government stock investing for the Trust Fund, the Federal Budget, and the Economy*, Report of the Special Committee on Aging, U.S. Senate (Washington, DC).

Willems, W. 1992. "Investment activities of the SVB (The Netherlands)", in: *Planning and financing in the nineties*, Proceedings of the Sixth Seminar for Actuaries in Social Security (The Netherlands, Social Security Council).

Williams, C.A., Jr. 1991. *An international comparison of worker's compensation*, Huebner International Series on Risk, Insurance and Economic Security (Norwell, Massachusetts, Kluwer Academic Publishers).

—. 1997. "Private versus state systems for industrial accidents and invalidity insurance in the UK", in: *The Geneva Papers on Risk and Insurance, Issues and Practice* (Geneva), No. 84, July.

World Bank. 1994. *Averting the old-age crisis: Policies to protect the old and promote growth* (New York, Oxford University Press).

Zalm, G. 1992. "Long-term economic development and social security", in: *Planning and financing in the nineties*, Proceedings of the Sixth Seminar for Actuaries in Social Security (The Netherlands, Social Security Council).

Zayatz, T. 1999. "Social security disability insurance program workers' experience", in: *Actuarial Study No. 114* (Baltimore, Social Security Administration).

INDEX

Note: Page numbers in **bold** refer to major text sections, those in *italic* to tables, figures and boxes. Subscript numbers appended to page numbers indicate endnotes, the letter *g* a glossary entry.

account balances *see* balances
accrual basis (financial statements) 91
accrual rate, annual (DB schemes) 161
acquired immune deficiency syndrome (AIDS) 131
active insured persons *see* insured population
actuarial balance *53*, 151, 483*g*
actuarial liability **172–5**, 241–2, 483*g*
actuarial services, organization 23–4
actuarial work **3–13**
    interrelationships between social security schemes and environment *see* social security schemes
    social security-specific models, need for **3–6**
actuaries, role 13, **14–24**
    actuarial services, organization 23–4
    ad hoc support and other related fields 21–3
        ad hoc support 22
        performance indicators 22
        social security agreements 22–3
        statistical reports 22
    at reform stage 19–21
        amendments to scheme 20
        structural reform of system 20–21
    reviews of ongoing schemes **17–19**
        analysis of past results 17–18
        financing recommendations 19
        other recommendations 19
        revision of assumptions and methods 18
        short-term projections 21
    valuation of new schemes **14–17**
        benefit provisions 15–16
        financing provisions 16–17
        legal vs actual coverage 15
adjustments to schemes *see* modifications
administrative expenses *153*
    analysis 95–6, *95*, 325–7, *327*
    DC schemes 438
    Demoland 324, 325–7, *326*, *327*, *347*, *349*
    ILO standards 421
    projection 21, 142, 144
    unemployment insurance 301–2
administrative mechanisms (setting revenue levels) 40
adoption 287
Africa 11, 21, 423
age differential, married couples 4
aggregate approach (valuation) 122, *122*, 132
agreements, social security 22–3
agriculture 206
AIDS (acquired immune deficiency syndrome) 131
amendments to schemes *see* modifications
American Academy of Actuaries 40
analysis of past results *see* experience analysis
annexes (reports) 312, *312*
annual accrual rate (DB schemes) 161
annuities 428–9, 430–31, 433–4, 435, 483*g*
    purchasing with provident fund

Index

balances 184–5
annuities certain 431
annuity factor (PAYG schemes) 177–8
appeals, benefit-related 421
Argentina *436*
assumptions 18, *312*, 314–15
  for major treatment *see* Demoland; employment injury benefits; pension schemes
automatic mechanisms (setting revenue levels) 40
average rate of return (investments) *97–8*
average replacement rates (pension schemes) 151

babies, sex ratios *376*
balance, actuarial *53*, 151, 483*g*
balance factor (employment injury rating systems) 443–4, *443*, 449, *450*
balance sheets (financial statements) 90, *92*
balances (DC schemes) 439
balances (provident funds) **183–6**
  converting into pension credits 185–6
  freezing 184
  paying out 183
  purchasing annuities with 184–5
bank deposits *see* investments
Barbados *141*
base run (pension valuation process) 36–7
Bédard, Michel xxiii
benefit expenditure *see* expenditure
benefits 15–16, *312*, 313–14
  ILO standards 418–21
  for major coverage *see* individual types of benefit
Binet, Gylles xxii
Bolivia 176
bonds *see* investments
Bühlmann-Straub model (employment injury benefits) 445–7, *446*
building block approach (investment return) *139*
Bulgaria *74*
business cycles, and unemployment insurance 292–4

Canada 23, 450
  Ontario 448

parental benefits 287
Quebec *154*, 267
unemployment insurance 23–4, 307$_2$
Canada Pension Plan *51–2*, 53, 85
Caribbean 21, 423
  investments *141–2*
cash basis (financial statements) 91
cash benefits, short-term *see* short-term cash benefits
cash refund annuities 431
catchment ratio 152, 483*g*
ceilings, insurable earnings 75, 129, *129*, *153*
census data 291
Central America 423
child supplement (widows' pensions) 367
children 4, *8*
  dependency ratio (Demoland) 334–5, *335*
  survivorship benefits *see* survivorship benefits
Chile 89$_2$, 176, *436*
  conversion of DB to DC scheme 20, 170, *171*
Cichon, Michael xxii
claims
  duration (unemployment insurance) 294, 297–8
  limiting (employment injury benefits) 442–3, *442*
closed-group method (valuation) 46
cohort 483*g*
cohort approach (valuation) 121–2
cohort component method (population projections) 105, 107
Colombia 89$_2$, *436*
compliance rate 483*g*
constituent capitals, assessment 483*g*
construction industry 206
continuity of contributions risk (DC schemes) 427
continuity of employment risk (DC schemes) 426–7
contribution rates 16–17, 19, 484*g*
  Demoland 318, 322–3, *323*, 357–9
    employment injury benefits 322, *323*, 357, *357*, *358*
    pension schemes 49–50, 322–3, *323*, 351–2, 357–9, *357*, *358*, *359*

Index

short-term cash benefits 322, *323*, 357, *357, 358*
employment injury benefits *449*
  Demoland 322, *323*, 357, *357, 358*
  full funding 197–9, 209–11
  PAYG 196–7, 198–9
pension schemes *47*, 148
  conversion of provident funds into DB schemes 180, 181
  Demoland *49–50*, 322–3, *323*, 351–2, 357–9, *357, 358, 359*
  flexibility 30–31
  GAP system *50*, 53–4
  modifications 166
  reserve ratio system 48, *49–50*, 53
  scaled premium system 47–8, *47*
  short-term cash benefits (Demoland) 322, *323*, 357, *357, 358*
contributions 16, 21
  density 4, 87–8, 129–30, 342, *342*, 438–9, 484*g*
  see also financing
contributions, pension schemes
  base (formula) *64*
  base run 36
  collection rate 140, 142, *143*
  DC schemes 438–9
  Demoland *326, 351, 359*
  density 4, 87–8, 129–30
  experience analysis 93
  modifications 165–6
contributors, pension schemes 36, 37, *60–61*
  ratio to pensioners (Demoland) 349, *350*, 353, *353*, 354, *354*
contributors' ratio 150, 484*g*
Conventions *see* ILO (standards)
cost *see* expenditure
coverage *see* insured population
covered earnings *see* earnings (insurable)
credibility (employment injury rating systems) 444–7, *446*
credits 86–7, 130–31, *401*, 486*g*
  conversion from DB to DC schemes 173, *173*
  converting provident fund balances into 185–6
  Demoland *88*, 342–3, *343*
  special 178

cross-subsidization, between income groups 15

data *80*
  employment injury benefits 267, *268–9*, 444–5
  labour force *70–71*, *80*, *380–82*
  salary scales *125*
  short-term cash benefits 282–3, 291–2
  tables (examples) *see* tables
  see also records; reports; statistics
data maintenance systems, appraisal 81–2
databases *312*, 314–15
  for major treatment *see* Demoland (database and scheme-specific assumptions); employment injury benefits; pension schemes (data and information base)
  maternity benefits 282–3
DB pension schemes *see* defined-benefit pension schemes
DC pension schemes *see* defined-contribution pension schemes
death benefit (employment injury benefits) 346, 348, *349*
Decent Work initiative (ILO) v
defined-benefit (DB) pension schemes 425, 484*g*
  annual accrual rate 161
  conversion from a provident fund *see* provident funds
  conversion to a DC scheme **170–76**, 423
    Chile 20, 170, *171*
    liability at conversion **172–5**
    scheme-specific assumptions 173–5
    specific considerations 176
  see also defined-contribution (DC) pension schemes
defined-contribution (DC) pension schemes **423–39**, 484*g*
  assumptions 437–9
    accumulation period 437–9
    payout period 439
  benefits **430–36**
    adjustment of annuities in payment 435
    compulsory annuities 434
    disability benefits 436
    individual life annuities 433–4

Index

periodic payments 430–33
programmed withdrawals 432, 434–5
survivorship benefits 436
conversion from a DB scheme *see* defined-benefit pension schemes
projections 439
rationale for **423–6**
  economic growth 425
  individual saving 424
  pensions are transfers 424
  rate of return 426
  retirement burden 425
  savings and investment 425
risks **426–30**
  accumulation period 426–8
  government 430
  pensioners 428–9
  regulation 429–30
state guarantees 436–7
demographic environment, interrelationships with social security schemes 4–5, *6*, 7–9, *8*
reports 312, *312*
see also Demoland; individual demographic variables; pension schemes (various); population
demographic ratio 150, 484g
Demoland 318–19
contributions/rates *see* contribution rates; contributions
for specific treatment of individual branches *see* employment injury benefits; pension schemes; short-term cash benefits
Demoland, report **319–72**
actuarial valuation **328–32**
  demographic and economic developments, modelling 329–30
  financial systems 331–2
  income and expenditure, projection 330–31
comparison with previous valuation 353, *353*
  PAYG cost rate 353, *353*
  ratio of pensioners to contributors 353, *353*
cost projections **345–52**
  employment injury benefits 345, 347–9, *348–9*

pensions **349–52**
short-term benefits 345, 346–7, *347*
database and scheme-specific assumptions 330–31, **339–45**
  contributions, density 342, *342*
  demographic assumptions 343–5
  insurable earnings 85, *85*, 341–2, *341*, 367
  insured population 339–41, *340–41*
  past credits *88*, 342–3, *343*
  pensions in payment on valuation date 343, *368–71*
demographic frame **332–5**
  fertility 332, *333*
  migration 334, *334*
  mortality 333, *333*
  population projection, general *147*, 329, 334–5, *335*, 337
economic projections *148*, **335–9**
  economic growth 329, 337–8, *338*
  inflation 329, 336, 337–8, *338*
  interest rates 336, *338*, 339
  wages 338–9, *338*
executive summary **322–4**
  administrative expenses 324
  contribution rates, recommended 322–3, *323*
  costs, future evolution 322
  financial autonomy of three branches 322
  investment policy 324
  modifications to scheme, effects 323–4
  pensions, adjustment 324
  reserves, reallocation 322
financing strategy **356–9**
  contribution rates 357–9
  reallocation of reserves 356–7, *356*
labour market projections
  employment 329, 336–7
  labour force 329, 336–7, *336*, 337
  unemployment 336, *337*
legal provisions 368
modifications to scheme, effects **359–63**
  minimum pension *168*, 323, 359–60, *360*
  retirement age *160*, 361–2
  sickness benefits (qualifying conditions) 362–3
  survivorship pensions 360–61, *360*

see also pension schemes
  (modifications)
 other issues **363–7**
  differentiation of (amount of)
   pensions 366–7
  indexation of pensions 319, 353, 366
  investment policy 363–4, *364*
  self-employed persons, coverage 318,
   365–6, *365*
  statistics, maintenance 367
 present situation and performance,
  analysis **325–8**
  administrative expenses 325–7, *326*,
   327
  investment results *326*, 327–8, *327*
  revenue and expenditure 325, *326*
 scheme-specific assumptions *see*
  Demoland, report (database and
  scheme-specific assumptions)
 sensitivity analysis 354–5
Denmark 11
dependency ratios 334–5, *335*
deterministic models 57–9, *58*, 484*g*
differential rating systems (employment
 injury benefits) **203–6, 440–48**
 balance factor 443–4, *443*
 classification structure 205–6
 credibility 444–7, *446*
 database and responsiveness 447–8,
  447
 large claims, limiting 442–3, *442*
 risk/rate relativities 440–48, *441*
disability *see* invalidity
diseases, occupational *see* occupational
 diseases
divorce 5, *6*, *8*, 9
dollar-weighted rate of return
 (investments) *97*
Dominica 186
Drouin, Anne xxi

earnings
 classes, redistribution between (pension
  schemes) 31–2
 distribution **126–8**, *128*, *394*
 investment *see* investment return
 reference 76, 77, 161–2, 486*g*
 replacement rates 15
 test at retirement 163–4
 see also wages

earnings, insurable 15
 Demoland 85, *85*, 341–2, *341*, 367
 employment injury benefits 193–6, *194*,
  199, *199*
 pension schemes *see* pension schemes
  (assumptions, scheme-specific);
  pension schemes (data and
  information base)
 tables (examples) *400*
economic environment, interrelationships
 with social security schemes 4, 5, *6*,
 7, *8*, 9–11
 reports 311–12, *312*
 see also Demoland; individual
  economic variables; pension
  schemes (various)
economic growth *6*, 10, *153*
 Demoland 318, 329, 337–8, *338*
 projection 110–12, *111*
 sensitivity analysis 154
 see also gross domestic product
economic sectors (employment injury
 rating systems) 203–6
economically active population 484*g*
EIOD (employment injury and
 occupational diseases) schemes *see*
 employment injury benefits
eligibility conditions
 ILO standards 417
 pension schemes *61*, 75, 158–9
 sickness benefits 286, 324, 362–3, 417
 unemployment insurance 294, 297–8,
  417
 see also legal provisions
eligibility factor (employment injury
 rating systems) *452*
employed persons (definition) 485*g*
employed population, projection *60*, 63
employers (employment injury rating
 systems) 203–6, 448–50, *451–2*, 453–
 4
 small 208, 448, *449*, 450
employment 10, *108*, *111*, 112, *153*
 data *80*, 383–8
 Demoland 329, 336–7, *337*
 sensitivity analysis 154
employment injury benefits **189–278,
 440–70**
 database **454–61**
  circumstances of accident 456–7

Index

data, credibility 444–5
differential rating systems 447–8, *447*
incapacity benefits (permanent) 459–60
incapacity benefits (temporary) 457–9
injured worker, identification 455–6
medical expenses and rehabilitation benefits 258–60, 267, *268–9*
survivorship benefits 460–1
ILO standards 414, 417, 418, 419
rehabilitation benefits *see* employment injury benefits (medical expenses and rehabilitation benefits)
reports *see* reports (employment injury benefits)
survivorship benefits *see* survivorship benefits
see also invalidity/pensions
employment injury benefits, Demoland 331–2, *370–71*
contributions/rates 318, 322, *323*, *326*, 357, *357*, *358*
expenditure 325, *326*, 347–9, *348–9*
investment earnings *326*, 327–8
reserve 322, 325, *326*, 356–7, *356*, 371–2, *372*
employment injury benefits, financial and rating systems **191–211**
assessment of constituent capitals 483*g*
contribution rate *see* contribution rates
experience-rating systems **207–9**
experience ratio *451–2*
nature of systems 207–8
retrospective programmes 207, 208–9, 453–4
experience-rating systems, prospective programmes 207, 208, **448–53**
balance factor 449, *450*
other employers 448–50, *451–2*
prevention groups 450, 453
small employers 208, 448, *449*, 450
financial systems **192–201**
actuary's role 201
basic concepts **193–6**
constant record 195, *195*
full funding *see* full funding
funds, sources 192–3
mixed systems 199–201
PAYG 196–7, 198–9, 209–11

rating systems **202–6**
differential rates *see* differential rating systems
uniform rates 203
see also risk
employment injury benefits, incapacity cash benefits (temporary) **212–32**
assumptions **217–25**
benefit recipients, evolution of numbers 220–21, *220*, *221*
benefits, basic amount 223–4
continuation table 221–2, *222*
duration of incapacity 218–19, *218*, *219*, *232*
new injuries, number 224–5
database 457–9
experience analysis **225–31**
deviations **226–31**, *228*, *229*, *230*
projection *224*, 225–6, *225*
financial projections, methodology **213–17**
benefits for injuries occurring after valuation date 216–17
benefits for injuries occurring before valuation date 214–16
legal provisions 212–13
employment injury benefits, incapacity (permanent) **233–55**
assumptions **242–51**
basic amount of benefits related to new awards 251
future awards **248–51**, *249*, *250*
terminations of pensions in payment (mortality) 243–5, *244*, 252–3, 468, 469
terminations of pensions in payment (recovery) **245–8**, *246*, *247*, *254–5*
database 459–60
financial projections **235–42**
future awards for future injuries 240–41
future awards for past injuries 239–40
pensions in payment at valuation date 236–8
present value of new awards 238–9, 252
successive liabilities 241–2
ILO standards 419

Index

legal provisions 233–5
employment injury benefits, medical expenses and rehabilitation benefits **256–78**
  assumptions **267–78**
    development factors, graduated 274–6, *275*
    development factors, observed *270–74*, **270–74**
    raw data 267, *268–9*
    tests 276–8, *276–7*
  database 258–60, 267, *268–9*
  financial projections **260–67**
    Demoland 346, 348–9, *348*, *349*
    injuries after valuation date 266–7
    injuries before valuation date **261–6**
  legal provisions 256–8
  statistical reporting 260
  see also short-term cash benefits (sickness benefits)
employment injury and occupational diseases (EIOD) schemes *see* employment injury benefits
England 432–3
equities *see* investments
exchange rates *395*
executive summaries 311, *312*
  Demoland *see* Demoland
expenditure
  cost rates 484*g*
  ILO standards 421
  for major treatment *see* individual expenditures
expenses, medical *see* employment injury benefits (medical expenses and rehabilitation benefits)
experience analysis 17–18
  for major treatment *see* employment injury benefits (incapacity cash benefits); pension schemes (experience analysis)
experience-rating systems
  employment injury benefits *see* employment injury benefits (financial and rating systems)
  unemployment insurance 306–7

FACTS (International Financial and Actuarial Service) 5, 328

family benefit, ILO standards 414, 417, 419, 420
females *see* women
fertility rates 5, *6*, 7, *60*, 103, *106*, *111*, *153*
  data *80*, *376*
  Demoland 332, *333*
  and maternity benefits 283, 286
  sensitivity analysis 152, *154*
  see also demographic environment; reproductive behaviour
fertility trends, reports 312
financial equilibrium *43–4*, *153*, 193
financial reporting *312*, 313–14, *397*
financial statements **90–93**, *312*
financing 16–17, 18–19
  for major treatment *see* defined-benefit schemes; defined-contribution schemes; Demoland; employment injury benefits (various); full funding; pay-as-you-go; pension schemes (various); provident funds
  systems 485*g*
  unemployment insurance (UI) **302–7**
  see also contributions; investments
findings and recommendations (pension schemes), presentation 37
fiscal environment, interrelationships with social security schemes 5, *6*, *8*, 11–12
fishing industry 206
foreign (non-national) residents 420
forestry 206
formulae, employment injury benefits financial and rating systems
  differential rating systems 203–4, *204*, 443, 444–6
  experience rating systems *451*, *452*
  full funding 197–8, 210
  mixed financial systems 199–200
  PAYG 196, 210
  uniform rating systems 203
incapacity cash benefits (temporary)
  benefit recipients, evolution 220–21, *220*, *221*
  duration of incapacity 218–19, *219*, *232*
  experience analysis 226–7, *226*
  injuries occurring after valuation date 216–17

Index

injuries occurring before valuation date 214–16
incapacity (permanent), and survivorship benefits
  future awards for future injuries 240–41
  future awards for past injuries 239–40
  pensions in payment at valuation date 236–8, 467
  present value of new awards 238–9, 252
  successive liabilities 241–2
  terminations of pensions in payment 244, 252–3
medical expenses and rehabilitation benefits **261–7**
  development factors, observed 270
  injuries after valuation date 266–7
  injuries before valuation date **261–6**
formulae, pension schemes *64–8*
  benefit expenditure *64*
  benefits, amount 75–6, *76*
  contribution base *64*
  coverage rates *119*
  covered population *64–6*
  earnings distribution 127–8
  earnings-related schemes 181–2
  employment *108*
  financial equilibrium *43–4*
  financing *43–5, 51–3*
  interest rates *109*
  investment earnings (Demoland) 328
  modifications 161–2
  new entrants and re-entrants *122*
  partial funding 44–5, 54
  PAYG systems *44*, 149
  population projection 105–7, *106*
  productivity *108*
  provident fund balances, converting into pension credits 185
  rate of return *97–8*
  reference earnings 77
  reform scenarios 167
  reserve *99*
  salary scales *123–4, 125–6*
  transition from active status to pensioners 66–7
  transition from active to active 67–8
  transition from pensioner to pensioner 68
  unemployment *108*
  wages *108–9*
formulae, short-term cash benefits
  sickness and maternity benefits 283–5, *284*
  unemployment insurance 294–6, 299–300, 304–5
formulae, symbols **471–82**
freezing provident fund balances 184
full funding 485g
  employment injury benefits **197–9**
  contribution rates 197–9, 209–11
  mixed systems (with PAYG) 199–201
  reserve 199, *199, 200*, 201
  pension schemes *see* pension schemes (financial systems)
  see also financing
funding ratio 151, 485g

GAP *see* general average premium
GDP *see* gross domestic product
general average premium (GAP) *44, 50*, 53–4, 148, 150–51, 352, *352*, 485g
  effect of scheme modifications 168–9, *168*, 360, *360*, 361
  see also premium financing
Germany 10
governance context (social security), reports 312, *312*
government, role in financing social security schemes *6, 8*, 11–12, 29, 40
  minimum guarantees 11–12, 40, 149, 182, 430, 436–7
  table (example) 396
grants, in lieu of pension 78
Great Britain 432–3
Grenada 186
gross domestic product (GDP) *60, 80*, 151, *392–3*, 485g, 487g
growth *see* economic growth
guarantees *see* government
Guyana 318[1]
  see also Demoland

health services 9, 259
hospitals 259, 417, 418
husbands *see* men

Index

ILO (International Labour Organization/Office) vi, 24, 47, 307_1, *312*
  Decent Work initiative v
  definitions 115_7, 415–16
  International Financial and Actuarial Service (FACTS) 5, 328
  models *60–61*, 62, *64*, 105–7, *106*, *128*, 328
ILO (International Labour Organization/Office), standards (ILO Conventions and Recommendations) 78, 193, 290, 313, 316, **413–22**
  adjustment of benefits 419
  contingencies covered 313, 415–16
  Convention No. 102 79, *160*, 290, 313, 361, 414
  Convention No. 168 290, 294, 297, 298, 313
  form and duration of benefits 79, 297–8, 419–20
  general remarks 413
  medical care 414, 417–18, 419–20
  miscellaneous 420–21
  personal scope of protection 416–17
  qualifying periods 79, 297, 417
  rates of periodical cash benefits 418–19
  see also legal provisions
implicit pension debt concept 172, *172*
inactive insured persons *see* insured population
incapacity benefits *see* employment injury benefits (various)
income rate 485*g*
indexation *8*, 16, 78, *79*, 137–8
  Demoland 319, 353, 366
  see also inflation
India 423
individual account balances (DC schemes) 439
individual savings schemes 181
industrial accident (ILO definition) 415
infants, sex ratios *376*
inflation 4, *6*, *8*, *61*, *80*, 114, *153*, *395*
  Demoland 318, 329, 336, 337–8, *338*
  sensitivity analysis 154, *154*
  see also indexation
informal-sector workers, coverage *74*
injury benefits *see* employment injury benefits

insurable earnings *see* earnings (insurable)
insurance credits *see* credits
insured population 4–5, 27–9, 63, 144_2, 485*g*
  catagories of insured persons 72, *74*, 318
  coverage rate *60*, 117–18, *119*, 150, 484*g*
  earnings *see* earnings (insurable)
  legal provisions 15
  pension schemes *see* pension schemes (assumptions, scheme-specific); pension schemes (characteristics); pension schemes (data and information base)
  tables (examples) *398–402*
  unemployment insurance 294, 295–7
insured population, active 119, *120*, 144_2, 148, 483*g*
  comparison with previous valuation 353, 354, *354*
  database 82, *82*, 339–41, *340*, *341*
  Demoland 318, 329, *337*
    comparison with previous valuation 353, 354, *354*
    database 339–41, *340*, *341*
  movement to inactive 63, 329
insured population, inactive 82, *82*, 83, *120*, 121, 144_2, 485*g*
  Demoland 329, 340, *340*, 367
  movement from active 63, 329
  see also re-entrants
interest rates 4, 5, *6*, *8*, *80*, *109*, *153*
  projection 114–15, 336, *338*, 339
  sensitivity analysis *154*
  tables (examples) *395*
  see also investments
intergenerational transfers 32–3
International Financial and Actuarial Service (FACTS) 5, 328
International Labour Office *see* ILO
International Social Security Association (ISSA) vi
invalidity 4, *6*, 9
  definition 74, 164
invalidity pensions *61*
  Demoland *147*, 343, *344*, 346, 348, *349*, *350*, *351*, *369*, *370*, 371–2, *372*
  disability incidence rates 154

Index

experience analysis 94
ILO standards 414, 417, 419
incidence and termination 132–4, *135*
  see also mortality
tables (examples) *403, 404, 407, 411–12*
  see also employment injury benefits
investment return *58*, 138–40, *139–40*
  analysis 93–4, **96–8**, *97–8*, 154, 327–8, *327*
  Caribbean *141–2*
  DC schemes 437–8
  Demoland *326*, 327–8, *327, 351, 359*
  projection 21, *351, 359*
  risk 181, 182–3, 427–8
investments
  DC schemes 425, 427–8
  policy 18, 324, 363–4, *364*
  value 99–100
  see also financing; interest rates
Iraq 186
ISSA (International Social Security Association) vi

Jamaica *141*
Japan 23, *52*
joint life annuities 431

Kuwait 45–6, *46*

labour force 484*g*
  data *70–71, 80, 380–82*
  Demoland 318, 329, 336–7, *336, 337*
  participation rates *5, 8, 80, 111*, 318, 336–7, *336, 382*
  projection *60*, 63, *108, 111*, 112, 329, 336–7, *336, 337*
labour standards *see* ILO (standards)
large claims (employment injury benefits), limiting 442–3, *442*
large families, redistribution mechanisms 32
law *see* legal provisions
legal provisions
  employment injury benefits 212–13, 233–5, 256–8
  legal vs actual coverage 15
  modifications 19–20, 156, *312*, 315
  pension schemes *143*, 156
    data and information base *see*
pension schemes (data and information base)
reports 312–13, *312*, 315, 368
tables (examples) *397*
unemployment insurance 290
see also eligibility conditions; ILO (standards)
legislation *see* legal provisions
liability, actuarial **172–5**, 241–2, 483*g*
life annuities 431, 433–4
life expectancy 7, *104*, *153*, *154*, 312, 361
  DC schemes 432–4
  sensitivity analysis 152
  see also mortality/rates
loans (pension schemes) 183
lump-sum payments 181, *403*

McGillivray, Warren R. xxii–xxiii
macroeconomic *see* economic
Malaysia 423
males *see* men
manufacturing sector 206
marriage breakdown 5, *6, 8,* 9
marriage rates 4, *6, 8, 80, 379*
married couples, age differential 4
married insured persons, redistribution mechanisms 32
maternity benefits *see* short-term cash benefits (maternity benefits)
maximum pensions 77, 163
medical care, ILO standards 414, 417–18, 419–20
medical expenses *see* employment injury benefits (medical expenses and rehabilitation benefits)
men
  age differential with wives 4
  contributions, density *342*
  credits *88, 343, 401*
  employment *337, 383–4, 385–6*
  insurable earnings *85, 341, 400*
  insured population *340, 398, 402*
  invalidity *344, 350, 351, 369, 370, 372, 404, 407, 411*
  labour force 318, 336–7, *336, 337, 380–81, 382*
  life expectancy *104, 154,* 361
  marriage rates *379*
  maternity benefits 287
  migration *378*

Index

mortality rates 333, *333*, 377
pensioners, ratio to contributors (Demoland) 349
pensions *351*, *369*, *404*, *406*, *409*
population *337*, *375*
self-employment *387–8*
survivorship benefits 323, 360–61, *360*, *369*, *372*, *404–5*, *408*
unemployment 336, *337*, 354, *389–91*
Mexico *436*
migrant workers, social security agreements 22–3
migration 6, 7, *60*, *80*, 153, *378*
  Demoland 334, *334*
  projection 104–5, *106*, *111*
  sensitivity analysis 152, *154*
  trends, reports 312
  see also demographic environment
minimum benefits 418–19
minimum pensions 77–8, 178
  Chile *436*
  DC schemes 436–7, *436*
  Demoland *168*, 319
  modification 163, *168*, 323, 359–60, *360*
mining 202, 206
mixed (PAYG and full funding) systems (employment injury benefits) 199–201
modelling
  Demoland 329–30
  pension schemes 35, 36, 105–7, *106*
  for major treatment *see* pension schemes (modelling)
models
  Bühlmann-Straub model (employment injury benefits) 445–7, *446*
  deterministic 57–9, *58*, 484g
  ILO *60–61*, 62, *64*, 105–7, *106*, *128*, 328
  social security-specific, need for **3–6**
  socio-economic actuarial (SEA) models 5, 6
  stochastic 57–9, *58*, 487g
modifications to schemes
  ILO standards 419
  legal provisions 19–20, 156, *312*, 315
  for major treatment *see* Demoland; pension schemes (modifications)
  survivorship benefits 165, 360–61, *360*

Monte-Carlo method (stochastic models) 59
mortality 6, *60*, 103–4, *104*, 107, *111*, 312
  employment injury benefits (terminations of pensions in payment) 243–5, 252–3, 468, 469
  see also demographic environment; invalidity pensions; life expectancy
mortality rates 4, 5, *61*, *80*, 131
  Demoland 333, *333*, 343
  gender-specific 333, *333*, 377

new entrants to schemes 4, *82*, 84, 121–2, *122*, 144$_2$, *402*, 486g
new-money rate approach (investment return) *139–40*
newborns, sex ratios 376
non-insured employed persons (Demoland) *337*
non-national residents 420
non-parametric income distribution *128*

occupational diseases
  ILO definition 415–16
  for major treatment *see* employment injury benefits
occupational pension schemes 4, 27–8, 29, 30, 33
  see also private sector
old-age pensions *see* pension schemes
Ontario, Canada 448
open-group (projection) method (valuation) 27–8, 46, 121
orphans *see* survivorship benefits

parametric income distribution *128*
partial funding (pension schemes) **46–54**
  general average premium (GAP) 44, 50, 53–4
  reserve ratio system 45, 48, *49–50*, *51–2*, 53
  scaled premium system 45, 47–8, *47*, 486–7g
participation factor (employment injury rating systems) 452
past insurance credits *see* credits
past results, analysis *see* experience analysis
pay-as-you-go (PAYG) financing
  cost rate 486g

505

Index

short-term benefits 281, 305
see also financing
pay-as-you-go (PAYG) financing, employment injury benefits 196–7, 209–11
  contribution rates 196–7, 198–9
  mixed systems (with full funding) 199–201
pay-as-you-go (PAYG) financing, pension schemes 39, 42, *44*, 45, 94, 148, 149, 150
  annuity factor 177–8
  base run 37
  Demoland *148*, 322, *351*, 352, 353–5, *353*, *354*, *355*, *359*
  monitoring 178–9
  Sweden **176–9**
PAYG financing *see* pay-as-you-go financing
pension debt overhang *172*
pension schemes **25–187**
  DB schemes *see* defined-benefit pension schemes
  DC schemes *see* defined-contribution pension schemes
  ILO standards 414, 417, 419
  interrelationships with environment *see* social security schemes
  occupational 4, 27–8, 29, 30, 33
  public (definition) 486g
  reports *see* reports
  tables (examples) *see* tables
pension schemes, assumptions, scheme-specific **117–45**
  administrative expenses, future level 142, 144
  contribution collection rate 140, 142, *143*
  conversion from DB to DC schemes 173–5
  indexing rate 137–8
  insurable earnings, projection 36, *60*, 63, **124–30**, 148, 438
    contributions, density 129–30
    earnings distribution **126–8**
    earnings growth *123–4*, **124–6**, *125–6*, *153*
    total versus insurable earnings 129, *129*
  insurance credits, accumulation 130–31

insured population, development *64–6*, **117–24**
  components 119–21, *120*, 144$_2$
  coverage rate 117–18, *119*
  new entrants and re-entrants 121–2, *122*, 144$_2$
  invalidity incidence and termination 68, 132–4, *135*
  see also mortality
investment return *58*, 138–40, *139–40*
  interest rates 138
  investment type 140
mortality rates 131
  retirement behaviour 35, 36, 68, 131–2, *133*
  selection 35–6
survivorship benefits, entitlement 134, 136–7
  average age of spouse *61*, 136, *137*
  children 136–7, *137*
  probability of having spouse at time of death *61*, 136, *137*
  see also survivorship benefits
pension schemes, characteristics **27–33**
  broad coverage and mandatory participation 27–9
  experience, relevance 28
  links with the general economic context 28
  no underwriting 28–9
  open-group method 27–8, 46, 121
  funding flexibility 30–31
  government sponsorship 29
  see also government
  redistribution mechanisms 31–3, 77
    between earnings classes 31–2
    between generations 32–3
    between workers with different career patterns 32
    in favour of married insured persons and large families 32
  self-financing 29–30
pension schemes, data and information base **69–89**
  data collection and analysis 34–5
  Demoland 330–31
  general demographic and economic data 80–81
  legal provisions **72–80**
    benefit, amount **75–9**

506

Index

contingencies covered 73–4
coverage 72, *74*
covered earnings 74–5
eligibility conditions 75
financing provisions 79–80
unclear/ineffective 73
scheme-specific data *71*, **81–9**
  beneficiaries 88–9
  contributions, density 87–8
  credits 86–7, *88*
  earnings level **84–6**, *85*
  institution's data maintenance system 81–2
  insured persons at valuation date 83–4
  insured population **82–8**
  new entrants and re-entrants *82*, 84
statistical information, sources **69–72**
pension schemes, Demoland 368–70
  administrative expenses *326*
  contributions/rates *49–50*, 318, 322–3, *326*, 332
  cost projections 346, **349–52**
    demographic projections *147*, 349, *350*
    expenditure 330–31, 351–2, *351*, *359*
    financial projections *148*, 349, 351–2, *351*, *352*
    income 330–31, 351–2, *351*
  differentiation of (amount of) pensions 366–7
  expenditure, recent experience 325, *326*
  investment earnings *326*, 327–8
  PAYG rate *148*, 322
  ratio of contributors to pensioners 349, *350*, 353, *353*, 354, *354*
  replacement rates 318–19
  reserve *see* reserves
  results, reconciliation with previous valuations *155*
  revenue, recent experience 325, *326*
pension schemes, experience analysis 28, **90–101**
  administrative expenses 95–6, *95*
  financial indicators, key **93–5**
  financial statements **90–93**
    cash versus accrual basis 91
    financial reporting 91–3
  investment performance 93–4, **96–8**, *97–8*

reserve, determining value 99–101, *99*
  investments 99–100
pension schemes, financial systems **38–55**
  expenditure 38–9, *39*, 41, *64*, 94, 148, 151, *153*
    tables (examples) *403*, *404*
  objectives 40–41
  revenue 39–40, 41, *42*, *153*
    see also individual sources
  types of systems **41–54**
    full funding 45–6, *46*, **176–9**
    partial funding *see* partial funding
    PAYG *see* pay-as-you-go financing
pension schemes, modelling 4–5, *6*, **56–68**
  definition of model 56–7
  deterministic versus stochastic models 57–9, *58*
  objectives 59, 62
  structure **62–8**
    demographic environment *60–61*, 62, 63
    economic environment *60–61*, 63
    future development of scheme 63
    ILO projection model *60–61*, 62, *64*
    mathematical structure 64–8
    see also formulae (pension schemes)
pension schemes, modifications, valuation of 35, **158–69**
  benefits **158–65**
    earnings test at retirement 163–4
    eligibility conditions (contribution requirements) 158–9
    invalidity, definition 164
    minimum and maximum pensions 163, *168*
    pension formula 161–2
    pensions in payment 162–3, 429, 435
    retirement age 159–61, *160*
    survivorship benefits 165
  contributions 165–6
    contribution rate 166
    salary base 166
  other considerations 167
  presenting effect of modifications 167–9, *168*
  reserves 100, *101*
  see also Demoland; pension schemes (structural reform considerations)

507

pension schemes, projections, frames for
102–16
demographic frame **102–7**
fertility 103, *106*, *111*
migration 104–5, *106*, *111*
mortality 103–4, *111*
standard model 105–7, *106*
macroeconomic frame **107–15**
economic growth 110–12, *111*
inflation 114
interest rates 114–15
labour force, employment and
unemployment *108*, *111*, 112
other considerations 115
wages 112–14, *113*
pension schemes, results and sensitivity
analysis **146–57**
indicators, calculation **149–52**
demographic indicators 149–50, *153*
financial indicators 150–52, *153*
see also individual indicators
reconciliation with previous valuation
155, 156–7
results 36–7, **146–9**
demographic projections 146, *147*,
148
financial projections 146, 148–9, *148*
sensitivity analysis 37, 152–6, *154*, 354–5
pension schemes, structural reform
considerations 20–21, **170–87**
converting a DB scheme into a DC
scheme **170–76**
Chile 20, 170, *171*
liability at conversion **172–5**
specific considerations 176
converting a provident fund into a DB
scheme **179–87**
alternatives **183–6**
countries that have converted 186–7
differences between provident funds
and pension schemes **180–83**
general considerations 179–80
Swedish pension reform **176–9**
actuarial intervention 177–9
new scheme 176–7
see also pension schemes
(modifications)
pension schemes, valuation process **34–7**
additional simulations 37

assumptions and indicators, selection
35–6
base run and results analysis 36–7
data collection and analysis 34–5
findings and recommendations,
presentation 37
model building and adjustments 35
model, feeding 36
preparatory work 34
report, writing 37
sensitivity analysis 37
pensionable age *see* retirement age
pensioners, old age 36, *61*, 88–9
ratio to contributors (Demoland) 349,
350, 353, *353*, 354, *354*
Perez-Montas, Hernando iii
periodic payments (DC schemes) 430–33
fixed 430–31
selection of system 432–3
variable 431–2
permanent incapacity benefits *see*
employment injury benefits
(incapacity, permanent)
perpetuities 430
Peru 89_2
phased (or programmed) withdrawals
(DC schemes) 432, 434–5
Plamondon, Pierre xxi
Poland 20
population
coverage *see* insured population
data *70*, *80*, 375–9
projection 105–7, *106*, 329, 334–5, *335*,
337
see also demographic environment
Portugal 300
premium financing 292, 302–4, 438
scaled premium system *45*, 47–8, *47*,
486–7g
see also general average premium
(GAP)
premium rates (unemployment insurance)
305–6
preparatory work (valuation process) 34
prevention groups (employment injury
rating systems) 450, 453
private sector 191–2
see also occupational pension schemes
productivity 6, *60*, *108*, *111*
programmed (or phased) withdrawals

(DC schemes) 432, 434–5
projection (open-group) method
 (valuation) 27–8, 46, 121
provident funds 486g
 balances **183–6**
provident funds, conversion into a DB
 scheme 21, **179–87**
 alternatives **183–6**
 countries that have converted 186–7
 differences between provident funds
  and pension schemes **180–83**
 general considerations 179–80
public pension schemes *see* pension
 schemes
public sector (employment injury rating
 systems) 206

qualifying periods *see* eligibility
 conditions
Quebec, Canada *154*, 267

rate of return *see* investment return
rating systems, employment injury
 benefits *see* employment injury
 benefits (financial and rating
 systems)
re-entrants to schemes *82*, 84, 121–2, *122*,
 144$_2$, 486g
 see also insured population (inactive)
real estate *see* investments
recommendations (actuarial) 19, 37, *312*,
 316
Recommendations (ILO) *see* ILO
 (standards)
reconciliation of results with previous
 valuations *155*, 156–7
records 183, 195, *195*
 see also data
recovery, permanent incapacity
 pensioners **245–8**, *246*, *247*, *254–5*
redistribution mechanisms *see* pension
 schemes (characteristics)
reference earnings 76, *77*, 161–2, 486g
reform of schemes 19–21
 for major treatment *see* pension
  schemes (structural reform
  considerations)
 reports *312*, 315
regulation risk (DC schemes) 429–30
rehabilitation benefits *see* employment

injury benefits (medical expenses and
 rehabilitation benefits)
remarriage, and survivorship pensions
 248
replacement rates 15, 37, 151, 318–19,
 486g
reports 22, 37, **311–72**
 communicating results 317
 Demoland *see* Demoland
 see also data; records
reports, employment injury benefits **461–70**
 incapacity benefits (permanent) **464–9**,
  465
 incapacity benefits (temporary) **461–4**,
  462, *463*
 medical expenses and rehabilitation
  benefits 260
 survivorship benefits 464–7, 469–70
reports, structure **311–16**, *312*
 analysis of present situation and
  performance 312–14, *312*
 benefit experience *312*, 313–14
 financial status 91–3, *312*, 313–14,
  397
 legal provisions 312–13, *312*, 368
 annexes 312, *312*
 conclusions and recommendations *312*,
  316
 demographic trends 312, *312*
 economic context 311–12, *312*
 executive summaries 311, *312*
 Demoland *see* Demoland
 governance context 312, *312*
 projections *312*, 314–15
  database and assumptions *312*, 314–15
  methodology *312*, 314
  modified legal provisions and reform
   proposals *312*, 315
  sensitivity analysis (status quo
   results) *312*, 315
  status quo projection results *312*,
   315
reproductive behaviour *8*, *9*
 see also fertility rates
reserve ratio system (pension schemes)
 48–53, 148, 151, 486g
 Demoland *49–50*, *148*, 322, 332, 351–2,
  351, *359*

Index

experience analysis 94–5
formulae 45, *51–2*
reserves 486g
   Demoland 319, 322, 325
   employment injury benefits
      Demoland 322, *326*, 332, 356–7, *356*, 371–2, *372*
      full funding 199, *199*, *200*, 201
      mixed systems *200*, 201
   pension schemes 41, *42*, 148, 152
      Demoland *148*, 322, *326*, *351*, 356–7, *356*, *359*
      determining value 99–101, *99*
   short-term cash benefits (Demoland) 325, *326*, 331, 356, *356*
   unemployment insurance 305–6
responsiveness (employment injury rating systems) 447–8, *447*
results 17–18, 307
   pension schemes *see* pension schemes (results and sensitivity analysis)
   presentation *see* reports
retail industry 206
retirement
   definition 73
   earnings test at 163–4
retirement age 16, 183
   Demoland *160*, 318, 344, 361–2
   ILO standards 361, 415
   modifications 159–61, *160*, 361–2
   sensitivity analysis 154
retirement behaviour *6*, *8*, 9, 35, 36, 131–2, *133*, 344
retirement pensions *see* pension schemes
retirement rates 4, 5, 9, *61*, 131–2, *133*
reviews of ongoing schemes *see* actuaries
revision (review process) 18
risk
   conversion of provident funds into DB schemes 181, 182–3
   DC schemes *see* defined-contribution pension schemes
   investments 181, 182–3, 427–8
   lack of underwriting 28–9
   see also employment injury benefits (financial and rating systems)
rural workers, coverage 74

Saint Kitts and Nevis 186
Saint Lucia 186

Saint Vincent and the Grenadines 186
salaries *see* earnings; wages
scaled premium system *45*, 47–8, *47*, 486–7g
SEA (socio-economic actuarial) models 5, 6
seasonal workers 286, 324, 362–3
securities *see* investments
self-employment *74*, *80*, 318, *357*, 365–6, *365*, *387–8*
self-financing characteristic of pension schemes 29–30
sensitivity analysis 37, 152–6, *312*, 315, 354–5, *355*
service sector (employment injury rating systems) 206
services (actuarial), organization 23–4
sex ratios (newborns) *376*
Seychelles 186–7
shares *see* investments
short-term cash benefits **279–308**
short-term cash benefits, Demoland
   administrative expenses *326*, *347*
   contributions/rates 318, 322, *323*, *326*, 331, 357, *357*, *358*
   cost projections 345, 346–7, *347*
   expenditure 325, *326*
   investment earnings *326*, 327–8
   reserve 325, *326*, 331
   reserve, reallocation 322, 331, 356, *356*
   revenue 325, *326*
short-term cash benefits, maternity benefits **281–7**
   cost projections **283–5**, *284*, **286–7**, 345, 347, *347*
   database 282–3
   and fertility rates 283, 286
   financial system 281–2
   ILO standards 414, 417, 418, 420
short-term cash benefits, sickness benefits **281–7**
   cost projections **283–6**, *284*, 287
   Demoland 345, 346–7, *346*, *347*
   new schemes 285
   seasonal workers 286
   data 282
   eligibility conditions 286, 324, 362–3, 417
   financial system 281–2
   ILO standards 414, 417, 418, 419–20

Index

see also employment injury benefits (medical expenses and rehabilitation benefits)
short-term cash benefits, unemployment insurance (UI) 24, **288–308**
  benefits, projection, administration costs 301–2
  benefits, projection (first method) **294–9**
    benefit rate 294, 298–9
    claims, average duration 294, 297–8
    eligibility, rate of 294, 297
    insured population 294, 295–7
  benefits, projection (second method) **299–301**
    average benefit per week 300, 301
    ratio of beneficiaries to unemployed 299, 300
  business cycles 292–4
  data 291–2
  eligibility conditions 294, 297–8, 417
  expertise and background of actuaries 289–90
  financing **302–7**
    experience rating 306–7
    premium financing 292, 302–4
    premium rates 305–6
    reserves, projection 305–6
    revenues, projection 304–5
  ILO standards 414, 417, 420, 421
  insurance concepts 288–9
  legal provisions 290
  results, validation 307
  see also unemployment
short-term projections 21
sickness benefits see short-term cash benefits (sickness benefits)
Singapore 176
small employers (employment injury rating systems) 208, 448, *449*, 450
smoothing techniques *99*, 100
social (behavioural) environment, interrelationships with social security schemes 4, 5, *6*, *8*, 9
  see also individual social variables
social governance, actuary's role 13
social security
  definitions 13_1, 487g
  ILO standards 414–15

social security schemes, interrelationships **7–13**, *8*
  with demographic environment 4–5, *6*, 7–9, *8*
  with economic environment 4, 5, *6*, 7, *8*, 9–11
  with fiscal environment 5, *6*, *8*, 11–12
  with social (behavioural) environment 4, 5, *6*, *8*, 9
social security-specific models, need for **3–6**
socio-economic actuarial (SEA) models 5, *6*
South America 423
Spain 308_6
spouses
  age differential 4
  survivorship benefits see survivorship benefits
statements, financial **90–93**
statistical reporting see reports
statistics **69–72**, 367
  see also data
statutory mechanisms (setting revenue levels) 40
stochastic models 57–9, *58*, 487g
stocks see investments
structural reform see reform of schemes
subsidies see government
summaries, executive 311, *312*
  Demoland see Demoland
survey data 291
survivorship benefits **233–53**, *369–71*
  average age of spouse *61*, 136
  Demoland *137*, *344*, 345
  children *61*, 136–7, *408*
  Demoland *137*, *147*, *344*, 345, *350*, 367, *370*, *371*, *372*
  cost projections (Demoland) 346, *351*
  database 460–61
  DC schemes 436, 438
  eligibility 134, 136–7, *137*, 417
  experience analysis 94
  financial projections *61*, **235–42**
    future awards 239–41, 248–51
    pensions in payment at valuation date 236–8
    present value of new awards 238–9, 252
    successive liabilities 241–2

Index

formulae *see* formulae (employment injury benefits)
ILO standards 414, 416, 417, 419, 420, 421
legal provisions 235
men 323, 360–61, *360*, *369*, *372*, *404–5*, *408*
modifications 165
  Demoland 360–61, *360*
probability of being married at time of death *61*, 136
  Demoland *137*, *344*, 345
redistribution mechanisms 32
remarriage 248
reports 464–7, 469–70
tables (examples) *403*, *404–5*, *408*
technical reserve (Demoland) 371–2, *372*
terminations of pensions in payment 243, 245, 248
suspension of benefits (ILO standards) 420–21
Sweden 20
  parental benefits 287
  pension reform **176–9**
    actuarial intervention 177–9
    new scheme 176–7
  symbols (formulae) **471–82**

tables (examples) **373–412**
  employment *383–8*
  exchange rates *395*
  financial reporting *397*
  general information *374*
  gross domestic product *392–3*
  income distribution *394*
  inflation *395*
  insured population *398–402*
  interest rates *395*
  invalidity pensions *403*, *404*, *407*, *411–12*
  labour force *380–82*
  legal provisions *397*
  old-age pensions *403*, *404*, *406*, *409–10*
  population, general *375–9*
  public finances *396*
  survivorship benefits *403*, *404–5*, *408*
  unemployment *389–91*
  wages *392*
taxation 12

technical reserve (Demoland) 332, 371–2, *372*
temporary incapacity benefits *see* employment injury benefits (incapacity cash benefits)
terminal funding *197*, 199, 487g
tests
  earnings at retirement 163–4
  medical expenses and rehabilitation benefits 276–8, *276–7*
  sensitivity analysis 37, 152–6, *312*, 315, 354–5, *355*
time-weighted rate of return (investments) *97*
transfers, intergenerational 32–3
transitional pensions 178
transportation industry 206
Trinidad and Tobago *141*
Turkey 74

UI *see* short-term cash benefits (unemployment insurance)
UN (United Nations) 70, 103, *104*, 107, 333
underwriting 28–9
unemployment 6
  data 80, *389–91*
  definitions 115$_7$, 416, 487g
  Demoland 336, *337*
  projection *60*, 63, *108*, *111*, 112
  see also short-term cash benefits (unemployment insurance)
unemployment insurance *see* short-term cash benefits (unemployment insurance)
unemployment rates 80, 300, 318, 336, *337*, *391*
  sensitivity analysis *154*, 354
unfunded liability 174, 487g
uniform rating systems (employment injury benefits) 203
United Kingdom 17, 23, 432–3
United Nations Population Council 70
United Nations (UN) 103, *104*, 107, 333
United States 23, 157$_3$
  actuarial balance *53*, 151
  American Academy of Actuaries 40
  business cycles 293
  disability pensions 134
  employment injury benefits 191

financial systems *52–3*
invalidity incidence rates *135*
mortality 103
savings rate 10
unemployment insurance 306
unemployment rate 300
urbanization 9
Uruguay *436*

valuation process *see* pension schemes (valuation process)
variable annuities 431
wage share at GDP *60*, 487g
wages 4, 5, *6*, *8*, 10–11, *80*, *153*
   Demoland 318
   formulae *108–9*
   ILO distribution model *128*
   projection 5, 10–11, *60*, 112–14, *113*
      Demoland 329–30, 336, 338–9, *338*
      salary base, extension 166
      salary scales *123–4*, 124–6, *125–6*, 486g
   sensitivity analysis 154, *154*, 355, *355*
   tables (examples) *392*
   see also earnings
Wales 432–3
wholesale industry 206
widowers, survivorship benefits 323, 360–61, *360*, *369*, *372*, *404*, *408*
widows *see* survivorship benefits
wives *see* women
women
   age differential with husbands 4
   contributions, density *342*
   credits *88*, *343*, *401*
   employment *337*, *383–4*, *385–6*
   fertility 103, *106*, *111*, *376*
   insurable earnings *85*, *341*, *400*
   insured population *340*, *398*, *402*
   invalidity *344*, *350*, *351*, *369*, *370*, *372*, *404*, *407*, *412*
   labour force 318, 336–7, *336*, *337*, *380–81*, *382*
   life expectancy *104*, *154*, 361
   marriage rates *379*
   maternity benefits *see* short-term cash benefits (maternity benefits)
   migration *378*
   mortality rates 333, *333*, *377*
   pensioners, ratio to contributors (Demoland) 349
   pensions *351*, *369*, *404*, *406*, *410*
   population *337*, *375*
   self-employment *387–8*
   survivorship benefits *see* survivorship benefits
   unemployment 336, *337*, 354, *389–91*
World Bank 172, *172*

youth dependency ratio (Demoland) 334–5, *335*

Zelenka, Valentin 47